Real Skills

with Readings

*Sentences and Paragraphs for College,
Work, and Everyday Life*

Real Skills

with Readings

Sentences and Paragraphs for College, Work, and Everyday Life

Susan Anker

With illustrations by Suzy Becker

Bedford/St. Martin's   *Boston* ◆ *New York*

For Bedford/St. Martin's

Senior Developmental Editor: Beth Castrodale
Developmental Editor: Karin Halbert
Production Editor: Deborah Baker
Production Supervisor: Jennifer Peterson
Senior Marketing Manager: Rachel Falk
Editorial Assistant: Christina Gerogiannis
Copyeditor: Janet Renard
Text Design: Claire Seng-Niemoeller
Cover Design: Billy Boardman
Composition: Stratford Publishing Services, Inc.
Printing and Binding: R. R. Donnelley & Sons Company

President: Joan E. Feinberg
Editorial Director: Denise B. Wydra
Editor in Chief: Karen S. Henry
Director of Marketing: Karen Melton Soeltz
Director of Editing, Design, and Production: Marcia Cohen
Managing Editor: Elizabeth M. Schaaf

Library of Congress Control Number: 2006926014

Manufactured in the United States of America.

1 0 9 8 7 6
f e d c b a

For information, write: Bedford/St. Martin's, 75 Arlington Street, Boston, MA 02116
(617-399-4000)

ISBN-10: 0–312–45708–1 ISBN-13: 978–0–312–45708–2 (*Real Skills*)
    0–312–43284–4   978–0–312–43284–3 (*Real Skills with Readings*)
    0–312–43153–8   978–0–312–43153–2 (Instructor's Annotated Edition)

Acknowledgments

Mitch Albom. "What's Patriotic?" From the *Detroit Free Press*, July 3, 2005. Copyright © Knight Ridder/Tribune (KRT) Media Services, Inc. Reprinted with permission. All Rights Reserved.

Russell Baker. "The Plot against People." From the *New York Times*, June 18, 1968. Copyright © 1968 by the New York Times Company. Reprinted by permission.

David Brooks. "Boys of Summer." From the *New York Times*, July 31, 2005. Copyright © 2005 by the New York Times Company. Reprinted by permission.

Tucker Carlson. "You Idiot! If You Believe What You See on TV, All Men Are Morons." From *Reader's Digest*, January 2003, pp. 33–34. Copyright © 2003 by the Reader's Digest Association, Inc. Reprinted with permission.

Cindy Chupack. "The End." From *The Between Boyfriends Book* by Cindy Chupack. Copyright © 2003 by the author and reprinted by permission of St. Martin's Press, LLC.

Chitra Banerjee Divakaruni. "Common Scents." This article first appeared in *Salon.com*, June 26, 1997. An online version remains in the *Salon* archives at www.salon.com. Reprinted with permission.

Patrice Gaines. "Healing the Wounds of Crime." Bedford/St. Martin's wishes to thank the Crisis Publishing Co., Inc., the publisher of the magazine of the National Association for the Advancement of Colored People, for the use of this material, which was first published in the July/August 2002 issue of *Crisis*.

Dianne Hales. "What Your Car Says about You." First appeared in *Parade* magazine, May 15, 2006. Copyright © 2006 by Dianne Hales. Reprinted by permission of the author. All rights reserved.

Grace Hsiang. "'FOBs' vs. 'Twinkies.'" From Pacific News Service. Posted on www.alternet.org, April 15, 2005. Printed on August 2, 2005. Copyright © 2005 Independent Media Institute. Reprinted by permission. All rights reserved.

Real Simple. "Saving Gas." From *Real Simple*, August 21, 2002, p. 42. Copyright © 2001. Reprinted by permission of Time, Inc. All rights reserved, Time, Inc.

David Oliver Relin. "Who's Killing Kids' Sports?" From *Parade* magazine, August 7, 2005. Copyright © 2005 Parade. Reprinted by permission of the author. All rights reserved.

Carolyn Foster Segal. "The Dog Ate My Disk, and Other Tales of Woe." From the *Chronicle of Higher Education*, August 11, 2000. Reprinted by permission of the author.

Joseph Sobran. "Patriotism or Nationalism?" From www.sobran.com, October 16, 2001. Copyright © 2006 Griffin Internet Syndicate, www.griffnews.com. Reprinted with permission.

Preface for Instructors

Real Skills: Sentences and Paragraphs for College, Work, and Everyday Life is the third and newest text in the Anker series of books. This carefully sequenced series (with *Real Skills* focusing on sentences and paragraphs, *Real Writing* focusing on paragraphs and essays, and *Real Essays* focusing on the essay) demonstrates to students that writing competence is needed for success not only in college but also at work and in everyday life.

Real Skills shares the class-tested features of the other books in the Anker series, motivating students with the message that writing is an essential and achievable skill. These features include an emphasis on writing's relevance to the real world (with profiles of successful students and more), on the four basics of different types of writing, and on the four most serious errors. At the same time, *Real Skills* reimagines these highly praised features to address the most pressing needs of students in the sentence-to-paragraph-level course. First, it helps students develop strategies to solve problems that might cause them to drop out. It then gives students all the tools they need to write well in college, at work, and in everyday life, breaking writing and grammar concepts down into their most basic elements.

Also, special features of *Real Skills*, from an integrated approach to learning styles to instructive and humorous illustrations, make the book ideal for teaching the most basic skills.

Features

Offers a Simplified, Hands-on Approach to Grammar and Editing

In *Real Skills*, an emphasis on examples over terminology, along with plenty of practice, helps students learn and master essential grammar concepts, from basic parts of speech to proper verb usage and sentence construction. Additionally, color coding of subjects and verbs in the first grammar unit helps students visualize and understand the functions of these important parts of speech.

Also, *Real Skills*, like the other books in the Anker series, concentrates first, with fuller coverage and lots of practice, on the errors identified by teachers across the country as the most serious: fragments, run-ons and comma splices, subject-verb agreement problems, and verb tense problems. It then offers extensive coverage of other standard grammar, punctuation, spelling, and mechanics topics. Finally, "Find and Fix" charts throughout the grammar chapters provide visual instruction that helps students identify and correct grammar problems, making them better editors of their own writing.

Helps Students Understand — and Use — Their Learning Preferences

First, a learning-styles questionnaire in Chapter 3 helps students find their predominant learning style and suggests how to use that learning style to read and study, to write, and to take tests. Then, activities later in the book, including fun collaborative exercises and games, get students to use their learning style as they apply and practice writing and grammar concepts. These activities are marked with special icons matched to the various learning styles. Throughout the book, humorous color illustrations by a renowned illustrator, humorist, and author engage students of all learning styles, helping them understand writing and grammar concepts while making these concepts less intimidating and onerous.

Motivates Students and Prepares Them to Succeed in the Writing Course — and Beyond

Chapter 1, "Staying in College: Advice from Those Who've Been There," aims to promote student retention. Written with a board of student advisers who at one time dropped out of college but later achieved academic success, the chapter provides a step-by-step process for identifying and solving problems that might cause students to drop out. Topics covered include financial constraints; difficulties balancing college, work, and family responsibilities; and lack of preparation. Through inspirational profiles, these experienced students encourage newer ones to stay in school despite challenges and offer advice for success.

Next, Chapter 2, "Doing Well in College: Strategies for Success," helps students understand — and meet — academic expectations, with advice on getting organized, managing time, reading effectively, taking good notes, taking tests, and thinking critically.

Throughout the book, examples, assignment topics, and exercises are drawn from real-world situations, showing the relevance of good writing to college, work, and everyday life.

Offers Clear, Accessible Coverage of Writing and Reading

A focus on the "four basics" of each type of paragraph keeps the writing instruction simple, highlighting the most important elements students need to understand about a rhetorical strategy before they can use it successfully. The "four basics" lists are followed by model paragraphs color-coded to show these features. Also, step-by-step writing checklists and outlines help students write complete, organized, and well-thought-out papers.

Chapter 2 introduces students to basic reading skills, such as finding the main point and support and understanding important textbook features. And eighteen selections at the end of *Real Skills with Readings* give students more reading practice and provide springboards for writing. These readings are accompanied by marginal questions to encourage close reading, comprehension questions, critical reading questions, and writing assignments. Finally, an appendix on building vocabulary helps students become better readers and writers.

Helps ESL Students and Speakers of Nonstandard English Become Better Writers

Written with the help of ESL specialists, a comprehensive chapter addresses ESL students' most common grammar concerns, paying special attention to verbs (with extensive charts and examples) and offering plenty of practices to help build grammar skills.

Additionally, "language notes" throughout the grammar coverage highlight issues that can be especially challenging for ESL students, Generation 1.5 students, and other speakers of nonstandard English.

Gives Practice and Advice for Tests

Review tests at the end of each writing and grammar unit help instructors check students' knowledge of concepts presented in the text. These tests include questions like those on major standardized tests, such as the Florida College Basic Skills Exit Test and the Texas Higher Education Assessment (THEA), helping students to prepare for such exams. Also, an appendix of test-taking advice and strategies provides further test preparation. This appendix covers such topics as how to review for a test, how to reduce test anxiety, and how to approach different kinds of questions typically included on exams. It also provides special preparation for essay exams, with advice on how to meet standards presented on a rubric.

Ancillaries

Print Resources for Instructors and Students

- **Instructor's Annotated Edition of *Real Skills*.** Gives practical page-by-page advice on teaching with *Real Skills* and contains answers to all exercises and suggestions for using the other ancillaries.
- **Practical Suggestions for Teaching *Real Skills*.** An ideal resource for teachers new to teaching or to *Real Skills*. Contains information and advice on bringing the real world into the classroom, using computers, teaching ESL students, responding to the most difficult student papers, and more.

- **Additional Resources to Accompany *Real Skills*.** Supplements the instructional materials in the text with a variety of transparency masters, planning forms, handouts, and other reproducibles for classroom use.

- *Teaching Developmental Writing: Background Readings*, **Third Edition.** This professional resource, edited by Susan Naomi Bernstein, cochair of the Conference on Basic Writing, offers essays on topics of interest to basic writing instructors, along with editorial apparatus pointing out practical applications for the classroom.

- **Quick Reference Card with writing, editing, and academic success tips.** Students can prop this handy card up next to their computers for easy reference while they're writing, editing, and studying.

- *The Bedford/St. Martin's ESL Workbook.* Covers grammar issues for multilingual students with varying English-language skills and cultural backgrounds. Instructional introductions are followed by illustrative examples and exercises.

- *From Practice to Mastery* (study guide for the Florida Basic Skills Exit Tests in reading and writing). Gives students all the resources they need to practice for—and pass—the Florida tests in reading and writing. It includes pre- and post-tests, abundant practices, and clear instruction in all the skills covered on the exams.

New Media Resources for Instructors and Students

- **Book Companion Site at <bedfordstmartins.com/realskills>.** Provides additional resources for instructors as well as resources that help students with writing and grammar. Included are grammar exercises written especially for *Real Skills*. Thousands of additional exercises are available on Exercise Central, at **<bedfordstmartins.com/exercisecentral>**.

- **<bedfordstmartins.com/susananker>.** Includes a videotaped message from Susan Anker that tells the story of her series. Also provides tools for finding the right Anker text, helpful instructional resources, and more.

- *Make-a-Paragraph Kit* **CD-ROM.** This fun, interactive CD-ROM, coming in spring of 2007, includes an "Extreme Paragraph Makeover" animation teaching students about paragraph development as well as exercises that get students to build their own paragraphs. It also includes a set of audiovisual tutorials on the four most serious errors and additional grammar practices.

- *Exercise Central to Go: Writing and Grammar Practices for Basic Writers.* This student CD-ROM includes hundreds of practice items to help basic writers build their writing and editing skills and provides audio instructions and instant feedback. Drawn from the popular online Exercise Central resource, the practices have been extensively class-tested. No Internet connection is necessary.

- *Testing Tool Kit: A Writing and Grammar Test Bank.* This CD-ROM allows instructors to create secure, customized tests and quizzes from nearly two thousand questions covering forty-seven topics. It also includes ten prebuilt diagnostic tests. Charts on the inside front covers of the *Practical Suggestions* and *Additional Resources* print ancillaries correlate topics from *Testing Tool Kit* with chapters in *Real Skills* so that you can use the CD to support your teaching with the text.

- *Re: Writing* at **<bedfordstmartins.com/rewriting>**. Collects the most popular and widely used free online resources from Bedford/St. Martin's in an easy-to-navigate Web site. Offerings include writing and grammar exercises, model documents, and instructor resources.

- *Real Skills* **content for course management systems.** Content includes tests and quizzes from the *Testing Tool Kit* CD-ROM; writing, grammar, and research resources from Bedford/St. Martin's popular *Re:Writing* Web site; and topics for online chats and discussion boards. This content is ready for use in Blackboard, WebCT, and other popular course management systems. For more information about Bedford/St. Martin's course management offerings, visit **<bedfordstmartins.com/cms>**.

- *Comment.* This Web-based peer-review tool allows instructors to respond to student writing quickly and easily. Students can also use *Comment* to respond to each other's work. For more information, visit **<comment.bedfordstmartins.com>**.

Ordering Information

To order any of the ancillaries for *Real Skills*, please contact your Bedford/St. Martin's sales representative, e-mail sales support at **<sales_support@bfwpub.com>**, or visit our Web site at **<bedfordstmartins.com>**.

   Use these ISBNs when ordering the following supplements packaged with your students' books:

Real Skills with Readings and

- Quick Reference Card: ISBN-10: 0–312–46131–3/ ISBN-13: 978–0–312–46131–7

- *The Bedford/St. Martin's ESL Workbook:* ISBN-10: 0–312–46132–1/ ISBN-13: 978–0–312–46132–4

- *From Practice to Mastery* (for Florida): ISBN-10: 0–312–46133–X/ ISBN-13: 978–0–312–46133–1

- *Make-a-Paragraph Kit* CD-ROM: ISBN-10: 0–312–46134–8/ ISBN-13: 978–0–312–46134–8

- *Exercise Central to Go* CD-ROM: ISBN-10: 0–312–46263–8/ ISBN-13: 978–0–312–46263–5

continued

Real Skills and

- Quick Reference Card: ISBN-10: 0–312–46135–6/
  ISBN-13: 978-0–312–46135–5
- *The Bedford/St. Martin's ESL Workbook:* ISBN-10: 0–312–46136–4/
  ISBN-13: 978-0–312–46136–2
- *From Practice to Mastery* (for Florida): ISBN-10: 0–312–46137–2/
  ISBN-13: 978-0–312–46137–9
- *Make-a-Paragraph Kit* CD-ROM: ISBN-10: 0–312–46138–0/
  ISBN-13: 978-0–312–46138–6
- *Exercise Central to Go* CD-ROM: ISBN-10: 0–312–46264–6/
  ISBN-13: 978-0–312–46264–2

Acknowledgments

I must bracket the acknowledgments with special thanks to Beth Castrodale, who is nominally my editor but in reality a full-fledged coauthor.

As with *Real Writing* and *Real Essays*, *Real Skills* is the product of many people's voices and hard work. I am grateful to them all and apologize in advance if I have neglected to mention any of the many people who collaborated with me.

Reviewers

Instructors on our Editorial Advisory Board have graciously offered insightful suggestions that are reflected on every page of *Real Skills*. Members of the advisory board, several of whom have special expertise in teaching ESL and Generation 1.5 students, are Erick J. Alburez, SUNY Farmingdale; Sally Gearhart, Santa Rosa Junior College; Shelly Hedstrom, Palm Beach Community College; Catherine Hutcheson, Troy University; William Kenah, Long Beach City College; Luli Lopez-Merino, Palm Beach Community College; Sandra Roy, San Antonio College; Valerie Russell, Valencia Community College; and Cheli J. Turner, Greenville Tech.

Others who provided useful guidance include Gary Bennett, Santa Ana College; Rhonda Carroll, Pulaski Technical College; Gigi Derballa, A-B Tech; Kristen di Gennaro, Pace University; Connie Gulick, TVI Community College; Levia Hayes, Community College of Southern Nevada; Sylvia A. Holladay; Janice McIntyre, Kansas City Community College; Tracy A. Peyton, Pensacola Junior College; Timothy L. Roach, St. Louis Community College, Forest Park; Tamara Shue, Georgia Perimeter College; and Leslie St. Martin, College of the Canyons.

Students

I worked with a remarkable group of students to craft the advice in Chapter 1 on how to stay in school despite myriad challenges and problems. These student advisers are

- Alessandra Cepeda, Bunker Hill Community College; University of Massachusetts, Boston
- Marcus Aurelius De Volder, Pima Community College East; University of Arizona
- Mary Gallery, McLennan Community College; Baylor University
- Irene Kabigting, City College of San Francisco
- Rick Reyes, San Antonio College

Contributors

First and foremost, I am lucky to have worked with illustrator/humorist/author Suzy Becker, my dear friend and a remarkable and talented person. Her ability to render the world a friendlier and funnier place buoys me and will no doubt do the same for students navigating the formidable sea of grammar.

As always, Mark Gallaher created excellent apparatus for the readings despite repeated computer betrayals. Connie Gulick contributed material on learning styles, and Sally Gearhart helped with the ESL chapter and language notes. Several people contributed to the extensive exercise program: Lynette Ledoux, Julie Nichols, Tamra Orr, Sandra Roy, and Bruce Thaler. Patti Levine-Brown of Florida Community College wrote the vocabulary appendix, and Adam Moss of DeVry South Florida helped create the test-taking appendix. Warren Drabek and Sandy Schechter worked to secure text permissions, and Linda Finigan helped with art research and cleared art permissions. Finally, Eddye Gallagher, Lynette Ledoux, and Connie Gulick contributed to *Practical Suggestions for Teaching Real Skills*, and Lynette Ledoux, Julie Nichols, and Bruce Thaler wrote exercises for *Additional Resources* and Exercise Central.

Bedford/St. Martin's

In addition to Beth Castrodale, Karin Halbert has contributed immensely to this book and others in the series. She found superb readings and, for *Real Skills*, coordinated the huge exercise program, carefully editing the exercises as well. Christina Gerogiannis ran review programs, helped collect readings, coordinated permissions, and assisted with ancillaries, among other tasks. Deborah Baker, taking the baton from Kerri Cardone, ably coordinated the tricky production of the book, and Janet Renard copyedited the manuscript with her usual thoroughness and care. Claire Seng-Niemoeller again pulled together various textual elements into a cohesive, attractive design. Billy Boardman created yet another colorful cover with great flair; Tom Macy and Brian Fraley produced a colorful brochure; and Martha Friedman helped with the art research program.

Members of the New Media group—including Nick Carbone, Katie Schooling, Tari Fanderclai, Harriet Wald, Coleen O'Hanley, Daniel Cole, and Cate Kashem—imagine, create, and produce great learning tools that I could never conceive myself. Many thanks to them.

In marketing, I benefit greatly from the regular and smart input of Karen Melton Soeltz, Jane Helms, and Rachel Falk. In sales, I am indebted to some old friends who candidly share their sales wisdom: Doug Bolton, Bill Soeltz, Ed Tiefenthaler, and Steve Patrick. Some newer friends—Cindy Rabinowitz and Dennis Adams, among others—also helped shape the book. These people and others help us maintain a strong bridge between the content and the audience.

Finally, thanks to other members of the editorial team who provided valuable suggestions throughout the development of this book: Denise Wydra, Karen Henry, David Mogolov, and Joan Feinberg, president of Bedford/St. Martin's, whose singular insights inform every Bedford/St. Martin's book.

And back to the bracket and my brace: Beth Castrodale, my editor. Her fingerprints are all over and through all of my books, particularly this one, in which she did as much writing as editing, all quickly and brilliantly. She is the star of our own "mission impossible."

Thanks also to my husband, Jim Anker, himself a publisher, who understands the vicissitudes of writing and publishing.

—Susan Anker

Contents

Introduction for Students

How to Use Real Skills

The best advice we can give you is, "Get everything you can from this writing class. Your future may well depend on how much you learn." If you want to succeed in college, if you want to get a good job, and if you want to be taken seriously in your everyday life, learn to write well. Without decent writing skills, getting what you want will be difficult, so take this opportunity to learn as much as you can about good writing.

This introduction will explain how to use this book. It describes how the book is organized, how to find information in it, and how to use it to improve your writing. It's worth taking a few minutes to read these few pages.

How *Real Skills* Is Organized

The book has eight units:

- **Unit One (Chapters 1–3)** helps you gear up for success in this course and others, with advice from other students about how to stay in school; information about and practice in getting organized, managing your time, and reading and studying effectively; and a test that indicates your learning style, with advice about how to use it to read, write, and study for tests.

- **Unit Two (Chapters 4–9)** walks you through the stages of the writing process, providing examples, practices, and step-by-step, practical advice about how to write good paragraphs. The last chapter in this unit helps you move from writing paragraphs to writing essays.

- **Unit Three (Chapters 10–15)** introduces you to the four most serious grammar errors, the ones that people notice most. With lots of practices and visual guides, these chapters teach you how to edit your writing to eliminate these four kinds of errors. Avoiding just these four will improve your grades! Also, these chapters (and the rest of the chapters in the book) give you a chance to apply your learning style through activities that are instructive and, yes, fun!

- **Unit Four (Chapters 16–21)** covers other grammar issues, again with many helpful visuals and practices.

- **Unit Five (Chapters 22–24)** gives you techniques for combining and improving your sentences, giving them variety and different rhythms to make your writing more interesting.
- **Unit Six (Chapters 25–27)** helps you with spelling and choosing words that best express your meaning.
- **Unit Seven (Chapters 28–32)** covers punctuation, with an emphasis on how to use commas correctly. It also has instruction on capitalizing words.
- **Unit Eight (Chapters 33–42;** in *Real Skills with Readings* **only)** is a collection of eighteen readings and writing assignments that will improve both your reading and writing skills.

Finally, *Real Skills* has appendices to help you to succeed on tests, build your vocabulary, and get a job. The final appendix includes forms that you can use to quickly organize your writing.

How to Find Information in *Real Skills*

There are many different ways to find information in this book.

TABLE OF CONTENTS   This tool, at the beginning of the book (pp. xiii–xix), lists each chapter's title and the major points covered in the chapter, with page numbers.

INDEX   One of the fastest ways to find anything is to look it up in the index at the back of the book (pp. I-1–I-6). The index is more detailed than the table of contents and lists every topic covered in the book in alphabetical order, with page numbers.

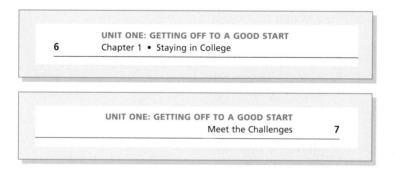

HEADINGS AT THE TOPS OF PAGES   Headings run along the top of every page. The headings on the left-hand pages tell you the unit you are in (for example, Unit One: Getting Off to a Good Start) followed by the chapter number and name; the headings on the right-hand pages repeat the unit name and tell you the particular section of the chapter that you're in.

CHART OF CORRECTION SYMBOLS   At the back of the book is a chart of the symbols that your instructors may use to indicate writing and grammar problems in your work.

LIST OF USEFUL CHARTS   On the inside of the back cover is a list of charts and quick reference tools that you will find helpful as you write and edit.

How to Use the Features of *Real Skills* to Improve Your Learning and Writing

Here are some regular features of *Real Skills* and how they can help you.

ILLUSTRATIONS   The illustrations throughout the book, drawn by a very well-known author/illustrator, are not only funny but they also will help you learn and remember the material, in the same way you remember a place you've actually seen better than one you've just read about.

LEARNING STYLE ICONS/"PRACTICE TOGETHER" ACTIVITIES   Chapter 3 has a test you can take to identify your learning style. It also introduces four icons (symbols) for each learning style that you can use to find activities later in the book that help you apply your learning style preference. Doing these activities can improve your understanding of chapter information.

The learning styles and the icons that go with them are repeated in each chapter as a reminder. Also, each chapter ends with fun group activities keyed to the different learning styles. These "Practice Together" items help cement your learning.

■ **LEARNING STYLES:** Look for activities in this chapter that are matched to your learning style. If you don't know your learning style, take the test on pages 26–28.

👁 Visual

👂 Auditory

📖 Reading/writing

✋ Kinesthetic (movement)

⬛⬛ FOUR BASICS OF CLASSIFICATION

1. It makes sense of a group of people or things by sorting them into useful categories.
2. It has a purpose for sorting.
3. It includes categories that follow a single organizing principle (for example, to sort by size, by color, by price, and so on).
4. It gives detailed examples or explanations of things that fit into each category.

The FALLING in LOVE DIET

1 Over the past several years, three kinds of diets have been **2** very popular in this country. **3** The first one was the low-fat diet. **4** Dieters had to limit their fat intake, so they stayed away from foods like nuts, fatty meats, ice cream, and fried foods. They could eat lots of low-fat food like pasta, bread, fruits, and vegetables, as well as lean meat, fish, and chicken. **3** The second kind of diet was the low-carbohydrate plan. **4** The first popular low-carb diet was the Atkins plan. Under this plan, dieters could eat all the fatty meats, butter, cheese, and nuts they wanted. Some

FOUR BASICS OF WRITING/COLOR CODING (remember the number four: writing basics).   Chapter 8 (Developing Your Paragraph) shows nine useful ways to develop your ideas. Discussion of each method begins with a list of the four basic characteristics of that type of writing, followed by a color-coded example that demonstrates the four basics. Reviewing these examples as you write will help you learn how to structure your paragraphs or essays. The four basics are repeated in the reader (Unit Eight).

FOUR MOST SERIOUS ERRORS (remember the number four: most serious errors) Concentrate hard on the chapters in Unit Three. Avoiding the four (just four!) errors covered in this unit will definitely improve your writing.

"FIND AND FIX" CHARTS Visual charts throughout the grammar chapters show how to find and correct particular grammar errors in your own writing.

FIND: Read each sentence in your writing carefully, stopping at periods.

The groom sneezed ten times. (During) the wedding.

- Circle any preposition that begins a word group.
- In this word group, underline any subject and double-underline any verb.
- If a subject or verb is missing, or if there is not a complete thought, there is a fragment. The word group in this example is a fragment: It doesn't have a subject, a verb, or a complete thought.

⬇

FIX: Correct the fragment by connecting it to the sentence either before or after it. Or make the fragment into its own sentence.

The groom sneezed ten times,ᵈ During the wedding.

He interrupted the wedding vows.
The groom sneezed ten times. ~~During the wedding.~~

- If the prepositional phrase comes first, a comma must follow it.

During the wedding, the groom sneezed ten times.

CHAPTER REVIEW CHART   At the end of most grammar chapters, a final chart summarizes various ways to find and fix errors. Use these charts to review grammar issues and to edit your writing before turning it in for a grade.

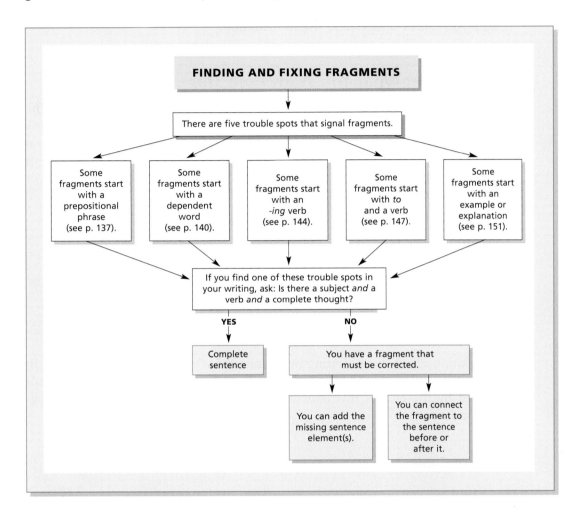

UNIT TESTS   Your instructor may assign the tests that are at the end of Units Two through Seven. Even if the tests aren't assigned, you should take them to make sure you understand the material covered in a unit.

LANGUAGE NOTES   These notes appear throughout the grammar chapters. Make sure to read them because they point out misunderstandings about grammar that cause many students to make mistakes.

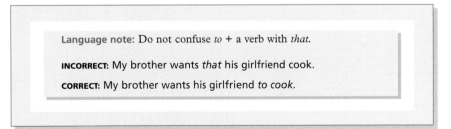

LEARNING JOURNALS   Each chapter ends with a Learning Journal prompt that asks you to write briefly about something you didn't understand in the chapter or to come up with a question that you would like to ask your teacher. These short writing assignments help you focus on areas where you need more help, either by reviewing part of the book or by asking your teacher.

MARGINAL PROMPTS IN READINGS   If you are using the version of the book with Unit Eight (Readings), notice that for each reading there are questions in the margins as well as questions at the end. The marginal questions help you understand the reading as you go along, so that you don't finish and realize you didn't understand the information.

How to Get What You Want from This Course

Aside from a good grade, what do you want to get from this course? Think about your writing, what teachers have told you about it, and what you think your main problems are. In the spaces below, first list what you think your three biggest writing problems are, being as specific as possible. For example, "grammar" is too big a problem; try to focus on a specific error you have been marked down for.

Writing Problems

_____

_____

_____

Now think about those writing problems and what you want to improve. In the spaces below, list three specific skills you want to have noticeably improved by the end of this course. Keep them in mind throughout the semester or term.

Course Goals

_____

_____

_____

_____

Unit One
Getting Off to a Good Start

1

Staying in College

Advice from Those Who've Been There

You may have many reasons for attending college, but here's one good reason for *staying* and graduating: Over a forty-year career, a college graduate is likely to earn about 73 percent more than someone with only a high school education (College Board, *Education Pays 2005,* October 2005).

But many students drop out, especially in their first year. In this chapter you'll meet five students who had doubts about whether to stay in college. The difficulties they faced may be similar to your own. All the students were the first in their families to attend college, and each of them needed to work while attending school. At some point, most of them dropped out of school temporarily. When they returned, they had a better idea of how to persist despite challenges.

VOCABULARY: Underline any words in this chapter that are new to you.

Meet the Students

Alessandra Cepeda

University of Massachusetts, Boston

I started college after high school, but money was an issue. After nine years, I returned to college.

DEGREES EARNED: A.A. and World Study Certificate, Bunker Hill Community College

CURRENTLY STUDYING: Psychology as a major and math as a minor

WANTS TO BECOME: A middle school math teacher

REASON FOR STAYING IN COLLEGE DESPITE THE PRESSURES: In college, I experienced new cultures, I developed my leadership abilities, and I helped my community.

ADVICE TO NEW STUDENTS: If you want to succeed in life, education and determination are the keys.

Marcus Aurelius De Volder

University of Arizona

I started college right after high school and hated it. After more than ten years, I returned for a second try.

DEGREES EARNED: A.A., A.S., Pima Community College

CURRENTLY STUDYING: Psychology

WANTS TO BECOME: A professional in the field of psychology

REASON FOR STAYING IN COLLEGE DESPITE THE PRESSURES: I started college after high school but dropped out and worked for several years at a good job. After being laid off, however, I knew I wouldn't get a comparable job without a college degree. I was offered a chance to go back to school, and I decided to see if it was something I wanted to do. I am very glad I went back. I wish everyone had the chance to attend college and get from it what I did. After receiving an associate's degree, I felt a pride I hadn't realized was missing.

ADVICE TO STUDENTS: Hold on tight. College is where you will learn the knowledge that will advance your career, any career. Don't be afraid to be laughed at. Ask the questions you need answered, no matter what they are. Finally, as Britain's former prime minister Winston Churchill said, "Never give in."

Mary Gallery

Baylor University

I took one year off after high school, then started college for a short time. After ten years, I started college again.

DEGREES EARNED: A.A., A.S., McLennan Community College

CURRENTLY STUDYING: Math

WANTS TO BECOME: A college math professor

REASON FOR STAYING IN COLLEGE DESPITE THE PRESSURES: Although work experience is valuable, it does not give you the edge in the workplace that a degree does. The fact that you have a degree shows potential employers that you have the ability to stay motivated, to maintain discipline, and to finish what you start. Realizing that I could never obtain the satisfying career or quality of life I desired without a degree was by far my greatest motivator to stay on task and get my first degrees. It continues to motivate me at Baylor.

ADVICE TO STUDENTS: Although many people may be supportive of you, you are the only one who can make your dream a reality. Never give up on yourself. Also,

- Make a chart that breaks your degree plan into semesters or some other digestible steps. Then, check off the steps as you complete them, making notes about what you've learned. It will give you great satisfaction to visualize your progress.

- Look outside of the box! Sometimes, resourcefulness will be your greatest tool. Tape lectures, and use the time you spend driving to work to listen to them. While waiting in the doctor's office, read your notes or assignments.

- Keep an open mind. You will probably have to adjust your study habits to fit the greater demands of college. Study with friends from your classes. Not only are friends a valuable resource in case you need to miss class, but they may also offer a different view or insight into difficult topics.

Irene Kabigting

City College of San Francisco

I started college but took a semester off after having a child.

DEGREES EARNED: None, yet

CURRENTLY STUDYING: Finance

WANTS TO BECOME: Chief financial officer for a company

REASON FOR STAYING IN COLLEGE DESPITE THE PRESSURES: After working for a very professional nonprofit organization, I've realized that the executives for this firm and many others that I've worked with have a degree, and I want to be an executive.

ADVICE TO STUDENTS: Worry more about your degree. The more seriously you take it, the sooner you'll be done, the sooner you will get to your dream career, and the more money you'll have.

Ricardo (Rick) Reyes

San Antonio College

I went from high school to the Marine Corps, where I served for twelve years. A back injury forced my retirement from the Marines and caused me to go to college to find a new career.

DEGREES EARNED: None, yet

CURRENTLY STUDYING: Art and history

WANTS TO BECOME: A high school teacher

REASONS FOR STAYING IN COLLEGE DESPITE THE PRESSURES: I gave my country my life for twelve years; now it's time for me to be selfish and earn my degree.

ADVICE TO STUDENTS: Study hard and earn your grades. In the long run, you will look back and be glad that you achieved a goal that many others are chasing!

Meet the Challenges

Alessandra, Marcus, Mary, Irene, and Rick came up with a list of the challenges they have faced in college. We present that list here for two reasons: to show you that you are not alone in feeling the pressure to drop out, and to alert you to obstacles that you may face as you work toward your degree. Knowing that these five students have stayed in school may help you stay as well.

Challenges Facing Students

FAMILY/PERSONAL ISSUES	SCHOOL ISSUES
Lack of (or difficulty keeping) child care	Poor performance in classes
Family violence	Not knowing how to study
Lack of support for college (Family members may think it's a waste of time.)	Feeling lost/overwhelmed
	Feeling alone/not fitting in
Personal health problems	**FINANCIAL ISSUES**
Sickness/neediness of family member	Not enough money to live on
Partner's loss of job	Lack of financial assistance
Inability to manage time	Time conflicts with work
Transportation problems	

Following are case studies of two students who are considering dropping out of college. The case studies blend the experiences of Alessandra, Marcus, Mary, Irene, Rick, and other students who have faced difficulties in college. Read the stories carefully, thinking about any experiences that are like your own.

Case Study: Tim Krader

Tim is twenty-seven years old and a first-year student at San Gabriel Community College. He started college right after high school but dropped out partway through the first semester to take a full-time job. He has returned to school because an injury prevented him from continuing in the job. Although Tim regrets losing his job, he now wants to finish college and teach history.

Excited to have a solid goal to pursue, Tim started the year very motivated. He now finds, though, that going to college is more challenging than he had thought, in a variety of ways. First, because he is older than many of his classmates, he doesn't have much in common with them. He is serious about his classes and wants to learn. In contrast, some of the younger students often skip classes or come in late and just waste time until the class ends. They don't do the work and blame the teacher when they fail tests or assignments. Tim hasn't made any friends and feels isolated.

He also lacks confidence. He's been out of school for a long time and isn't sure he can pick up what he used to know about being a student. Also, he's the first in his family to go to college, so he doesn't have anyone to give him advice or reassure him. His wife and children are supportive and proud of his decision to go back to school, but they don't really understand how much time it takes to do homework and to study. They feel neglected at times, and Tim feels guilty.

Tim has taken a part-time job, but he doesn't make as much as he did before, and money is really tight. He's not sure it's fair to his family to continue in this way, barely able to make it financially. Some months, he has had to overspend on his credit card to pay bills, even though he knows he won't be able to make the credit card payment and will therefore be charged high late fees. Then, last week, the family's car broke down, and repairing it will cost almost five hundred dollars.

Finally, there's the whole question of how to get everything done. Because of his injury, Tim has to see a doctor often, and he's in frequent pain, which makes many daily tasks difficult: driving, sitting in class, and concentrating on his schoolwork. Between medical appointments, school, work, and his family, Tim is just overwhelmed. He wants a degree and a good job, but staying in school is so hard he just doesn't know if he can do it—or even if it's worth the struggle. He is leaning toward dropping out, just for a while.

Case Study: Rosita Andrade

Rosita is nineteen and came to the United States from Brazil when she was nine. She graduated from high school a year ago and wants to become a nurse. She enrolled at Brickport Community College, where she is pursuing an associate's degree in nursing, after which she hopes to work part-time while studying to become a registered nurse. She wants to specialize in pediatric nursing.

Rosita and her one-year-old daughter live with Rosita's parents, her grandmother, and her brothers and sisters. Her parents think that going to college is a huge waste of time and money, and that Rosita should be concentrating on learning domestic skills, such as cooking, cleaning, and keeping a good home. Despite their opinions, Rosita is determined to be a nurse.

At college, Rosita quickly makes friends with other Latino students. She finds that many students seem to have their own, exclusive groups, and most seem confident about fitting in at college. Rosita isn't as confident, and many of her friends share her insecurities about being in college, studying, and getting good grades.

English is not her native language, and while she is doing fairly well in math, she is struggling in her other courses, especially English. The formal English her teacher expects is different from the way of speaking she is used to, and she's not good at grammar. Rosita is approaching the middle of her first semester, and her grades in most of her courses are not good.

On top of that, Rosita has a full-time job that takes her an hour to get to by public transportation. Between working, going to class, and taking care of her daughter, she can't find time to study. She tries to study after everyone else has gone to bed, but sometimes she's just too tired. Recently, she hasn't been able to sleep at all because she's so anxious about everything. She can't tell her family, though, since they already think school is a waste. She just doesn't see a way to fit everything in; plus, she's not even doing well. She's thinking that her family is right about college.

Use Problem Solving to Find Solutions

Fortunately, you can take certain steps to solve problems that are getting in the way of your success in college. Read the descriptions of each step and complete all the practices. Your instructor might want you to work in small groups.

Step 1. Identify the Problems

You may think you already know what your problems are. Sometimes, though, you can get a better understanding of your situation by thinking about each challenge you face and writing it down. Say your family thinks college is a waste of time *and* they won't help with child care; write these down as two separate problems.

> **PRACTICE 1**

List problems that you have that are similar to those listed in "Challenges Facing Students" (p. 6) and described in the case studies (pp. 6–8).

_____

_____

Add any other challenges you have in staying in school.

_____

_____

Step 2. Identify People and Resources That Can Help

Once you have identified the basic problems, think about who and what might help you solve them. Be creative, and identify as many possibilities as you can; you can always rule some out later.

PRACTICE 2 . . . .

In the left column of the following chart, the students profiled earlier in this chapter list some common challenges of college. On the right are people and resources that might help with each problem. Working with other students or on your own, suggest additional resources for the problems listed. Then, add problems of your own, drawing on ideas from Practice 1. Add resources for these, too. Don't forget to think about Web resources, either those that accompany this book (see **<bedfordstmartins.com/realskills>**) or those you can find by doing a search. For financial aid advice, see **<www.students.gov>** or **<www.finaid.org>**; for writing help, see **<www.nutsandboltsguide .com>** or **<www.bcc.ctc.edu/writinglab>**; and for advice on family problems, see **<www.uc.edu/psc/Family.html>**.

PROBLEMS/ CHALLENGES	PEOPLE/RESOURCES THAT MIGHT HELP
Poor performance in class(es)	• *A trusted teacher* • *An academic adviser or counselor* • *Students who are doing well* • *The tutoring center* • *Class notes* *Your ideas for help:* _____ _____
Money trouble	• *The financial aid office* • *The Internet (for information on scholarships and grants)* • *Work contacts* *Your ideas for help:* _____ _____
Time problems	• *Time management/study skills programs* • *Use of commuting time* • *Master schedules on Web sites, like those at <www.myfreecalendar.com>* *Your ideas for help:* _____ _____

PROBLEMS/ CHALLENGES	PEOPLE/RESOURCES THAT MIGHT HELP
Trouble with English language	• Units 3–7 and the "Language notes" in this book • Other resources accompanying this book Your ideas for help: _____ _____
Feelings of isolation	• Other students in class • A trusted teacher • College organizations • Mentors at school or work Your ideas for help: _____ _____
Health problems	Your ideas for help: _____ _____
Family pressures/ problems	Your ideas for help: _____ _____
Work problems	Your ideas for help: _____ _____
Other problems	Your ideas for help: _____ _____

Step 3. List Possible Solutions

Once you've identified resources to solve your problem, figure out exactly what you need to do to make the best use of the resources.

PRACTICE 3 . . . .

Working with other students or on your own, pick at least three problems from the chart in Practice 2 and write a solution for each using one or more of the resources from the right-hand column of the chart.

PROBLEM	POSSIBLE SOLUTION: WHAT I NEED TO DO
EXAMPLE: *Poor performance in classes*	*Make an appointment to talk with an instructor I feel comfortable with, like Professor Hills.*

. . . .

Step 4. Act

Even the best solutions won't help you if you don't act on them. Make a plan for following through on your ideas, and stick to it. If a solution that sounded great on paper doesn't work out, don't be frustrated—try another one until you succeed. Also, don't go it alone: find a partner to talk to. You and your partner can help each other stick to your plans.

PRACTICE 4 . . . .

Make a plan for acting on the solutions you came up with in the previous practice. In the left column, list the problems, and in the right column, list the actions that you will take over the next two weeks to carry out your solutions.

PROBLEM	ACTIONS TO TAKE, WHEN
EXAMPLE: *Poor performance in classes*	*Today, I will make an appointment to talk with Professor Hills.*
	Tomorrow, I'll ask Krystal if she'd like to study together once a week.
	By the end of this week, I will visit the tutoring center. (Call today to find out the hours and what I need to bring.)

PROBLEM	ACTIONS TO TAKE, WHEN
_____	_____
_____	_____
_____	_____

PRACTICE 5

On another piece of paper, write a commitment to yourself about staying in school: Why is it important? Why is it difficult? What will you do to try to continue your education without taking a leave? You can draw on ideas from the previous practices.

Include your telephone number and e-mail address, and exchange copies of your commitment with at least two people in class. If any of you miss more than one class in a row, contact that person. At the end of the semester, update your commitments, exchange the updated versions, and set a date when you will contact one another in the next semester.

Finally, these words from Alessandra, Marcus, Mary, Irene, and Rick:

Don't be a victim! Don't drop out without trying everything!

If we got through college, you can, too.

■ **TIP:** For good tips on time management, reading and study skills, and more, visit <www.sarc.sdes.ucf.edu/learningskills.html>.

Chapter Review

1. What are the four steps you can take to solve problems? _____

   _____

   _____

2. Which of the two case-study people did you relate to more? Why?

   _____

3. What resources will you use to address challenges you face?

   _____

■ **TIP:** For help with building your vocabulary, see Appendix B.

4. **VOCABULARY:** Go back to any new words that you underlined in this chapter. Can you guess their meanings now? If not, look up the words in a dictionary.

2

Doing Well in College

Strategies for Success

OUT with the OLD...

Get Organized with a Course Notebook

It is possible to get through high school without being organized; it is not possible to do so in college. Don't wait to get organized—the longer you put it off, the harder it will be. Many students stuff course materials into their pockets, backpacks, purses, or books, where they get crumpled or misplaced. Instead, get a three-ring binder to keep papers organized and in one place. The binders usually come with dividers that you can label. The table on page 14 shows one way you might organize your notebook, with suggestions for labeling the dividers. To tie the notebook more directly to your class, you might choose labels different from these. Two items that you should definitely include are the course syllabus and a course calendar.

If your instructor wants you to keep a journal, add a divider for your journal entries.

VOCABULARY: Underline any words in this chapter that are new to you.

Manage Your Time

You need to keep calendars to manage your time in college, work, and everyday life. There are two kinds of calendars that are particularly useful: a course calendar and a general calendar.

▪▪ FOUR BASICS OF USING CALENDARS FOR TIME MANAGEMENT

1. Make a calendar for each course and put it in the course notebook.

Suggested Organization for Your Course Notebook

DIVIDER/TITLE	CONTENTS
First divider: General Course Information	• Course syllabus and course/college policies (regarding absences, plagiarism, and so on) • List of student e-mail addresses • Other general course or college information
Second divider: Course Calendar	• A month-by-month schedule for course work (see p. 15 for an example)
Third divider: Class Handouts/Worksheets	• Any papers your instructor gives you
Fourth divider: Papers (If your instructor wants you to keep a portfolio of your work, you could title this divider "Writing Portfolio.")	• Drafts of papers • Revisions of papers • Comments from peer reviewers (Keep all of your drafts and revisions for the whole semester.)
Fifth divider: Tests	• All returned tests (Look back at returned tests to understand what you got wrong and to study for final exams.)
Sixth divider: Group Work	• Names, phone numbers, and e-mail addresses of group members • Written activities done as part of group work
Seventh divider: Notes	• Notes about lectures • Notes about readings • Notes about assignments • Notes about things you want to remember

MANAGEMENT LOOP

2. Keep a master calendar that has both course work and other life activities scheduled.

3. Check the calendars each day as part of your routine activities (over coffee, during a meal, or at some other regular time).

4. Update the calendars regularly and stick to them. If they don't work, figure out why.

Make a Course Calendar

A course calendar plots all the work you need to do for a course so that you can see what needs to be done, and when. Following is an example of a monthly calendar that you would put in the notebook for an English course.

English 098, Tuesday/Thursday, 8:30–10:00 a.m.
Professor Murphy
Office hours: T/Th, 11:00–12:30, and by appointment

		1	2	3	4	5
		8:30–10:00: Class. Draft due, illustration.	12:00: Study with Genie. Study for test on fragments (Ch. 11).	8:30–10:00: Class. Test, fragments.		Work on revising illustration.
6	7	8	9	10	11	12
	Read Ch. 13 of textbook.	8:30–10:00: Class.	11:30: Appt. at writing center.	8:30–10:00: Class. Final illustration due.		
13	14	15	16	17	18	19
	Study for test on subject-verb agreement (Ch. 13).	8:30–10:00: Class. Test, subject-verb agreement.		8:30–10:00: Class. 11:00: appt. with Prof. Murphy. Start description.		
20	21	22	23	24	25	26
	Read Ch. 14 of textbook.	8:30–10:00: Class. Draft due, description.		8:30–10:00: Class.	Work on revising description.	
27	28	29	30	31		
	Study for test on past-tense verbs (Ch. 14).	8:30–10:00: Class. Test, past-tense verbs.		8:30–10:00: Class. Final description due.		

You can make weekly calendars as well as monthly ones, and there are many good online calendars that you can download for free (see **<www.calendar.yahoo.com>**). Online calendars are particularly good because you can update them easily and neatly. If you use an online calendar, though, print out paper copies to keep in your notebook.

PRACTICE 1

Using your syllabus, make a calendar for the current month in this course. Make a copy of it that you will use in Practice 2.

Make a General Calendar

A course calendar helps you manage time for course work, but to keep track of everything you need to do in your life, you should also keep a general calendar that includes both your course work and every other commitment you have. Be sure to leave some unscheduled time for rest, fun, and unexpected events. Following is part of the calendar you just saw, with additional appointments and tasks filled in. The student who made the calendar is taking two courses, working, and caring for a two-year-old daughter, Lottie.

If you don't want to make two separate calendars, make one master calendar with all of your college, work, and everyday life commitments, and keep a copy in each of your course notebooks.

		1	**2**	**3**	**4**	**5**
12:00–6:00: Work.	8:00–4:00: Work.	8:30–10:00: English. Draft due, illustration.	8:00–4:00: Work.	8:30–10:00: English. Test, fragments.	8:00–4:00: Work.	Work on revising illustration.
7:00: Mom, dinner.	5:00: Pick up Lottie, day care.	12:00–6:00: Work.	12:00: Study with Genie.	11:00: Food shopping.	5:00: Pick up Lottie, get present for birthday party.	Clean, do laundry.
9:00: Illustration draft.	8:00–9:30: Study for math test.	7:00–10:00: Math. Test, Chs. 5–6.	4:30: Doctor. 5:30: Pick up Lottie.	12:00–6:00: Work.		6:00: Lottie to party.
			8:00: Study for English test, fragments. Math homework.	7:00–10:00: Math.		

PRACTICE 2

Using the copy of your course calendar from Practice 1, fill in the rest of your responsibilities and assign times.

Make the Most of Your Class Time

Use your time in class well. You are paying for college, so wasting time can mean wasting money. Following is some advice that has helped other students succeed in class.

FOUR BASICS OF USING CLASS TIME WELL

1. Go to every class, get there on time, and stay the entire period.
2. Sit near the front, where you are more likely to be involved.
3. Be an active participant (especially since many instructors grade partly on class participation).
4. **If there is something you don't understand, ask your instructor.**

■ **TIP:** For good tips on time management, reading and study skills, and more, visit **<www.sarc.sdes.ucf.edu/learningskills.html>**.

Improve Your Reading Skills

Good reading skills are essential to your success in college. This section will give you some strategies that will help you understand anything you read.

FOUR BASICS OF GOOD READING

1. Find the main point.
2. Find the support for the main point.
3. Highlight or underline, and make notes.
4. Review what you have read and written, and test your understanding.

Find the Main Point and Support

Identifying the main point and support in a reading is necessary to understand the author's message.

■ **TIP:** For more on main point and support, see Chapter 6.

Main Point

The **main point** of a reading is the major message that the writer wants you to understand. It is usually introduced early, so read the first few sentences (for a short reading) or paragraphs (for a longer reading) with special care. If the writer has stated the main point in a single sentence or a couple of sentences, highlight or double-underline those. You will remember the main point better if you write it in your own words, either in your notes or in the margin of the reading.

PRACTICE 3

Read the paragraph that follows and double-underline or highlight the main point. In the space after the paragraph, write the main point in your own words.

Congress often takes from the poor and gives to the rich, as members demonstrated recently. In December 2005, Congress approved budget cuts that shaved money mainly from Medicare,

Medicaid, and the federal student loan program. These programs serve those who are most needy, such as senior citizens, the poor, and students. Congress justified the cuts by saying that it needed to reduce the huge national deficit. A month later, however, huge tax cuts exceeding the budget cuts took effect, benefiting the most wealthy 20 percent of Americans. Do members of Congress think the average citizen is too stupid to understand what's happening? Our elected officials want us to believe that they are working for us, but they are really just helping themselves and their wealthy, powerful friends.

MAIN POINT: _____

_____

■ **TIP:** Many students find that reading aloud improves their understanding.

Support

The **support** in a reading is the information that shows, explains, or proves the main point. To understand the main point fully, you need to be able to identify the support. If you highlighted the main point, use a different color marker to highlight the support. If you double-underlined the main point, underline the support, perhaps using a different color pencil. Using different colors will help you when you review the material for class, a writing assignment, or a test.

PRACTICE 4

Reread the paragraph in Practice 3 and underline or highlight the three sentences that directly support the main point. Then, briefly state the support in your own words.

SUPPORT: _____

_____

_____

PRACTICE 5

Bring in a piece of writing with the main point and support underlined or highlighted in different colors. It can be an advertisement, an e-mail from a friend, a magazine or newspaper story, or anything you like.

When you have finished reading an assignment, review the parts you high-lighted or underlined and answer two questions:

1. What point does the author want me to "get"?
2. What does he or she say to back up that point?

If you can't answer these two questions, review the reading again. You need to know the answers to be able to participate in class discussion, do a writing assignment, or take a test.

PRACTICE 6 . . . .

Read the paragraphs that follow, highlighting or underlining the main point and the five sentences that most directly support the main point.

Consolidated Machinery offers excellent employee benefits, such as generous family leave programs and a menu of insurance plans. The family leave program offers paid two-week leaves to new parents, both mothers and fathers. These leaves are automatic, meaning that employees don't have to apply for them. Leave for new parents may be extended, without pay, for an additional four weeks. Employees may also apply for a one-week paid leave for a family emergency or a death in the immediate family. These leaves are part of what makes the company family-friendly.

The company also offers several insurance plans: two different HMOs[1] and several options of Blue Cross/Blue Shield. The company pays half of the insurance premiums for general health insurance. It also pays the entire cost of dental insurance for employees and their dependents. If employees would rather have child care benefits than dental benefits, they can put the money that would have gone to dental care toward day care. These programs are expensive, but Consolidated Machinery has found that the additional costs are more than covered by employee loyalty and productivity.

[1]HMOs: *Health maintenance organizations; health care plans that restrict patients to certain doctors to save costs.*

Know How to Read Textbooks

Textbooks have special features to help you understand what is important. Here are some common ones.

- ## Major Headings indicating main points.
- ### Smaller Headings signaling information that explains or supports the main points.
- *Even Smaller Headings* signaling more details about the main points.
- Words in **boldface** indicating important concepts or vocabulary.
- Notes in the margin, giving you extra information or advice to help you understand or find something.
- Charts, lists, and boxes presenting or reviewing important information.
- Checklists showing the important steps of a process.
- End-of-chapter summaries, reviews, or questions about key information in the chapter.

> **PRACTICE 7** . . . .

Working with a partner or by yourself, find the special features in Chapter 4 of this book, referring to the preceding list. List the features; then, answer the questions that follow.

FEATURES: _____

_____

_____

_____

1. What information is in lists? _____

_____

2. What are three major things Chapter 4 wants to explain? _____

_____

3. What features would you use to review Chapter 4? _____

_____

. . . .

After you have read and highlighted a textbook chapter, review your highlighting and write a few notes, in your own words, about what is important. Also, note what you do not understand and ask your instructor about it. This kind of reading takes some time, but it will help you learn the content and will save you lots of time when you are studying for a test: All you have to do is review your highlighting and your notes, and read any end-of-chapter reviews. The extra time you spend will help you get a better grade. Again: **If there is something you don't understand, ask your instructor!**

Take Careful Notes in Class

At the start of every class, write the date at the top of a fresh piece of note-paper and take careful notes throughout the class, writing clearly so you can read what you've written later. After class, put your notes for the day in the "notes" section of your course notebook.

The most important part of taking notes in class is listening carefully for what is important. Don't try to write down everything your instructor says, or you won't be able to listen well. Instructors often give clues about what is most important. Here are some things to listen for:

- "There are three (or some other number) important points here."
- "It is significant that . . ."
- "Remember, . . ."
- "What's important about this is . . ."
- "Listen carefully, because this is important."
- "You need to know that . . ."
- "This will be on the test."
- "First, . . ." "Second, . . ." "Finally, . . ."
- "For example, . . ." "For instance, . . ."
- "Let me explain."

You should also write down the following:

- Things your instructor writes on the board.
- Any answers to which the instructor responds, "That's exactly right!" or "Good answer!"
- Any answers an instructor gives to a question that he or she has com-plimented by saying, "That's a very good question!"

■ **TIP:** You might find it helpful to use abbreviations or symbols as you take notes, like *ex* for *example*, + for *and*, and *bc* for *because*.

EXAMPLE OF CLASS NOTES

2/2/07

Pronouns (Ch. 17)

> *replace nouns in sentences*
> *ex: Carrie loves Mr. Big. ~~Carrie~~ makes bad decisions about men.*
>   *She*
> *(She = pronoun)*
> *have to agree in number (??) I don't understand what this means. <u>ASK</u>*
> *<u>subject pronouns</u>: subject of sentence (I, we, you, he, she, it, they, who)*
> *ex: <u>They</u> went to the game.*

object pronouns: receive action or part of prep. phr. (me, us, you, him, her, it, them, whom)

ex: Tommy gave them tickets.

Isaiah went with them.

At the end of class, or later on the same day, read your notes. Then, highlight or underline the points that you think are most important so that they will be easy to review when you are studying for a test. You can also use asterisks (*) or stars to mark the most important points.
If there is something you don't understand, ask your instructor!

PRACTICE 8

Take careful notes during the next class. Then, exchange notes with another student to compare what each of you wrote. Talk about the differences, and ask your instructor about anything that you both don't understand.

Know How to Take Tests

Many students do poorly on tests because they do not listen to or read the directions carefully. Make sure you know what you're supposed to do.

FOUR BASICS OF TAKING TESTS

1. Listen to spoken directions.
2. Survey the whole test before starting, and budget your time.
3. Read the written directions carefully.
4. **If there is something you don't understand, ask your instructor!**

Because taking tests is so important, Appendix A of this book provides a longer discussion of how to succeed on tests, including advice on how to answer various types of questions.

Listen to Spoken Directions

When you receive a test, listen to what your instructor says about it before you begin. Your instructor may give you important information about the test that is not written anywhere. He or she might tell you whether you can use a dictionary or calculator, or point out corrections in test questions or instructions.

Survey the Whole Test before Starting

Before you begin, look over the whole test to see what kinds of questions it has and how much each item is worth. Then, figure out how much time you will spend on each section and plot a strategy. Start with easy questions you can answer quickly, but leave enough time to do the harder questions that are worth more points. Also, try to leave enough time to do a final check of your work. For an example of a student's time budget for a test, see Appendix A.

Read the Written Directions Carefully

Each part of a test has its own directions that you must read carefully. Underline or highlight the words that tell you what to do, as shown in the following examples.

1. Read three of the paragraphs and change all the present-tense verbs to the past tense, making other changes that the past tense requires.
2. In each of the following sentences, write the correct form of a verb in each blank. Choose from the list of verbs at the start of the section.
3. Choose one of the following topics and outline an answer, writing a complete topic sentence, three major support points, and examples of each major support point.
4. Read the following paragraphs and underline any errors. Then, write the correction above the error. There are five errors.
5. Rewrite each of the following topic sentences, making at least two improvements. Then, explain what you did and why.

Think Critically

In all college courses, instructors expect you to think about the content and question it rather than just remembering and repeating it. This ability to think carefully and ask questions is called **critical thinking**. Asking questions is the mark of an intelligent, responsible person. And in college and other situations, asking the right questions will help you learn more about any subject—and about yourself. It will also help prevent you from being taken advantage of.

When approaching a college subject, or an important policy or other communication at work or in daily life, ask the following questions.

■■ FOUR BASIC CRITICAL THINKING QUESTIONS
1. Do I understand the message or point?
2. Do I agree with it?
3. What does it mean to me?
4. How does it relate to other things I am studying, have learned, or have experienced?

> **PRACTICE 9** . . . .
>
> Apply the critical thinking questions to something important in your life,
> such as a school or work policy or document, or something that a partner or
> friend has said. Write your answers on a separate piece of paper.
>
> . . . .

Chapter Review

1. Where will you get your course notebook? What dividers will you use for
   this class? _____

2. What is the difference between a course calendar and a general calendar? _____
   _____
   _____ Have you ever kept either kind? Will you use a
   paper or an online calendar? _____

3. Which of the Four Basics of Using Class Time Well do you have the most
   trouble with? Why? What can you do to change your behavior?
   _____

4. What are the Four Basics of Good Reading? _____
   _____
   _____

5. List five common features of textbooks. _____
   _____
   _____

6. What are the Four Basics of Taking Tests? _____
   _____
   _____
   _____

7. What is critical thinking? _____
   What are the Four Basic Critical Thinking Questions? _____

8. **VOCABULARY:** Go back to any new words that you underlined in this chapter. Can you guess their meanings now? If not, look up the words in a dictionary.

■ **TIP:** For help with building your vocabulary, see Appendix B.

3

Understanding Your Learning Style

Ways to Use Your Strengths

VOCABULARY: Underline any words in this chapter that are new to you.

People learn in different ways, and knowing how you learn best will help you succeed in college. This chapter has a questionnaire that will tell you what your learning style is. It then suggests ways to use that style in your college classes.

Find Your Learning Style

■ **TIP:** To complete the questionnaire online and get automatic results, visit <www.vark-learn.com>.

For each item on the following questionnaire, circle the answer that is *most* like what you would do. There are no right or wrong answers.

VARK QUESTIONNAIRE ON LEARNING STYLES

1. You are about to give directions to a friend who is staying in a hotel in town and wants to visit you at home later. She has a rental car. Would you
   a. draw a map for her?
   b. tell her the directions?
   c. write down the directions (without a map)?
   d. pick her up at her hotel?

2. You are not sure whether a word is spelled *dependent* or *dependant*. Would you
   c. look it up in a dictionary?
   a. see the word in your mind and choose it by the way it looks?
   b. sound it out in your mind?
   d. write both versions on paper and choose one?

3. You have just planned a great trip, and your friend wants to hear about it. Would you

   b. phone him immediately and tell him about it?

   c. send him a copy of the printed itinerary?

   a. show him on a map of the world?

   d. share what you plan to do at each place you visit?

4. You are going to cook something as a special treat for your family. Do you

   d. cook something familiar without a recipe?

   a. look at the pictures in a cookbook for ideas?

   c. look for a particular recipe in a cookbook?

5. Your job is to help a group of tourists learn about parks in your state. Would you

   d. drive them to a park?

   a. show them slides or go to a Web site that has pictures?

   c. give them some booklets on parks?

   b. give them a talk on parks?

6. You are about to buy a new CD player. Other than price, what would most influence your decision?

   b. the salesperson telling you what you want to know

   c. reading about it in a consumer magazine

   d. trying it out at the store

   a. it looks very cool

7. Recall a time when you learned how to do something, like playing a board game. Try to avoid using a physical skill like riding a bike. How did you learn best? By

   a. looking at pictures, diagrams, or charts.

   c. reading written instructions.

   b. listening to somebody explaining it.

   d doing it or trying it.

8. You have a knee problem. Would you prefer that the doctor

   b. tell you what is wrong?

   a. show you a diagram of what is wrong?

   d. use a model to show you what is wrong?

9. You are about to learn to use a new computer program. Would you

   d. sit at the keyboard and play with the program's features?

   c. read the manual?

   b. phone a friend and ask questions about it?

10. You are staying in a hotel and have a rental car. You would like to visit friends whose addresses/locations you don't know. Would you like them to

   a. draw you a map?

   b. tell you the directions?

    c. write down the directions (without a map)?

    d. pick you up at the hotel?

11. Aside from price, what would most influence your decision to buy a particular kind of textbook?

    d. the fact that you used a copy before

    b. a friend talking about it

    c. quickly reading parts of it

    a. the way it looks (color, photographs, and so on)

12. What would most influence your decision to go see a new movie?

    b. You heard a review of it on the radio.

    c. You read a review of it.

    a. You saw a preview of it.

13. You prefer a teacher who uses

    c. textbooks, handouts, readings.

    a. diagrams, charts, and slides.

    d. field trips, labs.

    b. discussions, guest speakers.

Now, count how many *a*'s you circled and write that number in the blank beside the *V* (visual) below. Put the number of *b*'s you circled beside the *A* (auditory), put the number of *c*'s you circled beside the *R* (read/write), and put the number of *d*'s you circled beside the *K* (kinesthetic). Circle the letter next to your highest score. This is your strongest learning style. If you have two scores that are the same, that just means that you have two equally strong learning styles, as many people do.

__ **V** 👁 Visual

__ **A** 👂 Auditory

__ **R** 📖 Read/write

__ **K** 👣 Kinesthetic (movement)

Use Your Learning Style in College

To figure out how to apply your learning style in college, look at the following sections and read the one that matches your style. If you have a preference for more than one learning style, read all the sections that apply. Note the symbols that will be used throughout the book for your learning style.

Visual

Visual learners learn best by drawing, looking at images, or "seeing" things as they read, write, and listen. Visual activities in this book are indicated by the symbol 👁 .

Using Your Learning Style	
To read/study →	• Draw pictures or diagrams of concepts. • Use colored highlighters to mark what you want to remember. • Note headings in texts, and look at diagrams, charts, graphs, maps, pictures, and other visuals. • Write symbols that mean something to you in the margins. (For example, write exclamation points by the most important information in a chapter.) • Make your own flowcharts or time lines. • Make outlines in different-colored inks.
To write →	• Use mapping or clustering to get ideas. (See p. 44.) • Use charts or outlines to plan, write, and revise. (See Chapter 8.) • Use correction symbols to edit. (See the symbols at the back of this book.)
To take a test →	• Highlight important information, or put checks or other symbols by it. • Make a flowchart or outline of your answers.

Support for Your Learning Style in This Book

Look for the 👁 symbols to find activities related to your learning style. Also, note
  • Information in boxes, charts, and diagrams.
  • Color-coded sentence parts in Unit 3.
  • Find and Fix charts throughout the grammar chapters.
  • Illustrations of writing and grammar concepts.
  • References to audiovisual tutorials in electronic supplements.

Auditory

Auditory learners learn best by hearing things. Auditory activities in this book are indicated by the symbol .

Using Your Learning Style	
To read/study →	• Read aloud notes, texts, handouts, and so on. • Tape lectures and class discussions (but don't forget to take notes, too). Later, you can listen to the recordings. • Listen to course-related audio CDs or tapes. • Talk to other students about course material.

	• Work with other students to prepare for class, complete activities, and so on.
To write →	• Get ideas by talking to yourself or others.
	• Read your writing aloud as you draft.
	• Read your writing aloud as you revise and edit.
To take a test →	• Read the directions and test items aloud in a quiet whisper.
	• Read your answers aloud in a quiet whisper.

Support for Your Learning Style in This Book

Look for the 🎧 symbols to find activities related to your learning style. Also, note

- Read Aloud prompts that encourage you to say and hear information.
- References to audiovisual tutorials in electronic supplements.

📖 Read/Write

Read/write learners learn best by reading and writing throughout a course. Read/write activities in this book are indicated by the symbol 📖.

📖 Using Your Learning Style

To read/study →	• Read headings, summaries, and questions in books.
	• Put what you read into your own words.
	• Take careful notes from books and lectures, and read them later.
	• Keep and read all handouts.
	• Highlight when you read.
	• Describe charts, diagrams, maps, and other visuals in writing.
To write →	• Freewrite or brainstorm to get ideas. (See pp. 43–44.)
	• Keep a journal. (See p. 45.)
	• Read and reread what you write, making notes for revision.
	• Revise your writing several times.
To take a test →	• Read and highlight the directions.
	• Write an outline for essay questions, or write quickly and revise.
	• Reread your answers carefully.

Support for Your Learning Style in This Book

Look for the 📖 symbols to find activities related to your learning style. Also, note

- Headings and boldfaced information.
- Written instructions and lists.
- Writing prompts.
- Chapter reviews.

Kinesthetic (Movement)

Kinesthetic learners learn by doing and by moving around. Kinesthetic activities in this book are indicated by the symbol .

Using Your Learning Style	
To read/study →	• Stand up when you read or study.
	• Take short breaks and walk around.
	• Underline or highlight readings, or make notes—do something.
	• Make flash cards to study course material.
	• Make puzzles, like crosswords, to help you remember important concepts.
	• Make your own study guides.
	• Relate information to your own experiences.
	• Mark examples in texts that are relevant to you.
	• Write out questions that you have and ask them.
	• Work with other students to prepare for class, complete activities, and so on.
To write →	• Imagine your topic as a movie to get ideas.
	• Think of ideas for writing as you walk.
	• Imagine what pictures could express your ideas.
	• Write ideas or details for a paper on sticky notes, and move the notes around.
	• Create a writing notebook with different pockets for different kinds of ideas or writing.
	• Write and ask questions about your topic.
To take a test →	• Breathe deeply and regularly throughout the test.
	• Stand up and walk to a different part of the room (after asking your instructor for permission).
	• Calculate the time you will spend on each part of the test, and time yourself.
	• Stand and take a deep breath as you review your answers.

Support for Your Learning Style in This Book

Look for the symbols to find activities related to your learning style.

Chapter Review

1. What is your strongest learning style? If you have two that are about equally strong, list both. _____

2. Review the section(s) you read on using your learning style in college. Without looking back at the material, write down two ways to apply your learning style in the following tasks.

To read/study: _____

To write: _____

To take a test: _____

■ **TIP:** For help with building your vocabulary, see Appendix B.

3. **VOCABULARY:** Go back to any new words that you underlined in this chapter. Can you guess their meanings now? If not, look up the words in a dictionary.

Unit Two
Writing Paragraphs

4

Understanding the Basics of Good Writing

How to Write in College and Other Formal Settings

College writing requires formal English, just as certain occasions require formal dress.

Understand the Basics of Good Writing

Good writing has four basic features.

📖 **VOCABULARY:** Underline any words in this chapter that are new to you.

▪▪ FOUR BASICS OF GOOD WRITING

1. It considers the readers (the audience).
2. It achieves the writer's purpose.
3. It includes a main point.
4. It has details that support the main point.

Audience and Purpose: Getting What You Want from Your Words

Your **audience** is the person who will read what you write. When you write, always have a real person in mind as a reader. Think about what that person knows and what he or she needs to know to understand the point you want to make.

👁 Draw the audience for something you wrote recently.

Your **purpose** is your reason for writing. In college, and often at work, your purpose is to show something, to explain something, or to convince someone.

What you say and how you say it may be very different for two different audiences or purposes. Suppose you had a bad morning and were late for work. In an e-mail to a friend, you might tell what happened in a humorous and informal way. But an e-mail to your boss explaining why you were late would be more formal and serious. For example, read the two e-mails that follow.

JAKE'S E-MAIL TO A FRIEND

> **PURPOSE: TO INFORM AND ENTERTAIN**
>
> Out late last nite, good time!! Late for work again. Caught my toe on a corner and it was ugly like a melon with a toenail. No shower, ugly there 2. One clean shirt but ript it. Had 2 find a stapler 2 hold together. Then roadwork!!!! So late, gotta get a good story together for the bossman. He got no humor, ya no?

JAKE'S E-MAIL TO A BOSS

> **PURPOSE: TO EXPLAIN LATENESS AND AVOID GETTING INTO TROUBLE**
>
> Mr. Janus,
>
> I apologize for being late today, and I owe you an explanation. As I was getting ready to leave this morning, I injured my toe, and it swelled up right away. I had to ice it until it would fit inside my shoe. I was only a little late leaving my house, but then traffic on Hastings Road was down to one lane because of construction. This slowed traffic and made me late. I would have called, but my cell phone was dead. I can make up the time I missed by not taking lunch today. Thank you for your consideration.

As these examples show, we speak to our friends differently than we speak to people in authority (like employers or instructors)—or we should. We also speak to our children, our parents, and other audiences in different ways. Jake's e-mail to his friend uses **informal English** (like *2* instead of *to* and *bossman*) because friends can be casual with each other and because his purpose is just to inform or entertain. In contrast, Jake's e-mail to his boss, a person in authority, uses **formal English** (with a serious tone and correct grammar and spelling) because the relationship is more formal. Also, the purpose is serious: to avoid getting into trouble.

In college, at work, and in everyday life when you are speaking or writing to someone in authority for a serious purpose, use formal English. Otherwise, you won't achieve your purpose, whether that is to pass a course, to get and keep a good job, or to solve a personal problem (like being billed on your credit card for a purchase you didn't make or reporting a landlord who doesn't turn on your heat). Formal English gives you power in these situations, so it is important to know how to use it. This book will give you practice in writing and speaking formal English and also in hearing it so that it sounds right to you.

PRACTICE 1 . .

Working in a small group, list three situations in each setting where you would use formal English. Do not repeat the examples presented earlier.

COLLEGE: _____

WORK: _____

EVERYDAY LIFE: _____

■ **TIP:** For more practice with writing for a formal audience, see the editing exercises at the end of Chapters 10–15, or visit Exercise Central at <bedfordstmartins.com/realskills>.

PRACTICE 2 . .

The following description of an evening's activities was written by a young man who is away at college to his grandmother (his audience), who is older and very traditional. She worries that the people he's meeting at school could have a bad influence on him. His purpose is to reassure her that he's having a positive experience.

Read the description and rewrite it as if the young man were writing to his best friend, whom he wants to make laugh. Have fun.

> **Last night, I went out with a group of new friends. First, we had a good dinner, and then we went to another place to continue our discussion. I had a very good time and am happy to have such nice new friends to spend an evening with.**

READ ALOUD

Stand and read your rewritten descriptions to the rest of the class. Vote on which is the funniest.

Main Point and Support

Your **main point** is what you want to get across to your readers about a topic or situation. In college, instructors usually expect you to state your main point in a sentence. You may also include main-point statements in writing you do at work. Here is the main-point statement in Jake's e-mail to his boss (p. 36):

> I apologize for being late today, and I owe you an explanation.

You back up such statements by providing **support**: details that show, explain, or prove your main point. In Jake's e-mail, the support consisted of the reasons he was late: He injured his toe, and then he ran into a construction delay during his commute. Providing enough support for your main point helps you get your ideas across and makes sure you are taken seriously.

■ **TIP:** For more on main point and support, see Chapters 2 and 6.

Understand What a Paragraph Is

A **paragraph** is a short piece of writing that presents a main point and supports it. A paragraph has three parts:

1. A **topic sentence** that states your main point.
2. **Body sentences** that support (show, explain, or prove) your main point.
3. A **concluding sentence** that reminds readers of your main point and makes an observation.

Here is an example of a paragraph:

Indentation marks start of paragraph

Topic sentence with main point

Body sentences with support

Concluding sentence

> Although they didn't exist a few years ago, blogs, short for *Web logs,* are now an important part of many people's lives. There are thousands of blogs on as many topics as you can think of. The topics range from cars to entertainment to medicine to important national and international events. Many people use blogs as diaries, to record their opinions, feelings, and whatever they feel like saying. Others use blogs as a source of news, instead of reading newspapers or watching television news. People visit blogs before buying things to learn what others think about certain products and their prices. Want to find out what others think about a DVD? You can probably find any number of blogs on the subject. Blogs have exploded in current culture, and new ones appear every minute. If you haven't visited a blog, give it a try, but be careful: You might get completely hooked, like the ten million people who write and read blogs every day.

READ ALOUD

Stand and read the example paragraph.

Paragraphs can be short or long, but for this course, your instructor will probably want you to have at least three to five body sentences in addition to your topic and concluding sentences. When you write a paragraph, make sure that it includes the following basic features.

FOUR BASICS OF A GOOD PARAGRAPH

1. It has a topic sentence that includes the main point the writer wants to make.
2. It has detailed examples (support) that show, explain, or prove the main point.
3. It is organized logically, and the ideas are joined together so that readers can move smoothly from one idea to the next. (See Chapter 7 for more details.)
4. It has a concluding sentence that reminds readers of the main point and makes a statement about it.

Understand the Writing Process

The following chart shows the basic steps of the **writing process**—the stages you will move through to produce a good piece of writing. It also shows the parts of this book where you can get more information on each step.

GET IDEAS (See Chapter 5.)

- Find and explore your topic (prewrite).

WRITE (See Chapter 6.)

- State your main point (topic sentence).
- Give details to support your point (support).
- Make an outline of your ideas.
- Write a draft.

REWRITE (See Chapter 7.)

- Reread your draft, making notes about what would make it better.
- Rewrite your draft, making changes you noted (and more).
- Reread the new draft, making sure it is as good as you can make it.

EDIT (See Units 3–7.)

- Read your paper for grammar, punctuation, and spelling errors.

Practice Together

Working with a few other students, practice what you have learned in this chapter.

1. Each group member should write an informal note to a friend about something that happened in this or another class recently. It should be at least five sentences long. Then, exchange papers with a group member and rewrite his or her note so that it addresses a parent or grandparent. If you have time left, give examples of the changes you made, and explain why you made them.

2. A coworker has cleaned up his or her workspace. With your group members, create a dialogue with the coworker in which you praise or criticize

LEARNING STYLES: Look for activities in this chapter that are matched to your learning style. If you don't know your learning style, take the test on pages 26–28.

👁   Visual

🎧   Auditory

📖   Reading/writing

👣   Kinesthetic (movement)

the cleanup. Pick two members to read the dialogue aloud in front of the class.

3. Were you ever in an accident? Share accident stories in your group, and choose the most interesting storyteller to be interviewed in front of the class by a volunteer "reporter." The storyteller's group should tell the class how the story and the language used to tell it changed from the original telling to the interview.

4. With your group, pick a paragraph from this book or another available text. Then, draw a diagram of a sandwich on a piece of flip-chart paper, with a top and bottom bun and room in the middle for fillings. Take turns "making a sandwich" from the paragraph by writing the main point on the top bun, the support points where the fillings should go, and the concluding sentence on the bottom bun.

5. A friend calls just as the scene shown in the following photo appears on TV. Each group member should write a description of the scene that will make the friend laugh. Then, take turns reading the descriptions aloud. Which is the funniest?

Chapter Review

1. What is the word for the person or people who read your writing?

   _____ Highlight this word where it first appears in this chapter.

2. What is *purpose* in writing? _____

3. In your own words, explain what formal English is and why it is important. _____

_____

_____

4. In the most recent piece of writing you did (in college or not), who was your audience and what was your purpose? _____

_____

5. Label the topic sentence, body sentences, and concluding sentence in the following paragraph.

   The full moon affects many people in strange ways. For example, people who get migraine headaches often find out that the headaches started on the morning after a full moon. In hospitals for the criminally insane, doctors and nurses make note of an upcoming full moon because the patients often become much more violent at that time. To avoid problems, the hospitals take special precautions and increase security. Hospital emergency rooms also report an increase in the number of accident victims during a full moon. There are many opinions about why a full moon affects people in odd ways, but we do know that it is not just a symbol of romance; it is also a time of great stress for many.

6. **VOCABULARY:** Go back to any new words that you underlined in this chapter. Can you guess their meanings now? If not, look up the words in a dictionary.

■ **TIP:** For help with building your vocabulary, see Appendix B.

5

Narrowing and Exploring Your Topic

How to Decide What to Write About

Narrow Your Topic

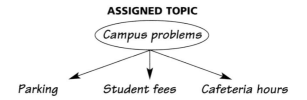
VOCABULARY: Underline any words in this chapter that are new to you.

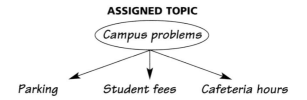
IDEA JOURNAL: Write about some things you care about in life.

Your **topic** is what you are going to write about. Often, instructors assign a general topic that you need to make more specific so that you can write about it in a paragraph or short essay. To **narrow** a topic, break it into smaller parts that interest you.

ASSIGNED TOPIC

Campus problems

Parking   Student fees   Cafeteria hours

PRACTICE 1 . . . .

Choose three of the following general topics and, on a separate sheet of paper, write three narrower topics for each one. Then, select the narrowed topic that interests you most and write it in the space provided.

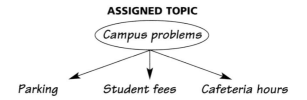
You may want to diagram the topics, as in the "campus problems" example.

Any issue you care about	Someone you admire
Being a single parent	Something you do well
A campus problem	Something you enjoy

A class you enjoyed   Something you fear

Family traditions   Stresses on students

A favorite time of day   Worries about college

A personal goal   Your best subject in school

NARROWED TOPIC THAT INTERESTS YOU MOST: _____

· ·

Explore Your Topic

To get ideas to write about, use the **prewriting techniques** described in
the following sections. Writers rarely use all the techniques shown here, so
choose the ones that work best for you after you have tried them out. Use a
prewriting technique to get ideas at any time during your writing: to narrow or explore your topic or to add details and explanations after you have
begun writing a paragraph or essay.

The examples in the rest of this chapter show a community college
student, Patti Terwiller, using different prewriting techniques to get ideas
about the topic *a lesson I learned*. She narrowed her topic to *how I learned
self-respect*.

Freewrite

Freewriting is like having a conversation with yourself on paper.
Just start writing about your topic, and continue nonstop for
five minutes. Don't worry about how you write or whether your
ideas are good. Just write.

> *Got tired of my boyfriend pushing me around, making all the decisions, not
> caring what I thought. Just let it happen because I wanted to keep him.
> Mean to me, rude to friends, late or didn't show up. Borrowed money. At a
> party he started hitting on[1] someone else. Told him I had to go home.
> Before that, let him get away with stuff like that. He said no just wait baby.
> Something snapped and I got home on my own. He's history[2] and I'm kind
> of sad but it's okay.*

[1]**hitting on:** *approaching another person with romantic
intentions (slang)*

[2]**history:** *part of the past
(slang)*

You can also have a
conversation with yourself
aloud. Think about your topic
for a moment and then talk
through some of your ideas,
recording them on tape or on
computer.

PRACTICE 2 ·

Freewrite about your narrowed topic from Practice 1.

· ·

👁 Draw a picture of a story you want to tell, or illustrate some of your ideas.

Brainstorm

Brainstorming is listing all the ideas you can think of without worrying about how good they are. You can brainstorm by yourself or by talking to others. Again, here's Patti Terwiller on her narrowed topic, *how I learned self-respect*.

> *Always tried to please everyone, especially my boyfriends*
> *Thought everything was fine*
> *Thought love was about keeping guys happy, not myself*
> *Always got dumped anyway, couldn't figure it out*
> *Finally I just blew up, I don't really know what happened*
> *Glad it did*
> *My boyfriend was surprised, so was I*
> *He had no respect for me at all, I didn't respect myself*
> *My friends all told me but I never listened*
> *That party everything changed*
> *Never again*

Map or Cluster

To map, or cluster, write your narrowed topic at the top or in the center of a page. Then, write ideas about the topic that occur to you around or under your narrowed topic—anything you can think of. As details about those ideas come to you, write those around or under the ideas.

PRACTICE 3 . . . .

Using either a blank sheet of paper or the mapping form at the back of this book or online (at **<bedfordstmartins.com/realskills>**), create a map or cluster to explore your narrowed topic from Practice 1.

. . . .

Keep a Journal

Set aside a regular time to write in a journal. You can keep your journal on a computer or in a notebook or other small book. Write about

- Your personal thoughts and feelings.
- Things that happen to you or to others.
- Things you care about but don't really understand.

Real Skills has two kinds of journal assignments. **Idea journals**, near the start of chapters, give you ideas that you might turn into papers later. **Learning journals**, at the end of chapters, prompt you to write for one minute about the information in the chapter.

PRACTICE 4 . . . .

Each day over the next week, write at least ten lines about your narrowed topic in a journal. At the end of the week, reread what you have written and write a few sentences about it.

. . . .

Use the Internet

The Internet can be a great source of ideas. Type your narrowed topic into Google or another search engine. Visit some of the sites that come up and write down any new ideas you get about your topic. Or visit a blog (meaning *Web log,* a kind of Web journal) related to your topic, and write down ideas. For links to different types of blogs, try Blogcatalog.com—go to its home page and click on the Browse tab to find a list of categories.

IMPORTANT NOTE ABOUT THE INTERNET AND WRITING: The Internet is a re-source for all kinds of things, including papers that you can download and turn in as your own. It's tempting, but doing so is called *plagiarism* and is one of the worst errors you can make in college. Students who plagiarize may be given a failing grade automatically or may even be suspended or dismissed from college. Also, keep in mind that most instructors are expert in detecting plagiarism, and many are using the Internet and software tools to do so, so don't take the risk.

> **PRACTICE 5** . .
>
> Use the Internet to get ideas for your topic. Save sites that interest you by using the "bookmark" or "favorites" feature in the browser you use to view the Internet.

■ **LEARNING STYLES:** Look for activities in this chapter that are matched to your learning style. If you don't know your learning style, take the test on pages 26–28.

👁 Visual

🗣 Auditory

📖 Reading/writing

👣 Kinesthetic (movement)

By now, you should have some good ideas about your narrowed topic. You will use them in the next chapters as you write your own paragraph.

Practice Together

Working with a few other students, practice what you have learned in this chapter.

1. Pick a topic that you all agree on and write it on the board. (It can be one of your narrowed topics from Practice 1.) Then rotate to another group's topic and write down three ideas about it. Keep rotating until you get back to your topic. What ideas would you use? 🗣 📖 👣

2. To write about the topic *annoying habits*, pick several habits and then decide which is most annoying; write this habit on the top of a piece of paper: that is your narrowed topic. Then, each student should use a method of prewriting that he or she likes and come up with some ideas about the topic. As a group, review all of the ideas and agree on ten that you would use in a paper about that annoying habit. 🗣 📖

3. Agree on a television or movie character that you like or dislike. Use mapping to say why you like or dislike the character. Or draw a cartoon of the person. You can use word or thought balloons to show things about the person that you like or dislike. 👁

4. Look around and agree to write about one thing you can all see. One person should go to the board and write down the group's ideas about how to describe the object to someone who is not in the room. 👁 👣

5. Write about what the woman in the photo on the left is feeling and what might have happened to her. Or write about a time when you had this same expression on your face. Before you begin, start by listing some ideas. Then, circle the ones that you

think are best. Read what you have written to other members of your group. Or imagine another expression, draw it, and write about what caused it. 👁 ✍ 📖

Chapter Review

1. How can you narrow a topic? _____

2. Which prewriting technique worked best for you? Why?

   _____

3. **VOCABULARY:** Go back to any new words you underlined in this chapter. Can you guess at their meanings now? If not, look up the words in a dictionary.

📖 **LEARNING JOURNAL:** Write for two minutes about which prewriting techniques you liked or disliked using and whether the ones you liked helped you get ideas.

■ **TIP:** For help with building your vocabulary, see Appendix B.

6

Writing Your Paragraph

How to Put Your Ideas Together

📖 **VOCABULARY:** Underline any words in this chapter that are new to you.

📖 **IDEA JOURNAL:** Write about a time you wanted to convince someone but didn't. What did you want to convince the person of?

■ **TIP:** The main point of an essay is the thesis statement. For more information, see Chapter 9.

Make a Point

Every piece of writing should have some point. Your **topic sentence** presents that point, and is usually the first or the last sentence of the paragraph. In this book, the examples will have the topic sentence first. Many people find that putting the topic sentence first helps them set up the rest of the paragraph.

In the following paragraph, the topic sentence (main point) is underlined.

<u>Caring for my first accident victim as a student nurse was the toughest job I ever had.</u> A young mother, Serena, had been admitted to the intensive care unit after her car collided head-on with a truck. She had suffered a head injury, a collapsed lung, and a broken arm. I knew that my supervisor, a kind and highly skilled nurse, would be with me the whole time, but I was afraid. I'd never assisted with a patient who was so severely injured. After Serena was wheeled into the ICU, the medical team began working on her immediately. While the doctor and senior nurses gave Serena blood and administered other care, I managed the medical pumps and kept a detailed record of everything that was being done to help her. In the end, we stabilized Serena, and my supervisor complimented me for being so calm and responsible. I'll never forget how hard that time was, but it gave me confidence that I carry into every new day at work.

One way to write a topic sentence is to use the following basic formula:

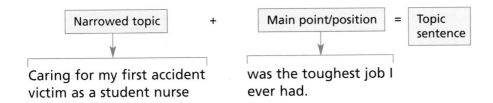

| Narrowed topic | + | Main point/position | = | Topic sentence |

Caring for my first accident victim as a student nurse   was the toughest job I ever had.

If you have trouble coming up with a main point about your topic, look back over your prewriting. For example, to write her topic sentence, Patti Terwiller, the student introduced in Chapter 5, reviewed her prewriting about how she learned self-respect (see pp. 43–45). She realized that the lesson she learned through a painful experience with her boyfriend could be applied to all of her relationships. Here is her topic sentence:

I finally learned self-respect in relationships.

PRACTICE 1

Reread the prewriting you did in Chapter 5. What is the point that you want to make about your narrowed topic? Think about why the topic interests you or is important to you.

POINT YOU WANT TO MAKE ABOUT YOUR NARROWED TOPIC: _____

> Pair up with another student, and read your prewritings aloud. Talk about what points each of you might want to make.

A good topic sentence has four necessary features.

FOUR BASICS OF A GOOD TOPIC SENTENCE

1. It has a single main point stated in a sentence.
2. It is something that you can write about in a paragraph, not too broad or too narrow.
3. It is something that you can say something about, not a simple fact.
4. It is a confident statement, not weak or starting with *I think, I hope,* or *In this paper I will.*

> Read aloud all the Four Basics lists in this chapter.

TWO MAIN POINTS   Daily exercise can keep the mind alert, and eating right aids weight loss.

[How could the writer cover this in only one paragraph?]

REVISED   Daily exercise keeps the mind alert.

TOO BROAD   Sports are popular in every culture.

[How could the writer cover this in only one paragraph?]

TOO NARROW	Basketball is popular at my gym.
	[What else is there to say?]
REVISED	Playing a team sport has taught me important lessons.
SIMPLE FACT	Fashions change every year.
	[What else is there to say?]
REVISED	Two of last year's hot fashions are now "out."
WEAK	Until students get real benefits for the activity fees they pay, I think that the college should lower these fees.
	[*I think* weakens the statement.]
REVISED	Until students get real benefits for the activity fees they pay, the college should lower these fees.

PRACTICE 2 . . . .

Review the Four Basics of a Good Topic Sentence on page 49. Then, read the following topic sentences and, to the left of each, write the number of the basic that is missing. Be ready to say why you chose a certain number.

> **EXAMPLE:** __4__ I think that video games help people in some ways.

— 1. Video games take mental skill, and they are coming down in price.

— 2. The census[1] is taken every ten years.

— 3. There are many religions in this world.

— 4. The Christian religion

— 5. In this paper, I hope to show that Wal-Mart hurts small businesses.

[1]census: *a regular population count*

PRACTICE 3 . . . .

Decide whether each of the following sentences is too broad or okay, and write *B* (broad) or *OK* in the space to the left of the sentence. Think about whether you could write a good paragraph about the sentence. Rewrite any that are too broad.

> **EXAMPLE:** __B__ I like programs on Comedy Central.
>
> **REWRITE:** On Jon Stewart's *The Daily Show*, news is entertaining.

— 1. People love their pets.

— 2. Colleges offer many different kinds of degree programs.

— 3. My grandmother saved things that most people would have thrown out.

___ 4. I love all kinds of food.

___ 5. Donald Trump is entering into a new venture: online higher education.

PRACTICE 4 . . . .

Narrow each of the following topics. Then, circle the one that interests you most and write a possible topic sentence for it.

EXAMPLE:

TOPIC: Favorite pastimes

NARROWED: (movies)   walking   cooking

TOPIC SENTENCE: *I enjoy seeing movies because they take me out of my every-*

day life.

1. **TOPIC:** Things you're good at

   NARROWED: _____

   TOPIC SENTENCE: _____

2. **TOPIC:** Benefits of an education

   NARROWED: _____

   TOPIC SENTENCE: _____

3. **TOPIC:** Difficulties you have overcome

   NARROWED: _____

   TOPIC SENTENCE: _____

. . . .

Here, again, is student Patti Terwiller's topic sentence:

> **TOPIC SENTENCE:** I finally learned self-respect in relationships.

After rereading her topic sentence and prewriting, Patti thought of a way to make the sentence more specific.

> **REVISED:** One evening in May, I finally learned to practice self-respect in my relationships.

PRACTICE 5 . . . . . .

Using your narrowed topic from Chapter 5 (Practice 1, p. 42) and the point you want to make about it (Practice 1 of this chapter), write a topic sentence. Your first try may not be perfect, so review the Four Basics of a Good Topic Sentence (p. 49), and rewrite the topic sentence to make it clearer, more specific, or more confident.

NARROWED TOPIC: _____

TOPIC SENTENCE: _____

REWRITTEN: _____

. . . .

Support Your Point

You might think that you don't have much power or choice in your writing, but you do. To make sure that people see things your way, provide good **support**: detailed examples that show what you mean.

In the paragraph on page 48, the support consists of the events that happened on the day that the student nurse cared for her first accident victim. The events show how important the day was for the writer's growth as a nurse.

▪▪ FOUR BASICS OF GOOD SUPPORT

1.   It relates to your topic sentence.
2.   It tells your readers what they need to know to understand your point.
3.   It uses details that show, explain, or prove your main point.
4.   The details don't just repeat your main point; they explain it.

READ ALOUD

Read the following two paragraphs, which start with the same topic sentence. They were addressed to a financial aid officer by a student seeking tuition assistance.

> Financial aid is key to my goal of getting a college degree. My family can't help me. I have worked, but I don't have enough money to pay tuition. If I can get financial aid, I know that I will succeed in college because I will work very hard. Going to college is very important to me, but I will not have enough money without financial aid.

> Financial aid is key to my goal of getting a college degree. I am the oldest of six children, and although my mother works two jobs to support us, she cannot help me with tuition. My mother did not graduate

from high school, but she has always made us work hard in school so that we could go to college and have a better life. Like my mother, I have worked two jobs through high school to save for college, but they both pay the minimum wage, and my savings will not cover tuition. If I can get financial assistance, I know that I will succeed in college. Even with two jobs, I have maintained good grades. It has not been easy, but I am very motivated. I often get only three hours of sleep per night, but that's worth the sacrifice if I can achieve my dream of getting a college degree. I will continue to work hard, and I know from experience that hard work pays off. Financial aid will not be wasted on me.

PRACTICE 6 . . . .

1. Why is the second paragraph more convincing? _____
   _____

2. What details does the second paragraph give that the first doesn't? ____
   _____
   _____

3. What impression from the writer do you have from the first paragraph?
   From the second paragraph? _____

4. Why is the second paragraph more likely than the first to result in a financial aid offer? _____
   _____

. . . .

Putting yourself in the role of the reader helps you make sure that you provide support that will appeal to him or her. The second paragraph provides details that are likely to make the financial aid officer more understanding of the writer's situation.

The main support that you provide for a topic sentence is known as **primary support**. Good writers also provide **details** about the primary support to help readers understand the main point.

Patti Terwiller reread her prewriting and did some more to get additional details about her story. Then, after rereading her topic sentence, she chose the support points that most clearly explained her main point, numbering them according to when they happened. After each point, she wrote in additional details.

IDEA JOURNAL: What would you say about yourself if you were applying for financial aid?

■ **TIP:** Try prewriting to get detailed examples that support your point. See Chapter 5 for details.

[2]put up with: *to tolerate*

> **TOPIC SENTENCE:** *One evening in May, I finally learned to practice self-respect in my relationships.*
>
> **PRIMARY SUPPORT POINT 1:** *Used to put up with*[2] *anything to keep my boyfriend happy.*
>
> **DETAILS:** *He could be late, or drunk, or rude, and I'd put up with it. Could call me names around his friends or ignore me, and that was okay. I just wanted to keep him.*
>
> **PRIMARY SUPPORT POINT 2:** *One night at a party, he was ignoring me as usual, but then something happened.*
>
> **DETAILS:** *He started making out with another girl. Something inside me snapped—knew I didn't need this.*
>
> **PRIMARY SUPPORT POINT 3:** *I spit in his face and walked out.*
>
> **DETAILS:** *He was screaming, but I didn't look back, and I didn't answer his calls.*

PRACTICE 7

Write three primary support points for each of the following topic sentences. Then, pick one of the topics and write two supporting details for each primary support point. You may want to use a separate sheet of paper.

1. _____ (fill in yourself) is an important role model for me.

    _____

    _____

    _____

2. An important lesson I have learned is _____ (fill in yourself).

    _____

    _____

    _____

3. _____ (fill in yourself) is the most important thing in the world to me.

    _____

    _____

    _____

PRACTICE 8 . . . .

On a separate sheet of paper, write your topic sentence from Practice 5 and three or four primary support points. Then, add at least two supporting details for each primary support point. Try prewriting to get ideas, and choose the ideas that show or explain your main point most effectively.

. . . .

Make a Plan

Once you have your topic sentence and support points, you are ready to write, but it's easier to write if you have a plan, or outline. As you make an outline, try to shape your support into sentences.

In the following outline, Patti turned her primary support and supporting details into complete, separate sentences. Notice also how Patti changed some of her support as she made her outline. All along as you write, you can change what you want to say if you come up with better ideas or words.

I. **TOPIC SENTENCE:** *One evening in May, I finally learned to practice self-respect in my relationships.*

   A. **SUPPORT SENTENCE 1:** *I always put up with anything my boyfriend did because I was afraid he might leave me.*
      1. **DETAILS:** *He was always late and drunk. I never said anything.*
      2. **DETAILS:** *He never had any money, and around his friends he ignored me or was totally rude.*

   B. **SUPPORT SENTENCE 2:** *At a party, he was ignoring me, as usual, but then something happened.*
      1. **DETAILS:** *Right in front of me, he was coming on to[3] another girl.*
      2. **DETAILS:** *I could feel something inside me snap.*

   C. **SUPPORT SENTENCE 3:** *I knew I didn't need this.*
      1. **DETAILS:** *I spit in his face.*
      2. **DETAILS:** *Then, I walked out. He was screaming, but I didn't look back. I haven't answered his calls.*

---

[3]**coming on to:** *showing romantic interest in (slang)*

Sometimes, it is useful to outline writing that you have already done. This gives you a quick, visual way to see if you have too many details for one support sentence but not enough for another.

■ **TIP:** For more advice on organizing your ideas, see Chapter 7.

PRACTICE 9 . . . .

Write an outline of your paragraph using Patti's as an example.

. . . .

Write a Draft

Working with your outline, you are ready to write a first draft of your paragraph. Write it in complete sentences, using the details you have developed to support your topic sentence. Include your topic sentence and a concluding sentence.

You will have as many chances as you want to make changes in your draft. The important thing now is to make sure that you express your ideas in full sentences, in paragraph form.

▪▪ FOUR BASICS OF A GOOD DRAFT

1. It has a topic sentence and a concluding sentence.
2. The first sentence, often the topic sentence, is indented.
3. The paragraph has complete sentences that start with capital letters.
4. It has details that show, explain, or prove the main point.

A **concluding sentence** is the last sentence in the paragraph. It reminds readers of the main point and makes a comment based on what is in the paragraph. Do not just repeat your main point.

Notice how the topic sentence and concluding sentence from the paragraph on page 48 are connected:

TOPIC SENTENCE: Caring for my first accident victim as a student nurse was the toughest job I ever had.

CONCLUDING SENTENCE: I'll never forget how hard that time was, but it gave me confidence that I carry into every new day at work.

In her concluding sentence, the writer reminds readers that the job was difficult but makes a new point about the experience: It gave her confidence.

    PRACTICE 10 . . . .

Read the following two paragraphs and write a concluding sentence for each.

1. A good mentor can mean the difference between success and failure. Fortunately for me, I found a good one in Professor Robinson. He was my English teacher during my first year in college, and without him, I would not have lasted. After four weeks of classes, I was ready to drop out. I was not doing well in my course work, and I was exhausted from working, going to class, and trying to do homework. Because he seemed like he cared about his students, I went up to him after class and told him I was leaving school. I said I'd try again later. Professor Robinson asked me to come to his office, where we talked for over an hour. He said he would help me in his class, and he would arrange a meeting with my other teachers, too. He also said that I should go to the tutoring cen-

ter for free extra help. He urged me to stay until the end of the semester and then decide whether or not to leave. I got lots of extra help from some of my teachers, and I was surprised that they were willing to spend so much time with me. I also made friends at the tutoring center, and we began to help each other out. I am proud to say that I stayed and passed all of my courses.

CONCLUDING SENTENCE: _____

_____

2. Even the best doctors can't know everything these days. There are so many people around the world publishing so many new medical findings that no one could ever hope to keep up with them all. I learned about doctors' limitations when my daughter was not responding to medication for her asthma. I went onto the Internet, to Webmd.com, and found many useful links. I printed out the information and called my daughter's pediatrician. I was afraid he would be offended that I had been questioning my daughter's treatment. But he wasn't at all; he was pleased that I had found new studies and possible medications. He seemed to respect me, not just as the parent but as someone who could do research to help my daughter.

CONCLUDING SENTENCE: _____

_____

_____

· ·

READ ALOUD

Listen carefully as you or another student reads Patti's draft paragraph. Notice how she made changes from her outline, including adding a concluding sentence.

> One evening in May, I finally learned to practice self-respect in my relationships. I had always put up with anything my boyfriend did because I was afraid he might leave me. He was always late and drunk, but I never said anything. He never had any money, and around his friends he either ignored me or was totally rude. At a party, he was ignoring me, as usual, but then something happened. Right in front of me, he was hitting on another girl. Something inside me snapped, and I knew I didn't need this. I spit in his face and walked out. He was screaming, but I didn't look back. I haven't answered his calls; he's history. I have learned about self-respect.

PRACTICE 11 . .

On a separate piece of paper, write a draft paragraph. Use your outline as a guide, but make any changes that you think will improve your draft, including adding more details and changing your topic sentence or concluding sentence.

Practice Together

LEARNING STYLES: Look for activities in this chapter that are matched to your learning style. If you don't know your learning style, take the test on pages 26–28.

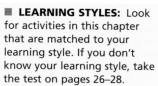 Visual

 Auditory

 Reading/writing

Kinesthetic (movement)

Working with a few other students, practice what you have learned in this chapter.

1. Agree on something that is a problem on campus, and write a topic sentence: _____ is a huge problem on this campus. Then, discuss examples of the problem. List these examples and agree on three or four that best support your point. Together, write a paragraph that includes the topic sentence, the best support, and a concluding sentence.

2. Each group member should draw an unusual hat. Then, the group should choose one drawing as the most unusual and discuss the details that make it so strange. Agree on three or four of the details and write them down. Together, write a paragraph that describes the most unusual hat, including the details.

3. As a group, pick a paragraph (perhaps one from this chapter). Then, each person should draw a picture of the paragraph, labeling its parts. When you're done, compare drawings. How are they similar or different?

4. Choose a group member to write a topic sentence on the board. Then, move to another group's topic sentence and write a supporting statement under it. Continue rotating and adding support until you come back to your own group's topic sentence. Discuss the support with your group. What other support might you add? What might you drop?

5. Contrast two ways of life. You can use the picture on the left or choose two other groups that you are familiar with (city residents/country residents, young people/old people, males/females). As a group, come up with examples of each group's way of life. Then, have each person write a paragraph contrasting the groups, using the examples for support.

Chapter Review

1. Using the headings in this chapter, list the steps in writing a paragraph.

2. What is a topic sentence? Highlight the answer in this chapter.

3. What are some words that can weaken your topic sentence? _____

    _____

4. What is support in writing? Highlight the answer in this chapter.

5. What is the point of making a plan? _____

    _____

6. What is a concluding sentence, and what should it do? Highlight the answers in this chapter.

7. **VOCABULARY:** Go back to any new words that you underlined in this chapter. Can you guess at their meanings now? If not, look up the words in a dictionary.

LEARNING JOURNAL: Write for two minutes, completing and explaining this sentence: When I went to write my paragraph, I _____.

■ **TIP:** For help with building your vocabulary, see Appendix B.

7

Improving Your Paragraph

How to Make It the Best It Can Be

Understand What Revision Is

Revision means "re-seeing." When you revise, you read your writing with fresh eyes and think about how to improve your support. You also try to order and connect your ideas in a way that makes your meaning clear to readers.

◼️ **FOUR BASICS OF REVISION**

1. Take a break from your draft (at least a few hours).
2. Get feedback (comments and suggestions) from someone else.
3. Improve your support, deciding what to add or drop.
4. Make sure your ideas are ordered and connected in a way that readers will understand.

The rest of this chapter focuses on steps 2–4.

Get Feedback

Getting feedback from a reader will help you improve your first draft. Also, giving other people feedback on their writing will build your own understanding of what good writing is.

Exchanging papers with another student to comment on each other's writing is called *peer review*. Although it may feel awkward at first, that feeling will wear off as you give and get more peer review.

Use the following questions to get and give feedback. Although peer review may be done in writing, it is best to work face-to-face with your partner so that you can discuss each other's comments and ask any questions.

QUESTIONS FOR A PEER REVIEWER

- What is the main point (topic sentence)?
- Is there enough support for the main point? Where could there be more support?
- Do any parts seem unrelated to the main point?
- Are there places where you have to stop and reread something to understand it? If so, where?
- Could the concluding sentence be more forceful?
- What do you like best about the paper?
- Where could the paper be better? What improvements would you make if it were your paper?
- If you were getting a grade on this paper, would you turn it in as is?
- What other comments or suggestions do you have?

■ **TIP:** Peer review guides for different kinds of papers are available at <bedfordstmartins.com/realskills>.

Improve Your Support

Peer comments will help you see how you might improve your support. Also, underline the examples you use to support your point, and ask: Are there any examples that don't really help make the point? What explanations or examples could I add to make my writing clearer or more convincing?

To practice answering these questions, read what a seller posted on Craigslist.com about her iPod:

> The silver iPod Mini I am selling is great. I need an iPod with more memory, but this is very good. I got it for Christmas, and it was a great gift. It is lightweight and in good condition because it is fairly new. It holds a charge for a long time and can hold a lot of iTunes. It comes with the original case. The price is negotiable. This is a great deal! Contact me for more details.

PRACTICE 1 . . . .

Working with another student or students, answer the following questions.

1. What is the seller's main point? _____

2. Underline the one sentence that has nothing to do with the main point.

3. Circle any words that do not provide enough information. List three of these terms and say what details would be useful.

_____

_____

_____

■ **TIP:** The following are three good online writing labs: <owl.english.purdue.edu>, <web.missouri.edu/ ~writery>, and <grammar.ccc.commnet .edu/grammar>.

4. Rewrite the seller's main point/topic sentence to make it more convincing.

_____

_____

PRACTICE 2 . . . .

Read the two paragraphs that follow and underline the sentence that does not relate to the main point.

¹service learning: *education that combines course work and community service*

1. Service learning¹ provides excellent opportunities for college students. While students are helping others, they are learning themselves. For example, a student in the medical field who works at a local free clinic provides much-needed assistance, but he is also learning practical skills that relate to his major. He learns about dealing with people who are afraid, who don't know the language, or who are in pain. He might meet someone he likes. When he has to write about his experience for class, he has something real and important to write about. And for many students, working for an organization provides a strong sense of community and purpose. Students have as much to gain from service learning as the organizations they work for.

2. Before choosing roommates, think about your own habits so that you find people whom you can stand living with. For example, if you regularly stay up until 1:00 a.m., you probably shouldn't get a roommate who wants quiet at 10:00 p.m. If you are very sloppy and like it that way, don't live with people who demand that you wash every dish every day or clean up after yourself every morning. Cleaning is one of those chores that most people hate. If you want to share all expenses, think about how you will handle discussions on how money should be spent. How much do you want to spend every month, and on what kind of things? Roommates are great for many reasons, but only if you can live with them.

PRACTICE 3 . . . .

To each of the five sentences, add two sentences that give more details.

EXAMPLE: Modern life is full of distractions.

E-mails and instant messages demand our attention.

Even bathrooms and grocery carts have advertising.

1. _____ (your favorite music group) creates music that has an important message.

_____

_____

2. _____ (your favorite sport) is the most exciting sport today.

_____

_____

3. Every family has unique traditions that they carry on from one generation to the next.

_____

_____

4. Fast-food restaurants are not completely unhealthy.

_____

_____

5. One person's junk is another person's treasure.

_____

_____

Check the Arrangement of Your Ideas

After you have improved your support by cutting sentences that do not relate to your main idea and adding more details and examples, check that you've ordered and linked your ideas in a way that readers will understand. This process is called improving your writing's **coherence**.

There are three common ways to organize ideas: by time order, space order, and order of importance. Each of these arrangements uses words that help readers move smoothly from one idea to the next. These words are called **transitions**.

Time Order

Use **time order** to present events according to when they happened, as in the following paragraph. Time order is useful for telling stories.

READ ALOUD

Read the following paragraph aloud, paying attention to the order of ideas and words that link one idea to the next.

Michael Jackson's trial was a spectacle that dragged on for almost four months and involved more than 140 witnesses. First, the

²**prosecution:** *a person or group taking legal action against someone else*

³**testimony:** *evidence; reports*

⁴**pedophilia:** *sexual activity with children*

prosecution² presented its case, calling witnesses who gave testimony³ that made Jackson seem guilty of horrible acts of pedophilia.⁴ During this time, Jackson seemed like a monster, with each witness adding to the negative picture. After the prosecution finished presenting its case, the defense began. The witnesses for the defense, including several Hollywood stars, painted a very different picture. Their Jackson was a kind, generous man who loved children in a healthy way. After all the witnesses were done, the jury had to decide which was the real Jackson: child molester or unfairly persecuted star? Finally, after seven days of deliberation, the jury found Jackson not guilty on all counts, ending a trial that had become a circus.

The paragraph describes the order of events in the trial, moving from the prosecution to the defense to the jury decision. Time transitions move the reader from one event to the next.

Circle the time transitions in the paragraph on Michael Jackson.

Time Transitions

after	finally	next	soon
as	first	now	then
before	last	second	when
during	later	since	while

PRACTICE 4 . . . .

In each item in this practice, the first sentence begins a paragraph. Put the rest of the sentences in the paragraph in time order, using 1 for the first event, 2 for the second event, and so on. Be ready to explain why you ordered the sentences the way you did.

EXAMPLE: The annual sale of designer bridal gowns at the bridal warehouse was about to start, and the atmosphere was tense.

_5_ The women ran to where their favorite designers' items were displayed and threw as many dresses as they could hold into one another's arms.

_2_ Groups planned their strategy for when the doors opened.

_3_ As the guard approached to open the doors, the crowd pushed forward to get inside.

_1_ Hundreds of women crowded outside of the door two hours before opening time.

_4_ When the doors opened, the women flooded in, holding onto others in their group so they wouldn't be parted.

1. Edward VIII, King of Britain, gave up his throne in 1936 after what was considered scandalous behavior.

___ Their relationship was a problem because the British constitution did not allow royals to marry divorced individuals.

___ After he gave up the throne, Edward became Duke of Windsor, and he and Wallis were free to marry.

___ Edward fell madly in love with Wallis Simpson, a commoner and an American divorcée.

___ After the marriage, the couple lived most of their lives in France.

___ Edward and Wallis were so in love that Edward gave up his throne in order to marry her.

2. Sally Ride, one of the first American woman astronauts, was very qualified for the job.

___ In 1978, she was accepted into the astronaut training program, one of only thirty-five selected from the eight thousand applicants.

___ Later, at Stanford University, she earned four degrees.

___ To become an astronaut, she had to undergo very difficult physical training.

___ Born in 1951, she was a star junior tennis player.

___ In 1983, she became the first American woman to orbit Earth.

. . . .

Space Order

Use **space order** to present details in a description of a person, place, or thing.

READ ALOUD

Stand and read the following paragraph aloud, paying attention to the order of ideas and words that link one idea to the next.

> Thirteenth Lake in the Adirondacks of New York is an unspoiled place of beauty. Because the law protects the lake, there are no homes on it, and only nonmotorized boats like canoes and kayaks are allowed. I often just sit at the end of the lake and look out. In front of me, the water is calm and smooth, quietly lapping against the shore. Near the shore, wild brown ducks, a mother

leading a line of six or seven adorable ducklings, paddle silently, gliding. Farther out, the water is choppy, forming whitecaps as the wind blows over it. On each side are trees of all sorts, especially huge white birches hanging out over the water. From across the water, loons call to each other, a clear and hauntingly beautiful sound. Beyond the lake are mountains as far as the eye can see, becoming hazier in the distance until they fade out into the horizon. I find peace at Thirteenth Lake, always.

The paragraph describes what the writer sees, starting near and moving farther away. Other ways of using space order are far to near, top to bottom, and side to side. To move readers' attention from one part of the lake to another, the writer uses space transitions.

Circle the space transitions in the paragraph on Thirteenth Lake.

Space Transitions		
above	beyond	next to
across	farther	on the side
at the bottom/top	in front of	over
behind	in the distance	to the left/right/side
below	inside	under
beside	near	

PRACTICE 5

The first sentence of each item below begins a description. Put the phrases that follow it in space order, using 1 for the first detail, 2 for the second details, and so on. There can be more than one right order for each item. Be ready to explain why you used the order you did.

EXAMPLE: **The apartment building I looked at was disgusting.**

_1_ trash scattered all over the front steps

_3_ boarded-up and broken windows

_4_ tattered plastic bags waving from the roof

_2_ front door swinging open with no lock

1. For once, my blind date was actually good-looking.

___ tanned, muscular arms

___ flat stomach

___ long, straight brown hair

___ dark brown eyes and a nice smile

___ great legs in tight jeans

2. As the police officer drove toward the accident site, she made note of the scene.

___ another police car stopped on the right, in the breakdown lane

___ another car in the middle of the road, its smashed hood smoking

___ two cars spun off to the left, between the northbound and southbound lanes

___ witnesses standing to the right of the police car, speaking to an officer

. . . .

Order of Importance

Order of importance builds up to the most important point, putting it last. When you are writing or speaking to convince or persuade someone, order of importance is very effective.

READ ALOUD

Stand and read the following paragraph aloud, paying attention to the order of ideas and words that link one idea to the next.

The Toyota Prius is definitely the next car I will buy because it is affordable, safe, and environmentally friendly. A new Prius costs a little over $20,000, which is reasonable for a new car. I cannot afford a new Prius, but the model has been out for several years, so I can buy a used one for somewhere between $14,000 and $16,000. I will need to get a car loan, but it will be a good investment. More important than the price is the safety record of the Prius, which is good. *Consumer Reports* rates the car as very safe. Most important to me, however, is that it is a "green" car, making it better for the environment than a regular car. It runs on a combination of electric power and gasoline, which means that it gets higher gas mileage than cars with standard gasoline engines. On the highway, the 2006 Prius gets fifty-one miles a gallon, and in the city the mileage is about forty-four miles per gallon. Because I believe that overuse of gasoline is harmful to the environment, I want to drive a car that does the least harm.

The paragraph states the writer's reasons for wanting to buy a Prius. He ordered the reasons according to how important they are to him, starting with the least important and ending with the most important. Transitions signal the importance of his ideas.

In the paragraph on the Prius, circle the transitions that indicate importance.

Importance Transitions

above all	more important	most
best	most important	one reason/another reason
especially	another important	worst

> **PRACTICE 6** . . . .

The first sentence of each item below begins a paragraph. Put the sentences that follow it in order of importance, using 1 for the first detail, 2 for the second detail, and so on. There can be more than one right order for each item, although the most important detail should be last. Be ready to explain why you used the order you did.

EXAMPLE: **Making at least one friend at college is important for several reasons.**

_4_ There is someone who makes you feel a part of the college community.

_1_ There is someone to sit with and talk to.

_3_ There is someone to work with to study material.

_2_ There is someone to give you assignments you miss.

1. Laughter is a great thing.

___ It's fun to have fun.

___ Laughter reduces built-up stress and releases tension.

___ It's important to see the humor in life.

___ People who laugh regularly live longer.

2. Executive salaries in this country are out of control.

___ Often, executive salaries are not tied to a company's performance.

___ In the United States, the average salary of CEOs[5] of big companies is more than a hundred times the average worker's.

___ In Japan, CEOs' salaries are about ten times higher than workers'.

___ High executive salaries and poor company performance can lower workers' salaries and benefits and even lead to job losses.

[5]**CEOs:** _chief executive officers—leaders of corporations_

Even if you are not using time, space, or importance orders, use transitions to link your ideas. The following are some other ways to use transitions:

PURPOSE	TRANSITIONS
To give an example	for example, for instance, for one thing/ for another, one reason/another reason
To add information	also; and; another; in addition; second, third, and so on
To show contrast	although, but, however, in contrast, instead, yet
To indicate a result	as a result, because, so, therefore

Check for the Four Basics of a Good Paragraph

When you revise your draft, check that it has these basic features.

▪▪ FOUR BASICS OF A GOOD PARAGRAPH

1. It has a topic sentence that includes the main point the writer wants to make.
2. It has detailed examples (support) that show, explain, or prove the main point.
3. It is organized logically, and the ideas are joined together so that readers can move smoothly from one idea to the next.
4. It has a concluding sentence that reminds readers of the main point and makes a statement about it.

Read student Patti Terwiller's draft paragraph, which you first saw in Chapter 6. Then, read the revised draft with her changes. The colors in the revised paragraph, matched to the Four Basics of a Good Paragraph, show how she used the basics to revise. Notice that most of Patti's changes involved adding detailed examples (the words in red). She also added transitions (underlined), especially time transitions, since her paragraph is organized by time order. She also crossed out words or phrases she didn't like.

PATTI'S DRAFT

> One evening in May, I finally learned to practice self-respect in my relationships. I had always put up with anything my boyfriend did because I was afraid he might leave me. He was always late and drunk, but I never said anything. He never had any money, and around his friends he either ignored me or was totally rude. At a party, he was ignoring me, as usual, but then

continued

something happened. Right in front of me, he was hitting on another girl. Something inside me snapped, and I knew I didn't need this. I spit in his face and walked out. He was screaming, but I didn't look back. I haven't answered his calls; he's history. I have learned about self-respect.

PATTI'S REVISED DRAFT

One hot, steamy evening in May, I finally learned to practice self-respect in my relationships. I had always put up with anything my boyfriend did because I was afraid he might leave me. He was always late and drunk, and he was often abusive, but I never said anything. He never had any money, and around his friends he either ignored me or was totally rude, calling me disrespectful names and cursing at me. At a party in May, he was ignoring me, as usual. ~~but then something happened~~ Then, right in front of me, he ~~was hitting on~~ started seriously kissing another girl. Next, they were all over each other. And then, my boyfriend smirked right at me. Something inside me snapped. ~~and I knew I didn't need this.~~ I felt my blood rush to my face, and a powerful pressure in my chest roared up and exploded. I gritted my teeth for a moment, holding back the force. Then, I narrowed my eyes, spit right in his face, and hissed, "No way." As I ~~walked~~ stormed out, he was screaming to me, but I didn't look back. Since that night, I haven't answered his calls or believed his sweet-talking messages. ~~he's history.~~ I have learned I don't need him or anyone like him who doesn't treat me right. What I do need is self-respect, and now I have it.

> **PRACTICE 7** ·

With a partner, read the first and revised drafts aloud. Talk about why the revised draft is better, and be specific. For example, don't just say, "It has more examples." Discuss why the examples make Patti's experience come alive. Then, answer the following questions.

1. What emotions was Patti feeling? _____

   What words showing those emotions are in the revised draft but not in the first draft? _____

_____

2. What sentence describes what her boyfriend did to anger her the most?

_____

3. What two sentences do you think have the most emotion? _____

_____

PRACTICE 8 . . . .

Revise your own draft, thinking about how Patti made her paragraph stronger. Take an especially close look at your topic and concluding sentences, revising them at least once more. Use the following checklist as a guide.

CHECKLIST: REVISING YOUR WRITING

☐ My paragraph fulfills the assignment.

☐ My topic sentence expresses my main point, with confidence.

☐ The body sentences have detailed examples that show, explain, or prove my main point.

☐ The sentences are organized logically, and transitions link my ideas together.

☐ My concluding sentence reminds readers of my main point and ends the paragraph on a strong note.

☐ This paragraph is the best I can do, and I am ready to turn it in for a grade.

Edit Your Paragraph

After you revise your paragraph, you are ready to edit it. When you edit, you read your writing not so much for ideas, as you do when revising, but for correctness of grammar, punctuation, spelling, and word choice.

Units 3 through 7 contain information that will help you edit your writing. As you work through the chapters in these units, you will learn what errors are most noticeable to people and practice how to edit your writing for correct grammar, punctuation, spelling, and word choice. When you learn to edit, you are learning how to use formal English, the English you need to succeed in college, at work, and in parts of your everyday life.

Practice Together

■ **LEARNING STYLES:** Look for activities in this chapter that are matched to your learning style. If you don't know your learning style, take the test on pages 26–28.

  Visual

Auditory

Reading/writing

Kinesthetic (movement)

Working with a few other students, practice what you have learned in this chapter.

1. Have group members draw a picture of their draft paragraphs so that a viewer can tell what the paragraph is about. Then, have members take turns holding up their pictures, while the others say what they think the paragraph is about. Do the writers agree? What details or examples could they add to their paragraphs to make them clearer?

2. Act out your draft paragraphs for each other. Members who are watching should take notes and write a short paragraph on what they think is being acted out. Then, the watchers should read their paragraphs aloud. Finally, the author of the original paragraph should read it out loud. Compare the original version to the audience descriptions. If the audience didn't "see" the paragraph as the writer intended it, how could the paragraph be made clearer?

3. With your group, decide whether to tell a story or describe a scene (for instance, your classroom). Each person should add at least one sentence to the story, until you have a paragraph of several sentences. Make sure that each sentence after the first includes a time transition (if you are telling a story) or a space transition (if you are describing a scene).

4. As a group, write a paragraph, putting each sentence on a separate index card. Then, shuffle the cards and exchange them with another group. Each group should put the other group's sentences in a logical order, adding transitions. Then, write the sentences in order on a separate piece of paper and return it to the original group.

5. Take turns telling what your favorite clothes or shoes are and why. Then, have each group member write a paragraph about what makes a piece of clothing or pair of shoes a favorite, drawing pictures of the clothes or shoes if they like. Next, have group members take turns reading their paragraphs aloud. Others should suggest at least three ways in which each paragraph could be improved, referring to the checklist on page 71.

Chapter Review

1. What does *revision* mean? _____ Reread and highlight the paragraph where it is defined.

2. Getting _____ from a reader will help you improve your first draft.

3. What are three ways to organize your writing? Highlight them where they appear in the chapter.

4. What purpose do transitions serve? _____

   _____

5. How is editing different from revising? _____

   _____

6. **VOCABULARY:** Go back to any new words that you underlined in this chapter. Can you guess at their meanings now? If not, look up the words in a dictionary.

LEARNING JOURNAL:
Write for two minutes to complete the following sentences:
I think the weakest part of my writing is _____ because _____. I think I most need to improve _____.

■ **TIP:** For help with building your vocabulary, see Appendix B.

8

Developing Your Paragraph

Different Ways to Present Your Ideas

📖 **VOCABULARY:** Underline any words in this chapter that are new to you.

📖 **IDEA JOURNAL:** Write about a time when someone didn't understand what you meant.

In this course and other college classes, instructors will expect you to express your ideas in logical patterns so that what you say or write is clear. Understanding how to use these patterns will be helpful in all areas of your life.

COLLEGE	Tests and papers require you to understand and use these patterns.
WORK	E-mails, reports, memos, and oral and written communication with coworkers/bosses often follow these patterns.
EVERYDAY LIFE	Whenever it's important that someone understand your point in speech or writing, you have to use these patterns well.

The rest of this chapter contains the following elements related to each of the nine common patterns of development:

- **The Four Basics of the pattern:** A summary of the essential characteristics of the pattern.
- **An example for analysis:** A paragraph written using the pattern, showing the Four Basics. Following the paragraph are some questions about its structure and content.
- **Practice outlines:** Outlines for paragraphs that you fill in. You are given a topic sentence, and you provide the support and a concluding sentence.
- **A writing assignment**.
- **A checklist:** A set of statements to help you evaluate the paragraph you wrote for the assignment.

Narration

Narration is telling a story of an event or experience and showing why it is important through details about the experience.

▪▪ FOUR BASICS OF NARRATION

1. It reveals something of importance (your main point).
2. It includes all of the major events of the story (support).
3. It gives details about the major events, bringing the event or experience to life for your readers.
4. It presents the events using time order (according to when things happened).

READ ALOUD

Read all of the example paragraphs in this chapter aloud.

1 Winning the jackpot does not always bring happiness. A couple from Newport, Kentucky, won more than $60 million in the Powerball lottery a few years ago and imagined that they would live out their dreams. **2** One of the first things that happened after they won was that they separated, ending their long marriage. **3** Apparently, they had different dreams, and they could not agree on how to live anymore. They had been happy together without the money, but now they found they could not get along. **2** Then, two years after winning the jackpot, the man was found dead at home. **3** Since winning, he had been arrested for drunk driving and not paying child support. His dream of moving to Australia never came about. **2** Meanwhile, the woman quit her job and bought a big new house. A year after she moved in, a body was found in the house, belonging to a man dead from a drug overdose. After that, she bought another house, where she lived for three years. **3** During that time, she lost contact with former friends and was involved in a legal dispute. **2** Finally, five years from the time she and her former husband won the lottery, she too was found dead in her home, where she had been dead for several days. This couple's experience should be a lesson to people that money does not bring happiness.

— Events in time order

1. Underline the **topic sentence**.
2. What is important about the event/experience? _____

_____

3. What detail made the biggest impression on you? Why? _____

■ **TIP:** To complete this chapter, you will need to know about prewriting (Chapter 5); writing the main point (topic sentence), supporting that point, and planning/outlining (Chapter 6); and using transitions and revising (Chapter 7). For longer readings that follow the patterns described in this chapter, see Unit 8 (if you are using *Real Skills with Readings*).

■ **TIP:** Appendix D has additional blank outlines that you can use to plan paragraphs.

4. Circle the **transitions**.

5. Name one way the paragraph could be better. _____

_____

Outline a Narration Paragraph

Fill in the two outlines with events and details that support the topic sentence. Try prewriting to get ideas, and arrange the events according to time order.

1. **TOPIC SENTENCE:** When I was (fill in age), I learned that (fill in a word) is important.

   FIRST EVENT: _____

       DETAILS: _____

   SECOND EVENT: _____

       DETAILS: _____

   THIRD EVENT: _____

       DETAILS: _____

   CONCLUDING SENTENCE: From that time on, I _____.

2. **TOPIC SENTENCE:** The (funniest, saddest, most emotional, most embarrassing, or scariest) thing that I ever (saw, experienced) was _____.

   FIRST EVENT: _____

       DETAILS: _____

   SECOND EVENT: _____

       DETAILS: _____

   THIRD EVENT: _____

       DETAILS: _____

   CONCLUDING SENTENCE: Every time I remember that time, I think

   _____.

Write a Narration Paragraph

Write a narration paragraph, using one of the outlines you developed, one of the following topics, or a topic of your own. Then, complete the narration checklist that follows the list of topics.

- An experience or event you witnessed
- An experience or event that you will remember for a long time
- A school experience you liked or had fun with

- The plot of a movie you liked
- A time you helped a friend or family member in trouble
- An unusual news story
- A rumor that is going around

- Something important that is happening in your town/city

- A story told in the lyrics of a song you like

👁 Draw pictures to illustrate your narration. Include one drawing for each of the major events.

CHECKLIST: EVALUATING YOUR NARRATION PARAGRAPH

- ☐ My topic sentence states what is important about the event or experience.

- ☐ I have included all the important events with details so that readers can understand what happened.

- ☐ The paragraph has *all* of the Four Basics of Narration (p. 75).

- ☐ I have included transitions to move readers smoothly from one event to the next.

- ☐ I have reread the paragraph, making improvements and checking for grammar and spelling errors.

- ☐ This is the best I can do.

Illustration

Illustration uses examples to show, explain, or prove a point.

▪▪ FOUR BASICS OF ILLUSTRATION

1. It has a main point to illustrate.
2. It gives specific examples to show, explain, or prove the point.
3. It gives details to support the examples.
4. It uses enough examples to get the point across.

1 When buying a new computer printer, there are several factors to consider in addition to price. **2** For example, the cost of ink cartridges varies from one kind of printer to another, ranging from $15 to more than $50. **3** The higher price does not necessarily mean that the cartridge produces more copies, so it is important to find out both the cost of the cartridge and the average number of copies it prints. **2** Another factor is the speed of copying. **3** Print speeds can range from two to eleven copies a minute, even for printers that cost about the same price. Slow printing time can be both frustrating and limiting to your productivity, so it makes sense to look at how fast the machine does what you want it to do. **2** A third factor is the quality of the printing, in both black-and-white and color. **3** An inexpensive printer is no bargain if you can hardly read what it prints. Before buying any printer, learn about your options from reliable sources. *Consumer Reports*, for example,

Enough examples to make the writer's point

Enough examples to make
the writer's point

has side-by-side comparisons of different printer models and their features, and it even makes recommendations.

1. Underline the **topic sentence**.
2. In your own words, what is the point the writer wants to make?

_____

_____

3. Circle the **transitions**.
4. What is another example the writer might give? _____

_____

Outline an Illustration Paragraph

Fill in the two outlines with examples and details that support the topic sentence. Try prewriting to get ideas.

1. **TOPIC SENTENCE:** I am a good _____ (cook, friend, athlete, driver, worker, student . . .).

    FIRST EXAMPLE: _____

       DETAILS: _____

    SECOND EXAMPLE: _____

       DETAILS: _____

    THIRD EXAMPLE: _____

       DETAILS: _____

    CONCLUDING SENTENCE: I am proud of _____

       because_____ .

2. **TOPIC SENTENCE:** Today's college students have many _____

       _____ (challenges, stresses, roles . . .).

    FIRST EXAMPLE: _____

       DETAILS: _____

    SECOND EXAMPLE: _____

       DETAILS: _____

    THIRD EXAMPLE: _____

       DETAILS: _____

    CONCLUDING SENTENCE: Going to college is not easy, (and, but, so)

       _____

       _____ .

Write an Illustration Paragraph

Write an illustration paragraph on a separate sheet of paper, using one of the outlines you developed, one of the following topics, or a topic of your own. Then, complete the illustration checklist that follows the list of topics.

- Why you like a certain kind of music
- What makes a class good
- Some things that annoy you
- What you hope to get from a college education
- The benefits of something you do regularly

- Examples of junk e-mail
- Examples of bad television
- Examples of deceptive advertising
- Examples of dreams you've had that you remember
- Examples of rude behavior

CHECKLIST: EVALUATING YOUR ILLUSTRATION PARAGRAPH
☐   My topic sentence states my point.
☐   I have several detailed examples that support my point.
☐   The paragraph has *all* of the Four Basics of Illustration (p. 77).
☐   I have included transitions to move readers smoothly from one example to the next.
☐   I have reread the paragraph, making improvements and checking for grammar and spelling errors.
☐   This is the best I can do.

Description

Description creates a strong impression of your topic: It shows how the topic looks, sounds, smells, tastes, or feels.

▪▪ FOUR BASICS OF DESCRIPTION

1. It creates a main impression—an overall effect or image—about the topic.
2. It uses specific examples to create the impression.
3. It supports the examples with details that appeal to the senses: sight, hearing, smell, taste, and touch.
4. It brings a person, place, or object to life for the readers.

1 Late at night, the ocean near my grandmother's house always fills me with wonder. **2** It is dark, lit only by the moon. **3** When the

Examples and details bring the subject to life

Examples and details bring the subject to life

moon is full, the light reflects off the water, bouncing up and shining on the waves as they start to break. When the clouds cover the moon, the darkness is complete. The world stands still and silent for a moment. **2** Then, I hear the waves **3** coming toward me, swelling, breaking, and bursting into surf that I can't see. I hear them gently go back, only to start again. **2** Gulls call in the distance. **3** During the day, their call sounds raw, but at night it softens and sounds like a plea. **2** Now that I'm in touch with my senses, I am hit with a smell of salt and dampness that **3** seems to coat my lungs. **2** I stand completely still, just experiencing the beach, as if I've become a part of the elements. The experience always calms me and takes away the strains of everyday life.

1. What impression does the writer want to create?_____

_____

2. Underline the **topic sentence**.
3. Underline the **example** that makes the strongest impression on you.

   Why did you choose this example? _____

4. Add another sensory detail to one of the examples.
5. Try rewriting the topic sentence.

Outline a Description Paragraph

Fill in the two outlines with examples and details that support the topic sentence. Try prewriting to get ideas.

1. **TOPIC SENTENCE:** My room is _____.

   FIRST EXAMPLE: _____

      DETAILS: _____

   SECOND EXAMPLE: _____

      DETAILS: _____

   THIRD EXAMPLE: _____

      DETAILS: _____

   CONCLUDING SENTENCE: Looking around my room, you can tell _____

   _____.

2. **TOPIC SENTENCE:** The _____ on this campus is _____.

   FIRST EXAMPLE: _____

      DETAILS: _____

   SECOND EXAMPLE: _____

      DETAILS: _____

THIRD EXAMPLE: _____

DETAILS: _____

CONCLUDING SENTENCE: Every time I'm there, I think _____

_____ .

Write a Description Paragraph

Write a description paragraph, using one of the outlines you developed, one of the following topics, or a topic of your own. Then, complete the description checklist that follows the list of topics.

- A favorite food
- A photograph
- Your dream house
- A section of the college library
- An alien being

- A home of the future
- A scary person
- A scene that makes you feel threatened
- A pet

👁 Draw a picture of what you are describing.

CHECKLIST: EVALUATING YOUR DESCRIPTION PARAGRAPH
☐   My topic sentence includes the main impression I want to create for readers.
☐   I include examples that show the readers what I mean.
☐   The paragraph has *all* of the Four Basics of Description (p. 79).
☐   I have included transitions to move readers smoothly from one example to the next.
☐   I have reread the paragraph, making improvements and checking for grammar and spelling errors.
☐   This is the best I can do.

Process Analysis

Process analysis either explains how to do something (so that readers can do it) or how something works (so that readers understand it).

▪▪ **FOUR BASICS OF PROCESS ANALYSIS**

1. It tells readers either how to do the steps of the process or to understand how it works.

2. It includes the major steps in the process.

3. It explains each step in detail.

4. It presents the steps in the order they happen (time order).

Readers told how to do something

Steps presented in the order they need to happen

People always ask for the recipe for simplest cookie I make, and I'm always a little embarrassed to give it to them. **1** Here is how to make delicious cookies with almost no effort. **2** First, buy two ingredients: a roll of sugar-cookie dough from your supermarket's refrigerated section and a bag of mini peanut butter cups. Cut the roll into half-inch slices and then cut each slice in half. Next, roll the pieces into balls. Then, grease a mini-muffin pan and put the balls in the pan. Start baking the dough according to the directions on the sugar-cookie package. When the cookies are about three minutes from being done, take them out. Press a peanut butter cup into the center of each ball and return the cookies to the oven until they are golden brown. When they are cool, pop them out of the muffin pans. These cookies are so easy to make that even little children can help. Enjoy!

1. Underline the **topic sentence**.
2. How many steps does the writer describe? _____
3. Could you perform the process after reading the paragraph? If not,

   where do you need more information? _____
4. Circle the **transitions**.
5. Which of the four basics does this paragraph lack? _____
   Revise the paragraph so that it includes this basic.

Outline a Process Analysis Paragraph

Fill in the two outlines with the steps in the process and detailed explanations of them. Try prewriting to get ideas, and organize the steps according to time order.

1. **TOPIC SENTENCE:** Learning how to _____

   (something you do well) isn't hard if you _____

   _____ .

   FIRST STEP: _____

      EXPLANATION: _____

   SECOND STEP: _____

      EXPLANATION: _____

   THIRD STEP: _____

      EXPLANATION: _____

   CONCLUDING SENTENCE: _____ takes some practice
      and concentration, but anyone can do it.

2. **TOPIC SENTENCE:** To avoid losing your temper, try these steps.

    FIRST STEP: _____

        EXPLANATION: _____

    SECOND STEP: _____

        EXPLANATION: _____

    THIRD STEP: _____

        EXPLANATION: _____

    CONCLUDING SENTENCE: Getting angry doesn't usually help anyone, so learning to manage your anger is important.

Write a Process Analysis Paragraph

Write a process analysis paragraph, using one of the outlines you developed, one of the following topics, or a topic of your own. Then, complete the process analysis checklist that follows the list of topics.

- How to use a cell phone
- How to find a book in a library
- How to make someone (a partner, a coworker, a teacher) mad
- How find information on the Web
- How to make something
- How to fail a test
- How to get a bargain
- How to make a good impression at a job interview
- How to find a job

CHECKLIST: EVALUATING YOUR PROCESS ANALYSIS PARAGRAPH

☐ My topic sentence tells readers what the process I'm writing about is.

☐ I have included all of the major steps and details about them.

☐ The paragraph has *all* of the Four Basics of Process Analysis (p. 81).

☐ I have included transitions to move readers smoothly from one step to the next.

☐ I have reread the paragraph, making improvements and checking for grammar and spelling errors.

☐ This is the best I can do.

Classification

Classification sorts people or things into categories so that they can be understood.

■■ FOUR BASICS OF CLASSIFICATION

1. It makes sense of a group of people or things by sorting them into useful categories.
2. It has a purpose for sorting.
3. It includes categories that follow a single organizing principle (for example, to sort by size, by color, by price, and so on).
4. It gives detailed examples or explanations of things that fit into each category.

The FALLING in LOVE DIET

1 Over the past several years, three kinds of diets have been 2 very popular in this country. 3 The first one was the low-fat diet. 4 Dieters had to limit their fat intake, so they stayed away from foods like nuts, fatty meats, ice cream, and fried foods. They could eat lots of low-fat food like pasta, bread, fruits, and vegetables, as well as lean meat, fish, and chicken. 3 The second kind of diet was the low-carbohydrate plan. 4 The first popular low-carb diet was the Atkins plan. Under this plan, dieters could eat all the fatty meats, butter, cheese, and nuts they wanted. Some people were eating a whole pound of bacon for breakfast with eggs and butter. However, they could not eat bread, pasta, or most fruits. On this plan, people lost a lot of weight quickly, but many found that they could not stick with a diet that didn't allow carbs. The South Beach diet was also a low-carb plan, but not quite as strict as the Atkins diet, at least after the first two weeks. 3 The third diet plan, one that has been around for a long time, is Weight Watchers. 4 It requires that dieters eat smaller portions of most foods: everything in moderation. Points are assigned to foods, and dieters must stay within a certain number of points each day. High-calorie foods have a high number of points, and many vegetables have no points. Americans have spent millions on these diet plans, but the obesity rate continues to increase. It seems that the "right" kind of diet, one that allows people to lose weight and keep it off, has yet to be invented.

1. Underline the **topic sentence**.
2. What are the categories? _____

_____

3. Circle the **transitions**.

4. What is the purpose of the classification? _____

5. What is the organizing principle? _____

6. Rewrite the concluding sentence to improve it.

> 👁 Draw a diagram of this paragraph, using labeled boxes for the different parts.

Outline a Classification Paragraph

Fill in the two outlines with the categories and detailed examples or explanations of what fits into them. Try prewriting to get ideas.

1. **TOPIC SENTENCE:** Like most people, I have several different kinds of _____ (friends, shoes, moods...).

    FIRST CATEGORY: _____

        EXAMPLE/EXPLANATION OF WHAT FITS INTO THE CATEGORY: _____

    _____

    SECOND CATEGORY: _____

        EXAMPLE/EXPLANATION OF WHAT FITS INTO THE CATEGORY: _____

    _____

    THIRD CATEGORY: _____

        EXAMPLE/EXPLANATION OF WHAT FITS INTO THE CATEGORY: _____

    _____

    CONCLUDING SENTENCE: Even though my _____ are

    different, they are all _____ to me.

2. **TOPIC SENTENCE:** The Web site Doctors.com lists a variety of doctors and services.

    FIRST CATEGORY: _____

        EXAMPLE/EXPLANATION OF WHAT FITS INTO THE CATEGORY: _____

    _____

    SECOND CATEGORY: _____

        EXAMPLE/EXPLANATION OF WHAT FITS INTO THE CATEGORY: _____

    _____

    THIRD CATEGORY: _____

        EXAMPLE/EXPLANATION OF WHAT FITS INTO THE CATEGORY: _____

    _____

    CONCLUDING SENTENCE: I don't know how reliable the site is, but it does

    _____

    _____.

Write a Classification Paragraph

Write a classification paragraph, using one of the outlines you developed, one of the following topics, or a topic of your own. Then, complete the classification checklist that follows the list of topics.

- Kinds of music
- Kinds of attitudes
- Kinds of bad habits
- Kinds of television programs
- Kinds of drivers
- Kinds of cars
- Kinds of clutter in your room/home
- Kinds of students
- Kinds of snacks
- Kinds of smells

CHECKLIST: EVALUATING YOUR CLASSIFICATION PARAGRAPH

☐ My topic sentence tells readers what I'm classifying.

☐ I have stated the categories and given examples of what is in them.

☐ The paragraph has *all* of the Four Basics of Classification (p. 84).

☐ I have included transitions to move readers smoothly from one category to the next.

☐ I have reread the paragraph, making improvements and checking for grammar and spelling errors.

☐ This is the best I can do.

Definition

Definition explains what a term or concept means.

▪▪ FOUR BASICS OF DEFINITION

1. It tells readers what is being defined.
2. It gives a clear definition.
3. It gives examples to explain the definition.
4. It gives details about the examples that readers will understand.

1 Propaganda 2 is information that is promoted to support certain views or messages. It can come in many forms, but its purpose is to persuade us to see things a certain way. 3 For example, the president of the United States may give televised speeches to con-

vince us that some policy or action he supports is right. **4** We may get mailings on the subject. People who agree with the president's message may speak in favor of it on talk shows or in interviews. **3** Religious organizations may spread propaganda about the importance of certain actions (or avoiding certain actions). **4** For example, many churches sent positive messages to their members about the religious importance of the movie *The Chronicles of Narnia*. Churches urged their members to see the movie and even had their own showings, hoping the film would increase church attendance. **3** Propaganda can be good, as when a health organization sends information about how to avoid unhealthy behavior and follow good habits, or bad, as when one political group publishes false or exaggerated information to attack another group. Because we are surrounded by propaganda, it is important that we think about who is behind the message and whether we believe the information.

1. Underline the **topic sentence**.
2. What is the term being defined? _____
3. In your own words, what does the term mean? _____
4. Give another example that would help define the term. _____
   _____
5. Add a transition that would be useful.

Outline a Definition Paragraph

Fill in the two outlines with a definition and examples and details that explain the definition. Try prewriting to get ideas.

1. **TOPIC SENTENCE:** Education is _____.

   FIRST EXAMPLE: _____

       DETAILS: _____

   SECOND EXAMPLE: _____

       DETAILS: _____

   THIRD EXAMPLE: _____

       DETAILS: _____

   CONCLUDING SENTENCE: The word *education* may mean different things

       to different people, but to me it means _____.
   (Don't just repeat the definition in your topic sentence.)

2. **TOPIC SENTENCE:** A responsible person is someone who _____.

    FIRST EXAMPLE: _____

        DETAILS: _____

    SECOND EXAMPLE: _____

        DETAILS: _____

    THIRD EXAMPLE: _____

        DETAILS: _____

    CONCLUDING SENTENCE: Responsible people are _____.
    (Don't just repeat the definition in your topic sentence.)

Write a Definition Paragraph

Write a definition paragraph, using one of the outlines you developed, one of the following terms, or a topic of your own. Then, complete the definition checklist that follows the list of topics.

- Blogs
- Democracy
- Success
- Goal-oriented
- A good student
- Ethical
- Frugal
- Fantasy
- Collaboration
- Mentor

CHECKLIST: EVALUATING YOUR DEFINITION PARAGRAPH
☐   My topic sentence tells readers what I'm defining and gives a basic definition.
☐   I have given examples and details that show readers what the term means as I am defining it.
☐   The paragraph has *all* of the Four Basics of Definition (p. 86).
☐   I have included transitions to move readers smoothly from one example to the next.
☐   I have reread the paragraph, making improvements and checking for grammar and spelling errors.
☐   This is the best I can do.

Comparison and Contrast

Comparison shows the similarities among people, ideas, situations, and things; **contrast** shows the differences.

▪▪ FOUR BASICS OF COMPARISON AND CONTRAST

1. It has subjects (usually two) that are enough alike to be usefully compared or contrasted.

2. It serves a purpose—either to help readers make a decision about two subjects or to understand them.

3. It gives several points of comparison and/or contrast.

4. It uses one of two organizations: **point-by-point** or **whole-to-whole**.

POINT-BY-POINT	WHOLE-TO-WHOLE

1. First point of comparison
   Subject 1
   Subject 2
	1. Subject 1
	   First point of comparison
	   Second point of comparison
	   Third point of comparison

2. Second point of comparison
   Subject 1
   Subject 2
	2. Subject 2
	   First point of comparison
	   Second point of comparison
	   Third point of comparison

3. Third point of comparison
   Subject 1
   Subject 2	

   1 Greenline Bank **2** suits my needs much better than **1** Worldly Bank does. **3** For one thing, there aren't any hidden charges at Greenline. For example, customers get free checking even if they keep a low balance in their accounts. Since I don't usually have much in my checking account, this is important for me. In contrast, to get free checking at Worldly Bank, customers must have a minimum balance of three thousand dollars. That would mean that I pay for every check I write, and I don't need that charge. Another way that Greenline Bank is better is that it offers low interest rates on loans. If I need a loan for something like a new car, for example, the bank's rate of interest on that would be 9 percent. Wordly Bank would charge 17.5 percent for the same loan. Over a three-year period, the difference between 9 percent and 17.5 percent is huge. Another difference between the two banks is that

Greenline Bank is a small, local bank. People know me when I walk in, and I feel I can trust them. I also believe that giving Greenline my business helps the local economy in some small way. In contrast, Worldly Bank is huge. The people in the local office are polite in a businesslike way, but I don't feel as if I know them. Worldly Bank as a whole is the fourth largest bank in the country, so I know that my little account means nothing to it. Because of these differences, I am a loyal Greenline Bank customer.

1. Underline the **topic sentence**.

2. Is the purpose to help make a choice or to understand? _____

3. Does the paragraph compare or contrast? _____

4. What kind of organization does it use? _____

5. What are the points of comparison? _____

_____

Outline a Comparison/Contrast Paragraph

Fill in the two outlines with the points of comparison and/or contrast between the two subjects. Try prewriting to get ideas, and save the most important point of comparison or contrast for last.

1. **TOPIC SENTENCE:** I had no idea how different high school and college would be.

   FIRST POINT OF CONTRAST

       HIGH SCHOOL: _____

       COLLEGE: _____

   SECOND POINT OF CONTRAST

       HIGH SCHOOL: _____

       COLLEGE: _____

   THIRD POINT OF CONTRAST

       HIGH SCHOOL: _____

       COLLEGE: _____

   CONCLUDING SENTENCE: While high school is _____,

       college is _____.

2. **TOPIC SENTENCE:** _____ (falling in love, learning to drive, the first week of a new job . . .) can be just like

   _____

SUBJECT 1

   FIRST POINT OF COMPARISON: _____

   SECOND POINT OF COMPARISON: _____

   THIRD POINT OF COMPARISON: _____

SUBJECT 2

   FIRST POINT OF COMPARISON: _____

   SECOND POINT OF COMPARISON: _____

   THIRD POINT OF COMPARISON: _____

   CONCLUDING SENTENCE: The important thing about both is that

_____

_____.

Write a Comparison/Contrast Paragraph

Write a comparison or contrast paragraph, using one of the outlines you developed, one of the following topics, or a topic of your own. Then, complete the comparison/contrast checklist that follows the list of topics.

- Yourself and a sister or brother
- The job you have/the job you want
- Two bosses
- Two places you have lived
- Clothes for a job interview/clothes for a weekend
- Yourself now/yourself ten years ago
- Your life now/what you want it to be
- Two pets
- Two photographs of your family
- A good student/a bad student

CHECKLIST: EVALUATING YOUR COMPARISON/CONTRAST PARAGRAPH

☐ My topic sentence tells readers what my subjects are and whether I am comparing them, contrasting them, or both.

☐ I have detailed points of comparison or contrast between the two subjects.

☐ The paragraph has *all* of the Four Basics of Comparison and Contrast (p. 89).

☐ I have included transitions to move readers smoothly from one point or subject to the next.

☐ I have reread the paragraph, making improvements and checking for grammar and spelling errors.

☐ This is the best I can do.

Cause and Effect

A **cause** is what makes something happen. An **effect** is what happens as a result of something.

A ring diagram is useful to show causes and effects of something.

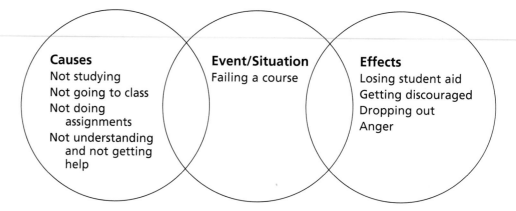

Causes
Not studying
Not going to class
Not doing assignments
Not understanding and not getting help

Event/Situation
Failing a course

Effects
Losing student aid
Getting discouraged
Dropping out
Anger

FOUR BASICS OF CAUSE AND EFFECT

1. The main point reflects the writer's purpose: to explain causes, effects, or both.

2. If the purpose is to explain causes, it gives real causes, not just things that happened before. For example, just because you ate a hot dog before you got the flu doesn't mean the hot dog caused the flu.

3. If the purpose is to explain effects, it gives real effects, not just things that happened after. For example, getting sick wasn't the effect of eating the hot dog; it just happened after you ate the hot dog.

4. It gives readers detailed examples or explanations of the causes and/or effects.

1 Cigarette smoking has at least three important negative effects. 3 The first is that it is annoying to others. Nonsmokers who have to inhale secondhand smoke have every right to be annoyed. 4 The bad-smelling smoke coats people's hair and clothing and is dangerous to their health. 3 Another negative effect of smoking is that it supports an industry that is careless about people's health. 4 The courts have proved that the tobacco industry knew about the extreme dangers of nicotine and hid the findings from the public. The industry also spent billions of dollars per year on advertisements specifically directed to young people. The courts have stopped such advertising, but much damage has been done al-

ready, as indicated by the number of young people who smoke. New reports show that the tobacco industry has a scheme to target women with flavored cigarettes. Big Tobacco doesn't care that smoking kills; it needs people to smoke in order to produce big profits. That leads to the most dangerous effect of smoking: 3 It is potentially fatal to the smoker, 4 causing damage to the heart and lungs that can lead to cardiovascular disease and cancer. The effects of smoking are all negative: Who can say anything positive about this habit?

1. Underline the **topic sentence**.
2. What is the writer's purpose? _____

    _____

3. What are the three effects? _____

    _____

4. Rewrite the topic sentence to improve it.
5. Rewrite the concluding sentence to improve it.

Outline a Cause/Effect Paragraph

Fill in the two outlines with the detailed examples or explanations of causes or effects. Try prewriting to get ideas, and save the most important cause or effect for last.

1. **TOPIC SENTENCE:** Several factors caused me to break up with my last

    _____ (boyfriend/girlfriend/spouse).

    FIRST CAUSE: _____

        DETAILS: _____

    SECOND CAUSE: _____

        DETAILS: _____

    THIRD CAUSE: _____

        DETAILS: _____

    CONCLUDING SENTENCE: Ending the relationship wasn't easy, but _____

        _____.

2. **TOPIC SENTENCE:** I never expected so much to happen as a result of my

    decision to _____.

    FIRST EFFECT: _____

        DETAILS: _____

    SECOND EFFECT: _____

        DETAILS: _____

THIRD EFFECT: _____

DETAILS: _____

CONCLUDING SENTENCE: All of this reminded me that _____

_____ .

Write a Cause/Effect Paragraph

Write a cause/effect paragraph, using one of the outlines you developed, one of the following topics, or a topic of your own. Then, complete the cause/effect checklist that follows the list of topics.

- Causes of laughter
- Causes of annoyance
- Causes of cheating
- Causes of stress
- Causes of anxiety

- Effects of exercise
- Effects of overeating
- Possible effects of cheating
- Effects of getting a degree
- Effects of having a job you like

CHECKLIST: EVALUATING YOUR CAUSE/EFFECT PARAGRAPH
☐ My topic sentence includes my topic and whether I am writing about causes, effects, or both.
☐ I have written details about causes or effects so my readers will understand them.
☐ The paragraph has _all_ of the Four Basics of Cause and Effect (p. 92).
☐ I have included transitions to move readers smoothly from one cause or effect to the next.
☐ I have reread the paragraph, making improvements and checking for grammar and spelling errors.
☐ This is the best I can do.

Argument

Argument takes a position on an issue and gives detailed reasons that defend or support it. You use argument to persuade someone to see things your way and/or to take an action. Being able to argue well is important in every area of your life.

▪▪ FOUR BASICS OF ARGUMENT

1. It takes a strong and definite position.
2. It gives good reasons and evidence to defend the position.

3.   It considers opposing positions.

4.   It has energy from start to finish.

1 The minimum wage in this country must be raised for the benefit of all our citizens. 2 For one thing, the wage, now $5.15, has not been increased since 1997, almost a decade ago; in that time, inflation[1] has continued to grow, so the spending power of the minimum wage is less than it was before it was raised. In other words, people can buy much less with today's minimum wage than they were able to in 1995, when the minimum wage was $4.25. 3 Some people believe that an increase in the minimum wage would cause mass layoffs. However, studies done after the last wage increase show that no jobs were lost, even in small businesses. 2 In fact, the studies found that employers actually made money after the wage increase because of increased productivity and morale and decreased absenteeism. This is a good reason to raise the wage. Most important, raising the minimum wage would help get people off welfare and help them become productive members of our society. For example, although the many single mothers on welfare can get financial assistance for child care from the federal government, this assistance is minimal. As a result, poor mothers may have to limit their work hours or leave their jobs altogether because of lack of adequate child care. Higher wages would allow such people to hold on to their jobs, to get child care, and to build a better life overall for themselves and their families. Better wages would also increase workers' self-esteem; nobody likes to feel like a charity case. It's time to act now to make life better for millions of poor people—and for Americans as a whole.

[1]**inflation:** *an increase in the prices of goods and services*

Argument has energy from start to finish.

1.   Underline the **topic sentence**.

2.   What is the topic? _____ What is the writer's position?

    _____

3.   What four reasons does the writer give to support the position?

    _____

    _____

4.   Name one thing the writer could do to make the paragraph stronger.

    _____

    _____

5.   Rewrite the topic sentence to make it more persuasive.

Outline an Argument Paragraph

Fill in the two outlines with reasons, and details about the reasons, that support the position in the topic sentence. Try prewriting to get ideas, and save the most important reason for last.

1. **TOPIC SENTENCE:** Tuition should not be raised next year.

   FIRST REASON: _____

   DETAILS: _____

   SECOND REASON: _____

   DETAILS: _____

   THIRD REASON: _____

   DETAILS: _____

   CONCLUDING SENTENCE: If the tuition is higher next year, _____

   _____ .

2. **TOPIC SENTENCE:** It should be (legal/illegal) for the government to listen in on U.S. citizens' phone conversations without having to get a warrant.

   FIRST REASON: _____

   DETAILS: _____

   SECOND REASON: _____

   DETAILS: _____

   THIRD REASON: _____

   DETAILS: _____

   CONCLUDING SENTENCE: _____

Write an Argument Paragraph

Write an argument paragraph, using one of the outlines you developed, one of the following topics, or a topic of your own. Then, complete the argument checklist that follows.

- Using the phrase *Merry Christmas* versus *Happy Holidays*
- Raising the minimum wage or keeping it as it is
- Why you should get a raise
- Why you should get a higher grade
- Banning/allowing junk food in schools
- Lowering/raising the drinking age
- Making smoking illegal
- Why the parking lot at your school or business should be enlarged
- Why you should be allowed to retake a test

CHECKLIST: EVALUATING YOUR ARGUMENT PARAGRAPH

- ☐ My topic sentence states my topic and a strong position on that topic.

- ☐ I have given solid reasons, and details about them, to support my position.

- ☐ My paragraph has *all* of the Four Basics of Argument (pp. 94–95).

- ☐ I have included transitions to move readers smoothly from one reason or example to the next.

- ☐ I have reread the paragraph, making improvements and checking for grammar and spelling errors.

- ☐ This is the best I can do.

Practice Together

Working with a few other students, practice what you have learned in this chapter.

1. One student should start a story, saying one sentence about what a character did or experienced. He or she should then ask, "What happened next?" The next person should add a sentence to the story and ask another person, "What happened next?" Keep going until you have finished the story. Each person should contribute at least two sentences. 𝄞

2. Each person should think of a well-known person, place, or thing and write a description of it without naming it. Then, each person should stand up and read his or her description. The others should guess what the person, place, or thing is. 𝄞 📖 ⤺

3. With your group, choose a process and draw a flowchart for it on a sheet of poster paper. Examples of processes could be signing up for classes, making Jell-O, or sending an e-mail. When everyone is done, all groups should hang their flowcharts on the wall. Students should look at others' flowcharts and see if they can think of any steps or details to add. 👁 𝄞 📖 ⤺

4. As a group, pick something by which to classify people in your class, such as age, major, height, length of hair, or favorite activity. Then, have each group take turns physically sorting people in the room by the chosen organizing principle. For example, if the organizing principle is age, a group might ask students ages twenty and younger to stand at one side of the room and those ages twenty-one and older to stand at the other side. To find people who fit your category, you may have to call out questions. 👁 𝄞 ⤺

<aside>
■ **LEARNING STYLES:** Look for activities in this chapter that are matched to your learning style. If you don't know your learning style, take the test on pages 26–28.

👁   Visual

𝄞   Auditory

📖   Reading/writing

⤺   Kinesthetic (movement)
</aside>

5. The words on the T-shirt shown in the photo below define *Dad.* Each person in the group should choose a role he or she plays in life (friend, parent, student, spouse, partner, and so on). Members should take turns saying their role and giving at least three detailed examples of how they play that role. Then, discuss what method of development you would use to write paragraphs about your roles. 👁 ✍

6. Find two things in the room that are of the same kind but slightly different (like watches, textbooks, sweaters, or shoes). On a sheet of paper, make columns headed "Similarities" and "Differences" and come up with as many points of comparison and contrast as you can find. 👁 ✍ 📖

DAD
is a verb.
like catch and hug and listen.
it is not just something you are.
it is something you do.
like laugh and read and play.
are you doing anything more important?
have you been a dad today?

AdCouncil.org

for more ideas call 800-790-DADS or visit www.fatherhood.org

National Fatherhood Initiative

7. With your group, pick an event or situation and draw a ring diagram of causes and effects, as shown on page 92. Each person in the group should supply at least two causes or effects. 👁 🖊 📖

8. As a group, pick a controversial issue, such as one of those listed on page 96. Then, pick one side of the issue. Each member should call out one reason for taking that side. (One person in your group should be writing down all of the answers.) When you have at least five reasons for that side, take up the opposing view. Each member should call out one reason for the opposite argument, until you have at least five reasons. Finally, present both sides of the issue to the class. 🖊 📖

Chapter Review

1. Choose three of the ways to develop paragraphs and list one way that

   you have used or might use each of them. _____

2. List the four basics of each method of development you chose. _____

   _____

3. On a separate piece of paper, briefly define each of the nine ways to develop paragraphs.

4. **VOCABULARY:** Go back to any new words that you underlined in this chapter. Can you guess their meanings now? If not, look up the words in a dictionary.

📖 **LEARNING JOURNAL:** Write for two minutes about what you've learned about developing paragraphs. Write down any questions you still have and ask your instructor.

■ **TIP:** For help with building your vocabulary, see Appendix B.

9

Moving from Paragraphs to Essays

How to Write Longer Papers

Understand Essay Structure

VOCABULARY: Underline any words in this chapter that are new to you.

IDEA JOURNAL: Write about two different experiences that happened on the same day.

An essay has multiple paragraphs and three necessary parts:

ESSAY PART	CONTENTS/PURPOSE OF THE PART
1. An **introduction**	includes a thesis statement that states the main point. The introduction is usually the first paragraph.
2. A **body**	includes at least three paragraphs. Each paragraph begins with a topic sentence that supports the thesis statement. Each topic sentence is supported by examples and details in the rest of the paragraph.
3. A **conclusion**	reminds readers of the main point, just as the concluding sentence of a paragraph does. The conclusion in an essay is usually the last paragraph. It summarizes the support and makes an observation.

The following diagram shows how the parts of an essay relate to the parts of a paragraph.

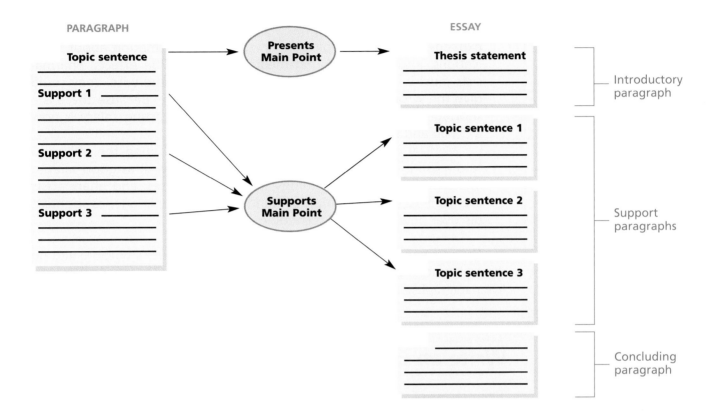

READ ALOUD

Read the following essay aloud, using different voices for the introduction, body, and conclusion.

Demand for medical professionals is high, and it is expected to grow over the next decade. Although physicians are always needed, medicine offers many other kinds of jobs that provide satisfaction and good salaries.

One of the high-demand professions is that of radiology technician. These professionals perform ultrasounds, take X rays, and do mammograms and magnetic resonance imaging (MRI) tests. Radiology technicians must operate expensive, sensitive machines with great care and accuracy. They must also have good people skills because they will encounter patients who are nervous about tests. The average starting salary for these technicians is $30,000.

Another high-demand profession is nursing. With the average age of Americans on the rise, many more nurses are needed to supply good health care to the aging population. Registered nurses are in short supply all over the United States, and hospitals are competing with each other to hire them. These nurses provide a wide range of patient care, such as documenting symptoms, administering medicines,

Thesis statement

Introduction

Body paragraphs

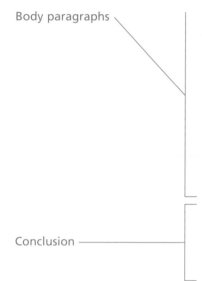

Body paragraphs

and working with physicians. Registered nurses' average starting salary is $43,000, and many of them can expect to be offered large bonuses when they agree to accept a position.

The highest demand in the medical field is for pharmacists. Pharmacists dispense drugs prescribed by doctors, but their role has expanded as more people rely on them for information about medications, interactions among medications, and side effects. Pharmacists must be precise and must read carefully; otherwise, they could give the wrong medication or the wrong dosage. Because there is a shortage of trained pharmacists, the average starting salary is now $75,000 and rising.

Conclusion

Medical careers offer many advantages, including the ability to find a job in almost any area of the country as well as good salaries and benefits. Trained radiology technicians, nurses, and pharmacists are likely to remain in high demand as more people age, as scientists discover new cures, and technology advances.

Essays can be short or long, depending on the writer's purpose and on the assignment. In this course, you may be asked to write essays that have five paragraphs: an introduction, three body paragraphs, and a conclusion.

Write an Essay

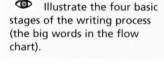 Illustrate the four basic stages of the writing process (the big words in the flow chart).

The process of writing an essay is the same process you have used to write a paragraph. The steps in this section will help you write an essay, but if you need more explanations and practices, go back to Chapters 5–7, which have more details about each of the steps.

> **GET IDEAS (See Chapter 5.)**
> • Narrow and explore your topic (prewrite).

> **WRITE (See Chapter 6.)**
> • State your main point (thesis statement).
> • Write topic sentences for each major point supporting the thesis statement, and write paragraphs that support each topic sentence.
> • Make an outline or plan of your ideas.
> • Write a draft.
> • Reread your draft, taking notes about what would make it better.

> **REWRITE (See Chapter 7.)**
> - Rewrite your draft, making changes you noted (and more).
> - Reread the new draft, making sure it as good as you can make it.

> **EDIT (See Units 3–7.)**
> - Read your paper for grammar, punctuation, and spelling errors.

Narrow Your Topic

Just as you have done for paragraphs, you often need to narrow a general essay topic to a smaller one.

Because essays are longer than paragraphs, essay topics can be a little more general than paragraph topics, but not a lot more. The topic still needs to be narrow enough that you can make your main point about it in a few paragraphs. You can use prewriting (see Chapter 5) to get ideas for a narrower topic.

The following examples show how the topic for an essay is a little broader than one for a paragraph.

ASSIGNED GENERAL TOPIC		NARROWED FOR AN ESSAY		NARROWED FOR A PARAGRAPH
Student stress	→	Managing work and college	→	Studying for a test
Television programs	→	Reality TV	→	*Survivor*
Gender differences	→	Male/female speech patterns	→	Male/female movie preferences

PRACTICE 1 . . . .

Narrow the following five general topics to good essay topics. Think about whether you could make a point about the topic *and* support that point in three paragraphs.

1. Professional sports; **NARROWED ESSAY TOPIC:** _____

2. Vacation; **NARROWED ESSAY TOPIC:** _____

3. Personal goals; **NARROWED ESSAY TOPIC:** _____

4. Helping others; **NARROWED ESSAY TOPIC:** _____

5. Things that annoy you; **NARROWED ESSAY TOPIC:** _____

As you narrow your topic, you usually get some ideas about why that topic is important to you (or what is interesting about it) and what you want to say about it. Make a note of those ideas so that you can use them to write a thesis statement.

Write a Thesis Statement

The **thesis statement** usually includes both the narrowed topic and the main point the writer wants to make about it.

Narrowed topic	+	Main point	=	Thesis statement

Swimming benefits more parts of the body than most other exercises.

PRACTICE 2

Write a thesis statement for each of the following essay topics. After you've written each thesis statement, circle the topic and underline the main point.

1. How drinking affects driving ability; **THESIS:** _____

2. Annoying things about cell phone users; **THESIS:** _____

3. Kinds of fast-food restaurants; **THESIS:** _____

4. Some differences between what men like and what woman like; **THESIS:**

_____

5. Kinds of summer activities; **THESIS:** _____

PRACTICE 3

Write a thesis statement for each of the narrowed topics you wrote for Practice 1.

1. **NARROWED TOPIC:** _____

   THESIS: _____

2. **NARROWED TOPIC:** _____

   THESIS: _____

3. **NARROWED TOPIC:** _____

   THESIS: _____

4. **NARROWED TOPIC:** _____

   THESIS: _____

5. **NARROWED TOPIC:** _____

   THESIS: _____

You may have to rewrite your thesis statement several times, first after you write it and again as you read and revise your essay. Because the thesis statement sets up the whole essay, it must clearly state the main point that the essay will support.

PRACTICE 4 . . .

Rewrite three of the thesis statements you wrote for Practice 3. Think about how someone else would react to the original statement, and strongly state what you want to show, explain, or prove about your topic.

1. _____

2. _____

3. _____

Support Your Thesis Statement and Write Topic Sentences

Each body paragraph in an essay presents a different point that supports your thesis statement. The point of each paragraph is expressed in a topic sentence. Then, the rest of the sentences in the paragraph show, explain, or prove the topic sentence.

Using a prewriting technique is an excellent way to find support. You practiced these ways to get ideas (freewriting, brainstorming, mapping or clustering, journal writing, and using the Internet) in Chapter 5. If you need to review them, go back to that chapter. When you have completed your prewriting, read what you have written and select the ideas that will best support your thesis: You will turn these into topic sentences. You also need details and examples that will show, explain, or prove the support.

PRACTICE 5 . . . .

On a separate piece of paper, use a prewriting technique to get ideas to support your thesis and explain the support. Use one of the thesis statements you wrote for Practice 4.

PRACTICE 6 . . . .

Choose three points from your prewriting that support your thesis. Turn each support point into a topic sentence, and add details that explain the topic sentences.

1. **SUPPORT POINT:** _____

   TOPIC SENTENCE: _____

   _____

   DETAILS THAT EXPLAIN THE TOPIC SENTENCE: _____

2. **SUPPORT POINT:** _____

   TOPIC SENTENCE: _____

   _____

   DETAILS THAT EXPLAIN THE TOPIC SENTENCE: _____

3. **SUPPORT POINT:** _____

   TOPIC SENTENCE: _____

   _____

   DETAILS THAT EXPLAIN THE TOPIC SENTENCE: _____

Make a Plan

When you have chosen the best support for your thesis and have written topic sentences for each major support point, decide the order in which you should present the support. Three common ways to organize your ideas are time order, space order, and order of importance. For a review of these organization methods, see Chapter 7. Also, you will need to think of ideas for your introduction and your conclusion.

The planning stage is a good time to think of ideas for your introduction and conclusion. The introduction includes your thesis statement and previews what you will show, explain, or prove in the rest of your essay. It should let readers know what your purpose is and make them want to read the rest of the essay. The conclusion should both remind readers of your main point and make an observation based on what you have written. For examples of an introduction and conclusion, see the essay on pages 101–02.

Design your own essay-planning form.

PRACTICE 7 . . . .

Using your work from Practices 4 and 6, fill in the blanks that follow. For each topic sentence, write sentences for the supporting details. At the top, indicate what order of organization you are using and why.

ORDER OF ORGANIZATION: _____

REASON FOR USING THIS ORDER: _____

THESIS STATEMENT: _____

    OTHER IDEAS FOR INTRODUCTORY PARAGRAPH: _____

_____

TOPIC SENTENCE 1: _____

    SUPPORTING DETAILS (1 SENTENCE FOR EACH DETAIL): _____

_____

TOPIC SENTENCE 2: _____

    SUPPORTING DETAILS (1 SENTENCE FOR EACH DETAIL): _____

_____

TOPIC SENTENCE 3: _____

    SUPPORTING DETAILS (1 SENTENCE FOR EACH DETAIL): _____

_____

CONCLUSION REMINDING READERS OF MAIN POINT AND MAKING AN

OBSERVATION: _____

. . . .

Write, Revise, and Edit

The next step is to write your essay, using the outline you created and referring to the following basics of a good draft. Make sure to indent each paragraph. (If you are using a computer, you can do this with the tab key.)

■■ FOUR BASICS OF A GOOD DRAFT

1. It has an introduction that gets readers interested and includes a thesis statement.
2. It has a topic sentence for each paragraph supporting the thesis.
3. It has examples and details to support each topic sentence.
4. It has a conclusion that reminds readers of the main point and makes an observation.

PRACTICE 8 . . . .

Using your outline from Practice 7, write a draft essay.

. . . .

Get feedback on your draft by asking another student to answer the Questions for a Peer Reviewer on page 61. After taking a break, reread your draft essay, thinking about the feedback you received.

PRACTICE 9 . . . .

Revise your draft, using the following checklist as a guide. Or, if you prefer, write and revise an essay based on one of the Fifty Popular Essay Topics in the list that follows the checklist.

CHECKLIST: EVALUATING YOUR ESSAY
☐ My essay fulfills the assignment and includes *all* of the Four Basics of a Good Draft (p. 107).
☐ In the introduction, my thesis statement expresses my main point with confidence.
☐ The body paragraphs have good topic sentences that support the thesis statement.
☐ Detailed examples show, explain, or prove the points made in the topic sentences.
☐ The paragraphs are organized logically, and I've included transitions to move readers smoothly from one idea to the next.
☐ My concluding paragraph reminds readers of my main point and ends on a strong note.
☐ I have reread the essay, making improvements and checking for grammar and spelling errors.
☐ This essay is the best I can do, and I am ready to turn it in for a grade.

FIFTY POPULAR ESSAY TOPICS

Family traditions

Identity theft

Greediness

Cheating

Something I think is wrong

Moral values

Society today

Why college students don't vote

Vivid dreams

Something I would go to jail for

Mistakes

First love

Becoming (or being) a parent

Family feuds

Things that frighten me (or make me laugh)

FIFTY POPULAR ESSAY TOPICS

What I read in a month

Religious traditions

Effects of being popular/ unpopular

A first date

Belongings I would save from a fire

The kind of person I want to be

How to waste time

When does a child become an adult?

What I really care about

I wish someone would...

If I won the lottery,...

Losing gracefully

If I could be anyone,...

Things I would put in a time capsule

Star athletes' salaries

A statement of my beliefs

When I graduate, I hope...

Dear Mr. President,...

Job interviews

Favorite Web sites

My first best friend

Something I will regret for a long time

Something I will remember for a long time

Things I save

Procrastination

Why do I need to learn grammar?

Things I want to gain from college

How to stand up for your rights

Pets

When I wasn't treated fairly

What I expect in a friend

A news event that got my attention

The generation gap

How to fight stress

I wish I had more time to...

TOPIC 37: HOW TO WASTE TIME

1. PICK A TOPIC.
2. CHANGE IT.
3. CHANGE IT AGAIN.
4. REPEAT STEPS 2+3.

Practice Together

Working with a few other students, practice what you have learned in this chapter.

1. Pick one of the Fifty Popular Essay Topics and, as a group, narrow the topic, write a thesis statement, and list three major support points. Then, have someone in your group stand up and read your thesis statement and support to the class. Class members should call out other support that they can think of.

2. As a group, create a diagram or picture of the essay on pages 101–02. You might show the essay as a sandwich, making the thesis statement and introduction the top bun, the support the fillings, and the conclusion the bottom bun. When all groups are done, post your visuals on the wall so that people can see one another's work.

■ **LEARNING STYLES:** Look for activities in this chapter that are matched to your learning style. If you don't know your learning style, take the test on pages 26–28.

👁 Visual

🗣 Auditory

📖 Reading/writing

👣 Kinesthetic (movement)

3. Have each person read aloud the draft he or she wrote for Practice 8. Then, have other group members say at least one thing they liked about the draft and give at least two suggestions for improvement.

4. In your group, discuss what the billboard in the following picture means and whether it is effective. (Or choose another advertisement or billboard that you are all familiar with and discuss that.) If you were writing an essay about the billboard or the topic it deals with, what would your thesis statement be? What kind of support would you include? Present your ideas to the rest of the class.

Chapter Review

1. What are the three parts of an essay? _____

2. A thesis statement includes _____.

3. The major support for the main point is expressed in _____.

4. What are three ways to organize an essay? _____

5. What are some ways to improve an essay when you revise? _____

_____

_____

■ **TIP:** For help with building your vocabulary, see Appendix B.

6. **VOCABULARY:** Go back to any new words that you underlined in this chapter. Can you guess their meanings now? If not, look up the words in a dictionary.

LEARNING JOURNAL: Write for two minutes, completing and explaining this sentence: I don't feel that I really understand _____.

Unit Two Test
Writing Paragraphs

Read the following three paragraphs and circle the correct answers to the questions after each one.

1 After seventy-eight years, a nice, hot bath was certainly in order for the Mount Rushmore National Memorial in South Dakota. 2 In July 2005, the faces of presidents that are carved into the mountain got their first washing ever — a difficult but necessary process. 3 First, enormous pressure washers were placed behind the carved faces of George Washington, Thomas Jefferson, Theodore Roosevelt, and Abraham Lincoln. 4 The presidents' faces appear in that order from left to right. 5 The heavy machines and their companion hoses had to be brought to the top of the monument by helicopter. 6 Once the machines were in place, cleaning technicians began their dangerous job. 7 Hanging from harnesses anchored on top of the sculpture, workers sprayed the monument with over seven thousand gallons of boiling water every day. 8 No soap, chemicals, whiteners, or bleach were used, just the water shooting from a hose. 9 _____ three weeks of washing, the workers had removed thick layers of dirt, algae, and lichen that were damaging the rocks. 10 The lichen, combining algae and fungus, were particularly harmful because their roots were digging holes in the rocks. 11 When the lichen die and fall away, water then collects, freezes, and expands in the holes, causing the rocks to crack. 12 The faces of Mount Rushmore are now brighter than they have been in many years. 13 _____, however, the cleaning has helped ensure that the monument will be around for the generations of tomorrow.

1. Which sentence from the paragraph is the topic sentence?
   a. Sentence 1   c. Sentence 9
   b. Sentence 2   d. Sentence 12

2. Which of the following sentences provides primary support?
   a. Sentence 1   c. Sentence 4
   b. Sentence 3   d. Sentence 8

3. Which of the following sentences is a supporting detail?
   a. Sentence 1   c. Sentence 11
   b. Sentence 5   d. Sentence 13

4. Which of the following sentences does not provide primary or secondary support for the topic sentence?
   a. Sentence 4   c. Sentence 10
   b. Sentence 9   d. Sentence 11

5. Which of the following sentences would be a good alternative topic sentence for the paragraph?

a. Thick layers of dirt, algae, and lichen were removed from Mount Rushmore National Memorial in July 2005.

b. The process was not easy, but Mount Rushmore National Memorial recently received a much-needed cleaning for the first time in its seventy-eight-year history.

c. Mount Rushmore National Memorial is a more enjoyable place to visit now that the monument has been cleaned.

d. The faces of Mount Rushmore National Memorial were being damaged by thick layers of dirt, algae, and lichens.

6. Which transition, inserted into blank 9, would aid coherence?

a. Since   c. Instead of

b. Above all   d. After

7. Which transition, inserted into blank 13, would aid coherence?

a. Most important   c. While

b. For instance   d. Soon

8. What method of development does this paragraph use?

a. argument   c. comparison and contrast

b. process analysis   d. definition

9. What order of organization does it follow?

a. time order   c. order of importance

b. space order

1 Many of us are living longer than we otherwise would have thanks to scientists like Sir Richard Doll. 2 Doll's research played an important role in making people aware of the connection between smoking and lung cancer, emphysema, heart attacks, and many other health problems. 3 He also proved that electrical power lines do not cause cancer. 4 It seems hard to believe today, but in the first half of the twentieth century, few people suspected that smoking could cause such serious consequences. 5 When Doll and other scientists began their search for the cause of lung cancer in 1947, they initially believed that it was caused by automobile exhaust or by the tar in road paving. 6 _____, Doll's numerous interviews with people who had lung cancer clearly showed that cigarette smoking was the most likely cause. 7 Published in 1950, the results of Doll's initial study sparked a worldwide campaign against smoking. 8 In 1954, the United Kingdom's health minister called a press conference to publicize Doll's research and warn the public of the dangers of smoking. 9 Since then, the number of smokers worldwide has dramatically decreased. 10 For example, in 1954, around 80 percent of British adults smoked. 11 Today, that number is down to about 26 percent. 12 In 2004, Doll published his fifty-year follow-up study of forty thousand British doc-

tors. **13** The study found that, on average, smoking over a lifetime short-ened a person's life span by ten years. **14** In 2005, Doll died of heart fail-ure at the age of ninety-two. **15** He himself had quit smoking in 1950, after smoking for nineteen years.

10. Which sentence from the paragraph is the topic sentence?

   a. Sentence 2   c. Sentence 5

   b. Sentence 4   d. Sentence 13

11. Which of the following sentences provides primary support?

   a. Sentence 1   c. Sentence 10

   b. Sentence 7   d. Sentence 14

12. Which of the following sentences is a supporting detail?

   a. Sentence 2   c. Sentence 7

   b. Sentence 3   d. Sentence 10

13. Which of the following sentences does not provide primary or second-ary support for the topic sentence?

   a. Sentence 3   c. Sentence 7

   b. Sentence 4   d. Sentence 8

14. Which of the following sentences would be a good alternative topic sen-tence for the paragraph?

   a. By establishing the dangers of smoking, Sir Richard Doll helped many people live healthier and longer lives.

   b. After publishing his first study on smoking and lung cancer in 1950, Sir Richard Doll conducted a fifty-year follow-up study, publishing the results in 2004.

   c. Several scientists, including Sir Richard Doll, studied the possible link between smoking and lung cancer, emphysema, heart attacks, and many other health problems.

   d. Sir Richard Doll, who himself quit smoking in 1950, died of heart failure in 2005 at the age of 92.

15. Which transition, inserted into blank 6, would aid coherence?

   a. However   c. Furthermore

   b. For example   d. Worst of all

   1 Not all computer hackers—those who break into computer sys-tems—are criminals; some hackers aim to help companies, not hurt them. **2** Today, many companies are hiring "white-hat" hackers to help them improve their security systems. **3** Paid to try to break into a com-pany's computer system, a white-hat hacker informs the company of weaknesses in its network. **4** _____, the weaknesses can be patched before being discovered by criminal "black-hat" hackers. **5** Sometimes, a white-hat hacker can even save a company money by pointing out that an expensive security tool isn't actually necessary.

6 The bank that I work for thought its computer files were secure until it hired my brother Erik, a white-hat hacker, to find out for sure. 7 Within only two days, Erik had accessed the bank's most secure files from his home computer. 8 He reported back to bank officials about the network's weaknesses and helped them fix the problems. 9 Erik sometimes finds it difficult to enjoy strolling through a museum because he is most interested in figuring out how to hack into the museum's security system. 10 Security programs continually get better at hiding information, but that only makes the black-hat hackers who want to steal that information more creative. 11 _____, the business for white-hat hackers is booming these days.

16. Which sentence from the paragraph is the topic sentence?
   a. Sentence 1   c. Sentence 6
   b. Sentence 4   d. Sentence 10

17. Which of the following sentences provides primary support?
   a. Sentence 1   c. Sentence 4
   b. Sentence 2   d. Sentence 8

18. Which of the following sentences is a supporting detail?
   a. Sentence 1   c. Sentence 7
   b. Sentence 6   d. Sentence 9

19. Which of the following sentences does not provide primary or secondary support for the topic sentence?
   a. Sentence 3   c. Sentence 8
   b. Sentence 5   d. Sentence 9

20. Which of the following sentences would be a good alternative topic sentence for the paragraph?
   a. Erik found it relatively easy to break into the computer network of the bank that had hired him.
   b. White-hat hackers like Erik have trouble enjoying museums because they feel they must figure out the museums' security systems.
   c. Many companies do not realize how easy it might be to break into their network.
   d. Although they have a bad reputation, not all hackers are criminals.

21. Which transition, inserted into blank 4, would aid coherence?
   a. In contrast   c. Then
   b. In addition   d. Nearby

22. Which transition, inserted into blank 11, would aid coherence?
   a. As a result   c. Later
   b. Most important   d. Nevertheless

■ **TIP:** For advice on taking tests, see Appendix A.

Unit Three

Editing for the Four Most Serious Errors

10
The Complete Sentence

Key Parts to Know

The Four Most Serious Errors

This unit focuses first on four grammar errors that people most often notice in writing.

THE FOUR MOST SERIOUS ERRORS

1. Fragments (Chapter 11).
2. Run-ons and comma splices (Chapter 12).
3. Subject-verb agreement problems (Chapter 13).
4. Verb problems (Chapters 14 and 15).

If you can avoid these four—just four—kinds of errors, your writing will improve. This chapter reviews the basic sentence parts that you will need to know to avoid or correct these errors, and more.

VOCABULARY: Underline any words in this chapter that are new to you.

IDEA JOURNAL: Write about a time when you were sick.

An audiovisual tutorial on finding and fixing the four most serious errors is available on a CD that comes with this book.

Understand What a Sentence Is

A **sentence** is the basic unit of written communication. A complete sentence in formal English has a **subject**, a **verb**, and a **complete thought**. Sentences are also called **independent clauses** because they make sense by themselves, without other information.

> Language note: In English, subjects cannot be left out of sentences.
>
> **INCORRECT**   **Called** Stephan last night.
>
> **CORRECT**   *I* **called** Stephan last night.

None of the following examples is a sentence.

_____ **invented** the telephone in 1876.

The Great Wall of China _____ the largest manmade structure in the world.

The movie *Million Dollar Baby*, which won several Oscars,[1] _____ Hilary Swank.

[1]**Oscars:** *film-industry awards given every year to the best movie, best actor, and so on*

The first example is missing a subject, the second is missing a verb, and the third is not a complete thought. Here they are as complete sentences:

Alexander Graham Bell invented the telephone in 1876.

The Great Wall of China is the largest manmade structure in the world.

The movie *Million Dollar Baby*, which won several Oscars, **starred** Hilary Swank.

■ **TIP:** In all the sentence examples in this chapter, subjects are light blue and verbs are red.

> Language note: Formal English has many sentence patterns, but all of them build on just three basic structures.
>
> 1. Subject   Verb
>   ↓   ↓
>   **Deshawn paints.**
>
> 2. Subject   Verb   Direct object
>   ↓   ↓   ↓
>   **Deshawn painted** three houses last summer.
>
> A **direct object** receives the action of a verb.
>
> 3. Subject   Verb   Direct object   Indirect object
>   ↓   ↓   ↓   ↓
>   **Deshawn gave** the extra paint to Rudy.
>
> An **indirect object** is the person or thing to whom or for whom the action is performed.

👁 ✍ In a piece of your own writing, highlight the subjects in one color and the verbs in another.

Find Subjects

A **subject** is the word or words that a sentence is about. Subjects can be **nouns** (people—Alexander Graham Bell; places—the Great Wall of China; or things—The movie *Million Dollar Baby*). They can also be **pronouns** (like *I, you, he/she, it, we, they*).

■ **TIP:** For more on nouns, see Chapter 16. For more on pronouns, see Chapter 17.

A **simple subject** is just the one noun or pronoun that the sentence is about.

The summer-school students were taking final exams.

A **complete subject** includes all the words that describe the simple subject.

The summer-school students were taking final exams.

PRACTICE 1 . . . .

Each of the following items is missing a subject. For each item, add a subject to make a complete sentence.

EXAMPLE: My _____car_____ broke down last week.

1. The _____ told me that the repairs would cost $1,400.

2. _____ should just buy a new car, according to my sister.

3. _____ is embarrassed to be seen in a beat-up station wagon.

4. The brown _____ is peeling off in several places.

5. The _____ hasn't worked all summer.

6. A/an _____ made a big dent in the side door.

7. Last month, a/an _____ cracked the windshield.

8. _____ agreed to look at new cars this weekend.

9. A new _____ would be my dream car.

10. However, a used _____ is closer to my price range.

PRACTICE 2 . . . .

Underline the simple subject in each of the following sentences.

EXAMPLE: Airport security has changed the way many people dress for travel.

1. My father was always told to dress nicely when flying.

2. He used to wear a suit to the airport.

3. Today, he dresses differently because of tight airport security.

4. The metal detector is often triggered by a piece of clothing or an accessory.

5. The traveler may have to remove his or her coat, belt, and shoes.

6. This process often slows down the security line.

7. You may have noticed an "airport-friendly" label on some shoes and clothing.

8. An airport-friendly item contains no metal.

9. My dad now wears airport-friendly flip-flops to the airport.

10. A flip-flop is less formal but easier to slip on and off than a dress shoe.

PRACTICE 3

In each of the following sentences, underline the complete subject.

> **EXAMPLE:** <u>The common mosquito</u> is one of the most unpopular creatures on earth.

1. These annoying insects have bothered people for thousands of years.

2. The female mosquitoes are the ones that bite.

3. The hungry pests are attracted to body heat and certain chemicals.

4. Human sweat contains one of these chemicals, lactic acid.

5. Mosquitoes also like the smell of perfume.

6. Some scientists recently made an interesting discovery.

7. Their discovery, however, is good news only for some people.

8. Some lucky people produce certain chemicals.

9. These special chemicals keep mosquitoes away from them.

10. For the rest of us, bug spray is the best defense.

PRACTICE 4

Each of the following items is missing a complete subject. Turn each item into a sentence by adding a complete subject.

> **EXAMPLE:** *My Uncle Brian got*
> ~~Got~~ excited when he saw the sale advertised in the
> ^
> newspaper.

1. Was 30 percent off the regular price.

2. Forgetting everything else, rushed to the store.

3. Was packed with shoppers.

4. Fought his way to the counter to make his purchase.

5. Is now his favorite toy.

📖 📖 Read aloud any sections of this book that are assigned as homework. Make up your own examples and say them aloud.

. . . .

Singular and Plural Subjects

Singular means one, and *plural* means more than one. Sentences can have singular or plural subjects.

SINGULAR   Elizabeth Blackwell was the first woman doctor in the United States.

[There is one noun: *Elizabeth Blackwell.*]

PLURAL   Elizabeth Blackwell and her sister Emily were both doctors.

[There are two separate nouns: *Elizabeth Blackwell* and *her sister Emily.*]

The Blackwell sisters started a women's medical college in the late 1800s.

[There is one plural noun: *The Blackwell sisters.*]

Language note: In the present tense, verbs for third-person singular subjects (like *Bob, he, she,* or *it*) end in *-s* or *-es.*

Singular   Singular
subject   verb
↓   ↓

Perry hates vegetables.

Plural   Plural
subject   verb
↓   ↓

The **boys hate** vegetables.

For more on verb tense, see Chapters 14 and 15.

PRACTICE 5 . . . .

In each of the following sentences, underline the complete subject. In the space to the left of each item, write "S" if the subject is singular. If the subject is plural, write "P."

EXAMPLE: $\underline{\quad P \quad}$ Many people use the Internet every day.

— 1. College students spend an average of 15.1 hours online weekly, according to one survey.

— 2. On average, male students spend slightly more time online than female students do.

— 3. Google.com and ESPN.com are among students' most frequently visited Web sites.

— 4. Despite its many advantages, the Internet makes some people nervous.

— 5. Some Internet users are concerned about losing their privacy.

— 6. My mother and my grandmother refuse to make online purchases.

— 7. My mother likes to see a product before buying it.

— 8. Grandma and many other people feel uncomfortable using their credit cards online.

— 9. Eventually, online shopping sites may become more popular than traditional retail stores.

— 10. For now, though, many people prefer to go online just for information.

PRACTICE 6 . .

Write five sentences using plural subjects.

Prepositional Phrases

A common mistake is to think that the subject of the sentence is in a **prepositional phrase**, which starts with a **preposition** and ends with a noun (the object of the preposition).

Prepositional phrase

In the hall closet, I found my birthday gifts.

Preposition   Object of preposition

You might think that the words *hall closet* are the subject of the sentence, but—*and this is very important*—**the subject of a sentence is** <u>**never**</u> **in a prepositional phrase.**

To find prepositional phrases, look for prepositions.

Common Prepositions

about	before	except	of	to
above	behind	for	off	toward
across	below	from	on	under
after	beneath	in	out	until
against	beside	inside	outside	up
along	between	into	over	upon
among	by	like	past	with
around	down	near	since	within
at	during	next to	through	without
because of				

Write sentences with these prepositions and then say them aloud.

> **Language note:** *In* and *on* can be tricky prepositions for people whose native language is not English. Keep these definitions and examples in mind:
>
> *in* = inside of (in the box, in the office) or within a period of time (in January, in the fall, in three weeks)
>
> *on* = on top of (on the table, on my foot), located in a certain place (on the page, on Main Street), or at a certain time (on January first)
>
> If you get confused by what prepositions to use in common English phrases, see Chapter 21.

To make sure that you don't confuse the noun in the prepositional phrase (the object of the preposition) with the subject of the sentence, try crossing out the prepositional phrase.

Prepositional phrase

~~After the graduation party~~, Duane and Sally went out dancing.

Preposition   Object of preposition

Many sentences have more than one prepositional phrase. To find the subject, cross out all the prepositional phrases.

~~At the Apollo Theater in New York City~~, many famous African American musicians got their start.

Some ~~of the big future stars~~ were Count Basie, Billie Holiday, Ella Fitzgerald, and Aretha Franklin.

~~In the 1970s, after some years of slow business,~~ the theater closed.

~~After major remodeling,~~ the theater reopened ~~in 1985~~.

> **PRACTICE 7** . . . .

In the following paragraph, cross out any prepositional phrases and underline the subject of each sentence.

(1) Without a doubt, crows are intelligent birds. (2) Crows in the Pacific Northwest steal food using both violence and trickery. (3) Crows from this region violently attack other crows for food. (4) Sometimes, however, the thief simply sneaks a bite of another bird's food. (5) Curious about this behavior, scientists at the University of Washington observed a group of fifty-five crows. (6) After thirty months, the researchers made an interesting discovery. (7) The crows are rough and aggressive while stealing from distant relatives and nonrelatives. (8) However, crows in the same family steal by using trickery instead of violence. (9) Like most humans, these birds are nicer to members of their family than to nonrelatives.

Find Verbs

The **main verb** in the sentence either tells what the subject does or connects it to another word that describes it.

Clarence Birdseye invented frozen foods in 1923.

[*Invented* tells what Birdseye, the subject, did.]

By 1930, he was ready to sell his product.

[*Was* connects the subject to a word that describes him: *ready*.]

Action Verbs

Action verbs show the subject *doing* something.

Alvaro set his mug of coffee in the microwave.

After one minute, he took it out, but the coffee wasn't hot enough.

He put the coffee back in for thirty seconds.

Unfortunately, it exploded.

PRACTICE 8 . . . .

In each of the following sentences, fill in the blank with the correct action verb from the list below.

ACTION VERBS

charge	earn	install	wanted
developed	go	suggested	withdrew
drink	hated	threatened	

> 👁 📖 Write a sentence with an action verb and then draw it.

EXAMPLE: After a heavy snowstorm, some hardware stores ___*charge*___ more than usual for snow shovels.

1. Several years ago, the president of a major soda company _____ a similar scheme.

2. The president _____ to raise the price of soda on hot days.

3. People _____ more soda in warm weather than in cold weather.

4. The company, therefore, would _____ more money.

5. The president _____ a plan.

6. The company would _____ thermometers on vending machines.

7. At a certain temperature, the price of soda from the vending machine would _____ up.

8. Unfortunately for the president, the company's customers _____ his idea.

9. On Internet chat rooms, many people _____ never to buy the company's soda again.

10. The president quietly _____ his idea, but a lot of people never forgot it.

PRACTICE 9 . . . .

In the following paragraph, double-underline the action verb in each sentence.

(1) I lost most of my hair years ago. (2) Upset about my baldness, I complained to my close friends. (3) Some friends teased me about my shiny head. (4) However, most people ignored it. (5) After a while, I forgot about my embarrassment. (6) Then, I heard an ad on the radio for a new miracle drug. (7) According to the ad, the drug replaces lost

hair. (8) Then, I read about a new laser treatment for baldness. (9) I rejected both ideas as too good to be true. (10) I now accept my baldness, my right-handedness, my poor eyesight, and the rest of myself as well.

. . . .

Linking Verbs

Linking verbs connect the subject of the sentence to a word or words that describe it. Some words can be either action verbs or linking verbs, depending on how they are used.

> **ACTION VERB**   Mario **tasted** the lasagna.
>
> [Mario *does* something: he *tasted* the lasagna.]
>
> **LINKING VERB**   The lasagna **tasted** delicious.
>
> [The lasagna doesn't *do* anything. *Tasted* links lasagna to a word that describes it: *delicious*.]

👁 🖐 Draw a linking verb or act out its function.

In the following sentences, the linking verbs are red and the words describing the subject are in italics.

Joseph McCarthy **was** *a powerful senator from Wisconsin.*

He **felt** *certain* that many people in America were communists.[2]

McCarthy **seemed** *unable to think of anything other than finding what he called "disloyal persons."*

Even normal citizens **appeared** *dangerous* to McCarthy.

[2]**communists:** *members of the Communist Party, which was considered a threat to the United States, especially in the middle of the twentieth century*

Common Linking Verbs

FORMS OF BE	FORMS OF SEEM AND BECOME	FORMS OF SENSE VERBS
am	become, becomes, became	appear, appears, appeared
are		
is	seem, seems, seemed	feel, feels, felt
was		look, looks, looked
were		smell, smells, smelled
		taste, tastes, tasted

> **Language note:** The verb *be* is required in English to complete sentences like the following:
>
> | **INCORRECT** | Tonya well now. |
> |---|---|
> | **CORRECT** | Tonya **is** well now. |

PRACTICE 10

In each of the following sentences, underline the subject, double-underline the linking verb, and circle the word or phrase that describes the subject.

EXAMPLE: Melissa's tennis opponent looked tired.

1. Now, Melissa felt confident.

2. Her mind became focused on her opponent's weaknesses.

3. Her serves were stronger than ever.

4. Suddenly, her opponent appeared more alert.

5. He seemed serious and aggressive.

6. Melissa became upset with herself.

7. Tennis was great fun.

8. But only winning seemed satisfying.

9. Keeping her goal in mind, she looked determined.

10. After playing a strong match, Melissa was the new national champion.

Helping Verbs

Helping verbs help the main verb by adding another word or words.

Thumbelina **can hold** her breath for one hundred seconds.

[*Can* is the helping verb, and *hold* is the main verb.]

In the following sentences, the helping verbs are in italics and the main verbs are bold.

Her friends *are* **hoping** that she can win the breath-holding contest.

She almost *did* **win** last year.

She *might* **win** the grand prize this year.

The same person *has* **won** several years in a row.

Common Helping Verbs

FORMS OF *BE*	FORMS OF *HAVE*	FORMS OF *DO*	OTHER
be	have	do	can/could
am	has	does	may/might/must
are	had	did	should/will/would
been			
being			
is			
was			
were			

Language note: The words in the "Other" column are also called *modal auxiliaries*. If you have trouble using them correctly, see Chapter 21.

INCORRECT	His dog ~~will~~ might bark.
CORRECT	His dog might bark.

Using helping verbs in negative statements and questions can also be tricky. Chapter 21 shows how to form such statements.

> Make up sentences with helping verbs, saying them aloud.

PRACTICE 11 . . . .

In each of the following sentences, double-underline the complete verb (the linking verb or the helping verb plus the main verb) and circle the linking or helping verb.

EXAMPLE: In my nursing class this semester, I (am) learning some interesting facts about famous people.

1. Alexander the Great, Benjamin Franklin, and other familiar figures throughout history have suffered from gout.

2. Gout is a common form of arthritis.

3. The condition is most common among men over the age of forty.

4. People with gout are troubled by terrible pain in their big toes and other joints.

5. The number of people with gout has doubled since 1969.

6. People from all parts of society can have gout, not just the rich.

7. Gaining thirty pounds or more after the age of twenty-one can double a person's risk for gout.

8. According to a recent study, gout is seen most often among men with a diet high in meat and seafood.

9. People with gout should watch their diets carefully.

10. Gout is treated with medications and rest.

Decide If There Is a Complete Thought

Even when a group of words has a subject and a verb, it may not have a complete thought.

> **Because their team won the championship.**
>
> [There is a subject (*team*) and a verb (*won*), but you can't tell what is going on without more information.]

In the following examples, the added words (in italics) create a complete thought.

> *The students went* wild because their team won the championship.
>
> Because their team won the championship, *the students went* wild.

READ ALOUD

Read the following sentences aloud and ask if there is a complete thought.

> Who sat next to me in class.
>
> Damon saved the game.

A word group that has a subject and a verb but that is not a complete thought is called a **dependent clause**. It is not a sentence because it is *dependent* on another set of words for meaning.

PRACTICE 12 . .

Two of the following items contain complete thoughts, and eight do not. In the space to the left of each item, write "C" for complete thought or "I" for incomplete thought. If you write "I," add words to make a sentence.

EXAMPLE: <u>I</u> *I got several*
<u>Several</u> speeding tickets last year.
                                    ^

___ 1. The cost of my car insurance.

___ 2. After I paid the speeding tickets.

___ 3. The speed limit in my town.

___ 4. It is twenty-five miles per hour.

___ 5. Even though my friends make fun of me.

___ 6. If they had paid $225 in speeding fines.

___ 7. Another speeding ticket.

___ 8. When aggressive drivers follow me too closely.

___ 9. Sometimes, impatient drivers honk their horns at me.

___ 10. Continue driving exactly at the speed limit.

PRACTICE 13 . .

Write five sentences of your own. Each should have a subject and a verb, and each should express a complete thought.

Edit for Sentence Elements in College, Work, and Everyday Life

EDITING REVIEW 1: COLLEGE . .

The following paragraph is similar to one you might find in a college psychology textbook. Underline the simple subject and double-underline the complete verb of each sentence. Cross out any prepositional phrases. The first sentence has been marked for you.

(1) <u>People</u> ~~with obsessive-compulsive disorder~~ <u><u>have</u></u> rituals, or repeated behaviors. (2) For instance, they may check a stove several times to make sure it's turned off. (3) These people may not feel in control of

their actions. (4) In their minds, their actions may prevent something terrible. (5) They feel less anxious as a result. (6) Symptoms of obsessive-compulsive behavior are varied. (7) People may clean their homes, their clothing, or themselves dozens or even hundreds of times during the day. (8) Another ritual may involve touching or not touching certain items. (9) Also, sufferers might repeat certain words, phrases, or expressions. (10) In most cases, people with the disorder are aware of the unreasonable nature of their behavior.

EDITING REVIEW 2: WORK/USING FORMAL ENGLISH

■ **TIP:** For advice on using formal English, see Chapter 4. For advice on avoiding slang, see Chapter 25.

Rewrite the following memo, revising incomplete sentences by adding a subject or a verb, or by adding words to create a complete thought. Then, change informal language to formal language. The first sentence has been edited for you. You should find six cases of informal language.

DATE: July 10, 2006

TO: Jon Smithson

FROM: Katya Stein

SUBJECT: Salary Raise

(1) Your supervisor, Eduardo Lopez, recently met with me to ~~give me the 411 on~~ *talk about* your projects. (2) Your work performance in the past year. (3) I am psyched to inform you of a raise in your salary. (4) Will be upped by 5 percent. (5) Will begin with your next paycheck. (6) Your achievements.

- (7) Completed additional training by attending company classes.
- (8) Evening classes in process technology at San Jacinto Community College.
- (9) Twenty hours of overtime.
- (10) After we reorganized responsibilities in your department.
- (11) When two members of your department took off.
- (12) Awesome leadership skills.
- (13) Organizing events for the company barbecue.

(14) Are too appreciated.

In the following paragraph, revise incomplete sentences by adding a subject or a verb, or by adding words to create a complete thought. Three sentences are correct; write "C" next to them. The first sentence has been edited for you.

(1) Although a teen's first car may be old and unreliable, *she probably remembers it with affection.* (2) A car represents a step toward adulthood. (3) Freedom from parental controls. (4) My first car was my grandmother's old car. (5) An ancient, unattractive, canary-yellow Oldsmobile. (6) Because the air conditioner was broken, (7) Dented and rusty in spots. (8) Embarrassed to be seen driving it. (9) Called it the "junk-mobile." (10) Nevertheless, driving the junk-mobile was better than riding with Mom, taking the school bus, or walking to school.

Write and Edit Your Own Work

ASSIGNMENT 1: WRITE . .

Tell about a time in your life when something didn't happen the way you expected it to. What was good about the experience, and what was bad about it? How did it change you? When you are done, check that each sentence has a subject, a verb, and a complete thought.

ASSIGNMENT 2: EDIT . .

Check for subjects, verbs, and complete thoughts in sentences from a paper you are writing for this course or another course, or from a piece of writing from your work or everyday life.

Practice Together

Working with a few other students, practice what you have learned in this chapter.

1. Have each group member write a sentence on a sheet of paper. Then, pass your sentences to another member of the group. Members should

take turns calling out subjects and verbs in the sentences they received, and they should say whether or not there is a complete thought. If a sentence is not complete, discuss what needs to be added. 🎧 📖 🖐

2. Break into pairs. Have each student explain to the other what a complete sentence is. Then, have each one say a complete sentence. Finally, use the verb *look* as an action verb in one sentence and as a linking verb in another sentence. 🎧

3. Have a group member write a complete sentence on the board. Have another student add a sentence to the first, continuing the idea. Keep going until all group members have written at least one sentence. Together, read aloud what you have written and agree on whether or not the sentences are complete. Also, identify the action, linking, and helping verbs. 🎧 📖 🖐

4. Have each group member draw a picture that shows some kind of action. Then, exchange your pictures with another person in the group. Each person should write a sentence describing what is happening in the other's picture. Then, the drawer and the writer should stand up, say the sentence together, and name the subject and the verb. 👁 🎧 📖 🖐

5. For each term in this chapter, make a flash card with an example of the term, a sample sentence, and, if you like, drawings. Use the flash cards to study with students in your group. 👁 🎧 📖 🖐

6. Create a study guide for this chapter, recording important terms and examples. Use the guide to study with other students in your group. 🎧 📖

■ **LEARNING STYLES:** Look for activities in this chapter that are matched to your learning style. If you don't know your learning style, take the test on pages 26–28.

👁 Visual

🎧 Auditory

📖 Reading/writing

🖐 Kinesthetic (movement)

Chapter Review

1. What are the three necessary elements of a sentence in formal written English? _____ Write a complete sentence, identifying the complete subject and the complete verb.

2. What is the difference between a simple subject and a complete subject?

_____

_____ Underline where these terms are first defined in the chapter.

3. The subject of a sentence is never in _____.

4. Highlight where action verbs, linking verbs, and helping verbs are defined in this chapter, and write a sentence for each kind of verb.

LEARNING JOURNAL:
Write for two minutes about something in this chapter that confuses you.

■ **TIP:** For help with building your vocabulary, see Appendix B.

5. A dependent clause has a _____ and a _____ but is not _____

_____.

6. **VOCABULARY:** Go back to any new words that you underlined in this chapter. Can you guess their meanings now? If not, look up the words in a dictionary.

11

Fragments

Sentences That Are Missing a Key Part

Understand What Fragments Are

A **fragment** is a group of words that is missing one or more parts of a complete sentence.

FRAGMENT	To the store.
	[*Who* is doing *what*? You can't tell without more information.]
SENTENCE	Dara **drove** to the store.
	[A subject, *Dara*, and an action verb, *drove*, make the fragment a complete sentence. Now you know *who did what*.]

READ ALOUD

Stand up and read the following word groups aloud, pausing at the periods. Is there a difference in the way you say the fragment and the sentence? If you read only the words in *italics*, would they be a complete thought?

FRAGMENT	I am going to a concert on Friday. *At Memorial Arena.*
SENTENCE	I am going to a concert on Friday at Memorial Arena.
FRAGMENT	Jack loves Florida. *Because it is warm.*
SENTENCE	Jack loves Florida because it is warm.
FRAGMENT	Penny broke her leg. *Snowboarding last week.*
SENTENCE	Penny broke her leg snowboarding last week.

VOCABULARY: Under-line any words in this chapter that are new to you.

■ **TIP:** In all the sentence examples in this chapter, subjects are light blue and verbs are red.

👁 Draw a fragment. The picture at the start of the chapter (p. 135) may give you some ideas.

📖 Complete and support the statement "I am a good _____." You are applying for a job in the financial aid office of your college.

In the Real World, Why Is It Important to Correct Fragments?

In writing, a fragment is one of the grammar errors that people notice most, and it can make a bad impression on bosses, clients, and instructors.

Read aloud Jeremy Trail's written response to the following job-interview question, pausing at all periods. Can you hear the fragments?

> How would you complete and support the statement "I am a good _____"?
>
> **JEREMY TRAIL'S ANSWER:**
>
> I am a good listener. This trait serves me well in all areas of my life. At work, for example. I listen carefully to directions. To do the job right. I listen to all customers, even older people. Who talk very slowly and repeat themselves. Listening carefully takes patience. I listen quietly and wait for people to finish. I also listen to my colleagues. To hear what they think and how we can work together. Being a good listener is key to being a good worker. I believe this ability to listen makes me a good candidate. For the position at Stillmark Company.
>
> **EMPLOYER'S RESPONSE TO JEREMY'S ANSWER:**
>
> Jeremy's writing had several errors. He may be able to listen, which is important, but he can't write correctly, and that's important in the job, too. When I read applicants' answers, I'm looking for ways to narrow the field of candidates. With Jeremy's answer, I found a way. He wouldn't be hired.

🎧 👁 An audiovisual tutorial on finding and fixing the four most serious errors, including fragments, is available on a CD that comes with this book.

Learning how to avoid or correct fragments is important because it will prevent you from being in a situation such as Jeremy's, in which he was ruled out for a job right away.

■ PRACTICE 1 ·

There are five fragments in Jeremy's writing. Looking for subjects, verbs, and complete thoughts in each word group, underline what you think are the fragments.

· ·

■ **TIP:** To do this chapter, you need to understand the following terms: *sentence*, *subject*, *verb*, *preposition*, and *prepositional phrase*. (For review, see Chapter 10.)

The following section will explain how to find and fix five common types of fragments.

Find and Correct Fragments

Trouble Spot 1: Fragments That Start with a Prepositional Phrase

IDEA JOURNAL: Write about a time when you learned something new.

FIND: Read each sentence in your writing carefully, stopping at periods.

The groom sneezed ten times. (During) **the wedding.**

- Circle any preposition that begins a word group.
- In this word group, underline any subject and double-underline any verb.
- If a subject or verb is missing, or if there is not a complete thought, there is a fragment. [The word group in this example is a fragment: It doesn't have a subject, a verb, or a complete thought.]

FIX: Correct the fragment by connecting it to the sentence either before or after it. Or make the fragment into its own sentence.

The groom sneezed ten times, *d* **During the wedding.**

He interrupted the wedding vows.
The groom sneezed ten times. ~~During the wedding.~~

- If the prepositional phrase comes first, a comma must follow it.

During the wedding, the groom sneezed ten times.

■ **TIP:** For a list of common prepositions, see page 123.

Make your own find-and-fix charts for each type of fragment.

PREPOSITIONAL-PHRASE FRAGMENTS

Last week, I found a starfish. *At the beach.*

Free parking is available. *Behind the mall.*

I met Joe on Chester Street. *By the stop sign.*

FRAGMENT JOINED TO SENTENCES

Last week, I found a starfish at the beach.

Free parking is available behind the mall.

I met Joe on Chester Street by the stop sign.

PREPOSITIONAL-PHRASE FRAGMENTS

I visited the Super Duper Dollar Store. *In the Emerald Square Mall.*

I am taking a three-week luxury cruise with Carnival Cruise Lines. *With my mother.*

FRAGMENTS MADE INTO THEIR OWN SENTENCES

I visited the Super Duper Dollar Store. It is in the Emerald Square Mall.

I am taking a three-week luxury cruise with Carnival Cruise Lines. My mother is coming along.

The word groups in italics have no subject (remember that the subject is *never* in the prepositional phrase). Also, they have no verb and no complete thought.

PRACTICE 2

In the following items, circle any preposition that appears at the beginning of a word group. Then, correct fragments by connecting them to the previous or the next sentence.

> **EXAMPLE:** (After) a ten-year study of people ages seventy and older,
> A group of scientists reached some interesting conclusions.

1. Among older people. Those with close friends tend to live longer.

2. Through their research. The scientists also learned that the older people with the most good friends lived the longest.

3. Having close family ties did not affect the life span. Of the people studied.

4. This may come as a surprise To most of us.

5. Before the study was published. Many people believed that staying close to family members would help a person live longer.

6. The researchers interviewed over fourteen hundred people. During the study.

7. They gathered their data. By interviewing the participants every year for the first four years of the study.

8. Over the remaining six years. Researchers talked with the participants twice.

9. This study sends a clear message. About our older relatives and friends.

10. For a long, healthy life. Friendship is important.

■ **TIP:** For more practice, visit Exercise Central at <**bedfordstmartins.com/ realskills**>.

PRACTICE 3 . . . .

Each of the following items is a fragment beginning with a prepositional phrase. Turn each fragment into a complete sentence by adding the missing sentence elements.

EXAMPLE: With six parties to attend, *, Amy was tired.*

1. By herself.

2. Out of the six parties.

3. At those parties.

4. During high school.

5. With a few close friends.

6. After graduation.

7. In the future.

8. Since meeting these new people.

9. Through meeting new people and doing new things.

10. At the next party.

PRACTICE 4 . . . .

In the following paragraph, eight of the ten items include a fragment that starts with a prepositional phrase. Underline any fragment and then correct it either by adding the missing sentence elements or by connecting it to the previous or the next sentence. Two sentences are correct; write "C" next to them.

(1) After eating a meal. You should wait for a while before going swimming. (2) Most of us have heard this warning since we were young. We might even repeat it to our own children. (3) At the pool. Children wait impatiently for their food to digest. (4) They take the warning seriously, believing that muscle cramps caused by food might lead to drowning. (5) From a review of the available statistics. It now appears that this warning is a myth. (6) Of drownings in the United States. Less than 1 percent occurred right after the victim ate a meal, according to one study. (7) With alcohol use involved. The story is different. (8) Among one hundred young people who drowned in the state of Washington one

year. Twenty-five percent had been drinking heavily. (9) In California. Forty-one percent of drowning deaths one year were alcohol-related. (10) So, you should no longer be afraid of swimming after eating, unless you had some alcohol. With your meal.

PRACTICE 5 . . . .

Using the list of common prepositions on page 123, write five complete sentences that either start or end with a prepositional phrase.

. . . .

Trouble Spot 2: Fragments That Start with a Dependent Word

Look out for word groups that begin with one of the following words; there might be a fragment.

Common Dependent Words		
after	if	what(ever)
although	since	when(ever)
as	so that	where
because	that	whether
before	though	which
even though	unless	while
how	until	who/whose

FIND: Read each sentence in your writing carefully, stopping at periods.

Don't get me anything from the bakery. (Unless) you see something with a lot of chocolate.

- Circle any dependent word that begins a word group.
- In this word group, underline any subject, and double-underline any verb.
- If a subject or verb is missing, or if there is not a complete thought, there is a fragment. [The word group in this example is a fragment: It has a subject and a verb, but it's not a complete thought.]

> **FIX: Correct the fragment by connecting it to the sentence either before or after it. Or make the fragment into its own sentence.**
>
> Don't get me anything from the bakery, ^u Unless you see something with a lot of chocolate.
>
> *However, if you see something*
> Don't get me anything from the bakery. ~~Unless you see some~~
> *with a lot of chocolate, ignore these instructions.*
> ~~thing with a lot of chocolate.~~
>
> • If the dependent word group comes first, a comma must follow it.
>
> Unless you see something with a lot of chocolate, don't get me anything from the bakery.

DEPENDENT-WORD FRAGMENTS

Amy **got** to the club. *After I went home.*

She **went** home to change. *Because she was uncomfortable.*

FRAGMENTS JOINED TO A SENTENCE

Amy **got** to the club after **I went** home.

She **went** home to change because **she was** uncomfortable.

DEPENDENT-WORD FRAGMENTS

IBM, *which is the company I want to work for.*

Rob **is** known for having tantrums at airports. *Whenever his flight is delayed.*

FRAGMENTS MADE INTO THEIR OWN SENTENCES

There **are** some big **companies** nearby, like IBM, which is the one **I want** to work for.

Rob **is** known for having tantrums at airports. **He gets** upset whenever his **flight is** delayed.

The words in italics have a subject and a verb, but they don't make sense alone; they are **dependent**, meaning that they depend on other words for their meaning. They are called *dependent clauses*.

PRACTICE 6 . .

In the following items, circle any dependent word or words that appear at the beginning of a word group. Then, correct any fragment by connecting it to the previous or the next sentence. Four sentences are correct; write "C" next to them.

EXAMPLE: (If) monkeys live on the rock of Gibraltar, ~~The~~ t rock will ~~stay under British rule.~~

1. Even though it is just a legend, the British take this statement seriously.

2. The government of Gibraltar pays for the care and feeding of the colony's nearly 240 monkeys. Which the legend calls "Barbary apes."

3. The legend says that the monkeys must be allowed to wander freely. Therefore, they are not confined to any specific area.

4. Whether they are in search of candy bars, fruit trees, shady places, or human toys. The monkeys wander everywhere.

5. They have even learned to entertain tourists so that they can get bits of food.

6. Because tourists love it. The monkeys pose for cameras and act like they are snapping a picture.

7. They also steal ice cream cones from children. When the kids are not careful.

8. The monkeys particularly enjoy potato chips, candy, and ice cream. Although they now suffer from tooth decay.

9. Because they are Europe's last free-ranging monkeys, they are also Gibraltar's biggest tourist attraction.

10. While many Gibraltar residents think the monkeys are pests. Most people feel they just have to live with them.

PRACTICE 7 . .

Each of the following items is a fragment that begins with a dependent word. Turn each fragment into a complete sentence by adding the missing sentence elements.

, I had to give it up.

EXAMPLE: Though I had a credit card for several years/

1. When I had the credit card.

2. Although I tried to be careful with my spending.

3. Because the credit card made it so easy to borrow money.

4. After I ran up a huge credit card debt.

5. Until I paid off my debt.

6. After I became debt-free.

7. Unless a person has self-discipline.

8. Before I got my new debit card.

9. Which draws money from my checking account.

10. Even though my debit card helps me control my spending.

PRACTICE 8 · ·

All but one of the numbered items in the following paragraph include a fragment that begins with a dependent word. Underline the fragments and then correct them either by adding the missing sentence elements or by connecting them to the previous or the next sentence. Write "C" next to the one correct item.

(1) If a person is not very active. That person is likely to be overweight. (2) Since my boss, Ms. Lynch, believes this theory. She does everything as actively as possible. (3) Although she has her own parking spot close to the door. She parks as far away as possible and takes the stairs instead of the elevator whenever she can. (4) She even has a treadmill in her office. So that she can exercise while working at her computer. (5) When she walks to work. She keeps a pace of 3.7 miles an hour. (6) Whenever people visit her office. They can exercise on the second treadmill installed next to her own. (7) All this treadmill exercise could make Ms. Lynch exhausted. However, she says the result is exactly the opposite. (8) She is healthy and slim. Which certainly shows that being active can help with weight control.

> **PRACTICE 9** . . . .
>
> Using the list of common dependent words on page 140, write five complete sentences that either start or end with a dependent clause.

. . . .

Trouble Spot 3: Fragments That Start with an *-ing* Verb

FIND: Read each sentence in your writing carefully, stopping at periods.

Charlie stood on his toes in the crowd. ⃝Trying to see the passing parade.

- Circle any *-ing* verb that starts a word group.
- In this word group, underline any subject and double-underline any verb.
- If a subject or verb is missing, or if there is not a complete thought, there is a fragment. [The word group in this example is a fragment: It doesn't have a subject, and it's not a complete thought.]

FIX: Correct the fragment by connecting it to the sentence either before or after it. Or make the fragment into its own sentence.

Charlie stood on his toes in the crowd, *, trying* **~~Trying~~ to see the passing parade.**

Charlie stood on his toes in the crowd. *He was trying* **~~Trying~~ to see the passing parade.**

- Usually, you will need to put a comma before or after the fragment to join it to the complete sentence.

-ING VERB FRAGMENTS

I will be up late tonight. *Studying for finals.*

I get plenty of daily exercise. *Walking to the bus stop.*

FRAGMENTS JOINED TO SENTENCES

I will be up late tonight studying for finals.

I get plenty of daily exercise walking to the bus stop.

-ING VERB FRAGMENTS

Gerard swims for three hours each day. *Training for the regionals.*

Maya took a plane instead of the bus. *Wanting to get home as fast as possible.*

FRAGMENTS MADE INTO THEIR OWN SENTENCES

Gerard swims for three hours each day. He is training for the regionals.

Maya took a plane instead of the bus. She wanted to get home as fast as possible.

PRACTICE 10 . . . .

In the following items, circle any *-ing* verb that appears at the beginning of a word group. Then, correct any fragment either by adding the missing sentence elements or by connecting it to the previous or the next sentence. One item contains no fragment; write "C" next to it.

EXAMPLE: (Writing) in his spare time, Albert Einstein published four important physics papers while working at a patent[1] office in Switzerland.

[1]**patent:** *protection of ownership rights to an invention*

1. Working an eight-hour shift six days a week. Einstein somehow found time to follow his true passion.

2. Examining patents by day. He revised the basic laws of physics at night.

3. Einstein's day job may have helped his scientific career. Remaining outside the academic community had its advantages.

4. Being at a university. He might have found others ignoring his advanced ideas.

5. Reviewing inventions at the patent office might also have been helpful. In keeping his mind active.

6. Taking a university job. He eventually entered the academic world, where he produced the general theory of relativity.

7. The Nobel Prize committee found Einstein's theory of relativity too extreme. Refusing Einstein the prize for that accomplishment.

8. Awarding him the Nobel Prize for his other contributions. The committee told Einstein not to mention relativity in his acceptance speech.

9. Ignoring the committee. He mentioned it anyway.

10. Perhaps people should pay more attention to dreamers. Forming brilliant ideas where they are least expected.

PRACTICE 11

Each of the following items is a fragment beginning with an *-ing* verb. Turn each fragment into a complete sentence by adding the missing sentence elements.

EXAMPLE: **Typing at his computer,** *, Patrick was keeping Shawn awake.*

1. Pretending he did not hear his roommate's loud typing.

2. Turning from side to side.

3. Stuffing cotton in his ears.

4. Getting louder and louder.

5. Sounding like mice tap-dancing.

6. Clearing his throat to get his noisy roommate's attention.

7. Smiling as he continued typing.

8. Yelling at his roommate to stop.

9. Stopping his typing.

10. Sleeping soundly before his roommate began typing again.

PRACTICE 12

In the following paragraph, eight items include a fragment that begins with an *-ing* verb form. Underline any fragment and then correct it either by adding the missing sentence elements or by connecting it to the previous or the next sentence. Write "C" next to the two correct items.

(1) Tens of millions of Americans try online dating every year. Making it one of the most popular paid services on the Internet. (2) Three economists recently researched an online dating service. Revealing some interesting facts. (3) Filling out a personal profile is one of the first steps in online dating. The information people provide is often hard to believe.

(4) Describing their appearance. Only 1 percent of those studied said their looks were less than average. (5) Looks were the most important personal feature. Ranking first for both women and men. (6) Hearing this fact. Most people are not surprised. (7) Women who posted photos got higher interest. Receiving twice as many e-mail responses than those who did not post photos. (8) Having plenty of money seems to increase men's chances of finding a date. Men who reported high incomes received nearly twice the e-mail responses as men with low incomes. (9) Going beyond looks and income. Most relationships last because of the personalities involved. (10) Accepting online dating despite some participants' focus on looks and money. Many single people say that it is no worse than other ways of meeting people.

PRACTICE 13 . .

Write five complete sentences that either start or end with an *-ing* verb.

Trouble Spot 4: Fragments That Start with *to* and a Verb

FIND: Read each sentence in your writing carefully, stopping at periods.

We went to at least five music stores. To find the guitar Colin wanted.

- Circle any *to*-plus-verb combination that starts a word group.
- In this word group, underline any subject, and double-underline any verb.
- If a subject or verb is missing, or if there is not a complete thought, there is a fragment. [The word group in this example is a fragment: It doesn't have a subject, and it's not a complete thought.]

> **FIX: Correct the fragment by connecting it to the sentence either before or after it. Or make the fragment into its own sentence.**
>
> *to*
> We went to at least five music stores, To find the guitar Colin wanted.
>
> *It took us a long time to*
> We went to at least five music stores, To find the guitar Colin wanted.

Word groups consisting only of *to* and a verb are also called **verbal phrases** or **infinitives**. They don't have a subject, and they don't function as a verb.

TO + VERB FRAGMENTS

Christiane went home last week. *To help her mother move.*

Hundreds of people were waiting in line. *To get tickets.*

FRAGMENTS JOINED TO SENTENCES

Christiane went home last week to help her mother move.

Hundreds of people were waiting in line to get tickets.

-ING VERB FRAGMENTS

Barry spent an hour on the phone waiting. *To talk to a customer service representative.*

Leah wrote several letters to politicians. *To build support for the pedestrian-rights bill.*

FRAGMENTS MADE INTO THEIR OWN SENTENCES

Barry spent an hour on the phone waiting. He wanted to talk to a customer service representative.

Leah wrote several letters to politicians. She hoped to build support for the pedestrian-rights bill.

Language note: Do not confuse *to* + a verb with *that*.

INCORRECT: My brother wants *that* his girlfriend cook.

CORRECT: My brother wants his girlfriend *to cook*.

PRACTICE 14 . . . .

In the following items, circle any verbal phrase (*to* + a verb) at the beginning of a word group. Then, correct fragments by connecting them to the previous or the next sentence. Two items contain no fragments; write "C" next to them.

EXAMPLE: At the age of twelve, Paul G. Allen used an aluminum
tube. To build his first rocket.

1. To fuel the rocket. He used zinc and sulfur from his chemistry set.

2. To launch the rocket. He lit the fuel mixture.

3. Unfortunately, he should have used a stronger metal. To prevent the burning fuel from melting the rocket.

4. To get on with his life. Allen accepted the failure.

5. He later achieved success as a cofounder of Microsoft. To become a billionaire must have been very satisfying for Allen, who never lost his interest in rockets.

6. His wealth has made it possible to pursue his interest. To build bigger and better rockets, it takes a lot of money.

7. To help build the rocket *SpaceShipOne*. Allen invested a large amount of money.

8. *SpaceShipOne* won a $10 million prize for being the first privately financed vehicle. To send a person into space.

9. What Allen learned as a businessman may have helped him. To find the designer and test pilots who made *SpaceShipOne* a success.

10. To create the best space craft. He knew he had to hire the best people for the job.

PRACTICE 15 . . . .

Each of the following items is a fragment beginning with a verbal phrase (*to* + a verb). Turn each fragment into a complete sentence by adding the missing sentence elements.

EXAMPLE: To improve my tennis skills, *, I signed up for tennis lessons.*

1. To win a game against my sister.

2. To avoid hitting the ball out of bounds.

3. To hit the ball where my opponent cannot get to it.

4. To keep from getting bored during practice.

5. To take care of the pain that developed in my elbow.

6. To do the exercises the physical therapist recommended.

7. To avoid making the injury worse.

8. To stay occupied while I could not play tennis.

9. To play well right after my elbow had healed.

10. To surprise my sister with my improved tennis skills.

PRACTICE 16

In the following paragraph, most items include a fragment that begins with a verbal phrase (*to* + a verb). Underline any fragment and then correct it either by adding the missing sentence elements or by connecting it to previous or the next sentence. Two items are correct; write "C" next to them.

(1) To make cars more comfortable and convenient to drive. Engineers have designed many high-tech features. (2) Seat heaters were invented. To keep people warm while driving in cold weather. (3) However, some seat heaters are programmed. To switch off after fifteen minutes without warning the driver. (4) To stay warm on a long trip. The driver must remember to keep turning the seat heater back on. (5) To some people, these cars may be too convenient. One car's computer has seven hundred possible commands. (6) To avoid bothering their neighbors at night. Some people want to stop their cars from honking when they lock the doors. (7) Many people do not know that it is fairly easy. To turn off some of a car's features. (8) Some people carefully study their cars' systems. To change the programming. (9) To make programming changes on one's own car is risky. It may cause the car's warranty to be lost. (10) It is probably easiest for people who own these complicated cars. To simply enjoy their high-tech conveniences.

PRACTICE 17 . .

Write five complete sentences that begin or end with *to* and a verb.

Trouble Spot 5: Fragments That Start with an Example or Explanation

---

FIND: Read each sentence in your writing carefully, stopping at periods.

I can tell you about a lot of bad dates I had. Like the one when I was taken to a funeral.

- Circle any word group that is an example or explanation. Look for words like *especially*, *for example*, *for instance*, *like*, and *such as*.
- In this word group, underline any subject, and double-underline any verb.
- If a subject or verb is missing, or if there is not a complete thought, there is a fragment. [The word group in this example is a fragment: It has a subject and a verb, but it's not a complete thought.]

FIX: Correct the fragment by connecting it to the sentence either before or after it. Or make the fragment into its own sentence.

I can tell you about a lot of bad dates I had,^, l Like the one when I was taken to a funeral.

The
I can tell you about a lot of bad dates I had. ~~Like the one when I~~ was taken to a funeral,^*was especially memorable.*

- When you add a fragment to a complete sentence, you may need to add a comma, as in the first corrected example.

FRAGMENTS STARTING WITH AN EXAMPLE OR EXPLANATION

I would like to get new boots. *Like the ones Sheila wore last night.*

I get lots of offers from credit card companies. *Such as Visa and MasterCard.*

FRAGMENTS JOINED TO SENTENCES

I would like to get new boots like the ones Sheila wore last night.

I get lots of offers from credit card companies such as Visa and Master-Card.

FRAGMENTS STARTING WITH AN EXAMPLE OR EXPLANATION

It is hard to stay in and study. *Especially during the summer.*

Some people cook entirely from scratch, even if it takes all day. For example, Bill.

FRAGMENTS MADE INTO THEIR OWN SENTENCES

It is hard to stay in and study. It is especially hard during the summer.

Some people cook entirely from scratch, even if it takes all day. Bill is one such person.

PRACTICE 18

In the following paragraph, most items include a fragment that begins with an example or an explanation. Underline any fragment and then correct it either by adding the missing sentence elements or by connecting it to the previous or the next sentence. Two items contain no fragment; write "C" next to them.

(1) One major fast-food chain is making changes to its menu. Like offering fresh apple slices. (2) The company still mostly sells traditional fast food. For example, double cheeseburgers. (3) The company is trying to offer its customers healthier food. Such as fresh fruit and salads. (4) The cause of the change seems to be public opinion. Like complaints about high-calorie fast-food meals. (5) Many people are blaming fast-food companies for Americans' expanding waistlines. Especially those of children. (6) Consumers love to eat fatty foods. However, they also like to blame fast-food restaurants when they gain weight. (7) This particular restaurant is discovering that healthy food can be profitable. Earning about 10 percent of its income from fresh salads. (8) There are limits to how far the company will go to make its food healthier. For instance, with its apple slices. (9) Apple slices are certainly healthy. However, they are less healthy when dipped in the sugary sauce the company packages with the slices. (10) The company followed the advice of its taste testers.

Who, in the case of apple slices, greatly preferred the slices dipped in the sugary sauce.

PRACTICE 19 . . . .

Write five complete sentences that include examples or explanations.

. . . .

Edit Fragments in College, Work, and Everyday Life

Complete the editing reviews as instructed, referring to the chart on page 157.

EDITING REVIEW 1: COLLEGE . . . .

The following paragraph is similar to one you might find in a college nursing textbook. Underline the fragments you find and correct them either by adding the missing sentence elements or by connecting them to the previous or the next sentence. Two sentences are correct; write "C" next to them. The first numbered item has been edited for you.

(1) Like doctors and physical therapists, nurses must study the structure, Of the body and the way it functions. (2) Anatomy is the study of the structures that make the body work. Such as the skeleton, tissue, muscles, and organs. (3) Studying how these elements of the body function is called *physiology*. (4) To care for patients. Nurses must understand the body's structures and how they work together. (5) Studying disorders of the structures and functions of the body is called *pathophysiology*. (6) These disorders produce disease. For example, diabetes, which can produce kidney failure, blindness, and other serious conditions. (7) A solid understanding of medical terminology is necessary. To communicate with doctors about patients' disorders. (8) Looking at a long list of common medical terms. You might feel overwhelmed. (9) Most medical terms, however, can be broken into three parts. The prefix, the root, and the suffix. (10) To improve your understanding of medical terminology. You might find it helpful to study a chart of common prefixes, roots, and suffixes used in medical language.

EDITING REVIEW 2: WORK . .

In the following business letter, underline the fragments and correct them either by adding the missing sentence elements or by connecting the fragment to the previous or the next sentence. Write "C" next to the one item that is correct. The first item has been edited for you.

Shawn Brendan

Ballis Engineering Company

8175 NASA Road

Clear Lake, TX 75016

Dear Mr. Brendan:

(1) We hope that your company is pleased with the project we completed for you in January. Two oak wall units. (2) The units, which measured 8' × 10', were installed in your conference room. On January 18, 2005.

(3) Looking through our records. I realize that we have not received payment for the project. (4) For your convenience. I have attached another copy of our invoice #4590, dated January 10, 2005. (5) We would appreciate immediate payment of the amount owed. Which is $1,500. (6) So that we can close the accounting on all work done in the first half of the year. We would like to receive the payment as soon as possible.

(7) Thank you for your attention to this matter. (8) Since we wish to maintain our good working relationship. We hope the issue will be resolved soon. (9) If you have any questions or concerns. Please contact me at (817) 555-3499. (10) I look forward. To hearing from you soon.

Sincerely,

Alex Shubikov, Manager

EDITING REVIEW 3: EVERYDAY LIFE/USING FORMAL ENGLISH . . . .

A friend of yours wants to send the following letter about problems on her street to a city councilor. Before she does, she wants your help in revising it so that she'll make the best impression possible. Underline the fragments that you find. Then, correct them and revise informal or inappropriate language so that it is suitable to address a public official. The first numbered item has been edited for you. In addition to this item, you should find eight cases of informal language.

> ■ **TIP:** For advice on using formal English, see Chapter 4. For advice on avoiding slang, see Chapter 25.

Dear Councilor Vargas,

(1) As a longtime resident of 5 Rosemont Way in this city, I have seen my neighborhood ~~go down the toilet~~. *decline* (2) But not one damn person in the city government seems to care. Although different residents on this street have complained at least ten separate times to city councilors.

(3) The sidewalks are messed up bad and have caused several residents to injure themselves. Such as my son. (4) Also, trash pickup is unreliable and inconsistent. With the trucks coming at 8:00 a.m. one time and at noon another time. (5) As a result, residents don't know the right time. To leave out their trash. (6) If they leave it out too late. It sits around all day getting smelly. (7) It ain't pretty!

(8) Worst of all, most streetlights are busted up bad and never get repaired. Even when only one or two are left burning. (9) Hanging out at the bus in the morning darkness. My daughter is very afraid. (10) Because of her fears, I have driven her to school myself. On several occasions.

(11) Thirty residents of the Rosemont neighborhood, including me, have organized. To draw up a full list of our beefs. (12) We gonna go to the press with the list. Unless we get a satisfactory response from your office within seven days.

Sincerely,

Sheree Niles

Write and Edit Your Own Work

ASSIGNMENT 1: WRITE . . . .

Write a paragraph about the two most important things you hope to gain from going to college. Then, read your writing carefully, stopping at periods and looking for the five fragment trouble spots. Use the chart on page 157 to help you revise any fragments that you find.

ASSIGNMENT 2: EDIT . . . .

Using the chart on page 157, correct fragments in a paper you are writing for this course or another course or in a piece of writing from your work or everyday life.

. . . .

Practice Together

■ LEARNING STYLES: Look for activities in this chapter that are matched to your learning style. If you don't know your learning style, take the test on pages 26–28.

 Visual

Auditory

 Reading/writing

Kinesthetic (movement)

Working with a few other students, practice what you have learned in this chapter.

1. Write five fragments on a sheet of paper, putting each one on a separate line and leaving room between them. Then, exchange papers with another student and complete each other's fragments.

2. With a few other students, write a five-item test for one or more of the five fragment trouble spots. Use any kinds of questions or format you want. Give your test to another team to take.

3. Share your responses to "I am a good _____" (p. 136) with a group of students. Have them comment, and make changes based on their comments. Read your revised response aloud to the class.

4. Listen to a popular song and write down some of the lyrics. What fragments do you hear? Bring in the lyrics and read them to your teammates. Have them find the fragments.

5. Draw the concept of a fragment for someone who knows no words. (The visual at the start of this chapter may give you an idea.)

6. Create a study guide for this chapter, recording important terms and examples. Use the guide to study with other students in your group.

Chapter Review

1. What are the five fragment trouble spots? Highlight where they first appear in this chapter.

2. The two ways to correct a fragment are _____
_____. Highlight where this information appears in the book.

3. **VOCABULARY:** Go back to any new words that you underlined. Can you guess their meanings now? If not, look up the words in a dictionary.

LEARNING JOURNAL: Write for two minutes completing the sentence, "I need more practice on _____ from this chapter."

Create your own review chart.

■ **TIP:** For help with building your vocabulary, see Appendix B.

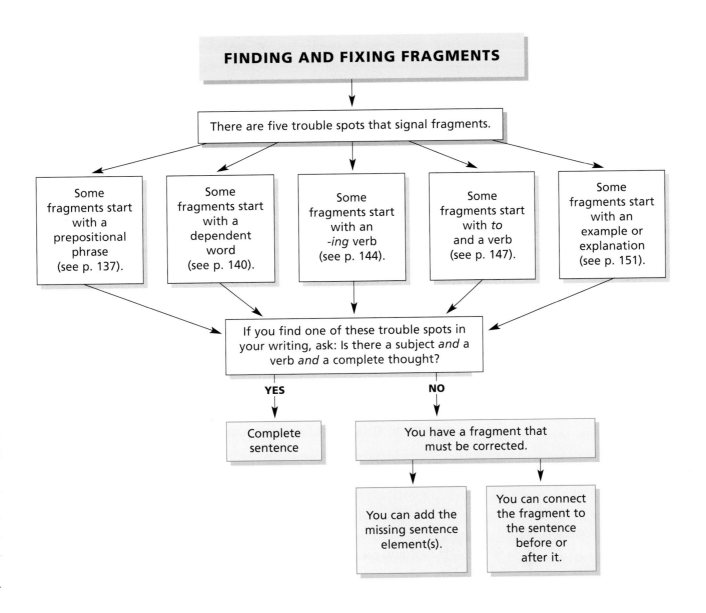

FINDING AND FIXING FRAGMENTS

There are five trouble spots that signal fragments.

Some fragments start with a prepositional phrase (see p. 137).

Some fragments start with a dependent word (see p. 140).

Some fragments start with an *-ing* verb (see p. 144).

Some fragments start with *to* and a verb (see p. 147).

Some fragments start with an example or explanation (see p. 151).

If you find one of these trouble spots in your writing, ask: Is there a subject *and* a verb *and* a complete thought?

YES

Complete sentence

NO

You have a fragment that must be corrected.

You can add the missing sentence element(s).

You can connect the fragment to the sentence before or after it.

12

Run-Ons and Comma Splices

Two Sentences Joined Incorrectly

Understand What Run-Ons and Comma Splices Are

📖 **VOCABULARY:** Under-line any words in this chapter that are new to you.

📖 **IDEA JOURNAL:** Write about a bad habit you broke.

Sometimes, two complete **sentences** can be joined to make one sentence.

TWO COMPLETE SENTENCES JOINED CORRECTLY

Complete sentence   Complete sentence

The **bus was** late, so many **people went** home.

Complete sentence   Complete sentence

Drivers were on strike, but few **passengers knew** it.

Complete sentences that are not joined correctly are either run-ons or comma splices.

Complete sentence   Complete sentence

RUN-ON My **aunt has** several dogs **she has** no other pets.

A **run-on** occurs when two complete sentences are joined without any punctuation.

158

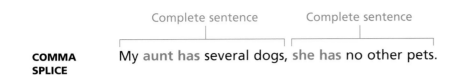

COMMA SPLICE   My aunt has several dogs, she has no other pets.

■ **TIP:** In the sentence examples in this chapter, subjects are light blue and verbs are red.

A **comma splice** occurs when two complete sentences are joined by only a comma instead of a comma and one of the following words: *and, but, for, nor, or, so, yet.*

In the Real World, Why Is It Important to Correct Run-Ons and Comma Splices?

Although run-ons and comma splices may not be noticeable in spoken language, they are confusing in writing. Like fragments, they make a bad impression.

Read Jenny Kahn's response to the following question, which was on an application for a job as a veterinarian's assistant.

Why do you think you are qualified to work with people and their pets?

JENNY KAHN'S ANSWER:

Growing up, I had many pets, there were always dogs and cats in our house. My parents made sure I was responsible for my animals I had to feed, comb, and bathe them regularly. I also had to take them to the vet once a year for their shots, I often talked to other people in the waiting room about their pets. Some people were very upset about their sick pets, I tried to calm them down with reassuring words. Pets, too, get nervous in the vet's waiting room, so they have to be calmed down. If you work with animals, you have to have some experience you also have to be quiet and gentle or you are going to scare the pet and its owner.

VETERINARIAN'S RESPONSE TO JENNY'S ANSWER:

My assistants work with animals and their owners in my office, but they also have to do a good deal of writing. They write up the patients' histories, and they update files. They also write memos to our clients and to companies who sell us supplies. Jenny's answer has many confusing sentences. Her writing might reflect badly on me. It might even be dangerous if I could not understand what she has written. I cannot hire her.

PRACTICE 1 . . . .

There are five run-ons or comma splices in Jenny's answer to the job-application question. Looking for complete sentences, underline what you think are the errors.

PRACTICE 2 . . . .

Five of the following sentences are correct, and the others are either run-ons or comma splices. In the blank to the left of each sentence, write "C" if the sentence is correct, "CS" if it is a comma splice, and "RO" if it is a run-on.

> **EXAMPLE:** _CS_ Two young scientists met in a conference room in 1973, they were working in the new field of computer networks.

___ 1. They wanted to connect separate computer networks this was not possible at the time.

___ 2. They argued out loud, wrote on a chalkboard, and sketched on a yellow pad.

___ 3. Two days later, they felt they had the start of a good technical paper, they did not realize that it was the beginning of today's Internet.

___ 4. Vinton G. Cerf and Robert E. Kahn received the 2004 A. M. Turing Award for their work, the Turing Award is like the Nobel Prize for the computer field.

___ 5. The Turing Award is named for a British mathematician who cracked German codes during World War II.

___ 6. Few people have ever heard of Cerf and Kahn; some believe the Internet was invented by a large company like Microsoft.

___ 7. Cerf and Kahn developed a way to group computer data into packages, each package could be sent to any computer in the world.

___ 8. To decide whose name would appear first on their research article, they tossed a coin.

___ 9. Other scientists have also been given credit for helping to develop the Internet, these scientists' inventions were very important as well.

___ 10. Cerf and Kahn did not gain much fame for their invention, and they earned no money from it.

■ **TIP:** For more practice, visit Exercise Central at <**bedfordstmartins.com/ realskills**>.

Find and Correct Run-Ons and Comma Splices

FIND: Read each sentence in your writing carefully.

The fire spread quickly the ground was dry.

- To see if there are two complete sentences, underline the subjects and double-underline the verbs.
- If no punctuation joins the sentences, there is a run-on. If only a comma joins the sentences, there is a comma splice. [The previous example is a run-on.]

TIP: Before going on in this chapter, you may want to review the following terms from Chapter 10: *sentence, subject,* and *verb.*

FIX: There are three ways to fix run-ons or comma splices.

- Add a period or semicolon (;).
- Add a comma and a coordinating conjunction.
- Add a subordinating conjunction (dependent word).

An audiovisual tutorial on finding and fixing the four most serious errors, including run-ons and comma splices, is available on a CD that comes with this book.

The rest of this chapter explains each of the three ways to fix run-ons and comma splices.

Add a Period or a Semicolon

Notice how periods and semicolons are used between complete sentences.

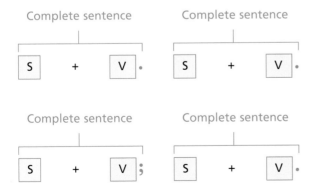

Correct a run-on or comma splice by adding a period or a semicolon.

FIND: Read each sentence in your writing carefully.

I <u>went</u> to the concert it <u>was</u> great.

- To see if there are two complete sentences, underline the subjects and double-underline the verbs.
- If no punctuation joins the sentences, there is a run-on. If only a comma joins the sentences, there is a comma splice. [The example is a run-on.]

FIX: Add a period or semicolon (;).

I went to the concert. It was great.

I went to the concert; it was great.

RUN-ON	Students crowded the tiny library they were studying for final exams.
CORRECTED WITH A PERIOD	Students crowded the tiny library. They were studying for final exams.
CORRECTED WITH A SEMICOLON	Students crowded the tiny library; they were studying for final exams.
COMMA SPLICE	Children played in the park, they loved the merry-go-round.
CORRECTED WITH A PERIOD	Children played in the park. They loved the merry-go-round.
CORRECTED WITH A SEMICOLON	Children played in the park; they loved the merry-go-round.

PRACTICE 3 . . . .

For each of the following items, indicate in the space to the left whether it is a run-on ("RO") or a comma splice ("CS"). Then, correct the sentences by adding a period or a semicolon. Capitalize letters as necessary to make two sentences.

EXAMPLE: <u>RO</u> One type of ant has an especially useful skill it can

fall from a tall tree and land right where it wants to.

___ 1. The *Cephalotes atratus* ant is common in Central and South America, it lives in trees about a hundred feet above the forest floor.

___ 2. Sometimes, these ants fall off their branches high winds or animals can make them fall.

___ 3. Most of the time, the ants do not fall straight to the ground they land on the tree trunk instead.

___ 4. The ants can easily rejoin their colony from the tree trunk, it takes them about ten minutes to return to the same branch.

___ 5. The ants do not want to fall to the ground, that can be a dangerous place for them.

___ 6. On the ground, they can lose their way they can also be eaten quickly.

___ 7. Researchers videotaped some falling ants, the video showed that the ants fall in three separate stages.

___ 8. The first stage is straight down, the ant has no control in this stage.

___ 9. Next, the ant quickly adjusts its position it lines up its stomach with the tree trunk.

___ 10. It then changes its direction it goes toward the tree trunk and lands on it.

READ ALOUD

To find run-ons and comma splices, read sentences aloud, coming to a complete stop only when there is a period. Pause when you come to a comma, and don't let your voice drop.

> **PRACTICE 4** · ·

In the following paragraph, identify each item as a run-on ("RO"), a comma splice ("CS"), or correct ("C") in the blank before each item. Then, correct each run-on or comma splice by adding a period or a semicolon. Capitalize letters as necessary when you make new sentences. There are four correct items.

___ (1) People who are likable are often more successful than others.

___ (2) Being likable is an important quality no matter where you work, likable employees are often promoted over others who do their job equally well but are less pleasant to be around. ___ (3) People want to be around likable coworkers, they make everyone feel better emotionally and physically. ___ (4) According to business experts, likable employees share several characteristics. ___ (5) For example, a likable person is friendly he or she makes other people feel liked and welcome. ___ (6) One business writer suggests acting like a greeter wherever you are, you might think of yourself as a hostess welcoming guests into a party or a restaurant. ___ (7) The likable person is also sensitive to other people's wants and needs it makes people comfortable to feel understood. ___ (8) Honesty is another quality that makes a person likable. ___ (9) Most people can detect a liar, seeing through someone who is telling a lie or acting fake. ___ (10) Sincerity is important at work it's also respected in everyday dealings with others.

PRACTICE 5 . .

Write three pairs of two complete sentences. Then, join the pairs with either a period or a semicolon.

> **EXAMPLE:** The hikers ate lunch in the field; they had been walking
>
> since daybreak.

Add a Comma and a Coordinating Conjunction

You can add a comma and a **coordinating conjunction** between two complete sentences. Remember the seven coordinating conjunctions by using the acronym *fanboys*: (**f**or, **a**nd, **n**or, **b**ut, **o**r, **y**et, **s**o.)

The Unforgettable FANBOYS!

Sentence 1	Coordinating conjunction	Sentence 2
	, **f**or	
	, **a**nd	
	, **n**or	
	, **b**ut	
	, **o**r	
	, **y**et	
	, **s**o	

To correct a run-on or comma splice with a coordinating conjunction, follow these steps:

FIND: Read each sentence in your writing carefully.

Don lives on Main Street he works downtown.

- To see if there are two complete sentences, underline the subjects and double-underline the verbs.
- If no punctuation joins the sentences, there is a run-on. If only a comma joins the sentences, there is a comma splice. [The example is a run-on.]

FIX: Separate the sentences with a comma and a coordinating conjunction.

- Choose the conjunction that makes sense in the sentence. (A comma splice already has a comma, so just add a coordinating conjunction.)

, and
Don lives on Main Street he works downtown.

but
Don lives on Main Street, he works downtown.

RUN-ONS

His used cars are too expensive I bought mine from another dealer.

Computers are her first love she spends a lot of time gardening.

CORRECTED

His used cars are too expansive, *so* I bought mine from another dealer.

Computers are her first love, *yet* she spends a lot of time gardening.

COMMA SPLICES

I would spend an extra day in Chicago, I simply don't have the free time.

Jane is in charge of invoicing, her sister runs the lingerie department.

CORRECTED

I would spend an extra day in Chicago, *but* I simply don't have the free time.

Jane is in charge of invoicing, *and* her sister runs the lingerie department.

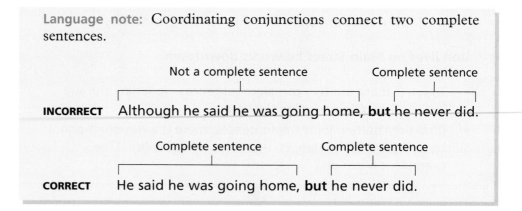

Language note: Coordinating conjunctions connect two complete sentences.

	Not a complete sentence	Complete sentence

INCORRECT Although he said he was going home, **but** he never did.

	Complete sentence	Complete sentence

CORRECT He said he was going home, **but** he never did.

> **PRACTICE 6** . . . .

All of the following items are run-ons or comma splices. First, underline the subject and double-underline the verb in each part. Then, correct the error by adding a comma, if necessary, and the appropriate coordinating conjunction from the two choices in parentheses.

> **EXAMPLE:** The black-capped chickadee's <u>name</u> <u><u>makes</u></u> perfect
>
>   *, for*
> sense its <u>song</u> <u><u>sounds</u></u> like "chick-a-dee." (but, for)
>   ^

1. Most birds use their songs to attract mates the chickadee also sings for another reason. (or, but)

2. The chickadee has many enemies, the hawk and the owl are two of the most dangerous. (so, and)

3. Chickadees are protective of their flock they use their song to warn other chickadees of danger. (so, for)

4. The song tells other chickadees of a nearby enemy it also tells more than that. (nor, yet)

5. The chickadee's call can have a different number of "dees" at the end the number of "dees" sends a message to the rest of the flock. (but, and)

6. A call might end with many "dees," it might end with just a few. (for, or)

7. A call ending with many "dees" warns of a small enemy fewer "dees" signal a larger enemy. (and, nor)

8. Chickadees are small and fast, larger and slower animals are not a big threat. (for, so)

9. A call ending with a large number of "dees" brings many chickadees to the area to dive-bomb the enemy fewer "dees" draw fewer chickadees. (yet, and)

10. The chickadee is good at driving enemies out of its territory it knows how to use its song for protection. (so, for)

PRACTICE 7 . . . .

Two of the following items are correct sentences; the other eight are either run-ons or comma splices. First, underline the subject and double-underline the verb in each part (if there are two parts). Then, fix the incorrect items by adding a comma, if necessary, and an appropriate coordinating conjunction. Write "C" next to the two correct sentences.

> **EXAMPLE:** Kids today have fewer toys to choose from than in the
> _____ *for* _____
> past, toy makers are making fewer products.
>   ^

1. Large discount chains are keeping toy prices low this makes it difficult for toy companies to make a profit.

2. Children still like traditional toys, newer gadgets are often more popular.

3. Today, many kids play video games they also spend a lot of time on the Internet.

4. Traditional dolls are still popular, many children prefer dolls that sing, dance, tell jokes, and play games on command.

5. Some simple toys still become kids' favorites discount stores often copy these toys.

6. The discount stores can sell the copies at a lower price, the copied toys often become big hits.

7. The original toys often cannot compete against the cheaper copies.

8. One toy company has decided to increase sales by making toys for adults as well.

9. The company calls one of its creations "Money Man" the doll looks like a company's chief financial officer with cash strapped around its waist.

10. The "Boss Man" doll comes with a happy-face mask it also has a separate angry-face mask.

PRACTICE 8 . .

Some items in the following paragraph are run-ons or comma splices. Correct each error by adding a comma, if necessary, and a coordinating conjunction. Two sentences are correct; write "C" next to them.

(1) Bette Nesmith Graham was a secretary in the 1950s her typing skills were poor. (2) She needed more income she took a second job decorating bank windows for the holidays. (3) While painting windows, she noticed some artists painting over their mistakes. (4) She decided to bring a small bottle of paint to her secretarial job she could paint over her typing errors. (5) She soon needed more paint the other secretaries wanted to use the fluid, too. (6) She experimented with other fluids at home, she also asked her son's chemistry teacher for advice. (7) She started selling an improved fluid in 1956, she called it Mistake Out. (8) In the 1960s, she changed the name to Liquid Paper it was the same product. (9) Graham eventually sold her Liquid Paper business for $47.5 million in 1979. (10) Hardly anybody today uses a typewriter, reports show that people still use correction fluid on about 42.3 million pages a year.

PRACTICE 9 . .

Write three pairs of two complete sentences. Join the pairs with a comma and a coordinating conjunction.

EXAMPLE: He doesn't have much money left, for he spent it on the gift.

. . . .

Add a Subordinating Conjunction (Dependent Word)

Finally, to fix a run-on or comma splice, you can add a dependent word (also called a *subordinating conjunction*) to one of the two complete sentences to make it a dependent clause.

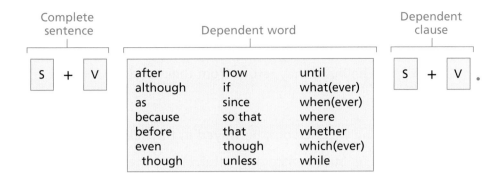

To correct a run-on or comma splice with a subordinating conjunction, follow these steps:

FIND: Read each sentence in your writing carefully.

I cannot go tonight, I have a class.

- To see if there are two complete sentences, underline the subjects and double-underline the verbs.
- If no punctuation joins the sentences, there is a run-on. If only a comma joins the sentences, there is a comma splice. [The example above is a comma splice.]

⬇

FIX: Add a subordinating conjunction.

- Choose the conjunction that makes sense in the sentence.

because
I cannot go tonight, **I have a class.**

RUN-ONS

Day care is free at our college I can afford to go to school.

She lost her job her company outsourced her position.

CORRECTED

Because day care is free at our college, I can afford to go to school.

She lost her job *after* her company outsourced her position.

COMMA SPLICES

He was nervous, he stayed in the delivery room.

The deck will be built, they return from their vacation in June.

CORRECTED

Even though he was nervous, he stayed in the delivery room.

The deck will be built *before* they return from their vacation in June.

When the dependent clause starts the sentence, add a comma after it, as in the first corrected examples in each of the previous groups. When the dependent word is in the middle of the sentence, you don't need a comma.

READ ALOUD

In the following examples, the dependent clauses are in italics. Read them in a softer voice so you can hear the difference.

1. Jonah learned to play the trumpet *because his father is a trumpeter.*
2. *Although Jonah was the best trumpeter the instructor had ever heard,* the band class was already filled.

> Illustrate a sentence from this chapter that has a dependent clause and a complete sentence. Use colors, word size, or other means to show that one clause is less important than the other.

> **PRACTICE 10** . . . .

All of the following items are run-ons or comma splices. First, underline the subject and double-underline the verb in each part. Then, correct the error by adding the appropriate subordinating conjunction from the two choices in parentheses. If a dependent clause starts the sentence, it should be followed by a comma.

>   *If you*
> **EXAMPLE:** You feel tired all the time, you are not alone. (if, that)

1. Most people understand the importance of a good night's rest, about half of all Americans do not get enough sleep. (because, even though)

2. We are busy sleep often becomes our least important concern. (how, when)

3. You have had a long week with little sleep, you might sleep late on the weekend. (after, so that)

4. Many people try to catch up on lost sleep this is not possible, according to doctors. (although, if)

5. Coffee, tea, and soda can keep you alert they contain caffeine. (because, after)

6. Studies have not proved that caffeine is harmful to most people's health, it is a poor substitute for sleep. (though, when)

7. Your pillow might be the problem you have trouble sleeping. (until, if)

8. You prefer a soft or a firm pillow, it should not be too flat. (whether, because)

9. A supportive pillow is important for restful sleep, pillow experts suggest a simple test. (before, because)

10. You fold a pillow in half, it should unfold itself instantly. (after, whichever)

PRACTICE 11 . . . .

Two of the following items are correct sentences; the other eight are either run-ons or comma splices. First, underline the subject and double-underline the verb in each part. Then, correct the errors by adding a subordinating conjunction from the chart on page 169. If a dependent clause starts the sentence, it should be followed by a comma. Write "C" next to the two correct items.

> **EXAMPLE:** *If you* ~~You~~ <u>dream</u> of driving a Ferrari or a Porsche, <u>it</u> <u>may</u>
> ^
> be possible.

1. Few people can afford such expensive cars some companies are offering them for rent.

2. You might be interested in this service you want to feel rich and famous for a day.

3. Rental times are flexible, you can rent a fancy car for as short as a few hours or as long as several months.

4. Most of these companies are in Beverly Hills similar companies have opened in other major cities as well.

5. It may seem surprising, but 70 percent of the companies' renters are women.

6. Many of these women rent the cars they want to surprise their husbands or boyfriends with a gift.

7. A Ferrari is like a racecar the driver changes gears by pulling a pair of paddles behind the steering wheel.

8. The driver hits the gas pedal, it feels like being in a rocket.

9. Because it goes so fast, the car has specially designed brakes.

10. The rental period ends, the driver must return to normal life at normal speed.

PRACTICE 12 . .

In the following paragraph, correct any run-ons or comma splices by adding a subordinating conjunction. Four sentences are correct; write "C" next to them.

(1) Most people buy a new cell phone, they pay close attention to the phone's features. (2) However, many people do not know what to do with their old cell phone. (3) Some charities accept old cell phones their owners no longer want them. (4) The charities usually send the old phones to a recycling company the phones are taken apart and sometimes rebuilt. (5) Some people would prefer to receive money for their old phone. (6) Recycling companies can sell used phones after replacing old parts, many of these companies will pay people for their old cell phones. (7) Most old cell phones are worth only $2 to $20, that is better than nothing. (8) If a cell phone cannot be rebuilt, the recycling company can still make money on the gold and other metals inside the phone. (9) Recycling companies can also remove arsenic, nickel, zinc, lead, and other harmful chemicals from the inside of an old cell phone. (10) These chemicals are harmful to the environment, more people should consider recycling their old cell phones.

PRACTICE 13 . .

Write three complete sentences that contain a dependent clause that starts with a subordinating conjunction. When the dependent clause comes first, be sure to put a comma after it.

EXAMPLE: Although I parked illegally for just ten minutes, I found a ticket on my car when I returned.

Edit Run-Ons and Comma Splices in College, Work, and Everyday Life

Complete the editing reviews as instructed, referring to the chart on page 177.

EDITING REVIEW 1: COLLEGE

The following paragraph is similar to one you might find in a college biology textbook. Revise the paragraph, correcting run-ons and comma splices. In addition to the first sentence, which has been marked for you, two more sentences are correct; write "C" next to them.

(1) *C* Scientists classify gibbons, orangutans, chimpanzees, and gorillas as modern apes. (2) With the exception of the gibbon, apes are larger than monkeys. (3) Apes have more complex brains than monkeys, apes' brains are larger in relation to the size of their body. (4) All apes can swing their bodies from tree branches, only gibbons move primarily by swinging from trees. (5) This method of movement is called *brachiation* the term comes from the Latin word for "arms." (6) Gibbons have weakly developed legs and long, muscular arms, brachiation is a particularly efficient type of movement. (7) Gibbons are good acrobats they can cover up to fifty feet in one swing, at a speed of about thirty-five miles per hour. (8) The other three groups of apes also have short legs and long arms, they rest much of their body weight on their knuckles. (9) As a result, their bodies are partially erect even when on all fours. (10) This body position supports the theory of evolution the theory argues that this posture of the apes led to the erect posture of human beings.

EDITING REVIEW 2: WORK/USING FORMAL ENGLISH

Find and correct the run-ons and comma splices in the following paragraph, which describes a company's policy regarding visitors. Then, revise informal language. The first sentence has been corrected for you. In addition to this sentence, you should find seven cases of informal language.

(1) Safety is a ~~big deal~~ *Because safety* *top priority* at Alpha Chemical, the following visitor policy must be followed at all times. (2) Visitors may not park in the employee lot they gotta use the visitor spaces near the east entrance on St. James Street. (3) Visitors must sign in at the front lobby, they will

■ TIP: For advice on using formal English, see Chapter 4. For advice on avoiding slang, see Chapter 25.

receive a visitor's badge. (4) All visitors must provide photo identification and the stuff about their visit. (5) They watch a brief safety flick, visitors will be given protective eyewear, a lab coat, and any other necessary safety things. (6) Visitors must also sign a legal release the release states that they are OK about the risk of entering a chemical plant. (7) Visitors must be accompanied by an employee at all times, no children are allowed into the facility. (8) Munchies are not allowed in any laboratory areas. (9) For security reasons, personal stuff such as purses and briefcases are not allowed in laboratory areas, these items must be left at the front desk or in personal office areas. (10) You may have questions about this policy, if so, contact the Human Resources Department.

EDITING REVIEW 3: EVERYDAY LIFE

Correct run-ons and comma splices in the following paragraph. Aside from the first sentence, which has been marked for you, six sentences are correct; write "C" next to them.

C
(1) The tradition of the Olympic torch relay has a long and interesting history. (2) The ancient Greeks used fire in their religious rituals a sacred flame was always kept burning in front of major temples. (3) In Olympia, where the ancient Olympic Games took place, extra flames were lit during the competition. (4) Fire was part of the original Olympics, the torch relay is a modern tradition. (5) Several months before the start of each Olympic Games, relay runners carry the torch from the ancient site of Olympia to the host city for that year's competition. (6) The torch reaches the opening ceremonies, it is used to light the Olympic flame.

(7) The Olympics celebrate friendship and world peace, you might be shocked by the dark history of the first torch relay. (8) The tradition was started by Adolf Hitler in 1936. (9) The games that year were held in Berlin, Hitler believed the torch relay would show off the glory and power of Nazi Germany. (10) Today, the relay has a much different purpose it unites the world in friendship and excitement for the upcoming games.

(11) The torch is usually carried by runners, the relays for several early Olympics were held entirely on foot. (12) However, other methods of transportation are often used. (13) The torch has been conveyed by horseback, steamboat, Indian canoe, and skis, it has even traveled by satellite. (14) The torch is often carried by athletes, celebrities, or politicians ordinary people can also serve as torchbearers. (15) The nomination process is open to the public most people chosen to be torchbearers have shown some kind of heroism or made a positive contribution to their community. (16) No matter how the torch travels or who carries it, it is an inspiring part of Olympic tradition.

Write and Edit Your Own Work

ASSIGNMENT 1: WRITE

Write a paragraph describing the perfect job for you. When you have finished, read your paragraph carefully, using the chart on page 177 to correct any run-ons or comma splices that you find.

ASSIGNMENT 2: EDIT

Using the chart on page 177, correct run-ons or comma splices in a paper you are writing for this course or another course, or in a piece of writing from your work or everyday life.

■ **LEARNING STYLES:** Look for activities in this chapter that are matched to your learning style. If you don't know your learning style, take the test on pages 26–28.

👁 **Visual**

🎧 **Auditory**

📖 **Reading/writing**

👣 **Kinesthetic (movement)**

Practice Together

Working with other students, practice what you have learned in this chapter.

1. Pair up with one other student and read the following lists. Each of you should pick two sentences from List 1 and join them with the most logical sentences from List 2, saying the joined sentences out loud. Then, on a sheet of paper, create run-ons by writing your sentences without commas or other punctuation. Take turns fixing each other's sentences by adding the correct punctuation and conjunctions as needed. 🎧 📖 👣

LIST 1	**LIST 2**
It was a really fun month.	The fruits will not be good.
Your plant's leaves are diseased or destroyed by insects.	She said the biggest was finishing school.
I knew that the little Suzuki cruiser had to be mine.	We saw many cool shows.
We asked Dawn about her biggest challenges.	It was the only bike that fit me perfectly.

2. On your computer screens, each of you should call up a paragraph that you wrote recently. Put your cursor at the end of each sentence and hit the enter or return key so that each sentence is on separate line. Then, each of you should go to another's computer to see if you can identify run-ons or comma splices in the sentences displayed. Tell the writer about any errors that you find.

3. A long sentence is not a run-on or a comma splice as long as word groups are joined correctly. As a group, make a long sentence by having each person say a sentence that could be connected to another. Someone should write the sentences as they're said. Then, read the long sentence together and add any coordinating conjunctions, subordinating conjunctions, or punctuation as needed. Discuss whether it is a good idea to write such a long sentence.

4. As a group, figure out a way to act out a run-on or a comma splice using everyone in the group to represent words, sentences, or punctuation. (Members can hold up signs to indicate their parts.) Or you might act out fixing a run-on or comma splice. Act out your sentence for the class.

5. Together, make notes about all the ways to correct run-ons and comma splices. Write examples for each way.

Chapter Review

1. A _____ is two complete sentences joined without any punctuation.

2. A _____ is two complete sentences joined by only a comma instead of a comma and *and, but, for, nor, or, so,* or *yet.*

3. What are the three ways to fix a run-on or comma splice? _____

_____

_____

■ **TIP:** For help with building your vocabulary, see Appendix B.

4. **VOCABULARY:** Go back to any new words that you underlined. Can you guess their meanings now? If not, look up the words in a dictionary.

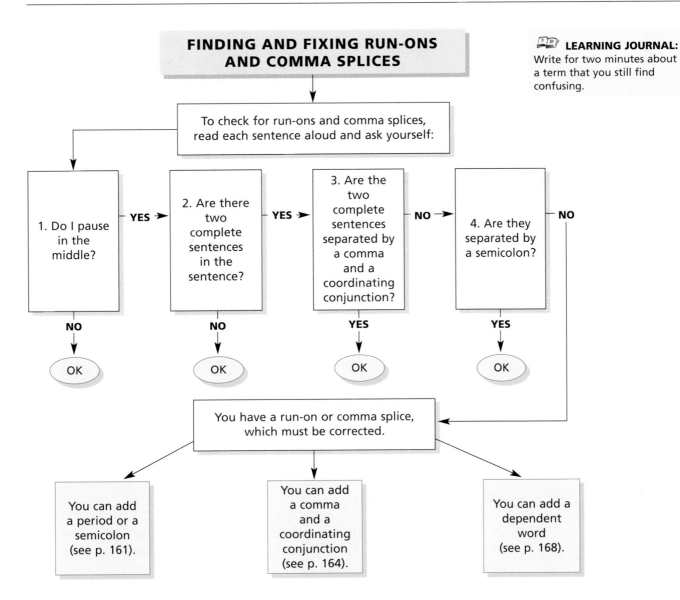

FINDING AND FIXING RUN-ONS AND COMMA SPLICES

LEARNING JOURNAL: Write for two minutes about a term that you still find confusing.

To check for run-ons and comma splices, read each sentence aloud and ask yourself:

1. Do I pause in the middle? — **YES** → 2. Are there two complete sentences in the sentence? — **YES** → 3. Are the two complete sentences separated by a comma and a coordinating conjunction? — **NO** → 4. Are they separated by a semicolon? — **NO**

1. **NO** → OK
2. **NO** → OK
3. **YES** → OK
4. **YES** → OK

You have a run-on or comma splice, which must be corrected.

You can add a period or a semicolon (see p. 161).

You can add a comma and a coordinating conjunction (see p. 164).

You can add a dependent word (see p. 168).

13

Subject-Verb Agreement Problems

Subjects and Verbs That Don't Match

📖 **VOCABULARY:** Underline any words in this chapter that are new to you.

📖 **IDEA JOURNAL:** Write about a favorite gift you have received.

■ **TIP:** In the sentence examples and charts in this chapter, subjects are light blue and verbs are red.

Understand What Subject-Verb Agreement Is

In any sentence, the **subject and the verb must match—or agree**—in number. If the subject is singular (one person, place, or thing), then the verb must also be singular. If the subject is plural (more than one), the verb must also be plural.

SINGULAR	The library computer crashes often.
	[The subject, *computer*, is singular—just one computer—so the verb must take the singular form: *crashes*.]
PLURAL	The library computers crash often.
	[The subject, *computers*, is plural—more than one computer—so the verb must take the plural form: *crash*.]

In the present tense, verbs for third-person singular subjects (like *Bob, he, she,* or *it*) end in *-s* or *-es*.

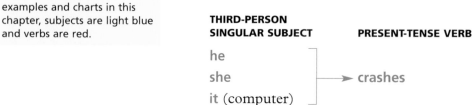

THIRD-PERSON SINGULAR SUBJECT	PRESENT-TENSE VERB
he	
she	➔ crashes
it (computer)	

178

PRACTICE 1 . . . .

In each of the following sentences, circle the correct form of the verb. Then, write the subject and the verb in the blank next to the sentence.

EXAMPLE: *cell phone rings* Jason's cell phone (ring / (rings)) in the doc-

tor's office.

_____ 1. Jason (jumps / jump) from the examining table.

_____ 2. He (searches / search) his pockets for his ringing phone.

_____ 3. Signs (tells / tell) patients to turn off their cell phones in the hospital.

_____ 4. Cell phones (causes / cause) problems with medical equipment.

_____ 5. However, doctors (believes / believe) that the risk is much lower than they once thought.

_____ 6. Now, many hospitals (allows / allow) the use of cell phones in certain areas.

_____ 7. People (wants / want) to talk to family and friends when they are in the hospital.

_____ 8. Jason (feels / feel) guilty about forgetting to turn his phone off.

_____ 9. The phone (falls / fall) out of his pocket.

_____ 10. Quickly, Jason (puts / put) the phone back in his pocket just as the doctor enters the examining room.

PRACTICE 2 . . . .

For each subject, fill in the blank with the correct present-tense form of the verb.

EXAMPLE: **to write**   I   _write_

                          he   _writes_

                          they   _write_

1. **to practice**   you   _____

                     we   _____

                     she   _____

2. **to ride**   he   _____

            we   _____

            they   _____

3. **to play**   we   _____

            I   _____

            he   _____

4. **to give**   they   _____

            she   _____

            you   _____

5. **to clean**   he   _____

            she   _____

            they   _____

6. **to drive**   he   _____

            we   _____

            they   _____

7. **to lose**   we   _____

            he   _____

            I   _____

8. **to bring**   they   _____

            you   _____

            she   _____

9. **to sing**   I   _____

            they   _____

            he   _____

10. **to let**   you   _____

            she   _____

            they   _____

PRACTICE 3 . . . .

In each of the following sentences, fill in the blank with the correct present-tense form of a verb of your choice.

    EXAMPLE: Some people ___*say*___ that I am cheap.

1. I _____ my money wisely.

2. Many people _____ only one side of a sheet of paper.

3. I _____ on both sides.

4. I never _____ a new car until the old one dies.

5. I _____ my spare change in a big paint bucket.

6. I _____ birthday presents instead of buying them.

7. My friends _____ the thoughtful gifts.

8. In my opinion, store brands _____ just as good as famous brands of food.

9. Coupons also _____ me save money on my groceries.

10. My husband always _____ that a penny saved is a penny earned.

In the Real World, Why Is It Important to Correct Subject-Verb Agreement Errors?

When Danny Alvarez filled out his application for admission to Eastside College, he had to write about his reasons for choosing that particular college. Read his paragraph aloud. Can you hear the problems with subject-verb agreement?

Briefly tell us why you chose Eastside College.

DANNY'S ANSWER:

I knows Eastside College is the best college in the area. My sister Beth and my sister Angel attends it now. My older sister study in the nursing school, and my younger sister want to be a paralegal in a lawyer's office. Both sisters likes the college fine and feels they gets a good education there. I hopes to get an associate's degree in drafting; my drafting teacher in high school and my high school counselor also recommends Eastside College for this line of work.

continued

> **THE RESPONSE OF EASTSIDE COLLEGE'S REGISTRAR TO DANNY'S ANSWER:**
> We get hundreds of applications each semester, and, of course, we cannot accept them all. Therefore, we must choose those candidates who seem most prepared for college work. The mistakes in Danny's response make me think he is not ready for college at this time.

PRACTICE 4 . .

There are nine subject-verb agreement errors in Danny's response. Looking at the subjects and verbs in each sentence, underline what you think are the errors.

Find and Correct Errors in Subject-Verb Agreement

■ **TIP:** To do this chapter, you need to understand the following terms: *subject, verb, prepositional phrase,* and *dependent clause.* (For review, see Chapter 10.)

> **FIND: Read each sentence in your writing carefully, looking for subjects and verbs. Make sure that the verb matches the form of the subject, looking for the trouble spots detailed later in this chapter.**
>
> • The verb is a form of *be, have,* or *do.*
> • Words or phrases come between the subject and the verb.
> • The sentence has a compound subject.
> • The subject is an indefinite pronoun.
> • The verb comes before the subject.

> **FIX: If you find a subject-verb agreement error, fix it by matching the verb to the form of the subject.**

🎬 👁 An audiovisual tutorial on finding and fixing the four most serious errors, including subject-verb agreement problems, is available on a CD that comes with this book.

The Verb Is a Form of *Be, Have,* or *Do*

The verbs *be, have,* and *do* do not follow the regular patterns for forming singular and plural forms; they are **irregular verbs**.

Forms of the Verb Be *in the Present Tense (Happening Now)*

SINGULAR (ONE ONLY)			PLURAL (TWO OR MORE)	
	IF THE subject IS	…THEN THE verb IS	IF THE subject IS	…THEN THE verb IS
First person	I	am	we	are
Second person	you	are	you	are
Third person	he/she/it	is	they	are

Forms of the Verb Be *in the Past Tense (Happening before Now)*

SINGULAR (ONE ONLY)			PLURAL (TWO OR MORE)	
	IF THE subject IS	…THEN THE verb IS	IF THE subject IS	…THEN THE verb IS
First person	I	was	we	were
Second person	you	were	you	were
Third person	he/she/it	was	they	were

Language note: Some nouns that don't end in -*s* are plural and need plural verbs. For example, *children* and *people* don't end in -*s*, but they indicate more than one, so they are plural.

| INCORRECT | These children is making me crazy. |
| CORRECT | These children **are** making me crazy. |

For more on irregular plural forms of nouns, see Chapter 16.

 Put sticky notes on the verb charts in this chapter so that you can refer to them later.

To correct an agreement problem in a sentence with the irregular verb *be,* follow these steps:

FIND: Read each sentence in your writing carefully, looking for forms of the irregular verb *be*.

At Christmastime, the shopping <u>malls</u> <u><u>was</u></u> busy.

- Underline the subject and double-underline the *be* verb.
- If the subject is singular, then the verb must also be singular.
- If the subject is plural, then the verb must also be plural. [In the example sentence, the subject is plural but the verb is singular.]

> **FIX: Revise any forms of *be* that don't agree.**
>
>   *were*
> **At Christmastime, the shopping malls was busy.**
>   ^

INCORRECT

You *is* the fastest driver.

Most **books** in this library *is* hard.

CORRECT

You *are* the fastest driver.

[The second-person singular, *you*, takes *are* as the verb.]

Most **books** in this library *are* hard.

[The third-person plural, *books*, takes *are* as the verb.]

PRACTICE 5 . . . .

In each of the following sentences, fill in the correct form of *be*. Make sure that the verb agrees with the subject.

EXAMPLE: I ___*am*___ a customer at the Internet café near my friend

Nadine's apartment.

1. She _____ a customer there, too.

2. We _____ addicted to *The Sims*, a computer role-playing game about daily life.

3. It _____ fun to create and control the everyday lives of our characters.

4. They _____ not like most video game characters.

5. Instead, they _____ realistic people who eat, sleep, work, pay bills, and spend time with family and friends.

6. They _____ citizens of a virtual town called Alphaville.

7. In Alphaville, I _____ a famous movie star who lives in a mansion next to Nadine's character.

8. She _____ a bank robber who owns a pet tiger.

9. In the online version of *The Sims*, you _____ able to interact with players around the world.

10. Last week, Nadine _____ excited to learn that she was playing with people from Germany.

■ **TIP:** For more practice, visit Exercise Central at <**bedfordstmartins.com/realskills**>.

Forms of the Verb Have *in the Present Tense (Happening Now)*

SINGULAR (ONE ONLY)			PLURAL (TWO OR MORE)	
	IF THE subject IS	...THEN THE verb IS	IF THE subject IS	...THEN THE verb IS
First person	I	have	we	have
Second person	you	have	you	have
Third person	he/she/it	has	they	have

To correct an agreement problem in a sentence with the irregular verb *have*, follow these steps:

 Copy the chart above and write a sentence for each singular and plural form.

FIND: Read each sentence in your writing carefully, looking for forms of the irregular verb *have*.

The male elephant <u>have</u> several miles to roam in that park.

- Underline the subject and double-underline the *have* verb.
- If the subject is singular, then the verb must also be singular. [In the sentence example, the subject is singular but the verb is plural.]
- If the subject is plural, then the verb must also be plural.

⬇

FIX: Revise any forms of *have* that don't agree.

                has
The male elephant ~~have~~ several miles to roam in that park.
          ^

INCORRECT

I *has* the right to see my records.

They *has* the parking permit.

CORRECT

I *have* the right to see my records.

[The first-person singular, *I*, takes *have* as the verb.]

They *have* the parking permit.

[The third-person plural, *they*, takes *have* as the verb.]

PRACTICE 6 . .

In each of the following sentences, fill in the correct form of *have*. Make sure that the verb agrees with the subject.

EXAMPLE: I ___*have*___ a new puppy named Betty.

1. She _____ beautiful eyes.

2. We _____ another puppy whose name is Rusty.

3. He _____ a gentle personality.

4. Like many people, I _____ a soft spot for puppies from the animal shelter.

5. It _____ many puppies and kittens in need of good homes, but the older animals are often overlooked.

6. We _____ a neighbor who adopted four older dogs that had been in the shelter for over a year.

7. They _____ a good home now.

8. We _____ no concerns about all the animals, but some neighbors complain about the noise.

9. Occasionally, you _____ to cover your ears when all the dogs are barking.

10. Now that we _____ two puppies, I _____ a fantasy of adopting some older dogs, too.

Forms of the Verb Do in the Present Tense (Happening Now)

SINGULAR (ONE ONLY)			PLURAL (TWO OR MORE)	
	IF THE subject IS	...THEN THE verb IS	IF THE subject IS	...THEN THE verb IS
First person	I	do	we	do
Second person	you	do	you	do
Third person	he/she/it	does	they	do

To correct an agreement problem in a sentence with the irregular verb *do*, follow these steps:

 Referring to the chart on page 186, repeat the subjects and forms of *do* aloud. Then, say the different forms in sentences.

FIND: Read each sentence in your writing carefully, looking for forms of the irregular verb *do*.

In their company, computers does the bookkeeping automatically.

- Underline the subject and double-underline the *do* verb.
- If the subject is singular, then the verb must also be singular.
- If the subject is plural, then the verb must also be plural. [In the example sentence, the subject is plural but the verb is singular.]

↓

FIX: Revise any forms of *do* that don't agree.

               do
In their company, computers ~~does~~ the bookkeeping automatically.
               ^

INCORRECT

She always *do* her assignments on time.

They *does* not like to swim.

CORRECT

She always *does* her assignments on time.

[The third-person singular, *she*, takes *does* as the verb.]

They *do* not like to swim.

[The third-person plural, *they*, takes *do* as the verb.]

PRACTICE 7 . . . .

In each of the following sentences, fill in the correct form of *do*. Make sure that the verb agrees with the subject.

    EXAMPLE: I ___*do*___ everything at the last minute, unlike my friend

    Kevin.

1. He _____ all his assignments early.

2. My other friends are like me; they _____ their work late, too.

3. We _____ understand the importance of starting early.

4. When you _____ an entire paper the night before a deadline, you run out of time for revising and editing.

5. I _____ my best to start assignments early, but it's easy to get distracted.

6. Thinking that the paper can wait, I _____ the dishes or the laundry instead.

7. We _____ not understand how Kevin is so good at managing his time.

8. In addition to night classes and his full-time job, he even _____ volunteer work on weekends.

9. He _____ not have a secret way of adding extra hours to the day; he simply creates a written schedule and sticks to it.

10. He _____ well in all of his classes, so it really _____ pay to be organized.

PRACTICE 8

In the following paragraph, correct problems with subject-verb agreement. If a sentence is correct as written, write "C" next to it. There are five correct sentences.

(1) My family have trouble finding time to eat dinner together. (2) We do our best. (3) Our busy schedules is hard to work around, however. (4) We are aware of the importance of regular family meals. (5) Scientists has found interesting benefits to such meals. (6) One study are especially revealing. (7) According to this study, teenagers does less drinking and smoking if they eat with family members an average of five to seven times weekly. (8) Family mealtime also has a link to eating disorders. (9) A teen girl are less likely to be anorexic or bulimic if she regularly eats meals with her family. (10) Family dinners even does wonders for children's language development. (11) Mealtime is more important to children's vocabulary than play, story time, and other family activities. (12) Of course, long discussions is more useful for vocabulary skills than one-phrase comments like "Eat your vegetables." (13) Vegetables is certainly important, too, and children eat more of them when dining with their families. (14) Like most people, you probably has a busy schedule. (15) Nevertheless, family dinners are clearly well worth the time.

Language note: The verbs *be*, *have*, and *do* cause problems for people who use only one form of the verb in casual conversation: *You is the nicest* (incorrect); *He is the nicest* (correct). In college and at work, use the correct form of the verbs as shown in this chapter.

PRACTICE 9

Write six sentences: two using a form of *be*, two using a form of *have*, and two using a form of *do*. Refer to the tables earlier in this chapter to make sure that the subjects agree with the verbs.

Words Come between the Subject and the Verb

A prepositional phrase or a dependent clause often comes between the subject and the verb. Even when the subject and the verb are not next to each other in the sentence, they still must agree.

A **prepositional phrase** starts with a preposition and ends with a noun or pronoun:

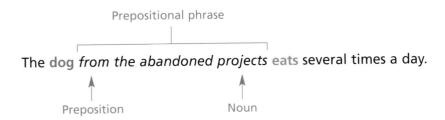

Prepositional phrase

The **dog** *from the abandoned projects* **eats** several times a day.

Preposition   Noun

A **dependent clause** has a subject and a verb but does not express a complete thought. When a dependent clause comes between the subject and the verb, it usually starts with the word *who*, *whose*, *whom*, *that*, or *which*.

Dependent clause

The **woman** *who won two million dollars* **was** homeless.

Subject   Verb

Remember, the subject of a sentence is never in a prepositional phrase or dependent clause.

■ **TIP:** For a list of common prepositions, see page 123.

🎧 Read the sentence about the dog aloud without the prepositional phrase (in italics). Then, read it with the prepositional phrase. Repeat until it sounds right both with and without the phrase.

To correct an agreement problem when the subject and the verb aren't next to each other in a sentence, follow these steps:

FIND: Read each sentence in your writing carefully.

The <u>man</u> who grew those giant tomatoes <u><u>win</u></u> at the fair every year.

- Underline the subject and double-underline the verb.
- Cross out any words between the subject and verb (a preposi-tional phrase or dependent clause).
- If the subject is singular, then the verb must also be singular. [In the example sentence, the subject is singular but the verb is plural.]
- If the subject is plural, then the verb must also be plural.

FIX: Revise any verb forms that don't agree.

The man who grew those giant tomatoes <u>win</u> *wins* at the fair every year.

READ ALOUD

Stand up and read the following sentences aloud, emphasizing the subject and the verb and mentally crossing out the words between them.

INCORRECT

The best deal with the greatest savings *are* at that store.

Items for sale *includes* a baby carriage.

The chef who studied at one of their schools *make* good money.

Some county records that burned in the fire *was* replaced.

CORRECT

The best deal ~~with the greatest savings~~ *is* at that store.

Items ~~for sale~~ *include* a baby carriage.

The chef ~~who studied at one of their schools~~ *makes* good money.

Some county records ~~that burned in the fire~~ *were* replaced.

PRACTICE 10 . . . .

In each of the following sentences, underline the subject and cross out the prepositional phrase between the subject and the verb. Then, circle the correct form of the verb.

> **EXAMPLE:** The <u>workers</u> ~~on the boat~~ (waits / (wait)) for the guests to come on board.

1. Waves from the bay (hits / hit) the dock hard.

2. The deck of the boat (leans / lean) to the side.

3. The people on the deck (grabs / grab) the rail for support.

4. Strong gusts of wind (blows / blow) in from the water.

5. One of the guests (asks / ask) the captain if it is safe to go out in this weather.

6. The sailor at the controls (says / say) that everything is fine.

7. The ride across the bay (goes / go) smoothly at first.

8. Then, dark clouds in the sky (covers / cover) the sun without warning.

9. The boats on the water (turns / turn) back toward the dock.

10. The passengers on board (thanks / thank) the crew for getting them back safely.

PRACTICE 11 . . . .

In each of the following sentences, underline the subject and cross out the dependent clause. Then, circle the correct form of the verb.

> **EXAMPLE:** <u>People</u> ~~who travel a lot~~ (appreciates / (appreciate)) helpful advice.

1. Tips that save money or improve comfort (is / are) always welcome.

2. Flights that are overbooked (is / are) common around holidays.

3. Passengers who volunteer to travel on a later flight (receives / receive) a free ticket.

4. Travel agents who save you money (is / are) worth their fees.

5. The people who you sit near on a plane (is / are) important to your comfort.

6. A conversation that includes a few kind words (makes / make) strangers more polite to each other.

7. A person whose seat back is pushing into your knees (is / are) very annoying.

8. A passenger whom you have befriended (moves / move) the seat up when asked.

9. People who want to avoid lost luggage (carries / carry) all their bags with them on the plane.

10. A traveler who follows these tips (has / have) a more comfortable flight.

PRACTICE 12 . . . .

In each sentence of the following paragraph, cross out any prepositional phrases or dependent clauses that come between the subject and the verb. Then, correct all verbs that do not agree with their subjects. Three sentences are correct; write "C" next to them.

(1) Baby strollers that you see today is fancier than ever before. (2) The safety of the stroller is still important, of course. (3) However, features that increase the baby's comfort is becoming more popular. (4) The seat in some strollers are adjustable. (5) Babies who like to sleep in their strollers are able to lie flat on their backs. (6) Strollers with an adjustable seat is not cheap. (7) A certain type of these strollers cost $850. (8) However, the popularity of these products continue to grow. (9) One expert on stroller marketing makes an interesting point. (10) Many of today's new parents wants their strollers to make a statement. (11) Statements that express something about the parents' lifestyle is best. (12) A stroller with a designer label show off the parents' wealth. (13) Strollers that keep the baby very high off the ground shows the parents' desire to be close to their child. (14) Sometimes, parents who want to make several statements owns more than one stroller.

PRACTICE 13 . .

Write six sentences in which the subject and the verb are not next to each other—three with a prepositional phrase and three with a dependent clause. Then, make sure that the subject and verb in each sentence agree. Crossing out the prepositional phrase or dependent clause may be helpful.

EXAMPLE: Gasoline, ~~which is very expensive in Europe~~, costs five

cents a gallon in Saudi Arabia.

The Sentence Has a Compound Subject

If two (or more) subjects are joined by *and*, they form a **compound** (plural) subject, which requires a plural verb.

| Subject 1 | + | *and* | + | Subject 2 | = | Plural subject requiring plural verb |

> 👁 📖 Write your own formula, illustrating it if you'd like.

Plural subject

The fire **truck** and the **ambulance take** the freeway.

If two (or more) subjects are connected by *or* or *nor*, they are actually considered separate, and the verb agrees with whatever subject is closer to it.

| Subject 1 | + | *or or nor* | + | Subject 2 | = | Separate subjects (use verb that agrees with last subject) |

Singular subject

The fire **truck** or the **ambulance takes** the freeway.

Plural subject

Neither the fire **truck** nor the **ambulances take** the freeway.

To correct an agreement problem when there is a compound subject, follow these steps:

FIND: **Read each sentence in your writing carefully, looking for compound subjects.**

Two soldiers or an officer always wait at the door.

- Underline the subjects and double-underline the verb.
- Circle the *and*, *or*, or *nor* between the subjects.
- If the circled word joins the subjects to make them plural, a plural verb is needed. If the word separates the subjects, the verb must agree with the subject that is closer to the verb. [In the example sentence, *or* separates the subjects, so the verb must agree with *officer* (singular).]

FIX: **Revise any verb forms that don't agree.**

waits
The soldiers or an officer always ~~wait~~ at the door.

INCORRECT

The **Girl Scouts** and their **leader** *buys* the leftover cookies.

Neither his **children** nor his **dog** *like* him very much.

CORRECT

The **Girl Scouts** and their **leader** *buy* the leftover cookies.

[The subject is plural.]

Neither his **children** nor his **dog** *likes* him very much.

[The verb agrees with the closest subject, *dog*.]

PRACTICE 14 . . . .

In each of the following sentences, circle the word that joins the two parts of the compound subject. Then, choose the correct form of the verb.

EXAMPLE: My bedroom (and) the library (is / (are)) two places that I expect to be fairly quiet.

1. Loud conversations or music (makes / make) it hard to study.

2. Music and loud voices (is / are) common in my house.

3. My sister and I (runs / run) downstairs to see who is being so loud.

4. As usual, my brother Leo and his friend (is / are) listening to the stereo and playing a video game at the same time.

5. The stereo and the television (is / are) so loud that I can barely hear myself think.

6. My sister and I (looks / look) at each other.

7. An angry complaint or a dirty look (is / are) not a good solution.

8. A bribe or a gentle request (works / work) much better.

9. Leo and his friend (agrees / agree) to my offer.

10. A new video game and a new CD (is / are) their prize for being quiet the rest of the evening.

PRACTICE 15 . . . .

In each of the following sentences, circle the word that joins the two parts of the compound subject. Then, fill in the correct present-tense form of the verb in parentheses.

> **EXAMPLE:** Motorcycles (and) minibikes known as "pocket rockets"
>
> ___are___ (**be**) for people who like to go fast.

1. Mostly older children and teens _____ (*ride*) pocket rockets.

2. A bike or a skateboard _____ (*be*) not fast enough for them.

3. So these teens or brave parents _____ (*buy*) something with more speed.

4. A toy store or an auto parts store _____ (*be*) where most people buy their pocket rockets.

5. Unclear laws or careless drivers _____ (*make*) these miniature motorcycles controversial.

6. Many cities and states _____ (*have*) laws against riding pocket rockets on the street.

7. Accidents or noise complaints _____ (*have*) caused some areas to ban the small motorcycles.

8. Speeding or other traffic violations _____ (*create*) problems, too.

9. Neither sidewalks nor streets _____ (*be*) safe when people do not follow traffic laws.

10. Pocket rockets and motorcycles _____ (*require*) knowledge of traffic rules and great care while driving.

PRACTICE 16

In the following paragraph, correct problems with subject-verb agreement. Three sentences are correct; write "C" next to them.

(1) Diet and exercise is important parts of a healthy lifestyle. (2) Unfortunately, laziness or bad habits controls the way we eat in many cases. (3) Doctors and nutritionists recommends starting every day with a healthy breakfast. (4) On busy mornings, however, a doughnut or a muffin seem easier than more nutritious options. (5) A healthy lunch or dinner are easier to prepare than many people think. (6) However, frozen food or fast food seems easier than preparing a fresh, healthy meal. (7) As a result, our health and wallets suffer. (8) At a fast-food restaurant, fries and a drink comes in a combination meal. (9) Most children and adults orders the combination meal, even when they want only a hamburger. (10) In many cases, the easiest choice or the most familiar choice is not the best choice for our health.

PRACTICE 17

Write five sentences with compound subjects (for example, *my mother and I*). Then, make sure that the subject and verb in each sentence agree.

The Subject Is an Indefinite Pronoun

Indefinite pronouns, which refer to unspecified people or objects, are often singular, although there are exceptions.

Indefinite Pronouns

ALWAYS SINGULAR (USE THE *IS* FORM OF *BE*)		
anybody	everyone	nothing
anyone	everything	one (of)
anything		somebody
each (of)	neither (of)	someone
either (of)	nobody	something
everybody	no one	

MAY BE SINGULAR OR PLURAL (USE THE *IS* OR *ARE* FORM OF *BE*)	
all	none
any	some

 Listen for indefinite pronouns as subjects on the radio or television news.

Nobody wants to tell him the bad news.

[*Nobody* is always singular, so it takes the singular verb *wants*.]

Some of the soldiers **stay** on base over the weekend.

[In this case, *some* is plural, referring to some (more than one but less than all) of the *soldiers*, so it takes the plural verb *stay*. It might help to think of "*some* of the soldiers" in this case as "they."]

When putting on makeup, **some is** enough if you use it wisely.

[In this case, *some* is singular, so it takes the singular verb *is*.]

Often, an indefinite pronoun is followed by a prepositional phrase or a dependent clause; remember that the subject of a sentence is never found in either of these. To choose the correct verb, you can cross out the prepositional phrase or dependent clause to focus on the indefinite pronoun. If words come between the indefinite-pronoun subject and the verb, mentally cross them out.

To correct agreement problems in sentences with indefinite pronouns, follow these steps:

FIND: Read each sentence in your writing carefully, looking for indefinite-pronoun subjects.

<u>Everyone</u> in this house <u>read</u> the Sunday paper.

- Underline the subject and double-underline the verb.
- Cross out any words that come between the subject and the verb.
- If the subject is singular, then the verb must also be singular. [In the example sentence, the subject is singular but the verb is plural.]
- If the subject is plural, then the verb must also be plural.

> **FIX: Revise any verb forms that don't agree.**
>
> *reads*
> **Everyone in this house read the Sunday paper.**
> ^

INCORRECT

Anyone in the choir *sing* better than I do.

Both of them *is* graduates of this college.

Someone, whom I cannot remember at the moment, always *leave* early.

Many who buy tickets early *feels* cheated when a concert is canceled.

CORRECT

Anyone ~~in the choir~~ *sings* better than I do.

[The subject is *anyone*, which takes a singular verb.]

Both ~~of them~~ *are* graduates of this college.

[The subject is *both*, which always takes a plural verb.]

Someone, ~~whom I cannot remember at the moment~~, always *leaves* early.

[*Someone* is always singular.]

Many ~~who buy tickets early~~ *feel* cheated when a concert is canceled.

[The subject is *many*, which is always plural.]

> **PRACTICE 18** . . . .

In each of the following sentences, circle the verb that agrees with the subject.

EXAMPLE: One of my daughters (wants / want) her own pet.

1. Everyone (thinks / think) that this is a good chance to teach her responsibility.

2. No one (knows / know) why, but she is not interested in puppies and kittens.

3. Someone in her class (owns / own) a goldfish and some Sea Monkeys.

4. Either (makes / make) a good first pet.

5. Everybody who has raised Sea Monkeys (tells / tell) me that they are inexpensive and easy to care for.

6. One of my daughter's friends (thinks / think) that the small creatures are related to monkeys.

7. Neither of my children (believes / believe) this.

8. Each of the tiny animals (is / are) actually a type of shrimp.

9. Everybody (loves / love) to watch the little shrimp wiggle around in the water.

10. Everyone who (enjoys / enjoy) Sea Monkeys can thank Harold von Braunhut, who started selling the shrimp eggs in 1957.

PRACTICE 19 . .

Write five sentences that each include one of the indefinite pronouns from the chart on page 197. Then, make sure that the subject and the verb in each sentence agree.

The Verb Comes before the Subject

In most sentences, the subject comes before the verb. However, the verb comes *before* the subject in questions and in sentences that begin with *here* or *there*. To find the subject and verb, turn these sentences around.

Which **is** the **prize** that you won? The **prize** that you won **is**...

Where **are** the **envelopes**? The **envelopes are**...

Notice that turning a question around means answering it.

Language note: For reference charts and practices on forming questions and negative statements, see Chapter 21.

Here **is** the **magazine** I promised to bring you. The **magazine** I promised to bring you **is** here.

There **are** several **pictures** on the wall. Several **pictures are** on the wall.

FIND: Read each sentence in your writing carefully, looking for questions and sentences that begin with *here* or *there*.

Where is the carpenter's tools?

Here is the carpenter's tools.

- Turn the sentences around and underline the subjects.

The carpenter's <u>tools</u> is where?

The carpenter's <u>tools</u> is here.

- Ask if the subject is singular or plural. If it's singular, it needs to have a singular verb, and if it's plural, it needs to have a plural verb. [In the example sentences, the subject is plural but the verb (*is*) is singular.]

FIX: Revise any verb forms that don't agree.

      are
Where ~~is~~ the carpenter's tools?

      are
Here ~~is~~ the carpenter's tools.

INCORRECT

Which company *deliver* your boxes?

There *is* the paint brushes I brought you.

CORRECT

Which company *delivers* your boxes?

[Answer: UPS *delivers*...]

There *are* the paint brushes I brought you.

[The paint brushes *are* there.]

PRACTICE 20 . . . .

In each of the following items, underline the subject and circle the correct verb.

EXAMPLE: When (are)/ is) <u>we</u> leaving for vacation?

1. (Is / Are) you excited?

2. Where (is / are) the theme park?

3. How far away (is / are) it?

4. When (is / are) we going to arrive?

5. What (is / are) your favorite ride?

6. There (is / are) five roller coasters in the park.

7. Which ones (does / do) you want to ride?

8. Here (is / are) the brochure showing the fastest one.

9. Why (does / do) everyone go to the theme park in the evening?

10. There (is / are) so many people lined up for rides then.

PRACTICE 21 . . . .

In each of the following sentences, underline the subject and circle the correct verb.

EXAMPLE: Here (are /(is) our <u>cabin</u>.

1. There (is / are) a lake around the corner.

2. Here (is / are) the boat that we can use on the lake.

3. Where (is / are) the keys to the boat?

4. There (is / are) a family of birds nesting on the lake.

5. (Is / Are) their cries what we hear every night?

6. There (is / are) the small kitchen where we will cook.

7. Here (is / are) the phone number of the cabin's owner.

8. There (is / are) some maps of the area.

9. (Is / Are) there good hiking trails around?

10. Here (is / are) the bed that I want to nap on before we do anything else.

PRACTICE 22 . . . .

In the following paragraph, correct problems with subject-verb agreement. Three sentences are correct; write "C" next to them.

(1) Here are the farm stand we were telling you about. (2) It sells the freshest fruits and vegetables that you will ever taste. (3) The corn is picked fresh every morning. (4) Where is the fields in which it is grown? (5) Here is tomatoes loaded with flavor. (6) Is the watermelons in that box too big for one person to carry? (7) Here are homemade ice cream fresh from the freezer. (8) Where are the prize-winning cherry pies? (9) There are an apple pie that is still steaming from the oven. (10) There are no space in the car for all that I want to eat.

PRACTICE 23 . . . .

In the following paragraph, correct problems with subject-verb agreement. Three sentences are correct; write "C" next to them.

(1) Here is some common questions about traveling to New York City: (2) Do a trip to the city have to be expensive? (3) How much does most hotels cost? (4) Is cheap hotels available in safe areas? (5) Where does travelers on a tight budget stay? (6) People who worry about these questions are often pleasantly surprised to learn about hostels. (7) A hostel is an inexpensive type of lodging in which travelers share dormitory-style rooms. (8) There is many benefits of staying in a hostel. (9) Most hostels are quite safe, clean, and affordable; plus, they offer you the chance to meet interesting travelers from all over the world. (10) What else does budget-minded travelers need?

PRACTICE 24 . . . .

Write five questions or sentences that begin with *here* or *there*, making sure that the verb agrees with the subject.

. . . .

Edit Subject-Verb Agreement Problems in College, Work, and Everyday Life

Complete the editing reviews as instructed, referring to the chart on page 208.

EDITING REVIEW 1: COLLEGE

The following passage is similar to one you might find in a criminal-justice textbook. Correct problems with subject-verb agreement. Four sentences are correct; write "C" next to them. The first sentence has been edited for you.

(1) Members of a law enforcement agency collects evidence before making an arrest. (2) There is three main types of evidence: testimonial, documentary, and physical evidence. (3) Someone who has firsthand knowledge of a crime provide testimonial evidence. (4) As its name suggests, documentary evidence consists of written documents as well as audio and video recordings. (5) Physical evidence, in contrast, is an object or a material that might link a suspect to the scene of a crime. (6) Fingerprints and DNA is physical evidence. (7) Other examples of physical evidence includes drugs, weapons, and fibers from clothing. (8) Generally, testimonial evidence and documentary evidence are not as reliable as physical evidence.

(9) The Fourth Amendment of the U.S. Constitution regulate the collection of evidence. (10) To obtain a search warrant, a law-enforcement officer have to give a good reason, or probable cause. (11) However, a search warrant is not always required. (12) For example, an officer do not need a warrant to search for marijuana fields by helicopter. (13) In certain situations, an officer have the authority to search a car without a warrant. (14) There is many citizens who disagree with such exceptions. (15) Neither security nor freedom are worth sacrificing for the other, they believe.

EDITING REVIEW 2: WORK/USING FORMAL ENGLISH

TIP: For advice on using formal English, see Chapter 4. For advice on avoiding slang, see Chapter 25.

Correct the subject-verb agreement errors in the following grant-application letter. Then, revise informal language. The first sentence has been corrected for you. In addition to this sentence, you should find four cases of informal language.

Maura Vogel

Grant Manager

Tri-State Foundation

429 Woodland Ridge Boulevard

Fort Wayne, IN 46803

Dear Ms. Vogel:

(1) The Volunteer Center of Northern Indiana ~~wish~~ *wishes* to apply for a Tri-State Foundation Community Development Grant.

Our Mission: (2) The Volunteer Center, which serves Allen, Whitley, Noble, and DeKalb counties, are a nonprofit organization. (3) The center supports volunteerism in the area by hooking up various organizations with volunteers. (4) The 150 organizations that turn to us for help includes animal shelters, youth programs, hospitals, and soup kitchens. (5) There is many people who are unsure about where to volunteer their time and energy. (6) Everyone who come to us are referred to an organization that need their help.

Purpose of Grant: (7) The Volunteer Center seek a $10,000 grant from the Tri-State Foundation. (8) How does we plan to spend the dough? (9) The Volunteer Center now operate on an $800,000 annual budget. (10) One-eighth of our funds come from grants. (11) Currently, however, no funds is used for training our volunteers or communications staff. (12) Newsletters and our Web site gives potential volunteers the 411 on volunteer opportunities. (13) With a Tri-State Foundation Community Grant, we plan to train our peeps to communicate this information more effectively. (14) We also hopes to purchase new software and computers to improve the quality of our newsletters and Web site.

(15) I looks forward to your response.

Sincerely,

Marcus Owens

EDITING REVIEW 3: EVERYDAY LIFE . . . .

Correct problems with subject-verb agreement in the following essay. Eight sentences are correct; write "C" next to them. The first sentence has been edited for you.

(1) There *are* is few natural disasters more destructive than a hurricane. (2) The winds of a hurricane usually forms over a warm ocean into a spiral shape. (3) A typical hurricane measures about three hundred miles across. (4) The hurricane's center, which is usually twenty to thirty miles wide, are called the *eye*. (5) The eye of a hurricane is its calmest spot. (6) The winds near the eye of a hurricane is the strongest. (7) In fact, some hurricanes has winds of up to 250 miles per hour near the eye.

(8) Major hurricanes, like Hurricane Katrina, has destroyed entire communities. (9) Hurricane winds cause much of the damage. (10) However, floods that are caused by a hurricane is often more destructive than the wind. (11) A wall of water called a storm surge build up in front of a hurricane. (12) The tide sometimes rises more than twenty-five feet when the storm surge reaches land. (13) The violent waves and high water is extremely dangerous.

(14) The amount of damage from a hurricane depend on the storm's strength. (15) There is five categories of hurricanes. (16) Category 1 is the weakest. (17) A Category 1 hurricane have wind speeds of 74 to 95 miles per hour. (18) Hurricanes in this category causes some flooding but generally only minor damage. (19) Roofs and trees is damaged during a Category 2 hurricane. (20) However, most buildings does not

receive much damage. (21) Anything over a Category 2 are considered a major hurricane. (22) These hurricanes result in major damage and severe flooding. (23) With wind speeds over 150 miles per hour, a Category 5 hurricane result in widespread destruction.

(24) How does scientists measure the strength of a hurricane? (25) There is several methods. (26) Satellites and ground stations measure hurricane conditions whenever possible. (27) At other times, people flies small planes right into a hurricane. (28) Air Force members who fly into a storm is called Hurricane Hunters. (29) They collect information on wind speeds, rainfall, and air pressure. (30) The National Hurricane Center in Miami, Florida, use this information to predict the hurricane's strength and path. (31) Anyone who understands the incredible power of hurricanes admire the bravery of these men and women.

Write and Edit Your Own Work

ASSIGNMENT 1: WRITE

Write a paragraph about an important purchase you have made or hope to make. Then, edit the paragraph to make sure that all subjects and all verbs agree. Revise any subject-verb agreement problems that you find using the chart on page 208.

ASSIGNMENT 2: EDIT

Using the chart on p. 208, edit subject-verb agreement errors in a paper you are writing for this course or another course, or in a piece of writing from your work or everyday life.

Practice Together

Working with a few other students, practice what you have learned in this chapter.

1. Each person should think of a subject and write it down. Then, take turns saying your subjects and the forms of *be*, *have*, and *do* that agree with them.

2. As a group, make up a funny sentence. Have each person write it down. Then, discuss a way that you could illustrate agreement between the subject and the verb. Make a sketch to show this. At the end of the activity, groups should post their sketches on the wall so that others can see. 👁 🎧 📖 👣

3. As a group, write a set of sentences on one sheet of paper, with each group member contributing a sentence or two. Then, exchange sheets with another group. In the sentences you receive, change singular subjects to plural subjects and plural subjects to singular subjects, making sure that the verbs agree. Then, return the sentences to the group that gave them to you. 🎧 📖 👣

4. As a group, write a set of questions on one sheet of paper, with each group member contributing one or two. Then, exchange sheets with another group. Change the questions you receive to statements, making sure the subjects and verbs agree. Then, return the questions to the group that gave them to you. 🎧 📖 👣

5. Create a study guide for this chapter, recording important rules and examples. Use the guide to study with other students in your group. 🎧 📖

Chapter Review

1. In any sentence, the subject and the verb must match—or agree—in

   _____.

2. What are the five trouble spots for subject-verb agreement? _____

   _____

   _____

   _____

3. Write three subjects and present-tense forms of *be*, *have*, and *do* that

   agree with the subjects. _____

4. Write four examples of indefinite pronouns. _____

5. **VOCABULARY:** Go back to any new words that you underlined. Can you guess their meanings now? If not, look up the words in a dictionary.

■ **LEARNING STYLES:** Look for activities in this chapter that are matched to your learning style. If you don't know your learning style, take the test on pages 26–28.

👁 Visual

🎧 Auditory

📖 Reading/writing

👣 Kinesthetic (movement)

📖 **LEARNING JOURNAL:** Complete this sentence: My biggest problem with subject-verb agreement is _____.

■ **TIP:** For help with building your vocabulary, see Appendix B.

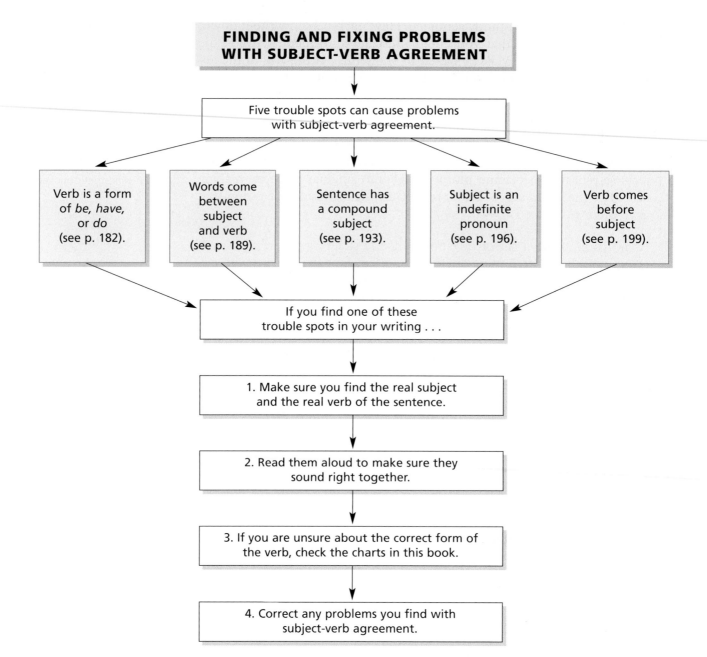

FINDING AND FIXING PROBLEMS WITH SUBJECT-VERB AGREEMENT

Five trouble spots can cause problems with subject-verb agreement.

Verb is a form of *be, have,* or *do* (see p. 182).

Words come between subject and verb (see p. 189).

Sentence has a compound subject (see p. 193).

Subject is an indefinite pronoun (see p. 196).

Verb comes before subject (see p. 199).

If you find one of these trouble spots in your writing . . .

1. Make sure you find the real subject and the real verb of the sentence.

2. Read them aloud to make sure they sound right together.

3. If you are unsure about the correct form of the verb, check the charts in this book.

4. Correct any problems you find with subject-verb agreement.

14

Verbs

The Past Tense

ALFREDO P. ZAPP
Founder of ZAPP'S
Born 1863 · Zapped 1929

Understand Regular Verbs in the Past Tense

Verb tense tells *when* the action of a sentence occurs. Use the **past tense** to describe actions that happened in the past. To form the past tense of most **regular verbs**, add **-ed**. For verbs that end in *e*, just add a **-d**.

📖 **VOCABULARY:** Underline any words in this chapter that are new to you.

	REGULAR VERBS → -ED	REGULAR VERBS ENDING WITH -E → -D
Present/past	learn/learn**ed**	move/move**d**
	pass/pass**ed**	smoke/smoke**d**
	finish/finish**ed**	hire/hire**d**
	start/start**ed**	fire/fire**d**
	work/work**ed**	stare/stare**d**
	laugh/laugh**ed**	rescue/rescue**d**
	play/play**ed**	excuse/excuse**d**

For regular verbs that end with a consonant and a *-y* change the *-y* to an *-i* before adding *-ed*.

Present/past	worry/worr**ied**	hurry/hurr**ied**
	cry/cr**ied**	party/part**ied**
	try/tr**ied**	study/stud**ied**

TIP: Consonants are *b, c, d, f, g, h, j, k, l, m, n, p, q, r, s, t, v, w, x, z,* and *sometimes y*.

👁 Draw a timeline showing the present and past.

> **Language note:** Remember to include needed endings on present-tense and past-tense verbs, even if they are not noticed in speech.
>
> **PRESENT TENSE**   Nate listen**s** to his new iPod wherever he goe**s**.
>
> **PAST TENSE**   Nate listen**ed** to his iPod while he walk**ed** the dog.
>
> If you have trouble forming the present or past tense, see Chapter 21 for reference charts and additional practices.

In the Real World, Why Is It Important to Use the Correct Tense?

Stanley "Steamer" Mahoney works as a unit supervisor for Zapp's Electronics, a manufacturing company. Recently, he applied for an opening in the company's management training program. Steamer followed up his interview with the company's vice president by sending this e-mail:

STEAMER'S E-MAIL:

Dear Mr. Kirby,

Thank you for meeting with me. I know you examine my qualifications thoroughly before our discussion. I hope yesterday you also learn personally how much I want to be a manager. I work hard to get this far in our company, but as a manager, I need to know more than what I experience over the years.

I am ready to begin!

Thank you,

Stanley "Steamer" Mahoney

THE VICE PRESIDENT'S RESPONSE:

Both management and the employees under Steamer respect him. He is smart, fair, and dedicated, but his poor grammar has always been a problem. The errors in this e-mail convince me that, as a manager, Steamer would not represent the company's high overall standards. Reluctantly, I have denied Steamer's application to this year's management training program.

📖 **IDEA JOURNAL:** Write about something that really makes you angry.

READ ALOUD

Stand up and read Steamer's e-mail aloud. Listen for the errors without worrying about how they should be corrected.

> ■ **TIP:** To do this chapter, you may want to review the terms *subject* and *verb* from Chapter 10.

PRACTICE 1

Find and underline the four verb-tense errors in Steamer's e-mail.

PRACTICE 2

In each of the following sentences, underline the verb. Then, in the blank next to each sentence, write *present* if the verb is in the present tense; write *past* if the verb is in the past tense.

EXAMPLE: ___*past*___ Randall finally <u>mailed</u> the forms.

_____ 1. This library subscribes to most major newspapers.

_____ 2. Shana cooked dinner every night last week.

_____ 3. I traveled to Chicago on the midnight plane.

_____ 4. The baby needs his breakfast right now.

_____ 5. Riding my bike relaxes me more than anything else.

_____ 6. Bernie lived in South Korea for several years.

_____ 7. Our dog learns new tricks quite easily.

_____ 8. The blizzard covered the city in two feet of snow.

_____ 9. Alex carried his injured friend down the mountain.

_____ 10. Giving to those in need rewards us with great satisfaction.

PRACTICE 3

In the following paragraph, underline the verb in each sentence. Then, change each verb to the past tense.

(1) I like the small bank around the corner from my old house. (2) My checking account includes no fees. (3) Conveniently, the bank stays open on weekends. (4) Because of its small size, I receive excellent customer service. (5) Only four tellers work at that branch. (6) They all recognize me. (7) They even talk to me about more than just the weather. (8) Sometimes, I need to meet with someone from the bank.

■ **TIP:** For more practice, visit Exercise Central at <bedfordstmartins.com/realskills>.

(9) The bank president agrees to meet with me at any time. (10) For these reasons, I hate switching to a large bank in my new neighborhood.

PRACTICE 4 . .

In the following paragraph, fill in the correct past-tense form of each verb in parentheses.

(1) Roman _____ (*trust*) his computer completely. (2) He _____ (*use*) it for several years without any problems. (3) The computer's hard drive _____ (*store*) all of Roman's important files. (4) He _____ (*appreciate*) how quickly it _____ (*connect*) to the Internet. (5) Last Wednesday, Roman _____ (*turn*) on his computer and _____ (*try*) to open the draft of his research paper. (6) The computer _____ (*display*) a confusing message on the screen and didn't open the file. (7) Roman _____ (*repeat*) his attempt several times. (8) The computer _____ (*fail*) each time, still showing the same error message. (9) Roman was _____ (*worry*), so he called several of his friends to ask for advice. (10) Finally, Alicia _____ (*suggest*) a small company that _____ (*repair*) broken hard drives. (11) The company's owner _____ (*estimate*) a cost of $950 if his technicians _____ (*recover*) the information on the hard drive. (12) Roman _____ (*complain*) about the high cost, but he _____ (*decide*) to pay the fee. (13) He _____ (*wait*) a week before the company _____ (*call*). (14) They _____ (*save*) most of the information on the hard drive, including the file containing his research paper. (15) Roman _____ (*purchase*) a new hard drive, along with an extra one on which he _____ (*perform*) regular backups of his work from then on.

PRACTICE 5 . .

Write five sentences using the past tense of the following five verbs: *ask, like, reach, stay,* and *touch.*

Understand Irregular Verbs in the Past Tense

Irregular verbs do not follow the regular pattern of adding *-d* or *-ed* for the past tense. Practice using these verbs.

Irregular Verb Forms

BASE VERB	PAST TENSE	BASE VERB	PAST TENSE
be (am/are/is)	was/were	have/has	had
become	became	hear	heard
begin	began	hide	hid
bite	bit	hit	hit
blow	blew	hold	held
break	broke	hurt	hurt
bring	brought	keep	kept
build	built	know	knew
buy	bought	lay	laid
catch	caught	lead	led
choose	chose	leave	left
come	came	let	let
cost	cost	lie	lay
dive	dived/dove	light	lit
do	did	lose	lost
draw	drew	make	made
drink	drank	mean	meant
drive	drove	meet	met
eat	ate	pay	paid
fall	fell	put	put
feed	fed	quit	quit
feel	felt	read	read
fight	fought	ride	rode
find	found	ring	rang
fly	flew	rise	rose
forget	forgot	run	ran
freeze	froze	say	said
get	got	see	saw
give	gave	sell	sold
go	went	send	sent
grow	grew	shake	shook

(continued)

An audiovisual tutorial on finding and fixing the four most serious errors is available on a CD that comes with this book.

BASE VERB	PAST TENSE	BASE VERB	PAST TENSE
show	showed	strike	struck
shrink	shrank	swim	swam
shut	shut	take	took
sing	sang	teach	taught
sink	sank	tear	tore
sit	sat	tell	told
sleep	slept	think	thought
speak	spoke	throw	threw
spend	spent	understand	understood
stand	stood	wake	woke
steal	stole	wear	wore
stick	stuck	win	won
sting	stung	write	wrote

PRACTICE 6 . . . .

In the following paragraph, fill in each blank with the past-tense form of the irregular verb in parentheses.

1. This spring, my friends _____ (*run*) in the Relay for Life to help fight cancer.

2. They all _____ (*make*) sure to get into shape for the run.

3. Katelyn _____ (*begin*) the relay for the team.

4. A strong runner, she _____ (*go*) for about an hour.

5. The team _____ (*choose*) Deanna to run the next section of the race.

6. Unfortunately, she _____ (*hurt*) her knee while warming up.

7. Although I had only planned on cheering from the sidelines, I _____ (*have*) on workout clothes and running shoes.

8. I _____ (*get*) ready to take Deanna's place as quickly as I could.

9. A tired Katelyn _____ (*give*) the baton to me.

10. My hour on the track was challenging, but I _____ (*grow*) a lot from the experience.

PRACTICE 7

In each sentence of the following paragraph, fill in the correct past-tense forms of the irregular verbs in parentheses.

(1) Last semester, Andrew _____ (take) a course in zoology. (2) At the end of the semester, he _____ (go) to the zoo to apply for an internship. (3) A few days later, he _____ (get) a phone call from the director of the zoo's internship program. (4) She _____ (say) that the position was his. (5) Over the summer, the zoologists _____ (teach) him about their day-to-day life. (6) He _____ (spend) a lot of time in the baby-animal nursery, his favorite exhibit. (7) He _____ (see) the birth of two tiger cubs. (8) He even _____ (feed) the tiny cubs from a bottle. (9) The internship _____ (pay) very little. (10) However, Andrew _____ (find) the experience to be invaluable.

With another person, make a list of five past-tense irregular verb errors that you have heard before (for example, "he knowed" instead of "he knew").

PRACTICE 8

In the following paragraph, change each irregular present-tense verb to the past tense.

(1) A few years ago, I fall into debt. (2) Unfortunately, my computer's printer breaks just then. (3) Through a quick Internet search, I find a company that sells printers at a very low cost. (4) I give the company a call and speak to one of its sales representatives. (5) Then, I understand the reason for the low prices. (6) The salesperson says that the company puts new parts into used printers. (7) I buy one of these printers from the company. (8) At that time, I tell everyone about my possible mistake. (9) But over the last few years, my wonderful printer make me a believer in used products.

PRACTICE 9

Write five sentences using the past tense of five irregular verbs from the table on pages 213–14.

Understand Four Very Irregular Verbs

The Verb *Be*

Be is tricky because its singular and plural forms are different, both in present and past tenses.

Present and Past Tense Forms *of* Be

	SINGULAR		PLURAL	
	PRESENT →	PAST TENSE	PRESENT →	PAST TENSE
First person	I am →	I was	we are →	we were
Second person	you are →	you were	you are →	you were
Third person	he/she/it is →	he was	they are →	they were

■ **TIP:** In the chart above, and in later charts and sentence examples, subjects are light blue and verbs are red.

PRACTICE 10 . . . .

In each of the following sentences, fill in the blank with the correct past-tense form of *be*—either *was* or *were*.

EXAMPLE: The smashed egg ___was___ on the kitchen floor.

1. Caroline _____ too small to ride the roller coaster.

2. The books _____ on the shelf gathering dust.

3. My cousins _____ at the party on Saturday night.

4. The fans _____ angry at the team's star player.

5. I _____ wet, muddy, and tired.

6. There _____ eight ducklings swimming behind their mother.

7. The students _____ quiet throughout the entire lecture.

8. _____ you hoping to eat the last piece of pie?

9. The store _____ empty during the big game.

10. You _____ late for our appointment yesterday.

PRACTICE 11 . . . .

In the following paragraph, fill in each blank with the correct past-tense form of *be*.

(1) When our electricity bill for last month arrived, we _____ surprised. (2) The bill _____ for $3,218. (3) I _____ sure that this impossibly high amount _____ wrong. (4) Right away, my roommate and I _____ on the phone with the electric company. (5) The representatives with whom we spoke _____ of no help. (6) Each of them said that we _____ wrong and had to pay the bill. (7) A friend of mine who works for a cable company _____ much more helpful. (8) She _____ eager to give us advice. (9) If we continued complaining politely and regularly, she _____ sure that the company would correct the bill. (10) After a month of polite complaints and letters, we _____ pleased to receive a corrected bill of $218, which we immediately paid.

PRACTICE 12

Write five sentences using the past tense of *be*. Use a mix of singular and plural subjects, referring to the table on page 216 if you need help.

The Verb *Have*

Present and Past Tense Forms of **Have**

	SINGULAR		PLURAL	
	PRESENT →	PAST TENSE	PRESENT →	PAST TENSE
First person	I have →	I had	we have →	we had
Second person	you have →	you had	you have →	you had
Third person	he/she/it has →	he had	they have →	they had

■ **TIP:** *Have* is used in the past participle, covered in Chapter 15.

PRACTICE 13

In each of the following sentences, circle the correct form of *have*: present or past tense.

EXAMPLE: Yesterday, the rental car company (have / had) no cars available.

1. You (have / had) to see the car Tad is picking us up in tomorrow.

2. Before it burned down, Dominique's house (have/had) the best view of the mountains.

3. Estella (have/had) a cold last week.

4. The bus Sal takes to work every day (has/had) exhaust problems.

5. I am sorry that you (have/had) trouble finding me at last night's concert.

6. Beryl is healthy because she (has/had) a good diet.

7. Yesterday morning, Marco got soaked because he (have/had) no umbrella.

8. Because we live on a busy street, we (have/had) trouble parking next to our house.

9. At last week's chess match, Jonathan (have/had) seven victories.

10. Our dog Fritz likes the woods because he (has/had) lots of squirrels to chase there.

. . . .

Can/Could and Will/Would

People mix up the past and present tense forms of these tricky verbs. The verb *can* means *able*. Its past-tense form is *could*. The verb *will* expresses a plan. Its past-tense form is *would*.

PRESENT TENSE	He can play poker daily. [He is able to play poker daily.]
	He will play poker daily. [He plans to play poker daily.]
PAST TENSE	He could play poker daily. [He was able to play poker daily.]
	He would play poker daily. [He planned to play (and did play) poker daily.]

■ **TIP:** See Chapter 10 for more on helping verbs.

In these examples, *can, could, will,* and *would* are helping verbs followed by the main verb *play*. Notice that the main verb is in the base form (*play*). It does not change from present to past.

	CAN/COULD		WILL/WOULD	
	PRESENT	**PAST**	**PRESENT**	**PAST**
First person	I/we can	I/we could	I/we will	I/we would
Second person	you can	you could	you will	you would
Third person	he/she/it can	he could	he will	he would
	they can	they could	they will	they would

PRACTICE 14 . . . .

📓 📖 Make up a sentence for each of the forms from the chart on page 218 and read them aloud.

In each of the following sentences, circle the correct verb.

> **EXAMPLE:** This morning, Dane said that he (can / (could)) teach himself how to use our new digital camera.

1. He always thinks that he (can / could) do everything on his own.

2. I told Dane that I (will / would) read the manual for him.

3. He answered that I (will / would) be wasting my time.

4. Several hours and many fuzzy pictures later, he admitted that he (can / could) not figure out how to use the camera's fancy features.

5. I decided that I (will / would) help him.

6. Next week, it (will / would) not be my fault if our vacation photographs turn out fuzzy.

7. I wish that he (will / would) have listened to me in the first place.

8. After reading the manual myself, I showed him how he (can / could) take better pictures.

9. Now he (can / could) use the camera like a professional.

10. On our vacation, he (will / would) appreciate my help.

PRACTICE 15 . . . .

In the following paragraph, fill in each blank with the correct form of the helping verb *can/could* or *will/would*.

   (1) Learning to ride a bike _____ be difficult for a child. (2) When my daughter Carlita started learning, she _____ fall over every time. (3) Even with training wheels, she _____ not keep her balance. (4) I hoped that she _____ keep trying, but I didn't want to force her. (5) Luckily, Carlita refused to quit and said that she _____ practice every day. (6) Soon, she _____ balance with the help of the training wheels. (7) Bikes like Carlita's _____ have their training wheels easily removed. (8) This morning, I asked Carlita if I _____ take the training wheels off. (9) She said that she _____ be ready for the challenge.

(10) This afternoon, I _____ take off the training wheels. (11) As she tries to balance without them, I _____ hold her shoulders and run alongside her. (12) When I first let go, I know that she _____ probably fall. (13) We will keep trying until she _____ zip around the neighborhood all by herself. (14) I wish that I _____ keep her from falling, but I know that it's just part of the learning process. (15) Soon, I _____ have to go through this whole process again with Carlita's younger sister.

PRACTICE 16 . . .

Write two sentences using the present-tense helping verb *can* and two sentences using the present-tense helping verb *will*, leaving a space after each sentence. Then, in the space below each sentence, rewrite each sentence in the past tense using *could* or *would*.

> **EXAMPLE:** I can drive to the game after work.
>
>   I could drive to the game after work.

Edit Past-Tense Errors in College, Work, and Everyday Life

Complete the editing reviews as instructed, referring to the chart on page 225.

EDITING REVIEW 1: COLLEGE . .

The following paragraphs are similar to those you might find in a criminal-justice textbook. Correct problems with past-tense verb forms so that the paragraphs are correctly written in the past tense. Two sentences are correct; write "C" next to them. The first sentence has been edited for you.

CASE STUDY: ARMED ROBBERY

(1) One late night in St. Louis, Missouri, in 1996, an elderly woman
came
~~come~~ out of a convenience store. (2) In the dark, she do not notice the young man next to her car. (3) As she fumbled with her keys, the man grabbed her from behind. (4) He hold a gun to her head and demanded her purse. (5) Before she had time to respond, the attacker hitted her

with the gun and run off. (6) The attacker was found, and he goes to jail for armed robbery.

(7) In 1996, a group of social scientists studyed eighty-six criminals like this one in St. Louis. (8) The researchers wondered if the fear of punishment can prevent crimes motivated by money. (9) Many of the criminals was afraid of being caught. (10) Nevertheless, they see a greater possibility of success than of punishment. (11) When they thought about the risk of punishment, they will only work more quickly to finish the crime. (12) Why did the risk of punishment fail to stop these offenders? (13) Many of them was broke and living on the streets. (14) Generally, they believed that sooner or later they will be caught. (15) But their day-to-day life is so difficult that they feared prison less than they feared being broke.

EDITING REVIEW 2: WORK/USING FORMAL ENGLISH

Correct the tense errors in the following job-application letter. Then, revise informal language. The first sentence has been corrected for you. Outside of this sentence, you should find five cases of informal language.

■ **TIP:** For advice on using formal English, see Chapter 4. For advice on avoiding slang, see Chapter 25.

Jana Thoms

421 Rose Street

Campbell, CA 95008

Dear Ms. Thoms,

(1) Your advertisement for a personal private investigator, which I ~~see~~ *saw* in the March 31 issue of *The Campbell Times*, ~~catched~~ *caught* my eye. (2) I'm totally psyched about the position and will like to apply for it.

(3) Last year, I graduate from Whitley University with a B.S. in administration of justice. (4) Throughout my four years, I studied a bunch of techniques for collecting and examining evidence. (5) In particular, I gain extensive experience with high-technology surveillance equipment. (6) Some of my profs was experienced detectives who taught us the most up-to-date methods of evidence collection and analysis.

(7) In addition to my classroom studies, last year I were an intern with a private investigation firm in San Francisco. (8) I worked with all kinda clients with many kinds of problems. (9) By the end of the internship, I can handle large cases on my own. (10) For each case, I begun by looking in my training manual for the best techniques. (11) If a technique that I needed were not in the manual, I usually can figured out the problem myself. (12) When I can not do that, I learned quickly with assistance from my supervisors.

(13) Thank you for considering me for the position. (14) I can do a F2F at your convenience.

Sincerely,

Lydia Casselles

EDITING REVIEW 3: EVERYDAY LIFE . .

In the following paragraphs, correct problems with past-tense verb forms. Five sentences are correct; write "C" next to them. The first sentence has been edited for you.

THE NOBLE FORK

(1) The first humans ~~use~~ *used* tools as early as 2.5 million years ago. (2) The fork, however, is not around until fairly recently. (3) For most of human history, people simply eat with their fingers. (4) The first forks, which were invented by the ancient Greeks, were not for eating. (5) When Greek servers carved meat, food sometimes slipped and fall off the plate. (6) With a fork, however, the servers can firmly hold the meat in place.

(7) Around A.D. 700, royalty in the Middle East begin to use forks at meals. (8) Wealthy people enjoyed a variety of foods, and forks keep their fingers grease-free. (9) In the eleventh century, a wealthy man in Venice married a princess from the Middle Eastern city of Byzantium. (10) She taked many things to Venice, including two cases of forks. (11) The princess make people angry when she refused to eat with her

fingers. (12) The Italians thought she was a snob and refused to use this new eating tool. (13) It was not until the sixteenth century that Italians used forks regularly.

(14) In 1533, another marriage bring forks to France. (15) Catherine de Médicis, from Italy, married Henry II, future king of France. (16) She introduced forks to the French royalty. (17) As in Italy, the tool is unpopular once again. (18) Eventually, however, forks that were made of silver and gold become a symbol of wealth and luxury. (19) Today, forks could be made of expensive material, or they might be made of inexpensive plastic, aluminum, or steel.

Write and Edit Your Own Work

ASSIGNMENT 1: WRITE

Write a paragraph about one of your strong points and how it has helped you. Try to include irregular verbs in the past tense and helping verbs. Then, using the chart on page 225, revise any verb errors you find.

ASSIGNMENT 2: EDIT

Using the chart on page 225, correct verb errors in a paper you are writing for this course or another course, or in a piece of writing from your work or everyday life.

Practice Together

Working with a few other students, practice what you have learned in this chapter.

1. One student should make a statement in the present tense (for example, *I am hungry*). The next student should tell the others what the first person said (*She said she was hungry*). All students should write down both sentences as they are said. Keep going until everyone has said at least one present-tense sentence and one past-tense sentence.

2. As a group, make up a funny sentence in the past tense. Have each group member write it down. Then, discuss how you could illustrate the past-tense action. Make a sketch to show this. At the end of the activity, groups should post their sketches on the wall so that others can see.

3. As a group, write a set of present-tense sentences on one sheet of paper, with each group member contributing a sentence or two. Then, exchange sheets with another group. In the sentences you receive, change verbs to the past tense. Next, return the sentences to the group that gave them to you.

4. With your group, write a paragraph describing the events of a movie, putting verbs in the present tense. (The movie should be one that everyone has seen.) Switch paragraphs with another group and change each other's verbs to the past tense.

5. Create a study guide with important verb forms and examples. Use the guide to study with other students in your group.

Chapter Review

1. The past tense is used to describe _____.

2. To form the past tense of most regular verbs, add ____ or ____.

3. _____ do not follow the pattern described in question 2. Write three examples of irregular verbs: _____

4. The past tense of can is _____, and the past tense of will is _____.

5. **VOCABULARY:** Go back to any new words that you underlined. Can you guess their meanings now? If not, look up the words in a dictionary.

LEARNING JOURNAL: Write for two minutes about something you still find confusing about past-tense verb forms.

■ **TIP:** For help with building your vocabulary, see Appendix B.

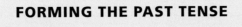

FORMING THE PAST TENSE

Regular Verbs

Use an *-ed* ending for most regular verbs.

clean   → clean**ed**
explain → explain**ed**
toss   → toss**ed**

Use a *-d* ending for verbs that end in *e*.

excite   → excite**d**
like   → like**d**
promote → promote**d**

For verbs that end with a consonant + *y*, change the *-y* to an *-i* before adding *-ed*.

comply   → compl**ied**
cry   → cr**ied**
rely   → rel**ied**
supply   → suppl**ied**

Irregular Verbs

Refer to the past-tense forms
of irregular verbs on pages 213–14.

Be careful with very irregular verbs:
be, have, can/could, and *will/would.*
See the charts on pages 216–18.

15

Verbs

The Past Participle

■ **TIP:** In the sentence examples and charts in this chapter, subjects are light blue and verbs are red.

Understand the Past Participle

The **past participle** is a past-tense verb form that uses a helping verb.

Past-tense verb

PAST TENSE   Bees swarmed around the hive all last summer.

[Bees swarmed in the past but no longer swarm.]

Helping verb   Past participle

PAST PARTICIPLE   Bees have swarmed around the hive all summer.

[Bees have swarmed in the past and may continue to swarm.]

Use the Past Participle Correctly

Past Participles of Regular Verbs

For **regular verbs,** add a helping verb (often a form of *have*) plus *-d* or *-ed* to the base form of the verb to make the past participle.

PAST TENSE	PAST PARTICIPLE (WITH HELPING VERB)
I collected	I **have** collected
you collected	you **have** collected
he/she/it collected	he/she/it **has** collected

PAST TENSE	PAST PARTICIPLE (WITH HELPING VERB)
we collect**ed**	we **have** collect**ed**
you collect**ed**	you **have** collect**ed**
they collect**ed**	they **have** collect**ed**

IDEA JOURNAL: Write about a very small object.

PRACTICE 1

In each of the following sentences, underline the helping verb *have* and double-underline the past participle.

    EXAMPLE: Connor and Billy <u>have</u> <u><u>finished</u></u> the repairs on your car.

1. We have stayed friends since elementary school.

2. Professor Adjani said that everyone has passed the exam.

3. The three partners have worked hard to make their business a success.

4. Because they have practiced for weeks, the band is ready for the show.

5. My husband has remembered our anniversary every year.

6. Brian has needed a haircut for quite a while.

7. I have used four vacation days already this year.

8. She has not forgotten the favor that she owes me.

9. Monique has learned how to play that hit song on her guitar.

10. My sister has borrowed my car for the weekend.

■ **TIP:** To do this chapter, you may want to review the terms *subject, verb,* and *helping verb* from Chapter 10.

PRACTICE 2

Rewrite each of the following sentences to use the helping verb *has* or *have* plus the past participle form of the verb.

    EXAMPLE: April hoped to become a dancer.

      April has hoped to become a dancer.

1. Your friends knocked on the door three times already.

_____

2. Kelly impressed her English instructor.

_____

3. You washed the dishes every night this week.

_____

4. Because of my injury, I stayed on the sidelines for the entire game.

_____

5. Our supervisor repeated the instructions four times.

_____

6. They owned that dog for more than ten years.

_____

7. I wanted to speak with you all morning.

_____

8. I helped them as much as I could.

_____

9. Since January, Lauren needed a new car.

_____

10. For years, Silvio collected shells.

_____

PRACTICE 3 . . . .

In each of the following sentences, underline the helping verb and fill in the correct past-participle form of the verb in parentheses.

> **EXAMPLE:** Angela <u>has</u> _renewed_ (_renew_) her magazine
>
> subscription.

1. Everyone has _____ (_order_) dessert.

2. I have _____ (_travel_) too far to turn back now.

3. The mosquitoes have _____ (_bother_) us all weekend.

4. Lindsey has always _____ (_hope_) to move to California.

5. We have _____ (_watch_) this movie three times.

6. Maria has _____ (_wait_) for him before.

7. Tonya has _____ (_decide_) to join the ski club.

8. The zoo has _____ (_close_) for the winter.

9. James has _____ (_train_) his hamster to do tricks.

10. They have _____ (_arrive_) early for the concert.

Write five sentences of your own that use the helping verb *has* or *have* followed by the past participle form of a regular verb.

Past Participles of Irregular Verbs

Endings of **irregular verbs** do not follow a regular pattern in the present, past, and past participle forms.

PRESENT TENSE	PAST TENSE	PAST PARTICIPLE (WITH HELPING VERB)
I drive	I **drove**	I **have driven**
you drive	you **drove**	you **have driven**
he/she/it drives	he/she/it **drove**	he/she/it **has driven**
we drive	we **drove**	we **have driven**

Irregular Verb Forms

BASE VERB	PAST TENSE	PAST PARTICIPLE
be (am/are/is)	was/were	been
become	became	become
begin	began	begun
bite	bit	bitten
blow	blew	blown
break	broke	broken
bring	brought	brought
build	built	built
buy	bought	bought
catch	caught	caught
choose	chose	chosen
come	came	come
cost	cost	cost
dive	dived/dove	dived
do	did	done
draw	drew	drawn
drink	drank	drunk
drive	drove	driven
eat	ate	eaten

(continued)

Practice saying the past participles of irregular verbs aloud until they sound familiar to you.

BASE VERB	PAST TENSE	PAST PARTICIPLE
fall	fell	fallen
feed	fed	fed
feel	felt	felt
fight	fought	fought
find	found	found
fly	flew	flown
forget	forgot	forgotten
freeze	froze	frozen
get	got	gotten
give	gave	given
go	went	gone
grow	grew	grown
have/has	had	had
hear	heard	heard
hide	hid	hidden
hit	hit	hit
hold	held	held
hurt	hurt	hurt
keep	kept	kept
know	knew	known
lay	laid	laid
lead	led	led
leave	left	left
let	let	let
lie	lay	lain
light	lit	lit
lose	lost	lost
make	made	made
mean	meant	meant
meet	met	met
pay	paid	paid
put	put	put
quit	quit	quit
read	read	read
ride	rode	ridden
ring	rang	rung
rise	rose	risen
run	ran	run

BASE VERB	PAST TENSE	PAST PARTICIPLE
say	said	said
see	saw	seen
sell	sold	sold
send	sent	sent
shake	shook	shaken
show	showed	shown
shrink	shrank	shrunk
shut	shut	shut
sing	sang	sung
sink	sank	sunk
sit	sat	sat
sleep	slept	slept
speak	spoke	spoken
spend	spent	spent
stand	stood	stood
steal	stole	stolen
stick	stuck	stuck
sting	stung	stung
strike	struck	struck, stricken
swim	swam	swum
take	took	taken
teach	taught	taught
tear	tore	torn
tell	told	told
think	thought	thought
throw	threw	thrown
understand	understood	understood
wake	woke	woken
wear	wore	worn
win	won	won
write	wrote	written

PRACTICE 5 . . . .

Rewrite each of the following sentences to use the helping verb *has* or *have* plus the past participle form of the verb.

> **EXAMPLE:** Nat sang in the choir for many years.
>
> *Nat has sung in the choir for many years.*

1. We gave ourselves plenty of time.

_____

2. Lily ate at this restaurant often.

_____

3. Dan came to class after all.

_____

4. José and I were friends since high school.

_____

5. I rode horses for more than fourteen years.

_____

6. Everybody forgot your big mistake.

_____

7. So far, Melissa caught no fish.

_____

8. Ashley found several nice apartments for rent.

_____

9. He chose you because of your honesty.

_____

10. The president spoke for about thirty minutes.

_____

PRACTICE 6

In each of the following sentences, fill in either *has* or *have* plus the past participle form of the verb in parentheses.

EXAMPLE: This tree _has grown_ (*grow*) too big for our front yard.

1. We _____ (*spend*) too much money on restaurants this month.

2. I think that I _____ (*lose*) my favorite hat.

3. So far, Kendrick _____ (*read*) that book three times.

4. Julio is a good friend whom we _____ (*know*) for many years.

5. The baby _____ (*eat*) most of his dinner.

6. The band _____ (*wear*) different uniforms for each parade.

7. You _____ (*meet*) Marci before.

8. He _____ (*shut*) all the windows in the building.

9. The leaves _____ (*fall*) from most of the trees.

10. I _____ (*begin*) to look for a new job.

PRACTICE 7

Write five sentences of your own that use the helping verb *has* or *have* followed by the past participle form of an irregular verb.

Present Perfect Tense

The **present perfect tense** is formed as follows.

| Present tense of *have* (helping verb) | + | Past participle | = | Present perfect tense |

It is used to describe two kinds of actions:

1. Some action that started in the past and is still going on:

   The **families have vacationed** together for years.

2. Some action completed at an unspecified time in the past, or something that has just happened:

   The **package has arrived**.

Note the difference in meaning between the past tense and present perfect tense.

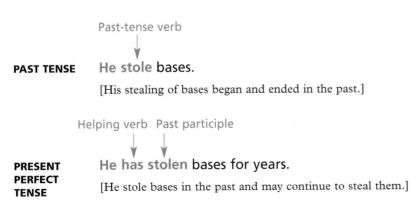

Past-tense verb

PAST TENSE　　He stole bases.

[His stealing of bases began and ended in the past.]

Helping verb　Past participle

PRESENT PERFECT TENSE　　He has stolen bases for years.

[He stole bases in the past and may continue to steal them.]

📝 Working with another student, discuss the difference in meaning between the past tense and present perfect tense.

👁 Draw and illustrate your own time line.

Helping verb   Past participle

He **has** recently **stolen** bases.

[At some unspecified point in the past, he stole bases.]

Present perfect

Present (now)

Past ◄—————————————————► Future

Language note: Be careful not to leave out *have* when it is needed for the present perfect. Time-signal words like *since* and *for* may mean that the present perfect is required.

INCORRECT	I been driving since 1985.	We been waiting for two hours.
CORRECT	I **have** been driving since 1985.	We **have** been waiting for two hours.

For reference charts and additional practices on the present perfect tense, see Chapter 21.

Present Perfect Tense (have + *past participle*)

	SINGULAR	PLURAL
First person	I **have finished**	we **have finished**
Second person	you **have finished**	you **have finished**
Third person	he/she/it **has finished**	they **have finished**

INCORRECT

Since 2004, he *traveled* to five continents.

We *worked* together for three years now.

Antiwar protests *became* common in recent years.

CORRECT

Since 2004, he *has traveled* to five continents.

[He completed his traveling at some unspecified point in the past.]

We *have worked* together for three years now.

[They still work together.]

Antiwar protests *have become* common in recent years.

[They continue to be common.]

PRACTICE 8 . . . .

In each of the following sentences, circle the correct verb tense—past or present perfect.

> **EXAMPLE:** Lately, fantasy camps (became /(have become)) popular among people who can afford them.

1. Many people (went / have gone) to summer camp when they were children.

2. Now, fantasy camps (gave / have given) people a chance to attend camp as adults.

3. In 1988, a camp called Air Combat USA (opened / has opened) to the public.

4. Since then, it (offered / has offered) more than twelve thousand campers the opportunity to fly a fighter jet with the assistance of an experienced combat pilot.

5. In recent years, the Rock 'n' Roll Fantasy Camp (was / has been) one of the most well-attended adult camps.

6. There, campers (played / have played) their musical instruments with world-famous rock stars from the 1960s and '70s.

7. Many of these campers (played / have played) an instrument for many years.

8. The Rock 'n' Roll Camp (allowed / has allowed) them to perform with legendary musicians.

9. Other adults (always wanted / have always wanted) to shoot hoops with a professional basketball player, and basketball camps give them a chance to do just that.

10. These camps (found / have found) that people will pay a lot of money to live out their fantasies for a few days.

■ **TIP:** For more practice, visit Exercise Central at <**bedfordstmartins.com/ realskills**>.

PRACTICE 9 . . . .

In the following paragraph, fill in each blank with the correct past or present perfect tense of the verb in parentheses.

(1) Before there were health clubs, people rarely _____ (*have*) problems getting along with each other during workouts. (2) Back then, in fact, most people _____ (*work*) out by themselves. (3) Today, health clubs and gyms _____ (*become*) popular places to exercise. (4) In these physically stressful settings, some people _____ (*forget*) how to be polite to others. (5) When we were young, we all _____ (*learn*) to take turns when playing with other children. (6) Our parents _____ (*tell*) us to treat others as we would like to be treated ourselves. (7) But in health clubs, some people _____ (*complain*) about customers who refuse to share the equipment. (8) Gym employees say that they _____ (*notice*) an increase in the number of arguments between members. (9) Yesterday, I _____ (*see*) one woman push another woman off a treadmill that they both had been waiting for. (10) To create a more pleasant atmosphere, some gyms _____ (*post*) rules and suggestions for their customers. (11) Most people always _____ (*consider*) it to be common courtesy to clean up after themselves. (12) Now, health clubs _____ (*begin*) to require that exercisers wipe up any perspiration that they leave on equipment. (13) It seems that the need to stay in shape _____ (*create*) mental as well as physical stress for some people. (14) However, it is important to always keep in mind the basic rules of polite behavior that our parents _____ (*teach*) us when we were young.

PRACTICE 10 . . .

Write a short paragraph that uses the past and present perfect tenses.

. . . .

Past Perfect Tense

The **past perfect tense** is used to show two actions completed in the past, one before the other.

| Past tense of *have* (helping verb) | + | Past participle | = | Past perfect tense |

Note the difference in meaning between the past tense and past perfect tense.

Past-tense verb

PAST TENSE   In March 1954, runner **Roger Bannister broke** the four-minute mile record.

[One action (breaking the four-minute mile) occurred in the past.]

Helping verb   Past participle

PAST PERFECT TENSE   Within a month, **John Landy had broken** Bannister's record.

[Two actions (Bannister's and Landy's races) occurred in the past, but Bannister's action was completed before Landy's action started.]

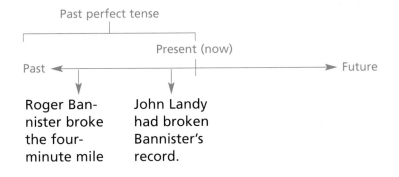

Past perfect tense

Present (now)

Past ←→ Future

Roger Bannister broke the four-minute mile

John Landy had broken Bannister's record.

Present Perfect Tense (had + *past participle*)

	SINGULAR	PLURAL
First person	I **had driven**	we **had driven**
Second person	you **had driven**	you **had driven**
Third person	he/she/it **had driven**	they **had driven**

READ ALOUD

Stand up and read the following two sentences and give the reason for the use of the perfect tense in each case.

PRESENT PERFECT TENSE   We *have collected* aluminum cans for our club.

| PAST PERFECT TENSE | Before Columbus arrived, the Native Americans already *had built* an advanced civilization. |

PRACTICE 11 . .

In each of the following sentences, circle the correct verb tense.

EXAMPLE: Before we left for our camping trip, we (talked/
(had talked)) about the wildlife at Moosehead Mountain.

1. I decided not to mention the rattlesnake that (scared/had scared) me on last year's trip.

2. I never (was/had been) afraid of snakes until I came that close to one.

3. On this year's trip, we (saw/had seen) something even more frightening than a snake.

4. As my friends and I (planned/had planned), we took a long hike after setting up our tent.

5. By the time we returned to the campsite, the sun (went/had gone) down.

6. Near the tent, we (heard/had heard) a low growl.

7. Suddenly, we (saw/had seen) a dark shadow running into the woods.

8. We realized that a bear (visited/had visited) our campsite.

9. Frightened but tired, we (tried/had tried) to get some rest.

10. When the sun finally came up, we saw that the bear (stayed/had stayed) away, but we (got/had gotten) little sleep.

PRACTICE 12 . .

Write five sentences of your own in the present perfect tense. Then rewrite each sentence in the past perfect tense.

EXAMPLE: You have been working on the project for several months.

You had been working on the project for several months.

PRACTICE 13 . . . .

In the following paragraph, fill in each blank with the correct form of the verb in parentheses. Use whichever form of the verb is logical—simple past tense, present perfect tense, or past perfect tense.

(1) Ever since he learned to talk, our six-year-old son Christopher _____ (*show*) an interest in the business world. (2) Last week, he said that he _____ (*decide*) to start a business of his own. (3) We _____ (*become*) used to eager statements like this. (4) When Christopher was five years old, he _____ (*ask*) for a larger allowance. (5) In return, he _____ (*offer*) to do more chores. (6) Before I decided what extra chores to give him, he already _____ (*make*) all the beds in the house. (7) So by the time Christopher asked for his own business, I _____ (*be*) expecting it. (8) I _____ (*tell*) him that he could open a lemonade stand. (9) Before I even finished telling him my ideas, he _____ (*come*) up with a plan of his own. (10) For his products, Christopher _____ (*choose*) fresh lemonade and cookies. (11) With my help, he _____ (*make*) the lemonade and _____ (*bake*) the cookies. (12) I asked whether he _____ (*decide*) on a price for his products. (13) He _____ (*settle*) on twenty-five cents for each cup of lemonade and a dime for each cookie. (14) He set up the stand on a corner where he _____ (*notice*) many dog walkers. (15) To increase his business, he _____ (*add*) free dog biscuits to give to his customers. (16) So far this week, he _____ (*earn*) $14.75. (17) I _____ (*enjoy*) watching Christopher run the lemonade stand. (18) He _____ (*learn*) that work can be fun and rewarding. (19) I also _____ (*notice*) an improvement in his math and people skills. (20) For many years, lemonade stands _____ (*teach*) children valuable lessons.

Passive versus Active Voice

In sentences that use the **passive voice**, the subject is acted on—it receives the action of the verb. The passive voice is formed as follows:

Be form (helping verb) + Past participle = Passive voice

Be form (helping verb)   Past participle

PASSIVE   Houses were destroyed by the tsunami.

[*Houses* did not act; they were acted upon by the tsunami.]

In sentences that use the **active voice**, the subject performs the action.

ACTIVE   The tsunami destroyed the houses.

Whenever possible, use the active voice. Use the passive voice only when you do not know the specific performer of an action or when you want to emphasize the receiver of the action.

👁 🖐 Act out or draw one sentence in the active voice and one in the passive voice.

■ **TIP:** See page 229 for the various forms of *be*.

Language note: Avoid confusing passive voice and the present perfect tense, which does not use *been* except in sentences with *be* as main verb.

INCORRECT   My aunt and uncle have been trained the dogs.

CORRECT   My aunt and uncle **have trained** the dogs. (present perfect)

CORRECT   The dogs **have been trained**. (passive)

EXAMPLES OF THE CORRECT USE OF ACTIVE AND PASSIVE VOICE

ACTIVE   After the fight, the police took him away.

[We know that the police took him away.]

PASSIVE   After the fight, he was taken away.

[We do not know who took him away.]

PASSIVE   The old bridge was demolished this morning by engineers.

[The important point is that the bridge was demolished.]

PASSIVE   The chemical elements are arranged by their atomic weights.

[Scientific and technical reports frequently use the passive since the focus is often on the subject.]

Move over, he've comes OXYGEN!

Language note: Other languages, such as Russian and Korean, form the passive voice differently. If your first language is not English, note that the *be* verb—not the past participle that follows it—shows the time of the action.

EXAMPLES   The assignment **is** explained every   (*is* = present)
day.

Yesterday the assignment **was**   (*was* = past)
explained.

PRACTICE 14 · · · · · · · · · · · · · · · ·

In each of the following sentences, underline the verb. In the blank space provided, write "A" if the sentence is in the active voice or "P" if the sentence is in the passive voice.

EXAMPLE: __A__ Many parents <u>assume</u> that their children will stop

eating when they are full.

___ 1. Scientists recently studied this assumption.

___ 2. In the study, children were given more food than necessary.

___ 3. The children almost always ate all the food on their plates.

___ 4. Their level of hunger made no difference.

___ 5. In another study, similar conclusions were drawn.

___ 6. Parents and their children were observed during a typical meal.

___ 7. The parents of overweight children served much larger portions.

___ 8. Often, the overweight children were told to finish everything on their
plates.

___ 9. Healthier children were given much smaller amounts of food.

___ 10. The children who served themselves ate the most appropriate amount
of food.

PRACTICE 15 · · · · · · · · · · · · · · · ·

Each of the following sentences is in the passive voice. Rewrite each sentence in the active voice.

The three of us made plans for the outdoor concert.
EXAMPLE: ~~The plans for the outdoor concert were made by the~~

^

~~three of us.~~

1. The tickets to the concert at the campground were gotten by Matthew.

2. The dinner was planned by me.

3. The driving was done by Sean.

4. Unfortunately, the wrong directions were gotten by him.

5. Several wrong turns were made.

6. When we arrived, our tent was set up by Sean and Matthew.

7. Meanwhile, dinner was prepared by me.

8. The three-course meal was enjoyed by everyone.

9. While we waited for the concert to begin, we were joined by several other friends.

10. Wonderful music was played all evening by the band.

> **PRACTICE 16** . .

Write five sentences of your own in the active voice.

Edit Past-Participle Errors in College, Work, and Everyday Life

Complete the editing reviews as instructed, referring to the chart on page 247.

> **EDITING REVIEW 1: COLLEGE** . .

The following paragraphs are similar to those you might find in a history-of-science textbook. Correct problems with the use of past participles, the present perfect tense, and the past perfect tense. Four sentences are correct; write "C" next to them. The first sentence has been edited for you.

        created
(1) Few scientific theories have ~~create~~ as much controversy as the theory of evolution. (2) In 1860, Charles Darwin has published *The Origin of Species.* (3) The book presented evidence that Darwin has collected on a five-year voyage along the coast of South America. (4) Darwin argued that life on earth had began slowly and gradually. (5) He believed

that each species of animals, including humans, developed from previous species. (6) This theory contradicted the Bible's account of creation.

(7) For more than a century now, people had been divided on whether evolution should be taught in public schools. (8) The first court trial on evolution had been in 1925. (9) Earlier, in the small town of Dayton, Tennessee, a biology teacher named John T. Scopes assigned a textbook that described the theory of evolution. (10) The book said that humans had came from earlier forms of life. (11) Earlier that year, a state law titled the Butler Law has banned the teaching of evolution, so Scopes was arrested. (12) Although Scopes's lawyer made an impressive case against the constitutionality of the Butler Law, Scopes was found guilty and the law remained intact. (13) In 1967, the U.S. Supreme Court ruled the Butler Law unconstitutional. (14) However, recent court cases in Kansas, Ohio, and Pennsylvania have showed that Americans are still divided on whether to teach creationism, evolution, or both in public schools. (15) Ever since the Scopes trial, people fought over the issue in courtrooms across the country.

EDITING REVIEW 2: WORK/USING FORMAL ENGLISH . . . .

In the following business report, correct problems with past participles, the present perfect tense, and the past perfect tense. Then, revise informal language. The first sentence has been corrected for you. Outside of this sentence, you should find five cases of informal language.

■ TIP: For advice on using formal English, see Chapter 4. For advice on avoiding slang, see Chapter 25.

STATUS REPORT: Lydia Castrionni

Date: 9/18/05

I. NEW DATABASE TRAINING

(1) On Monday, a new database system was ~~chose~~ *chosen* and installed by the Information Technology Department. (2) This week, I have spended mucho time becoming familiar with the new system. (3) After I have read the user's manual, I attended the all-day training session on Tuesday. (4) On Wednesday, I helped Ajay Shah with the new system because he blew off the training session. (5) I have make a lot of progress learning

the system. (6) However, this has took a lot of time away from my regular projects.

II. CUSTOMER SERVICE TASKS

(7) By the end of last week, I have logged thirty-five customer-service calls. (8) Twenty-five of the beefs involved problems with software. (9) All the software problems has been handled at the time of the call. (10) The other ten complaints were from people who had experience problems with their hardware. (11) So far, I have resolve half of these calls. (12) Five of these calls were handle at the time of the call. (13) I submitted service requests for the other five, but I had no time to follow up on those requests yet. (14) I had expect to take care of all the customer service calls last week, but the database training slowed me down big time. (15) I am certain the remaining problems will been resolved early next week. (16) OK?

> **EDITING REVIEW 3: EVERYDAY LIFE** . . . .

In the following paragraphs, correct problems with the use of past participles, the present perfect tense, and the past perfect tense. Five sentences are correct; write "C" next to them. The first sentence has been edited for you.

(1) A recent study shows that Americans have ~~start~~ *started* watching more sports on television rather than actually playing them. (2) One reason may be that people have not feel like leaving their homes during these times of economic and political turbulence. (3) Another reason may be that they might had been discouraged at some point in the past, so they have left the playing to the professionals. (4) Neither of these reasons, however, makes a whole lot of sense. (5) Playing sports had always been and always will be better than watching them.

(6) Companionship is a persuasive reason to play sports. (7) Throughout human history, people have gather together to form teams. (8) Families have play against each other. (9) Men have went head-to-head against women. (10) Even entire communities had teamed up for a bit of friendly competition with neighboring towns or villages. (11) You

don't have to be a professional; there is nothing like a good game to lift the spirits.

(12) It has been no mystery why playing sports makes people feel great. (13) The health benefits have spoke for themselves. (14) For a long time, people didn't know why they enjoyed exercise so much. (15) Then, in the 1970s, scientists had discovered endorphins, chemicals that produce a pleasant feeling after a workout. (16) In addition, scientists have find a direct connection between regular exercise and a longer life. (17) Healthy people usually have had less stress, a benefit that may add years to their life.

(18) Some argue that watching sports on television also provides companionship. (19) Cheering for the same team, for example, has brung people closer together and made friends out of enemies. (20) Likewise, when it has come to older people, scientists now say that simply meeting with friends makes the elderly healthier and happier. (21) However, no one who had played in an exciting basketball game would argue that watching the sport is more thrilling than actually doing it. (22) There is something about direct participation that has made the experience more satisfying.

Write and Edit Your Own Work

ASSIGNMENT 1: WRITE

Write a short letter to the editor of your school or city newspaper complaining about or complimenting some service. Try to include past participles, the present perfect tense, and the past perfect tense. Then, revise any verb errors you find using the chart on page 247.

ASSIGNMENT 2: EDIT

Using the chart on page 247, correct verb errors in a paper you are writing for this course or another course, or in a piece of writing from your work or everyday life.

■ **LEARNING STYLES:** Look for activities in this chapter that are matched to your learning style. If you don't know your learning style, take the test on pages 26–28.

👁   Visual

🎧   Auditory

📖   Reading/writing

👣   Kinesthetic (movement)

Practice Together

Working with a few other students, practice what you have learned in this chapter.

1. Play the "one-upping" game. One person should start by listing a few interesting things that he or she has done, beginning with *I have*—for example, *I have flown a plane, I have traveled to ten different countries, I have built a clock.* The next person should make similar statements, trying to outdo the previous person. Keep going until everyone has had a turn. When you are done, vote on the most interesting fact. The person who said it should stand up and tell the rest of the class. 🎧 👣

2. As a group, organize the irregular verbs on pages 229–31 into categories according to how they change from present tense to past tense to past participle. For example, you might separate out all the words that don't change at all (for example, *cost, hit*) and all the words that change a vowel each time (for example, *sing, sang, sung*). Record your answers. When you're done, tell the rest of the class how you organized your findings and then share them. 🎧 📖

3. Each group member should draw a diagram or illustration comparing the present tense with the past tense and the past participle. When you're done, share and discuss your drawings with the group. 👁 🎧

4. Create a study guide for this chapter with examples of the various verb tenses and forms. Use the guide to study with other students in your group. 🎧 📖

Chapter Review

1. A past participle is a verb form that uses a _____ .

2. _____ do not follow a regular pattern in the present, past, and past participle forms.

3. Write the formula for the present perfect tense: _____

   _____

4. The past perfect tense is used to show _____ , one before the other.

5. In the passive voice, the subject _____ of the verb.

6. **VOCABULARY:** Go back to any new words that you underlined. Can you guess their meanings now? If not, look up the words in a dictionary.

📖 **LEARNING JOURNAL:** Take two minutes to write about anything in this chapter that still confuses you.

■ **TIP:** For help with building your vocabulary, see Appendix B.

FORMING THE PAST PARTICIPLE

Regular Verbs

Helping verb (often a form of *have*)   +

Base verb   +   *-d* or *-ed*

have listen**ed**
have walk**ed**
have promot**ed**

Irregular Verbs

Helping verb (often a form of *have*)   +

Irregular past participle

For a list of irregular past participles, see pages 229–31.

have eaten
have sat
have known

Present Perfect

Present tense of *have*   +   Past participle

Use for
1. Some action that started in past and is still going on.
2. Some action completed at an unspecified time in the past or something that has just happened.

Past Perfect

had   +   Past participle

Used to show two actions completed in the past, one before the other.

Lana **had left** by the time Sheila arrived.

Unit Three Test
Editing for the Four Most Serious Errors

Part 1

Following are two paragraphs and one essay. Read them carefully and circle the correct answers to the questions that follow them. Use some of the reading strategies from Chapter 2.

    1 Many tourists says that they love buying products from New York City's street vendors. **2** In some cases, the vendors are set up illegally, but they are one of New York City's top tourist attractions. **3** For as long as anyone can remember, street vendors have line the city's sidewalks. **4** Recently, however, they have become more popular and numerous than ever. **5** The vendors sell everything from fake silk ties to cell phones to African wooden masks they also sell inexpensive "designer" items. **6** Imitation designer handbags, watches, and sunglasses are among the most popular items. **7** Most shoppers are aware that the vendors' versions are fake. **8** However, few people <u>has</u> thousands of dollars to spend on a real Rolex watch or Gucci purse. **9** If the fake version is a good copy. **10** Many shoppers are happy to get such a bargain.

1. Which of the following changes is needed in sentence 1?
   a. Change "tourists" to "tourist."
   b. Join it to sentence 2 to avoid a fragment.
   c. Change "says" to "saying."
   d. Change "says" to "say."

2. Which of the following changes is needed in sentence 3?
   a. Join it to sentence 4 to avoid a fragment.
   b. Join it to sentence 2 to avoid a fragment.
   c. Change "can" to "will."
   d. Change "line" to "lined."

3. Which of the following should be used in place of the underlined word in sentence 8?
   a. having   c. haves
   b. have   d. have had

4. Which of the following changes is needed in sentence 9?
   a. Divide it into two sentences because it is a run-on.
   b. Change "is" to "are."
   c. Join it to sentence 10 to avoid a fragment.
   d. Change "version" to "versions."

5. Which of the following sentences should be revised because it is a run-on?

   a. Sentence 2   c. Sentence 6

   b. Sentence 5   d. Sentence 8

1 Over the past century, a number of French adventurers have become famous for some rather odd accomplishments. 2 One of these men was the first to walk across Niagara Falls on a tightrope, another walked from Paris to Moscow on stilts. 3 In 1952, Alain Bombard float aimlessly in a rubber lifeboat across the Atlantic Ocean for 65 days. 4 His trip, which has started off the coast of Morocco, finally landed him in Barbados, near the coast of Venezuela. 5 He brung along emergency food and water in a sealed container. 6 At the end of his journey, however. 7 The seal was reported to be unbroken. 8 Amazingly, he drank only seawater and ate only plankton (tiny sea creatures) and raw fish. 9 Bombard said that, at first, the mix of raw fish and plankton had tasted like lobster soup, but he quickly grew bored with it. 10 He later summed up the experience as a "starving, thirsty hell." 11 After his journey, he became a spokesperson for the Bombard line of lifeboats and a deputy representing France at the European Parliament. 12 Bombard died in 2005 at the age of eighty.

6. Which of the following sentences should be revised because it is a run-on?

   a. Sentence 1   c. Sentence 3

   b. Sentence 2   d. Sentence 10

7. Which of the following changes is needed in sentence 3?

   a. Change "float" to "floats."

   b. Join it to sentence 2 to avoid a fragment.

   c. Change "float" to "floating."

   d. Change "float" to "floated."

8. Which of the following changes is needed in sentence 4?

   a. Join it to sentence 5 to avoid a fragment.

   b. Divide it into two sentences because it is a run-on.

   c. Change "has started" to "had started."

   d. Change "landed" to "had landed."

9. Which of the following changes is needed in sentence 5?

   a. Divide it into two sentences because it is a run-on.

   b. Join it to sentence 4 to avoid a fragment.

   c. Change "brung" to "brought."

   d. Change "brung" to "brang."

10. Which of the following changes is needed in sentence 6?
    a. Join it to sentence 5 to avoid a fragment.
    b. Join it to sentence 7 to avoid a fragment.
    c. Avoid the preposition at the beginning of the sentence.
    d. Divide it into two sentences because it is a run-on.

1 Scientists are using California's James Reserve as a new type of environmental laboratory the reserve is home to more than thirty rare and endangered species. 2 To gather detailed information about what goes on in the thirty-acre area under study, scientists are using the latest technology. 3 They place more than one hundred sensors, robots, cameras, and computers among the trees and bushes of the area. 4 Many of these devices are wireless. 5 Most is also small, about the size of a deck of cards. 6 The instruments measure wind speed, rainfall, light, temperature, humidity, and pressure. 7 In addition, they can track wind speeds and tell when an animal is nearby. 8 Among other things. Scientists are trying to distinguish between normal environmental changes and changes caused by human activity. 9 So far, they have take and compared many measurements.

10 The James Reserve is just one environmental landscape that scientists are beginning to explore with new technology. 11 A group of researchers has planned to give the Hudson River in New York a close look as well. 12 Floating robots and wireless sensors will measure and, hopefully, help to improve the Hudson's water quality. 13 Sensor stations are also planned throughout North America to trace the continent's history. 14 Scientists hope to discover how the continent evolve over time. 15 They also plan to map the area below the surface of the earth. 16 The Pacific Ocean's natural events will be tracked by sensors, cameras, and floating robots.

17 This revolution in environmental knowledge is now possible because of small, energy-efficient electronic devices such as cameras, radios, computers, and batteries. 18 They can automatically go to sleep most of the time, they can then wake up when necessary to check nearby sensors and send the data to networked computers. 19 Scientists who use these devices hope to help preserve the earth. 20 Some people say that the knowledge gained by new technology will change environmental science similar to the way that MRI tests and CAT scans have change medical science.

21 Many of the devices being used to detect environmental events will remain in place permanently. 22 This will allow scientists to track environmental changes over time and better understand how humans are changing the planet. 23 Scientists who are working on such projects have some specific goals. 24 They want to learn more about the effects of pollution. Such as pesticides, fertilizer, acid rain, and air pollution. 25 Many scientists say that the knowledge gained by these projects will change the way we treat the earth.

11. What revision should be made to the underlined section in sentence 1?
    a. No change is necessary.   c. laboratory: the reserve
    b. laboratory, the reserve   d. laboratory. The reserve

12. What revision should be made to the underlined section in sentence 3?
    a. No change is necessary.   c. has place
    b. have placed   d. placing

13. What revision should be made to the underlined section in sentence 5?
    a. No change is necessary.   c. are
    b. am   d. were

14. What revision should be made to the underlined section in sentence 8?
    a. No change is necessary.   c. things; scientists
    b. things, scientists   d. things scientists

15. What revision should be made to the underlined section in sentence 9?
    a. No change is necessary.   c. taken
    b. taked   d. took

16. What revision should be made to the underlined section in sentence 14?
    a. No change is necessary.   c. evolving
    b. had evolved   d. has evolved

17. What revision should be made to the underlined section in sentence 18?
    a. No change is necessary.   c. time; they
    b. time: they   d. time they

18. What revision should be made to the underlined section in sentence 20?
    a. No change is necessary.   c. changed
    b. changing   d. changes

19. What revision should be made to the underlined section in sentence 23?
    a. No change is necessary.   c. haves
    b. has   d. having

20. What revision should be made to the underlined section in sentence 24?
    a. No change is necessary.   c. pollution; such
    b. pollution, such   d. pollution. Such

Part 2

Circle the correct choice for each of the following items.

1. If an underlined portion of this item is incorrect, select the revision that fixes it. If the item is correct as written, choose d.

When you <u>are dressed properly.</u> You can be <u>comfortable</u> in cold weather.
      A   **B**   **C**

 a. is   c. comfortable. In

 b. properly, you   d. No change is necessary.

2. Choose the correct word(s) to fill in the blank.

 Apple slices or celery sticks _____ a quick, healthy snack for kids.

 a. makes   c. making

 b. make   d. to make

3. Choose the item that has no errors.

 a. Stopping to catch my breath. I realized that I had already missed the bus.

 b. Stopping to catch my breath; I realized that I had already missed the bus.

 c. Stopping to catch my breath, I realized that I had already missed the bus.

4. Choose the correct word(s) to fill in the blank.

 Someone he knows from high school _____ for *Late Night with Conan O'Brien*.

 a. writes   c. writing

 b. write   d. has wrote

5. Choose the item that has no errors.

 a. Charlie has a great new wheelchair it can climb stairs.

 b. Charlie has a great new wheelchair; it can climb stairs.

 c. Charlie has a great new wheelchair, it can climb stairs.

6. If an underlined portion of this item is incorrect, select the revision that fixes it. If the item is correct as written, choose d.

 Jane and Amanda <u>take</u> <u>turns cutting</u> the <u>lawn for</u> their grandmother.
        A **B**   **C**

 a. takes   c. lawn. For

 b. turns, cutting   d. No change is necessary.

7. Choose the item that has no errors.

 a. The heavy winds knocked down the big tree, that I had climbed as a child.

 b. The heavy winds knocked down the big tree. That I had climbed as a child.

 c. The heavy winds knocked down the big tree that I had climbed as a child.

8. If an underlined portion of this item is incorrect, select the revision that fixes it. If the item is correct as written, choose d.

   My car's motor finally has <u>died</u>, I just <u>replaced</u> it with a new <u>motor that</u>
   　　　　　　　　　　　　　　A　　　　　　　B　　　　　　　　　　　C
   works quite well.

   a. died. I　　　　　　　　　c. motor. That
   b. replace　　　　　　　　　d. No change is necessary.

9. Choose the correct word to fill in the blank.

   I _____ to go to the movie alone when I learned that all my friends had seen it already.

   a. decided　　　　　　　　　c. decides
   b. decide　　　　　　　　　　d. deciding

10. Choose the item that has no errors.
    a. The light bulb over the front steps burned out, I tripped and fell.
    b. Because the light bulb over the front steps burned out I tripped and fell.
    c. Because the light bulb over the front steps burned out, I tripped and fell.

11. Choose the correct word to fill in the blank.

    The brothers who live next door _____ high school wrestling champions.

    a. am　　　　　　　　　　　c. is
    b. are　　　　　　　　　　　d. be

12. Choose the item that has no errors.
    a. Marcus has built a large cage. To house his pet rabbits.
    b. Marcus has built a large cage; to house his pet rabbits.
    c. Marcus has built a large cage to house his pet rabbits.

13. If an underlined portion of this item is incorrect, select the revision that fixes it. If the item is correct as written, choose d.

    I <u>loved</u> that little antique <u>shop unfortunately</u>, it went out of <u>business last</u>
    　　　A　　　　　　　　　　　　　B　　　　　　　　　　　　　　C
    week.

    a. loves　　　　　　　　　　c. business. Last
    b. shop. Unfortunately,　　　d. No change is necessary.

14. If an underlined portion of this item is incorrect, select the revision that fixes it. If the item is correct as written, choose d.

    Johann <u>typed</u> on his <u>laptop.</u> During the bus <u>ride</u> to his uncle's house.
    　　　　　A　　　　　　　B　　　　　　　　　　　C

a. type   c. ride. To

b. laptop during   d. No change is necessary.

15. Choose the correct word(s) to fill in the blank.

The cookbooks on this shelf _____ many good vegetarian recipes in them.

a. have   c. having

b. has   d. has had

16. Choose the item that has no errors.

a. There is no hotel rooms available over the holiday weekend.

b. There be no hotel rooms available over the holiday weekend.

c. There are no hotel rooms available over the holiday weekend.

17. If an underlined portion of this item is incorrect, select the revision that fixes it. If the item is correct as written, choose d.

Last month, you <u>borrowed</u> twenty <u>dollars. That</u> you <u>have</u> not paid back
                  A   B   C

yet.

a. borrow   c. has

b. dollars that   d. No change is necessary.

18. Choose the correct word to fill in the blank.

Before I took this class, I _____ not speak well in front of large groups.

a. will   c. could

b. can   d. would

19. If an underlined portion of this item is incorrect, select the revision that fixes it. If the item is correct as written, choose d.

The library <u>has</u> wireless Internet <u>access, this</u> allows me to work <u>there</u>
             A   B   C

without all my computer cables.

a. have   c. there, without

b. access; this allows   d. No change is necessary.

20. Choose the item that has no errors.

a. This child has received all the shots he needs he can register for our school.

b. This child has received all the shots he needs, so he can register for our school.

c. This child has received all the shots he needs, he can register for our school.

■ **TIP:** For advice on taking tests, see Appendix A.

Unit Four
Editing for Other Sentence Grammar

16

Nouns

Using Plural Forms

Understand What Nouns Are

A **noun** is a word that names a general or specific person, place, or thing. Nouns that name a specific person, place, or thing need to begin with capital letters.

📖 **IDEA JOURNAL:** Write about a favorite object or possession.

📖 **VOCABULARY:** Underline any words in this chapter that are new to you.

	GENERAL	SPECIFIC (PROPER NOUNS)
PERSON	politician	George W. Bush
PLACE	city	Chicago
THING	shoe	Reeboks

Nouns can be **singular**, meaning *one*, or **plural**, meaning *more than one*.

SINGULAR	PLURAL
politician	politicians
city	cities
shoe	shoes

Form Plural Nouns Correctly

Regular Plural Nouns

Most nouns form the plural by adding -*s*. Add -*es* to form the plural of singular nouns ending in -*s*, -*sh*, -*ch*, or -*x*.

👁 Draw a picture of one of the plural words in the list, or of a plural word in one of your own sentences.

SINGULAR	PLURAL	SINGULAR	PLURAL
apple	apple**s**	lunch	lunch**es**
bus	bus**es**	tax	tax**es**
calendar	calendar**s**	window	window**s**
dish	dish**es**		

> **Language note:** Standard English usually requires an *-s* ending for plurals of nouns that can be counted (for instance, *book, dollar*). Be careful not to drop the final *-s*.
>
> I found twenty dollar**s** on the street.
>
> For more on count versus noncount nouns, see pages 360–61.

PRACTICE 1 ...

In the blank next to each of the following singular nouns, write the plural form.

EXAMPLE: pencil ___*pencils*___

1. character _____

2. envelope _____

3. couch _____

4. poet _____

5. wish _____

6. poster _____

7. pickle _____

8. loss _____

9. ash _____

10. fox _____

Irregular Plural Nouns

Certain nouns form the plural irregularly, meaning that there are no rules to follow. The easiest way to learn irregular plurals is to use them and say them aloud to yourself. Here are some common examples:

SINGULAR	PLURAL	SINGULAR	PLURAL
child	children	ox	oxen
foot	feet	person	people
goose	geese	tooth	teeth
man	men	woman	women
mouse	mice		

Other irregular plurals follow certain patterns.

1. **Nouns Ending in -y.** Usually, to make these plural, change the *y* to *ie* and add -*s*. However, when a vowel (*a, e, i, o,* or *u*) comes before the *y,* just add a final -*s*.

SINGULAR	PLURAL
city	cit**ies**
key	key**s** [Vowel (*e*) comes before *y*]
lady	lad**ies**
ruby	rub**ies**
workday	workday**s** [Vowel (*a*) comes before *y*]

2. **Nouns Ending in -f or -fe.** Usually, to make these words plural, change the *f* to *v* and add -*es* or -*s*.

SINGULAR	PLURAL
calf	cal**ves**
half	hal**ves**
hoof	hoo**ves**
life	li**ves**
shelf	shel**ves**
thief	thie**ves**
wife	wi**ves**

   Exceptions to this rule include the plurals of such words as *cliff* (*cliffs*), *belief* (*beliefs*), and *roof* (*roofs*).

3. **Hyphenated Nouns.** In this case, two or three words are joined with hyphens (-) to form a single noun. Usually, the -*s* is added to the first word.

SINGULAR	PLURAL
attorney-at-law	attorneys-at-law
commander-in-chief	commanders-in-chief
runner-up	runners-up
sister-in-law	sisters-in-law

READ ALOUD

In each of the following sentences, the first bold noun is singular, and the second bold noun is the plural of the same word. When you read the sentences aloud, can you hear the difference in the nouns?

The **peach** tree was loaded with beautiful, juicy **peaches**.

This **child** will not sit where the other **children** are sitting.

The **thief** stole the jewels, dropped from the window, and joined the other **thieves**.

> **Language note:** Two of the preceding sentences use the word *the* before the noun (*The peach tree*, *The thief*). *The*, *a*, and *an* are called *articles*. If your native language doesn't use such words, check all nouns in your writing to see if they need an article (*a*, *an*, or *the*). To be clear on which article to use with which nouns, see Chapter 21.
>   Also, in English, abstract or nonspecific nouns do not use articles.
>
> **EXAMPLES**   **Beauty** is defined in many ways.
>
>   **Laws** are important.

A final word: The plurals of some words (like *deer*, *fish*, and *species*) are the same as their singular forms.

    I saw a deer in my yard this morning. [*Deer* is singular in this case.]

    Several deer ran across the road. [*Deer* is plural in this case.]

PRACTICE 2 ·

In each of the following sentences, correct plural nouns that are formed incorrectly. Two sentences are correct; write "C" next to them.

                                                    nations

EXAMPLE: Although Spain was one of the first ~~nationes~~ to explore

              North America, England settled it first.

1. The people who arrived in Jamestown in 1607 were willing to face many difficultys.

2. However, the settlers were poorly prepared for their new lifes.

3. Among the group were craftsmen, soldiers, and breeders of animals, such as oxes.

4. Others were people of wealth, gentlemans who had never done physical labor.

5. After the first winter, only 38 of the original 120 pioneers had survived.

6. In particular, many wifes and children had died.

7. Captain John Smith pulled the survivors together and kept the colony going for many more dayes, until five hundred more people arrived.

8. In 1609, however, supplys ran dangerously low, and the weather was bad.

9. To make matters worse, Jamestown was built on a swamp and bugs were everywhere.

10. My sister have been researching the settlement for three years.

PRACTICE 3

In the following paragraph, edit incorrectly formed plural nouns. Two sentences are correct; write "C" next to them.

> **EXAMPLE:** **Since ancient times, bread has been an important part**
> *lives*
> **of people's ~~lifes.~~**
> ⌃

(1) Archaeologists have found loafs of bread in Egyptian tombs. (2) Sometimes, the bread was placed on shelfs in the tombs. (3) In the British museum, visitors can see this bread as well as grains of wheat found in the tombs. (4) Originally, bread was baked only in the home by womens. (5) Soon, however, men set up bread-baking shops, and bakerys were born. (6) For the Greeks and Romans, color was one of the most important qualitys of bread. (7) Good bread had to be white, which is why wifes used wheat only from certain places. (8) In ancient Greece, citys competed to make the best bread. (9) Politicians in Athens insisted that authors record the names of the greatest bakers. (10) Through these writers, we have come to know the importance of bread in early societys.

Edit Nouns in College, Work, and Everyday Life

EDITING REVIEW 1: COLLEGE

The following paragraph is similar to one you might find in a nursing textbook. Correct problems with plural nouns. Three sentences are correct; write "C" next to them. The first sentence has been edited for you.

newborns
(1) In delivery rooms, doctors and nurses evaluate the health of ~~newbornes~~ at one, five, and sometimes ten minutes following birth.
(2) The purpose of the evaluation is to identify babys who need immediate care. (3) There are several quick wayes to test a baby's initial health. (4) Parents have probably heard of the APGAR test, which stands for <u>a</u>ctivity, <u>p</u>ulse, <u>g</u>rimace, <u>a</u>ppearance, and <u>r</u>espiration. (5) Infants receive zero to two points in each area. (6) For example, no activity points are given to a baby whose arms and leges are limp and unmoving. (7) A baby whose limbes are flexed and moving slightly receives one point. (8) A baby whose arms, legs, and feets are moving actively receives two points. (9) Infants with a total score of seven to ten points are considered normal, and those scoring three points or fewer need immediate medical attention. (10) These evaluations indicate how well infants are adjusting to their new lifes.

EDITING REVIEW 2: WORK . . . .

Correct problems with plural nouns in the following memo. Two sentences are correct; write "C" next to them. The first sentence has been edited for you.

DATE: September 15, 2006

TO: Shipping Department Employees

FROM: James McCarter, President

SUBJECT: Vacation Leave

seasons
(1) As you know, October 15 to December 31 is one of our busiest and most profitable ~~seasones~~. (2) Boxs are already beginning to pile up in the warehouse. (3) As a result, we need to have as many peoples as possible on the shipping floor during that period. (4) Several major holidayes fall within this time, so many of you will want to take vacation days. (5) We want to accommodate your plans, but we need plenty of advance warning. (6) All vacation requestes for that time must be submitted by October 1 so that coverage can be scheduled. (7) If you

are willing to work extra shiftes, please notify your supervisor. (8) As usual, managers must sign all vacation request forms. (9) If you have any questiones, please see your supervisor or call Human Resources at extension 15. (10) Best wishs to all of you this season.

EDITING REVIEW 3: EVERYDAY LIFE

Correct problems with plural nouns in the following essay. Three sentences are correct; write "C" next to them. The first sentence has been edited for you.

(1) Every summer, carnivals come to many small ~~townes~~ *towns* across America. (2) As larger amusement parks have become more popular, small traveling carnivals have lost some of their excitement. (3) However, many familys still enjoy an old-fashioned day at the fair.

(4) Carnival attractions fall into three main categorys: amusement rides, games, and performances. (5) Ferris wheeles, small roller coasters, and various spinning machines are among the most popular rides. (6) For the younger childrens, there might be bumper cars, merry-go-rounds, or ponys to ride. (7) At the carnival's game boothes, players might throw darts at balloons or shoot fake guns at toy ducks. (8) The prizes are usually stuffed animals, such as bears or deers, and some winners go home with real goldfishes. (9) For visitors who don't like rides or just need a break, a tent is often set up for performers such as knife throwers. (10) The knife thrower's assistant stands against a board while the thrower hurls knifes into the board. (11) Between acts, there might be clowns and monkies to keep the audience laughing.

(12) Because everything must be packed into trailers, traveling carnivals cannot compete with large theme parks on the basis of size or number of attractions. (13) However, most carnivals offer an embarrassment of richs. (14) With such a wide range of activitys, there's something for everyone.

Write and Edit Your Own Work

ASSIGNMENT 1: WRITE

Write a paragraph describing where items are in a local store. Be sure to use some plural nouns. When you're done, check the plurals against the rules in this chapter, correcting any mistakes that you find.

ASSIGNMENT 2: EDIT

Using this chapter as a guide, edit problems with plural nouns in a paper you are writing for this course or another course or in a piece of writing from your work or everyday life.

Practice Together

■ LEARNING STYLES: Look for activities in this chapter that are matched to your learning style. If you don't know your learning style, take the test on pages 26–28.

  Visual

  Auditory

  Reading/writing

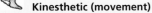 Kinesthetic (movement)

Working with a few other students, practice what you have learned in this chapter.

1. Have one group member write a singular noun on top of a blank sheet of paper. Then, he or she should pass the paper to the next person, who should make the noun plural and write another singular noun for the next person to make plural. Continue until you get back to the first person. Take turns calling out sentences that use the plural nouns.

2. With your group, choose an interesting photograph or painting, perhaps one of the images from Unit 2 of this book. Then, write "singular" and "plural" as headings on a blank sheet of paper. Together, name the things you could see or touch if you were able to climb into the photo or painting. Start with singular things. Then, name the plural things. Write down the words for these nouns under the proper heading. Post your pictures and word lists at the front of the room for others to see.

3. With your group, make up a story that uses plural forms of at least four of the following words: *boss, child, cloud, deer, dog, factory, foot, glass, idea, life, ox, ribbon, tooth, woman.* Choose one person to write down the story and another to read it to the rest of the class. Vote for your favorite story.

Chapter Review

1. A _____ is a word that names a general or specific person, place, or thing.

2. Nouns can be _____, meaning *one*, or _____, meaning *more than one*.

3. Most nouns form the plural by adding _____.

4. Certain nouns form the plural irregularly. Write five irregular plurals:

   _____

5. **VOCABULARY:** Go back to any new words that you underlined in this chapter. Can you guess their meanings now? If not, look up the words in a dictionary.

LEARNING JOURNAL: Which words form plurals in a way that you didn't expect? Write for two minutes about what you've learned.

■ **TIP:** For help with building your vocabulary, see Appendix B.

17

Pronouns

Using Substitutes for Nouns

I've always been bad with names

SHE

HE

📖 **VOCABULARY:** Underline any words in this chapter that are new to you.

📖 **IDEA JOURNAL:** Write about a time when you helped someone.

Understand What Pronouns Are

Pronouns replace nouns or other pronouns in a sentence so that you do not have to repeat them.

$\qquad$ *his*
Earl loaned me ~~Earl's~~ lawn mower.

[The pronoun *his* replaces *Earl's*.]

$\qquad$ *She*
You know Tina. ~~Tina~~ is my best friend.

[The pronoun *she* replaces *Tina*.]

The noun or pronoun that a pronoun replaces is called the **antecedent**. In most cases, a pronoun refers to a specific antecedent nearby.

Antecedent

I removed my photo albums and papers from the basement. It flooded just an hour later.

Pronoun replacing antecedent

Common Pronouns

PERSONAL PRONOUNS	POSSESSIVE PRONOUNS	INDEFINITE PRONOUNS	
I	my	all	many
me	mine	another	much
you	your/yours	any	neither
she/he	hers/his	anybody	nobody
her/him	hers/his	anything	none
it	its	both	no one
we	our/ours	each	nothing
us	our/ours	either	one
they	their/theirs	everybody	several
them	their/theirs	everyone	somebody
		everything	someone
		few	something

PRACTICE 1 . . . .

In each of the following sentences, circle the pronoun, underline the noun to which it refers, and draw an arrow from the pronoun to the noun.

EXAMPLE: Black bears in Nevada are facing a problem because people have moved into (their) territory.

1. Nevada's bears used to have trouble getting enough pinyon nuts, a staple of their diet.

2. About ten years ago, the bears discovered a new source of food that they can find more easily.

3. Garbage is a bear treat, and it is found in many urban areas.

4. Trash cans are easy to open, and they offer a constant source of food.

5. The urban bear gets little exercise because it can find garbage so easily.

6. Bears that eat garbage are taller and heavier than average, making them even more frightening to the people living nearby.

7. City managers have contacted Jon Beckman, a bear researcher, and asked him for advice.

■ **TIP:** For more practice, visit Exercise Central at <**bedfordstmartins.com/realskills**>.

8. Beckman recommends that cities require bear-proof trash containers; they are one of the best long-term methods of keeping bears away from urban areas.

9. However, when bears are first kept out of garbage cans, they might break into cars and houses.

10. Bears have even been found napping in houses after eating until their stomachs are full.

. . . .

Find and Correct Pronoun Problems

Make Pronouns Agree

A pronoun must agree with (match) the noun or pronoun it refers to in number: Both must be singular (one) or plural (more than one).

The Riccis opened *their* new store yesterday.

[*Their* agrees with *Riccis* because both are plural.]

If a pronoun refers to a singular noun, it must also match that noun in gender: *he* for masculine nouns, *she* for feminine nouns, and *it* for genderless nouns.

Louella brushed *her* cat.

[*Her* agrees with *Louella* because both are singular and feminine.]

Language note: Notice that pronouns have gender (*he/she, him/her, his/her/hers*). The pronoun must agree with the gender of the noun it refers to.

INCORRECT	My sister is a doctor. *He* works at County General Hospital.
CORRECT	My sister is a doctor. *She* works at County General Hospital.
INCORRECT	Carolyn went to see *his* boyfriend.
CORRECT	Carolyn went to see *her* boyfriend.

Also, notice that English has different forms for subject and object pronouns (see p. 279).

Two types of words often cause errors in pronoun agreement: indefinite pronouns and collective nouns.

Indefinite Pronouns

An **indefinite pronoun** does not refer to a specific person, place, or thing. Indefinite pronouns often take singular verbs.

Indefinite Pronouns

ALWAYS SINGULAR

anybody	everyone	nothing
anyone	everything	one (of)
anything	much	somebody
each (of)	neither (of)	someone
either (of)	nobody	something
everybody	no one	

MAY BE SINGULAR OR PLURAL

all	none
any	some

When you see or write a sentence that has an indefinite pronoun, choose the word that goes with this pronoun carefully.

FIND: Read each sentence in your writing carefully.

<u>Someone</u> left (her/their) earring in the ladies' room.

Underline any indefinite pronouns. Often, an indefinite pronoun's antecedent will be singular, as in this example.

CHOOSE: Choose the pronoun that agrees with the indefinite pronoun.

Someone left (her/their) earring in the ladies' room.

The singular pronoun *her* correctly refers to the single indefinite pronoun *someone*.

INCORRECT

The priests assembled in the hall. Each had *their* own seat.

Almost no one likes to hear a recording of *their* voice.

CORRECT

The priests assembled in the hall. Each had *his* own seat.

[The singular pronoun *his* matches the singular pronoun *each*.]

Almost no one likes to hear a recording of *his* voice.

[The singular pronoun *his* matches the singular pronoun *no one*.]

NOTE: Although it is grammatically correct, using a masculine pronoun (*he, his,* or *him*) alone to refer to a singular indefinite pronoun, such as *no one,* is considered unfair to women. Here are two ways to avoid this problem:

1. Use the phrase *his or her.*

   Almost no one likes to hear a recording of *his or her* voice.

2. Change the sentence so that the pronoun refers to a plural noun or pronoun.

   People don't usually like to hear recordings of *their* voices.

PRACTICE 2

In each of the following sentences, circle the indefinite pronoun. Then, fill in the blank with the correct form of the pronoun that replaces the circled word.

   EXAMPLE: In the 1800s, (any) Americans who loaded up ___*their*___ covered wagons to move west did not have an easy time.

1. Everyone who traveled with a wagon train had _____ daily chores.

2. Nobody could just sit back in _____ seat and relax.

3. Nothing got done on _____ own.

4. Anyone who chose to bring _____ cows along had to be sure to milk them.

5. All of the children had to do _____ tasks before dinner.

6. Each boy helped _____ father gather wood or care for the horses, while each girl helped _____ mother prepare dinner.

7. Some of the children would gather berries for _____ dessert.

8. One of them might find a new plant and gather the seeds to take to _____ new home in Oregon.

9. Some of the older people helped by shaking out _____ blankets and quilts to get rid of the dust.

10. Everybody was expected to help _____ neighbor get food.

Circle the correct pronoun or group of words in parentheses.

(1) Anyone who is entering the job market must make a good impression with (his or her / their) writing skills. (2) Everyone should start by updating (their / his or her) résumé and proofreading it carefully. (3) Some potential employers say that (he or she spends / they spend) only six to eight seconds deciding whether to seriously consider a résumé. (4) If anything on a résumé suggests that the candidate was too lazy to proofread, (it / they) will probably cause that person to be eliminated from consideration. (5) Nobody should send a résumé without (his or her / their) cover letter. (6) Although some people are tempted to use the same cover letter for every job that (they apply / he or she applies) for, that is not a good idea. (7) Managers want to hire someone who shows that (they are / he or she is) interested in and knowledgeable about the specific position. (8) Finally, each potential employer might also ask you to fill out (their / his or her) application form. (9) Everybody who fills out these forms should use (their / his or her) neatest handwriting. (10) Nobody wants to lose a job offer because of (his or her / their) résumé, cover letter, or application, so it is worth the time and effort to make these documents flawless.

Collective Nouns

A **collective noun** names a group that acts as a single unit.

Common Collective Nouns

audience	company	group
class	crowd	jury
college	family	society
committee	government	team

Collective nouns are often singular, so when you use a pronoun to refer to a collective noun, it too must usually be singular.

 Draw your own wall poster of one or more of the charts in this chapter. Pick a mistake that you often find in your writing, and include a new example of your own.

> **FIND: Read each sentence in your writing carefully.**
>
> **The <u>company</u> sold (its/their) largest warehouse.**
>
> Underline any collective nouns.

⬇

> **CHOOSE: Choose the pronoun that agrees with the collective noun.**
>
> **The company sold (its/their) largest warehouse.**
>
> The singular pronoun *its* correctly refers to the collective noun *company*.

INCORRECT

The class was assigned *their* first paper on Monday.

The team won *their* first victory in ten years.

CORRECT

The class was assigned *its* first paper on Monday.

[The class as a whole was assigned the paper, so the meaning is singular, and the singular pronoun *its* is used.]

The team won *its* first victory in ten years.

[The team, acting as one, had a victory, so the singular pronoun *its* is used.]

If the people in a group are acting separately, however, the noun is plural and should be used with a plural pronoun.

The audience shifted in *their* seats.

[The people shifted at different times in different seats. They weren't acting as one.]

Draw a collective noun in two ways: acting as a unit and acting separately.

PRACTICE 4 . . . .

Circle the antecedent and fill in the correct pronoun (*its* or *their*) in each of the following sentences.

EXAMPLE: The (class) of 1969 showed ___*its*___ school spirit at the homecoming pep rally last night.

1. When the band began playing _____ opening song, everyone stopped talking.

2. Recognizing the school fight song, the crowd leaped to _____ feet and began cheering.

3. The music continued for ten minutes before the audience sat down in _____ seats.

4. The jazz choir performed next, but _____ sounded slightly off-key.

5. Everyone wanted the band to return and play _____ most famous march.

6. At that moment, the football team would make _____ entrance onto the field.

7. First, however, the dance troupe gave _____ usual energetic performance.

8. At last, the entire brass section of the band made _____ way onto the field.

9. The horns blasted the school song as the team ran onto the field wearing _____ new orange uniforms.

10. This year, the school hoped to win back _____ championship trophy.

> **PRACTICE 5** . . . .

In each of the following sentences, circle the correct pronoun in the parentheses.

(1) In March, the corporation made (their/its) decision to move to a new office in the town of Lawson. (2) The town council gave (their/its) wholehearted approval to the project. (3) The community invited the executives to (their/its) annual spring barbecue. (4) A construction company was chosen to build the factory, and (it/they) began the project in May. (5) Each department will now have (their/its) own kitchen facility. (6) The administrative group will have (their/its) choice of break rooms. (7) The board of directors moved into (their/its) offices yesterday, and the rest of the company will follow next week. (8) A large crowd will be invited to the grand opening, and (their/its) seats will be arranged around a green space in front of the building.

. . . .

Check Pronoun Reference

A pronoun should refer to only one noun, and it should be clear what that noun is.

FIND: Read each sentence in your writing carefully.

Brenda told Alicia that <u>she</u> needed a vacation.

When I went to park, <u>they</u> told me that the lot was full.

Underline any pronouns. Is it clear what words they refer to? [In these examples, it is not. In the first sentence, *she* could refer to Brenda or Alicia. In the second, it's not clear who *they* is.]

FIX: Replace the confusing pronouns with something more specific, or rewrite the sentence.

to take
Brenda told Alicia ~~that she~~ needed a vacation.
                              ^

              an attendant
When I went to park, ~~they~~ told me that the lot was full.
                            ^

CONFUSING

I put the shirt in the drawer, even though *it* was dirty.

[Was the shirt or the drawer dirty?]

If you can't find your doctor's office, *they* can help.

[Who's *they*?]

An hour before the turkey was to be done, *it* broke.

[What broke?]

CLEAR

I put the dirty shirt in the drawer.

If you can't find your doctor's office, *the information desk* can help.

An hour before the turkey was to be done, *the oven* broke.

Language note: In writing formal papers, do not use *you* to mean *people*.

INCORRECT	The instructor says that you have to turn in your homework.
CORRECT	The instructor says that **students** have to turn in **their** homework.

> **PRACTICE 6** . . . .

Edit each sentence to eliminate problems with pronoun reference. Some sentences may be revised in more than one way.

> **EXAMPLE:** When we were young, our babysitter gave my sister Jan
>   *Jan's*
>   and me a book that became one of ~~her~~ favorites.
>   ^

1. The babysitter, Jan, and I were fascinated by *Twenty Thousand Leagues Under the Sea,* and she is now studying marine biology.

2. I know very little about the ocean except for what it says in occasional magazine articles.

3. I enjoy visiting the aquarium and have taken a biology class, but it didn't focus on ocean life as much as I would have liked.

4. I did learn that it covers about 71 percent of the Earth's surface.

5. Both space and the ocean are largely unexplored, and it contains a huge proportion of all life on Earth.

6. They say that the ocean might contain as many as a million undiscovered species.

7. Jan says that they have found some very odd creatures in the ocean.

8. In Indonesia, they have found an octopus that uses camouflage and "walks" across the ocean floor on two legs.

9. According to marine biologists who made the discovery, it looks like a piece of seaweed bouncing along the sand.

10. Scientists say that it might help them develop better robot arms.

. . . .

A pronoun should *replace* the subject of a sentence, not *repeat* it.

FIND: Read each sentence in your writing carefully.

The insurance **agent**, ⟨she⟩ said that the policy covered a new roof.

- Underline the subject, double-underline the verb, and circle any pronouns.
- Ask what the pronoun refers to. [In this case, it's *agent*.]
- Ask if the subject and the pronoun referring to it share the same verb. [Here, they share the verb *said*.]
- Ask if the pronoun repeats the subject rather than replacing it. [Here, *she* repeats *agent*.]

FIX: Delete the repetitious pronoun.

The insurance agent,/ she said that the policy covered a new roof.

■ **TIP:** For more on subjects, verbs, and other sentence parts, see Chapter 10.

PRONOUN REPEATS SUBJECT

The doctor, *she* told me to take one aspirin a day.

The plane, *it* arrived on time despite the fog.

CORRECT

The doctor told me to take one aspirin a day.

The plane arrived on time despite the fog.

PRACTICE 7

Correct repetitious pronoun references in the following sentences.

> **EXAMPLE:** Many objects we use today ~~they~~ were invented by the
>
> Chinese.

1. Fireworks they were originally used by the Chinese to scare enemies in war.

2. The wheelbarrow, also invented in China, it was called the "wooden ox."

3. People who use paper fans to cool off they should thank the Chinese for this invention.

4. The Chinese they were the first to make kites, which were used both as toys and in wartime to fly messages over enemy lines.

5. A counting device called the *abacus* it was used for counting and led to the development of the calculator.

6. Many people, they don't know that spaghetti was first made in China, not Italy.

7. The oldest piece of paper in the world it was discovered near Xian, China.

8. In fact, paper money it was invented in China.

9. Chinese merchants they were using paper money in the ninth century.

10. Matches were also invented in China when a woman she wanted an easier way to start fires for cooking.

Use the Right Type of Pronoun

There are three types of pronouns: **subject** pronouns, **object** pronouns, and **possessive** pronouns. Note the pronouns in the following sentences.

Object   Subject

The horse kicked *her*, but *she* wasn't seriously hurt.

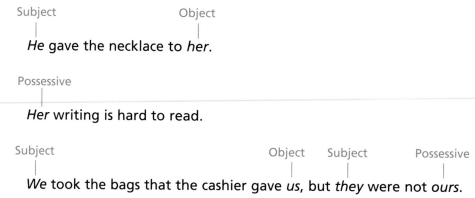

Subject   Object

He gave the necklace to *her.*

Possessive

Her writing is hard to read.

Subject   Object   Subject   Possessive

We took the bags that the cashier gave *us,* but *they* were not *ours.*

Pronoun Types

	SINGULAR			PLURAL		
	SUBJECT	**OBJECT**	**POSSESSIVE**	**SUBJECT**	**OBJECT**	**POSSESSIVE**
First person	I	me	my, mine	we	us	our, ours
Second person	you	you	your, yours	you	you	your, yours
Third person	he	him	his	they	them	their, theirs
	she	her	her, hers			
	it	it	its			

Subject Pronouns

A **subject pronoun** serves as the subject of a verb.

> *She* plays on the softball team.

> *I* changed the oil.

> **Language note:** Some languages omit subject pronouns, but English sentences always have a stated or written subject.
>
> **INCORRECT**   Hates cleaning.
>
> **CORRECT**   *He* hates cleaning.

Object Pronouns

An **object pronoun** either receives the action of the verb (that is, it is the object of the verb) or is part of a prepositional phrase (that is, it is the object of the preposition).

OBJECT OF THE VERB   Roberto asked *me* to copy the report.

[*Me* receives the action of the verb *asked.*]

Roberto gave *me* the report.

[*Me* receives the action of the verb *gave.*]

OBJECT OF THE PREPOSITION   Roberto gave the report to *me*.

[*Me* is part of the prepositional phrase *to me*.]

■ **TIP:** For more on preposi-tions, see Chapter 10.

Possessive Pronouns

Possessive pronouns show ownership. Because these pronouns already show ownership, you never need to put an apostrophe in them.

INCORRECT   That job is *your's*.

CORRECT   That job is *yours*.

PRACTICE 8 .. . . . .

In each of the following sentences, fill in the blank with an appropriate pro-noun. In some cases, there may be more than one correct choice. The clues in parentheses tell you what type of pronoun is needed.

EXAMPLE: Ms. Beau gave ___*her*___ (*possessive*) class a pop quiz.

1. _____ (*subject*) bought a new shirt for her sister.

2. The dog chewed on _____ (*possessive*) bone for nearly an hour.

3. We could hardly wait to watch _____ (*possessive*) favorite television program this week.

4. My uncle left _____ (*possessive*) tools in the back of my truck.

5. At the awards ceremony, the coach gave _____ (*object*) the trophy for best player on the soccer team.

6. _____ (*subject*) will pick up a pizza on his way home from class tonight.

7. My mother sent a card to _____ (*object*) asking when she will visit.

8. We asked _____ (*object*) to turn in their projects early.

9. _____ (*subject*) fixed the leaking faucet in the bathroom with her new wrench.

10. _____ (*subject*) sold seven boxes of cookies before they went home.

. . . .

Certain kinds of sentences can make choosing the right type of pronoun a little more difficult:

• Sentences that have more than one subject or object.

• Sentences that make a comparison.

• Sentences that use *who* or *whom*.

Pronouns Used with Compound Subjects and Objects

When a subject or object has more than one part, it is called **compound**. The parts are joined by *and* or *or*.

COMPOUND SUBJECT	Travis and *I* play soccer.
	[The two subjects are *Travis* and *I*.]
COMPOUND OBJECT	Becky made the candles for the boys and *me*.
	[The two objects are *boys* and *me*.]

To decide what type of pronoun is correct in compound subjects or objects, use the following chart.

FIND: Read each sentence in your writing carefully.

~~Daniella and~~ me go running every morning.

The waiter brought the dessert tray to Jack and I.

- Underline the subject(s), double-underline the verb, and circle any objects (words that receive the action of the verb).
- Ask if there is a compound subject or object. [*Daniella and me* is a compound subject, and *Jack and I* is a compound object.]
- Cross out one of the subjects or objects so that only the pronoun remains.
- Does the sentence sound right with just the pronoun as the subject or object? [In both examples, the answer is "no." *Me go running every morning* and *The waiter brought the dessert tray to I* both sound strange.]

FIX: Replace the incorrect pronoun with the correct one.

Daniella and ~~me~~ *I* go running every morning.

The waiter brought the dessert tray to Jack and ~~I~~ *me*.

INCORRECT

Harold and *me* like to go to the races.

The boss gave the hardest job to Rico and *I*.

I sent the e-mail to Ellen and *she*.

CORRECT

Harold and *I* like to go to the races.

[Think: *I* like to go to the races.]

The boss gave the hardest job to Rico and *me*.

[Think: The boss gave the hardest job to *me*.]

I sent the e-mail to Ellen and *her*.

[Think: I sent the e-mail to *her*.]

Many people make the mistake of writing *between you and I*. It should be *between you and me*.

The girl sat between you and I.
                                     ^me

■ **TIP:** When you are writing about yourself and someone else, always put yourself after everyone else. *My friends and I went to the movies,* not *I and my friends went to the movies.*

PRACTICE 9 . . . .

Circle the correct pronoun in each of the following sentences.

EXAMPLE: Carol went shopping with Josh and (I/(me)).

1. A tall fence stood between (he/him) and the angry bull.

2. After lunch, Gracie and (I/me) decided to go shopping.

3. Jon gave the new drawings to Marla and (I/me).

4. Mr. Edwards hopes that Dan and (she/her) will complete the project early.

5. Rajan and (he/him) met three friends for pizza.

6. For Carl and (we/us), the unpleasant day seemed to last forever.

7. The children rode to the park with my mother and (I/me).

8. My aunt sent (they/them) and (I/me) a photograph of the entire family.

9. I'm taking an art class with Marcella and (he/him).

10. Between you and (I/me), I think the new library is ugly.

PRACTICE 10 . . . .

Edit each sentence using the correct type of pronoun. Two sentences are correct; write "C" next to them.

EXAMPLE: Because Calico Jack was a famed pirate of the
                                        he
Caribbean, ~~him~~ and the crew of his ship *Vanity* were
                     ^

greatly feared and respected.

1. On a trip to the Bahamas, he and a woman named Anne Bonny fell in love.

2. Because women were considered bad luck on a ship, Anne disguised herself as a man and kept the secret between she and Calico Jack.

3. No one guessed that Calico Jack's new first mate was a woman, and her and the other pirates became friends.

4. With Calico Jack and she in command, the *Vanity* raided Spanish ships throughout the Caribbean.

5. On one ship, her and Calico Jack discovered Mary Read, another female sailor disguised as a man.

6. Her and Anne became good friends.

7. When Calico Jack learned of their friendship, him and Anne decided to let Mary sail on the *Vanity*.

8. Soon, she and Anne became known as two of the most dangerous pirates in the Caribbean.

9. Anne and Mary were skilled pirates and fierce fighters, but the British Navy finally captured they and their pirate crew in 1720.

10. The two women were sentenced to hang, but because they were pregnant, them and their babies were spared.

. . . .

Pronouns Used in Comparisons

A **comparison** describes similarities and differences between two things. It often includes the words *than* or *as*.

> Terrence is happier *than* Elena.

> Terrence is as happy *as* Carla.

Pronouns have specific meanings in comparisons, so be sure to use the right ones. To do so, mentally add the words that are missing.

Subject

Anne likes Internet games more than *I*.

[This sentence means "Ann likes Internet games more than I like them." You can tell by adding the missing words to the end: *more than **I like Internet games**.*]

Object
|
Ann likes Internet games more than *me*.

[This sentence means "Ann likes Internet games more than she likes me." You can tell by adding the missing words to the end: *more than **she likes** me*.]

FIND: Read each sentence in your writing carefully.

April studies more (than) me.

- Circle the word that signals a comparison (*than* or *as*).
- Ask what word or words could be added after the signaling word. [Here, *do* could be added.]
- Ask whether the sentence makes sense with the added word(s). [*April studies more than me do* does not make sense.]

⬇

FIX: Replace the incorrect pronoun with the correct one.

                            I (do)
April studies more than ~~me~~.
                          ^

INCORRECT

Bettina is taller than *me*.

I wish I could sing as well as *her*.

Your team is faster than *us*.

CORRECT

Bettina is taller than *I*.

[Think: Bettina is taller than *I* am.]

I wish I could sing as well as *she*.

[Think: I wish I could sing as well as *she* sings.]

Your team is faster than *we*.

[Think: Your team is faster than *we* are.]

READ ALOUD

In each of the following sentences, decide what words could be added to the end of each comparison. Speak the sentences, including the added words, aloud.

Dave drives as fast as I.

No one can make a better lasagna than we.

We decided that Alicia was a better candidate than he.

> **PRACTICE 11** . . . .

Edit each sentence using the correct pronoun type. One sentence is correct; write "C" next to it.

> **EXAMPLE:** No one is prouder of Lance Armstrong than ~~me~~.   *I*

1. Other Texans may be more famous than him, but Lance Armstrong has accomplished so much.

2. I wish that I had as much determination as him.

3. Few cyclists have won as many races as him.

4. Very few athletes have had as many problems as him, even though he won so many contests.

5. Against incredible odds, he survived surgery and chemotherapy for cancer and went on to compete against athletes who thought that they were better than him.

6. In July 2005, he won his seventh Tour de France, with the closest rider finishing more than four minutes later than him.

7. Athletes are in awe of Armstrong's determination and know that he can perform better than them under extreme pressure.

8. While I love cycling, I don't think I could ever be as good as he.

9. Cycling just seems to come more naturally to Lance Armstrong than to I.

10. Nevertheless, I owe my love of cycling to no one more than he.

. . . .

Who versus Whom

Who is always a subject; use it if the pronoun performs an action. *Whom* is always an object; use it if the pronoun does not perform any action.

WHO = SUBJECT	Dennis is the neighbor *who* helped us build the deck.
	[*Who* (*Dennis*) is the subject.]
WHOM = OBJECT	Carol is the woman *whom* I met at school.
	[You can turn the sentence around: *I met whom* (*Carol*) *at school. Whom* (*Carol*) is the object of the verb *met*.]

In most cases, for sentences in which the pronoun is followed by a verb, use *who*. When the pronoun is followed by a noun or pronoun, use *whom*.

The man (who/whom) called 911 was unusually calm.

[The pronoun is followed by the verb *called*. Use *who*.]

The woman (who/whom) I drove to the train was from Turkey.

[The pronoun is followed by another pronoun: *I*. Use *whom*.]

Whoever is a subject pronoun; *whomever* is an object pronoun.

PRACTICE 12 . . . .

In each sentence, circle the correct word, *who* or *whom*.

   EXAMPLE: Mary Frith was a thief (who/whom) lived in the 1600s.

1. She joined a gang of thieves (who/whom) were known as cutpurses.

2. People (who/whom) had money and jewelry carried the items in purses tied around their waists.

3. Mary and her gang would cut the purse strings, steal the purses, and find someone to (who/whom) they could sell the goods.

4. Mary, (who/whom) was not one to pass up a chance to make money, opened her own shop to sell the "used" goods.

5. She often sold items back to the people from (who/whom) she had stolen.

. . . .

Edit Pronouns in College, Work, and Everyday Life

Complete the editing reviews as instructed, referring to the chart on page 292.

EDITING REVIEW 1: COLLEGE . . . .

The following paragraph is similar to one you might find in a student handbook. Correct pronoun errors. Two sentences are correct; write "C" next to them. The first sentence has been edited for you.

students

(1) Sometimes, ~~a student~~ receives a grade for a course that is not what they expected. (2) To help students determine whether the grade is correct, they usually have a policy for challenging grades. (3) Although the policies may differ among schools, most schools require that students follow a series of steps. (4) First, anyone who is concerned about a grade should contact their instructor to ask for an explanation. (5) The student should provide copies of quizzes, tests, research papers, or other assignments as evidence. (6) If him or her and the instructor cannot reach a compromise, it might be brought to a higher authority, such as a department committee. (7) The committee will issue their ruling after contacting the student and instructor for information. (8) Based on the ruling, the original grade it will either stand or be changed. (9) No one is happier than us administrators when both parties feel they have been treated fairly. (10) Just remember: Students whom want to challenge a grade usually have a limited time in which to do so.

EDITING REVIEW 2: WORK

Correct pronoun errors in the following e-mail. Three sentences are correct; write "C" next to them. The first sentence has been edited for you.

Thursday, 2/2/2006, 12:09 p.m.

FROM: Thomas Hamson

TO: Juan Alvarez

CC: Alicia Newcombe

SUBJECT: New color printer

me

(1) On March 21, you asked Allegra Conti and I to look into purchasing a new color printer for our department. (2) This e-mail it presents our findings and recommendations.

(3) Two printers will meet our needs: the FX 235 and the AE 100. (4) It says that both handle 8½" × 11", 8½" × 15", and A4 size paper. (5) They are also able to print labels, photographs, and overhead transparencies. (6) It, however, has several capabilities not found in the AE 100. (7) The

FX 235 offers more flexibility for employees whom have unique needs. (8) For example, if Allegra wants to print something more quickly than me, the FX model offers a low-quality setting that prints documents at a higher speed. (9) Although the two printers are similarly priced, replacement ink cartridges for the FX 235 are 35 percent cheaper than cartridges for the AE 100. (10) It also has a better warranty.

(11) We read several reviews of both printers, and every reviewer recommends the FX as their top choice in our price range. (12) Additionally, the IT Department agrees that their favorite is the FX 235. (13) Today, I will bring you brochures for both printers. (14) Allegra and me will answer any additional questions you might have. (15) Please let us know when the company has made their decision.

EDITING REVIEW 3: EVERYDAY LIFE . . . .

Correct pronoun errors in the following passage. Three sentences are correct; write "C" next to them. The first sentence has been edited for you.

(1) The Internet is continually changing to meet the needs of the people ~~whom~~ *who* use it. (2) They originally thought it would be used primarily for business and research. (3) However, the Internet has become a place where people share his or her thoughts and opinions.

(4) In the past few years, for example, Web logs (blogs) have become an Internet craze. (5) Blogs, they began as online diaries where people could regularly post their thoughts and links to favorite Web sites for friends and family. (6) Today, many previously unknown bloggers are writing for huge audiences across the world. (7) They cover every topic imaginable, including politics, current events, sports, music, and technology. (8) Anyone using the Internet can start their own blog. (9) When a lot of people blog about a particular political or social controversy, it is called a blogstorm.

(10) More recently, another type of Web site—the wiki—has become popular among people whom like to share information. (11) People can

post information to a wiki or edit information that has already been posted. (12) For a class project, my partner and me evaluated an online encyclopedia's article about a wildlife refuge near our college. (13) Because the site is a wiki, her and me were able to edit outdated facts and add new information.

Write and Edit Your Own Work

ASSIGNMENT 1: WRITE

Write about a time when you worked with others to get something done. Be sure to use several pronouns. When you're done, use the chart on page 292 to check the pronouns, and correct any mistakes that you find.

ASSIGNMENT 2: EDIT

Using the chart on page 292, edit pronoun errors in a paper you are writing for this course or another course or in a piece of writing from your work or everyday life.

Practice Together

■ LEARNING STYLES: Look for activities in this chapter that are matched to your learning style. If you don't know your learning style, take the test on pages 26–28.

 Visual

 Auditory

 Reading/writing

 Kinesthetic (movement)

Working with a few other students, practice what you have learned in this chapter.

1. Play pronoun catch. Pick an object that can be tossed among group members, such as a set of keys, a pencil, or an eraser. Then, open your books to the list of common pronouns on page 269. The first "pitcher" should pick a pronoun from the list, call it out, and toss the object to another person. That person should use the pronoun in a sentence and then pick another pronoun and toss the object to a new person. Keep going until everyone in the group has used a pronoun in at least one sentence.

2. Underline every noun in the following paragraph and discuss as a group which nouns would be best to replace with pronouns. Then, pick a group member to write your revised paragraph on a sheet of paper. Post your paragraph at the front of the room.

One of the strangest tales from Irish history is the story of an ancient king, Conor, who was hit by a "brainball" (probably a metal ball on a chain) during a battle. The brainball caved in Conor's skull, but Conor still lived. A doctor said that if the brainball were taken out of Conor's skull, Conor would bleed to death. So Conor continued as a mighty king for years although Conor had a brainball stuck in Conor's head.

3. With your group, replace some of the pronouns in the following sentences with nouns to make the sentences clear. You may have to rewrite the sentences. 📖

   EXAMPLE: She told her that her hair was a mess.

   REVISED: Mary told Ellen that Ellen's hair was a mess.

   His father used to play football, and he told me he made a lot of money betting on the game.

   They were giving away doughnuts at the bakery.

   Although my bicycle hit the tree, it was not damaged.

   It won't work, and it has too many steps.

4. As an extra step to activity 3, pick one of your revised sentences and discuss what a picture of it would look like. Pass around a sheet of paper and draw a picture of the sentence. 👁

"IF LIFE GIVES YOU A BRAINBALL, MAKE a CROWN."
— Conor

Chapter Review

1. Pronouns replace _____ or other _____ in a sentence.

2. A pronoun must _____ (match) its antecedent (the noun or pronoun to which it refers) in number and in gender.

3. An _____ does not refer to a specific person, place, or thing. What are three examples of this kind of pronoun? _____

4. A _____ names a group that acts as a single unit. What are two examples? _____

5. If a pronoun repeats the subject of a sentence rather than replacing it, the pronoun should be _____ .

6. _____ pronouns serve as the subject of the verb. Give an example: _____ . _____ pronouns receive the action of a verb or are part of a prepositional phrase. Give an example: _____ . _____ pronouns show ownership. Give an example: _____

_____ .

LEARNING JOURNAL:
Write for two minutes, describing how you would explain pronoun agreement to someone who doesn't understand.

■ **TIP:** For help with building your vocabulary, see Appendix B.

7. When a subject or object has more than one part, it is described as _____.

8. Use *who* when the pronoun is followed by a _____. Use *whom* when the pronoun is followed by a _____.

9. **VOCABULARY:** Go back to any new words that you underlined in this chapter. Can you guess their meanings now? If not, look up the words in a dictionary.

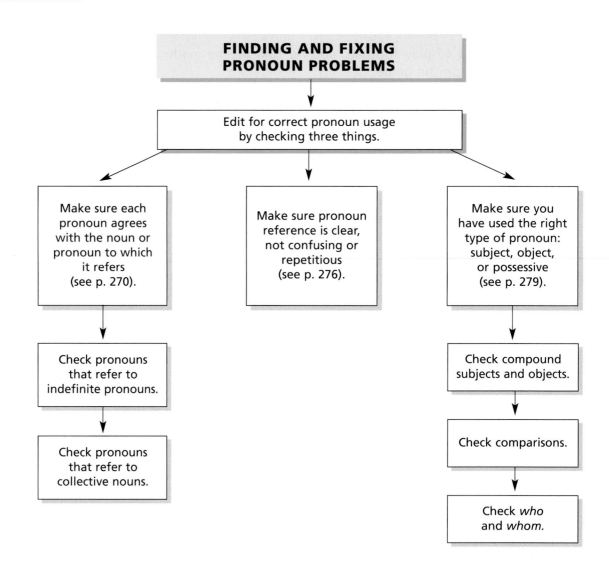

FINDING AND FIXING PRONOUN PROBLEMS

Edit for correct pronoun usage by checking three things.

Make sure each pronoun agrees with the noun or pronoun to which it refers (see p. 270).

Make sure pronoun reference is clear, not confusing or repetitious (see p. 276).

Make sure you have used the right type of pronoun: subject, object, or possessive (see p. 279).

Check pronouns that refer to indefinite pronouns.

Check compound subjects and objects.

Check pronouns that refer to collective nouns.

Check comparisons.

Check *who* and *whom*.

18

Adjectives and Adverbs

Using Descriptive Words

Understand What Adjectives and Adverbs Are

Adjectives describe nouns and pronouns. They add information about what kind, which one, or how many.

The *five new* students shared a *two-floor* house.

The *funny* movie made the *sad little* girls laugh.

Two large gray birds stood in the water.

> **Language note:** In English, adjectives are never plural unless they are numbers.
>
> **INCORRECT**   The three babies are *adorables*.
>
> [The adjective *three* is fine because it is a number, but the adjective *adorables* should not end in *-s* to indicate a plural noun.]
>
> **CORRECT**   The three babies are *adorable*.

Another way to describe a noun is with an adjective clause, a group of words (not just one word) that describes a noun.

ADJECTIVE (ONE WORD) AS MODIFIER   I am looking for a **helpful** person.

ADJECTIVE CLAUSE AS MODIFIER   I am looking for someone **who is helpful**.

📖 **IDEA JOURNAL:** How would describe yourself in a personal ad?

📖 **VOCABULARY:** Underline any words in this chapter that are new to you.

■ **TIP:** For more on nouns, see Chapter 16. For more on pronouns, see Chapter 17.

Often, adjective clauses can join two ideas smoothly:

TWO SENTENCES/IDEAS	That is the woman. Her son attends this class.
IDEAS JOINED	That is the woman **whose son attends this class**.

> **Language note:** Be aware that certain prepositions often follow certain adjectives. There is no logical explanation for many of these word combinations; you just have to remember them.
>
> **EXAMPLES**   I was **ashamed of** my behavior after the party.
>
> The boss was **happy about** my good performance.
>
> For more examples, see Chapter 21.

Adverbs describe verbs, adjectives, or other adverbs. They add information about how, how much, when, where, or why. Adverbs often end with -*ly*.

DESCRIBING A VERB	Mira sings *beautifully*.
	[*Beautifully* describes the verb *sings*.]
DESCRIBING AN ADJECTIVE	The *extremely* talented singer entertained the crowd.
	[*Extremely* describes the adjective *talented*.]
DESCRIBING ANOTHER ADVERB	Mira sings *very* beautifully.
	[*Very* describes the adverb *beautifully*.]

Note that both adjectives and adverbs can come either before or after the words they modify. Also note that you can use more than one adjective or adverb to modify a word.

PRACTICE 1 . . . .

■ **TIP:** For more on verbs and other sentence parts, see Chapter 10.

In each sentence, underline the word that is being described and fill in an appropriate adjective.

EXAMPLE: At the end of the day, I like to sit in my <u>*comfortable*</u>

<u>chair</u> and read a mystery book.

1. The _____ kitten hid under the couch during the storm.

2. _____ banners of pink, purple, and green hung across the stage.

3. Her favorite outfit included a _____ sweater.

4. Because the chef had added too much hot sauce, the chili was

  _____ .

5. The _____ baseball fans poured onto the field after their team

  won.

6. My neighbor's chicken is very _____ .

7. After waiting on hold for twenty minutes, the _____ customer

  slammed down the phone.

8. The old dress was _____, and all the buttons were missing.

9. After unloading the truck in the hot sun, Hank drank a _____

  soda.

10. Mary Lou was _____ when she won the chess game.

■ **TIP:** For more practice, visit Exercise Central at <**bedfordstmartins.com/ realskills**>.

PRACTICE 2 . . . .

In each sentence, underline the word that is being described and fill in an appropriate adverb.

  EXAMPLE: Because he was in a hurry, the man ____*quickly*____ paid his

  bill.

1. When I got out the tennis ball, my dog ran _____ into the yard.

2. The puppy _____ licked its mother's face.

3. We could not believe that Rita could dance so _____ .

4. Carol told Robert that his history notes were _____ helpful.

5. Gabe walked _____ on the ice.

6. We watched the turtle move _____ across the yard.

7. The defendant _____ told her story to the jury.

8. The car in front of me swerved _____ off the road.

9. Mr. Martin shouted _____ at the boys who were picking his

  apples.

10. Marcella drives _____ fast now that she has a sports car.

Use Adjectives and Adverbs Correctly

Choosing between Adjectives and Adverbs

Many adverbs are formed by adding -*ly* to the end of an adjective.

ADJECTIVE	ADVERB
The *fresh* vegetables glistened in the sun.	The house was *freshly* painted.
She is an *honest* person.	She answered the question *honestly*.

Draw a picture of one of the adjective/adverb sentences or of one of your own sentences that contains an adjective or adverb.

TIP: Note that nouns can be used as adjectives—for example, *City* traffic is terrible.

FIND: Read each sentence in your writing carefully.

The (quiet / quietly) ⟨child⟩ played in the yard.

The child ⟨played⟩ (quiet / quietly).

- Circle the word that is being described.
- Ask if this word is a noun or a verb, adjective, or adverb. [*Child* is a noun, and *played* is a verb.]

CHOOSE: Choose an adjective to describe a noun and an adverb to describe a verb, an adjective, or another adverb.

The (⟨quiet⟩ / quietly) child played in the yard.

The child played (quiet / ⟨quietly⟩).

INCORRECT

I was *real* pleased about the news.

We saw an *extreme* funny show last night.

We had a *peacefully* view of the lake.

CORRECT

I was *really* pleased about the news.

[An adverb, *really*, is needed to describe the verb *pleased*.]

We saw an *extremely* funny show last night.

[An adverb, *extremely*, is needed to describe the adjective *funny*.]

We had a *peaceful* view of the lake.

[An adjective, *peaceful*, is needed to describe the noun *view*.]

> **Language note:** The *-ed* and *-ing* forms of adjectives are sometimes confused. Common examples include *bored/boring*, *confused/confusing*, *excited/exciting*, and *interested/interesting*.
>
> **INCORRECT**   Janelle is interesting in ghosts and ghost stories.
>
> **CORRECT**   Janelle is interested in ghosts and ghost stories.
>
> **CORRECT**   Janelle finds ghosts and ghost stories interesting.
>
> Often, the *-ed* form describes a person's reaction, while the *-ing* form describes the thing being reacted to.

PRACTICE 3

In each sentence, underline the word that is being described, and then circle the correct adjective or adverb in the parentheses.

EXAMPLE: In the 1970s, <u>Richard O'Brien</u>, (**poor**/poorly) and unemployed, wrote a musical about a mad scientist from outer space.

1. The *Rocky Horror Picture Show* opened in London and audiences were (wild / wildly) enthusiastic.

2. Filmmakers decided that it would make a (successful / successfully) movie.

3. Just before the movie was to be released, the play opened in New York, and the reviews were (poor / poorly).

4. Because critics complained (constant / constantly) about the play, the movie didn't make much money at first.

5. The producer persuaded a theater in Greenwich Village to show the (unusual / unusually) film nightly at midnight.

6. Then, something interesting (slow / slowly) began to happen.

7. (Serious / Seriously) fans attended the movie every night and began dressing like the characters.

8. Soon the audience was (loud / loudly) shouting the lines, and watching the audience became entertaining in itself.

9. People covered their heads with newspapers during rainy scenes and danced (happy/happily) in the aisles during the theme song.

10. The movie is thirty years old, but (devoted/devotedly) fans still attend midnight showings at theaters across the country.

READ ALOUD

Read each of the following sentences aloud, emphasizing the bold words. Then, choose an adjective or adverb, as indicated, to fill in each blank, and read each sentence aloud again, with the additions.

I **swam** _____ across the pond. (Adverb)

The _____ **sunset** bathed the beach in a red glow. (Adjective)

The _____ old **house** scared the children. (Adjective)

If the train **arrives** _____, call me for a ride. (Adverb)

Using Adjectives and Adverbs in Comparisons

To compare two persons, places, or things, use the **comparative** form of adjectives or adverbs. This form often includes *than*.

Trina runs *faster* than I do.

Davio dances *more gracefully* than Harper does.

To compare three or more persons, places, or things, use the **superlative** form of adjectives or adverbs.

Trina runs the *fastest* of all our friends.

Davio is the *most graceful* of all the ballroom dancers.

Comparative and Superlative Forms

ADVERBS AND ADJECTIVES OF ONE SYLLABLE: Add *-er* to form the comparative and *-est* to form the superlative.

ADJECTIVE OR ADVERB	COMPARATIVE	SUPERLATIVE
tall	taller	tallest
fast	faster	fastest

Miguel is the tallest boy in the class.

ADJECTIVES ENDING IN -Y: Follow the same rule as for one-syllable words, but change the *-y* to *-i* before adding *-er* or *-est*.

ADJECTIVE OR ADVERB	COMPARATIVE	SUPERLATIVE
happy	happier	happiest
silly	sillier	silliest

That is the silliest joke I have ever heard.

ADVERBS AND ADJECTIVES OF MORE THAN ONE SYLLABLE: Add *more* to make the comparative and *most* to make the superlative.

ADJECTIVE OR ADVERB	COMPARATIVE	SUPERLATIVE
graceful	more graceful	most graceful
gracefully	more gracefully	most gracefully
intelligent	more intelligent	most intelligent
intelligently	more intelligently	most intelligently

Last night's debate was the most intelligent one I have ever seen.

■ **TIP:** Think of a syllable as a "beat": the word *ad-jec-tive* has three beats, or syllables.

■ **TIP:** For more on changing a final *-y* to *-i* when adding endings, and on other spelling changes involving endings, see Chapter 27.

Use either an ending (*-er* or *-est*) or an extra word (*more* or *most*) to form a comparative or superlative—not both at once.

Some say that Dale Earnhardt was the ~~most~~ greatest NASCAR driver ever.

Language note: Some languages, such as Spanish, always use words meaning *more* or *most* in comparisons, even when there is already the equivalent of an *-er* or *-est* ending on an adjective or adverb. If you do that when writing in English, pay special attention to this section and the practices.

PRACTICE 4 . . . .

In the blank next to each word, write the comparative form of the adjective or adverb.

EXAMPLES: tall   *taller*

beautiful   *more beautiful*

1. smart _____

2. strong _____

3. quietly _____

4. joyful _____

5. brief _____

6. wealthy _____

7. patiently _____

8. funny _____

9. thankful _____

10. normal _____

PRACTICE 5 . . . .

In the blank next to each word, write the superlative form of the adjective or adverb.

EXAMPLE: tall _____*tallest*_____

grateful __*most grateful*__

1. rich _____

2. glossy _____

3. proud _____

4. skillfully _____

5. sensible _____

6. cheap _____

7. bitter _____

8. hairy _____

9. impatiently _____

10. skinny _____

PRACTICE 6 . . . .

In each sentence, fill in the blank with the correct form of the adjective or adverb in parentheses.

> **EXAMPLE:** Some of the ___most interesting___ (*interesting*) inventions were accidental.

1. Ruth Wakefield, manager of the Toll House Inn, was baking butter cookies and wanted them to taste _____ (*sweet*) than other cookies.

2. She was out of baker's chocolate, so she cut a chocolate candy bar into the _____ (*small*) pieces possible.

3. She was certain that she would have the _____ (*tasty*) chocolate cookies she had ever eaten.

4. The chocolate was supposed to melt and make the cookies _____ (*delicious*) than regular butter cookies.

5. When she took the cookies out of the oven, she was the _____ (*surprised*) person in the inn.

6. The chocolate had not melted, and the cookies looked _____ (*strange*) than she had expected.

7. She served them anyway and her guests were the first to sample what became the _____ (*popular*) cookie in America.

8. She published her recipe, and everyone thought it made the _____ (*wonderful*) cookie ever baked.

9. The chocolate bar company responded _____ (*generous*) than she had hoped, offering her a lifetime supply of free chocolate if she allowed her recipe to be published on the chocolate bars' wrappers.

10. Today, Ruth Wakefield's Toll House chocolate chip cookies are one of the _____ (*favorite*) cookies in the United States.

> **PRACTICE 7** . . . .

Find and correct problems with comparative and superlative forms in the following paragraph. One sentence is correct; write "C" next to it.

(1) This summer, my family and I went to the most biggest amusement park in the state. (2) The first thing we saw was the wonderfulest gift shop that I have ever visited. (3) My little sister bought the most silliest red-and-yellow clown hat. (4) I was happy with a simple postcard showing a picture of the park. (5) Dad was hungry and got some chili that turned out to be more saltier than he imagined. (6) An hour later, we decided to ride the scarier ride in the park. (7) The line seemed to go on for miles, but it moved more quicklier than we had expected. (8) As we balanced on the edge of the first drop, I screamed loudlier than I had ever screamed before. (9) Everyone said it was the most bumpiest ride ever invented. (10) The end of the day came quickly, and I wish that we could have stayed more longer.

. . . .

Understanding *Good, Well, Bad,* and *Badly*

Good, well, bad, and *badly* do not follow the regular rules for forming comparatives and superlatives.

	COMPARATIVE	SUPERLATIVE
ADJECTIVE		
good	better	best
bad	worse	worst
ADVERB		
well	better	best
badly	worse	worst

Forms of Good, Well, Bad, *and* Badly

> ✍ If you had to act out *good/better/best* or *bad/worse/worst*, how would you show the differences?

People often get confused about whether to use *good* or *well*. *Good* is an adjective, so use it to describe a noun or pronoun. *Well* is an adverb, so use it to describe a verb or an adjective.

ADJECTIVE   Mike is a *good* person.

[The adjective *good* describes the noun *person*.]

ADVERB   He works *well* with others.

[The adverb *well* describes the verb *works*.]

Well can also be an adjective to describe someone's health.

INCORRECT   Mira is not feeling *good* today, so she might not sing *well*.

CORRECT   Mira is not feeling *well* today, so she might not sing *well*.

PRACTICE 8 . . . .

In each of the following sentences, underline the word that *good* or *well* modifies and then circle the correct word in parentheses.

EXAMPLE: Sometimes, recipes do not <u>work</u> (good/(well)).

1. In the past, some recipes didn't work because it was difficult to get (good/well) ingredients.

2. Not everyone's oven got hot enough to bake (good/well).

3. Also, many recipes were not written (good/well).

4. Instead of calling for a cup of flour, an old recipe might say, "Add enough flour until you can knead the dough (good/well)."

5. People interpreted this direction differently, so it was hard to end up with (good/well) dough.

6. In Boston, Fannie Farmer started a cooking school to teach home cooks how to cook (good/well).

7. At that time, the only people who formally learned to cook (good/well) were chefs.

8. She insisted that every recipe have a standard measurement so that the dish would always be (good/well).

9. Then, she wrote exact measurements for (good/well) recipes in her famous *Boston Cooking School Cook Book.*

10. Thanks to Fannie Farmer, we know that if we follow (good/well) directions, the results will be delicious.

PRACTICE 9 . .

In each of the following sentences, circle the correct comparative or superlative form of *good* or *bad* in parentheses, first underlining the word that is being described.

> **EXAMPLE:** When combined with regular exercise, a healthful diet is one of the (better/best) ways to stay fit.

1. Many people think that a salad is a (better/best) choice than a burger.

2. However, a salad loaded with high-fat cheese, bacon, and dressing could be (worse/worst) than a sensible turkey burger.

3. What is the (better/best) beverage to drink in the morning?

4. Orange juice is (better/best) than coffee, but it's healthier to eat an orange.

5. The (better/best) choice is plain water; your body loses fluid while you sleep and needs to be rehydrated in the morning.

6. What is the (worse/worst) type of breakfast food?

7. Doughnuts are obviously much (worse/worst) than cereal.

8. A fiber-rich food that contains B vitamins is among the (better/best) breakfast foods.

9. Bran flakes are good, but oatmeal is even (better/best).

10. Add some toasted pumpkin seeds and honey, and you'll have the (better/best) breakfast for your health.

Edit Adjectives and Adverbs in College, Work, and Everyday Life

Complete the editing reviews as instructed, referring to the chart on page 309.

EDITING REVIEW 1: COLLEGE . . . .

Edit the adjectives and adverbs in the following paragraph. Two sentences are correct; write "C" next to them. The first sentence has been edited for you.

(1) College tuition costs are ~~more~~ higher than ever before. (2) At Merriweather College, financial aid advisers are available to help students understand the different types of financial aid available. (3) The commonest types of aid include scholarships, loans, and military aid. (4) Scholarships exist for students who perform good in academics or athletics. (5) Scholarships are also available for students specializing in fields such as agriculture or nursing. (6) For many students, government loans are gooder than private loans. (7) Government loans don't require credit checks, and they usual offer the lowest interest rates. (8) The popularest loans are the Stafford and the Perkins. (9) Finally, students can enroll in Reserve Officers Training Corps (ROTC) for funds, and veterans can also obtain well tuition benefits. (10) Students with questions should contact the financial aid department, and a meeting with an adviser will be set up quick.

EDITING REVIEW 2: WORK . . . .

Edit the adjectives and adverbs in the following business letter. Two sentences are correct; write "C" next to them. The first sentence has been edited for you.

Mr. David Jones

Cooperative Canning Company

235 Paxton Boulevard

Philadelphia, PA 19104

Dear Mr. Jones:

(1) Thank you for interviewing me on Thursday and giving me such a
thorough
~~thoroughly~~ tour of your factory. (2) Your production line was one of the
efficientest I have seen in my years in the industry. (3) I was particular
impressed with the quality-control system. (4) As I said when we met, I
am real interested in the position of production manager. (5) I have fifteen years' experience in similar positions and a degree in mechanical
engineering. (6) My education and experience would help me operate
your good system even gooder. (7) I would also enjoy the challenge of
developing more newer methods for increasing production and improving plant safety.

(8) If you have questions or would like to interview me again, you
can reach me at (123) 555-1234. (9) I hope you consider me a well
candidate for your management team. (10) I am available to begin
immediate.

Sincerely,

Ty Manfred

EDITING REVIEW 3: EVERYDAY LIFE . . . .

Edit the adjectives and adverbs in the following essay. Three sentences are
correct; write "C" next to them. The first sentence has been edited for you.

new
(1) At military boot camps, ~~newly~~ recruits receive physical and psychological training. (2) Boot camps emphasize discipline and hard work
in a real intense environment. (3) Recruits are pushed to learn new responsibilities and skills quick. (4) Recently, this idea has been expanded,
and many people are paying hundreds of dollars to attend nonmilitary
boot camps.

(5) Juvenile boot camps teach respect and discipline to teenagers
who behave bad. (6) However, some people believe that forcing a teen

to attend boot camp causes even worser behavior. (7) Boot camps that teach life skills or hobbies to adults offer a pleasanter environment than military or juvenile boot camps. (8) At poker camp, for example, students spend several days learning to become a more good player. (9) At the end of the camp, the bestest player gets to join the World Poker Tournament. (10) At one writers' boot camp, participants work toward the goal of completing a screenplay in weeks. (11) Golf camp participants take lessons from some of the most greatest professional golfers. (12) The camp is challenginger than it sounds; between lessons, participants go through difficult drills. (13) Even Oprah is part of this most latest fad. (14) She has developed a well weight-loss program called Oprah's Boot Camp. (15) The program consists of a strictly diet and eight workouts a week.

(16) To some people, nothing sounds worst than boot camp. (17) Others, however, find that the strict environment is just what they need. (18) Boot camp can be incredible difficult, but the results are often worth the effort.

Write and Edit Your Own Work

ASSIGNMENT 1: WRITE

Describe your favorite place, using as many adjectives and adverbs as you can. When you're done, use the chart on page 309 to check the adjectives and adverbs. Correct any mistakes that you find.

ASSIGNMENT 2: EDIT

Using the chart on page 309, edit adjectives and adverbs in a paper you are writing for this course or another course or in a piece of writing from your work or everyday life.

Practice Together

Working with a few other students, practice what you have learned in this chapter.

1. One person in your group should say a noun, like *monster*. Then, the second person should add an adjective, and the third person should add another adjective. Keep going until everyone has supplied an adjective. Then, as a group, write a sentence that includes the noun and all the adjectives. Have someone read it to the class. 🎧 📖

2. Think of a well-known person, place, or thing. Then, as a group, write down several adjectives that describe the person, place, or thing. Have someone read your descriptions to the rest of the class. Can the class guess who or what you are trying to describe? If not, come up with more adjectives until someone guesses correctly. 🎧 📖

3. Each group member should draw a picture of some person, object, or activity that interests them. Then, members should take turns holding up their pictures. Other group members should each say one sentence that includes an adjective or adverb describing the picture. Keep going until each person's picture has been described. 👁 🎧 👣

4. Each group member should think of someone who excels at something: a friend, a relative, an athlete, or another professional. Then, he or she should think of an adjective or adverb for this person. Next, he or she should stand up and use the description in a statement, in a comparative sentence, and in a superlative sentence.

   EXAMPLE: My uncle is a *good* cook. My uncle cooks *better* than anyone else in my family. My uncle is the *best* cook in my family. 🎧 👣

Chapter Review

1. _____ describe nouns, and _____ describe verbs, adjectives, or other adverbs.

2. Adverbs often end in _____.

3. The comparative form of an adjective or adverb is used to compare how many people, places, or things? _____ It is formed by adding an _____ ending or the word _____.

4. The superlative form of an adjective or adverb is used to compare how many people, places, or things? _____ It is formed by adding an _____ ending or the word _____.

5. What four words do not follow the regular rules for forming compara-

   tives and superlatives? _____

6. *Good* is an (adjective / adverb) and *well* is an (adjective / adverb).

7. **VOCABULARY:** Go back to any new words that you underlined in this
   chapter. Can you guess their meanings now? If not, look up the words
   in a dictionary.

LEARNING JOURNAL:
Write for two minutes about
specific adjectives or adverbs
that have confused you. What
advice from this chapter will
help you remember the correct forms?

■ **TIP:** For help with
building your vocabulary,
see Appendix B.

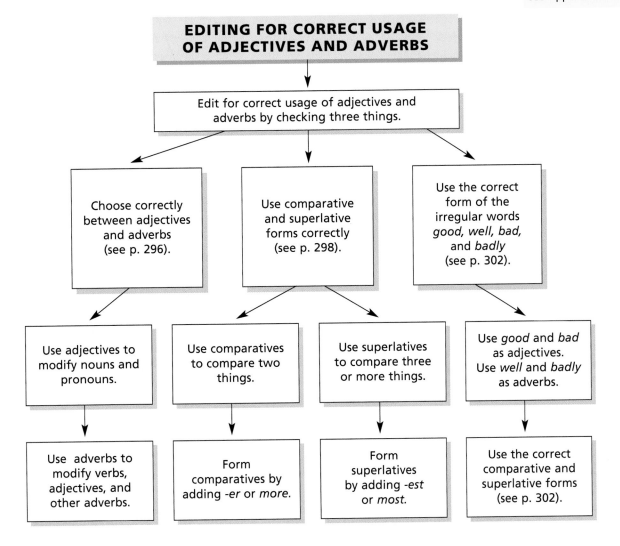

**EDITING FOR CORRECT USAGE
OF ADJECTIVES AND ADVERBS**

Edit for correct usage of adjectives and
adverbs by checking three things.

Choose correctly
between adjectives
and adverbs
(see p. 296).

Use comparative
and superlative
forms correctly
(see p. 298).

Use the correct
form of the
irregular words
good, well, bad,
and *badly*
(see p. 302).

Use adjectives to
modify nouns and
pronouns.

Use comparatives
to compare two
things.

Use superlatives
to compare three
or more things.

Use *good* and *bad*
as adjectives.
Use *well* and *badly*
as adverbs.

Use adverbs to
modify verbs,
adjectives, and
other adverbs.

Form
comparatives by
adding *-er* or *more.*

Form
superlatives
by adding *-est*
or *most.*

Use the correct
comparative and
superlative forms
(see p. 302).

19

Misplaced and Dangling Modifiers

Avoiding Confusing Descriptions

📖 **VOCABULARY:** Under-line any words in this chapter that are new to you.

📖 **IDEA JOURNAL:** Write about a time when you were confused about something and then overcame your confusion.

Understand What Misplaced Modifiers Are

Modifiers are words or word groups that describe other words in a sentence.

The man *who came in late* is Marla's father.

[The words *who came in late* modify *man*.]

Unless the modifier is near the words it describes, the sentence can be confusing or funny.

READ ALOUD 🗣️ 📖

The modifying words in the example sentences that follow are in italics. Read the sentences aloud and explain what they mean as written. The first one is explained for you.

A **misplaced modifier**, because it is not correctly placed in the sentence, describes the wrong word or words.

MISPLACED   Risa saw Sanjay's cat *painting her house.*

[Was Sanjay's cat painting Risa's house? No, Risa was painting her house, so the modifier must come right before or right after her name.]

CORRECT   *Painting her house*, Risa saw Sanjay's cat.

Four types of modifiers are often misplaced:

- **Modifiers such as *only*, *almost*, *hardly*, *nearly*, and *just*.**

  I ~~only~~ drove *only* thirty miles on my vacation.

  Carla ~~nearly~~ needed *nearly* ten cans of peaches.

- **Modifiers that start with *-ing* verbs.**

  Using a soft cloth, Taylor polished the car hood ~~using a soft cloth~~.

  Opening the closet, Candice found her daughter's hamster ~~opening the closet~~.

- **Modifiers that are prepositional phrases.**

  Catherine was carrying the luggage for her sister *to the taxi* ~~to the taxi~~.

  I found the bill in the drawer *from the dry cleaner* ~~from the dry cleaner~~.

- **Modifiers that are clauses starting with *who*, *whose*, *that*, or *which*.**

  Babysitters are the most popular *who play with children* ~~who play with children~~.

  I returned the shirt to the store *that was torn* ~~that was torn~~.

Language note: People whose native language is not English often confuse the word pairs *almost/most* and *too/very*.

Almost = nearly
Most = the largest share of

INCORRECT	Almost students had problems with that question.
CORRECT	Most students had problems with that question.
INCORRECT	We are most there.
CORRECT	We are almost there.

Too = more than desired
Very = extremely

INCORRECT	The weather today is too beautiful.
CORRECT	The weather today is very beautiful.
INCORRECT	It's very late to call.
CORRECT	It's too late to call.

Find and Correct Misplaced Modifiers

> **FIND: Read each sentence in your writing carefully.**
>
> (Megan) found the lost dog <u>driving to the store</u>.
>
> • Underline any modifying words.
> • Circle the word or words that are being modified.
> • Ask if the modifying words are close to what is being described. In this example, the answer is "no." [*Driving to the store* modifies *Megan*, but these words are next to *dog*.]

> **FIX: Move the modifying words next to what is being described.**
>
> *Driving to the store,*
> **Megan found the lost dog** ~~driving to the store~~.
>   ^   ^
>
> When the modifying words begin the sentence, they are followed by a comma.

PRACTICE 1 . . . .

Find and correct misplaced modifiers in the following sentences. Two sentences are correct; write "C" next to them.

> **EXAMPLE:** ~~Having a party in her backyard,~~ I often see my next-door
>   *having a party in her backyard.*
>   neighbor.
>   ^

1. I received an invitation to Mrs. Garcia's upcoming barbecue in the mail.

2. She had invited many guests who were bringing food.

3. Mrs. Garcia wanted to use her new grill who likes to barbecue.

4. In the oven, I decided to bake some beans.

5. I burned the beans losing track of time.

6. I gave the beans to my dogs which were ruined.

7. Mrs. Garcia fired up the grill in her backyard with the extra-large cooking racks.

8. The guests almost began arriving twenty minutes early.

9. Eating juicy burgers, everyone looked forward to having dessert.

10. I almost ate three pieces of the delicious lemon pie.

PRACTICE 2 . . . ·

Rewrite each of the following sentences, adding a modifying word or phrase according to the directions in parentheses.

EXAMPLE: Dylan came home with one book. (Add *only* to make the
sentence mean that Dylan brought home a single book.)

ANSWER: *Dylan came home with only one book.*

1. The instructions explain how to install the fan's blades. (Add *in the first paragraph* to make the sentence mean that the explanation was found in the first paragraph.)

_____

_____

2. James left a voice-mail message for his manager. (Add *who was sick* to make the sentence mean that James was sick.)

_____

_____

3. Lilly saw a beautiful butterfly. (Add *working in the garden* to make the sentence mean that Lilly was working in the garden).

_____

_____

4. Shari remembered to return the sweater to her sister. (Add *who is usually forgetful* to make the sentence mean that Shari is usually forgetful.)

_____

_____

5. He left the screen door open. (Add *nearly* to make the sentence mean that he almost left the door open.)

_____

_____

■ **TIP:** For more practice, visit Exercise Central at <**bedfordstmartins.com/ realskills**>.

6. Jon watched the hawk sitting in the tree. (Add *from the kitchen window* to make the sentence mean that Jon looked out of the kitchen window to watch the hawk).

_____

_____

7. Julia keeps a sweatshirt in her backpack. (Add *that is comfortable* to make the sentence mean that the sweatshirt is comfortable.)

_____

_____

8. The lifeguard thought that the waves were too high for the man. (Add *who was a poor swimmer* to make the sentence mean that the man was a poor swimmer.)

_____

_____

9. James has completed the entire lesson. (Add *nearly* to make the sentence mean that James is almost finished completing the lesson.)

_____

_____

10. Gracie and Crystal helped the tourist. (Add *who appeared to be lost* so that it describes the tourist.)

_____

_____

. . . .

Understand What Dangling Modifiers Are

A **dangling modifier** "dangles" because the word or words it is supposed to describe are not in the sentence. A dangling modifier is usually at the beginning of the sentence and seems to modify the noun after it, but it really doesn't.

DANGLING	*Looking under the dresser,* a dust ball went up my nose.
	[Was the dust ball looking under the dresser? No.]
CORRECT	*Looking under the dresser,* I inhaled a dust ball.
	[The correction adds the word being modified right after the opening modifier.]
CORRECT	While I was *looking under the dresser,* a dust ball went up my nose.
	[The correction adds the word being modified to the opening modifier itself.]

Find and Correct Dangling Modifiers

FIND: Read each sentence in your writing carefully.

Skating down the sidewalk, a fire erupted in a neighbor's trash can.

- Underline any modifying words. (Dangling modifiers often appear at the beginning of a sentence.)
- Ask if you can find the word or words being modified. [In this example, nothing is logically modified by *Skating down the sidewalk*. The fire couldn't be skating down the sidewalk.]

FIX: Add the word being modified right after the modifying words, or make it part of the modifying words. You might need to reword the sentence so that it makes sense.

I saw a fire erupt
Skating down the sidewalk, a ~~fire erupted~~ in a neighbor's trash can.
                                    ^

While I was skating
~~Skating~~ down the sidewalk, a fire erupted in a neighbor's trash can.
^

DANGLING   Buying stereo equipment online, shipping can cost more than the equipment.

[*Buying stereo equipment online* does not modify *shipping*.]

CORRECT   When buying stereo equipment online, you may find that the shipping costs more than the equipment.

[By adding *when* to the modifying words *buying stereo equipment online* and changing the second part of the sentence to *you may find that*, the correction makes the modifying words describe the right word: *you*.]

DANGLING   Eating at Jimmy's Restaurant, the pizza had a bug on it.

CORRECT   Eating at Jimmy's Restaurant, I found a bug on my pizza.

 Draw your own picture of a sentence with a dangling modifier. Then, draw the corrected sentence.

PRACTICE 3 · · · · · · · · · · · · · ·

Find and correct dangling modifiers in the following sentences. Two sentences are correct; write "C" next to them. It may be necessary to add new words or ideas to some sentences.

I found
EXAMPLE: Getting ready to audition for the talent show, the back-
                                                        ^
stage area ~~was~~ noisy.

1. Practicing my song, my costume made a ripping sound.

2. Terrified that something was wrong, the audition was about to start.

3. With fear closing my throat, I tried to find where the costume had torn.

4. Trying to help, the tiny dressing room was crowded.

5. Checking the whole costume, it was hard to see in the dimly lit dressing room.

6. Sensing my panic, the costume was checked again to reassure me.

7. Worried, the ripping sound still echoed in my head.

8. Trying to focus on my song, my costume still bothered me.

9. Pulling myself together, I went onstage.

10. Beginning to sing my song, the audience laughed as they noticed the hole in my dress.

PRACTICE 4 . . . .

Combine the sentence pairs, turning one sentence into a modifying word group.

EXAMPLE: **I walked slowly down the street. I ate an icy Popsicle.**

Walking slowly down the street, I ate an icy Popsicle.

1. We arrived early. We got good seats for the concert.

   _____

2. Tomas enjoyed the snack. He nibbled cheese and munched on peanuts.

   _____

3. Carlo wants to be a gymnast. He must practice every day.

   _____

4. I took a bowl out to the barn. I fed the kittens.

   _____

5. I was frightened by the spider. I almost dropped my can of soda.

   _____

6. Jackson found an old diary in the attic. He gave it to his uncle.

_____

7. I saw a strange parrot. It was sitting on a perch in the pet shop.

_____

8. I realized I was tired. I nearly fell asleep over my book.

_____

9. Gino was bored with the movie. He turned off the television.

_____

10. Anthony was startled by the strange sound. He ran back into the house.

_____

Edit Misplaced and Dangling Modifiers in College, Work, and Everyday Life

Complete the editing reviews as instructed, referring to the chart on page 322.

EDITING REVIEW 1: COLLEGE

The following paragraph is similar to one you might find in a criminal-justice textbook. Edit the modifiers in it. Two sentences are correct; write "C" next to them. The first sentence has been edited for you.

(1) Hoping to make their streets safer, *some communities are trying* new crime-fighting programs, ~~are being tried by some communities~~. (2) Community policing links police departments with local community groups, which is one of these new programs. (3) Identifying the problems that are most important to the community, goals are set. (4) Working together, the goals are easier to meet. (5) Actively involved with the people in their precincts, the program requires a strong commitment. (6) Often, officers set up mini-stations within neighborhoods. (7) Patrolling on foot rather than in cars, a sense of security and community is created. (8) Officers often sponsor local events who participate in community policing. (9) They are always

looking for ways with the community to establish better ties. (10) The partnerships help both the police and the people that are formed by these programs. (11) Community policing programs have reduced crime and improved the relationships between police departments and the communities they serve.

EDITING REVIEW 2: WORK

Edit the modifiers in the following e-mail. In addition to the first sentence, which has been marked for you, three sentences are correct; write "C" next to them.

Friday, 3/10/2006, 1:14 p.m.

FROM: Don Pimentel

TO: MiHiTech Customer Service

SUBJECT: Software problem with new laptop

Dear MiHiTech Customer Service:

(1) *C* On February 26, I purchased a laptop computer from MiHiTech. (2) Guaranteeing that the computer would be equipped with the most up-to-date word-processing software, I was pleased with my purchase.

(3) Opening the word-processing program, the computer comes with version 5.0 rather than version 6.0. (4) Because I use this computer for my home business, a program is important to me that can handle customers' files. (5) Because most of my customers use version 6.0, I am writing to request an updated version of the program. (6) If that is not possible, I would like to return my computer for a full refund.

(7) For the past five years, I have nearly used MiHiTech for all of my technology needs. (8) Resolving this issue, I can continue to shop at your store. (9) Please let me know your decision as soon as possible.

Sincerely,

Don Pimentel

EDITING REVIEW 3: EVERYDAY LIFE . . . .

Edit the modifiers in the following passage. Two sentences are correct; write "C" next to them. The first sentence has been edited for you.

(1) Invented in 2001, *iPods are now used by* an estimated twenty-two million people ~~now use an iPod.~~ (2) If you almost walk down any city street, you're sure to see someone wearing iPod headphones. (3) Looking around any college campus, iPods are seen everywhere.

(4) It's not hard to see why these gadgets are so popular. (5) Music fans can keep thousands of songs in their pocket by different artists. (6) Paying less than a dollar per song, endless hours of entertainment can be downloaded. (7) People especially love their iPods who ride public transportation. (8) Shutting out background noise, a bus or subway ride is more relaxing. (9) Popular among athletes, many people enjoy their exercise more. (10) Listening to music, talk programs, or audio books, time passes more quickly.

(11) Some people say that iPods are just a fad. (12) However, most people would disagree who own an iPod. (13) If the trend continues, soon everyone will nearly have iPods.

Write and Edit Your Own Work

ASSIGNMENT 1: WRITE . . . .

Write about a busy day, using as many modifying word groups as you can. When you're done, use the chart on page 322 to check for misplaced and dangling modifiers. Correct any mistakes that you find.

ASSIGNMENT 2: EDIT . . . .

Using the chart on page 322, edit modifiers in a paper you are writing for this course or another course or in a piece of writing from your work or everyday life.

Practice Together

Working with a few other students, practice what you have learned in this chapter.

1. Your instructor will give your group slips of paper that, together, will form a sentence with modifying words. As a group, decide the correct order for the sentence parts. Add capitalization and punctuation as needed. If your sentence needs words to make sense, add them to a separate slip and insert them. When you're done, call out, "Ready!" Then, have one group member stand up and read the sentence aloud. The first group to correctly form the sentence wins. 👁 ⑊ 📖 ⥇

2. Choose one of the following sentences and, as a group, draw a picture of what the sentence says. (It's best if each group chooses a different sentence.) Write the sentence at the bottom. Post the drawing and sentence on the wall. Next, groups should walk from drawing to drawing, copying the sentences and deciding on ways to correct them. 👁 ⑊ 📖 ⥇

I introduced myself to the woman who was walking a dog wearing a fur coat.

As a single mother, my son has no father figure in his life.

We found a dress at the thrift store with gold buttons.

The president of the company attended the party with her husband dressed in a blue gown.

3. **NOTE:** This activity requires a ten-person team—nine people to hold the word sheets and one person to call out the meanings.

Write each of the following words/word groups on a separate sheet of paper. (Write them large and dark enough so that people sitting at a distance can read them.)

[Ellen] [told] [her] [brother] [she] [bought] [the milk] [yesterday] [only]

Each person should hold a different sheet of paper. Then, another person should call out the following meanings one at a time. The paper holders should rearrange themselves to fit with the described meaning.

Ellen didn't tell other people (only her brother).

Ellen has one brother (her only brother).

Ellen's mother didn't buy any milk (only Ellen did).

Ellen didn't get the rest of the groceries (only the milk).

Ellen bought the milk recently (only yesterday).

It's not easy being married to the President.

Chapter Review

LEARNING JOURNAL:
Write for two minutes about misplaced and dangling modifiers you have found in your work, noting specific examples. How would you correct them?

1. _____ are words or word groups that describe other words in a sentence.

2. A _____ describes the wrong word or words.

3. Modifiers need to be placed _____ the words they describe.

4. When there is a _____, the word or words that are supposed to be modified are not in the sentence.

5. When you find a dangling modifier, add the word being modified _____ the opening modifier, or add the word being modified _____.

6. **VOCABULARY:** Go back to any new words that you underlined in this chapter. Can you guess their meanings now? If not, look up the words in a dictionary.

■ **TIP:** For help with building your vocabulary, see Appendix B.

EDITING FOR MISPLACED AND DANGLING MODIFIERS

A misplaced modifier modifies the wrong sentence element because it is incorrectly placed (see p. 310).

A dangling modifier is an opening word group that modifies an element that is not in the sentence (see p. 314).

Check the modifiers *only, almost, hardly, nearly,* and *just.*

Check opening modifiers, especially phrases and clauses.

Check prepositional phrases.

Check phrases beginning with *-ing* verb forms.

Check clauses beginning with *who, whose, that,* or *which.*

Edit to ensure that the sentence element to be modified is in the sentence and is as close as possible to the modifier.

20
Illogical Shifts
Avoiding Inconsistencies

Understand Consistent Tense

Tense is the time when an action takes place (past, present, or future). **Consistent tense** means that all verbs in a sentence that describe actions happening at the same time are in the same tense: all in the present, all in past, or all in the future.

INCONSISTENT	As soon as the actor *climbed* onto the life raft, the shark *leaps* from the water.
	[Both actions (the actor's climbing and the shark's leaping) happened at the same time, but *climbed* is in the past tense, and *leaps* is in the present tense.]
CONSISTENT, PRESENT TENSE	As soon as the actor *climbs* onto the life raft, the shark *leaps* from the water.
	[The actions and verb tenses are both in the present.]
CONSISTENT, PAST TENSE	As soon as the actor *climbed* onto the life raft, the shark *leaped* from the water.
	[The actions and verb tenses are both in the past.]

323

Find and Correct Inconsistent Tenses

■ **TIP:** To do this chapter, you need to know what subjects and verbs are. For a review, see Chapter 10.

FIND: Read each sentence in your writing carefully.

Although I like my old job, I took a new one because of its higher salary.

- Underline the verbs.
- Ask what tense each verb is in. [*Like* is in the present tense, and *took* is in the past tense.]
- Unless the actions take place at different times, the tenses must be consistent. [In the example, the actions took place in the past, so *like* is inconsistent.]

FIX: Replace the inconsistent verb with a form that is consistent.

liked
Although I ~~like~~ my old job, I took a new one because of its higher salary.

 IDEA JOURNAL: What things have changed recently in your life? What has stayed the same?

INCONSISTENT

Whenever I *go* to the store, I *left* the children with their aunt.

[*Go* is in the present tense, but *left* is in the past tense.]

June *pulled* out of the driveway just as the salesperson *arrives*.

[*Pulled* is in the past tense, but *arrives* is in the present tense.]

Good service *pleases* customers and *was* good for business.

[*Pleases* is in the present tense, but *was* is in the past tense.]

CONSISTENT

Whenever I *go* to the store, I *leave* the children with their aunt.

[Both verbs are in the present tense.]

Jane *pulled* out of the driveway just as the salesperson *arrived*.

[Both verbs are in the past tense.]

Good service *pleases* customers and *is* good for business.

[Both verbs are in the present tense.]

Language note: For summary charts on the various verb tenses, see Chapter 21.

PRACTICE 1 . .

In each of the following sentences, circle the correct verb tense.

(1) Although he wanted to be an artist, Rube Goldberg (begins/ began) his career as an engineer. (2) After six months, he left his job and (gets/got) a position as an office assistant at a newspaper. (3) In his free time, he drew cartoons and (submits/submitted) them to one of the newspaper's editors. (4) He continued submitting cartoons until the editor finally (agrees/agreed) to publish them. (5) Goldberg quickly gained fame as a sports cartoonist, but a different type of cartoon (becomes/became) his most famous creation. (6) In 1914, he sketched a funny-looking professor and (names/named) him Professor Lucifer Gorgonzola Butts. (7) Goldberg (begins/began) drawing comic strips that featured the professor's crazy inventions. (8) In one strip, for example, Goldberg (draws/drew) an automatic stamp licker consisting of a tiny robot, a bucket of ants, and an anteater. (9) Today, people use the term *Rube Goldberg* to describe any process that (is/was) unnecessarily complicated. (10) Goldberg died in 1970, but fans today still (enjoy/ enjoyed) his funny drawings.

> 👁 In this chapter and in your own writing, try highlighting all the verbs in one color. Then, check for shifts.

PRACTICE 2 . .

In the following paragraph, correct any unnecessary shifts in verb tense. Three sentences are correct; write "C" next to them.

(1) The first time I tried skydiving, I was terrified. (2) Even though I knew I was going to be jumping with an instructor, I got more and more nervous as the plane climb to ten thousand feet. (3) The side door was open so that I could see the fields far below me. (4) I think, "Why am I doing this?" (5) When my instructor gave the sign to jump, we leap out together and fell for what seemed like forever. (6) Then, the instructor activates my parachute, and I get pulled up suddenly. (7) After the parachute opened, I begin a graceful and relaxing landing. (8) That was the best part of all!

> ■ **TIP:** For more practice, visit Exercise Central at <**bedfordstmartins.com/ realskills**>.

Understand Consistent Person

Person is the point of view a writer uses: **first person** (the pronouns *I* or *we*), **second person** (the pronoun *you*), or **third person** (the pronouns *he*, *she*, *it*, or *they*). To find out which pronouns go with what person, see the table on page 280.

Consistent person means that the nouns and pronouns stay consistent.

INCONSISTENT PERSON	When *a customer* comes into the office, *you* can't tell where the reception area is.
	[The sentence begins with a third-person noun (*a customer*) but shifts to the second person (with the pronoun *you*).]
CONSISTENT PERSON	When *a customer* comes into the office, *he or she* can't tell where the reception area is.
	[The sentence stays with the third person.]
CONSISTENT PERSON, PLURAL	When *customers* come into the office, *they* can't tell where the reception area is.
	[The sentence stays with the third person.]

Find and Correct Inconsistent Person

FIND: Read each sentence in your writing carefully.

I had the right address, but to get to the office, <u>you</u> had to go around to the back.

- Underline all of the subject nouns and pronouns in the sentence.
- If pronouns with the same antecedent shift in person, there is an error. [The person could be first (*I*, *we*), second (*you*), or third (*he*, *she*, *it*, or *they*). In the example, *I* is a first-person pronoun and *you* is a second-person pronoun.]

FIX: Change the inconsistent pronoun.

I had the right address, but to get to the office, ~~you~~ had to go around to the back.

INCONSISTENT

Every *student* must learn how to manage *your* own time.

[The sentence shifts from third to second person.]

I like to go to crafts fairs because *you* can get good ideas for projects.

[The sentence shifts from first to second person.]

CONSISTENT

Every *student* must learn how to manage *his or her* time.

[The sentence stays in the third person. **NOTE:** This sentence could also be fixed by making the subject and the pronoun referring to it plural: *Students must learn to manage their own time.*]

I like to go to crafts fairs because *I* can get good ideas for projects.

[The sentence stays in the first person.]

PRACTICE 3 · ·

In the following sentences, correct any illogical shifts in person. There may be more than one way to correct some sentences.

> **EXAMPLE:** Drivers can follow some simple tips to help improve
>   *their*
>   ~~your~~ gas mileage.

1. Whether a person has a new car or an old one, you can still take some steps to save gas.

2. For example, I combine my errands so that you don't have to make a lot of separate trips.

3. A driver should also make sure that their trunk is empty because extra weight causes the car to use more gas.

4. Drivers can save fuel by taking the roof rack off your cars.

5. People should not drive aggressively or fast if you want to improve gas mileage.

6. I have been told to keep your engine tuned.

7. I know that keeping the tires inflated improves your gas mileage.

8. Every driver should read their owner's manual.

9. It tells drivers about correct tire inflation and gasoline quality so that your cars will be cheaper to run.

10. I also learned that changing the air filter regularly can increase your gas mileage by 10 percent or more.

. . . .

READ ALOUD

Read the following sentences aloud, emphasizing the words in bold. Can you hear the shifts in tense and person?

> We **hiked** for miles and miles, but we never **find** the secret cave.

> In the play, the king **kills** his brother and then **married** his brother's wife.

> I like scary movies because **you** can never tell what is going to pop out of the dark.

> **We** spent only a day in Lakilaw Park because **you** are not allowed to put up a tent there.

Edit Illogical Shifts in College, Work, and Everyday Life

Complete the editing reviews as instructed, referring to the chart on page 332.

> **EDITING REVIEW 1: COLLEGE** . .

Edit illogical shifts in the following paragraph, which is similar to one you might find in an anthropology textbook. Two sentences are correct; write "C" next to them. The first sentence has been edited for you.

(1) Around ten thousand years ago, early humans ~~learn~~ *learned* how to keep animals and grow crops. (2) Before then, all people were hunter-gatherers, and you survived on wild animals and plants. (3) The men used simple tools to hunt, while the women gather wild fruits, vegetables, honey, and birds' eggs. (4) Although hunter-gatherers moved about in search of food, the area you covered was relatively small. (5) Hunter-gatherer societies typically consisted of about twenty to fifty people, and tasks are shared by all. (6) In fact, sharing was critical to survival. (7) According

to archaeologists, people treat each other equally in hunter-gatherer societies. (8) Today, less than 0.1 percent of the world's population lives in a hunter-gatherer society. (9) When agriculture spread throughout the world, the hunter-gatherer way of life mostly ends. (10) Anthropologists know of a few groups that can still be considered hunter-gatherer societies, but you cannot find many people who are untouched by agriculture and industry.

EDITING REVIEW 2: WORK · · · · · · · · · · · · · · · · ·

Edit illogical shifts in the following paragraph. Outside of the first sentence, which has been marked for you, two sentences are correct; write "C" next to them.

(1) *C* In a typical marketing exchange, companies sell products, services, or ideas to buyers. (2) For example, an advertising agency might design and sold a logo to a start-up corporation. (3) Automobile manufacturers build cars, and then you sell them to customers. (4) Until the 1980s, many companies were satisfied with these one-time sales, and you did not focus on long-term customer relationships. (5) Today, however, marketing departments want to create repeat customers. (6) Automakers want to sell current customers your next car as well. (7) The ad agency might help the start-up organization place ads on radio and television. (8) When companies and buyers form long-term partnerships, you both benefit.

EDITING REVIEW 3: EVERYDAY LIFE · · · · · · · · · · · · · · · · ·

Edit illogical shifts in the following passage. Three sentences are correct; write "C" next to them. The first sentence has been edited for you.

(1) As people answer phones, review e-mail messages, and respond to text messages, *they* ~~you~~ become overwhelmed. (2) Many people answer messages while on vacation and worked extra hours on their days off. (3) Worse, overuse of technology may lower people's IQ and damaged their relationships.

(4) A recent British study found that excessive use of e-mail can actually lower a person's IQ score by about ten points. (5) In the study, workers who tried to juggle e-mail and voice-mail messages while working on other tasks score lower on IQ tests than those who focused on a single task. (6) Apparently, the distractions made the workers less alert and lowered your productivity.

(7) Other experts believe that technology leads to social isolation. (8) Some people, however, point out that technology helped them stay in touch with families and friends. (9) People must find a balance between being "connected" to work and connecting in meaningful ways with people outside of work.

Write and Edit Your Own Work

ASSIGNMENT 1: WRITE

Write about a past or current event that is significant to you. When you're done, check the verbs for consistency of tense and the nouns for consistency of person. Use the chart on page 332 as a guide, and correct any mistakes that you find.

ASSIGNMENT 2: EDIT

Using the chart on page 332, edit illogical shifts in a paper you are writing for this course or another course or in a piece of writing from your work or everyday life.

Practice Together

■ **LEARNING STYLES:** Look for activities in this chapter that are matched to your learning style. If you don't know your learning style, take the test on pages 26–28.

 Visual

Auditory

Reading/writing

Kinesthetic (movement)

Working with a few other students, practice what you have learned in this chapter.

1. Write a story that begins with this line: "I knew that my day was going to be great as soon as I got up." Pass a sheet of paper from person to person, and have each group member add a sentence to the story, making up an example of a good thing that happened. (Each person might take two turns to make the story detailed.) When the story is completed, one

person should read it aloud while the others listen for consistency of tense (past) and person (first). Group members should call out any errors that they find so that the reader can mark them. 🗣 📖 ✍

2. Read the following paragraph aloud, with each group member taking a different sentence. After each sentence is read, the reader should declare the sentence "consistent" or "inconsistent" in tense. If the sentence is inconsistent, the reader should call out the verbs that need to be changed and change them. Others should point out any verbs that the reader might have missed. 🗣 📖

Yesterday, I was crossing the street when I nearly got run over by a truck. The driver of the truck screeched to a halt and yells, "Get out of the way, stupid!" So I yell back at him. When he starts revving his truck up like he's going to run me over, I decided to get to the curb fast. I don't know what's wrong with the guy. My sister says he's probably in a bad mood because he's breaking up with his girlfriend.

3. Read the following paragraph aloud, with each group member taking a different sentence. After each sentence is read, the reader should declare the sentence "consistent" or "inconsistent" in person. If the sentence is inconsistent, the reader should call out the nouns that need to be changed and change them. Others should point out any nouns that the reader might have missed. 🗣 📖

Some doctors seem to think that they are more important than nurses, but nurses have a very tough job. In an office setting, you try your best to keep both patients and the doctor satisfied. However, the doctor may yell at you for things that are not your fault. At a hospital, nurses do most of the work, but you are not often recognized. Fortunately, nurses have each other to talk to when you run into problems. We need that support, because we just don't get any respect.

4. Divide your group into two smaller groups. Each group should describe the picture on page 58 in two different ways: in the present tense and in the past tense. (Pick a person to write down the stories.) Then, join the two groups and compare your stories. Is each story consistent in tense? 👁 🗣 📖

Chapter Review

1. _____ means that all verbs in a sentence that describe actions happening at the same time are in the same tense.

2. To fix sentences that are inconsistent in tense, replace inconsistent _____ with forms that are consistent.

■ **TIP:** For help with building your vocabulary, see Appendix B.

📖 **LEARNING JOURNAL:** Which is more difficult for you, keeping tense consistent or keeping person consistent? Write for two minutes about this, and think of ways that you could help yourself keep your writing consistent.

3. _____ means that the point of view of a piece of writing does not shift without reason.

4. To fix sentences that are inconsistent in person, replace inconsistent _____ so that they are consistent with the nouns they refer to.

5. **VOCABULARY:** Go back to any new words that you underlined in this chapter. Can you guess their meanings now? If not, look up the words in a dictionary.

EDITING FOR CONSISTENT TENSE AND PERSON

Make sure you have been consistent with verb tenses: Use all past-tense verbs for past-tense actions, and so on.

Make sure you have been consistent in point of view: Avoid shifts from first to second person, and so on.

Look especially for sentences that use *I* and *you* instead of the correct *I* and *I* (see page 326).

21

Formal English and ESL Concerns

Grammar Trouble Spots for Multilingual Students

Multiple Choice
PERSONALITY TEST

_____ is the international language.

(A) Love

(B) Money

(C) English

(D) Chocolate

MATCH YOUR ANSWER with the TYPE below:
A= Romantic B= Capitalist C= Realist
D= Chocoholic (No answer: No personality.)

Academic, or formal, English is the English you will be expected to use in college and in most work situations, especially in writing. If you are not used to using formal English, or if English is not your native language, this chapter will help you avoid the most common problems with key sentence parts.

NOTE: In this chapter, we use the word *English* to refer to formal English.

VOCABULARY: Underline any words in this chapter that are new to you.

Subjects

- **Every sentence in English must have a subject and a verb.** The most basic sentence pattern is **SUBJECT-VERB (S-V)**.

TIP: For more on using formal English, see Chapter 4. For more on English sentence patterns, see Chapter 10.

            S   V
EXAMPLE   The dog ate.

TIP: In this chapter, subjects are underlined, and verbs are double-underlined.

To find the subject in a sentence, ask, "Who or what is doing the main action of the sentence?" In the previous example, the answer is *the dog*. To find the verb in a sentence, ask, "The subject did what?" In the preceding example, the answer is *ate*.

Other English sentence patterns build on the **S-V** structure. One of the most common patterns is **SUBJECT-VERB-OBJECT (S-V-O)**. The object in the **S-V-O** pattern is called a **direct object** because it directly receives the action of the verb.

$$\begin{array}{ccc} S & V & DO \\ | & | & | \end{array}$$

EXAMPLE   The dog ate the food.

To find the direct object in a sentence, ask "What?" of the verb. For the preceding example, the question would be "Ate what?" The answer is *the food*.

• **A complete subject can be more than one word.** The complete subject includes all the words that make up the subject.

EXAMPLES   Smoky Mountain National Park is famous for its beauty.

The old apple tree produced a lot of fruit.

• **Some sentences can have more than one subject.** Consider these three cases:

1. Subjects joined by *and* or *or*.

EXAMPLES   Taxes **and** tests are not on anyone's list of fun things to do.

Tatiana **or** Bill will wash the car.

2. Sentences that are really two sentences joined with the words *and, but, for, or, so, nor,* or *yet*.

EXAMPLES   Kim went to English class, **and** Dan went to math.

Kim went to English class, **but** she was late.

3. Sentences joined by dependent words, such as *after, before, if, since, unless, until,* and *while*.

EXAMPLES   Dan went to math class **before** he ate lunch.

Dan did his homework **after** he ate.

IMPORTANT: The subject of a sentence can never be in a prepositional phrase. For more information, see pages 189–90.

■ **TIP:** For more on how to join sentences with these words, see Chapters 12 and 22.

👁 Use different colors to highlight the subjects, verbs, and objects in your writing. Then, check to make sure you've used the right order.

■ **TIP:** For a more complete list of dependent words, see page 140.

PRACTICE 1 . . . .

Underline the complete subjects in each sentence. If there is no subject, add one and underline it. If the sentence pattern is incorrect, rewrite the sentence using either the S-V or S-V-O pattern.

               Most people like
EXAMPLE: ~~Like~~ a good ghost story.
               ^

1. Recently, a professor similarities found between modern and ancient ghost stories.

2. Ghost stories from ancient Greece and Rome white, black, or gray spirits describe.

3. Modern ghost stories also spirits of this color have.

4. Also, ancient and modern ghosts often news bring.

5. Or may bring a warning.

6. Dogs and other pets always spirits see that humans can't.

7. In the scariest stories, want revenge.

8. Good stories of the present and past frightening details have.

9. Bring life to the tales.

10. For example, a severed hand a door may open.

■ **TIP:** For more practice, visit Exercise Central at <**bedfordstmartins.com/ realskills**>.

Pronouns

Pronouns replace nouns (or other pronouns) in a sentence so that you do not have to repeat them. There are three kinds of pronouns: subject pronouns, object pronouns, and possessive pronouns, and it is important not to confuse them.

    Subject pronouns serve as the subject of the verb in a sentence; remember, *every English sentence must have a subject.* **Object pronouns** either receive the action of the verb or are part of a prepositional phrase. **Possessive pronouns** show ownership. The following chart lists the type of pronouns.

■ **TIP:** For more on pronouns, see Chapter 17.

Pronoun Types

SUBJECT		OBJECT		POSSESSIVE	
SINGULAR	**PLURAL**	**SINGULAR**	**PLURAL**	**SINGULAR**	**PLURAL**
I	we	me	us	my/mine	our/ours
you	you	you	you	your/yours	your/yours
he/she/it	they	him/her/it	them	his/her/hers/its	theirs

NOTE: Most singular third-person pronouns (*he/she, him/her, his/hers*) show gender. *He, him,* and *his* are masculine. *She, her,* and *hers* are feminine.

Here are some examples of common pronoun errors, with corrections.

- **Confusing subject and object pronouns**

  Use a subject pronoun for the subject of the sentence, the word that performs the action.

INCORRECT	Joseph is in my class. **Him** failed the test.
	[*Him* is the subject of the verb *failed* in the second sentence. The sentence needs a subject pronoun: *he*.]
CORRECT	Joseph is in my class. **He** failed the test.
INCORRECT	My teacher is Professor Smith. I gave the homework to **she**.
	[In the second sentence, *I* is correct: It is a subject pronoun. *She* is not the subject of the verb *gave*. An object pronoun should be used: *her*.]
CORRECT	I gave the homework to **her**.

- **Confusing gender in pronouns**

  If the pronoun replaces a masculine noun, the pronoun must be masculine. A pronoun that replaces a feminine noun must be feminine.

INCORRECT	Gloriana is my cousin. **He** lives in Buenos Aires.
	[Gloriana is female, so the pronoun must be feminine: *she*.]
CORRECT	Gloriana is my cousin. **She** lives in Buenos Aires.
INCORRECT	The jacket belongs to David. Janice gave it to **her**.
	[David is male, so the pronoun must be masculine: *him*.]
CORRECT	The jacket belongs to David. Janice gave it to **him**.

- **Leaving a pronoun out**

  In some sentences, the subject is *it*. Remember, all English sentences have subjects, so do not leave the word *it* out.

INCORRECT	Is cold today.
	[The sentence has no subject.]
CORRECT	**It** is cold today.
INCORRECT	The soccer game was canceled. Will be played next week.
	[The second sentence has no subject.]
CORRECT	The soccer game was canceled. **It** will be played next week.

IDEA JOURNAL: Write about a time when you met a person who is important in your life.

Earlier, you learned that a common English sentence pattern is subject-verb-object. To find the direct object in a sentence, ask "What?" of the subject. Sometimes, the object is an object pronoun that cannot be left out.

INCORRECT   I skiied for the first time, and I liked very much.

[I liked what? An object pronoun is needed.]

CORRECT   I skiied for the first time, and I liked **it** very much.

- **Using a pronoun to repeat the subject**
  Pronouns are used to replace nouns or pronouns, not to repeat them.

INCORRECT   The driver **he** hit another car.

[*Driver* is the subject noun, and *he* just repeats it.]

CORRECT   The driver hit another car.

PRACTICE 2 . . . .

Using the chart of pronouns, fill in the blanks with the correct pronoun.

EXAMPLE: Bill and Jane are my neighbors, and ___*they*___ have a

toddler.

1. _____ is a boy.

2. _____ name is David.

3. Whenever Bill and Jane go out, I babysit for _____.

4. _____ walk to the park, eat ice cream, or play games.

5. _____ favorite question is "What's that?"

6. When David sees _____, he always smiles.

7. _____ makes me feel really good.

8. In some ways, David is _____ best friend.

9. If I ever have a child, _____ want him to be just like David.

10. Who is _____ best friend?

. . . .

Verbs

■ **TIP:** For more on the kinds of English verbs (action, linking, and helping), see Chapter 10. For more on irregular verb forms, see Chapters 14 and 15.

English verbs, like verbs in most other languages, have different tenses to show when something happened: in the past, present, or future.

Present (now)

Past ◄──────────────────┼──────────────────► Future

👁 For any of the charts with time lines in this chapter, draw a single time line contrasting the different situations. For example, for this chart draw one time line that includes the simple present, the simple past, and the simple future.

This section covers the most common tenses. The discussions of each tense start with a chart that tells you what time the tense is used for. The chart then shows how to use the tense in statements, negative sentences, and questions. You can use the verb charts both to learn tenses and to edit your own writing. Following the charts are lists of common errors to avoid.

The Simple Tenses

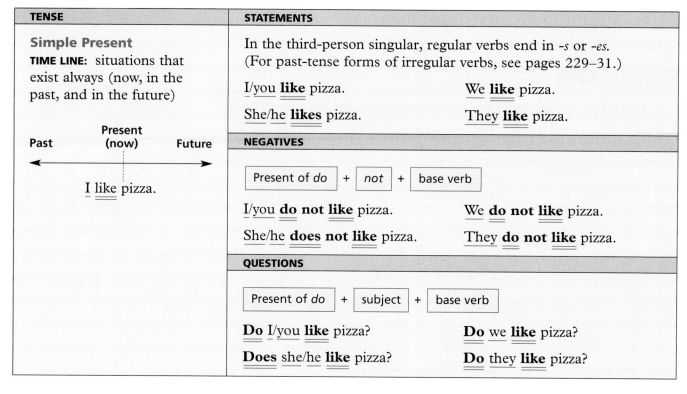

TENSE	STATEMENTS
Simple Present **TIME LINE:** situations that exist always (now, in the past, and in the future) **Past — Present (now) — Future** ◄────────────► I like pizza.	In the third-person singular, regular verbs end in *-s* or *-es*. (For past-tense forms of irregular verbs, see pages 229–31.) I/you **like** pizza. We **like** pizza. She/he **likes** pizza. They **like** pizza.
	NEGATIVES
	Present of *do* + *not* + base verb I/you **do not like** pizza. We **do not like** pizza. She/he **does not like** pizza. They **do not like** pizza.
	QUESTIONS
	Present of *do* + subject + base verb **Do** I/you **like** pizza? **Do** we **like** pizza? **Does** she/he **like** pizza? **Do** they **like** pizza?

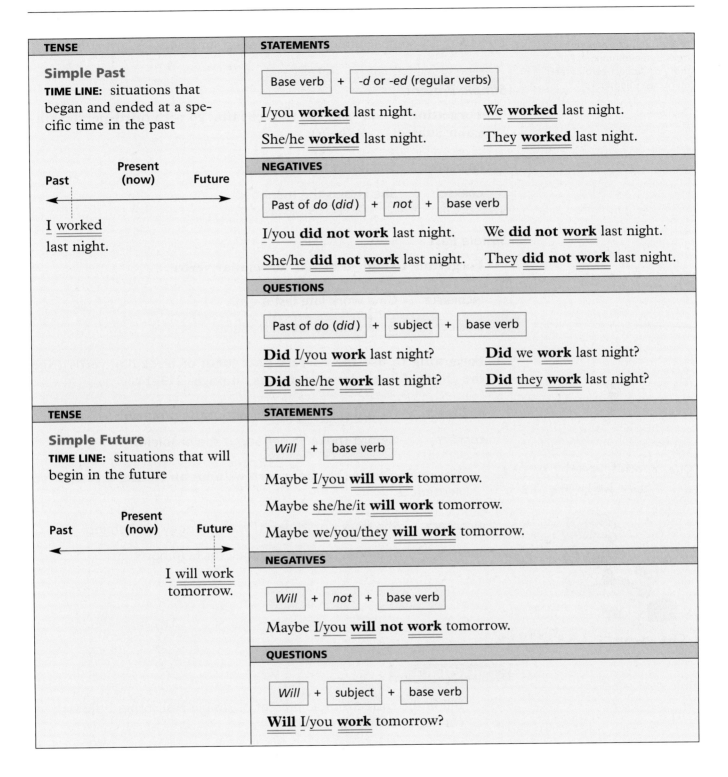

TENSE	STATEMENTS
Simple Past **TIME LINE:** situations that began and ended at a specific time in the past **Present** **Past (now) Future** ◄─────────┼─────────► I worked last night.	Base verb + -d or -ed (regular verbs) I/you **worked** last night. We **worked** last night. She/he **worked** last night. They **worked** last night.
	NEGATIVES
	Past of *do* (*did*) + *not* + base verb I/you **did not work** last night. We **did not work** last night. She/he **did not work** last night. They **did not work** last night.
	QUESTIONS
	Past of *do* (*did*) + subject + base verb **Did** I/you **work** last night? **Did** we **work** last night? **Did** she/he **work** last night? **Did** they **work** last night?
TENSE	**STATEMENTS**
Simple Future **TIME LINE:** situations that will begin in the future **Present** **Past (now) Future** ◄─────────┼─────────► I will work tomorrow.	*Will* + base verb Maybe I/you **will work** tomorrow. Maybe she/he/it **will work** tomorrow. Maybe we/you/they **will work** tomorrow.
	NEGATIVES
	Will + *not* + base verb Maybe I/you **will not work** tomorrow.
	QUESTIONS
	Will + subject + base verb **Will** I/you **work** tomorrow?

■ **TIP:** Subjects and verbs must agree in number. For more on subject-verb agreement, see Chapter 13.

Following are some common errors in using simple tenses.

Simple Present

- **Forgetting to add *-s* or *-es* to verbs that go with third-person singular subjects (*she/he/it*)**

INCORRECT	She know the manager.
CORRECT	She knows the manager.

Simple Past

- **Forgetting to add *-d* or *-ed* to regular verbs**

INCORRECT	Gina work late last night.
CORRECT	Gina worked late last night.

- **Forgetting to use the correct past form of irregular verbs (See the chart of irregular verb forms on pages 213–14.)**

INCORRECT	Gerard speaked to her about the problem.
CORRECT	Gerard **spoke** to her about the problem.

- **Forgetting to use the base verb without an ending for negative sentences**

INCORRECT	She does not [doesn't] wants money for helping.
CORRECT	She does not **want** money for helping.

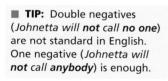

She doesn't want money for helping.

(She wants chocolate.)

PRACTICE 3 . . . .

Fill in the correct simple present or simple past form of the verb in parentheses after the blank.

EXAMPLE: Pop music ___*includes*___ (*include*) a wide range of music.

■ **TIP:** Double negatives (*Johnetta will **not** call **no one***) are not standard in English. One negative (*Johnetta will **not** call **anybody***) is enough.

1. It _____ (*cut*) across boundaries of age and race.

2. For example, people of all ages _____ (*enjoy*) a rock-and-roll beat.

3. Almost everyone _____ (*love*) to dance!

4. At first, rock-and-roll music _____ (*offend*) the older generations.

5. Parents _____ (*object*) to the sexual lyrics.

6. They _____ (*think*) it would be a bad influence on their children.

7. Many people _____ (*feel*) the same way about hip-hop when it first became popular.

8. Now, hip-hop _____ (*rank*) as the second-most-popular kind of music behind rock and roll.

9. However, some people _____ (*wonder*) if hip-hop glorifies crime and excessive wealth.

10. Critics argue that hip-hop often _____ (*miss*) the opportunity to deal with problems such as poverty and racism.

PRACTICE 4 . . . .

Rewrite the following sentences as indicated.

1. Sasha plays baseball with her sister.

   Make the sentence a question: _____

2. They go to the beach every weekend.

   Make the sentence a negative statement: _____

   _____

3. Chris baited the hook on the fishing line.

   Make the sentence a question: _____

4. They will enjoy that movie.

   Make the sentence a negative statement: _____

   _____

5. Rivka watched the tennis match.

   Make the sentence into a question: _____

The Progressive Tenses

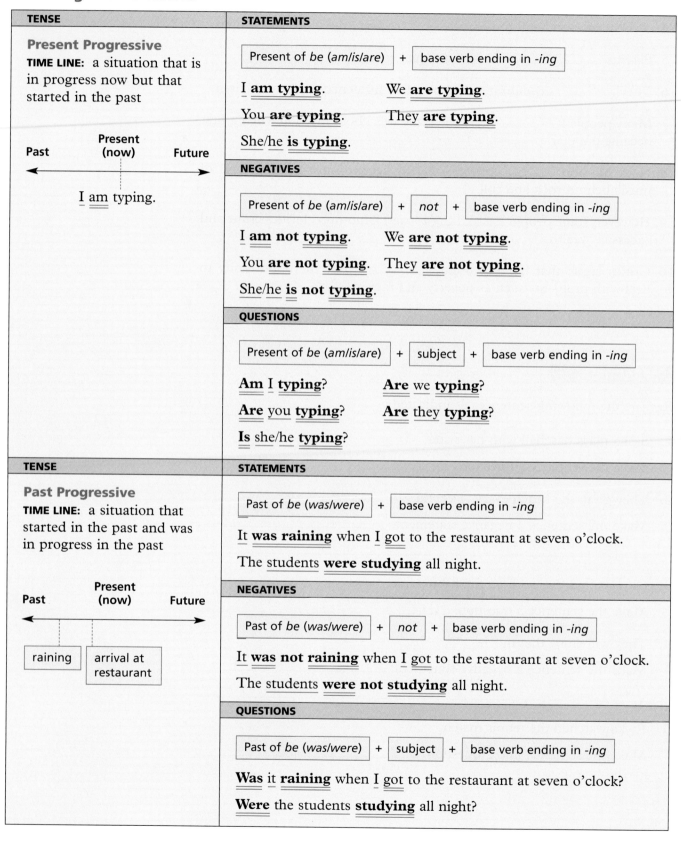

TENSE	STATEMENTS
Present Progressive **TIME LINE:** a situation that is in progress now but that started in the past ┌─────────────────────┐ Past **Present (now)** Future ◄─────┼──────────► I am typing.	Present of *be* (*am/is/are*) + base verb ending in *-ing* I **am typing**. We **are typing**. You **are typing**. They **are typing**. She/he **is typing**.
	NEGATIVES
	Present of *be* (*am/is/are*) + *not* + base verb ending in *-ing* I **am not typing**. We **are not typing**. You **are not typing**. They **are not typing**. She/he **is not typing**.
	QUESTIONS
	Present of *be* (*am/is/are*) + subject + base verb ending in *-ing* **Am** I **typing**? **Are** we **typing**? **Are** you **typing**? **Are** they **typing**? **Is** she/he **typing**?
TENSE	**STATEMENTS**
Past Progressive **TIME LINE:** a situation that started in the past and was in progress in the past Past **Present (now)** Future ◄─────┼──────────► [raining] [arrival at restaurant]	Past of *be* (*was/were*) + base verb ending in *-ing* It **was raining** when I got to the restaurant at seven o'clock. The students **were studying** all night.
	NEGATIVES
	Past of *be* (*was/were*) + *not* + base verb ending in *-ing* It **was not raining** when I got to the restaurant at seven o'clock. The students **were not studying** all night.
	QUESTIONS
	Past of *be* (*was/were*) + subject + base verb ending in *-ing* **Was** it **raining** when I got to the restaurant at seven o'clock? **Were** the students **studying** all night?

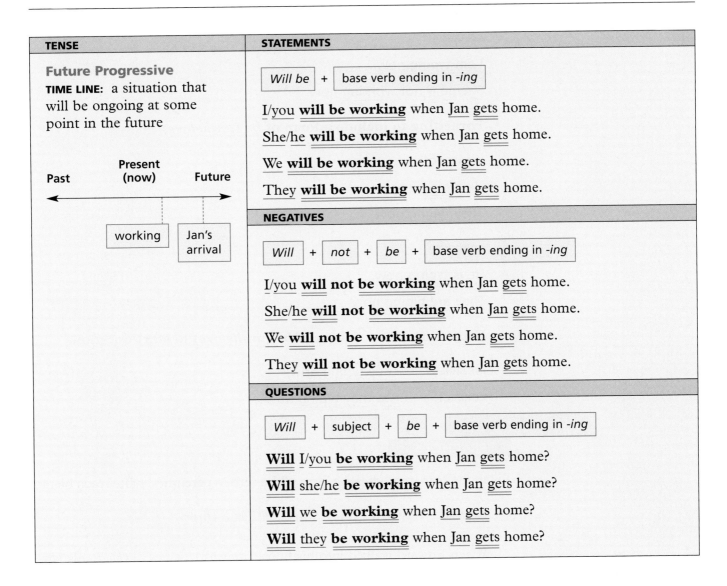

TENSE	STATEMENTS
Future Progressive **TIME LINE:** a situation that will be ongoing at some point in the future	Will be + base verb ending in *-ing* I/you **will be working** when Jan gets home. She/he **will be working** when Jan gets home. We **will be working** when Jan gets home. They **will be working** when Jan gets home.

Time line: Past — Present (now) — Future; working — Jan's arrival

NEGATIVES

Will + not + be + base verb ending in *-ing*

I/you **will not be working** when Jan gets home.

She/he **will not be working** when Jan gets home.

We **will not be working** when Jan gets home.

They **will not be working** when Jan gets home.

QUESTIONS

Will + subject + be + base verb ending in *-ing*

Will I/you **be working** when Jan gets home?

Will she/he **be working** when Jan gets home?

Will we **be working** when Jan gets home?

Will they **be working** when Jan gets home?

READ ALOUD

For each of the verb charts in this chapter, read at least three regular statements, three negative statements, and three questions aloud.

Following are some common errors in forming the present progressive.

- **Forgetting to add *-ing* to the verb**

  INCORRECT

  I am type now.

  She/he is not work now.

CORRECT

I am typing now.

She/he is not working now.

• **Forgetting to include a form of *be* (*am/is/are*)**

INCORRECT

He typing now.

They typing now.

CORRECT

He **is** typing now.

They **are** typing now.

• **Forgetting to use a form of *be* (*am/is/are*) to start questions**

INCORRECT   They typing now?

CORRECT   **Are** they typing now?

PRACTICE 5 . . . .

Fill in the correct progressive form of the verb in parentheses after each blank.

EXAMPLE: Edward's tooth was ___*hurting*___ (***hurt***).

1. When Edward walked into his house, he was _____ (*hold*) his jaw.

2. Tears were _____ (*stream*) down his face.

3. His mother asked him, "Why are you _____ (*cry*), Edward?"

4. "My tooth is _____ (*kill*) me!" he exclaimed.

5. "Did you do something to it while you were outside _____ (*play*)?"

6. "I don't think so," said Edward. "It was _____ (*throb*) last night when I was trying to sleep."

7. His mother looked around the room as if she were searching for something. "What are you _____ (*do*)?" he asked.

8. "I'm _____ (*try*) to find my keys," she said.

9. "Why?" asked Edward. "Where are you _____ (*go*)?"

10. "Don't worry," she said. "You're _____ (*come*), too. I'm _____ (*take*) you to the dentist."

Rewrite the following sentences as indicated.

1. Dan is mowing the grass.

    Make the sentence a question: _____

2. It was freezing this morning.

    Make the sentence a negative statement: _____

3. You are wearing a new dress.

    Make the sentence a question: _____

4. They are driving to the park.

    Make the sentence a negative statement: _____

5. Chad was working when you saw him.

    Make the sentence into a question: _____

Modal Auxiliaries/Helping Verbs

If you have taken an English-as-a-second-language (ESL) course, you might recognize the term **modal auxiliary**, a type of helping verb that expresses a writer's view about an action. As shown in the following chart, these helping verbs join with a main (base) verb to make a complete verb.

> ■ **TIP:** For more on helping verbs, see Chapter 10.

HELPING VERB (MODAL AUXILIARY)	STATEMENTS
General formulas For all modal auxiliaries. (More helping verbs shown on pp. 346–48.)	**Present:** Subject + helping verb + base verb Dumbo can fly. **Past:** Forms vary—see below.
	NEGATIVES
	Present: Subject + helping verb + *not* + base verb Dumbo cannot fly. **Past:** Forms vary—see below.
	QUESTIONS
	Present: Helping verb + subject + base verb Can Dumbo fly? **Past:** Forms vary—see below.

continued

HELPING VERB (MODAL AUXILIARY)	STATEMENTS
Can Means *ability*	**Present:** Beth **can** work fast. **Past:** Beth **could** work fast.
	NEGATIVES
	Present: Beth **can**not work fast. **Past:** Beth **could** not work fast.
	QUESTIONS
	Present: Can Beth work fast? **Past: Could** Beth work fast?
Could Means *possibility*. It can also be the past tense of *can*.	STATEMENTS
	Present: Beth **could** work fast if she had more time. **Past:** Beth **could** have worked fast if she had more time.
	NEGATIVES
	Can is used for present negatives. (See above.) **Past:** Beth **could not** have worked fast.
	QUESTIONS
	Present: Could Beth work fast? **Past: Could** Beth have worked fast?
May Means *permission* For past-tense forms, see *might*.	STATEMENTS
	Present: You **may** borrow my car.
	NEGATIVES
	Present: You **may not** borrow my car.
	QUESTIONS
	Present: May I borrow your car?
Might Means *possibility*. It can also be the past tense of *may*.	STATEMENTS
	Present (with *be*): Lou **might** be asleep. **Past** (with *have* + past participle of *be*): Lou **might** have been asleep. **Future:** Lou **might** sleep.

■ **TIP:** The past participle of regular verbs is *-d* or *-ed*. For past participle forms of irregular verbs, see Chapter 15.

HELPING VERB (MODAL AUXILIARY)	NEGATIVES
Might (*continued*) Means *possibility*. It can also be the past tense of *may*.	**Present** (with *be*): Lou **might** not be asleep. **Past** (with *have* + past participle of *be*): Lou **might** not have been asleep. **Future:** Lou **might** not sleep.
	QUESTIONS
	Might in questions is very formal and not often used.
Must Means *necessary*	**STATEMENTS**
	Present: We **must** try. **Past** (with *have* + past participle of base verb): We **must** have tried.
	NEGATIVES
	Present: We **must** not try. **Past** (with *have* + past participle of base verb): We **must** not have tried.
	QUESTIONS
	Present: Must we try? Past-tense questions with *must* are unusual.
Should Means *duty* or *expectation*	**STATEMENTS**
	Present: They **should** call. **Past** (with *have* + past participle of base verb): They **should** have called.
	NEGATIVES
	Present: They **should** not call. **Past** (with *have* + past participle of base verb): They **should** not have called.
	QUESTIONS
	Present: Should they call? **Past** (with *have* + past participle of base verb): **Should** they have called?

continued

HELPING VERB (MODAL AUXILIARY)	STATEMENTS
Will Means *intend to* (future) For past-tense forms, see *might*.	**Future:** I **will** succeed.
	NEGATIVES
	Future: I **will** not succeed.
	QUESTIONS
	Future: Will I succeed?
Would Means *prefer* or used to start a future request. It can also be the past tense of *will*.	**STATEMENTS**
	Present: I **would** like to travel. **Past** (with *have* + past participle of base verb): I **would** have traveled if I had the money.
	NEGATIVES
	Present: I **would** not like to travel. **Past** (with *have* + past participle of base verb): I **would** not have traveled if it hadn't been for you.
	QUESTIONS
	Present: Would you like to travel? *Or* to start a request: **Would** you help me? **Past** (with *have* + past participle of base verb): **Would** you have traveled with me if I had asked you?

Following are some common errors in using modal auxiliaries.

- **Using more than one helping verb**

INCORRECT	They **will can** help.
CORRECT	They **will** help. (future intention)
	They **can** help. (are able to)

- **Using *to* between the helping verb and the main (base) verb**

INCORRECT	Emilio **might to** come with us.
CORRECT	Emilio **might** come with us.

- **Using *must* instead of *had to* in the past**

INCORRECT	She **must** work yesterday.
CORRECT	She **had** to work yesterday.

- **Forgetting to change *can* to *could* in the past negative**

    INCORRECT   Last night, I **cannot** sleep.

    CORRECT   Last night, I **could** not sleep.

- **Forgetting to use *have* with *could/should/would* in the past tense**

    INCORRECT   Tara **should** called last night.

    CORRECT   Tara **should have** called last night.

- **Using *will* instead of *would* to express a preference in the present tense**

    INCORRECT   I **will** like to travel.

    CORRECT   I **would** like to travel.

PRACTICE 7 . . `. . . . . . . . . . . . . . . . . . . .`

Fill in modal auxiliaries (helping verbs) in the sentences below.

    EXAMPLE: When Carlos walked into the department store, a sales-clerk asked, "___*May*___ I help you?"

1. "Hi," said Carlos. "I _____ like to buy a gift for my girlfriend."

2. "Okay," said the clerk. "We have lots of nice things here. _____ you be more specific?"

3. Carlos shuffled his feet and said, "I know I _____ have thought of something before I got here, but I was hoping you might have some suggestions."

4. "Certainly," said the salesclerk, leading him to a large glass case. "She _____ like jewelry."

5. "Hmm," said Carlos. "Jewelry would be nice, but I _____ afford to spend over $50."

6. "That _____ be a problem," said the clerk. "We have some earrings for under $50."

7. "Really?" asked Carlos, obviously pleased. "_____ you show them to me?"

8. "Absolutely!" said the clerk. "What about these? She _____ like pearls. They're so delicate."

9. "Perfect!" exclaimed Carlos. "I _____ take them!"

10. "Excellent," said the clerk. "How _____ you like to pay?"

PRACTICE 8

Rewrite the following sentences as indicated.

1. You can tell me the secret.

   Make the sentence a question: _____

2. We might go to dinner on Friday.

   Make the sentence a negative statement: _____

   _____

3. They should leave the house before us.

   Make the sentence a question: _____

4. They could make breakfast.

   Make the sentence a negative statement: _____

5. Cathy would like to go sailing with us.

   Make the sentence into a question: _____

The Perfect Tenses

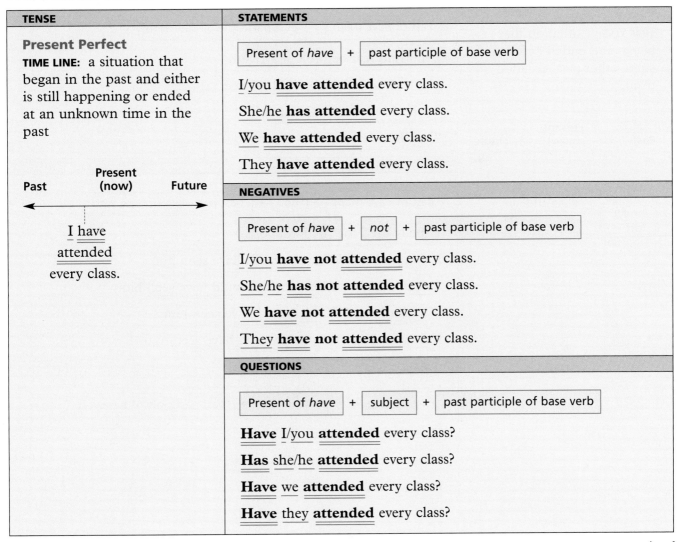

TENSE	STATEMENTS
Present Perfect **TIME LINE:** a situation that began in the past and either is still happening or ended at an unknown time in the past **Present** **Past (now) Future** I have attended every class.	Present of *have* + past participle of base verb I/you **have attended** every class. She/he **has attended** every class. We **have attended** every class. They **have attended** every class.
	NEGATIVES
	Present of *have* + *not* + past participle of base verb I/you **have not attended** every class. She/he **has not attended** every class. We **have not attended** every class. They **have not attended** every class.
	QUESTIONS
	Present of *have* + subject + past participle of base verb **Have** I/you **attended** every class? **Has** she/he **attended** every class? **Have** we **attended** every class? **Have** they **attended** every class?

continued

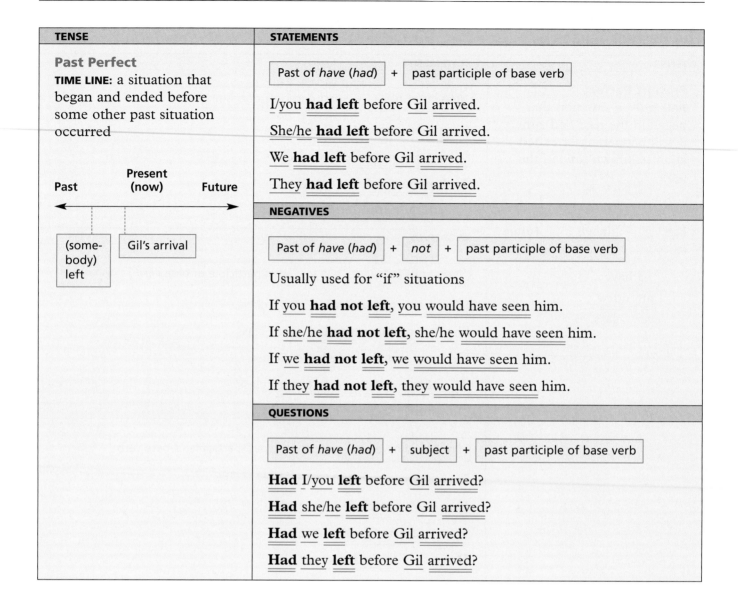

TENSE	STATEMENTS
Past Perfect **TIME LINE:** a situation that began and ended before some other past situation occurred	Past of *have* (*had*) + past participle of base verb I/you **had left** before Gil arrived. She/he **had left** before Gil arrived. We **had left** before Gil arrived. They **had left** before Gil arrived.

Past — Present (now) — Future

(somebody) left — Gil's arrival

	NEGATIVES
	Past of *have* (*had*) + *not* + past participle of base verb Usually used for "if" situations If you **had not left**, you would have seen him. If she/he **had not left**, she/he would have seen him. If we **had not left**, we would have seen him. If they **had not left**, they would have seen him.

	QUESTIONS
	Past of *have* (*had*) + subject + past participle of base verb **Had** I/you **left** before Gil arrived? **Had** she/he **left** before Gil arrived? **Had** we **left** before Gil arrived? **Had** they **left** before Gil arrived?

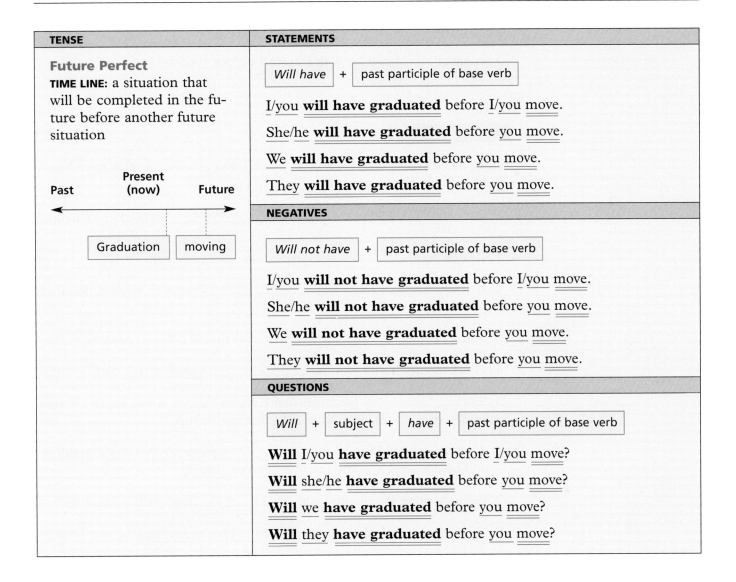

TENSE	STATEMENTS
Future Perfect **TIME LINE:** a situation that will be completed in the future before another future situation	*Will have* + past participle of base verb I/you **will have graduated** before I/you move. She/he **will have graduated** before you move. We **will have graduated** before you move. They **will have graduated** before you move.

Past — Present (now) — Future

Graduation | moving

NEGATIVES
Will not have + past participle of base verb I/you **will not have graduated** before I/you move. She/he **will not have graduated** before you move. We **will not have graduated** before you move. They **will not have graduated** before you move.

QUESTIONS
Will + subject + *have* + past participle of base verb **Will** I/you **have graduated** before I/you move? **Will** she/he **have graduated** before you move? **Will** we **have graduated** before you move? **Will** they **have graduated** before you move?

■ **TIP:** For more on the perfect tense, see Chapter 15. For lists of irregular verbs and their forms, see Chapters 14 and 15.

Following are some common errors in forming the perfect tense.

- **Using *had* instead of *has* or *have* for the present perfect**

  INCORRECT   We **had** lived here since 2003.

  CORRECT   We **have** lived here since 2003.

- **Forgetting to use past participles (with *-d* or *-ed* endings for regular verbs)**

  INCORRECT   She has attend every class.

  CORRECT   She has attend**ed** every class.

- **Using *been* between *have* or *has* and past of base verb**

  INCORRECT   I have **been** attended every class.

  CORRECT   I have attended every class.

INCORRECT	I will have **been** graduated before I move.
CORRECT	I will have graduated before I move.

PRACTICE 9

Fill in the correct perfect tense of the verb in parentheses after each blank. Add helping verbs as needed.

EXAMPLE: ___*Have*___ you ever ___*traveled*___ (*travel*) to Europe?

1. If so, where _____ you _____ (*be*)?

2. If you _____ not _____ (*go*), you should definitely plan a trip!

3. Some people _____ (*complain*) that it is too expensive.

4. However, my friend JoAnna _____ (*find*) a solution.

5. She _____ (*discover*) that Eastern Europe is less expensive than some other places, and it has a fascinating history.

6. The citizens of Prague _____ (*preserve*) the city's buildings and bridges, such as the famous Charles Bridge.

7. Before visiting Prague, JoAnna _____ (*see*) such a beautiful city.

8. Your next stop should be Poland. The main square in Krakow _____ (*survive*) since medieval times.

9. The Poles _____ (*open*) many fine hotels in the heart of the city.

10. If you don't believe me, call your travel agent for a brochure. By the time you finish reading it, you _____ (*change*) your mind.

PRACTICE 10

Fill in the blanks with the correct verbs, adding helping verbs as needed. Refer to the verb charts if you need help.

EXAMPLE: ___*Are*___ (*be*) you concerned about the future of our earth?

1. Research shows that the earth's temperature _____ (*rise*).

2. Many scientists _____ (*conclude*) that the rise in temperature is due at least in part to human activity.

3. When people drive their cars or heat their homes, they _____ (*produce*) gases that trap heat.

4. Before the Industrial Revolution, the atmosphere _____ (*keep*) these gases in check.

5. Now, high levels of these gases _____ (*overwhelm*) the environment.

6. Thus, the earth _____ (*become*) warmer.

7. As a result, glaciers _____ (*melt*).

8. Also, snow cover in the earth's Northern Hemisphere _____ (*decrease*).

9. Many scientists believe that if we continue to burn large amounts of coal, oil, and gas, we _____ (*destroy*) our planet.

10. However, one person _____ (*can* + *not*) possibly _____ (*stop*) the destruction, right?

11. Wrong—there are a variety of easy things you _____ (*do*) to help.

12. If just 10 percent of the people in our nation took small steps, it _____ (*make*) a big difference.

13. For example, _____ (*do*) you _____ (*drink*) coffee?

14. _____ you ever _____ (*think*) about how many disposable cups you use in a year?

15. You _____ (*bring*) a travel mug with you to the coffee shop.

16. _____ (*do*) your school or office _____ (*recycle*)?

17. You _____ (*start*) a program.

18. Keep in mind, however, that you _____ first _____ (*get*) permission.

19. You _____ also _____ (*buy*) recycled products, such as paper towels, tissue, and writing paper.

20. Finally, if we support energy sources such as solar and wind energy, we _____ (*help*) to sustain life on our planet for generations to come.

PRACTICE 11 . .

Fill in the blanks with the correct verbs, adding helping verbs as needed. Refer to the verb charts if you need help.

EXAMPLE: How many planets _____*are*_____ (*be*) in our solar system?

(1) For decades, the answer was "nine," but that _____ (*change*), at least according to scientists. (2) Since its discovery in 1930, Pluto _____ (*be*) considered a planet. (3) However, the recent discovery of an ice ball larger than Pluto made scientists wonder whether we _____ (*continue*) to label Pluto as a planet. (4) At a 2006 meeting of the International Astronomical Union, astronomers _____ (*vote*) to relabel Pluto as a "dwarf planet," decreasing the number of full-sized planets to eight. (5) The astronomers determined that to be a full-sized planet, an object _____ (*pass*) three tests. (6) First, it _____ (*be*) big enough to be shaped into a ball by the forces of gravity. (7) Second, it _____ (*orbit*) the sun. (8) Third, it _____ (*knock*) other objects out of the path of its orbit. (9) To be labeled a dwarf planet, an object simply _____ (*be*) round. (10) However, since people _____ (*consider*) Pluto a planet for nearly eighty years, many _____ (*continue*) to do so.

Gerunds and Infinitives

■ **TIP:** For other problems with verbs, see Chapters 14 and 15.

■ **TIP:** To improve your ability to write and speak standard English, read magazines and your local newspaper, and listen to television and radio news programs. Also, read magazines and newspaper articles aloud; this will help your pronunciation.

A **gerund** is a verb form that ends in *-ing* and acts as a noun. An **infinitive** is a verb form that is preceded by the word *to*. Gerunds and infinitives cannot be the main verbs in sentences; each sentence must have another word that is the main verb.

GERUND	Mika <u>loves</u> **swimming**.
	[*Loves* is the main verb, and *swimming* is a gerund.]
INFINITIVE	Mika <u>loves</u> **to run**.
	[*Loves* is the main verb, and *to run* is an infinitive.]

How do you decide whether to use a gerund or an infinitive? The decision often depends on the main verb in a sentence. Some verbs can be followed by either a gerund or an infinitive.

> ## Verbs That Can Be Followed by Either an Infinitive or a Gerund
>
> | begin | hate | remember | try |
> |-------|------|----------|-----|
> | continue | like | start | |
> | forget | love | stop | |

Sometimes, using an infinitive or gerund after one of these verbs results in the same meaning.

GERUND   Joan likes **playing** the piano.

INFINITIVE   Joan likes **to play** the piano.

Other times, however, the meaning changes depending on whether you use an infinitive or a gerund.

GERUND   Carla stopped **helping** me.

                       [This means that Carla no longer helps me.]

INFINITIVE   Carla stopped **to help** me.

                       [This means that Carla stopped what she was doing and helped me.]

> ## Verbs That Are Followed by an Infinitive Only
>
> | agree | decide | need | refuse |
> |-------|--------|------|--------|
> | ask | expect | offer | want |
> | beg | fail | plan | |
> | choose | hope | pretend | |
> | claim | manage | promise | |

Aunt Sally wants **to help**.

Cal hopes **to become** a millionaire.

> ## Verbs That Are Followed by a Gerund Only
>
> | admit | discuss | keep | risk |
> |-------|---------|------|------|
> | avoid | enjoy | miss | suggest |
> | consider | finish | practice | |
> | deny | imagine | quit | |

The <u>politician</u> <u>risked</u> **losing** her supporters.

<u>Sophia</u> <u>considered</u> **quitting** her job.

A FINAL NOTE: Gerunds and infinitives can serve as nouns. Make sure to use a gerund or infinitive, not the base form of a verb, when a noun is intended.

In the following sentence, the writer's intended meaning is that the act of gambling (a noun) can be addictive.

INCORRECT	<u>Gamble</u> <u>can be</u> addictive.
	[*Gamble* is a verb, but the subject must be a noun.]
CORRECT	**<u>Gambling</u>** <u>can be</u> addictive. Or **<u>To gamble</u>** <u>can be</u> addictive.
	[*Gambling* is a gerund and *to gamble* is an infinitive. Both serve as nouns here.]

PRACTICE 12 . .

Read the paragraph and fill in the blanks with either a gerund or an infinitive as appropriate.

EXAMPLE: Have you ever wanted ___*to start*___ (*start*) your own business?

(1) Every day, people imagine _____ (*work*) for themselves. (2) They might hate _____ (*feel*) like their efforts only benefit someone else. (3) If you are one of these people, stop _____ (*dream*) and start _____ (*make*) your dream come true.

(4) Try _____ (*picture*) yourself as the boss; are you self-motivated? (5) Will you enjoy _____ (*develop*) your own projects and _____ (*ensure*) they are done correctly? (6) Will you manage _____ (*stay*) organized and meet deadlines without someone else watching over you? (7) Are you certain you will like _____ (*be*) independent, having no one to praise or blame but yourself? (8) If you answered "yes" to all of the above, you are ready for the greatest adventure of your career. (9) To avoid _____ (*go*) into this process blindly, you must create a business plan. (10) For example, you should determine what you want _____ (*do*), what skills you possess, and how you might market your services.

Articles

Articles announce a noun. English uses only three articles—*a, an,* and *the*—and the same articles are used for both masculine and feminine nouns.

To use the correct article, you need to know whether the noun being announced is count or noncount. **Count nouns** name things that can be counted, and count nouns can be made plural, usually by adding *-s* or *-es*. **Noncount nouns** name things that cannot be counted, and they are usually singular. They can't be made plural.

COUNT/SINGLE	I got a **ticket** for the concert.
COUNT/PLURAL	I got two **tickets** for the concert.
NONCOUNT	The Internet has all kinds of **information**.
	[You would not say, *The Internet has all kinds of informations*.]

Here are some count and noncount nouns. This is just a brief list; all nouns in English are either count or noncount.

COUNT	NONCOUNT	
apple/apples	beauty	milk
chair/chairs	flour	money
dollar/dollars	furniture	postage
letter/letters	grass	poverty
smile/smiles	grief	rain
tree/trees	happiness	rice
	health	salt
	homework	sand
	honey	spaghetti
	information	sunlight
	jewelry	thunder
	mail	wealth

Use the chart that follows to determine when to use *a, an, the,* or no article.

Articles with Count and Noncount Nouns

COUNT NOUNS	ARTICLE USED
SINGULAR	
Identity known →	*the* I want to read **the book** on taxes that you recommended. [The sentence refers to one particular book: the one that was recommended.] I can't stay in **the sun** very long. [There is only one sun.]
Identity not known →	*a* or *an* I want to read **a** book on taxes. [It could be any book on taxes.]
PLURAL	
Identity known →	*the* I enjoyed **the books** we read. [The sentence refers to a particular group of books: the ones we read.]
Identity not known → or a general category	no article or *some* I usually enjoy **books**. [The sentence refers to books in general.] She found **some books**. [I don't know which books she found.]

NONCOUNT NOUNS	ARTICLE USED
SINGULAR	
Identity known →	*the* I put away **the food** we bought. [The sentence refers to particular food: the food we bought.]
Identity not known → or a general category	no article or *some* There is **food** all over the kitchen. [The reader doesn't know what food the sentence refers to.] Give **some food** to the neighbors. [The sentence refers to an indefinite quantity of food.]

PRACTICE 13 . . . .

Fill in the correct article (*a*, *an*, or *the*) in each of the following sentences. If no article is needed, write "no article."

EXAMPLE: When my dog Smitty died last year, I was overcome with
<u>no article</u> grief.

1. My parents bought him when I was _____ infant.

2. They thought it would be good for me to have _____ pet.

3. Because of Smitty, I have always loved _____ animals.

4. He was my best friend, and all of _____ other children in the neighborhood loved him too.

5. One time, he saved my cousin from drowning in _____ pond on our property.

6. We treated him like _____ king that day.

7. My mom baked him _____ dog-food cake.

8. _____ cake smelled horrible to us, but Smitty ate it all up.

9. He seemed to have _____ stomachache afterward.

10. Now, I smile when I think of _____ good times we had.

PRACTICE 14 . . . .

Edit the following paragraphs, adding, revising, or deleting articles as necessary.

          Motherhood
EXAMPLE: ~~The~~ motherhood is both rewarding and difficult.

    (1) In 2005, national study about motherhood was released. (2) The mothers from the variety of ages, ethnicities, and economic backgrounds were surveyed. (3) As it turns out, mothers from around the country have many of same attitudes and concerns.

    (4) Of mothers surveyed, most stated that they are happy in their role. (5) Likewise, most mothers believe that their role is important one. (6) Also, most feel the tremendous love for their children. (7) They admit they had never experienced the love so intensely before they had children.

(8) That is only part of a story, however. (9) These women also had few concerns. (10) About half of women surveyed said they didn't feel appreciated by the others. (11) In fact, some felt less valued as mothers than they did before they had the children. (12) Also more than half felt that society should do more for the mothers, children, and families.

(13) Biggest concerns of the mothers surveyed were education and safety. (14) The lower an income of the mother, the more she was concerned about education.

· ·

Prepositions

■ **TIP:** For more on prepositions, see Chapter 10.

A **preposition** is a word (such as *of, above, between, about*) that connects a noun, pronoun, or verb with other information about it. The correct preposition to use is often determined by idiom or common practice rather than by the preposition's actual meaning.

An **idiom** is any combination of words that is always used the same way, even though there is no logical or grammatical explanation for it. The best way to learn English idioms is to listen and read as much as possible and then to practice writing and speaking the correct forms.

Adjectives with Prepositions

Adjectives are often followed by prepositions. Here are some common examples.

afraid of	full of	scared of
ashamed of	happy about	sorry about/sorry for
aware of	interested in	tired of
confused by	proud of	
excited about	responsible for	

Peri is afraid *of* snakes.

We are happy *about* Dino's promotion.

Verbs with Prepositions

Many verbs consist of a verb plus a preposition (or adverb). The meaning of these combinations is not usually the meaning the verb and the preposition would each have on its own. Often, the meaning of the verb changes completely depending on which preposition is used with it.

You <u>must</u> **take out** the trash.   [*take out* = bring to a different location]

You <u>must</u> **take in** the exciting sights of New York City.   [*take in* = observe]

Sometimes, words can come between the verb and preposition; other times, this isn't logical in English. Here are some examples of combinations that can and can't be separated.

SEPARABLE VERB/PREPOSITION COMBINATIONS	
call off (cancel)	They *called off* the pool party. [They *called* **it** *off*.]
fill in (refill)	Please *fill in* the holes in the ground. [Please *fill* **them** *in*.]
fill out (complete)	Please *fill out* this application form. [Please *fill* **it** *out*.]
fill up (make something full)	Don't *fill up* the tank all the way. [Don't *fill* **it** *up* all the way.]
find out (discover)	Did you *find out* her name? [Did you *find* **it** *out*?]
give up (forfeit; stop)	Don't *give up* your place in line. [Don't *give* **it** *up*.] Don't *give up* the fight.
hand in (submit)	You may *hand in* your homework now. [You may *hand* **it** *in* now.]
lock up (secure)	Don't forget to *lock up* the house. [Don't forget to *lock* **it** *up*.]
look up (check)	I *looked up* the word in the dictionary. [I *looked* **it** *up*.]
pick out (choose)	Sandy *picked out* a dress. [She *picked* **it** *out*.]
pick up (take or collect)	When do you *pick up* the keys? [When do you *pick* **them** *up*?]
put off (postpone)	I often *put off* chores. [I often *put* **them** *off*.]

continued

SEPARABLE VERB/PREPOSITION COMBINATIONS

sign up (register for)	I want to *sign up* for the contest.
	[Please *sign me up* for the contest.]

INSEPARABLE VERB/PREPOSITION COMBINATIONS

call on (choose)	The teacher always *calls on* me.
drop in (visit)	*Drop in* when you are in the area.
fight against (combat)	He tried to *fight against* the proposal.
fight for (defend)	We need to *fight for* our rights.
go over (review; travel to)	He wants to *go over* our speeches.
	I want to *go over* to Lisa's place on Saturday.
grow up (mature)	All children *grow up.*

PRACTICE 15 . . . .

Edit the following sentences to make sure that the correct prepositions are used. Three sentences are correct; write "C" next to them.

EXAMPLE: Because fighting HIV/AIDS is important, we can't give
~~out~~ without a fight.
  _{up}

1. Organizations such as the Centers for Disease Control are fighting over an HIV/AIDS epidemic in the rural United States.

2. Many people put by testing because they have limited incomes and limited access to testing centers.

3. They might also be afraid at having their testing or HIV status discovered by the community.

4. Or they might be ashamed of practicing high-risk behavior.

5. However, finding off their HIV status is the first step toward life-saving treatment for those who are infected.

6. Getting tested amounts to being responsible in oneself.

7. Even so, being scared of the virus and of people's reactions is understandable.

8. The good news is there are clinics that allow patients to fill up test forms anonymously.

9. Patients can look up these clinics in the yellow pages or on the Web.

10. After calling a few and talking to the staff, picking one for is easy.

PRACTICE 16 . . . .

Edit the following paragraph to make sure that the correct prepositions are used. Three sentences are correct; write "C" next to them.

> **EXAMPLE:** I'm tired ~~with~~ *of* my dad's goofy sayings, such as "That's
>
> like putting lipstick on a pig."

(1) As a child, I was totally confused with these statements, but I never asked him to explain them because I was scared of looking stupid. (2) I was ashamed at the fact that I couldn't figure out what the sayings meant. (3) One day, when I was handing across an assignment to my teacher, I repeated one of my father's sayings to her. (4) "Don't put away until tomorrow what you can do today," I said. (5) She didn't seem surprised, so I asked, "You've heard of that?" (6) She said, "Yes, it's a well-known saying; look it out." (7) I did, and I found the saying in a book of common expressions. (8) Not wanting to give out just yet, I tried to find a few of my father's other sayings. (9) The odd ones weren't in the book! (10) I can't tell you how happy I was at this discovery.

. . . .

Write and Edit Your Own Work

ASSIGNMENT 1: WRITE . . . .

Write about a time when you were new to a group or situation and what you did to feel more comfortable. When you are done, check the order of words in your sentences and look for errors in the use of subjects, verbs, pronouns, and other sentence parts covered in this chapter.

> **ASSIGNMENT 2: EDIT** . . . .
>
> Using rules in this chapter, especially the verb charts, edit a paper you are writing for this course or another course or a piece of writing from your work or everyday life.

Practice Together

■ **LEARNING STYLES:** Look for activities in this chapter that are matched to your learning style. If you don't know your learning style, take the test on pages 26–28.

👁 Visual

🔊 Auditory

📖 Reading/writing

🦶 Kinesthetic (movement)

Working with a few other students, practice what you have learned in this chapter.

1. Play a game of subject, verb, and object. One person should be the subject of a sentence, one the verb, and one the object; these people should stand in S-V-O order. The first person should call out a subject, the second person should call out a verb that goes with the subject, and the third person should call out an object that goes with the verb. Try to make the sentence as funny as possible. Play at least three rounds, switching in different students if you have more than three people in your group. 🔊 🦶

2. Take turns calling out one of the pronouns from the list on page 335. The person who says the pronoun should gesture to illustrate the pronoun (for instance, pointing to himself or herself to illustrate *I*). Then, he or she should use the pronoun in a sentence. 🔊 🦶

3. As a group, write five statement-style sentences in different forms based on the verb charts throughout this chapter. Then, exchange sentences with another group, and rewrite each other's sentences first as negative statements then as questions. When both groups are done, have someone from each group stand up and read the rewritten sentences aloud. Check them against the charts for correctness. 🔊 📖 🦶

4. Have each person in the group draw a person, place, or thing (a noun). One at a time, hold up your drawings. The others should each say a sentence that uses the noun with the correct article. 👁 🔊 🦶

5. Have each person pick one adjective + preposition combination (p. 363) and one verb + preposition combination (p. 364). Then, take turns acting these out. The audience should try to guess what the actor intended. 🔊 🦶

Chapter Review

1. What is a pronoun? _____

What are the three types of English pronouns? _____

Use each of the types in a sentence. _____

2. Rewrite this sentence in the simple past and the simple future: Melinda picks flowers every morning.

Past: _____

Future: _____

3. Using the progressive tenses, rewrite this sentence first as a question, then in the past tense and in the future tense.

Chris is learning Spanish.

Question: _____

Past: _____

Future: _____

4. Edit the following sentences so that they use the modal auxiliary correctly:

Jennifer should to help her mother.

Yesterday, I can not worked.

5. Edit this sentence so that it uses the perfect tense correctly.

They have call an ambulance.

6. What is a gerund? _____

Write a sentence with a gerund in it. _____

7. What is an infinitive? _____

Write a sentence with an infinitive in it. _____

8. Give an example of a count noun. _____ Give an example of a noncount noun. _____ Use each of the nouns in a sentence, using the correct article. _____

_____

9. What is a preposition? _____

_____

Write a sentence using a preposition. _____

_____

10. **VOCABULARY:** Go back to any new words that you underlined in this chapter. Can you guess their meanings now? If not, look up the words in a dictionary.

LEARNING JOURNAL: Write for two minutes about something in this chapter that you'd like more practice with.

■ **TIP:** For help with building your vocabulary, see Appendix B.

Unit Four Test
Editing for Other Sentence Grammar

. . . .

Part 1   Following are two paragraphs and one essay. Read them carefully and circle the correct answers to the questions that follow them. Use some of the reading strategies from Chapter 2.

> **1** Yesterday, I nearly spent twenty minutes on my cell phone being a "cell phoney." **2** No one was on the other line, but I was talking anyway. **3** Pretending to carry on a conversation, my cell phone was held to my ear. **4** We hear people on their cell phones when we were just about anywhere. **5** How many of them are having an actual conversation? **6** Students in a communications class were asked if it had ever pretended to talk on a cell phone. **7** The class was surprised to find that everyone had faked a conversation at some point. **8** People might have fake conversations to avoid real conversations that might be unpleasant. **9** When some people walk on dark streets late at night, they feel safer by pretending to talk on their cell phone. **10** Other people use fake phone conversations to send a message to those around them. **11** A man might talk about his busy schedule to show that he works <u>more hard</u> than his coworkers. **12** Another person fakes an emergency call so that they can escape a bad date. **13** The next time you hear someone chatting on a cell phone, ask yourself if this person might be a "cell phoney."

1. Which of the following changes is needed in sentence 1?
   a. Change "spent" to "spend."
   b. Change "nearly spent" to "spent nearly."
   c. Change "minutes" to "minute."
   d. Change "phone" to "phoneses."

2. Which of the following sentences should be revised because it contains a dangling modifier?
   a. Sentence 2   c. Sentence 5
   b. Sentence 3   d. Sentence 9

3. Which of the following sentences should be revised because it contains an illogical shift in verb tense?
   a. Sentence 4   c. Sentence 11
   b. Sentence 9   d. Sentence 13

4. Which of the following changes is needed in sentence 6?
   a. Change "communications" to "communicationes."
   b. Change "were" to "was."
   c. Change "it" to "they."
   d. Change "phone" to "phones."

5. Which of the following should be used in place of the underlined words in sentence 11?
   - a. most hard
   - b. more harder
   - c. hardest
   - d. harder

1 If someone were asked on a quiz show to name the state where water skiing was invented, you might quickly guess Florida or Hawaii. **2** However, in Montana in 1922, nineteen-year-old Ralph Samuelson was the first person to ski on a lake. **3** Trying to use snow skis, he was unsuccessful at first. **4** He also tried using strips of wood from barrels, but him crashed into the water. **5** He knew he had to think of something else. **6** He soften some pine boards in his mother's copper kettle. **7** He figured that skiing would be <u>more easier</u> if he turned up the ends of the skis. **8** He was right. **9** He started jumping over waves and broke his first pair of skis. **10** That, however, did not stop him, and soon he wanted to try something more adventurous. **11** Greasing the ramp of a half-submerged raft with lard, he invented the first water-ski jump. **12** Samuelson invented a real fun sport that many people enjoy.

6. Which of the following changes is needed in sentence 1?
   - a. Change "If someone was asked" to "If she was asked."
   - b. Change "If someone was asked" to "If he was asked."
   - c. Change "you" to "he or she."
   - d. Change "quickly" to "quick."

7. Which of the following changes is needed in sentence 4?
   - a. Change "tried" to "tries."
   - b. Change "strips" to "stripses."
   - c. Change "him" to "he."
   - d. Change "crashed" to "crashes."

8. Which of the following sentences should be revised because it leaves out a past-tense verb ending?
   - a. Sentence 3
   - b. Sentence 6
   - c. Sentence 7
   - d. Sentence 11

9. Which of the following should be used in place of the underlined words in sentence 7?
   - a. most easy
   - b. easiest
   - c. more easy
   - d. easier

10. Which of the following changes is needed in sentence 12?
   - a. Change "invented" to "invents."
   - b. Change "real" to "really."
   - c. Change "fun" to "more fun."
   - d. Change "people" to "peoples."

1 Most college students have to spend their money careful. **2** Even so, they want having a nice lifestyle. **3** Luckily, with a little creativity, students can save money and have some of the things that you want.

4 For example, if your apartment nearly looks bare without plants, there is no need to spend a lot of money. **5** Just look in your kitchen. **6** Orange or lemon seeds will grow into trees in warm, sunny places. **7** If you like vines, a sweet potato in a glass of water will grow roots and leafs. **8** There are many ways to decorate your apartment inexpensive with plants grown from common foods.

9 Whether you need a table or a T-shirt, don't pass by thrift stores or yard sales, which have everything from furniture to belts. **10** Paintings, wall hangings, old desks, workout equipment, and even toys for childrens can be found there. **11** Anything that has never been used and is still in its box can make great gifts.

12 Finally, have a do-it-yourself attitude. **13** Anybody can sew his or her own clothes or make skin-care products from milk, oatmeal, honey, or other inexpensive ingredients. **14** Saving money every day, there might be enough for a great vacation after final exams.

11. What revision should be made to the underlined section of sentence 1?
    a. No change is necessary.
    b. more careful
    c. carefuller
    d. carefully

12. What revision should be made to the underlined section of sentence 2?
    a. No change is necessary.
    b. to have
    c. had
    d. did have

13. What revision should be made to the underlined section of sentence 3?
    a. No change is necessary.
    b. we want
    c. they want
    d. you wanted

14. What revision should be made to the underlined section of sentence 4?
    a. No change is necessary.
    b. looks nearly bare
    c. nearly looked bare
    d. looks bare nearly

15. What revision should be made to the underlined section of sentence 7?
    a. No change is necessary.
    b. leaf
    c. leafes
    d. leaves

16. What revision should be made to the underlined section of sentence 8?
    a. No change is necessary.
    b. more inexpensive
    c. inexpensively
    d. most inexpensive

17. What revision should be made to the underlined section of sentence 10?
    a. No change is necessary.
    b. childs
    c. childes
    d. children

18. What revision should be made to the underlined section of sentence 11?
    a. No change is necessary.   c. your
    b. his or her   d. their

19. What revision should be made to the underlined section of sentence 13?
    a. No change is necessary.   c. their
    b. your   d. my

20. What revision should be made to the underlined section of sentence 14?
    a. No change is necessary.
    b. If you save money every day
    c. When saving money every day
    d. By saving money every day

Part 2

Circle the correct choice for each of the following items.

1. Choose the correct word to fill in the blank.

   Mateo began cutting up the two _____ of bread for sandwiches.
   a. loafs   c. loafes
   b. loaves   d. loaveses

2. If an underlined portion of this item is incorrect, select the revision that fixes it. If the item is correct as written, choose d.

   My wife and I painted the shelves with two colors of paint.
           A   **B**   **C**
   a. My wife and me   c. colores
   b. shelfs   d. No change is necessary.

3. Choose the correct word to fill in the blank.

   I am _____ every time you call me.
   a. eating   c. eaten
   b. eat   d. eats

4. Choose the correct word(s) to fill in the blank.

   Each of the club members wanted a different design on _____ jacket.
   a. our   c. his or her
   b. their   d. its

5. Choose the item that has no errors.
   a. My brother plays the piano much better than me.
   b. My brother plays the piano much better than I.
   c. My brother plays the piano much more good than I.

6. If an underlined portion of this item is incorrect, select the revision that fixes it. If the item is correct as written, choose d.

   On the news this morning, they said that the traffic was bad.
                                   A   B   C

   a. the reporter   c. badly
   b. say   d. No change is necessary.

7. If an underlined portion of this item is incorrect, select the revision that fixes it. If the item is correct as written, choose d.

   Yesterday, the freezer it made a funny sound when I opened the door.
                       A   B   C

   a. the freezer   c. open
   b. funniest   d. No change is necessary.

8. Choose the correct words to fill in the blank.

   The team named _____ the most valuable players in the game.
   a. him and me   c. I and him
   b. he and I   d. me and he

9. Choose the correct word(s) to fill in the blank.

   When I saw the puppy by the side of the road, I _____ stopped the car.
   a. most quickly   c. quick
   b. quicker   d. quickly

10. Choose the correct word to fill in the blank.

    Tyrese should enter the contest because his essay is written _____.
    a. good   c. well
    b. better   d. bestest

11. Choose the correct word(s) to fill in the blank.

    Today's weather is _____ than yesterday's.
    a. stormiest   c. more stormy
    b. stormier   d. most stormy

12. If an underlined portion of this item is incorrect, select the revision that fixes it. If the item is correct as written, choose d.

    You should told me that you didn't like beards before I arranged your
                    A   B   C

    date with my hairy brother.
    a. should have told   c. arranging
    b. didn't liking   d. No change is necessary.

13. If an underlined portion of this item is incorrect, select the revision that fixes it. If the item is correct as written, choose d.

   This year's <u>entries</u> in the art contest <u>were</u> a <u>significant</u> improvement over
             A   **B**   **C**
   the previous year's.

   a. entrys
   b. was
   c. significantly
   d. No change is necessary.

14. Choose the item that has no errors.

   a. A taxi driver must know your way around the city.
   b. A taxi driver must know their way around the city.
   c. A taxi driver must know his or her way around the city.

15. If an underlined portion of this item is incorrect, select the revision that fixes it. If the item is correct as written, choose d.

   <u>Finishing my essay</u>, the <u>hours</u> went by <u>quickly</u>.
             A   **B**   **C**

   a. As I finished my essay
   b. houres
   c. quick
   d. No change is necessary.

16. Choose the item that has no errors.

   a. She baked the cake using her grandmother's recipe.
   b. Using her grandmother's recipe, the cake was baked.
   c. Using her grandmother's recipe, she baked the cake.

17. Choose the item that has no errors.

   a. Trying to get in shape, the gym was always crowded.
   b. The gym was always crowded, trying to get in shape.
   c. Because the students were all trying to get in shape, the gym was always crowded.

18. Choose the item that has no errors.

   a. Excited and happy, the award was given to the members of the drama club.
   b. The members of the drama club, excited and happy, were given the award.
   c. The members of the drama club were given the award excited and happy.

19. Choose the item that has no errors.

   a. Following the route he suggested, the main highway was barricaded.
   b. The main highway was barricaded, following the route he suggested.
   c. Although I followed the route he suggested, the main highway was barricaded.

20. If an underlined portion of this item is incorrect, select the revision that fixes it. If the item is correct as written, choose d.

She finished the <u>reports</u> and <u>turns</u> over the <u>forms</u> to her boss.
                   A   **B**   **C**

a. reportes

b. turned

c. formes

d. No change is necessary.

■ **TIP:** For advice on taking tests, see Appendix A.

Unit Five

Editing to Combine and Improve Sentences

22

Coordination

Joining Sentences with Related Ideas

Understand What Coordination Is

If all of your sentences are short, they will seem choppy and hard to read. One way to vary the rhythm of your writing is to combine two short sentences into one longer one through **coordination**. The two sentences should have closely related ideas.

VOCABULARY: Underline any words in this chapter that are new to you.

IDEA JOURNAL: What is your most important goal for this month? This year?

■ **TIP:** To do this chapter, you need to know what a sentence is. For a review, see Chapter 10.

TWO SENTENCES, UNRELATED IDEAS	It was very hot today. My neighbor called to ask me to stay with her baby.
	[These sentences shouldn't be combined because the ideas are not related.]
TWO SENTENCES, RELATED IDEAS	Today, my son got an iPod and a new computer. He's using them right now.
COMBINED THROUGH COORDINATION	Today, my son got an iPod and a new computer, *and* he's using them right now.
	[The sentences are joined with a comma and the coordinating conjunction *and*.]
COMBINED THROUGH COORDINATION	Today, my son got an iPod and a new computer; he's using them right now.
	[The sentences are joined with a semicolon.]
COMBINED THROUGH COORDINATION	Today, my son got an iPod and a new computer; *in fact*, he's using them right now.
	[The sentences are joined with a semicolon and *in fact*.]

Use Coordination to Combine Sentences

Using Coordinating Conjunctions

One method of combining sentences through coordination is to use a comma and a **coordinating conjunction** between them. You can remember what the coordinating conjunctions are by keeping the word *fanboys* in mind: **f**or, **a**nd, **n**or, **b**ut, **o**r, **y**et, **s**o.

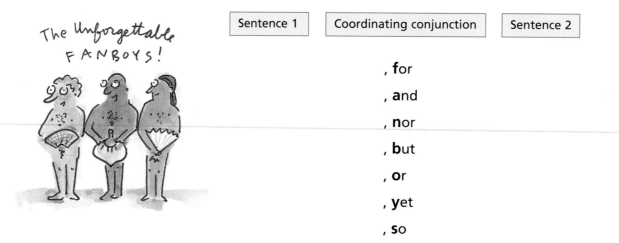

The Unforgettable FANBOYS!

Sentence 1	Coordinating conjunction	Sentence 2
	, for	
	, and	
	, nor	
	, but	
	, or	
	, yet	
	, so	

Don't use just any conjunction; choose the one that makes the most sense.

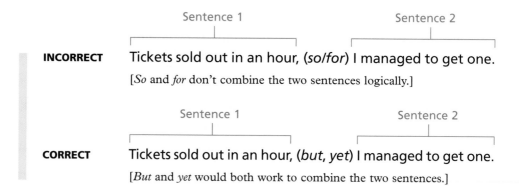

	Sentence 1		Sentence 2
INCORRECT	Tickets sold out in an hour, (*so/for*) I managed to get one.		

[*So* and *for* don't combine the two sentences logically.]

	Sentence 1		Sentence 2
CORRECT	Tickets sold out in an hour, (*but, yet*) I managed to get one.		

[*But* and *yet* would both work to combine the two sentences.]

Here are the meanings of the coordinating conjunctions and more examples of their use.

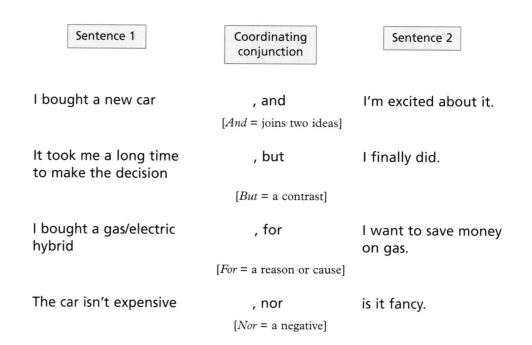

Sentence 1	Coordinating conjunction	Sentence 2
I bought a new car	, and	I'm excited about it.
	[*And* = joins two ideas]	
It took me a long time to make the decision	, but	I finally did.
	[*But* = a contrast]	
I bought a gas/electric hybrid	, for	I want to save money on gas.
	[*For* = a reason or cause]	
The car isn't expensive	, nor	is it fancy.
	[*Nor* = a negative]	

Sentence 1	Coordinating conjunction	Sentence 2
My friends will think the car is great	, or	they'll question my decision.
	[*Or* = alternatives]	
My friend Lisa is very worried about the environment	, so	she'll be very happy about my news.
	[*So* = a result]	
My friend Dan doesn't like hybrids	, yet	how can he argue with saving money and reducing pollution?
	[*Yet* = a contrast]	

 Draw a chart like the one shown here, with the conjunctions down the center, but leave each side blank. Then, fill in sentences on either side.

To figure out how to join two sentences using coordination, follow this advice:

FIND: Read each sentence in your writing carefully. Look for sentence pairs that are related.

Dan likes helping others. He decided to become a paramedic.

- Ask if the sentences would make sense if they were joined by a coordinating conjunction. [In this example, the answer is "yes."]
- If they would, you can join them.

CHOOSE: Join the sentences with a comma and a coordinating conjunction that makes sense.

Dan likes helping others. He decided to become a paramedic. *, so he*

The coordinating conjunction *so* indicates that Dan decided to become a paramedic *as a result of* the fact that he likes helping others.

TWO SENTENCES	JOINED THROUGH COORDINATION
Instant messaging is a great way to stay in touch with friends. It's fun.	Instant messaging is a great way to stay in touch with friends, *and* it's fun.
I wanted to go swimming after work. The pool was closed.	I wanted to go swimming after work, *but* the pool was closed.

TWO SENTENCES	JOINED THROUGH COORDINATION
You can drive to work with me. You can wait for the bus.	You can drive to work with me, *or* you can wait for the bus.

PRACTICE 1

In each of the following sentences, fill in the blank with an appropriate coordinating conjunction. There may be more than one correct answer for some sentences.

> **EXAMPLE:** Most workers receive only two to three weeks of vacation a year, ____*so*____ they choose their vacation destinations carefully.

1. Las Vegas is one of the hottest vacation spots in America, _____ it's not just because of the warm, sunny weather.

2. Las Vegas is famous for its casinos, _____ there is more to the city than many people think.

3. You can browse in the many shops, _____ you can relax in a cool swimming pool.

4. Hotel workers will treat you well, _____ they want you to spend your money in their restaurants and gaming areas.

5. You can take a tour to the Hoover Dam, _____ you might prefer to tour the Grand Canyon by helicopter.

6. Good meals are not hard to find, _____ do they have to be expensive.

7. Prime rib buffets start at around $7, _____ they are usually quite delicious.

8. Casinos compete fiercely for business, _____ they offer free attractions.

9. The MGM Grand Hotel has a lion's den, _____ the Bellagio presents a beautiful fountain show every fifteen minutes in the evenings.

10. Many tourists who visit Las Vegas don't like gambling, _____ they can have a wonderful time there.

PRACTICE 2 . . . .

Combine each pair of sentences into a single sentence by using a comma and a coordinating conjunction. In some cases, there may be more than one correct answer.

EXAMPLE: Instructors want students to be creative, ~~When~~ *, but when* it comes

to excuses, they prefer honesty.

1. Teachers hear a variety of interesting excuses. Some are more creative than others.

2. In the past, students claimed that the dog ate their homework. Students now say that the computer ate their file.

3. The due date for a major term paper approaches. Distant relatives die in surprising numbers.

4. The dearly departed grandmother remains one of the most frequently heard excuses. What instructor would be so cruel as to question a student's loss?

5. A noble excuse always sounds good. A student might claim that he had to shovel snow from an elderly neighbor's driveway.

6. Excuses involving animals can hit a soft spot in some instructors' hearts. Caring for a sick puppy would make an excellent excuse.

7. It's always best to be honest about a missed deadline. Students get caught more often than one would think.

8. One student claimed that she was at a funeral. Her professor, who happened to be watching a televised baseball game, saw the student catch a fly ball in the stands.

9. The professor did not accept the funeral excuse. He did not allow the student to make up the missed quiz.

10. As long as there are term papers due, there will be excuses. Many instructors will doubt them.

■ **TIP:** For more practice, visit Exercise Central at <**bedfordstmartins.com/ realskills**>.

Using Semicolons

Another method of combining related sentences is to use a **semicolon (;)** between them. Occasional semicolons are fine, but do not overuse them.

SENTENCE 1	;	SENTENCE 2
My favorite hobby is bike riding	;	it's the best way to see the country.
It's faster than running but slower than driving	;	that's the perfect speed for me.

A semicolon alone does not tell readers much about how the two ideas are related. Use a **conjunctive adverb** after the semicolon to give more information about the relationship. Put a comma after the conjunctive adverb.

Equal idea	Conjunctive adverb	Equal idea
	; afterward,	
	; also,	
	; as a result,	
	; besides,	
	; consequently,	
	; frequently,	
	; however,	
	; in addition,	
	; in fact,	
	; instead,	
	; still,	
	; then,	
	; therefore,	
I ride my bike a lot	; as a result,	I am in good enough shape for a long-distance ride.
My boyfriend wants me to go on a bike tour with him	; however,	I would find that stressful.
I ride my bike to relax	; therefore,	I suggested that he take a friend on the tour.

PRACTICE 3 . .

Join each pair of sentences by using a semicolon alone.

> **EXAMPLE:** Some foods are not meant to be eaten by themselves, *; macaroni*
>
> ~~Macaroni~~ would be no fun without cheese.

1. Homemade chocolate chip cookies are delicious. They're even better with a glass of cold milk.

2. A hamburger by itself seems incomplete. It needs a pile of fries to be truly satisfying.

3. Fries have another natural partner. Most people like to eat them with ketchup.

4. Apple pie is just apple pie. Add a scoop of vanilla ice cream, and you have an American tradition.

5. A peanut butter sandwich is boring. A little jelly adds some excitement.

PRACTICE 4 . .

Combine each pair of sentences by using a semicolon and a conjunctive adverb. In some cases, there may be more than one correct answer.

> **EXAMPLE:** Few people manage to survive being lost at sea for more *; however,*
>
> than a few weeks, Steven Callahan is one of those lucky few.

1. In January 1982, Steven Callahan set sail from the Canary Islands in a small homemade boat. The boat sank six days into his journey across the Atlantic.

2. Callahan was an experienced sailor. He was prepared for emergency situations.

3. Alone on a five-foot inflatable raft, he knew his chances for survival were slim. He was determined to live.

4. Callahan had just three pounds of food, eight pints of water, and a makeshift spear. He had a device that changes seawater into drinking water.

5. With his spear, Callahan was able to catch food. He lost a significant amount of weight.

6. Callahan suffered serious sunburn. He had to fight off sharks.

7. Several ships passed Callahan. Nobody on board saw him.

8. His raft sprang a leak thirty-three days before he was rescued. He did not give up hope.

9. For a total of seventy-six days, he drifted alone. Three fishermen found him.

10. Callahan possessed a tremendous will to live. He never gave up and lived to tell his tale.

. . . .

READ ALOUD

Read the following paragraph aloud. Can you hear how choppy it is? Then, read it a second time, trying to join some sentences with coordinating conjunctions.

> I am a cell phone addict. Every morning, I call my best friend. She answers right away. We talk for a few minutes. Then, I charge up my phone. I get ready for another day. At work, I can't use my cell. I make calls at lunch. I shut off my ringer for class. I turn it on as soon as I leave. Driving home, I call my best friend again.

Edit for Coordination in College, Work, and Everyday Life

Complete the editing reviews as instructed, referring to the chart on page 391.

EDITING REVIEW 1: COLLEGE . . . .

The following paragraph is similar to one you might find in a nursing textbook. Join the underlined sentences through coordination.

(1) Type 2 diabetes is also known as adult-onset or non-insulin-dependent diabetes. (2) Most diabetes cases are classified as Type 2 diabetes. (3) Ninety to 95 percent of diabetics have this type of the disease. (4) Without treatment, Type 2 diabetes can lead to a wide range of

complications. (5) <u>In fact, diabetes is the fifth-deadliest disease in the United States.</u> (6) <u>It can be controlled or even prevented by careful attention to diet and exercise.</u> (7) <u>Patients should be encouraged to exercise for thirty minutes daily.</u> (8) <u>They should be taught how to plan meals according to the American Diabetes Association's Diabetes Food Pyramid.</u> (9) <u>It is also important for patients to practice proper foot and skin care.</u> (10) <u>Diabetes can cause skin infections, particularly on the feet.</u> (11) <u>Without proper care, skin infections can lead to serious complications and even amputation.</u> (12) <u>Smoking is especially dangerous for people with diabetes.</u> (13) <u>Smokers should be provided with resources to help them quit.</u> (14) <u>Living with diabetes is not easy.</u> (15) <u>Patients can live long and healthy lives if they receive education and support in controlling the disease.</u>

EDITING REVIEW 2: WORK

In the following letter, join the underlined sentences through coordination.

Ms. Clara Martinez, Director

Personnel Office

Heart's Home Health

22 Juniper Drive

Greenfield, NM 87401

Dear Ms. Martinez:

(1) Please consider my application for the Certified Nursing Assistant position advertised in the *Daily Sun* last week. (2) <u>I am currently enrolled in the nursing program at Greenfield College.</u> (3) <u>This job would help me further develop skills in my field while letting me offer my services to your clients.</u> (4) My adviser, Dr. Wes Arrowsmith, praised your organization and encouraged me to apply.

(5) In May 2005, I became certified as a nurse's aide through Greenfield College, with sixty hours of work experience at Pine Manor Retirement Home. (6) <u>In my course work and practice, I learned to assist patients</u>

with basic hygiene procedures and meals. (7) <u>I monitored patients' vital</u> <u>signs and reported to the nurse on duty.</u> (8) I believe that in addition to these technical skills, my personality also makes me a strong candidate for the position. (9) <u>I bring a smile and a positive attitude to my nurs-</u> <u>ing assistant duties.</u> (10) <u>My cheerful nature makes me a strong team</u> <u>member.</u> (11) <u>Finally, I am fluent in Navajo, English, and Spanish.</u> (12) <u>I would be able to speak with all of your clients and assist staff with</u> <u>translation if needed.</u>

(13) If my background and qualifications meet your agency's needs, please contact me anytime at (505) 555-2322. (14) <u>I am very interested</u> <u>in joining the team at Heart's Home Health.</u> (15) <u>I hope to hear from</u> <u>you.</u> (16) Thank you for your time.

Sincerely,

Florence Redhouse

EDITING REVIEW 3: EVERYDAY LIFE

Join the underlined sentences through coordination.

(1) What did you do to prevent diabetes today? (2) <u>Did your break-</u> <u>fast consist of coffee and a doughnut?</u> (3) <u>Did you skip breakfast alto-</u> <u>gether?</u> (4) If so, you may be headed the way of 8.2 million Americans who have diabetes. (5) <u>This number may seem high.</u> (6) <u>It's actually</u> <u>quite low compared to the forty-one million Americans who have pre-</u> <u>diabetes, a condition that puts people at risk for developing diabetes in</u> <u>the future.</u> (7) Sadly, many of the hundreds of thousands of diabetes-related deaths each year could be prevented through diet and exercise.

(8) The death rate for people with diabetes is twice as high as for those without the disease. (9) <u>Diabetics have two to four times the risk</u> <u>of dying of heart disease or having a stroke.</u> (10) <u>They are fifteen to forty</u> <u>times more likely to have a limb amputated.</u> (11) Yet with careful man-agement, diabetes can usually be kept under control. (12) <u>People can</u> <u>use the categories of the American Diabetes Association's Diabetes</u>

Food Pyramid to select foods by calorie and sugar content. (13) They can plan meals according to their needs and preferences.

(14) Healthy lifestyles need to be supported through our mass media. (15) The media have a strong influence in our lives. (16) Advertising should promote a healthy diet instead of sugary, caffeinated sodas and greasy, salty fast foods. (17) Advertising has also promoted the idea that Americans can lose weight without work. (18) The message should be that exercise and a sensible diet are required—and worthwhile.

Write and Edit Your Own Work

ASSIGNMENT 1: WRITE

What have you done—or what would you like to do—to stay healthy? Describe the steps you have taken, or plan to take. When you are done, see if you can join any of the sentences using coordination. Use the chart on page 391 as a guide.

ASSIGNMENT 2: EDIT

Referring to the chart on page 391, use coordination to join sentences in a paper you are writing for this course or another course or in a piece of writing from your work or everyday life.

Practice Together

Working with a few other students, practice what you have learned in this chapter.

1. Half of the group should write three pairs of brief sentences that could be joined by a coordinating conjunction, putting a blank where the conjunction should go. **EXAMPLE:** *I like Tyler,* _____ *he likes me.* Someone from this group should read the sentences aloud to the other group, who should call out conjunctions that could fill in the blanks. Both groups should then discuss the answers, deciding if the conjunctions chosen make sense. Next, switch the groups so that the second group writes the sentences with the blanks and the first fills in the blanks. Time the responses to see which team comes up with the most logical conjunctions in the shortest time. 👁 👂 📖

■ **LEARNING STYLES:** Look for activities in this chapter that are matched to your learning style. If you don't know your learning style, take the test on pages 26–28.

👁 Visual

👂 Auditory

📖 Reading/writing

✍ Kinesthetic (movement)

2. Have each person write two sentences that could be joined through co-ordination, with space between them, on a sheet of paper. Here's an example, but use a different sentence: (1) *I want to learn surfing* (2) *I'm going to take lessons in Hawaii.* Then, have each person illustrate both sentences. When you're done, take turns holding up your pictures and asking others in the group to fill in appropriate punctuation and/or conjunctions. 👁 ✍ 📖 ✌

3. Have someone pick a coordinating conjunction and call it out. They will play the role of this conjunction in a sentence. Next, two other group members should stand on either side of the conjunction and say a sentence that could be connected by the conjunction. Finally, each person should read his or her part aloud. **EXAMPLE:** Person 1: *But.* Person 2: *I want to go the movies.* Person 3: *I have a cold.* Together: *I want to go to the movies, but I have a cold.* Next, let others play the conjunction and sentence parts. 👁 ✍ ✌

Chapter Review

1. _____ combines two short, related sentences into a longer one.

2. The coordinating conjunctions are _____.

3. A _____ is a punctuation mark that can join two sentences through coordination.

4. Use a _____ after a semicolon to give more information about the two sentences joined by the semicolon. List four conjunctive adverbs: _____

5. **VOCABULARY:** Go back to any new words that you underlined in this chapter. Can you guess their meanings now? If not, look up the words in a dictionary.

📖 **LEARNING JOURNAL:** Write for two minutes, describing how you would explain coordination to someone who doesn't know what it is.

■ **TIP:** For help with building your vocabulary, see Appendix B.

EDITING FOR COORDINATION

Coordination is a way to join two sentences with related ideas (see page 379).

There are two methods of combining sentences through coordination.

1. Use a comma and a coordinating conjunction (see p. 379).

2. Use a semicolon (;) or a semicolon and a conjunctive adverb followed by a comma (see p. 384).

The coordinating conjunctions are *for, and, nor, but, or, yet,* and *so* (see p. 379).

Some conjunctive adverbs are *also, however, in fact, instead, still, then,* and *therefore* (see p. 384).

23

Subordination

Joining Sentences
with Related Ideas

Understand What Subordination Is

 **VOCABULARY:** Under-
line any words in this chapter
that are new to you.

Like coordination, **subordination** is a way to combine short, choppy sentences with related ideas into a longer sentence. With subordination, you
put a dependent word (such as *after*, *although*, *because*, or *when*) in front of
one of the sentences. The resulting sentence will have one complete sentence and one dependent clause, which is no longer a complete sentence.

Before you join two sentences, make sure they have closely related ideas.

■ **TIP:** To do this chapter,
you need to know what a sentence is. For a review, see
Chapter 10.

TWO SENTENCES, UNRELATED IDEAS	I was hospitalized after a car accident. I had a pizza for lunch.
	[These two sentences shouldn't be combined because the ideas are not related.]
TWO SENTENCES, RELATED IDEAS	I was hospitalized after a car accident. My friends showed me how supportive they could be.
JOINED THROUGH SUBORDINATION	*When* I was hospitalized after a car accident,
	my friends showed me how supportive they could be.
	[The dependent word *when* logically combines the two sentences. The underlined word group is a dependent clause, and the second word group is a complete sentence.]

👁 Draw a picture of two
related things.

Use Subordination to Combine Sentences

Dependent words used to join two sentences through subordination are also
called **subordinating conjunctions**. Again, put a subordinating conjunction in front of one of the sentences to make that sentence a dependent
clause, which is not a complete sentence.

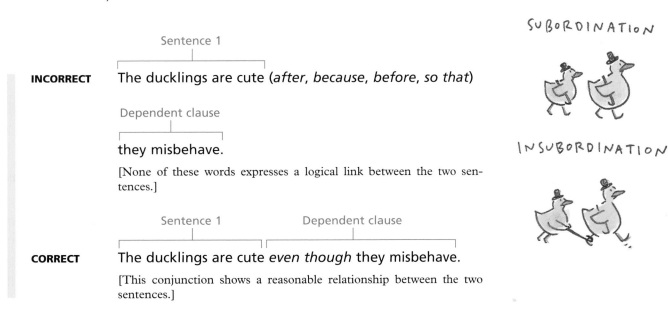

Sentence 1	Subordinating conjunction (dependent word)	Sentence 2 (now a dependent clause)

after	since
although	so that
as	unless
as if	until
because	when
before	where
even though	while
if	

■ **TIP:** The word *subordinate* means "lower in rank" or "secondary." In the workplace, for example, you are subordinate to your boss. In the army, a private is subordinate to an officer.

Choose the conjunction that makes the most sense with the two sentences.

Sentence 1

INCORRECT The ducklings are cute (*after, because, before, so that*)

Dependent clause

they misbehave.

[None of these words expresses a logical link between the two sentences.]

Sentence 1   Dependent clause

CORRECT The ducklings are cute *even though* they misbehave.

[This conjunction shows a reasonable relationship between the two sentences.]

When the complete sentence is before the dependent clause, do not use a comma. However, when the dependent clause is in front of the complete sentence, put a comma after it.

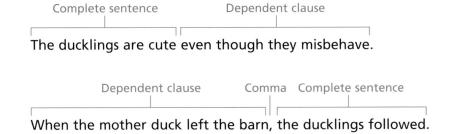

Complete sentence   Dependent clause

The ducklings are cute even though they misbehave.

Dependent clause   Comma   Complete sentence

When the mother duck left the barn, the ducklings followed.

🦢 You can practice combining sentences by using a magnetic poetry kit. Pick words to create sentences and then add conjunctions to join the sentences.

To figure out how to join two sentences using subordination, follow this advice:

FIND: Read each sentence in your writing carefully. Look for sentence pairs that are related.

My daughter studied hard. She made the honor roll at her school.

- Ask if the sentences would make sense if they were joined by a subordinating conjunction (such as *after*, *although*, *because*, or *until*). [In this example, the answer is "yes."]
- If they would, you can join them.

CHOOSE: Join the sentences with a subordinating conjunction that makes sense.

Because my   *, she*
My daughter studied hard. She made the honor roll at her school.

The subordinating conjunction *because* shows the cause-and-effect relationship between the sentences. Because the dependent clause begins the combined sentences, a comma is needed after it.

IDEA JOURNAL: What activities do you like to do with others, and what activities do you prefer to do alone? Why?

TWO SENTENCES	JOINED THROUGH SUBORDINATION
I raked the entire yard. I was very tired.	*After* I raked the entire yard, I was very tired.
You must drive with an adult. You have your driver's license.	You must drive with an adult *even though* you have your driver's license.
Patti works overtime. She will make an extra $200 this week.	*If* Patti works overtime, she will make an extra $200 this week.

PRACTICE 1 . . . .

In the following sentences, fill in the blank with an appropriate subordinating conjunction. In some cases, there may be more than one correct choice.

EXAMPLE: _____*Although*_____ most people vacation with family or friends, some people prefer traveling alone.

1. _____ you travel with a group, you must make compromises.

2. For instance, you won't be able to try that inviting Thai restaurant _____ everyone else in the group enjoys Thai food.

3. _____ you can split up for certain activities, it's silly to spend too much time apart on a group vacation.

4. You might also have to endure crankiness _____ travel can make people tired and irritable.

5. _____ you return from a family vacation, you might be more stressed out than you were before you left.

6. _____ you travel alone, you make your own plans and go at your own pace.

7. You can plan your activities _____ the entire vacation suits your own preferences.

8. _____ you spot an interesting shop, you don't have to ask any-one's permission to stop in and browse.

9. Vacationing alone also provides valuable private time _____ you are not distracted by others.

10. _____ family vacations make nice memories, everyone ought to vacation alone every now and then.

PRACTICE 2 . . . .

Combine each pair of sentences into a single sentence by using an appropriate subordinating conjunction either at the beginning of or between the two sentences. In some cases, there may be more than one correct answer.

EXAMPLE: *When* O.J. Simpson went on trial for murder, The entire nation *, the* tuned in to the live television coverage.

1. We are obsessed with the lives of celebrities. They often have to fight for their privacy.

2. A celebrity's marriage breaks up. We want to know why.

3. Photographers follow celebrities around. They can catch them in a newsworthy situation.

4. Ashlee Simpson believed no one was watching her yell at a fast-food worker. A camera at the restaurant caught everything.

5. The press reported Jude Law and Sienna Miller's relationship problems. The couple spoke out about their love for each other (though they later broke up).

6. Some celebrities disguise themselves in public. They can avoid the media.

7. Michael Jackson is constantly followed by photographers. He has reportedly disguised himself as a woman to escape the attention.

8. Most celebrity chasing is harmless. It is understandably annoying to celebrities.

9. Fascination with a celebrity can turn dangerous. An obsessive fan becomes a stalker.

10. Many people dream of fame and adoring fans. The cost of that fame can be high.

Turn each of the following into a complete sentence by filling in the blanks. Make sure that each word group you add includes a subject and a verb.

   EXAMPLE: **While Derek washed the dishes,** *I put away the laundry* .

1. Whenever Vincent goes to the dentist, _____

2. If _____, we will install a pool in the backyard.

3. Because a hurricane is heading toward our city, _____

   _____

4. The "no television" rule will remain in effect until _____.

5. Unless you turn the key all the way to the right, _____.

6. While _____, the rest of the hikers stayed at the camp.

7. Before _____, I must finish writing my term paper.

8. Blake drove all the way to Atlanta because _____.

9. George and Roxanne just bought a new fishing boat although _____

   _____.

■ **TIP:** For more practice, visit Exercise Central at <**bedfordstmartins.com/ realskills**>.

10. If I were Raoul, _____.

READ ALOUD

Read the following paragraph aloud. Can you hear how choppy it is? Then, read it a second time, trying to join some sentences with subordinating conjunctions.

> I am a good mechanic. My friends bring their cars to me. My best friend's car broke down. She had it towed to my house. I take apart old cars all the time. I had the right parts to fix her car. I made the repairs. She gave me a gift certificate for Circuit City. She didn't have to do this. I appreciated her kindness. I am always happy to help out when I can.

Edit for Subordination in College, Work, and Everyday Life

Complete the editing reviews as instructed, referring to the chart on page 401.

EDITING REVIEW 1: COLLEGE . . . .

The following paragraph is similar to one you might find in a history textbook. Join the underlined sentences through subordination.

(1) The explorer Christopher Columbus reached land in 1492. (2) He did not realize just how lost he was. (3) Sailing West from Spain, he and his crew had hoped to find a new sea route to India and the Far East. (4) They were greeted by natives of the island. (5) Columbus and his men mistakenly referred to them as Indians. (6) In reality, they were Arawaks, natives of the Caribbean islands where Columbus had landed. (7) The Arawaks were friendly and welcoming. (8) Columbus soon took some of them as prisoners, later bringing them back to Spain with him. (9) Describing them in his log, Columbus wrote, "They are artless and generous with what they have, to such a degree as no one would believe but him who had seen it." (10) He mistakenly assumed that the islands were rich in gold. (11) The Arawaks wore small gold ornaments in their noses. (12) The Arawaks also told Columbus of other islanders who wore gold bands around their arms and legs. (13) In March 1493, Columbus returned to Spain. (14) He was greeted as a hero.

EDITING REVIEW 2: WORK

In the following memo, join the underlined sentences by using subordination.

Date: September 1, 2006

To: All Employees

From: Jean Hachadourian, Human Resources

Re: Upcoming Change in Holiday Schedule

(1) President Nixon made Columbus Day a federal holiday in 1971. (2) Our offices have always been closed on the second Monday of October. (3) This week, however, our state legislature followed the lead of seventeen other states and voted to remove Columbus Day from the list of state-paid holidays. (4) This day will remain a federal holiday, with banks and post offices closed. (5) It will no longer be a state holiday.

(6) This is a state government office. (7) Columbus Day will not be on our holiday schedule next year. (8) The legislature has not yet decided which holiday should replace Columbus Day as a statewide day off. (9) The decision is announced next week. (10) We will issue a revised version of our holiday schedule. (11) Lawmakers are considering making our widely celebrated Harvest Day a state-funded holiday. (12) This decision is made. (13) The new holiday will fall in late September.

EDITING REVIEW 3: EVERYDAY LIFE

In the following student essay, join the underlined sentences by using subordination.

(1) The debate over Native American sports team names and mascots rages on. (2) I am a proud member of the Navajo tribe. (3) I think there are more important issues to argue about. (4) Others, however, see team names, symbols, and mascots representing Native Americans as offensive. (5) Protests have been held and teams have been boycotted. (6) The players themselves are not responsible. (7) Can't we lighten up a little? (8) Native American names for teams are a source of pride to many native people, so let's get rid of any images that are truly offensive, sit back, and enjoy the game.

(9) I hear someone argue that certain team names are offensive. (10) I am puzzled. (11) I think of team names such as the Braves or the Warriors as proud reminders of my people's heritage. (12) Europeans arrived on the continent. (13) Warriors were treated with great respect in native cultures, and they still are. (14) My high school basketball team, the Chieftains, went on to the national championship, and our name only added to our pride. (15) A sports team wants to call themselves the Indians to represent their strength. (16) I take the choice as a compliment. (17) In my view, people who oppose such team names and mascots are often far removed from present-day Native American culture. (18) There are numerous Native American tribes across the country. (19) Some people think of Native Americans as ghosts of the historical past, not as living people.

(20) Sports are meant to entertain. (21) Taking things too seriously just spoils the fun. (22) Native Americans on both sides of the issue should come together and decide which images are obviously offensive; those images should be removed. (23) Some teams, however, want to wear respectful symbols of my pride and heritage. (24) I say that they are welcome to do so.

. . . .

Write and Edit Your Own Work

ASSIGNMENT 1: WRITE . . . .

Think about something that defines you as a person (for example, *I am a good friend/employee/listener*). Write about what has made you this way, considering important people or events. When you are done, see if you can join any of the sentences through subordination. Use the chart on page 401 as a guide.

ASSIGNMENT 2: EDIT . . . .

Referring to the chart on page 401, use subordination to join sentences in a paper you are writing for this course or another course or in a piece of writing from your work or everyday life.

Practice Together

■ **LEARNING STYLES:** Look for activities in this chapter that are matched to your learning style. If you don't know your learning style, take the test on pages 26–28.

  Visual

  Auditory

  Reading/writing

  Kinesthetic (movement)

Working with a few other students, practice what you have learned in this chapter.

1. Half of the group should write three pairs of brief sentences that could be joined by a subordinating conjunction. **EXAMPLE:** *It snowed all night. School was canceled the next day.* Someone from this group should read the sentences aloud to the other group, who should call out as many subordinating conjunctions as possible that would work in the sentences. They should have ten seconds for each sentence. Next, switch the groups so that the second group writes the sentences and the first supplies subordinating conjunctions.

2. Have each person write two sentences that could be joined through subordination, with space between them, on a sheet of paper. Here's an example, but use a different sentence: (1) *Ed's tuxedo was too small.* (2) *He wore it to the wedding.* Then, each person should illustrate both sentences. When you're done, take turns holding up your pictures and asking others in the group to fill in appropriate subordinating conjunctions.

3. Play subordination catch. Pick an object that can be tossed among group members, such as a set of keys, a pencil, or an eraser. Then, open your books to the list of subordinating conjunctions on page 393. The first "pitcher" should pick a conjunction from the list, call it out, and toss the object to another person. That person should use the conjunction in a sentence and then pick another conjunction and toss the object to a new person. Keep going until everyone in the group has used a subordinating conjunction in at least one sentence.

Chapter Review

LEARNING JOURNAL: Use your journal as place to record short sentences that could be combined through subordination. Then, edit the sentences.

■ **TIP:** For help with building your vocabulary, see Appendix B.

1. _____ are dependent words that join two related sentences. List four subordinating conjunctions: _____

    _____

2. When a dependent clause begins a sentence, use a _____ to separate it from the rest of the sentence.

3. **VOCABULARY:** Go back to any new words that you underlined in this chapter. Can you guess their meanings now? If not, look up the words in a dictionary.

EDITING FOR SUBORDINATION

Subordination is a way to join two sentences with related ideas (see p. 392).

Join two sentences by adding a dependent word (such as *although*, *because*, *unless*, or *when*) in front of one of them. That sentence is now a dependent clause (see p. 392).

If the compete sentence comes before the dependent clause, do not use a comma.

If the dependent clause comes before the complete sentence, add a comma after the dependent clause.

24

Parallelism

Balancing Ideas

Understand What Parallelism Is

VOCABULARY: Underline any words in this chapter that are new to you.

IDEA JOURNAL: Do you use lists to help organize your life? Write about the kinds of lists you make—or might make.

Parallelism in writing means that similar parts of a sentence have the same structure: nouns are with nouns, verbs with verbs, and phrases with phrases.

READ ALOUD

Read the following sentences aloud, emphasizing the underlined parts. Can you hear the problems with parallelism? Can you hear how the corrections help?

NOT PARALLEL	Caitlin likes <u>history</u> more than <u>studying math</u>.
	[*History* is a noun, but *studying math* is a phrase.]
PARALLEL	Caitlin likes <u>history</u> more than <u>math</u>.
NOT PARALLEL	The performers <u>sang</u>, <u>danced</u>, and <u>were doing</u> magic tricks.
	[*Were doing* is not in the same form as the other verbs.]
PARALLEL	The performers <u>sang</u>, <u>danced</u>, and <u>did</u> magic tricks.
NOT PARALLEL	I would rather go <u>to my daughter's soccer game</u> than <u>sitting in the town meeting</u>.
	[*To my daughter's soccer game* and *sitting in the town meeting* are both phrases, but they have different forms. *To my daughter's soccer game* should be paired with another prepositional phrase: *to the town meeting*.]
PARALLEL	I would rather go <u>to my daughter's soccer game</u> than <u>to the town meeting</u>.

Use Parallel Structure

Parallelism in Pairs and Lists

When two or more items in a series are joined by *and* or *or*, use the same form for each item.

NOTE to SELF:
BRONCO
comes before
PIE-EATING
next time.

NOT PARALLEL	The state fair featured a <u>rodeo</u> and <u>having a pie-eating contest</u>.
	[*Rodeo*, the first of the pair of items, is a noun, so the second item should also be a noun. *Having a pie-eating contest* is more than just a noun, so the pair isn't parallel.]
PARALLEL	The state fair featured a <u>rodeo</u> and a <u>pie-eating contest</u>.
	[*Rodeo* and *pie-eating contest* are both nouns, so they are parallel.]
NOT PARALLEL	The neighborhood group picked up trash <u>from deserted property</u>, <u>from parking lots</u>, and <u>they cleaned up the riverbank</u>.
	[The first two underlined items in the list have the same structure (*from*...), but the third is different (*they cleaned*...).]
PARALLEL	The neighborhood group picked up trash <u>from deserted property</u>, <u>from parking lots</u>, and <u>from the riverbank</u>.
	[All items in the list now have the same *from*...structure.]

FIND: Read each sentence in your writing carefully. Look for lists of items.

Anique <u>works</u>, <u>takes classes</u>, and <u>she is a single parent with three children</u>.

- Underline each item in the list.
- Ask whether each item has the same structure as the others. [In the example sentence, the third item does not—it is not parallel.]
- Decide how the nonparallel item should be changed.

⬇

FIX: Change any nonparallel items so that they have the same structure as the other items.

Anique <u>works</u>, <u>takes classes</u>, and <u>she is a single parent with three children</u>.

Now, all the items start with a verb (*works, takes, is*).

🪶 While you're walking to class or a job, or while you're exercising, think about three questions you have about the work in this class or another one. Ask your instructor at least one of the questions.

PRACTICE 1

In each sentence, underline the parts of the sentence that should be parallel. Then, edit the sentence to make it parallel.

EXAMPLE: In 1964, two crew members and five tourists <u>boarded</u> the
S.S. *Minnow* and ~~were sailing~~ *sailed* from Hawaii for a three-
hour tour.

■ **TIP:** For more practice, visit Exercise Central at <**bedfordstmartins.com/ realskills**>.

1. On the television comedy *Gilligan's Island*, the title character was sweet, silly and he was clumsy.

2. The Skipper liked Gilligan and was tolerating his clumsiness most of the time.

3. The passengers included a friendly farm girl named Mary Ann and there was a science teacher called Professor.

4. Mary Ann gardened and was a cook.

5. Also on board was Ginger, an actress who liked singing and to perform plays for the castaways.

6. The millionaire Howells continually bragged about their money, education, and owning numerous vacation homes.

7. The seven castaways faced storms, wild animals, and they were attacked by natives of the island.

8. The professor designed inventions to help them escape or making living conditions more comfortable.

9. For three years they tried to escape the island, and for three years they were failing.

10. The show was canceled after three seasons, but reruns have kept *Gilligan's Island* in our homes and it is in our hearts since 1967.

Parallelism in Comparisons

Comparisons often use the words *than* or *as*. To be parallel, the items on either side of the comparison word(s) need to have the same structure. In the examples that follow, the comparison word(s) are circled.

NOT PARALLEL	Learning how to play the drums is (as hard as) the guitar.
PARALLEL	Learning how to play the drums is (as hard as) learning how to play the guitar.
NOT PARALLEL	Swimming is easier on your joints (than) a run.
PARALLEL	Swimming is easier on your joints (than) running.
OR	A swim is easier on your joints (than) a run.

LISTENING to someone learn how to play is the hardest.

To make the parts of a sentence parallel, you may need to add or drop a word or two.

NOT PARALLEL	A weekend trip can sometimes be (as restful as) going on a long vacation.
PARALLEL, WORD ADDED	**Taking** a weekend trip can sometimes be (as restful as) going on a long vacation.
NOT PARALLEL	Each month, my bill for day care is (more than) to pay my rent bill.
PARALLEL, WORDS DROPPED	Each month, my bill for day care is (more than) my rent bill.

👁 Draw one of these parallel sentences so that you show how the parts are parallel.

FIND: Read each sentence in your writing carefully. Look for comparisons.

Eating at McDonald's is (easier than) to fix a meal at home.

- Circle the comparison words.
- Underline the items being compared.
- Ask whether each item has the same structure. [In the example sentence, the items do not.]
- Decide how the nonparallel item should be changed.

⬇

FIX: Change any nonparallel item so that it has the same structure as the other item.

Eating at McDonald's is easier than ~~to fix~~ a meal at home.

fixing

Now, both items start with *-ing* verbs (*eating* and *fixing*).

> **PRACTICE 2** . . . .
>
> In each sentence, circle the comparison words and underline the parts of the sentence that should be parallel. Then, edit the sentence to make it parallel.
>
>   **EXAMPLE:** <u>Giving homemade gifts</u> is often (better than) <u>~~to buy~~ gifts.</u>
>   *buying*

1. To make a gift yourself takes more time than buying one.

2. More thought goes into creating a homemade gift than to pick up something at a store.

3. Most people appreciate homemade cookies more than getting a new sweater.

4. They think that making cookies or a loaf of bread is more thoughtful than to buy towels or a tie.

5. Making homemade gifts is generally not as expensive as the purchase of commercial gifts.

6. Homemade gifts send a message that thoughtfulness is better than spending money on an expensive gift.

7. Knitting a scarf will make a better impression than to buy an expensive one.

8. To receive a pretty tin filled with homemade fudge means more to most people than getting an expensive watch or piece of crystal.

9. Of course, sometimes finding a rare book or an antique vase is better than to make a pot holder.

10. Still, most people like a homemade gift more than opening a store-bought one.

. . . .

Parallelism with Certain Paired Words

When a sentence uses certain paired words, the items joined by these words must be parallel. Here are common ones:

both . . . and	neither . . . nor	rather . . . than
either . . . or	not only . . . but also	

NOT PARALLEL	Tasha *both* <u>cuts hair</u> *and* <u>she gives pedicures</u>.
PARALLEL	Tasha *both* <u>cuts hair</u> *and* <u>gives pedicures</u>.
NOT PARALLEL	We would *rather* <u>stay home</u> *than* <u>going dancing</u>.
PARALLEL	We would *rather* <u>stay home</u> *than* <u>go dancing</u>.

FIND: Read each sentence in your writing carefully. Look for paired words such as *either/or*, *neither/nor*, and *not only/but also*.

For homework I have (not only) <u>to study for a test</u> (but also) <u>I am writing two papers</u>.

- Circle the paired words.
- Underline the items that the paired words connect.
- Ask whether each item has the same structure. [In the example sentence, the items do not.]
- Decide how the nonparallel item should be changed.

FIX: Change any nonparallel item so that it has the same structure as the other item.

For homework I have not only to study for a test but also ~~I am~~
to write
writing two papers.
^

Now, both items start with *to* and a verb (*to study, to write*).

PRACTICE 3 . . . .

In each sentence, circle the paired words and underline the parts of the sentence that should be parallel. Then, edit the sentence to make it parallel. You may need to change one of the paired elements to make the sentence parallel.

EXAMPLE: For the Fourth of July, we wanted to (either) fly to Las Vegas (or) ~~we could~~ drive to Atlanta.

1. I would rather drive to Atlanta than to fly to Las Vegas.

2. Las Vegas is not only hot in the summer but also it is crowded on holi-day weekends.

3. My husband and I are neither gamblers nor do we drink alcohol.

4. Yet Las Vegas has both entertaining shows and has top-rated restaurants.

5. Nevertheless, we would rather go to Atlanta for a Braves game than be partying in Las Vegas.

6. In the end, however, we decided that staying at home would be both fun and we could relax.

7. As an added bonus, staying at home would not only cost less but also it would be less stressful.

8. We can either relax at our apartment's pool or shopping downtown would be fun.

9. My husband said that he would much rather relax at home than going on a stressful vacation.

10. I think that our plan sounds not only fun but also I think that it is smart.

> **PRACTICE 4** . . .

For each item, add the second part of the word pair and complete the sentence.

> **EXAMPLE:** Having a new kitten in the house is both fun
>
> _and exhausting_ .

1. Our new kitten, Tiger, is not only curious _____.

2. He would rather shred the sofa _____.

3. During the day, we must either lock him in the bedroom _____

    _____.

4. Trying to reason with Tiger is neither effective _____.

5. Still, having Tiger as my new friend is both a joy _____.

Edit for Parallelism in College, Work, and Everyday Life

Complete the editing reviews as instructed, referring to the chart on page 414.

EDITING REVIEW 1: COLLEGE

Fix problems with parallelism in the following paragraph, which is similar to one you might find in a criminal-justice textbook. The first sentence has been marked for you. Aside from this sentence, one other sentence is correct; write "C" next to it.

(1) Since the 1970s, law enforcement's approach to domestic violence calls has changed. (2) In the past, police often would neither make arrests nor would they record detailed information on the incident. (3) Resolving a domestic abuse call commonly involved "cooling off" the abuser by walking him around the block or to talk to him privately. (4) In the late 1970s, however, approaches to spousal abuse changed because of research findings and pressure from victims' advocates was increased. (5) Police agencies began to develop policies and programs for dealing with domestic incidents. (6) Today, police who respond to domestic violence reports usually follow not only formal department guidelines but also there are statewide policies. (7) In some states, the criminal-justice system attempts to protect abuse survivors by pursuing cases even if the alleged victim does not show up in court or is not wanting to press charges. (8) Despite increased training and developing clearer policies, police officers often face unclear situations. (9) For example, when they arrive on the scene, officers may find that the allegedly abusive spouse is absent or discovering that the partner who made the call says that nothing happened. (10) Most officers today would rather record every detail of a domestic incident than risking being charged with failing to enforce domestic violence laws.

EDITING REVIEW 2: WORK

Fix problems with parallelism in the following memo. The first sentence has been marked for you. Aside from this sentence, two other sentences are correct; write "C" next to them.

Date: August 14, 2006

To: All Employees

From: Glenda Benally, field administrative specialist,

Technical Services

Subject: Minutes of employee meeting, August 9, 2006

(1) Last week, Rhonda Schaeffer, personnel director from the main office, spoke to us about our new domestic violence policy. (2) Our company is committed to raising awareness of spousal abuse and to provide help for employees who are victims of domestic violence. (3) Rhonda defined domestic violence as abusive behavior between two people in an intimate relationship; it may include physical violence, economic control, emotional intimidation, or verbally abusing someone.

(4) Under the new program, Southwestern Oil and Gas will provide free counseling and referrals through the confidential Employee Assistance Program. (5) The company will also offer leave necessary for obtaining medical treatment, attending counseling sessions, or legal assistance. (6) Rhonda also outlined several procedures for the safety and protecting employees in the workplace. (7) She suggested documenting any threatening e-mail or voice-mail messages. (8) Employees who have a restraining order against a partner should keep a copy on hand at work and another copy should be given to the security office.

(9) Finally, if you know that a coworker is experiencing domestic violence, please consider asking if he or she would like to talk or you might suggest our counseling resources.

EDITING REVIEW 3: EVERYDAY LIFE . . . .

Fix problems with parallelism in the following essay. One sentence is correct; write "C" next to it. The first sentence has been edited for you.

(1) In most divorce cases, joint child custody or ~~when~~ generous visitation rights ~~are given~~ are in the best interests of the children. (2) How-

ever, in cases involving domestic violence, shared custody and visitation may endanger the abused spouse and the children. (3) As a result, many states now require training for judges, mediators, and for other court workers who handle domestic violence cases.

(4) Domestic violence affects not only the abused spouse but also the children are impacted. (5) A national study estimated that half of men who commit domestic violence not only abuse their wives but also are abusing their children. (6) Even if children do not see any violence, the effects of knowing it is happening can be as bad as to witness it directly. (7) The abuser may exercise damaging emotional control over the children during visits, and such behavior may be either difficult to document or it is ignored by the court.

(8) Visitation rights should be granted only if steps can be taken to protect the safety of both the children and for keeping the abused spouse safe. (9) A judge can make visitations safer by limiting the length of visits and to not allow overnight stays. (10) Visits should be supervised by a trained, court-appointed individual or an agency can do it. (11) Children should be sheltered from tension, conflict, and if there is potential violence between parents as much as possible. (12) Unsupervised visits should be allowed only after the abuser has completed a counseling program and he has been maintaining nonviolent relationships for a certain period of time.

Write and Edit Your Own Work

ASSIGNMENT 1: WRITE

Write about improvements that could be made to a system at school, at work, in government, or in your everyday life. When you are done, check your sentences for parallelism, correcting any mistakes that you find. Use the chart on page 414 as a guide.

ASSIGNMENT 2: EDIT

Using the chart on page 414, edit for parallelism a paper you are writing for this course or another course or a piece of writing from your work or everyday life.

Practice Together

Working with a few other students, practice what you have learned in this chapter.

1. The following are introductions to four lists of actions or qualities. Pick one of the introductions and have each group member add one action or quality to the list. Meanwhile, one person should record the listed items. **EXAMPLE:** *When you fall in love, you think about the other person all the time.* The person who adds the first item will set up a pattern that all the other group members will have to follow. After each person adds his or her item, group members should decide whether the item is parallel with the first person's. 🗣 📖

   When you fall in love, you . . .

   A good writer . . .

   To save money, you can . . .

   To get a good grade in this class, you need to . . .

2. Have everyone in the group write a word or phrase on a sticky note (for example, *the test, going to the movies, to eat cake*). Then, put all of the stickies on one sheet of paper. Each person should remove a sticky note (one that is not his or her own) and call out a list or comparison using the words provided. **EXAMPLE:** *Going to the movies is not as fun as playing video games.* 👁 🗣 📖 🖐

3. As a group, write at least four sentences that aren't parallel, drawing on examples from this chapter. Then, exchange your sentences with another group so that you can correct each other's sentences. When you're done, a person from each group should present the corrections to the two groups together, and everyone should discuss whether the corrections fix the problems. 🗣 📖 🖐

Chapter Review

1. _____ in writing means that similar parts of a sentence are balanced by having the same structure.

2. In what three situations do problems with parallelism most often occur?

   _____

3. List three paired words that occur in sentences that might not be parallel:

   _____

4. **VOCABULARY:** Go back to any new words that you underlined in this chapter. Can you guess their meanings now? If not, look up the words in a dictionary.

■ **TIP:** For help with building your vocabulary, see Appendix B.

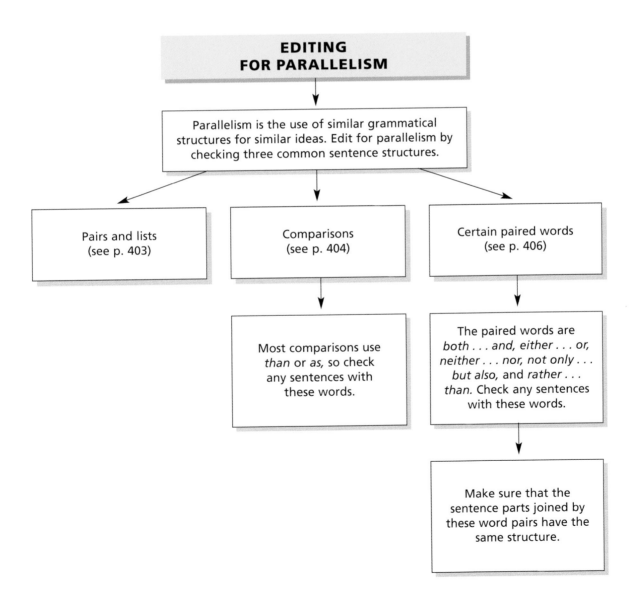

EDITING FOR PARALLELISM

Parallelism is the use of similar grammatical structures for similar ideas. Edit for parallelism by checking three common sentence structures.

Pairs and lists (see p. 403)

Comparisons (see p. 404)

Certain paired words (see p. 406)

Most comparisons use *than* or *as,* so check any sentences with these words.

The paired words are *both . . . and, either . . . or, neither . . . nor, not only . . . but also,* and *rather . . . than.* Check any sentences with these words.

Make sure that the sentence parts joined by these word pairs have the same structure.

Unit Five Test
Editing

Part 1

Following are two paragraphs and one essay. Read them carefully and circle the correct answers to the questions that follow them. Use some of the reading strategies from Chapter 2.

1 Carbonated soft drinks are refreshing and <u>delicious</u>. 2 Drinking too many of these beverages can be bad for your <u>health</u>. 3 Soft drinks can cause digestion problems, insomnia, and they make some people feel anxious. 4 Consuming large quantities of soft drinks increases levels of acid in the stomach. 5 All soft drinks are acidic to some degree, <u>or</u> dark colas are the most acidic of all soft drinks. 6 Increases in stomach acidity can inflame the stomach lining; in addition, the phosphorous in carbonated beverages interacts with stomach acid, causing indigestion, gas, and bloating. 7 Caffeinated soft drinks also act as a stimulant on the central nervous system. 8 As a result, too much soda can disrupt sleep, cause irritability, and increases in the heart rate can occur. 9 Studies have also shown that too much caffeine increases the risk of osteoporosis. 10 A cold soft drink can be a refreshing treat, too many carbonated beverages clearly can lead to serious health problems.

1. Which of the following should be used in place of the underlined words in sentences 1 and 2 to combine the sentences using coordination?

   a. delicious, or drinking
   c. delicious, while
   b. delicious, but drinking
   d. delicious, so

2. Which of the following should be used in place of the underlined word in sentence 5?

   a. but
   c. because
   b. for
   d. so that

3. Which of the following changes is needed in sentence 8?

   a. Change "As a result" to "Because."
   b. Change "cause irritability" to "irritability can occur."
   c. Change "increases in the heart rate can occur" to "increasing the heart rate."
   d. Change "increases in the heart rate can occur" to "increase the heart rate."

4. Which of the following sentences should be revised because it contains a problem with parallelism?

   a. Sentence 1
   c. Sentence 6
   b. Sentence 3
   d. Sentence 9

5. Which of the following changes is needed in sentence 10?
   a. Add "Because" to the beginning of the sentence and change "A" to "a."
   b. Add "Although" to the beginning of the sentence and change "A" to "a."
   c. Add "for" after the comma.
   d. Delete the comma.

1 I grew up in a small, isolated town in Oregon. **2** There wasn't much to do there, <u>but</u> my friends and I called it Dullsville. **3** I disliked the rocky scenery and found the cold weather depressing. **4** I couldn't wait to leave town. **5** I finally graduated from high school, I joined the Air Force and left Oregon. **6** While I was home years later for a visit, I was driving to my mother's house at sunset. **7** I gasped when I saw the beautiful orange sky, the snow-capped mountains, and the Columbia River was spectacular. **8** The beauty of the Columbia River Gorge took me by surprise. **9** I did not appreciate this beauty; until I had moved away. **10** I now realize that there are few places as beautiful as it is in my hometown.

6. Which of the following should be used in place of the underlined word in sentence 2?
   a. yet
   b. since
   c. although
   d. so

7. Which of the following changes is needed in sentence 5?
   a. Delete the comma.
   b. Add "yet" after the comma.
   c. Change "joined" to "was joining."
   d. Add "After" to the beginning of the sentence.

8. Which of the following sentences should be revised because it contains a problem with parallelism?
   a. Sentence 1
   b. Sentence 3
   c. Sentence 6
   d. Sentence 10

9. Which of the following changes is needed in sentence 7?
   a. Change "when" to "until."
   b. Change "the snow-capped mountains" to "the mountains were capped with snow."
   c. Change "the Columbia River was spectacular" to "the spectacular Columbia River."
   d. Change "and" to "but."

10. Which of the following changes is needed in sentence 9?
    a. Change the semicolon to a comma.
    b. Delete the semicolon.
    c. Change "until" to "because."
    d. Change "until" to "however."

1 Many of us dream of receiving an Academy Award or to win the Nobel Prize. 2 However, nobody wants to receive the Darwin Award. 3 This unwelcome award recognizes individuals who accidentally cause their own deaths in odd ways. 4 The purpose of the Darwin Award is not to make fun of tragedies but to make examples of people whose foolish actions are deadly.

5 Clement Vallandigham, who died in 1871, received a Darwin Award more than one hundred years after his death. 6 A lawyer, Vallandigham died while defending a client charged with murder. 7 To prove his client's innocence, Vallandigham decided to demonstrate how the alleged murder weapon could have gone off accidentally. 8 Indeed, the gun did go off Vallandigham was killed on the spot. 9 Vallandigham's client, however, was found innocent.

10 More recently, two men in Australia armed themselves with knives and went to a mobile home intending to stab the resident. 11 During the struggle, the attackers became confused. 12 The room was dark the attackers didn't notice the intended victim escape. 13 After the attackers frantically stabbed each other, one died at the scene and the other was hospitalized with critical injuries.

14 One of the most famous Darwin Award incidents, since discovered to be false, was said to have occurred in the Arizona desert. 15 As the story goes, the Arizona Highway Patrol discovered some mysterious, smoking wreckage in the side of a mountain. 16 An investigation revealed that an adventurous man had somehow obtained an Air Force rocket used to boost a jet's take-off power. 17 He attached it to his car, he ignited the rocket and sped down the highway. 18 Investigators estimated that his Chevy Impala reached a speed of about 300 miles per hour and traveled nearly four miles before it slammed into the side of the mountain. 19 The crash created a crater three feet deep and left nearly unidentifiable remains of both the car and the driver.

20 We all do foolish things yet, most of us live to laugh about our mistakes. 21 Few are unlucky enough to win a Darwin Award.

11. Which of the following should be used in place of the underlined section of sentence 1?
    a. No change is necessary.
    b. or, to win the Nobel Prize.
    c. or of winning the Nobel Prize.
    d. or, winning the Nobel Prize.

12. Which of the following should be used in place of the underlined section of sentence 8?

    a. No change is necessary.   c. off and Vallandigham

    b. off, and Vallandigham   d. off, if Vallandigham

13. Which of the following should be used in place of the underlined section of sentence 12?

    a. No change is necessary.

    b. The room was dark,

    c. Although the room was dark,

    d. Because the room was dark,

14. Which of the following should be used in place of the underlined section of sentence 17?

    a. No change is necessary.

    b. After he attached it to his car,

    c. Unless he attached it to his car,

    d. He attached it to his car, yet

15. Which of the following should be used in place of the underlined section of sentence 20?

    a. No change is necessary.   c. things, yet;

    b. things, yet   d. things; therefore,

Part 2

Circle the correct choice for each of the following items.

1. Choose the correct word to fill in the blank.

    Derrick wants a new computer, _____ he cannot afford one right now.

    a. so   c. and

    b. but   d. for

2. If an underlined portion of this item is incorrect, select the revision that fixes it. If the item is correct as written, choose d.

    <u>If</u> I were you, I would listen to Armand <u>until</u> he speaks <u>because</u> he is
    A   B   C

    usually right about financial issues.

    a. Because   c. although

    b. when   d. No change is necessary.

3. If an underlined portion of this item is incorrect, select the revision that fixes it. If the item is correct as written, choose d.

Allison <u>and</u> Brad wanted to give a gift that was meaningful and <u>thought-</u>
     A   **B**

<u>ful, but</u> they made hand-dipped chocolates.
   C

   a. nor   c. so
   b. they put thought into   d. No change is necessary.

4. Choose the correct word(s) to fill in the blank.

_____ a hurricane threatens the coastline, residents stock up on batteries and bottled water.

   a. Until   c. So that
   b. Although   d. When

5. Choose the item that has no errors.
   a. Our supervisor is neither organized nor does she know much.
   b. Our supervisor is neither organized, nor is she knowledgeable.
   c. Our supervisor is neither organized nor knowledgeable.

6. If an underlined portion of this item is incorrect, select the revision that fixes it. If the item is correct as written, choose d.

On Latisha's Caribbean vacation, she wanted to go <u>snorkeling</u>, <u>sailing</u>,
                                                 A   **B**

and <u>to swim</u>.
   C

   a. snorkel   c. swimming
   b. to sail   d. No change is necessary.

7. Choose the correct words to fill in the blank.

Lori's office duties include filing correspondence, typing letters, and _____.

   a. answering the telephone c. answer the telephone
   b. to answer the telephone d. she answers the telephone

8. Choose the correct word to fill in the blank.

The power went off on campus, _____ all classes were canceled.
   a. but   c. so
   b. yet   d. for

9. Choose the correct word(s) to fill in the blank.

   Julie ordered a hot fudge sundae _____ she claimed to be dieting.
   a. even though   c. since
   b. because   d. if

10. Choose the item that has no errors.
    a. If the sun rises, we will begin painting the barn.
    b. Although the sun rises, we will begin painting the barn.
    c. When the sun rises, we will begin painting the barn.

11. Choose the item that has no errors.
    a. Marvin dislikes beets, so he refuses to eat them.
    b. Marvin dislikes beets, but he refuses to eat them.
    c. Marvin dislikes beets, yet he refuses to eat them.

12. If an underlined portion of this item is incorrect, select the revision that fixes it. If the item is correct as written, choose d.

    Online, travelers can not only purchase airline tickets, but also they can
    $\qquad\quad$ A $\qquad\qquad\qquad\qquad\qquad$ B $\qquad$ C
    reserve hotel rooms.
    a. not   c. reserve
    b. but, also   d. No change is necessary.

13. Choose the item that has no errors.
    a. Franklin must have eaten the cake, in fact, he has frosting on his lips.
    b. Franklin must have eaten the cake; in fact, he has frosting on his lips.
    c. Franklin must have eaten the cake, in fact he has frosting on his lips.

14. If an underlined portion of this item is incorrect, select the revision that fixes it. If the item is correct as written, choose d.

    Daniel adores Marsilla; however, he likes neither her messy habits nor
    $\qquad\qquad\qquad$ A $\qquad\qquad\qquad\qquad\qquad\qquad\qquad\qquad$ B
    that she is a bad cook.
    $\qquad\qquad$ C
    a. Marsilla, however,   c. her bad cooking
    b. or   d. No change is necessary.

15. Choose the item that has no errors.
    a. Even though Sara dislikes politics, she ran for mayor.
    b. Even though Sara dislikes politics; she ran for mayor.
    c. Even though Sara dislikes politics she ran for mayor.

■ **TIP:** For advice on taking tests, see Appendix A.

Unit Six

Editing Words in Sentences

25

Word Choice

Using the Right Words

Understand the Importance of Choosing Words Carefully

When you talk with others, you show what you mean by the look on your face, your tone of voice, and your gestures. In writing, however, you have only the words on the page to make your point, so you must choose them carefully.

Two important tools will help you find the best words for your meaning: a dictionary and a thesaurus.

VOCABULARY: Underline any words in this chapter that are new to you.

IDEA JOURNAL: Write about a time when you felt misunderstood.

Dictionary

You need a dictionary, whether in traditional book form or in an electronic format. For not much money, you can get a good one that has all kinds of useful information about words: spelling, division of words into syllables, pronunciation, parts of speech, other forms of words, definitions, and examples of use.

The following is a part of a dictionary entry:

Spelling and end-of-line division	Pronunciation	Other forms	Definition	Example	Parts of speech

con • crete (kon'-krēt, kong'-krēt, kon-krēt', kong-krēt'), *adj., n., v.* **-cret • ed, -cret • ing,** *adj.* **1.** constituting an actual thing or instance; real; perceptible; substantial: *concrete proof.* **2.** pertaining to or concerned with realities or actual instances rather than abstractions; particular as opposed to general: *concrete proposals.* **3.** referring to an actual substance or thing, as opposed to an abstract quality: The words *cat, water,* and *teacher* are concrete, whereas the words *truth, excellence,* and *adulthood* are abstract....

—*Random House Webster's College Dictionary*

■ TIP: For online help with words, visit Merriam-Webster Online at <**www.m-w.com**>. You can use this site's dictionary and thesaurus features to look up words.

👁 If you are writing about an unfamiliar subject, consider looking up key words in an illustrated dictionary. (A librarian can help you find one.) The illustrations will help you understand and remember important information.

PRACTICE 1

Look up the following terms from this chapter in a dictionary. Then, in the blank following each word, write a brief definition.

1. synonym _____

2. vague _____

3. concrete _____

4. slang _____

5. wordy _____

6. cliché _____

Thesaurus

A thesaurus gives synonyms (words that have the same meaning) for the words you look up. Like dictionaries, thesauruses come in inexpensive and even electronic editions. Use a thesaurus when you can't find the right word for what you mean. Be careful, however, to choose a word that has the meaning you intend. If you are not sure how a word should be used, look it up in the dictionary.

> **Concrete,** *adj.* 1. Particular, specific, single, certain, special, unique, sole, peculiar, individual, separate, isolated, distinct, exact, precise, direct, strict, minute; definite, plain, evident, obvious; pointed, emphasized; restrictive, limiting, limited, well-defined, clear-cut, fixed, finite; determining, conclusive, decided.
>
> —J. I. Rodale, *The Synonym Finder*

Language note: Make sure to use the right kinds of words in sentences: Use a noun for a person, place, or thing. Use an adjective when you want to describe a noun.

INCORRECT   Everyone in the world wants happy.

[*Happy* is an adjective, but a noun is needed in this case.]

Smoking is not health.

[*Health* is a noun, but an adjective is needed in this case.]

CORRECT   Everyone in the world wants **happiness**.

Smoking is not **healthy**.

Avoid Four Common Word-Choice Problems

Four common problems with word choice can make it difficult for readers to understand you.

Vague Words

Your words need to create a clear picture for your readers. **Vague words** are too general to make an impression. The following are some common vague words.

Vague Words

a lot	dumb	old	very
amazing	good	pretty	whatever
awesome	great	sad	young
bad	happy	small	
beautiful	nice	terrible	
big	OK (okay)	thing	

When you see one of these words or another general word in your writing, try to replace it with a concrete, or more specific, word. A concrete word names something that can be seen, heard, felt, tasted, or smelled.

VAGUE	The cookies were good.
CONCRETE	The cookies were warm, chewy, and sweet and had a rich, buttery taste.

The first version is too general. The second version creates a clear, strong impression.

PRACTICE 2 . . . .

In the following sentences, underline any vague words. Then, edit each sentence by replacing the vague words with concrete ones. You may invent any details you like.

>   *Oak Meadow Mall   an entertaining place to spend the afternoon*
> **EXAMPLE:** ~~The mall~~ is ~~great~~.

If you are trying to describe a physical object, pick it up and touch it, if possible. This can help you add details about the object's texture, size, weight, and so on.

1. The interior design creates a nice atmosphere.

2. There are a lot of stores.

3. Pretty music is played on overhead speakers.

4. A Mexican restaurant serves good food.

5. I enjoy visiting the coffee shop for its great beverages.

6. If you don't want to shop, there are entertainment options and whatever.

7. At the spa, you can get many services.

8. One of the hairdressing shops offers many things.

9. Various entertainers perform on a small stage in the center of the complex.

10. The mall is the best attraction in my hometown.

■ **TIP:** For more practice, visit Exercise Central at <**bedfordstmartins.com/ realskills**>.

Slang

Slang, informal language, should be used only in casual situations. Avoid it when you write for college classes or at work.

SLANG

Let's *chill* this weekend.

Dude, let's leave now.

Sasha showed off her *bling* at the party.

This cell phone is *toast*.

EDITED

Let's *relax* this weekend.

Joe [or whoever], let's leave now.

Sasha showed off her *jewelry* at the party.

This cell phone is *broken*.

READ ALOUD

Imagine that you are a human resources officer who must hire someone for a customer-service position. The person you hire must communicate clearly and professionally. Read the following e-mail from a candidate for the job. What impression does it give you of the writer?

Dude,
I got the 411 on this gig from the local rag. I'm the man for the job, no doubt. Customer service is my game—I've been doin' it for five years. Drop me a line or you'll lose out big-time.

Later,
Bart Bederman

PRACTICE 3 . .

In the following sentences, underline any slang words. Then, edit the sentences by replacing the slang with language appropriate for a formal audience and purpose. Imagine that you are writing to your landlord.

              concern
    EXAMPLE: I have a beef about the condition of my apartment.

1. I am bummed about the kitchen.

2. I am creeped out by the mouse that lives under the refrigerator.

3. The previous tenant trashed the dishwasher, and the rinse cycle doesn't work.

4. The sides of the refrigerator are covered in gross green and black stains.

5. It would be cool if you could correct these problems.

6. I am also not down with the bathroom.

7. The mildew stains in the shower really freak me out.

8. I would give you mad props if you would fix the leaky faucets.

9. I hope it does not tick you off that I would like these problems taken care of as soon as possible.

10. I would be psyched if you could stop by and talk to me about these issues.

Wordy Language

Wordy language uses words when they aren't necessary. Sometimes, people think that using big words or writing long sentences will make them sound smart and important. However, using too many words in a piece of writing can make the point weaker or harder to find.

WORDY	*A great number of* students complained about the long registration lines.
EDITED	*Many* students complained about the long registration lines.
WORDY	*Due to the fact that* we arrived late to the meeting, we missed the first speaker.
EDITED	*Because* we arrived late to the meeting, we missed the first speaker.
WORDY	We can't buy a car *at this point in time.*
EDITED	We can't buy a car *now.*

Sometimes, sentences are wordy because some words in them repeat others, as in the bold parts of the first sentence below.

REPETITIVE	Our dog is **hyper** and **overactive**.
EDITED	Our dog is hyper.

Common Wordy Expressions

WORDY	EDITED
As a result of	Because
Due to the fact that	Because
In spite of the fact that	Although
It is my opinion that	I think (or just make the point)
In the event that	If
The fact of the matter is that	(Just state the point.)
A great number of	Many
At that time	Then
In this day and age	Now
At this point in time	Now
In this paper I will show that...	(Just make the point; don't announce it.)

PRACTICE 4 . . . .

In the following sentences, underline the wordy or repetitive language. Then, edit each sentence to make it more concise. Some sentences may contain more than one wordy phrase.

EXAMPLE: In this day and age, one of the most popular and well-liked forms of fiction is the romance novel.
         ^Today

1. Many people are of the opinion that romance novels follow a strict formula.

2. It is a true fact that a great number of successful romance novels share common elements.

3. The woman who is the heroine should be strong, independent, and beautiful.

4. The hero generally must be someone who is handsome and successful.

5. When the hero and heroine initially meet for the first time, there is usually a conflict between them.

6. At the same time, they must have an attraction to each other that is very strong in nature.

7. It is a well known fact that an obstacle will probably get in the couple's way and keep them apart.

8. As a result of this obstacle, it will appear that the hero and heroine have lost each other.

9. Due to the fact that readers expect a happy ending, the characters must conquer and overcome all obstacles and live happily ever after.

10. Writers who write romance novels are aware of the fact that these elements are necessary to the success of most romance novels.

Clichés

Clichés are phrases used so often that people no longer pay attention to them. To make your point clearly and to get your readers' attention, replace clichés with fresh, specific language.

Try the biscuit—she may not ask for the belly-rub.

JUNE WORKS LIKE A DOG.

CLICHÉS	EDITED
June *works like a dog.*	June works at least sixty hours every week.
This dinner roll is *as hard as a rock.*	This dinner roll would make a good baseball.

> *Common Clichés*
>
> | | |
> |---|---|
> | as big as a house | as light as a feather |
> | the best/worst of times | no way on earth |
> | better late than never | 110 percent |
> | break the ice | playing with fire |
> | the corporate ladder | spoiled brat |
> | crystal clear | spoiled rotten |
> | a drop in the bucket | starting from scratch |
> | easier said than done | sweating blood (or bullets) |
> | hard as a rock | work like a dog |
> | hell on earth | worked his or her way up the ladder |
> | last but not least | |

PRACTICE 5

In the following sentences, underline the clichés. Then, edit each sentence by replacing the clichés with fresh language that precisely expresses your meaning.

EXAMPLE: For every person who has his or her dream job, there are

a dozen other people who are ~~green with envy~~.
                                         envious

1. Are you stuck in a rut in your current job?

2. Perhaps you work like a dog but dislike what you do.

3. You might think that dream jobs are few and far between.

4. Finding your dream job, however, can be as easy as pie if you take the right approach.

5. Find a skill that you enjoy using and that is near and dear to your heart.

6. Maybe you can write songs that tug at the heartstrings.

7. Maybe your investigative skills leave no stone unturned.

8. Seek education and experience so that you can be the best that you can be.

9. Changing jobs may seem like playing with fire.

10. You might have to start from scratch, but getting your dream job is worth that effort.

A FINAL NOTE: Language that favors one gender over another or that assumes that only one gender performs a certain role is called *sexist*. Avoid such language.

> **SEXIST**   A doctor should politely answer *his* patients' questions.
>
> [Not all doctors are male.]
>
> **REVISED**   A doctor should politely answer *his or her* patients' questions.
>
> *Doctors* should politely answer *their* patients' questions.
>
> [The first revision changes *his* to *his or her* to avoid sexism. The second revision changes the subject to a plural noun (*Doctors*) so that a genderless pronoun (*their*) can be used.]

> ■ **TIP:** See Chapter 17 for more advice on using pronouns.

Edit for Word Choice in College, Work, and Everyday Life

Complete the editing reviews as instructed, referring to the chart on page 435.

EDITING REVIEW 1: COLLEGE

Edit the following paragraph, a student's response to an essay exam question, for word choice. Two sentences are correct; write "C" next to them. The first sentence has been edited for you.

(1) In the past few years, carbohydrates have ~~gotten a lot of flak from~~ *been criticized by* the media. (2) Popular diets made us believe that carbohydrates were really bad. (3) Some people decided that there was no way on earth they would ever eat pasta again. (4) Lately, however, a great number of dieters have changed their minds. (5) Carbohydrates are starting to be recognized as an important part of a healthy diet because they are the main source of energy for humans. (6) Current research demonstrates that while too many carbohydrates can be bad news, eliminating them completely is not wise. (7) The fact of the matter is that people should include healthy carbohydrates such as fruits, vegetables, and whole grains in their daily diets. (8) The overall key to good nutrition is eating balanced meals. (9) It is my opinion that people can eat many types of foods as long as they do so in moderation. (10) Maintaining a proper diet is easier said than done, but being fit as a fiddle is worth the work.

EDITING REVIEW 2: WORK . . . .

Edit the following business memo for word choice. One sentence is correct; write "C" next to it. The first sentence has been edited for you.

DATE: February 27, 2006

TO: All employees

FROM: Jason Connors

SUBJECT: Overtime pay

(1) It has come to my attention that some employees are ~~wigging out~~ *upset* about a lack of overtime hours. (2) Although I have covered this information in previous memos, I will attempt to do so again. (3) I hope this memo will make it crystal clear how overtime hours are assigned.

(4) Each month, two to five employees are asked to pull one all-nighter. (5) I rotate the names so that no one will become too beat. (6) If an employee cannot work overtime at that point in time, I move to the next name on the list and that employee must wait until the rotation reaches his or her name again. (7) It is my opinion that this is an effective technique; it has worked great for some time.

(8) I work like crazy to make sure that each employee has a chance to earn overtime at least twice a year. (9) I hope that we all agree about the fact that this policy is okay. (10) Please speak with me in the event that you have any further questions about overtime.

EDITING REVIEW 3: EVERYDAY LIFE . . . .

Edit the following essay for word choice. Outside of the first sentence, which has been marked for you, six sentences are correct; write "C" next to them.

(1) *C* The first year of college can bring many changes to students' lives. (2) Their academic responsibilities increase, and they may have to adjust to having roommates or a tighter schedule. (3) If they are working, going to school, and raising a family, they may be more likely to choose fast food than healthy stuff.

(4) Some students go out of their minds with worry about the "freshman fifteen," the average number of pounds some students gain during their first year in college, especially if they are young and live on campus. (5) The problem is not such a big deal for older students or those who live at home. (6) Such weight gain often happens due to the fact that students become overwhelmed by their new freedom. (7) Students who live on campus can stuff their faces in the cafeteria, at a friend's house, or at fast-food restaurants. (8) They might also keep bad food in their dorm rooms or desks. (9) For perhaps the first time in their lives, no one is telling them what, where, or when to eat.

(10) There are other reasons students—both young and older—might find themselves gaining weight during that first year. (11) Adjusting to an all new way of life is not cake. (12) Sometimes, students may feel bummed and eat more than they usually would.

(13) Does this mean that gaining weight during the first year of college is unavoidable? (14) It doesn't have to be if students follow a few simple rules. (15) Keep a regular meal schedule and avoid chowing down too quickly. (16) In spite of the fact that you should limit what you eat between meals, try to make healthy snack choices. (17) If you are feeling overwhelmed or lonely, call a friend or make an effort to meet other students in your dorm or class. (18) It's easier said than done, but it is possible to avoid the freshman fifteen.

Write and Edit Your Own Work

ASSIGNMENT 1: WRITE

Write about a time when you have had to choose your words carefully—for example, when having a tough conversation with a friend or coworker, when explaining something difficult to a child, or when breaking up an argument. When you're done, edit your writing for vague words, slang, wordiness, and clichés, referring to the chart on page 435.

ASSIGNMENT 2: EDIT . . . .

Using the chart on page 435, edit for word choice a paper you are writing for this course or another course or a piece of writing from your work or everyday life.

. . . .

Practice Together

LEARNING STYLES: Look for activities in this chapter that are matched to your learning style. If you don't know your learning style, take the test on pages 26–28.

👁 Visual

𝔶 Auditory

📖 Reading/writing

🐾 Kinesthetic (movement)

Working with a few other students, practice what you have learned in this chapter.

1. Pick one or two of the "good" things listed below. Have each group member call out a quality that makes the thing good. When everyone has had a turn, write a single sentence, as a group, that explains why the thing is good. 𝔶 📖

    good reason, good dog, good car, good job, good friend, good house

2. Have each group member draw a picture of something, including as many details as possible. Then, have each person pass his or her drawing to another. Group members should take turns describing the drawings they've been given, being as specific as possible. 👁 𝔶 🐾

3. Pick one of the following adjective-noun combinations and, as a group, write down as many descriptions of it as possible without naming the thing itself. Then, exchange lists with another group. Can each group guess what the other was trying to describe? 𝔶 📖 🐾

    Frightened child   Boring show
    Rich people   Lazy people
    Messy room

4. As a group, write four sentences that include slang or clichés. Then, exchange sentences with another group and correct each other's sentences. When you're done, a person from each group should present the corrections to the two groups together, and everyone should discuss whether the corrections fix the problems. 𝔶 📖 🐾

Chapter Review

1. What two tools will help you choose the best words for your meaning?

    _____

2. When you see a _____ word in your writing, replace it with a concrete, or more specific, word.

3. _____ should be used only in informal and casual situations.

4. _____ language uses words when they aren't necessary.

5. _____ are phrases used so often that people no longer pay attention to them.

6. **VOCABULARY:** Go back to any new words that you underlined in this chapter. Can you guess their meanings now? If not, look up the words in a dictionary.

LEARNING JOURNAL:
Write for two minutes about the word choice problems you have the most trouble with and how you might avoid them.

■ **TIP:** For help with building your vocabulary, see Appendix B.

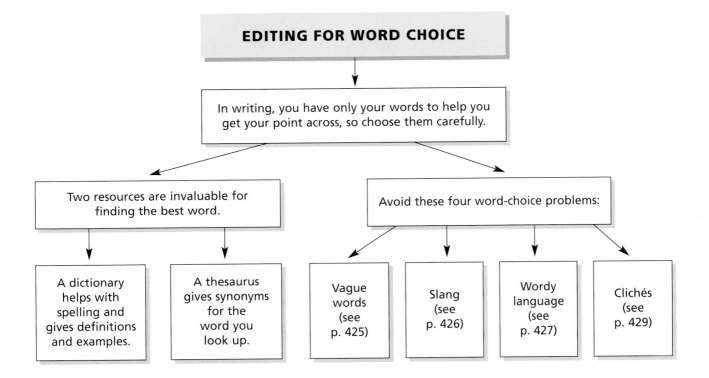

26

Commonly Confused Words

Avoiding Mistakes with Sound-Alikes

Understand Why Certain Words Are Commonly Confused

VOCABULARY: Underline any words in this chapter that are new to you.

IDEA JOURNAL: Many jobs call for good communication skills. What does this mean to you?

Certain words in English are confusing because they sound alike and may have similar meanings. In writing, words that sound alike may be spelled differently, and readers rely on the spelling to understand what you mean. Edit your writing carefully to make sure that you have used the correct words.

STRATEGIES FOR EDITING SOUND-ALIKES

1. **Proofread carefully.** Use the techniques discussed on page 451.
2. **Use a dictionary** to look up any words you are unsure of.
3. **Focus on finding and correcting mistakes** you make with the twenty-seven sets of commonly confused words covered in this chapter.
4. **Develop a personal list of sound-alikes that confuse you.** Before you turn in any piece of writing, consult your personal list to make sure you have used the correct words.

Use Commonly Confused Words Correctly

Study the different meanings and spellings of the following twenty-seven sets of commonly confused words. Complete the sentence after each set of words, filling in each blank with the correct word.

A/An/And

a: used before a word that begins with a consonant sound

A large brown bear pawed the tent.

an: used before a word that begins with a vowel sound

An egg on toast is delicious for breakfast.

and: used to join two words

Patrice *and* Dylan dated for three months.

In my favorite children's poem, *an* owl *and a* pussy-cat floated in *a* boat.

You will find _____ job if you have _____ impressive résumé _____ good personal skills.

■ **TIP:** The vowels in the alphabet are *a, e, i, o, u,* and sometimes *y.* All other letters are consonants.

Accept/Except

accept: to agree to receive or admit (verb)

Please *accept* my sincere apology.

except: but, other than

I like all the songs on this CD *except* the last one.

The store will *accept* all credit cards *except* the one I am carrying.

I cannot _____ the fact that I can use my card at every store _____ for my favorite ones.

Would you take a LIBRARY card? COLLEGE ID? SHOE STORE LICENSE? VIP?

Advice/Advise

advice: opinion (noun)

Can you give me some *advice* about which course to take?

advise: to give an opinion (verb)

A park ranger *advised* us not to approach wild animals.

Grandma *advised* us girls to wear dresses to the concert; her *advice* is sweet but old-fashioned.

You might think that my _____ is wrong, but I _____ you to listen to me.

■ **TIP:** To understand this chapter, you will need to know what nouns, verbs, adjectives, adverbs, and prepositions are. For a review, see Chapters 10, 16, and 18.

Affect/Effect

affect: to make an impact on, to change something (verb)

The rising gas prices will *affect* our vacation plans.

effect: a result (noun)

> The drought will have an *effect* on the citrus crop.

> The new retirement policy will *affect* all future employees, but it will have no *effect* on current employees.

> The realistic special _____ in the war film deeply _____ the audience.

Are/Our

are: a form of the verb *be*

> Those yellow roses *are* beautiful.

our: a pronoun showing ownership

> Have you seen *our* new car?

> *Are* you interested in seeing *our* vacation pictures?

> _____ new cats _____ shredding our furniture.

By/Buy

by: next to or before

> My trusty dog walks *by* my side.

> I must finish my essay *by* Tuesday.

buy: to purchase (verb)

> I need to *buy* a new washing machine.

> *By* the time I was eighteen, I was living on my own and saving to *buy* a new car.

> We are required to _____ our textbooks _____ the second day of class.

👁 Drawing pictures of words that confuse you can help you remember them better.

Conscience/Conscious

conscience: a personal sense of right and wrong (noun)

> Tiffany's *conscience* made her turn in the wallet she found.

conscious: awake, aware (adjective)

> I became *conscious* of a steadily increasing rattle in my car.

> We cannot sell this product in good *conscience* since we are quite *conscious* that it is addictive.

> The detectives were _____ of the fact that the suspect's _____ was bothering her.

■ **TIP:** Remember that one of the words is *con-science*; the other is not.

Fine/Find

fine: of high quality (adjective); feeling well (adverb); a penalty for breaking a law (noun)

Charles and Marilyn received a set of *fine* china as a wedding gift.

Mandy had only three hours of sleep, but she feels *fine*.

If you park in the faculty parking lot, expect a ten-dollar *fine*.

find: to locate, to discover (verb)

I need to *find* my car keys.

Did you *find* the book interesting?

I *find* that my grandmother's *fine* wood furniture looks great in my house.

Ahmand didn't _____ the rented DVD until yesterday, so he had to pay a _____ when he returned it.

> 🎵 If there is a word group that you find especially confusing, try making up a song that helps you remember the differences — for example, "When I see a fashion find, I feel just fine!"

Its/It's

its: a pronoun showing ownership

The jury has reached *its* verdict.

it's: a contraction of the words *it is* or *it has*

Did you know that *it's* snowing outside?

It's clear that the dog has injured *its* paw.

_____ difficult to forecast the track of a hurricane because of _____ unpredictable nature.

> ■ **TIP:** If you are not sure whether to use *its* or *it's* in a sentence, try substituting *it is*. If the sentence doesn't make sense with *it is*, use *its*.

Knew/New/Know/No

knew: understood, recognized (past tense of the verb *know*)

I *knew* you would get the job.

new: unused, recent, or just introduced (adjective)

I think Jill has a *new* boyfriend.

know: to understand, to have knowledge of (verb)

Do you *know* how to operate this DVD player?

no: used to form a negative

We have *no* more eggs.

I *know* that *no* job is too hard for this *new* employee.

I _____ that _____ faculty members would receive _____ computers this year. Didn't you _____ that?

■ **TIP:** For more practice with commonly confused words, visit Exercise Central at <**bedfordstmartins.com/ realskills**>.

Loose/Lose

loose: baggy, relaxed, not fixed in place (adjective)

The handle on this frying pan is *loose*.

lose: to misplace, to give up possession of (verb); to be defeated (verb)

I *lose* my mittens every winter.

Are we going to *lose* the game?

You will *lose* your trousers if your belt is too *loose*.

If your pet lizard gets _____ from its cage, you might _____ him forever.

READ ALOUD

Exaggerating the problem parts of commonly confused words can help you remember the differences. Read the following sentences, emphasizing the bold parts. Can you hear the differences?

I **acc**ept that you won't go with anyone **ex**cept me.

My advi**ce** is that you advi**se** him to leave early.

How did the storm **aff**ect you? Luckily, it had no **eff**ect on me.

Mind/Mine

mind: to object to (verb); the thinking or feeling part of one's brain (noun)

Do you *mind* if I change the TV channel?

I wanted to be a rock star, but I have changed my *mind*.

mine: belonging to me (pronoun); a source of ore and minerals (noun)

I'm afraid that the ringing cell phone is *mine*.

We visited an abandoned silver *mine* in Colorado.

The boss doesn't *mind* if I hire a friend of *mine* to clean our offices.

Enrique has made up his *mind* to move to Alaska and take over his grandfather's gold *mine*.

Do you _____ if I take that pen back from you? It's _____.

Of/Have

of: coming from; caused by; part of a group; made from (preposition)

One *of* the puppies is already weaned.

have: to possess (verb; also used as a helping verb)

We *have* two dogwood trees in our backyard.

You could *have* bought that computer for a lower price across town.

Three *of* our best basketball players *have* quit the team.

We should _____ asked one _____ the security guards for directions.

Passed/Past

passed: went by, went ahead (past tense of the verb *pass*)

We *passed* several slow-moving cars on the country road.

past: time that has gone by (noun); gone by, over, just beyond (preposition)

Jim has been an engineer for the *past* six years.

We accidentally drove right *past* our exit.

As we drove *past* the historic settlement, we felt that we had *passed* into a different era.

The speeding car _____ us on the right and then zoomed

_____ a parked police car. It was the third speeder we'd seen in the

_____ week.

Peace/Piece

peace: no disagreement; calm

The *peace* was disrupted when the cat attacked the dog.

piece: a part of something larger

All I had for breakfast was a *piece* of toast.

After that *piece* of chocolate fudge cake, I felt completely at *peace*.

Two signatures on a single _____ of paper began a new era of

_____ between the two lands.

SO MANY P's...

PEACE

PEAS

PIECE

Principal/Principle

principal: main (adjective) chief; head of a school or leader in an organization (noun)

The *principal* cause of the fire is still unknown.

Nobody likes to be summoned to the *principal's* office.

The request must be approved by a *principal* in the regional office.

principle: a standard of beliefs or behaviors (noun)

Her decision was based on strong moral *principles.*

We are seeking someone with high *principles* to be the next *principal.*

The _____ reason for the building's collapse is a simple _____ of physics.

Quiet/Quite/Quit

quiet: soft in sound; not noisy (adjective)

The children, for once, were *quiet.*

quite: completely, very (adverb)

It's *quite* foggy outside.

quit: to stop (verb)

Kenneth finally *quit* the band.

Once the birds *quit* singing, the forest grew *quiet* and *quite* eerie.

The mayor is _____ right; even if she _____ her job, she will not _____ her critics.

Right/Write

right: correct; in a direction opposite from left (adjective)

The *right* job is not so easy to find.

His office is two doors down on the *right.*

write: to put words on paper (verb)

You must *write* your name and address clearly.

Now is the *right* time to *write* your résumé.

Do you see the blue shaded box to the _____ of your name? That is the _____ place to _____ your job preference.

Set/Sit

set: a collection of something (noun); to place an object somewhere (verb)

What am I going to do with my old *set* of encyclopedias?

Please *set* those groceries on the counter.

sit: to be supported by a chair or other surface

I wish those children would *sit* down and be quiet.

Set down that broom. Let's *sit* down and choose a *set* of dishes for Felicia's wedding gift.

If we _____ the television on the top shelf, we can _____ on the sofa and see the screen clearly. We also need a _____ of good speakers.

Suppose/Supposed

suppose: imagine or assume to be true

I *suppose* you're right.

Do you *suppose* Jared has a girlfriend?

supposed: past tense of *suppose*; intended

We *supposed* that you had simply forgotten Chad's birthday.

I'm *supposed* to leave by 6:00 p.m.

Suppose you lost your job. Who is *supposed* to pay your bills?

I don't think we are _____ to leave those candles burning.

_____ they catch something on fire?

Than/Then

than: a word used to compare two or more things or persons

Cooper is a stronger bicyclist *than* Mitchell.

then: at a certain time; next in time

First, I was late to class; *then*, my cell phone rang during the lecture.

Back *then*, I was happier *than* I am now.

If you score higher _____ 90 percent on your exam, you are _____ ready to move on to the next course.

Their/There/They're

their: a pronoun showing ownership

My grandparents have sold *their* boat.

there: a word indicating location or existence

There are four new kittens over *there*.

they're: a contraction of the words *they are*

They're good friends of mine.

TIP: If you aren't sure whether to use *their* or *they're*, substitute *they are*. If the sentence doesn't make sense, use *their*.

There is proof that *they're* stealing from *their* neighbors.

We stopped by _____ house, but apparently _____ no longer living _____ .

Though/Through/Threw

though: however; nevertheless; in spite of

I bought the computer *though* it seemed overpriced.

through: finished with (adjective); from one side to the other (preposition)

After you are *through* with the computer, may I use it?

The tornado passed *through* the north side of town.

threw: hurled, tossed (past tense of the verb *throw*)

Elena *threw* her worn-out socks into the trash can.

Though Zak *threw* a no-hitter in his last baseball game, he said he was *through* with baseball.

_____ Shawn is usually calm, he _____ his alarm clock against the wall when he realized that it didn't go off. He slept _____ his eight o'clock class.

To/Too/Two

to: a word indicating a direction or movement (preposition); part of the infinitive form of a verb

We are driving *to* Denver tomorrow.

I tried *to* ride my bicycle up that hill.

too: also; more than enough; very (adverb)

I like chocolate *too*.

Our steaks were cooked *too* much.

That storm came *too* close to us.

two: the number between one and three

Marcia gets *two* weeks of vacation a year.

We are simply *too* tired *to* drive for *two* more hours.

If we wait even _____ more minutes for Gail, we will arrive at the dock _____ late _____ catch the early ferry.

Use/Used

use: to employ or put into service (verb)

Are you going to *use* that computer?

used: past tense of the verb *use*. *Used to* can indicate a past fact or state, or it can mean "familiar with."

Mother *used* a butter knife as a screwdriver.

Marcus *used to* play baseball for a minor league team.

I am not *used to* traveling in small airplanes.

You can *use* my truck if you are *used to* driving a standard transmission.

I _____ hem my pants with duct tape because it is so easy to

_____; however, I have grown _____ repairing my clothes with a

needle and thread.

Who's/Whose

who's: a contraction of the words *who is* or *who has*

May I tell her *who's* calling?

Who's been eating my cereal?

whose: a pronoun showing ownership

I don't know *whose* music I like best.

Whose car is parked in my flower bed? *Who's* responsible for this crime?

I don't know _____ supposed to work this shift, but we can check

to see _____ name is on the schedule.

> ■ **TIP:** If you aren't sure whether to use *whose* or *who's*, substitute *who is*. If the sentence doesn't make sense, use *whose*.

Your/You're

your: a pronoun showing ownership

Is this *your* dog?

you're: a contraction of the words *you are*

I hope *you're* coming to Deb's party tonight.

You're bringing *your* girlfriend to the company picnic, aren't you?

I think _____ right; _____ bingo card is a winner.

> ■ **TIP:** If you aren't sure of whether to use *your* or *you're*, substitute *you are*. If the sentence doesn't make sense, use *your*.

Edit Commonly Confused Words in College, Work, and Everyday Life

EDITING REVIEW 1: COLLEGE

Edit misused words in the following test instructions. Outside of the first sentence, which has been marked for you, two sentences are correct; write "C" next to them.

(1) *C* I hope that you are ready to take this test. (2) Please follow this advise carefully. (3) Your sure to do well if you do. (4) As you look threw the questions, keep in mine that there is only one right answer to each. (5) Take the time to read every question before answering it. (6) Its easy to miss an word here and there. (7) In the passed, students have rushed through the test and have regretted it. (8) You are allowed the full class hour to complete the test. (9) Use that time well, and you can't loose. (10) I no you will do a great job!

EDITING REVIEW 2: WORK

Edit misused words in the following excerpt from a job application. Only the first sentence, which has been marked for you, is correct.

(1) *C* Welcome to Gabler's Frozen Foods, and thank you for filling out a job application. (2) Your an important part of our business. (3) We hope that we will fine a job for you soon. (4) Be sure to right legibly so we can get in touch with you quickly. (5) Use a black or blue pen because its much easier to read then pencil. (6) It is important that you fill out every blank on the form to. (7) If you have references, please include there names and addresses on the back of the last page. (8) When you are finished, you are suppose to turn in the form at the front desk. (9) You will hear from a principle of the business within thirty days.

EDITING REVIEW 3: EVERYDAY LIFE . . . .

Edit misused words in the following essay. Two sentences are correct; write "C" next to them. The first sentence has been edited for you.

(1) Mars in the springtime is not the most pleasant place ^{to} ~~too~~ be.
(2) Daytime temperatures may be 68 degrees Fahrenheit, but nighttime temperatures are much lower then on Earth, sometimes dropping to 130 degrees below zero. (3) The fun doesn't stop their, however.

(4) On Earth, you probably except dust balls as part of life. (5) You might fine them under your desk or behind your computer monitor. (6) Believe it or not, dust balls also blow across the surface of Mars; there, however, they are as large as clouds. (7) Springtime on Earth usually brings some extra wind, but you might not no that it does the same thing on Mars. (8) During the spring, dust clouds known as dirt devils have been seen blowing they're way across Mars in several directions. (9) NASA's rover, *Spirit*, not only spotted them but took pictures of them two. (10) Experts at NASA went threw the pictures and created a twelve-minute black-and-white film.

(11) Watching a dust devil on film would certainly be much better then experiencing one in person. (12) These are not little dust storms like the ones that blow across are prairies and deserts. (13) Instead, dirt devils that have past measurement equipment have been recorded as being several miles high and hundreds of feet wide. (14) Brown sand an dust whip around at speeds of seventy miles per hour or more, and, as if that is not enough, some of these dust devils may also be full of miniature lightning bolts. (15) These dust storms are so powerful that they can be seen even from an orbiting spacecraft. (16) Scientists think the storms effect the surface of Mars, carving ridges into the planet.

(17) When it comes to dust devils, stick to the ones under you're bed. (18) Unless you haven't cleaned in a few decades, the dust you find there will be easier to clean up and not quiet so scary!

Write and Edit Your Own Work

ASSIGNMENT 1: WRITE . . . .

Write about a problem you have had in college, at work, or in everyday life. What did you do to try to solve it? When you're done, edit your writing, looking especially for commonly confused words.

ASSIGNMENT 2: EDIT . . . .

Using this chapter as a guide, edit commonly confused words in a paper you are writing for this course or another course or in a piece of writing from your work or everyday life.

. . . .

Practice Together

■ LEARNING STYLES: Look for activities in this chapter that are matched to your learning style. If you don't know your learning style, take the test on pages 26–28.

👁 Visual

👂 Auditory

📖 Reading/writing

🦶 Kinesthetic (movement)

Working with a few other students, practice what you have learned in this chapter.

1. Have one person pick a word group from this chapter and then read the words aloud, saying each one clearly. Others should write down the words they hear. Then, the reader should spell the words so that the others can compare what they wrote down to the actual spellings. Keep going until everyone has read at least one word group.

2. With your group, write five sentences that include the words *their, there,* and *they're,* only put blanks where these words would go. Then, exchange sentences with another group and fill in the blanks in each other's sentences. When you're done, a person from each group should present the answers to the two groups together, and everyone should discuss whether the additions are correct. 👂 📖 🦶

3. As a group, make up a song about one or more of the sets of commonly confused words. Think of lyrics that will help others remember the differences, and write them down. **EXAMPLE:** *The princi**pal** is not your **pal**, but she knows the princi**ples**.* Then, stand up and sing the song together for the class. You might vote on the best song. 👂 📖 🦶

4. As a group, pick one of the sets of commonly confused words, and draw pictures representing the different words. Then, exchange the pictures with another group. Each group should guess at the words represented, write them down, and use them in a sentence. The groups should then join up to discuss whether the answers are correct and what the other group had intended. 👁 👂 📖 🦶

Chapter Review

1. What are four strategies that you can use to avoid confusing words that sound alike or have similar meanings?

    _____

    _____

    _____

    _____

    _____

2. What are the top five commonly confused words on your list?

    _____

3. **VOCABULARY:** Go back to any new words that you underlined in this chapter. Can you guess their meanings now? If not, look up the words in a dictionary.

LEARNING JOURNAL: Write for two minutes about words you commonly confuse and how you might remember the differences.

■ **TIP:** For help with building your vocabulary, see Appendix B.

27

Spelling

Using the Right Letters

MISS PELL never MISSPELLS 'MISSPELL'

Understand the Importance of Spelling Correctly

VOCABULARY: Underline any words in this chapter that are new to you.

Some smart people are poor spellers. Unfortunately, spelling errors are easy to see. If you are serious about improving your spelling, you need to have a dictionary and a list of words you often misspell. When in doubt about a word's spelling, always look it up.

A **dictionary** contains the correct spellings of words, along with information on how they are pronounced, what they mean, and where they came from. The following are two popular Web sites with online dictionaries:

TIP: For a sample dictionary entry, see page 423.

- Merriam-Webster Online at **<www.m-w.com>**. If you are fairly sure how the beginning of a word is spelled, you can enter those letters and then an asterisk (*) in this site's search feature. You will then see a list of the words that begin with the letters you typed in. From the list, you can choose the word you want.

- Your Dictionary at **<www.yourdictionary.com>**. This site has dictionaries for business, computers, law, medicine, and other fields.

Keeping a **spelling list** of words you often misspell will help you edit your papers and learn how to write the words correctly. From this list, identify your personal spelling "demons"—the five to ten words that you misspell most frequently. Write these words, spelled correctly, on an index card, and keep the card with you so that you can look at it whenever you write.

Practice Spelling Correctly

Don't try to correct your grammar, improve your message, and check your spelling at the same time. Instead, do separate steps for each. Remember to check the dictionary whenever you are unsure about the spelling of a word and to add all the spelling mistakes you find to your personal spelling list.

Most word-processing programs have a **spell checker** that finds and highlights a word that may be misspelled and suggests other spellings. However, a spell checker ignores anything it recognizes as a word, so it will not help you find commonly confused words such as those discussed in Chapter 26. For example, a spell checker would not highlight any of the problems in the following sentences:

I am not *aloud* to do that.

[Correct: I am not *allowed* to do that.]

He took my *advise*.

[Correct: He took my *advice*.]

Did you feel the *affects*?

[Correct: Did you feel the *effects*?]

Use some of the following **proofreading techniques** to focus on the spelling of one word at a time.

- Put a piece of paper or a ruler under the line you are reading.
- Cut a "window" in an index card that is about the size of a long word (such as *misunderstanding*), and place it over your writing to focus on one word or phrase at a time.
- Proofread your paper backward, one word at a time.
- If you are using a computer, print out a version of your paper that looks different from a standard printed page: Make the words larger, make the margins larger, triple-space the lines, or do all of these. Read this version carefully.
- Exchange papers with a partner for proofreading, identifying only possible misspellings. The writer of the paper should be responsible for checking the words you have identified and correcting any that are actually misspelled.

After you proofread each word in your paper, look at your personal spelling list and your list of demon words one more time. If you used any of these words in your paper, go back and check their spelling again.

Read your paper aloud. This strategy will help you if you tend to leave words out.

PRACTICE 1 . .

Take the last paper you wrote—or one that you are working on now—and find and correct any spelling errors. Use any of the tools and techniques discussed in this chapter. How many spelling mistakes did you find? Were you

■ **TIP:** For more practice with spelling, visit Exercise Central at <**bedfordstmartins.com/ realskills**>.

surprised? How was the experience different from what you normally do to edit for spelling?

. . . .

Five Steps to Better Spelling

Step 1. Remember Ten Troublemakers

Writing teachers have identified the ten words in the following list as the words students most commonly misspell.

■ **IDEA JOURNAL:** What activities do you break into steps? How has that helped you?

INCORRECT	CORRECT
alot	**a l**ot
arguement	arg**um**ent
definate, defenite	defi**ni**te
develop**e**	develop
lite	lig**ht**
necesary, nesesary	ne**cess**ary
rec**ie**ve	rec**ei**ve
seperate	sep**a**rate
surprize, suprise	surprise
until**l**	until

Step 2. Defeat Your Personal Spelling Demons

Try some of the following techniques to defeat your spelling demons:

- Create an explanation or saying that will help you remember the correct spelling. For example, "*surprise* is no *prize*" may remind you to spell *surprise* with an *s*, not a *z*.
- Write the word correctly ten times.
- Write a paragraph in which you use the word at least three times.
- Ask a partner to give you a spelling test.

READ ALOUD

Say each separate part (syllable) of your spelling demons out loud so that you don't miss any letters (*dis-ap-point-ment, Feb-ru-ar-y, prob-a-bly*). You can also say each letter of the word out loud. See if there's a rhythm or a rhyme you can memorize.

■ **TIP:** Think of syllables as the number of "beats" a word has. The word *syllable* has three beats (*syl-la-ble*).

Step 3. Learn about Commonly Confused Words

Look back at Chapter 26, which covers twenty-seven sets of words that are commonly confused because they sound alike. If you can remember the differences between the words in each set, you will avoid many spelling mistakes.

Step 4. Learn Six Spelling Rules

The six rules discussed in this section can help you avoid or correct many of the spelling errors in your writing.

Before the six rules, here is a quick review of vowels and consonants.

VOWELS: a e i o u

CONSONANTS: b c d f g h j k l m n p q r s t v w x y z

The letter *y* can be either a vowel or a consonant. It is a vowel when it sounds like the *y* in *fly* or *hungry*. It is a consonant when it sounds like the *y* in *yellow*.

RULE 1: *I* before *e*
Except after *c*.
Or when sounded like *a*
As in *neighbor* or *weigh*.

piece (*i* before *e*)

receive (except after *c*)

eight (sounds like *a*)

EXCEPTIONS: either, neither, foreign, height, seize, society, their, weird

'I' before 'E'
except after 'C'
or when sounded like 'A'
as in 'neighbor' or 'weigh'
or when in 'weird'
like me.

You might say this rhyme out loud (or in your head) as you decide whether a word is spelled with an *ie* or an *ei*.

PRACTICE 2 ·

In the spaces provided, write more examples of words that follow Rule 1. Do not use words that have already been covered.

1. _____

2. _____

3. _____

4. _____

5. _____

6. _____

RULE 2: Drop the final *e* when adding an ending that begins with a vowel.

hop**e** + ing = hoping

imagin**e** + ation = imagination

Keep the final *e* when adding an ending that begins with a consonant.

> achieve + ment = achievement
> definite + ly = definitely

EXCEPTIONS: argument, awful, truly (and others)

> **PRACTICE 3** . .

For each item, circle the first letter in the ending, and decide whether it is a consonant or a vowel. Then, add the ending to the word and write the new word in the space.

1. fame + ous = _____

2. confuse + ing = _____

3. care + ful = _____

4. use + able = _____

5. nice + ly = _____

6. fate + ful = _____

7. dine + ing = _____

8. surprise + ing = _____

9. sense + less = _____

10. realize + ation = _____

RULE 3: When adding an ending to a word that ends in *y*, change the *y* to *i* when a consonant comes before the *y*.

> lonely + est = loneliest
> happy + er = happier
> apology + ize = apologize
> likely + hood = likelihood

Do not change the *y* when a vowel comes before the *y*.

> boy + ish = boyish
> pay + ment = payment
> survey + or = surveyor
> buy + er = buyer

EXCEPTIONS

1. When adding -*ing* to a word ending in *y*, always keep the *y*, even if a consonant comes before it: stud**y** + ing = stud**y**ing.
2. Other exceptions include *daily*, *said*, and *paid*.

PRACTICE 4 . .

For each item, circle the letter before the *y*, and decide whether it is a vowel or a consonant. Then, add the ending to the word, and write the new word in the space provided.

1. say + ing = _____

2. gray + er = _____

3. easy + ly = _____

4. healthy + er _____

5. beauty + ful = _____

6. play + ers = _____

7. lazy + est = _____

8. annoy + ance = _____

9. messy + ness = _____

10. fly + ing = _____

RULE 4: When adding an ending that starts with a vowel to a one-syllable word, double the final consonant only if the word ends with a consonant-vowel-consonant.

> t**rap** + ed = trapped
> d**rip** + ing = dripping
> **fat** + er = fatter
> **fit** + er = fitter

Do not double the final consonant if the word ends with some other combination.

VOWEL-VOWEL-CONSONANT	VOWEL-CONSONANT-CONSONANT
c**lean** + est = cleanest	sl**ick** + er = slicker
p**oor** + er = poorer	te**ach** + er = teacher
c**lear** + ed = cleared	**last** + ed = lasted

RULE 5: When adding an ending that starts with a vowel to a word of two or more syllables, double the final consonant only if the word ends with a consonant-vowel-consonant and the stress is on the last syllable.

ad**mit** + ing = admitting

cont**rol** + er = controller

oc**cur** + ence = occurrence

pre**fer** + ed = preferred

com**mit** + ed = committed

Do not double the final consonant in other cases.

problem + atic = problematic

understand + ing = understanding

offer + ed = offered

PRACTICE 5 . .

For each item, circle the last three letters in the main word, and decide whether they fit the consonant-vowel-consonant pattern. In words with more than one syllable, underline the stressed syllable. Then, add the ending to each word, and write the new word in the space provided.

1. talk + ing =_____

2. clap + ing = _____

3. thunder + ing = _____

4. drop + ed = _____

5. trip + ed = _____

6. appear + ance = _____

7. talent + ed = _____

8. mark + er = _____

9. begin + er = _____

10. danger + ous = _____

RULE 6: To make a plural or to change a verb form, add -s to most words, including words that end in *o* preceded by a vowel.

MOST WORDS	WORDS THAT END IN VOWEL PLUS *O*
book + s = book**s**	vid**eo** + s = videos
college + s = college**s**	ster**eo** + s = stereos
jump + s = jump**s**	rad**io** + s = radios

Add *-es* to words that end in *s*, *sh*, *ch*, or *x*, and *o* preceded by a consonant.

WORDS THAT END IN *S*, *SH*, *CH*, OR *X*	WORDS THAT END IN CONSONANT PLUS *O*
clas**s** + es = classe**s**	pota**to** + es = potatoes
pu**sh** + es = pushe**s**	he**ro** + es = heroes
ben**ch** + es = benche**s**	**go** + es = goes
fa**x** + es = faxe**s**	

EXCEPTIONS: pianos, solos (and others)

PRACTICE 6 . . . .

For each word, circle the last two letters, and decide which of the Rule 6 patterns the word fits. Add *-s* or *-es* and write the new word in the space provided.

1. phone _____

2. quilt _____

3. fox _____

4. glass _____

5. echo _____

6. splash _____

7. pencil _____

8. patio _____

9. dish _____

10. reach _____

. . . .

Step 5. Check a Spelling List

The following is a list of one hundred commonly misspelled words. Check this list as you proofread your writing.

One Hundred Commonly Misspelled Words

absence	convenient	height	receive
achieve	cruelty	humorous	recognize
across	daughter	illegal	recommend
aisle	definite	immediately	restaurant
a lot	describe	independent	rhythm
already	dictionary	interest	roommate
analyze	different	jewelry	schedule
answer	disappoint	judgment	scissors
appetite	dollar	knowledge	secretary
argument	eighth	license	separate
athlete	embarrass	lightning	sincerely
awful	environment	loneliness	sophomore
basically	especially	marriage	succeed
beautiful	exaggerate	meant	successful
beginning	excellent	muscle	surprise
believe	exercise	necessary	truly
business	fascinate	ninety	until
calendar	February	noticeable	usually
career	finally	occasion	vacuum
category	foreign	occurrence	valuable
chief	friend	perform	vegetable
column	government	physically	weight
coming	grief	prejudice	weird
commitment	guidance	probably	writing
conscious	harass	psychology	written

PRACTICE 7 . .

In the following paragraph, fill in each blank with the correct spelling of the base word plus the ending in parentheses. You may want to refer to Rules 2–5 on pages 453–456.

(1) Located near San Antonio, Texas, the Wild Animal Orphanage is one of the _____ (*big + est*) wildlife refuges in the country. (2) Since it _____ (*open + ed*) in 1983, the orphanage has cared for thousands of _____ (*unwant + ed*) exotic animals such as lions, tigers, bears, monkeys, and birds. (3) Most of these _____

(*neglect* + *ed*) animals are consequences of the exotic pet trade. (4) People can _____ (*easy* + *ly*) purchase wild animals from flea markets, classified ads, or Web sites. (5) However, few people have the space or the knowledge _____ (*need* + *ed*) to properly care for exotic animals, many of which end up _____ (*live* + *ing*) unhappy lives. (6) _____ (*Unfortunate* + *ly*), others are killed when breeders cannot find homes for them. (7) Tarzan, a lion cub, spent the first eighteen months of his life _____ (*unhappy* + *ly*) confined to a three-foot-by-four-foot cage in Cancun, Mexico. (8) He had only one toy for _____ (*amuse* + *ment*), a coconut shell. (9) Rescuers brought him to the Wild Animal Orphanage, and Tarzan is now _____ (*run* + *ing*) and _____ (*play* + *ing*) with other lions. (10) The orphanage offers public tours, _____ (*educate* + *ing*) people and _____ (*discourage* + *ing*) them from _____ (*purchase* + *ing*) animals meant to remain in the wild.

PRACTICE 8 . . . .

Find and correct any spelling mistakes in the following paragraph. You will find ten misspelled words. You may want to refer to Rules 1–6 on pages 453–457 or the list of commonly misspelled words on page 458.

(1) When I stopped by my freind Vanessa's cubicle at work, I noticed a small vase of beautiful flowers and two boxs of chocolates sitting on her desk. (2) "Who sent you flowers?" I asked her. (3) "I did," she admitted. (4) Vanessa thought they helped make her cubicle a better environment for studing some documents for a report she was writing. (5) "I beleive they help me while I'm thinking and writeing," she said. (6) At first, I thought Vanessa was jokeing. (7) Still, I bought some pink roses for my own desk. (8) I was aware of their lovely pink buds and delicate scent as I worked. (9) Even my accounting tasks seemed easyer than usual. (10) Fresh flowers in my work area definitly led to an improvment in my mood and concentration.

Edit Spelling Errors in College, Work, and Everyday Life

EDITING REVIEW 1: COLLEGE

Edit spelling errors in the following paragraph, which is like one you might find in an international relations textbook. One sentence is correct; write "C" next to it. The first sentence has been edited for you.

(1) The Channel Tunnel, or Chunnel, is the rail tunnel ~~connectting~~ *connecting* England and France. (2) Requireing ten individual contractors and thousands of workers, it was a challengeing project. (3) To complete this huge construction, a partnership had to be formed between two countrys with different languages, goverments, and sets of laws and safety codes. (4) England was definitly the more difficult country of the two. (5) For yeares, it had viewed itself as a seperate country from the rest of Europe. (6) It wanted to remain distinct, and this new connection to Europe made many English people uncomfortable. (7) Nevertheless, others saw the Chunnel as one of the best wayes to truely bring together the two countries. (8) Financeing the project was another one of the bigest obstacles. (9) The Chunnel cost billions of dollares, averaging $5 million each day of construction. (10) Ultimately, it cost seven hundred times more to develope than the Golden Gate Bridge in San Francisco, California.

EDITING REVIEW 2: WORK

Edit spelling errors in the following cover letter for a job application. Two sentences are correct; write "C" next to them. The first sentence has been edited for you.

Maya Collins

M & R Shipping

42 Park Forest Highway

Baton Rouge, LA 70816

Dear Ms. Collins:

(1) I am ~~writeing~~ *writing* in response to your classified ad in the *Baton Rouge*

Advocate. (2) The advertisment stated that you are looking for an office secratary for your shipping business. (3) I beleive I am the perfect person for the job. (4) I am both skiled and experienced in this kind of work. (5) I have worked at the front desk of three local businesses, where I greetted customers, answered phone calls, processed invoices, and managed the ordering of office supplys. (6) I am currently attendding Pearson Community College part-time, and my shedule meshs well with the hours you mentioned.

(7) My résumé is enclosed with this letter. (8) If nesessary, I can start work immediately. (9) I look forward to hearing from you.

(10) Sincerly,

Gina Thomasson

EDITING REVIEW 3: EVERYDAY LIFE . . . .

Edit spelling errors in the following paragraphs. Seven sentences are correct; write "C" next to them. The first sentence has been edited for you.

(1) Ask many of today's college students what a muscle car is and
you may ~~recieve~~ *receive* a blank look in return. (2) This is no surprize since the average student was born a decade after most companys quit making these cars.

(3) Muscle cars were very popular in the 1960s and early 1970s. (4) They had large engines and relativly small bodies, expecially when compared to the SUVs of today. (5) These cars were also fairly affordable, so they were not impossible to own. (6) The combineation of price and engine power made muscle cars popular with the younger crowd. (7) Unforunatly, these vehicles had so much power that they could be deadly in the hands of inexperienced drivers. (8) As a result, insurance premiums on muscle cars began skyrocketting. (9) The industry was also damaged by the 1973 oil crisis. (10) Suddenly, gas was extremly expensive and in short supply. (11) It simply became too costly to drive a muscle car.

(12) Now, more than thirty years later, car manufacturers are starting to bring back muscle cars. (13) Ford, Pontiac, and Dodge are makeing some new cars that will probly answer the wishs of some people who miss muscle cars. (14) These cars are fast, efficient, and come with a horsepower of at least 300. (15) They may still grab the attention of younger drivers. (16) However, with prices that usualy start at $27,000 and only go up, today's muscle cars may be meant only for the older crowd.

Write and Edit Your Own Work

ASSIGNMENT 1: WRITE

Write about an old trend that you see coming back (like muscle cars or a certain hairstyle or fashion). Do you like the trend or not? Why? When you're done, read each word carefully, looking for spelling errors.

ASSIGNMENT 2: EDIT

Using the rules and strategies from this chapter, edit spelling errors in a paper you are writing for this course or another course or in a piece of writing from your work or everyday life.

Practice Together

Working with a few other students, practice what you have learned in this chapter.

■ **LEARNING STYLES:** Look for activities in this chapter that are matched to your learning style. If you don't know your learning style, take the test on pages 26–28.

 Visual

 Auditory

 Reading/writing

 Kinesthetic (movement)

1. As a group, come up with at least three words that you all consider spelling demons. Write down the words and check the spellings in a dictionary. (If a dictionary is not available, your instructor may need to check the words.) Then, think of a rhyme or song that could help you remember each word. When all the groups are done, stand up and perform the rhymes or songs for the class. You might vote on the best creation.

2. As a group, draw a cartoon illustrating the rhyme "*I* before *e*/Except after *c*/Or when sounded like *a*/As in *neighbor* or *weigh*." You'll need to

talk about what types of details to include. When all groups are done, post your pictures on the wall and do a "gallery walk" so that everyone can see the other groups' work. 👁 ⭲ 📖 ✍

3. For each of the six spelling rules in this chapter, give three additional examples of words that can follow the rule. Write the words down and check the spellings against the rules. ⭲ 📖

4. Following is a list of words + endings. With your group, add the endings indicated, looking back at the rules in this chapter if you need to. Each person should write down the spelling of the word/ending combinations as they are discussed. When you're done, each person in the group should stand up, say one word + ending, and spell the combination.
    EXAMPLE: *Imagine + ation. I-m-a-g-i-n-a-t-i-o-n.* ⭲ 📖 ✍

    refer + ed = _____

    sad + er = _____

    merry + er = _____

    cope + ing = _____

    patrol + ing = _____

    separate + ly = _____

    acquit + al = _____

    integrate + ation = _____

    tomato + s = _____

Chapter Review

1. To improve your spelling, you need to have a _____ and _____

    _____ .

2. What are two proofreading techniques? _____

3. What are the five steps to better spelling?

    _____

    _____

    _____

    _____

    _____

4. For each of the six spelling rules in this chapter, write one word that

    shows how each rule works. RULE 1: _____; RULE 2:

📖 **LEARNING JOURNAL:**
Write for two minutes about the proofreading techniques you'd most like to try. What do you like about them? (Your journal is a good place to keep a record of your spelling demons.)

_____; RULE 3: _____; RULE 4: _____;

RULE 5: _____; RULE 6: _____.

■ **TIP:** For help with building your vocabulary, see Appendix B.

5. **VOCABULARY:** Go back to any new words that you underlined in this chapter. Can you guess their meanings now? If not, look up the words in a dictionary.

Unit Six Test
Editing Words in Sentences

Circle the correct choice for each of the following items.

1. If an underlined portion of this item contains an error or ineffective wording, select the revision that fixes the problem. If the item is correct as written, choose d.

    Barbara <u>use</u> to want to <u>buy</u> a new couch <u>and</u> a big-screen television, but
         A   B   C
    now she'd rather save up for a vacation.

    a. used   c. an
    b. by   d. No change is necessary.

2. If an underlined portion of this item contains an error or ineffective wording, select the revision that fixes the problem. If the item is correct as written, choose d.

    The <u>students</u> were <u>surprized</u> by the pop quiz, which they felt was <u>unfair</u>.
          A   B   C

    a. studentes   c. uncool
    b. surprised   d. No change is necessary.

3. If an underlined portion of this item contains an error or ineffective wording, select the revision that fixes the problem. If the item is correct as written, choose d.

    It took <u>hard work</u> to build <u>our log home</u>; however, we have never
               A   B
    <u>regreted</u> our decision to build our dream home ourselves.
     C

    a. blood, sweat, and tears   c. regretted
    b. our humble abode   d. No change is necessary.

4. Choose the correct word to fill in the blank.

    Two accidents _____ on the bridge at nearly the same time.
    a. happenned   c. hapenned
    b. happened   d. hapened

5. If an underlined portion of this item contains an error or ineffective wording, select the revision that fixes the problem. If the item is correct as written, choose d.

    Teresa's <u>conscience</u> has a significant <u>effect</u> on her moral <u>principles</u>.
             A   B   C

    a. conscious   c. principals
    b. affect   d. No change is necessary.

6. Choose the best word(s) to fill in the blank.

   During the news conference, the mayor admitted that he was _____ at the New Year's Eve party.

   a. wasted

   b. drunk and intoxicated

   c. intoxicated

   d. drunk as a skunk

7. If an underlined portion of this item contains an error or ineffective wording, select the revision that fixes the problem. If the item is correct as written, choose d.

   You will <u>receive</u> the report in two <u>seperate</u> parts; it is <u>definitely</u> quite
           A   B   C
   detailed.

   a. recieve   c. definitly

   b. separate   d. No change is necessary.

8. If an underlined portion of this item contains an error or ineffective wording, select the revision that fixes the problem. If the item is correct as written, choose d.

   Ben <u>fixed</u> our <u>benches</u> that were damaged by the <u>tornados</u>.
          A   B   C

   a. fixxed   c. tornadoes

   b. benchs   d. No change is necessary.

9. If an underlined portion of this item contains an error or ineffective wording, select the revision that fixes the problem. If the item is correct as written, choose d.

   I could <u>sense</u> that we were going to <u>loose</u> the game when the point guard
       A   B
   <u>passed</u> the basketball to the cheerleader.
    C

   a. since   c. past

   b. lose   d. No change is necessary.

10. If an underlined portion of this item contains an error or ineffective wording, select the revision that fixes the problem. If the item is correct as written, choose d.

    We hope that the city council will <u>develop</u> a plan to save the town's two
               A

    <u>prettyest</u> historic <u>churches</u>.
     B   C

    a. develope   c. churchs

    b. prettiest   d. No change is necessary.

11. If an underlined portion of this item contains an error or ineffective wording, select the revision that fixes the problem. If the item is correct as written, choose d.

Trey <u>flipped out</u> when his boss <u>reassigned</u> many of his <u>duties</u> to some-
        A   B   C
one else.

  a. became upset   c. tasks

  b. dished out   d. No change is necessary.

12. If an underlined portion of this item contains an error or ineffective wording, select the revision that fixes the problem. If the item is correct as written, choose d.

Now that the children have returned to school, it's just <u>too</u> <u>quite</u> in the
                                                    A   B C

house.

  a. its   c. quiet

  b. to   d. No change is necessary.

13. Choose the best word(s) to fill in the blank.

I _____ to pack all of my belongings before moving day.

  a. worked like a dog   c. worked a lot

  b. worked tirelessly   d. hustled

14. If an underlined portion of this item contains an error or ineffective wording, select the revision that fixes the problem. If the item is correct as written, choose d.

Steve finally <u>accepted</u> that <u>your</u> idea is better <u>than</u> his.
                  A   B   C

  a. excepted   c. then

  b. you're   d. No change is necessary.

15. Choose the best words to fill in the blank.

_____ that the speaker was being sarcastic.

  a. I think   c. In my opinion, I think

  b. I am of the opinion   d. I myself personally think

16. If an underlined portion of this item contains an error or ineffective wording, select the revision that fixes the problem. If the item is correct as written, choose d.

Can you <u>believe</u> that a robbery <u>occured</u> in my <u>peaceful</u> neighborhood
            A   B   C

last night?

  a. beleive   c. peacful

  b. occurred   d. No change is necessary.

17. Choose the best word(s) to fill in the blank.

The Fourth of July fireworks display was _____.

   a. great   c. nice

   b. way cool   d. loud and colorful

18. If an underlined portion of this item contains an error or ineffective wording, select the revision that fixes the problem. If the item is correct as written, choose d.

As we drove <u>through</u> town, we <u>past</u> many people <u>whose</u> homes had been
              A   B   C
damaged in the storm.

   a. threw   c. who's

   b. passed   d. No change is necessary.

19. Choose the best words to fill in the blank.

Tonia filed her taxes _____.

   a. in the nick of time

   b. just under the wire

   c. at the eleventh hour

   d. just before the midnight deadline

20. If an underlined portion of this item contains an error or ineffective wording, select the revision that fixes the problem. If the item is correct as written, choose d.

I am <u>definately</u> going to be in <u>a lot</u> of trouble if I don't finish my
           A   B
<u>argument</u> paper.
   C

   a. definitely   c. arguement

   b. alot   d. No change is necessary.

21. Choose the best words to fill in the blank.

When tourist traffic brings the highway to a standstill, many local residents _____.

   a. become irritated   c. get all worked up

   b. get bent out of shape   d. become irritated and annoyed

22. If an underlined portion of this item contains an error or ineffective wording, select the revision that fixes the problem. If the item is correct as written, choose d.

Marvin seems to take everyone's <u>advice</u> <u>except</u> <u>mind</u>.
                             A   B   C

   a. advise   c. mine

   b. accept   d. No change is necessary.

23. If an underlined portion of this item contains an error or ineffective wording, select the revision that fixes the problem. If the item is correct as written, choose d.

    Because of all the snowstorms this winter, the principal said that school
            A   **B**

    will be in session passed Memorial Day this year.
                     C

    a. Due to the fact of   c. past

    b. principle   d. No change is necessary.

24. Choose the best words to fill in the blank.

    While waiting for the results of the election, Mandy _____.

    a. was as nervous as a cat   c. was sweating bullets

    b. was not okay   d. was very nervous

25. If an underlined portion of this item contains an error or ineffective wording, select the revision that fixes the problem. If the item is correct as written, choose d.

    I knew that I should have followed my sister's advise to find a new job.
      A   **B**   **C**

    a. new   c. fine

    b. advice   d. No change is necessary.

26. If an underlined portion of this item contains an error or ineffective wording, select the revision that fixes the problem. If the item is correct as written, choose d.

    My neice is finally beginning to believe in herself.
        A   **B**   **C**

    a. niece   c. beleive

    b. begining   d. No change is necessary.

27. Choose the best word(s) to fill in the blank.

    Calculus is hard for many people, but for Jerome, it's _____.

    a. as easy as pie   c. no biggie

    b. quite easy   d. okay

28. If an underlined portion of this item contains an error or ineffective wording, select the revision that fixes the problem. If the item is correct as written, choose d.

    Are neighbors forgot that they were supposed to set out their garbage
     A   **B**   **C**

    can yesterday.

    a. Our   c. sit

    b. suppose   d. No change is necessary.

29. If an underlined portion of this item contains an error or ineffective wording, select the revision that fixes the problem. If the item is correct as written, choose d.

A popular <u>athlete</u> in high school, Andrew had trouble admitting to his
       A

<u>loneliness</u> at college <u>untill</u> now.
  B   C

  a. athelete   c. until

  b. lonelyness   d. No change is necessary.

30. If an underlined portion of this item contains an error or ineffective wording, select the revision that fixes the problem. If the item is correct as written, choose d.

I fell asleep <u>because</u> the <u>movie</u> was <u>awful.</u>
           A   B   C

  a. due to the fact that   c. boring and difficult to understand

  b. flick   d. No change is necessary.

■ **TIP:** For advice on taking tests, see Appendix A.

Unit Seven

Editing for Punctuation and Mechanics

28

Commas

,

Understand What Commas Do

A **comma** (,) is a punctuation mark that separates words and word groups to help readers understand a sentence.

READ ALOUD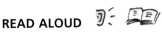

Stand up and read the following sentences aloud, pausing when there is a comma. How does the use of commas change the meaning?

NO COMMA	When you call Alicia I'll leave the house.
ONE COMMA	When you call Alicia, I'll leave the house.
TWO COMMAS	When you call, Alicia, I'll leave the house.

VOCABULARY: Underline any words in this chapter that are new to you.

IDEA JOURNAL: What do you do to relax?

Use Commas Correctly

Commas between Items in a Series

Use commas to separate three or more items in a series. The last item usually has *and* or *or* before it, and this should be preceded by a comma.

I put away my winter *sweaters, scarves, gloves,* and *hats*.

The candidates *walked to the stage, stood behind their microphones,* and *began yelling at each other*.

■ **TIP:** Some magazines, newspapers, and books do not use a comma before the final item. In college writing, however, it is always best to include it.

> **FIND: Read each sentence in your writing carefully. Look for series of items (lists).**
>
> **You can <u>go to the store</u> <u>go to the movies</u> or <u>stay at home</u>.**
>
> - Underline each item in a series.
> - Ask if there are three or more items. (If there are, commas are needed.) [In this example, the answer is "yes."]
> - Ask if there are commas separating the items. [In this example, the answer is "no."]

> **FIX: Add any commas that are missing. Make sure there is a comma after the final item (before *and* or *or*).**
>
> **You can go to the store, go to the movies, or stay at home.**

INCORRECT

I bought bread milk and bananas.

Dan will cook I will clean and Dara will do the laundry.

Tara likes to bike, and run.

CORRECT

I bought bread, milk, and bananas.

Dan will cook, I will clean, and Dara will do the laundry.

Tara likes to bike and run.

[No comma is necessary because there are only two items.]

 Visualize each thing in a series or list as you write it (*bread, milk, bananas*). This will help you separate the items and see where the commas should go.

PRACTICE 1 . . . .

Edit the following sentences by underlining the items in the series and adding commas where they are needed. One sentence is correct; write "C" next to it.

EXAMPLE: At the moment, I am <u>typing on my computer</u>, <u>listening to music</u>, and <u>tapping my toes</u>; doing more than one thing is called *multitasking*.

1. Multitasking is easier than ever thanks to gadgets such as cell phones laptop computers and portable music players.

2. There was a time when I could just sit in my easy chair put my feet on the coffee table and do nothing.

3. Sometimes, I miss the simpler days of record players black-and-white televisions and hula hoops.

4. People today feel the need to do two things or even three things at once.

5. Earlier today, I ate lunch watched the news and read a book at the same time.

6. Then, I walked the dog listened to the baseball game on my portable radio and called my sister on my cell phone.

7. Tonight, I will clean the house cook dinner and watch the children.

8. I get nervous when I see someone driving talking and applying makeup at the same time.

9. I try to avoid using my cell phone while driving eating or seeing a movie.

10. Do you believe that multitasking is useful simply annoying or downright dangerous?

■ **TIP:** For more practice with comma usage, visit Exercise Central at <**bedfordstmartins.com/ realskills**>.

Commas in Compound Sentences

A **compound sentence** contains two sentences joined by one of these words: *and, but, for, nor, or, so, yet.* Use a comma before the joining word to separate the two clauses.

■ **TIP:** The words *and, but, for, nor, or, so,* and *yet* are called coordinating conjunctions (see Chapter 22).

| Sentence | **,** | *and, but, for, nor, or, so, yet* | Sentence | **.** |

The toddler knocked over the oatmeal bowl, *and* then she rubbed the mess into her hair.

I love my criminal justice course, *but* the tests are very difficult.

You won't be at the meeting, *so* I'll tell you what we decide.

Language note: Remember that a comma alone cannot connect two sentences in English. This creates an error known as a *comma splice* (see Chapter 12). A comma is *not* needed if a coordinating conjunction joins two sentence elements that are *not* complete sentences.

■ **TIP:** For a review of sentences, subjects, and verbs, see Chapter 10.

FIND: Read each sentence in your writing carefully.

We would like to hire you (but) we don't have the right position.

- To decide whether the sentence is compound, underline the subjects, and double-underline the verbs. A compound sentence will have two subjects and two verbs.
- Ask if the sentence is compound. [The example is.]
- Circle the word that joins the sentences.
- If the sentence is compound and there is no comma before the joining word, a comma must be added. [A comma is needed in the example sentence.]

FIX: Put a comma before the word that joins the two sentences.

We would like to hire you, but we don't have the right position.

Walk as you read a few sentences with commas. When you get to a comma, stop walking. Then, continue walking until you get to another comma. What do the commas do?

INCORRECT

Jess is good with numbers and she's a hard worker.

Manuel hates to swim yet he wants to live by the water.

I meant to go, but couldn't.

CORRECT

Jess is good with numbers, and she's a hard worker.

Manuel hates to swim, yet he wants to live by the water.

I meant to go but couldn't.

[This sentence is not a compound, so a comma should not be used. *I meant to go* is a sentence, but *couldn't* isn't.]

PRACTICE 2 . . . .

Edit the following compound sentences by adding commas where they are needed. One sentence is correct; write "C" next to it.

EXAMPLE: Companies today realize the importance of diversity, but prejudice still exists in the workplace.

1. Many professions used to be dominated by men and the majority of those men were white.

2. Some workplaces still look like this but most do not.

3. Workplace diversity is now common yet discrimination still occurs.

4. Researchers recently conducted a survey of 623 American workers and the results revealed some alarming statistics.

5. Some respondents had been victims of prejudice over the previous year or they had overheard others making intolerant statements.

6. Thirty percent of respondents said that they had overheard statements of racial prejudice at their workplace, and 20 percent said that coworkers had made fun of others because of their sexual orientation.

7. Age discrimination is another problem for 20 percent of respondents reported prejudice against older workers.

8. The survey did not report on the characteristics of the respondents nor did it give details about the people expressing the prejudice.

9. The American workforce is more diverse than ever before and it will become even more diverse in the future.

10. This is a positive trend but steps need to be taken to eliminate prejudice in the workplace.

Commas after Introductory Words

Putting a comma after introductory words lets your readers know when the main part of the sentence is starting.

INTRODUCTORY WORD	*Luckily,* they got out of the burning building.
INTRODUCTORY PHRASE	*Until now,* I'd never seen a ten-pound frog.
INTRODUCTORY CLAUSE	*As I explained,* Jacob eats only red jelly beans.

PRACTICE 3

In each of the following sentences, underline any introductory word or word group. Then, add commas after introductory word groups where they are needed. One sentence is correct; write "C" next to it.

EXAMPLE: As many people know, stepping on a rusty nail can cause tetanus, a potentially deadly infection.

1. Yesterday I accidentally stepped on a nail.

2. Although the nail was not rusty I decided to call the hospital.

3. According to my doctor a shiny nail is just as likely to cause tetanus as a rusty one.

4. Though some people are unaware of it rust itself does not cause tetanus.

5. Apparently, tetanus is caused by bacteria that live in dust, soil, and human and animal waste.

6. Once the bacteria get deep enough inside a wound they begin growing as long as oxygen is not present.

7. Producing poisons that attack muscles all over the body, these bacteria kill an estimated fifty to one hundred people every year.

8. Fortunately nearly all children receive the tetanus vaccine.

9. However the vaccine's effects wear off after ten years.

10. Because of this the doctor recommended that I come in for a tetanus shot.

Commas around Appositives and Interrupters

■ **TIP:** For more on nouns, see Chapter 16.

An **appositive**, a phrase that renames a noun, comes directly before or after the noun.

> Claire, *my best friend,* sees every movie starring Johnny Depp.
> [*My best friend* renames *Claire.*]

> You should go to Maxwell's, *the new store that opened downtown.*
> [*The new store that opened downtown* renames *Maxwell's.*]

An **interrupter** is a word or word group that interrupts a sentence yet does not affect the meaning of the sentence.

> The baby, *as you know,* screams the moment I put her to bed.

> Mitch hit his tenth home run of the season, *if you can believe it.*

Putting commas around appositives and interrupters tells readers that these words are not essential to the meaning of a sentence. If an appositive or interrupter is in the middle of a sentence, put a comma before and after it.

Your pants, *by the way,* are ripped.

If an appositive or interrupter comes at the beginning or end of a sentence, separate it from the rest of the sentence with one comma.

By the way, your pants are ripped.

Your pants are ripped, *by the way.*

Sometimes, an appositive is essential to the meaning of a sentence. When a sentence would not have the same meaning without the appositive, the appositive should not be set off with commas.

The former seamstress *Rosa Parks* became one of the nation's greatest civil rights figures.

[The sentence *The former seamstress became one of the nation's greatest civil rights figures* does not have the same meaning.]

FIND: Read each sentence in your writing carefully.

Terrell ⟨my ex-brother-in-law⟩ likes to talk about himself.

- Underline the subject.
- Circle any appositive (which renames the subject) or interrupter (which interrupts the sentence).
- Ask if the circled words are essential to the meaning of the sentence. (If they aren't, commas should be used.) [In the example, the circled words aren't essential.]

FIX: Add any commas that are needed.

Terrell, my ex-brother-in law, likes to talk about himself.

INCORRECT

The actor, Marlon Brando, was very secretive.

Lila the best singer in my high school class is starring in a play.

He wore a clown suit to work believe it or not.

CORRECT

The actor Marlon Brando was very secretive.

Lila, the best singer in my high school class, is starring in a play.

He wore a clown suit to work, believe it or not.

> **PRACTICE 4** . . . .

Underline any appositives and interrupters in the following sentences. Then, use commas to set them off as needed. One sentence is correct; write a "C" next to it.

EXAMPLE: One of my favorite local shops is Melville's, a used book store.

1. The owner a very nice lady is Francine Smythe.

2. I suppose she named the bookstore after her favorite writer Herman Melville.

3. I have not however found any of Melville's books in her store.

4. Mrs. Smythe in any case is happy to order any book that she doesn't have in stock.

5. Melville's books, always excellent bargains, have given me great pleasure.

6. I once found a rare book on collecting antique glassware my favorite hobby.

7. My favorite part of the shop the basement is dimly lit and particularly quiet.

8. A bare lightbulb the only source of light hangs from a long cord.

9. The dim light is bad for my eyes of course but it gives the basement a cozy feel.

10. Melville's is closing next month sadly because a chain bookstore around the corner has taken away much of its business.

. . . .

Commas around Adjective Clauses

An **adjective clause** is a group of words that

- Often begins with *who*, *which*, or *that*.
- Has a subject and verb.
- Describes the noun right before it in a sentence.

If an adjective clause can be taken out of a sentence without completely changing the meaning, put commas around the clause.

| Noun | , | Adjective clause not essential to meaning | , | Rest of sentence. |

The governor, *who is finishing his first term in office,* will probably not be reelected.

Devane's, *which is the best bakery in the city,* is opening two more stores.

If an adjective clause is essential to the meaning of a sentence, do not put commas around it. You can tell whether a clause is essential by taking it out and seeing if the meaning of the sentence changes significantly.

| Noun | Adjective clause essential to meaning | Rest of sentence. |

Homeowners *who put their trash out too early* will be fined.

The jobs *that open up first* will be the first ones we fill.

■ **TIP:** For more on adjectives, see Chapter 18.

Use *who* to refer to a person; *which* to refer to places or things (but not to people); and *that* to refer to people, places, or things.

FIND: Read each sentence in your writing carefully.

The man <u>who stole Rick's car</u> was arrested.

Catherine <u>who is the fastest runner on our team</u> led the race.

- Underline any adjective clause (a word group that often begins with *who*, *which*, or *that*).
- Read the sentence without this clause.
- Ask if the meaning changes significantly without the clause. [In the first sentence it does, but in the second sentence, it doesn't.]

FIX: Add any commas that are needed.

The man who stole Rick's car was arrested.

[The meaning *does* change without the clause, so commas are not needed.]

Catherine,the fastest runner on our team,led the race.

[The meaning *does not* change without the clause, so commas are needed.]

INCORRECT

I like chess *which I learned to play as a child*.

The house, *that you like*, is up for sale.

Clive *who lives next door* grew a one-hundred-pound pumpkin.

CORRECT

I like chess, *which I learned to play as a child*.

The house *that you like* is up for sale.

Clive, *who lives next door*, grew a one-hundred-pound pumpkin.

PRACTICE 5

In the following sentences, underline the adjective clauses. Then, add commas where they are needed. Remember that if an adjective clause is essential to the meaning of a sentence, you should not use commas. Four sentences are correct; write "C" next to them.

EXAMPLE: A sushi restaurant in Chicago, which I read about in a magazine, offers some unusual dishes.

1. The restaurant's dishes which look like sushi are made of paper.

2. The restaurant's chef who is interested in technology makes images of sushi dishes on an ink-jet printer.

3. He prints the images on paper that people can eat.

4. The edible paper which tastes much like sushi is flavored with food-based inks.

5. Soybeans and cornstarch which are the main ingredients of the paper are also found in many other foods.

6. Customers can even eat the menu which they break up into a bowl of soup.

7. The chef sometimes seasons the menu which changes daily to taste like a main course.

8. He may season the menu to taste like the steak that is being served that day.

9. People who can afford the restaurant's high prices keep the place busy.

10. The chef has lately been testing scientific tools to see if he can make a meal that floats in the air.

Other Uses for Commas

Commas with Quotation Marks

Quotation marks (" ") are used to show that you are repeating exactly what someone said or wrote. Generally, use commas to set off the words inside quotation marks from the rest of the sentence. Notice the position of the commas in the following dialogue.

> "Pardon me," said a stranger who stopped me on the street.
>
> "Can you tell me," he asked, "where Newland Bank is?"
>
> I replied, "Yes, you're standing right in front of it."

■ **TIP:** For more on quotation marks, see Chapter 30.

> **PRACTICE 6**

In each of the following sentences, add or move commas as needed. Two sentences are correct; write "C" next to them.

> **EXAMPLE:** "I can't believe you're going," my friend Alyson said
>
> when I told her I would be leaving my job.

1. "It's not going to be the same here without you" she added.

2. "My new job isn't far away", I responded.

3. Alyson exclaimed "It won't be the same not seeing you every day, though!"

4. "I know," I replied.

5. "I think it would be a good idea" said Alyson, "if we had a going-away party for you."

6. I, said "That's a great idea."

7. Alyson cried, "I have another idea!"

8. "Wouldn't it be great", she asked "if we had a cake shaped like a file folder to represent your favorite job?"

> **∋** Speaking quoted conversations out loud can help you hear where both the commas and quotation marks should go.

9. "Not really," I replied "because I sure am sick of filing."

10. "I'm just joking" Alyson said with a laugh.

Commas in Addresses

Use commas to separate the parts of an address included in a sentence. However, do not use a comma before a zip code.

> My address is 421 Elm Street, Burgettstown, PA 15021.

If a sentence continues after the address, put a comma after the address. Also, when you include a city and a state in the middle of a sentence, use commas before and after the state name. If the state name is at the end of a sentence, put a period after it.

> We moved from Nashville, Tennessee, to Boulder, Colorado.

Commas in Dates

Separate the day from the year with a comma. If you give only the month and year, do not separate them with a comma.

> You must file your taxes no later than April 15, 2007.

> The next Supreme Court session begins in October 2007.

If a sentence continues after a date that includes the day, put a comma after the date.

> My grandmother was born on October 31, 1935, not far from where she lives now.

PRACTICE 7

In each of the following sentences, add, move, or delete commas as needed. Two sentences are correct; write "C" next to them.

> **EXAMPLE:** It was on November 10͵2004͵that we finally moved to San Francisco.

1. Michiko came here from Osaka Japan when she was four years old.

2. Were you living at 849 Livermore Avenue, Memphis, Tennessee 38104, last year?

3. I had my car's brakes fixed in July, 2004 and in January, 2005.

4. I will never forget March 18, 2002 because it was the day we met.

5. The snowstorm hit St. Paul Minnesota on February 3, 2005.

6. Since April 16 2000 the house at 2187 Court Place Tucson Arizona 85701 has had nobody living in it.

7. Leaving your job before June 2 2005, caused you to lose your health benefits.

8. Los Angeles, California, was my home until I moved here in December 2003.

9. I was driving to Houston, Texas on May 4, 2001 to see my parents.

10. They visited Camden Maine in September 1996 and have not been back since then.

Commas with Names

When a sentence "speaks" to someone by name, use a comma (or commas) to separate the name from the rest of the sentence.

Maria, could you please come here?

Luckily, Stan, the tickets have not sold out.

You can sit here, Phuong.

PRACTICE 8

In each of the following sentences, add commas as needed. One sentence is correct; write "C" next to it.

EXAMPLE: Alexandra, I gave the directions to you.

1. However David, you cannot come with the rest of us.

2. We need you to be part of this Eric.

3. Ryan please help me lift this box.

4. With all of my heart, Leanne, I wish you the best of luck.

5. Because I'm moving to Alaska Kevin you can have all of my Hawaiian shirts.

Commas with Yes or No

Put a comma after the word *yes* or *no* in response to a question or comment.

Yes, I understand.

PRACTICE 9 · ·

In each of the following sentences, add commas as needed. One sentence is correct; write "C" next to it.

EXAMPLE: No, we should not be doing this now.

1. Yes these curtains will brighten up the kitchen.

2. No there is nothing useful I can add to your statement.

3. Yes I will vote for your proposal.

4. With regrets no I will not be able to come to your party.

5. No, I don't know the answer.

Edit Commas in College, Work, and Everyday Life

EDITING REVIEW 1: COLLEGE · ·

Add or delete commas as needed in the following paragraph, which is like one you might find in a history-of-science textbook. It is about Marie Curie (1867–1934), the Nobel Prize–winning scientist known for discovering the element radium with her husband, Pierre. One sentence is correct; write "C" next to it. The first sentence has been edited for you.

(1) Marie, who went by the nickname Manya as a child, was finally on her way to her sister's home in Paris. (2) The winter journey which involved traveling for three days in an open carriage was very difficult. (3) She was so filled with joy however that she didn't care. (4) Her luggage was piled around her and she counted it often to make sure it was all there. (5) For five years, she had sent her earnings from her work as a governess to Bronya her sister to put her through medical school. (6) Bronya had graduated, and gotten married. (7) At last it was Man-

ya's turn to continue her education. (8) She shared her sister's apartment temporarily and then moved into a tiny attic room. (9) She ate little slept rarely and studied every minute. (10) "All my mind was centered on my studies" she wrote in her journal.

EDITING REVIEW 2: WORK . . . .

Add or delete commas as needed in the following memo. One sentence is correct; write "C" next to it. The first sentence has been edited for you.

DATE: August 29, 2006

TO: Kendra Landry

FROM: Benjamin Cooper

SUBJECT: Promotion

(1) For the past five years, you have been one of our most valued employees. (2) You have stocked shelves filled orders processed invoices and trained interns effectively. (3) You have been on time every day and you rarely use your sick days. (4) Your supervisor Cameron Lawson praises your performance often. (5) He has told me that you are the best floor manager in the company, and recommended you for a promotion. (6) For your hard work I am happy to promote you from floor manager to division manager. (7) Your new position which begins next week will pay an additional $4 per hour. (8) This raise will be effective on Monday September 5 2006. (9) You will also be granted an extra week of vacation time annually. (10) Congratulations Kendra and thank you again for your excellent service to our company.

EDITING REVIEW 3: EVERYDAY LIFE . . . .

Add or delete commas as needed in the following paragraphs. Two sentences are correct; write "C" next to them. The first sentence has been edited for you.

(1) When you first look up at the skyline of Malmö, Sweden, you might think you're dreaming. (2) You must be imagining the building, that looks like it came from the future. (3) However you pinch yourself

and find that you are wide awake. (4) The strange building which is real is one of the world's most unusual skyscrapers.

(5) On Saturday, August 27 2005, a different kind of apartment building joined Malmö's skyline. (6) Built by Santiago Calatrava a Spanish architect the building is nicknamed the "Turning Torso." (7) Over six hundred feet tall the Torso is made of nine stacked cubes. (8) What makes the building particularly unusual, however is that each of these cubes is slightly turned. (9) There is a full ninety-degree twist between the top, and the bottom of the building. (10) It looks like a giant hand reached down and gave the building a powerful turn. (11) The design is based on one of Calatrava's sculptures. (12) In the sculpture he shaped a human body twisting from head to toe.

(13) Already Calatrava's building has won several awards. (14) "There was a wish to get something exceptional" he told the media. (15) He added "I also wanted to deliver something technically unique." (16) The people, who choose to live in one of these apartments, will certainly have a great view. (17) The monthly rent payments are as high as $3,700 so the views had better be spectacular!

Write and Edit Your Own Work

ASSIGNMENT 1: WRITE

Write about a person who has strongly affected your life. Why has he or she been important? You might quote from a discussion you had with this person. When you're done, read your writing carefully, checking that you have used commas correctly.

ASSIGNMENT 2: EDIT

Using this chapter as a guide, edit for comma usage a paper you are writing for this course or another course or a piece of writing from your work or everyday life.

Practice Together

Working with a few other students, practice what you have learned in this chapter.

1. As a group, add commas to the following sentences. When you are done, have each person stand up and read a sentence aloud, pausing where the commas have been added. As each person reads, the others should double-check to make sure that the commas are in the right places.

    Roberto bought diet cola sunflower seeds raisins snack crackers and potato chips.

    I'd like ham and Swiss and Helen wants roast beef on rye.

    Donna my sister has seven children.

    Her children who are all in school like reading and math.

    No Karis you can't stay out until 11:00 p.m.

2. As a group, pick one of the following sentence pairs and compare the meanings of the first and second sentences in each pair by drawing a picture or diagram of them. How do the commas change the meanings? Present your explanations and drawings to the rest of the class.

    I took a busload of kids to the park; the kids who were interested in playing soccer ran to the field.

    I took a busload of kids to the park; the kids, who were interested in playing soccer, ran to the field.

    The men who had beards were allowed in first.

    The men, who had beards, were allowed in first.

3. Using the example on page 483 as a model, write a brief dialogue (ten lines or so) that includes a discussion between two or more characters. It should include the speakers' quotations and words about who's saying what. **EXAMPLE:** "Did you happen to see my little dog," the lady asked. "No," her neighbor said.

    Everyone should write down the lines as they are invented, discussing where to put commas and quotation marks. Finally, choose group members to perform the dialogue for the rest of the class.

Chapter Review

1. A comma (,) is a punctuation mark that _____ words and word groups to help readers understand a sentence.

2. Use commas

   • To separate three or more items in a _____.

   • To separate two _____ joined by *and, but, for, nor, or, so,* or *yet.*

   • _____ introductory words.

   • Around _____ (which rename a noun) and _____ (which interrupt a sentence).

   • Around _____ (which often begin with *who, which,* or *that;* have a subject and verb; and describe the noun right before them in a sentence).

3. What are two other uses of commas? _____

4. **VOCABULARY:** Go back to any new words that you underlined in this chapter. Can you guess their meanings now? If not, look up the words in a dictionary.

LEARNING JOURNAL: Write for two minutes about the mistake with commas that you make most often. Why do you think you make this mistake?

■ **TIP:** For help with building your vocabulary, see Appendix B.

29

Apostrophes

'

Understand What Apostrophes Do

An **apostrophe (')** is a punctuation mark that

- Shows ownership: *Susan's* shoes, *Alex's* coat

OR

- Shows that a letter (or letters) has been left out of two words that have been joined: *I + am = I'm; that + is = that's; they + are = they're.* The joined words are called *contractions.*

    Although an apostrophe looks like a comma **(,)**, it has a different purpose, and it is written higher on the line than a comma is.

    apostrophe **'**   comma **,**

VOCABULARY: Underline any words in this chapter that are new to you.

IDEA JOURNAL: Write about a time when you were jealous. Did you learn anything from the experience?

Use Apostrophes Correctly

Apostrophes to Show Ownership

- **Add -'s to a singular noun to show ownership even if the noun already ends in -s.**

    The president**'s** speech was shown on every television station.

    The suspect**'s** abandoned car was found in the woods.

    Travis**'s** strangest excuse for missing work was that his pet lobster died.

- **If a noun is plural (meaning *more than one*) and ends in -s, just add an apostrophe to show ownership. If it is plural but does not end in -s, add -'s.**

    Why would someone steal the camper**s'** socks?

    [There is more than one camper.]

TIP: For more on nouns, see Chapter 16.

The salesclerk told me where the girl**s'** shoe department was.

Men**'s** hairstyles are getting shorter.

- **The placement of an apostrophe makes a difference in meaning.**

My brother**'s** ten dogs went to a kennel over the holiday.

[One brother has ten dogs.]

My brother**s'** ten dogs went to a kennel over the holiday.

[Two or more brothers together have ten dogs.]

- **Do not use an apostrophe to form the plural of a noun.**

The fan**'s** were silent as the pitcher wound up for the throw.

Horse**'s** lock their legs so that they can sleep standing up.

- **Do not use an apostrophe with a possessive pronoun. These pronouns already show ownership (possession).**

My motorcycle is faster than your**'s**.

That shopping cart is our**'s**.

Draw a picture or diagram to show the difference in meaning between these two sentences.

TIP: For more on pronouns, see Chapter 17.

Possessive Pronouns

my	his	its	their
mine	her	our	theirs
your	hers	ours	whose
yours			

READ ALOUD

The most common error with apostrophes and pronouns is confusing *its* (a possessive pronoun) with *it's* (a contraction meaning "it is"). Whenever you write *it's*, test to see if it's correct by reading it aloud as *it is*.

PRACTICE 1 . . . .

Rewrite each of the following phrases to show ownership by using an apostrophe.

EXAMPLE: the baseball cards of my brothers *my brothers' baseball cards*

1. the motorcycle of my uncle _____

2. the essays of the students _____

3. the value of the necklace _____

4. the smile of James _____

5. the friendship of my sisters _____

PRACTICE 2

Edit the following sentences by adding -'s or an apostrophe alone to show ownership and by crossing out any incorrect use of an apostrophe or -'s.

> **EXAMPLE:** Our galaxy is the Milky Way, and astronomer's have
>
> made an interesting discovery about one of this galaxys
>
> stars.

1. What happen's when a galaxy loses one of it's star's?

2. Recently, one of the Milky Ways stars was observed flying out of the galaxy.

3. This was astronomers first discovery of a star escaping from a galaxy.

4. The stars high speed, 1.5 million miles per hour, is fast enough for it to escape the Milky Ways' gravity.

5. It is currently about 196,000 light-year's from the galaxys center.

6. The suns distance from the center of the galaxy is about 30,000 light years, which make's us fairly far out, too.

7. The stars official name is a long combination of letters and numbers, but some scientist's call it the Outcast.

8. According to some astronomers', the star almost got sucked into the black hole at the center of the Milky Way.

9. This near miss could have increased the Outcasts speed.

10. The star might not have been our's to begin with; perhaps it is just passing through the Milky Way.

■ **TIP:** For more practice with apostrophes, visit Exercise Central at <**bedfordstmartins.com/ realskills**>.

Apostrophes in Contractions

A **contraction** is formed by joining two words and leaving out one or more of the letters.

> Wilma**'s** always the loudest person in the room.
>
> [*Wilma is* always the loudest person in the room.]

> I**'**ll babysit so that you can go to the mechanic.
>
> [*I will* babysit so that you can go to the mechanic.]

When writing a contraction, put an apostrophe where the letter or letters have been left out, not between the two words.

> He does~~n~~**'**t understand the risks of smoking.

Language note: Contractions including a *be* verb (like *am*, *are*, or *is*) cannot be followed by the base form of a verb or another helping verb (like *can*, *does*, or *has*).

INCORRECT	I'm try to study.	He's can come.
CORRECT	**I'm trying** to study.	**He can** come.

Avoid contractions in formal papers for college. Some instructors believe that contractions are too informal for college writing.

Common Contractions

aren't = are not	she'll = she will
can't = cannot	she's = she is, she has
couldn't = could not	there's = there is
didn't = did not	they'd = they would, they had
don't = do not	they'll = they will
he'd = he would, he had	they're = they are
he'll = he will	they've = they have
he's = he is, he has	who'd = who would, who had
I'd = I would, I had	who'll = who will
I'll = I will	who's = who is, who has
I'm = I am	won't = will not
I've = I have	wouldn't = would not
isn't = is not	you'd = you would, you had
it's = it is, it has	you'll = you will
let's = let us	you're = you are
she'd = she would, she had	you've = you have

PRACTICE 3 . . . .

Write the following words as contractions, putting an apostrophe where the letter or letters have been left out.

   EXAMPLE: you + have = _____*you've*_____

1. there + is = _____

2. would + not = _____

3. it + is = _____

4. can + not = _____

5. you + will = _____

6. she + is = _____

7. I + am = _____

8. they + are = _____

PRACTICE 4 . . . .

Edit the following sentences by adding apostrophes where needed and crossing out misplaced apostrophes.

   EXAMPLE: There's a cute toddler next to me at the bus stop.

1. The little girl is dancing around the sidewalk, and shes certainly enjoying herself.

2. Ive got a lot of admiration for a mother who lets her daughter express herself so freely.

3. When they take a seat next to me on the bus, I think that wer'e going to have a great time together.

4. I quickly discover that Im wrong about that.

5. I ca'nt hear my own thoughts because the girl is singing so loudly.

6. Soon, I feel a sharp pain in my leg and realize that shes kicking me as hard as she can.

7. Then theres a hand reaching across my book, and the girls tearing a page out of it.

8. I expect her mother to stop this behavior, but she does'nt; in fact, she completely ignores it.

9. Im' a mother myself, so I hope you wont think that I dislike all children.

10. What I do dislike are parents who think its okay to let their children run wild.

Apostrophes with Letters, Numbers, and Time

- **Use -'s to make letters and numbers plural.**

  Should I type the www's to get to these Internet sites?

  The store was out of size 8's in that style.

- **Use an apostrophe or -'s when time nouns are treated as if they own something.**

  We took two weeks' vacation last year.

  This year's car models use less gas than last year's.

> **PRACTICE 5**

Edit the following sentences by adding apostrophes where needed and crossing out misplaced apostrophes.

EXAMPLE: The past few month's basketball schedule has been tough, and I could use several days' of vacation.

1. The last two weeks games had interesting scores.

2. All the scores had 3s' in them.

3. We win regularly because Renee, who spells her name with two es, is so good.

4. Luckily, Renee is going to be on next years team as well.

5. With a few months practice, we'll get even better.

Edit Apostrophes in College, Work, and Everyday Life

EDITING REVIEW 1: COLLEGE

Edit the following paragraph from a course syllabus, adding or deleting apostrophes as needed. One sentence is correct; write "C" next to it. The first sentence has been edited for you.

(1) During this course, you'll be given four tests and eight quizzes. (2) The point's from those exams will make up one-half of your overall grade. (3) You are allowed to take two makeup exams during the courses duration. (4) Please do'nt ask for more than that; there are no exceptions. (5) The other half of your grade will consist of point's for attendance, participation, homework, and two research papers. (6) All students papers and weekly homework must be turned in on time for full credit. (7) If you turn in others work as your's, you will have to leave the class. (8) Perfect attendance will earn 20 points, while 1 point will be taken off for each days absence. (9) Tutors will be available for help outside of class. (10) The research paper will be discussed four weeks before it's due date. (11) Even if you don't get all As, I hope this class will be a rewarding experience.

EDITING REVIEW 2: WORK

Edit the following paragraph from an employee handbook, adding or deleting apostrophes as needed. Two sentences are correct; write "C" next to them. The first sentence has been edited for you.

(1) This addition to the employee handbook further describes the company's dress code. (2) Its this businesss goal to have all employees look professional while on the job. (3) Most of you already dress appropriately, but weve been questioned about certain kinds of clothing by a number of people. (4) In order to address those employee's questions, we created these specific guidelines. (5) Please note that jeans, sweatpants, shorts, and overalls are'nt allowed. (6) Tank tops, T-shirt's with large and/or offensive logos, and Hawaiian shirts are also prohibited. (7) Womens skirts and dresses must be at knee length or below. (8) Most

shoes are acceptable, with the exception of flip-flops, sneakers, and slippers. (9) Of course, these rules do not apply to each summers company picnic. (10) We may revise this policy at next years annual procedures meeting. (11) Please contact Human Resources if you have any questions.

EDITING REVIEW 3: EVERYDAY LIFE

Edit the following brief article, adding or deleting apostrophes as needed. Outside of the first sentence, which has been marked for you, four sentences are correct; write "C" next to them.

(1) *C* When it comes to insects, small is indeed mighty. (2) Despite their tiny size, insects manage to build some of natures most fascinating and complex homes. (3) Using materials from their own bodies or from their surrounding environment, they build their homes anywhere from high up in trees to deep underground.

(4) For example, termites tall, complicated towers are the insect worlds equivalent to todays modern skyscrapers. (5) Considering the size of the construction workers, these towers are amazingly tall. (6) Some reach heights of fifteen feet or more, have twenty-inch-thick wall's, and are as hard as concrete. (7) Some termite homes have been around for more than fifty year's and contain millions of occupants.

(8) Inside these unique and complex towers are four main sections. (9) Fungus gardens and food storage rooms are on the upper levels, and living areas are closer to the ground. (10) The towers shapes vary, depending on the specific environment where they are built. (11) Towers in rain forest's, for example, are shaped like umbrellas to direct water away from the nest. (12) In the desert, the towers have long, thin tops and chimneys that cool down the nest for it's inhabitants.

(13) A towers internal chambers and tunnels are very complicated. (14) Amazingly, termite's are able to make their way from one place to another in complete darkness. (15) They like to stay at home, leaving their' amazing towers only to eat and mate. (16) Why, then, are several termites crawling in figure 8s on my floor?

Write and Edit Your Own Work

ASSIGNMENT 1: WRITE . . . .

Write about a party or other event that you attended recently, describing what people wore, said, or did. Make sure to use contractions in your descriptions (for example, *my friend's shoes, it's fun*). When you're done, read your writing carefully, checking that you have used apostrophes correctly.

ASSIGNMENT 2: EDIT . . . .

Using this chapter as a guide, edit for apostrophe usage a paper you are writing for this course or another course or a piece of writing from your work or everyday life.

. . . .

Practice Together

Working with a few other students, practice what you have learned in this chapter.

1. As a group, find and circle all the words with apostrophes in the following sentences and see if you can expand them into two words. If you cannot expand a word, leave it as it is. Each group member should write the contractions for the words that can be expanded on another sheet of paper, followed by the two words that formed them. Discuss how the expandable words with apostrophes are different from the words that cannot be expanded.

   They'll find an excuse not to go to the party, won't they?

   Don't you want to help with Mary's homework? She's a sweet girl.

   Henry's dream's a strange one.

   Go over to Ellen's mother's house, and she'll give you Ellen's notes.

   I'd like Newman's Own dressing on my salad.

2. Pick one of the following words and write it on a sheet of paper to be passed around the group. The first person should call out the word's plural form, the second person should call out the plural possessive form, and the third person should say the singular possessive form. Each person should call out the position of any -'s so that group members can make corrections if necessary. Then, pick a new word. Keep going until

LEARNING STYLES: Look for activities in this chapter that are matched to your learning style. If you don't know your learning style, take the test on pages 26–28.

Visual

Auditory

Reading/writing

Kinesthetic (movement)

each person has done at least two words. **EXAMPLE:** *Cat.* Plural: *Cats.* Plural possessive: *Cats'* (*s apostrophe*); Singular possessive: *Cat's* (*apostrophe s*). 📖 📖 ✎

boss, child, city, daughter, friend, man, parent, pet, school, shoe, tree, woman

3. Many business names end with -*'s*. Nick's, for example, could be short for Nick's Bar. Look through the yellow pages or the local newspaper and find examples of businesses that use the apostrophe correctly and examples of those that don't. Then, in a group in class, share your examples and discuss how to fix the incorrect ones. 👁 📖 📖

Chapter Review

1. An apostrophe (') is a punctuation mark that shows _____ or shows that a letter (or letters) have been left out of words that have been _____.

2. To show ownership, add _____ to a singular noun, even if the noun already ends in -*s*. For a plural noun, add an _____ alone if the noun ends in -*s*; add _____ if the noun does not end in -*s*.

3. Do not use an apostrophe with a _____ pronoun.

4. Do not confuse *its* and *it's*. *Its* shows _____; *it's* is a _____ meaning "it is."

5. A _____ is formed by joining two words and leaving out one or more of the letters. Use an apostrophe to show where _____ _____.

6. Use -*'s* to make letters and numbers _____.

7. Use an apostrophe or -*'s* when _____ are treated as if they own something.

8. **VOCABULARY:** Go back to any new words that you underlined in this chapter. Can you guess their meanings now? If not, look up the words in a dictionary.

📖 **LEARNING JOURNAL:** Write for two minutes about the mistake with apostrophes that you make most often. How can you avoid this mistake in the future?

■ **TIP:** For help with building your vocabulary, see Appendix B.

30

Quotation Marks

66 99

Understand What Quotation Marks Do

Quotation marks (" ") are used around **direct quotations**: someone's speech or writing repeated exactly, word for word.

DIRECT QUOTATION   Ellis said, "I'll finish the work by Tuesday."

Quotation marks are not used around **indirect quotations**: restatements of what someone said or wrote, not word for word.

INDIRECT QUOTATION   Ellis said that he would finish the work by Tuesday.

VOCABULARY: Underline any words in this chapter that are new to you.

IDEA JOURNAL: Think about a speaker, singer, or other performer who impressed you. What did he or she say or do that was special?

Use Quotation Marks Correctly

Quotation Marks for Direct Quotations

When you write a direct quotation, use quotation marks around the quoted words. These marks tell readers that the words used are exactly what was said or written.

1. "Did you hear about Carmela's date?" Rob asked me.

2. "No," I replied. "What happened?"

3. "According to Carmela," Rob said, "the guy showed up at her house in a black mask and cape."

4. I said, "You're joking, right?"

5. "No," Rob answered. "Apparently, the date thought his costume was romantic and mysterious."

Quoted words are usually combined with words that identify who is speaking, such as *Rob asked me* in the first example. The identifying words can come after the quoted words (example 1), before them (example 4), or in the middle (example 3). Here are some guidelines for capitalization and punctuation:

- Capitalize the first letter in a complete sentence that's being quoted, even if it comes after some identifying words (example 4).
- Do not capitalize the first letter in a quotation if it's not the first word in a complete sentence (*the* in example 3).
- If it is a complete sentence and its source is clear, you can let a quotation stand on its own, without any identifying words (example 5, second sentence).
- Attach identifying words to a quotation; these identifying words cannot be a sentence on their own.
- Use commas to separate any identifying words from quoted words in the same sentence.
- Always put quotation marks after commas and periods. Put quotation marks after question marks and exclamation points if they are part of the quoted sentence.

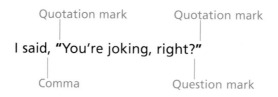

If a question mark or exclamation point is part of your own sentence, put it after the quotation mark.

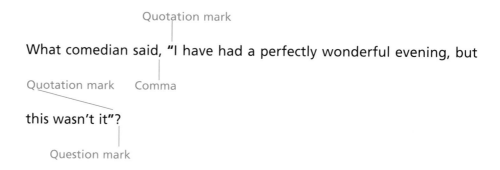

TIP: For more on commas with quotation marks, see page 483. For more on capitalization, see Chapter 32.

Read sentences with quotation marks aloud, making "air quotes" with your fingers at the beginning and end of quotations. This will help you understand and remember how quotation marks are used.

Setting Off a Quotation within Another Quotation

Sometimes, you may directly quote someone who quotes what someone else said or wrote. Put **single quotation marks (' ')** around the quotation within a quotation so that readers understand who said what.

The owner's manual said, "When the check-engine light comes on, see a mechanic immediately."

Quotation within a quotation

The owner told her mechanic, "The owner's manual said that I should 'see a mechanic immediately' when the check-engine light comes on, and the light is now on constantly."

No Quotation Marks for Indirect Quotations

When you report what someone said or wrote but do not use the person's exact words, you are writing an indirect quotation. Do not use quotation marks for indirect quotations. Indirect quotations often begin with the word *that*.

READ ALOUD

Read the following examples aloud, speaking the direct quotations as if you are speaking a character's part in a play. Can you hear the difference between the indirect and direct quotations?

INDIRECT QUOTATION

The man asked me how to get to the store.

Martino told me that he loves me.

Carla said that she won the lottery.

DIRECT QUOTATION

The man asked me, "How do I get to the store?"

"I love you," Martino whispered in my ear.

"I won the lottery!" Carla said.

PRACTICE 1 . . . .

For each of the following sentences, circle "I" if it is an indirect quotation or "D" if it is a direct quotation. In the blanks, write direct quotations as indirect, and indirect quotations as direct.

EXAMPLE: I / Ⓓ "I would rather send an e-mail than use the phone," said Johan.

Rewrite: *Johan said that he would rather send an e-mail than*

use the phone.

1. I / D Dana noted that phoning is more personal than e-mailing.

   Rewrite: _____

2. I / D Johan said, "I agree, but e-mail allows me to keep records of my conversations."

   Rewrite: _____

   _____

3. I / D Dana answered, "I don't see the point in keeping a record of asking someone to dinner."

   Rewrite: _____

   _____

4. I / D Johan responded that their date last week was a perfect example.

   Rewrite: _____

5. I / D Dana said, "I don't see your point."

   Rewrite: _____

6. I / D Johan asked, "Do you remember how late I was for dinner?"

   Rewrite: _____

7. I / D Dana said that she certainly remembered.

   Rewrite: _____

8. I / D Johan answered, "If we had arranged dinner by e-mail, I would have had the exact time in writing and wouldn't have been late."

   Rewrite: _____

   _____

PRACTICE 2 . . . .

Edit the following sentences by adding quotation marks and commas where needed.

> **EXAMPLE:** "Mr. Rivera will now answer questions from the audi-
> ence," said Dr. Sandler.

1. Robert exclaimed I cannot believe that you quit a fantastic job as president of a huge advertising agency.

2. That was not a question said Mr. Rivera but I will respond to it anyway.

3. Mr. Rivera continued I loved my job, but it left me with hardly any time to see my family."

4. So you gave up a great job just to be with your family? asked Mary Alice.

5. I consider myself very lucky Mr. Rivera responded.

6. My wife wanted to keep her job he said, and she's able to support our family.

7. Mr. Rivera admitted I never pictured myself in this position, but now that I am, I can't imagine otherwise.

8. About a year ago said Gerry you were quoted in a newspaper as saying There's nothing in the world like having a satisfying job.

9. Mr. Rivera laughed and then said I was exactly right, Gerry, and the most satisfying job I've ever had is the one I have now, being a stay-at-home dad.

10. Genine said With your permission, I'd like to quote you in our student newspaper as saying If your life changes, you sometimes are happiest if you change along with it.

PRACTICE 3 . . . .

Edit the following sentences by adding quotation marks where needed and crossing out quotation marks that are incorrectly used. One sentence is correct; write "C" next to it.

EXAMPLE: "Would you mind if I changed the channel?" asked
Katherine.

Draw a short cartoon that includes the characters' thoughts and words. Put their words in quotation marks.

1. You used the TV all last night, Evi complained.

2. Katherine said that "she was sorry, but that last night's game was important, too."

3. The show I'm watching, said Evi, is just as important to me.

4. Katherine explained that she used to have an agreement with her family.

5. Each week, she said, we signed up for time slots during which we had control of the television.

6. She said that "they worked out a compromise if two people wanted the same slot."

■ **TIP:** For more practice with quotation marks, visit Exercise Central at <**bedfordstmartins.com/ realskills**>.

7. What did you do if you couldn't reach an agreement? Evi asked.

8. We just kept discussing it, replied Katherine, and we always managed to work it out.

9. Evi thought it over and finally said that "the two of them could probably compromise after all."

10. You can watch tonight's game, but I get full control of the TV for the next two days, said Evi.

Quotation Marks for Certain Titles

When referring to a short work such as a magazine or newspaper article, a chapter in a book, a short story, an essay, a song, or a poem, put quotation marks around the title of the work.

NEWSPAPER ARTICLE	"City Disaster Plan Revised"
SHORT STORY	"The Swimmer"
ESSAY	"A Brother's Murder"

Usually, titles of longer works—such as novels, books, magazines, newspapers, movies, television programs, and CDs—are underlined or italicized. The titles of sacred books such as the Bible or the Koran are neither underlined, italicized, nor surrounded by quotation marks.

BOOK	The House on Mango Street or *The House on Mango Street*
NEWSPAPER	Washington Post or *Washington Post*
	[Do not underline, italicize, or capitalize the word *the* before the name of a newspaper or magazine, even if it is part of the title: I saw that in the *New York Times*. However, do capitalize and italicize *The* when it is the first word in titles of books, movies, and other sources.]

NOTE: When you write a paper for class, do not put quotation marks around the title.

> **PRACTICE 4** . .

Edit the following sentences by adding quotation marks around titles as needed. Underline any book, magazine, newspaper, or movie titles.

EXAMPLE: My doctor is also a writer, and his latest short story is titled "The Near-Dead."

1. He told me that his idea for that title came from James Joyce's short story The Dead, which was part of Joyce's book Dubliners.

2. I told my doctor that I love Joyce's works and once wrote an essay called The Dead Live On.

3. One of my band's most popular songs is The Day of the Living Dead, which we wrote to honor our favorite old movie, The Night of the Living Dead.

4. We also have a song called You Never Die, based on a poem I wrote titled Forever.

5. My doctor told me that our songs inspired him to write a story that he will call The Death of Death, which he plans to submit to the Atlantic Monthly magazine.

Edit Quotation Marks in College, Work, and Everyday Life

EDITING REVIEW 1: COLLEGE

Add or delete quotation marks as needed in the following paragraph, which is similar to one you might find in a history textbook. Commas may also need to be added. Outside of the first sentence, which has been marked for you, one other sentence is correct; write "C" next to it.

(1) You may know Orville and Wilbur Wright for their famous accomplishment: inventing and flying the world's first airplane. (2) Did you know, however, that they "began their careers as bicycle repairmen?" (3) As the newly invented bicycle began to sweep the nation, the brothers opened a repair shop because "they wanted to make sure people kept their new mode of transportation in good shape." (4) However, they later admitted that "working with bicycles kept them satisfied for only a short time." (5) As Wilbur wrote in a letter to a friend, The boys of the Wright family are all lacking in determination and push. (6) In search of a new hobby, Wilbur wrote a letter to the Smithsonian Institution and said that "he needed some information." (7) I have some pet theories as

to the proper construction of a flying machine, he wrote. (8) I wish to avail myself of all that is already known and then, if possible, add my mite to help the future worker who will attain final success. (9) He reassured the experts at the Smithsonian that "he and his brother were serious," not just simply curious. (10) "I am an enthusiast, but not a crank,", he added. (11) Even so, the brothers likely had no idea that they were close to achieving fame in aviation.

EDITING REVIEW 2: WORK

Edit the following work e-mail, adding or deleting quotation marks as needed. Commas may also need to be added. Three sentences are correct; write "C" next to them. The first sentence has been edited for you.

Mr. Cooperman:

(1) This afternoon, I spoke with Eileen Bosco about writing next month's feature article, tentatively titled "Where's the Beef? Corpus Christi's Best Steakhouses." (2) As a reminder of Elaine's excellent work, I am attaching a copy of her article on Texas diners, 830 Miles of Chicken Fried Steak. (3) She said that "she would be glad to take on another project." (4) In fact, she said My schedule just opened up, so the timing is perfect. (5) I gave her the details and asked her if she could finish the article within two weeks. (6) She said that "the deadline wouldn't be a problem for her."

(7) Elaine recently finished several articles for "Texas Monthly" magazine, and I am concerned that they might hire her full-time. (8) If possible, I'd like to keep her working for us. (9) Jenna Melton, who worked with Elaine on the diner article, told me, Elaine is a talented food writer, and we should hire her as a staff writer if a position opens up. (10) In the meantime, I told Elaine that we will consider giving her more regular assignments.

Best,

Tina Lopez

Edit the following essay, adding or deleting quotation marks as needed. You may also need to add commas. Outside of the first sentence, which has been marked for you, eight sentences are correct; write "C" next to them.

C
(1) Most people know that too much repeated sun exposure is harmful to their health. (2) Doctors continually warn us that "too much sun significantly increases the risk of skin cancer and other harmful conditions." (3) Nevertheless, people continue to bake in the sun for hours every spring and summer. (4) A group of dermatologists recently decided to investigate this behavior. (5) "We treat a lot of patients who have tans and get skin cancer" said Richard Wagner, a physician at the University of Texas Medical Branch. (6) We tell them to cut back, but they just can't seem to stop. (7) The researchers wanted to know if sunbathing had an addictive property to it, similar to drugs, cigarettes, or alcohol. (8) To find out, they surveyed 145 tanners on a Texas beach. (9) Their results, published in the journal "Archives of Dermatology," were far from conclusive but certainly fascinating.

(10) The researchers said that "more than one quarter of people they surveyed appeared to suffer from some kind of tanning addiction." (11) Some of the physicians think that the problem stems from the belief that a tan makes people look healthier, even though regular tanning rapidly ages the skin. (12) Others wonder if the problem is more complicated than that. (13) Earlier research has shown that people who are exposed to the ultraviolet light found in the sun produce more endorphins, natural brain chemicals that make a person feel content. (14) The endorphin buzz, Wagner said is what sunbathers are hoping to achieve.

(15) Regardless of why people continue to tan, tanning continues to be a serious health risk, for it increases the risk of skin cancer. (16) Wagner said that "tanning support groups would be beneficial, and he suggested modeling these after Alcoholics Anonymous."

Write and Edit Your Own Work

ASSIGNMENT 1: WRITE

Following the example on page 501, write a discussion between two people, adding quotation marks around their exact words. Pick an interesting situation, such as a first date, an argument, or an exchange of gossip. Make sure it is clear who is saying what. When you're done, read your writing carefully, checking that you have used quotation marks and other punctuation correctly.

ASSIGNMENT 2: EDIT

Using this chapter as a guide, edit quotation marks in a paper you are writing for this course or another course or in a piece of writing from your work or everyday life.

Practice Together

LEARNING STYLES: Look for activities in this chapter that are matched to your learning style. If you don't know your learning style, take the test on pages 26–28.

👁 Visual

🎧 Auditory

📖 Reading/writing

✋ Kinesthetic (movement)

Working with a few other students, practice what you have learned in this chapter.

1. Turn indirect quotations into direct quotations. One student should stand up and make a statement (for example, *I am hungry*) that the next student should turn into an indirect quotation (*She said that she is hungry*). The third student should change the indirect quotation into a direct quotation (*She said, "I am hungry."*). Meanwhile, someone should write the sentences on a flip chart or sheet of paper as they are spoken. When a set is complete, the group should look at the sentences to make sure that they are written and punctuated correctly. Then, start another round. Keep making up new statements until each person in the group has had at least two turns.

2. Divide a group of four into two-person teams. Each team should invent an interesting character and draw it on a sheet of paper (some ideas: a cowboy from outer space, a genius poodle, a monster who eats shoes). When both teams are done, say, "Go!" and then put your drawings down on the table. Together, imagine a conversation between the two characters, writing down some of the funniest lines. Share those lines with the class.

3. With a partner, write a play of five to ten lines using this style:

   Player 1: "Where are we going on vacation?"

   Player 2: "We are going to my favorite place: Adventure Time Fun Park." [and so on]

Then, exchange papers with another group and rewrite each other's plays as narrative dialogue (as on page 501), with quotation marks around direct quotations, as well as information about who is saying what. Each group should stand up and read what they've rewritten in front of the class, with each partner reading one person's lines. ⑩ 📖 👟

4. Form pairs. Within the pairs, students should interview each other on a controversial issue, such as the military draft, requiring individuals to purchase health insurance, or same-sex marriage. The interviewer should write up the interview using direct and indirect quotations. ⑩ 📖

Chapter Review

1. Quotation marks are used around _____: someone's speech or writing repeated exactly, word for word.

2. An _____ is a restatement of what someone said or wrote, not word for word.

3. Put _____ around a quotation within a quotation.

4. Put quotation marks around the titles of short works such as (give four examples) _____.

5. For longer works such as magazines, books, newspapers, and so on, either _____ or _____ the titles.

6. **VOCABULARY:** Go back to any new words that you underlined in this chapter. Can you guess their meanings now? If not, look up the words in a dictionary.

📖 **LEARNING JOURNAL:** In your own words, explain the difference between direct quotations and indirect quotations.

■ **TIP:** For help with building your vocabulary, see Appendix B.

31

Other Punctuation

Understand What Punctuation Does

VOCABULARY: Underline any words in this chapter that are new to you.

IDEA JOURNAL: What does success mean to you? (You can write about success in college, at work, or in your personal life.)

Punctuation helps readers understand your writing. If you use punctuation incorrectly, you send readers a confusing message—or, even worse, a wrong one. This chapter covers five punctuation marks that people sometimes use incorrectly.

Use Punctuation Correctly

Semicolon ;

Semicolons to Join Two Closely Related Sentences

Use a semicolon to join two very closely related sentences and make them into one sentence.

■ **TIP:** To do this chapter, you need to know what a complete sentence is. For a review, see Chapter 10.

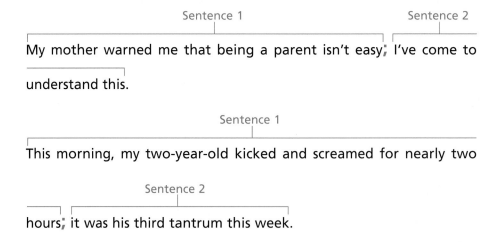

Sentence 1 | Sentence 2

My mother warned me that being a parent isn't easy; I've come to

understand this.

Sentence 1

This morning, my two-year-old kicked and screamed for nearly two

Sentence 2

hours; it was his third tantrum this week.

Semicolons When Items in a List Contain Commas

Use semicolons to separate items in a list that themselves contain commas. Otherwise, it is difficult for readers to tell where one item ends and another begins.

We drove through Pittsburgh, Pennsylvania; Columbus, Ohio; and Indianapolis, Indiana.

PRACTICE 1

Edit the following sentences by adding semicolons where needed and deleting or revising any punctuation that is incorrectly used.

> **EXAMPLE:** Manny had plenty to do Saturday afternoon;his big party
> was going to be that night.

1. He had visitors coming from as far away as Portland, Oregon, Butte, Montana, and Glasgow, Scotland.

2. Luckily, Manny's friend Emily arrived early to help clean and set up for the party.

3. The two of them vacuumed, dusted, put out bowls for popcorn, chips, and nuts, and cleared out the refrigerator for drinks.

4. Emily suggested that they play games, she shared several of her ideas with Manny.

5. In the end, they decided to play three games: find the orange, guess the number of pennies in a jar, and guess Manny's weight.

> **TIP:** For more practice with the punctuation covered in this chapter, visit Exercise Central at **<bedfordstmartins.com/ realskills>**.

> **TIP:** For more on using semicolons to join sentences see Chapter 22.

Colon   :

Colons before Lists

Use a colon to introduce a list after a complete sentence.

Complete sentence

The ten most popular baby names include some old-fashioned ones:

List

Emma, William, Hannah, and Jacob.

Complete sentence   List

It is impossible to escape three unpleasant facts of life: death, taxes,

and strangers' cell-phone conversations.

READ ALOUD

In this chapter, read the examples for semicolons, colons, parentheses, and dashes aloud, pausing when you see the punctuation marks. Can you hear how the punctuation marks make the sentences easier to read and understand?

Colons before Explanations or Examples

Use a colon after a complete sentence that introduces an explanation or example. If the explanation or example is also a complete sentence, capitalize the first letter after the colon.

👁 ✍ Labeling the parts of a sentence (as done here) can help you decide where punctuation should go.

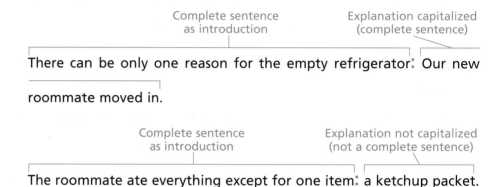

There can be only one reason for the empty refrigerator: Our new roommate moved in.

The roommate ate everything except for one item: a ketchup packet.

NOTE: A colon must follow a complete sentence. A common error is to place a colon after a phrase that includes *such as* or *for example*.

> **INCORRECT**
>
> Shara likes winter sports, such as: skiing, ice hockey, and snowshoeing.
>
> Hector has annoying habits, for example: talking loudly, singing with the radio, and interrupting others.
>
> **CORRECT**
>
> Shara likes winter sports: skiing, ice hockey, and snowshoeing.
>
> OR
>
> Shara likes winter sports, such as skiing, ice hockey, and snowshoeing.
>
> Hector has annoying habits: talking loudly, singing with the radio, and interrupting others.

Colons in Business Correspondence and before Subtitles

Use a colon after a greeting in a business letter and after the headings at the beginning of a memorandum. (Memos are used to share information within many businesses.)

Dear Ms. Ramirez:

To: All employees

From: Mira Cole

Colons are also used between the main title and subtitle of publications.

The book that Doug read is called *Technicolor: Race, Technology, and Everyday Life.*

PRACTICE 2 . . . .

Edit the following sentences by adding colons where needed and deleting or revising any punctuation that is incorrectly used.

> **EXAMPLE:** My three-year-old daughter, Courtney, has one problem;
> that makes traveling with her difficult; she is allergic to
> peanuts.

1. Because of her allergy, my wife and I always bring three things when we go on vacation with Courtney, medication, Courtney's medical information, and our doctor's emergency number.

2. We have to ask several questions about food: such as whether restaurant meals contain peanuts or whether a host's sandwiches contain peanut butter.

3. On our last vacation, a waitress made a serious mistake she was not aware that the restaurant used peanut oil in a dish that we ordered.

4. When Courtney started showing signs of an allergic reaction, there was only one thing to do, administer emergency medication to her.

5. Luckily, Courtney responded immediately, and her next words made us all laugh "Peanuts are not a friend."

. . . .

Using a bright color, highlight the punctuation in a newspaper or magazine article. Then, look back at how the punctuation is used.

Parentheses   ( )

Use parentheses to set off information that is not essential to the meaning of a sentence. Do not overuse parentheses. When you do use them, they should be in pairs.

My favorite dessert (and also the most difficult one to make) is cherry strudel.

The twins have stopped arguing (at least for now) about who should get the car on Saturday.

> **PRACTICE 3** . . . .

Edit the following sentences by adding parentheses where needed and deleting any that are incorrectly used.

EXAMPLE: In this age of casual dress (at least for most people , there are still times when (I feel most comfortable) wearing a suit.

1. Last year, I needed a new suit, but the suits I liked at stores were just too expensive some outrageously expensive.

2. I had heard about an excellent tailor who made custom suits that were fairly affordable about $300, on average.

3. This tailor, Mr. Shephard, measured me and had me try on several suits at least six to see what would work the best (given my height and body type.)

4. Together, we chose a gray suit with thin stripes called "chalk stripes" that looked really good on me.

5. Mr. Shephard was able to adjust (the suit) quickly in about a week, and it looks great on me.

. . . .

Dash   --

Use dashes as you use parentheses: to set off additional information, particularly information that you want to emphasize.

> The test -- worth 30 percent of your final grade -- will have forty questions.

> Over the holiday, the police officers gave huge tickets -- some as much as $300 -- to speeders.

A dash can also indicate a pause, much as a comma does but somewhat more forcefully.

> I want to go on vacation -- alone.

Make a dash by typing two hyphens together. Do not leave any extra spaces around a dash.

PRACTICE 4 . . . .

Edit the following sentences by adding dashes where needed and deleting any that are incorrectly used.

> **EXAMPLE:** People who live in cool, dry climates get more exercise than others -- at least that's what one study found.

1. This study matched the percentage of people in an area -- who meet the exercise recommendations of the Centers for Disease Control and Prevention -- with weather reports from all over the United States.

2. The recommendations are thirty minutes of moderate physical activity five to seven days a week or twenty minutes of energetic physical activity three to seven days a week; the exercise can be done anywhere indoors or outdoors.

3. Several states with cool climates Montana, Utah, Wisconsin, New Hampshire, and Vermont had the highest percentages -- of people who met the exercise requirements.

4. The areas with the lowest percentages -- of people meeting the exercise requirements Hawaii, North Carolina, Mississippi, and Puerto Rico all have hot and humid weather.

5. These unsurprising results few people like to exercise in hot, humid weather make me wonder why anyone even bothered to do this study.

. . . .

Hyphen   -

Hyphens to Join Words That Form a Single Description

Use a hyphen to join words that together form a single description of a person, place, or thing.

> The fourteen-year-old actor went to school while making the movie.
>
> The senator flew to Africa on a fact-finding mission.
>
> When will the company file its year-end report?

Hyphens to Divide a Word at the End of a Line

Use a hyphen to divide a word when part of the word must continue on the next line. Most word-processing programs do this automatically, but if you are writing by hand, you need to insert hyphens yourself.

> At the recycling station, you will be asked to sepa-
> rate newspapers from aluminum cans and glass.

If you are not sure where to break a word, look it up in a dictionary. The word's main entry will show you where you can break the word: *dic-tio-nary*. If you still aren't sure that you are putting the hyphen in the right place, don't break the word; write it all on the next line.

PRACTICE 5 . .

Edit the following sentences by adding hyphens where needed and deleting any that are incorrectly used.

> **EXAMPLE:** Nine-year-old Becky sometimes acts like she's two.

1. She is certainly a high achieving athlete, though.

2. She may be only nine, but she plays basketball like a twenty two year old professional.

3. Although Becky has a go-getter attitude, she is immature and a poor-loser.

4. That hasn't kept her from getting attention from high powered talent scouts.

5. Her league leading statistics are proving that she has tremendous-promise.

Edit Other Punctuation in College, Work, and Everyday Life

EDITING REVIEW 1: COLLEGE . .

The following paragraph is similar to one you might find in a psychology textbook. Edit it by adding or deleting punctuation as needed. One sentence is correct; write "C" next to it. The first sentence has been edited for you.

(1) What caused Hermann Rorschach to look at ink spilled on paper and see it as a way to test people's mental health is a mystery; there is little doubt, however, that his invention is useful. (2) Created almost a century ago; these inkblots are still being used by psychiatrists today. (3) When patients look at the inkblots, they see different patterns often, things that are quite unusual. (4) One psychiatrist wrote about a varied list of things seen by just one patient, animals, buildings, people, insects, and food. (5) Psychiatrists are trained to pay attention not only to the things patients see but also to how the patients describe what they see. (6) Both are quite telling about what is going on in the patient's mind at least that's what many experts believe. (7) Psychiatrists use the inkblots to help diagnose mental illnesses: such as schizophrenia, obsessive-compulsive disorder, and multiple-personality disorder. (8) The low tech inkblots can also reveal concerns, fears, and other personality traits. (9) Sadly, the man who came up with this unique testing method did not live long enough (to see it become widely used). (10) In 1922, he died at a relatively young age thirty-seven, shortly after he published findings about his inkblots. (11) We have him to thank for a very important improvement in psychiatry, a better understanding of people's mental states.

EDITING REVIEW 2: WORK

Edit the following memo by adding or deleting punctuation as needed. One sentence is correct; write "C" next to it. The first sentence has been edited for you.

To: All employees

From: Todd Grayson, Personnel Department

Re: Office picnic

(1) This is a reminder about this Friday's company picnic (our first) at Shelton Community Park. (2) Please plan to arrive at the park by 10:30 Friday morning, latecomers may not get the best parking. (3) We need each person to bring some food to share, snacks, desserts, side dishes,

casseroles, and salads. (4) Drinks will be brought by Jim Terrino, activity coordinator, Sally Bursal, head of administration, and Rita Perez, director of personnel. (5) Our tables will be set up by the east gate, and my nineteen year old son, Rob, will be directing you to the correct parking area. (6) Please remember to bring folding chairs, tables will be provided by the park. (7) Anyone who can't attend and I hope there won't be anyone on this list should let me know by the end of the day tomorrow. (8) I'm looking forward to this event.

EDITING REVIEW 3: EVERYDAY LIFE

Edit the following essay by adding or deleting punctuation as needed. Two sentences are correct; write "C" next to them. The first sentence has been edited for you.

(1) Many people would complain if they had to spend an entire day at the mall; if it was the Mall of America, however, the story would be different. (2) Located in the Twin Cities area of Bloomington, Minnesota, this mall has something for everyone. (3) There are places for people of all ages to spend time: more than five hundred stores, fifty restaurants, fourteen movie theaters with multiple screens, several concession areas, and great sound, eight nightclubs, a casino, a concert hall, and a bowling alley.

(4) The Mall of America is also home to Camp Snoopy the nation's largest indoor theme park, featuring thirty rides. (5) A four story Lego Imagination Center shows what can be made with thousands of plastic bricks. (6) If your kids like ocean creatures, there's something they have to see the Underwater Adventures Aquarium, where children can touch real sharks and stingrays.

(7) If this does not sound like enough fun; keep exploring. (8) Flight simulators give you a chance to feel what it would be like to fly. (9) The NASCAR Motor Speedway offers fast paced excitement for racing fans.

(10) The mall's latest addition is for visitors who are tired of walking the mall all 4.3 miles of it or who just need some rest. (11) In a new

store called MinneNAPolis, shoppers are offered a unique service the chance to take a nap. (12) The fee for this service is 70 cents per minute $42 per hour.

(13) My mother a very tough woman to please loves the Mall of America, and that says a lot. (14) Where else can you: shop, eat, see a movie, ride a Ferris wheel, pet a shark, and take a nap all in the same building?

Write and Edit Your Own Work

ASSIGNMENT 1: WRITE

Imagine that you are selling something—for example, your car or another possession, or a real or imaginary product. Write an advertisement for the item, including details about the item's features and benefits. If you can, invent a headline for the ad to get potential buyers' attention. When you're done, read your writing carefully, checking especially for punctuation errors.

ASSIGNMENT 2: EDIT

Using this chapter as a guide, edit punctuation errors in a paper you are writing for this course or another course or in a piece of writing from your work or everyday life.

Practice Together

Working with a few other students, practice what you have learned in this chapter.

1. Pick two or three of the punctuation marks covered in this chapter and, as a group, write a song or poem about each one. The song or poem should help someone remember how to use the punctuation mark. **EXAMPLE:** *With a hyphen, decide whether to join or divide.* When you're done, stand together and read or sing your work for the class.

2. With your group, write a paragraph that includes at least three of the punctuation marks covered in this chapter. (Each person might add a different sentence to the paragraph.) Then, have one member write the paragraph without the punctuation marks. Exchange the unpunctuated versions with another group and add the missing punctuation to each

■ **LEARNING STYLES:** Look for activities in this chapter that are matched to your learning style. If you don't know your learning style, take the test on pages 26–28.

👁 Visual

🗣 Auditory

📖 Reading/writing

🦶 Kinesthetic (movement)

other's paragraphs. Then, join the two groups together and discuss the answers. 👁️ 📖 ✍️

3. Pick one of the punctuation marks and prepare to "introduce" it to the other members of your group. (Imagine the mark stepping out of a limousine as you announce its arrival at a movie premiere.) First, draw a picture of the punctuation mark that you can hold up as you give your introduction. Make the drawing as interesting and funny as you can. You might even show it dressed for the big event. Then, come up with an introduction: a brief description, in your own words, of what the punctuation mark does and an example of a sentence it "stars" in. Group members should then stand up and present their punctuation marks. 👁️ 📖 ✍️

Chapter Review

1. Use a semicolon to _____ and make them into one sentence and to _____
_____.

2. A colon can be used after a complete sentence that introduces a _____ or an _____. A colon can also be used after a _____ in a business letter, after the _____ at the beginning of a memorandum, and between the main title and _____ of publications.

3. Use parentheses to set off _____
_____.

4. _____ also set off additional information, particularly information that you want to emphasize.

5. Use a hyphen to join words that together _____ and to _____ a word at the end of a line.

6. **VOCABULARY:** Go back to any new words that you underlined in this chapter. Can you guess their meanings now? If not, look up the words in a dictionary.

📖 **LEARNING JOURNAL:**
What is one useful piece of information you learned from this chapter? (You can also use your learning journal to record your punctuation errors and corrections for them.)

■ **TIP:** For help with building your vocabulary, see Appendix B.

32

Capitalization

Using Capital Letters

Understand Capitalization

Capital letters are generally bigger than lowercase letters, and they may have a different form.

CAPITAL LETTERS:	A, B, C, D, E, F, G, H, I, J, K, L, M, N, O, P, Q, R, S, T, U, V, W, X, Y, Z
LOWERCASE LETTERS:	a, b, c, d, e, f, g, h, i, j, k, l, m, n, o, p, q, r, s, t, u, v, w, x, y, z

Capitalize (use capital letters for) the first letter of

- Every new sentence.
- Names of specific people, places, dates, and things.
- Important words in titles.

📖 **VOCABULARY:** Underline any words in this chapter that are new to you.

📖 **IDEA JOURNAL:** If you could change one thing about the world, what would that be? Why?

Use Capitalization Correctly

Capitalization of Sentences

Capitalize the first letter of each new sentence, including the first word in a direct quotation.

> The police officer broke up our noisy party.

> He said, "Do you realize how loud your music is?"

■ **TIP:** To do this chapter, you need to know what a sentence is. For a review, see Chapter 10.

PRACTICE 1

Edit the following paragraph, changing lowercase letters to capital letters as needed. One sentence is correct; write "C" next to it.

(1) Mark Twain is well known for the books he wrote, but when he was alive, he was almost as famous for his clever sayings. (2) for instance, Twain once said, "a banker is a fellow who lends you his umbrella

when the sun is shining and wants it back the minute it begins to rain." (3) he also made people laugh when he stated, "get your facts first, and then you can change them as much as you please." (4) Along with Twain's humor came a touch of bitterness, as when he said, "always do right. This will gratify some people and astonish the rest." (5) People liked it best when Twain passed on comical advice, such as, "be respectful to your superiors, if you have any."

■ **TIP:** For more practice with capitalization, visit Exercise Central at **<bedfordstmartins.com/ realskills>**.

Capitalization of Names of Specific People, Places, Dates, and Things

Capitalize the first letter in names of specific people, places, dates, and things. Do not capitalize general words such as *college* as opposed to the specific name: *Witley College*.

People

Capitalize the first letter in names of specific people and in titles used with names of specific people.

👁 Draw two pictures: a specific person, place, or thing and a nonspecific version of the same noun.

SPECIFIC	NOT SPECIFIC
Patty Wise	my friend
Dr. Jackson	the physician
President George W. Bush	the president
Professor Arroyo	your professor
Aunt Marla, Mother	my aunt, my mother

The name of a family member is capitalized when the family member is being addressed directly or when the family title is replacing a first name.

Sit down here, Sister.

I wish Mother would see a doctor.

In other cases, do not capitalize.

My sister came to the party.

I'm glad that my mother is seeing a doctor.

Places

Capitalize the first letter in names of specific buildings, streets, cities, states, regions, and countries.

SPECIFIC	NOT SPECIFIC
the Seagram Building	that building
Elm Street	our street
Jacksonville, Florida	my town
Wisconsin	this state
the South	the southern part of the country
Chinatown	my neighborhood
Pakistan	her birthplace

Do not capitalize directions in a sentence: *Drive north for three miles.*

Dates

Capitalize the first letter in the names of days, months, and holidays. Do not capitalize the names of the seasons (winter, spring, summer, fall).

SPECIFIC	NOT SPECIFIC
Friday	today
July	summer
Martin Luther King Jr. Day	my birthday

Organizations, Companies, and Specific Groups

SPECIFIC	NOT SPECIFIC
Doctors Without Borders	the charity
Starbucks	the coffee shop
Wilco	his favorite band

Languages, Nationalities, and Religions

SPECIFIC	NOT SPECIFIC
English, Spanish, Chinese	my first language
Christianity, Judaism	her religion

The names of languages should be capitalized even if you aren't referring to a specific course: *I am studying economics and French.*

> **Language note:** Some languages, such as Spanish, French, and Italian, do not capitalize days, months, and languages. In English, such words must be capitalized.
>
> | | |
> |---|---|
> | **INCORRECT** | I study Russian every monday, wednesday, and friday from january through may. |
> | **CORRECT** | I study Russian every **Monday, Wednesday,** and **Friday** from **January** through **May.** |

Courses

SPECIFIC	NOT SPECIFIC
English 100	a writing course
Psychology 100	the introductory psychology course

Commercial Products

> Point to a few things around you that have a specific and general name. Say the specific and general names, for example: *Bic/pen*.

SPECIFIC	NOT SPECIFIC
Nikes	sneakers
Tylenol	pain reliever

PRACTICE 2

Edit the following sentences by adding capitalization as needed or removing capitalization where it is inappropriate.

EXAMPLE: Going to los angeles valley college gives me the chance to learn near one of the country's most exciting cities.

1. My favorite classes at College are Sociology, biology, and french.

2. On tuesdays and thursdays, I have a great class on shakespeare's Plays.

3. That Class is taught by professor John Sortensen, who happens to be my Uncle.

4. I decided to go to this College in the first place because uncle john recommended it.

5. On weekends, I can catch the Train into los angeles at the north hollywood station, which is not far from where I live.

6. Before it closed, I used to go to the carole and barry kaye museum, which displayed miniatures.

7. The Museum had a miniature Courtroom showing the o.j. simpson Trial and tiny Palaces furnished with chandeliers the size of rice.

8. I also like to visit the los angeles county museum of art, the craft and folk art museum, and an Automotive Museum that has some famous cars.

9. The City's Restaurants are another reason to visit often, and so far I have tried mexican, japanese, thai, italian, indian, argentinian, and, of course, chinese Food.

10. My Uncle was right about the city's great Cultural Attractions, but I have also made sure to see disneyland and two theme parks: universal studios and six flags magic mountain.

Capitalization of Titles

Capitalize the first word and all other important words in titles of books, movies, television programs, magazines, newspapers, articles, stories, songs, papers, poems, and so on. Words that do not need to be capitalized (unless they are the first or last word) include *the*, *a*, and *an*; the conjunctions *and*, *but*, *for*, *nor*, *or*, *so*, and *yet*; and prepositions.

> ■ **TIP:** For advice on punctuating titles, see Chapter 30. For a list of common prepositions, see Chapter 10.

Without a Trace is Marion's favorite television show.

Did you read the article titled "Humans Should Travel to Mars"?

We read *The Awakening*, a novel by Kate Chopin.

PRACTICE 3 . .

Edit the following paragraph by capitalizing titles as needed.

(1) "I married your mother because I wanted children," said Groucho Marx in the movie *horse feathers*. "Imagine my disappointment when you arrived." (2) One of the best-known comedians of all time, Marx got his first big break in show business costarring with his brothers in a 1924 Broadway comedy called *i'll say she is*. (3) As a team, the Marx Brothers followed up with more Broadway hits, including *animal crackers*. (4) They went on to make fifteen movies together, including *a night at the opera* and *a night in casablanca*. (5) In their

movie *duck soup*, Groucho Marx said to another character, "I got a good mind to join a club and beat you over the head with it." (6) After a successful movie career, Marx appeared in several radio shows, the most famous of which was the quiz show *you bet your life*. (7) Later, he brought *you bet your life* to TV. (8) Marx also wrote several books, including his autobiography *groucho and me*, which was published in 1959.

· ·

Edit for Capitalization in College, Work, and Everyday Life

EDITING REVIEW 1: COLLEGE · ·

Following is part of an instructor's handout for a history course. Edit it by capitalizing words as needed or by deleting unnecessary capital letters. The first sentence has been marked for you.

(1) This first unit of American History 101 will focus on the civil rights movement. (2) We will explore this movement from the Civil War until Current times. (3) Six of the eight weeks devoted to this unit will concentrate on the 1960s, when struggles for Civil Rights made daily headlines across the Nation. (4) we will learn about leaders such as Martin Luther King Jr., Rosa Parks, Malcolm X, and jesse jackson. (5) We will also examine the history of the Ku Klux Klan, the development of the National association for the advancement of Colored People, and the passage of the Civil Rights act of 1964. (6) As we work through the material, you will be given reading assignments from your textbook, *the American promise*. (7) A final exam covering the course material will be given on december 15 in howard hall. (8) Tutoring in this unit will be available through my Teaching assistants, Ms. Chambers and Mr. Carlin. (9) If you have any questions, please see me after class or during my Office Hours.

EDITING REVIEW 2: WORK . . . .

Following is a shipping document that a book publisher is using to fill an order. Edit it by capitalizing words as needed or by deleting unnecessary capital letters. The first sentence has been marked for you.

(1) $\overset{c}{\text{S}}$old to:

(2) mrs. Jean Stevens

(3) 1429 Statler blvd.

(4) westerville, Ohio 43081

(5) To be Delivered on or before saturday, September 19

(6) 12 copies of *Tom sawyer* by Mark Twain

(7) 12 copies of *the Scarlet Letter* by Nathaniel hawthorne

(8) 12 copies of *The Bluest eye* by Toni Morrison

(9) Send by way of the granger Distribution Company, Philadelphia, Pennsylvania

EDITING REVIEW 3: EVERYDAY LIFE . . . .

Edit the following essay by capitalizing words as needed or by deleting un-necessary capital letters. Four sentences are correct; write "C" next to them. The first sentence has been edited for you.

(1) You can live in the same $\overset{c}{\text{C}}$ity for years and completely miss see-ing a certain building. (2) You can overlook a particular house in a neighborhood that you've lived in for years. (3) However, can you imag-ine missing a four-hundred-foot Waterfall? (4) That is exactly what happened to officials at Whiskeytown National Recreation Area in cali-fornia. (5) In the Autumn of 2003, a park ranger found a waterfall that somehow had been missed for decades.

(6) Rumors had been circulating for years about some mysterious falls, and finally, russ Weatherbee, a park ranger, got curious. (7) he had no idea where to begin searching since the Park covers 42,500 acres. (8) While cleaning out an old cabinet, however, he discovered an old map showing the location of a waterfall about fifteen miles from Park Headquarters. (9) With this map in hand, he hiked to the spot and

found absolutely nothing. (10) Weatherbee was discouraged but not defeated. (11) While looking at some pictures of the area taken from a plane, he noticed something interesting less than a mile from the spot he had just explored. (12) He teamed up with a park Geologist, Brian Rasmussen, and together they headed back into the woods. (13) This time, the two of them found the Falls, which were later named Whiskeytown Falls.

(14) Although this waterfall is beautiful, not many People have had a chance to see it because of its remote location. (15) it is surrounded by deep ravines and thick undergrowth. (16) Park crews began cutting a two-mile path to the falls in 2005 and completed it the following Summer.

Write and Edit Your Own Work

ASSIGNMENT 1: WRITE

Pick three people, living or dead, whom you would like to meet. Write down the names and, under each, list at least three reasons why you would like to meet that person. Then, turn your notes into a paragraph about the three people you'd like to meet and why. When you're done, read your writing carefully, checking especially for capitalization errors.

ASSIGNMENT 2: EDIT

Using this chapter as a guide, edit capitalization errors in a paper you are writing for this course or another course or in a piece of writing from your work or everyday life.

■ **LEARNING STYLES:** Look for activities in this chapter that are matched to your learning style. If you don't know your learning style, take the test on pages 26–28.

👁 Visual

𝄆 Auditory

📖 Reading/writing

🖐 Kinesthetic (movement)

Practice Together

Working with a few other students, practice what you have learned in this chapter.

1. Have each person read one word from the following list out loud. Others should identify the word as specific or not specific. If it is not specific,

others should take turns listing specific substitutes. Keep going until the group has done at least five words.

drink	newspaper
food	singer
high school	*Shrek*
Hurricane Katrina	Statue of Liberty
instructor	World War II
a language	

2. As a group, think of specific substitutes (words that need to be capitalized) for the following nonspecific words. Have someone write down your responses. When you have finished, everyone in your group should stand up. The group that finishes first, with correct answers, wins.

an airport	a high school
a brand of coffee	a language
a brand of crackers	a pizza chain
a country with warm weather	a politician
a dark-haired actor	a popular cola
an electronic device	this state
a football team	a TV station
a funny movie	

3. As a group, create a list of movie titles (you can make up your own), but don't capitalize any of the words. Exchange lists with another group. Each group should decide which words should be capitalized in the list they received and which should not, making the capital letters extra large. Then, return the edited list to the group that wrote it. The groups should check each other's work.

Chapter Review

1. Capitalize the _____ of each new sentence.

2. Capitalize the first letter in names of specific _____, _____, _____, and _____.

3. Capitalize the first and last words and all other _____ in titles.

4. **VOCABULARY:** Go back to any new words that you underlined in this chapter. Can you guess their meanings now? If not, look up the words in a dictionary.

LEARNING JOURNAL: What problem with capitalization do you have most often? How can you edit more effectively for this problem in the future?

■ **TIP:** For help with building your vocabulary, see Appendix B.

Unit Seven Test
Editing for Punctuation and Mechanics

Circle the correct choice for each of the following items.

1. If an underlined portion of this item is incorrect, select the revision that fixes it. If the item is correct as written, choose d.

   "I love your record collection," said Barry, but does your old record
   <u>A</u>   <u>B</u>

   player work?"
   <u>C</u>

   a. collection",
   b. Barry, "but
   c. work"?
   d. No change is necessary.

2. Choose the correct item to fill in the blank.

   _____ no better place for nature study than your own backyard.

   a. Theres   c. There's
   b. Theres'   d. Theres's

3. Choose the correct item to fill in the blank.

   For my new home office, I bought _____.
   a. a desk, a chair, and a candy jar
   b. a desk, a chair and a candy jar
   c. a desk a chair, and a candy jar
   d. a desk a chair and a candy jar

4. If an underlined portion of this item is incorrect, select the revision that fixes it. If the item is correct as written, choose d.

   After breaking up with Edward, I will miss one thing; his great cooking.
   <u>A</u>   <u>B</u>   <u>C</u>

   a. After: breaking   c. thing: his
   b. Edward: I   d. No change is necessary.

5. Choose the correct item to fill in the blank.

   June told us that _____
   a. we have to be at the airport at 1:00 a.m.
   b. "we have to be at the airport at 1:00 a.m."
   c. 'we have to be at the airport at 1:00 a.m.'
   d. "we have to be at the airport" at 1:00 a.m.

6. If an underlined portion of this item is incorrect, select the revision that fixes it. If the item is correct as written, choose d.

Please <u>report to</u> Bradley <u>Pitt,</u> no relation to the movie <u>star on</u> Friday
      A   B   C
morning.

  a. report, to   c. star, on
  b. Pitt no   d. No change is necessary.

7. Choose the correct item to fill in the blank.

This is such a _____ train that I think we will arrive thirty minutes early.

  a. fast-moving   c. fast moving
  b. fastmoving   d. fast/moving

8. If an underlined portion of this item is incorrect, select the revision that fixes it. If the item is correct as written, choose d.

If the bike <u>you're</u> riding is <u>her's,</u> then <u>whose</u> bike does she use when she
               A   B   C
needs one?

  a. youre   c. who's
  b. hers   d. No change is necessary.

9. Choose the correct item to fill in the blank.

You are scheduled for _____, two literature courses, and Japanese.

  a. accounting 220   c. accounting-220
  b. accounting: 220   d. Accounting 220

10. If an underlined portion of this item is incorrect, select the revision that fixes it. If the item is correct as written, choose d.

Having put four <u>years</u> work into <u>his</u> invention so far, Mr. Hannyveld
                A   B
<u>isn't</u> about to give up now.
 C

  a. years'   c. is'nt
  b. his's   d. No change is necessary.

11. Choose the correct item to fill in the blank.

On _____ Randall told us he was moving to Denver, Colorado.

  a. May 13 2005,
  b. May 13, 2005
  c. May 13, 2005,
  d. May 13 2005

12. If an underlined portion of this item is incorrect, select the revision that fixes it. If the item is correct as written, choose d.

    When you get to the office it is easy to find, please sign in at the recep-
                A   B   C
    tion desk.
    a. (to the office)
    b. (it is easy to find)
    c. (at the reception desk)
    d. No change is necessary.

13. If an underlined portion of this item is incorrect, select the revision that fixes it. If the item is correct as written, choose d.

    please enter the Rockville Riders in the Thanksgiving Day relay race.
      A   B   C
    a. Please
    b. rockville riders
    c. Thanksgiving day
    d. No change is necessary.

14. Choose the correct item to fill in the blank.

    Margaret asked, "Did Antonia actually say, 'This contest is not
    _____
    a. fair?"
    b. fair'?"
    c. fair"?
    d. fair'"?

15. If an underlined portion of this item is incorrect, select the revision that fixes it. If the item is correct as written, choose d.

    I told my grandmother that she does not have to pay for me and all of
                                 A   B C
    my friends.
    a. that, she
    b. pay, for
    c. me, and
    d. No change is necessary.

16. Choose the correct item to fill in the blank.

    Dan's favorite book is _____.
    a. *Wine Tasting for Beginners Tips and Tricks*
    b. *Wine Tasting for Beginners, Tips and Tricks*
    c. *Wine Tasting for Beginners; Tips and Tricks*
    d. *Wine Tasting for Beginners: Tips and Tricks*

17. Choose the correct item to fill in the blank.

    By mistake, the payroll department added three extra _____ to my paycheck amount.
    a. 0's
    b. 0s
    c. 0s'
    d. '0s

18. If an underlined portion of this item is incorrect, select the revision that fixes it. If the item is correct as written, choose d.

An <u>article</u> titled <u>The Wild Web of China</u> is in today's <u>*New York Times*</u>.
  A   **B**   **C**

 a. "article"

 b. "The Wild Web of China"

 c. "New York Times"

 d. No change is necessary.

19. If an underlined portion of this item is incorrect, select the revision that fixes it. If the item is correct as written, choose d.

<u>If you</u> are a "<u>sun sneezer</u>" you will probably <u>sneeze as</u> soon as you go
 A   **B**   **C**
into the sunshine today.

 a. If, you   c. sneeze, as

 b. "sun sneezer,"   d. No change is necessary.

20. Choose the correct item to fill in the blank.

Our trip to Europe _____ will be expensive but worth every penny.

 a. --we're so excited about it--

 b. We're so excited about it.

 c. --we're so excited about it

 d. we're so excited about it

21. If an underlined portion of this item is incorrect, select the revision that fixes it. If the item is correct as written, choose d.

<u>Amy's</u> clothes sizes are so small that <u>she's</u> always shopping in the
 A   **B**
<u>childrens's</u> section.
 C

 a. Amys'   c. children's

 b. shes'   d. No change is necessary.

22. Choose the correct item to fill in the blank.

The Fourth of July _____ is a great time for parties.

 a. which is my favorite holiday

 b. , which is my favorite holiday,

 c. , which is my favorite holiday

 d. ; which is my favorite holiday,

23. Choose the correct item to fill in the blank.

Lara told us not be to late _____ she means it.

 a. and   c. , and

 b. ; and   d. : and

24. If an underlined portion of this item is incorrect, select the revision that fixes it. If the item is correct as written, choose d.

   People get <u>confused by</u> my address; <u>it's</u> 266 Lane Lane, <u>Seattle Wash-</u>
            A   **B**   **C**
   <u>ington</u>.
   - a. confused, by
   - b. its
   - c. Seattle, Washington
   - d. No change is necessary.

25. If an underlined portion of this item is incorrect, select the revision that fixes it. If the item is correct as written, choose d.

   Delegates came from many parts of the <u>country, including</u> Sacramento,
                                         A
   <u>California;</u> Champaign, <u>Illinois, and</u> Wilmington, Delaware.
       B   **C**
   - a. country: including
   - b. California,
   - c. Illinois; and
   - d. No change is necessary.

26. If an underlined portion of this item is incorrect, select the revision that fixes it. If the item is correct as written, choose d.

   <u>Its</u> frustrating that the bus took <u>its</u> time getting here today; <u>it's</u> certain
   A   **B**   **C**
   that I'll be late.
   - a. It's
   - b. it's
   - c. its
   - d. No change is necessary.

27. Choose the correct item to fill in the blank.

   "Sorry ＿＿＿＿＿ but you can't take the car this evening," Mrs. Davis said.
   - a. , Claire,
   - b. Claire,
   - c. Claire
   - d. , Claire

28. Choose the correct item to fill in the blank.

   When Arno gives the signal, do ＿＿＿＿＿ count to five, take a deep breath, and run for the nearest exit.
   - a. this
   - b. this,
   - c. this —
   - d. this:

29. Choose the correct item to fill in the blank.

   The meeting was called to order by ＿＿＿＿＿.
   - a. president Smith
   - b. president smith
   - c. President Smith
   - d. President smith

■ **TIP:** For advice on taking tests, see Appendix A.

30. Choose the correct item to fill in the blank.

"_____ Trina, I love you," Joe said.

a. Yes

b. Yes,

c. Yes:

d. Yes;

Unit Eight
Readings for Writers

33

Introduction to the Readings

In this part of the book, you will find eighteen essays (in Chapters 34–42) that demonstrate the types of writing you studied in Chapter 8 of this book.

These readings tell great stories, argue passionately about controversial issues, and present a wide range of perspectives and information. They can also provide you with ideas for your own writing, both in and out of school. Most important, they serve as models, offering you a chance to become a better reader and writer by seeing how others write.

How Can These Readings Help You?

Reading the essays in Unit Eight will help you develop several different abilities.

Your Ability to Write

The essays in Unit Eight are good examples of the types of writing you are doing in your writing course. By looking at how someone else states main ideas, provides supporting details, organizes ideas, and introduces and concludes an essay, you can gain a better sense of how you might write a similar type of essay. The essays can also help you choose writing topics: As you react to an author's ideas, you may discover ideas of your own to explore. It's a good idea to keep a reading journal to record these ideas.

Your Ability to Read Critically

To get the most out of what you read, you need to read critically. Critical reading means that you ask yourself why writers have made the points they did and whether you agree. To help you read critically, the essays in

Unit Eight contain many notes and questions. For more on critical reading, see Chapter 2.

Your Ability to Understand Other Experiences and Points of View

The authors of these readings vary in age, gender, race, culture, and experience, and their writing reflects their many differences. In a rapidly changing world, your ability to understand, appreciate, and interact with people whose outlooks differ from your own is essential.

Increasingly, employers value social skills, communication skills, and the ability to work as part of a team. Being able to understand new and different viewpoints can help you work well in a group. Another benefit may be more personal: As you read more and learn to see things through other people's eyes, you may discover new perspectives on your own life.

Your Ability to Help Yourself

Much practical information is in written form, either print or electronic. As a good reader, you will be able to find out whatever you need to know. The list of topics you can explore as a reader and a writer is endless: making money, investing, starting your own business, finding a job, raising a family, buying a car at the best price, protecting yourself from unfairness, and so on.

34

Narration

Each essay in this chapter uses narration to get its main point across to the reader. As you read these essays, consider how they achieve the four basics of good narration that are listed below and discussed in Chapter 8 of this book.

▣ FOUR BASICS OF NARRATION

1. It reveals something of importance (your main point).
2. It includes all of the major events of the story (support).
3. It gives details about the major events, bringing the event or experience to life for your readers.
4. It presents the events using time order (according to when things happened).

Elyzabeth Joy Stagg

From the Welfare Rolls, a Mother's View

In 1999, Elyzabeth Joy Stagg was a pregnant, jobless single mother, struggling to make ends meet and trying to earn a college degree. Her mixed feelings about her need to rely on welfare led her to write the following essay, which was published in *Newsweek*. After it appeared, Stagg received an outpouring of letters and support. She was delighted to hear that her narration had educated some of her readers about the real lives of welfare mothers.

Today, Stagg is the proud holder of a college degree and a registered nursing license. She is now a trauma-unit nurse and is glad that she can afford to buy the things her daughter and son need — "and some of the things they want." Although relieved that her previous financial hardships are behind her, she still remembers her days as a struggling parent. Her past, she feels, makes her more responsive to the needs of her patients, particularly those who are themselves struggling. She remains grateful for the help she received and says that her experience inspires her to do what she can to help others.

GUIDING QUESTION
What elements of the author's story change your perception of a typical welfare recipient?

PREDICT: At this point, what do you predict the author will write about?

SUMMARIZE: What has welfare taught Stagg (paragraphs 4 and 5)?

REFLECT: Do you share this opinion of those on welfare?

IDENTIFY: What is the main point of this paragraph?

I am a single mother of a three-year-old girl, and I'm expecting a son in November. My children have different fathers. I am a welfare mom, a burden to society. I live off your tax dollars. 1

I first went on welfare when I was pregnant with my daughter, after I lost my job and a house fire took nearly everything I owned. I was living in a hotel paid for by the Red Cross with no possessions, no job, and no boyfriend. 2

Since then, I've gotten temp jobs that pay enough to let me get off welfare, but when they end, I find myself struggling again. For the last several months I scoured[1] the classifieds[2] and sent out résumés to find a job that would coincide with day care and pregnancy. I ended up serving food part-time at a bar for minimum wage. I tried to supplement that income as best I could, even directing plays and giving swing-dance lessons, but somehow I never seemed to get ahead. Now, due to complications with my pregnancy, I can't work at all and depend totally on welfare. 3

Being on welfare has taught me a lot. I've learned to go to the grocery store when it's the least busy, so I don't get annoyed looks from the people behind me in line when I pay with coupons and food stamps. I've learned that when I meet with a caseworker periodically, I should get to the welfare office 45 minutes before it opens, or I'll be waiting all day. 4

The biggest lesson I've learned from being on welfare is that most people assume I don't want to work. When I list my job skills for the caseworkers, they can't seem to understand why I don't have a job. To them, and the rest of society, I am just one of the 7 million people on welfare who survive off less than 1 percent of the federal budget. 5

But I'm more than just a statistic. I graduated in the top 10 percent of my high-school class. I'm studying nursing at my community college. I've played the flute since I was five. My parents have been married thirty years. I can type more than eighty words a minute. I'm bilingual. I know half a dozen computer programs inside and out. I'm twenty-four years old. 6

Now that I'm unable to work, I live off the $265 a month I receive from TANF (Temporary Assistance to Needy Families), which doesn't even cover my rent. My utility bills get paid when I receive final disconnect notices and I can take the bills to a community agency for financial assistance. At the end of the month, when my daughter asks for an ice-cream cone I sometimes don't have the extra $2 to buy it for her. 7

I don't spend my money on anything I don't absolutely need. I borrow videos from the library. I take my daughter to garage sales to look for 8

[1]**scoured:** *searched thoroughly*   [2]**classifieds:** *newspaper advertisements that include job listings*

clothes. I've never bought an alcoholic drink or a cigarette in my life. I don't buy expensive steaks or junk food. I drive a small car that leaks when it rains.

I don't have the kind of relationship I want with either of my kids' fathers. Both men are more than ten years older than I. They've been unable to keep their promises to help me in whatever way I needed. My daughter's father comes in and out of our lives. When he's gone, we miss him. The father of the new baby and I broke up in May because we choose to live different lifestyles. I doubt he will participate in the baby's life when it is born.

I acknowledge that it was my having unprotected sex, and getting pregnant, that caused my situation. I don't regret becoming a mom, but I do regret the difficulties I've gone through as a result. My life isn't anything I'd hoped it would be. I find myself constantly having to make choices that force me to compromise what I really want. Do I struggle for a few more years to finish college, or do I work for little money the rest of my life?

My parents tell me I should give the new baby up for adoption. They wonder how I will possibly manage with two kids. I don't wonder. I'll do it because I have to and, more important, because I want to. They're my children, and I wouldn't leave them for anything. It boggles[3] my mind that there are so many parents out there who are not taking responsibility for their kids.

My daughter and my unborn child have forced me to grow up and taught me more about life than any other experience I can possibly think of. They've taught me patience, compromise, love, and that being a mom is a blessing. Although parenthood is often a struggle, I wouldn't trade it for anything.

I'm grateful for the help that welfare has given me in the past. It subsidized[4] my day care so I could go back to work and helped me return to school. I will continue to accept public assistance, but only until I can get back on my feet and make it on my own. I want more for my life. I want more for my children.

³**boggles:** *astonishes* ⁴**subsidized:** *gave money for*

9 ■ **IDEA JOURNAL:** Tell about a time something bad happened to you that was not your fault.

10

11

12

13 IDENTIFY/REFLECT: What decision does Stagg come to about public assistance in this paragraph? Based on what she writes in this essay, did you expect this decision?

_____

_____

_____

CHECK YOUR COMPREHENSION . . . .

1. Which of the following would be the best alternative title for this essay?
   a. "Battling the System"
   b. "Welfare Is Not My First and Final Choice"
   c. "We Have a Responsibility toward Our Children"
   d. "The Importance of Protected Sex"

2. The main idea of this essay is that
   a. people should not be rude to those on welfare.
   b. Stagg is a devoted and responsible parent.
   c. sometimes responsible people need public assistance.
   d. women with children have a right to public assistance.

3. According to the author, how do most people view welfare recipients?

   a. They think welfare recipients don't want to work.

   b. They have a fairly accurate view of welfare recipients.

   c. They think that anyone can reach a point when they will need welfare.

   d. They aren't very concerned about welfare recipients.

4. If you are unfamiliar with the following words, use a dictionary to check their meanings: *coincide* (para. 3); *statistic* (6).

READ CRITICALLY

1. Stagg provides a number of facts about herself in her first paragraph. What impression of her do these facts create? Why do you think that she creates this impression at the beginning of her essay?

2. How did the facts in the second paragraph change your first impression of Stagg? What other facts in the essay change that first impression?

3. What does Stagg mean by the sentence "But I'm more than just a statistic" (para. 6)? How does the rest of the essay demonstrate that she's "more than just a statistic"?

4. What specific examples of responsible behavior does Stagg provide?

5. What are the key events in Stagg's story? What details does she provide about one of these events?

WRITE

■ **TIP:** For a sample narration paragraph, see page 75.

1. Write about an experience that changed your impression of someone else or that changed someone else's impression of you.

2. Write a narration paragraph or essay that demonstrates "I am more than just a/an _____." Choose your own topic, such as "I am more than just a student taking a writing class, an older student, a pretty face, a waiter."

Brent Staples

A Brother's Murder

Brent Staples (b. 1951) was raised in Chester, Pennsylvania, an industrial city that had problems with poverty and violence. Staples escaped the life of the streets by earning his B.A. at Widener University (in Chester, where he later returned to teach) and then by leaving the East Coast to complete a Ph.D. in psychology at the University of Chicago. In 1985, Staples joined the staff of the *New York Times*, and in 1995, he published a memoir, *Parallel Time: Growing Up in Black and White*.

Staples frequently writes about issues of race, examining what it means to be a black male in contemporary American culture. In "A Brother's Murder" (from the *New York Times*, 1986), Staples questions the circumstances that drove him to leave home to obtain an education but led his brother Blake to stay behind and embrace the street life.

GUIDING QUESTION
What does Staples want us to learn from his brother's life and death?

It has been more than two years since my telephone rang with the news that 1 my younger brother Blake—just twenty-two years old—had been murdered. The young man who killed him was only twenty-four. Wearing a ski mask, he emerged from a car, fired six times at close range with a massive .44 Magnum, then fled. The two had once been inseparable friends. A senseless rivalry—beginning, I think, with an argument over a girlfriend— escalated from posturing,[1] to threats, to violence, to murder. The way the two were living, death could have come to either of them from anywhere. In fact, the assailant[2] had already survived multiple gunshot wounds from an incident much like the one in which my brother lost his life.

As I wept for Blake I felt wrenched backward into events and circum- 2 stances that had seemed light-years gone. Though a decade apart, we both were raised in Chester, Pennsylvania, an angry, heavily black, heavily poor, industrial city southwest of Philadelphia. There, in the 1960s, I was introduced to mortality,[3] not by the old and failing, but by beautiful young men who lay wrecked after sudden explosions of violence. The first, I remember from my fourteenth year—Johnny, brash lover of fast cars, stabbed to death two doors from my house in a fight over a pool game. The next year, my teenage cousin, Wesley, whom I loved very much, was shot dead. The summers blur. Milton, an angry young neighbor, shot a crosstown rival, wounding him badly. William, another teen-age neighbor, took a shotgun blast to the shoulder in some urban drama and displayed his bandages proudly. His brother, Leonard, severely beaten, lost an eye and donned a black patch. It went on.

I recall not long before I left for college, two local Vietnam veterans— 3 one from the Marines, one from the Army—arguing fiercely, nearly at blows about which outfit had done the most in the war. The most killing, they

IDENTIFY: Underline the sentence that best expresses the main point of paragraph 2.

■ **IDEA JOURNAL:** The author says, "The young think themselves immortal." What does this mean? Describe something that you or a friend did that showed you thought you were immortal.

[1]**posturing:** *acting tough*   [2]**assailant:** *attacker*   [3]**mortality:** *condition of eventually having to die*

meant. Not much later, I read a magazine article that set that dispute in context. In the story, a noncommissioned officer—a sergeant, I believe—said he would pass up any number of affluent, suburban-born recruits to get hard-core soldiers from the inner city. They jumped into the rice paddies[4] with "their manhood on their sleeves," I believe he said. These two items— the veterans arguing and the sergeant's words—still characterize for me the circumstances under which black men in their teens and twenties kill one another with such frequency. With a touchy paranoia[5] born of living battered lives, they are desperate to be *real* men. Killing is only machismo[6] taken to the extreme. Incursions[7] to be punished by death were many and minor, and they remain so: They include stepping on the wrong toe, literally; cheating in a drug deal; simply saying "I dare you" to someone holding a gun; crossing territorial lines in a gang dispute. My brother grew up to wear his manhood on his sleeve. And when he died, he was in that group— black, male and in its teens and early twenties—that is far and away the most likely to murder or be murdered.

IDENTIFY: Circle the transitions in paragraph 4.

REFLECT: Why does Staples give readers these details about his own life?

I left the East Coast after college, spent the mid- and late-1970s in   4
Chicago as a graduate student, taught for a time, then became a journalist. Within ten years of leaving my hometown, I was overeducated and "upwardly mobile," ensconced[8] on a quiet, tree-lined street where voices raised in anger were scarcely ever heard. The telephone, like some grim umbilical, kept me connected to the old world with news of deaths, imprisonings and misfortune. I felt emotionally beaten up. Perhaps to protect myself, I added a psychological dimension to the physical distance I had already achieved. I rarely visited my hometown. I shut it out.

As I fled the past, so Blake embraced it. On Christmas of 1983, I trav-   5
eled from Chicago to a black section of Roanoke, Virginia, where he then lived. The desolate public housing projects, the hopeless, idle young men crashing against one another—these reminded me of the embittered town we'd grown up in. It was a place where once I would have been comfortable, or at least sure of myself. Now, hearing of my brother's forays[9] into crime, his scrapes with police and street thugs, I was scared, unsteady on foreign terrain.[10]

I saw that Blake's romance with the street life and the hustler[11] image   6
had flowered dangerously. One evening that late December, standing in some Roanoke dive among drug dealers and grim, hair-trigger[12] losers, I told him I feared for his life. He had affected the image of the tough he wanted to be. But behind the dark glasses and the swagger, I glimpsed the baby-faced toddler I'd once watched over. I nearly wept. I wanted desperately for him to live. The young think themselves immortal, and a dangerous light shone in his eyes as he spoke laughingly of making fools of the policemen who had raided his apartment looking for drugs. He cried out as

---

[4]**paddies:** *fields*   [5]**paranoia:** *belief that people are out to get you*   [6]**machismo:** *aggressive male behavior*   [7]**incursions:** *attacks*   [8]**ensconced:** *settled comfortably*   [9]**forays:** *trips*   [10]**terrain:** *ground*   [11]**hustler:** *a person who makes money on the streets, often illegally*   [12]**hair-trigger:** *quick to respond to the slightest annoyance, insult, or challenge*

I took his right hand. A line of stitches lay between the thumb and index finger. Kickback from a shotgun, he explained, nothing serious. Gunplay had become part of his life.

I lacked the language simply to say: Thousands have lived this for you and died. I fought the urge to lift him bodily and shake him. This place and the way you are living smells of death to me, I said. Take some time away, I said. Let's go downtown tomorrow and buy a plane ticket anywhere, take a bus trip, anything to get away and cool things off. He took my alarm casually. We arranged to meet the following night—an appointment he would not keep. We embraced as though through glass. I drove away.

7

As I stood in my apartment in Chicago holding the receiver that evening in February 1984, I felt as though part of my soul had been cut away. I questioned myself then, and I still do. Did I not reach back soon or earnestly[13] enough for him? For weeks I awoke crying from a recurrent dream in which I chased him, urgently trying to get him to read a document I had, as though reading it would protect him from what had happened in waking life. His eyes shining like black diamonds, he smiled and danced just beyond my grasp. When I reached for him, I caught only the space where he had been.

8

REFLECT: Do you think that Staples did enough to help his brother? What would you have done?

_____

_____

_____

_____

[13]**earnestly:** *sincerely*

CHECK YOUR COMPREHENSION . . . .

1. Which of the following would be the best alternative title for this essay?

   a. "Their Manhood on Their Sleeves"

   b. "Pennsylvania's Inner Cities"

   c. "Why I Left the City"

   d. "Drug Dealers and Hair-Trigger Losers"

2. The main idea of this essay is that

   a. in order to survive, you must leave your past behind.

   b. many black males in the inner city are likely to kill or be killed trying to prove their toughness.

   c. killing is a glorified form of manhood.

   d. acting macho is a good way to protect yourself.

3. What group did Blake belong to?

   a. a violent street gang

   b. a group of drug dealers

   c. Vietnam veterans

   d. a group most likely to murder or be murdered

4. If you are unfamiliar with the following words, use a dictionary to check their meanings: *escalated* (para. 1); *wrenched, brash, donned* (2); *umbilical* (4); *desolate* (5); *swagger* (6); *recurrent* (8).

READ CRITICALLY . . . .

1. Why do you think Staples begins his narrative by telling about Blake's death? How did you feel when you read the opening of the essay? Why didn't the author mention his brother's death at the end of the essay?

2. Staples fills his narrative with details to help him tell his story. For example, in paragraph 6 he tells of "a line of stitches" in Blake's hand. Find another example of a vivid detail. What effect did it have on you as you read the story?

3. In this essay Staples also writes about his own life and how it differed from his brother's. What effect does this comparison between the lives of the two brothers have on the essay?

4. In quoting the veterans, Staples writes that "they jumped into the rice paddies with 'their manhood on their sleeves.'" What do you think he means by this phrase? How does it pertain to Blake?

5. In paragraph 3, Staples writes that young black men are "desperate to be *real* men." How do you think Staples would describe what it means to be a real man?

WRITE . . . .

■ **TIP:** For a sample narration paragraph, see page 75.

1. Write about how you relate to a brother or sister (or another family member or close friend). Present details in a clear order about an event (like a party or shopping trip) that describes the nature of your relationship (such as whether you get along or fight).

2. Write a paragraph or an essay that tells a story about a dramatic experience you have had. Be sure to tell what the incident is, why it's important, when it occurred, and who or what was involved. Include vivid details to help your reader experience the event as you did.

. . . .

35

Illustration

Each essay in this chapter uses illustration to get its main point across. As you read these essays, consider how they achieve the four basics of good illustration that are listed below and discussed in Chapter 8 of this book.

▪▪ FOUR BASICS OF ILLUSTRATION

1. It has a main point to illustrate.
2. It gives specific examples to show, explain, or prove the point.
3. It gives details to support the examples.
4. It uses enough examples to get the point across.

Dianne Hales

What Your Car Says about You

Dianne Hales is a writer specializing in mental health, fitness, and other issues related to the body and mind. She has written several college-level health textbooks. In her book *Just Like a Woman* (2000), she examines assumptions about the biological differences between women and men; she has also written a comprehensive overview of mental health, *Caring for the Mind* (1996), with her psychiatrist husband. Her most recent book is *Think Thin, Be Thin: 101 Psychological Ways to Lose Weight* (2004), written with Doris Wild Helmering. The American Psychiatric Association, the American Psychological Association, and the National Women's Political Caucus have all presented Hales with awards for her writing. She lives with her family in the San Francisco Bay area.

In "What Your Car Says about You," Hales takes a detour from her usual subjects of health and fitness. Using numerous examples, she illustrates the kinds of assumptions people make about each other based on the cars they drive.

GUIDING QUESTION
Do any of the points Hales raises in this essay surprise you? Do you see your-self as one of the people she describes?

Stud or dud? Sassy or shy? Trendy or traditional? Soccer mom[1] or sexy   1
mama? Before you say a word, your car broadcasts the answer. "Your car is the best way of advertising who you are and how well you're doing," says psychologist Carleton Kendrick of Millis, Mass. An analyst of auto trends, he notes that cars "are an extension of what we want to be"—whether that's successful, cool or just different.

According to a national survey by Roper,[2] almost half of Americans be-   2
lieve their cars match their personalities. And with more makes, models, sizes, styles, colors, and accessories available in every price range to buy or lease, any driver can make a vehicular[3] statement. "If cars were just about transportation, we would all drive the same thing," says Stephen Roulac, a business strategist in San Rafael, California. "Everybody expresses some-thing through their cars—even if they try not to."

Inkblots[4] on Wheels

REFLECT: How do you re-spond to Charles Kenny's points in this paragraph?

Most people think they choose a car rationally. Not so, says consumer psy-   3
chology expert Charles Kenny of Memphis. "Car choice comes from the right side of the brain—the emotional, irrational side. It's driven by psy-chological needs that most of us don't recognize. That's why you go to the dealer to buy a subcompact but end up driving home in a racier model with four on the floor.[5] The bottom line is, 'How does a car make you feel?'"

SUVs deliver the heady[6] feeling of being independent and above it all.   4
Convertibles epitomize[7] wind-in-the-hair freedom. Rugged off-roaders con-vey outdoor adventure—even if most rarely take on anything more formi-dable[8] than a speed bump.

"About 25 percent of people choose cars that make them feel powerful,"   5
says James Hazen, a psychologist in Wexford, Pennsylvania, who works in the auto industry. "They go for the big engines, the big tires. Some people want cars that look good and stand out. Others find comfort in blending in with all the other white Camrys on the road."

PREDICT: Pause after read-ing the first sentence of this paragraph. How do you think Hales will develop this point?

Colors, accessories, and origins also send signals. "People with red Cor-   6
vettes are different than those who opt for a power color like black," says Hazen. White minivan owners who buy a GPS (global positioning system) because they worry about getting lost are different from those who get roof racks because they ski. Import-car buyers are more likely to live in blue

---

[1]**Soccer mom:** *a typically suburban, upper-middle-class woman who drives her chil-dren to and from various activities*   [2]**Roper:** *a national polling firm*   [3]**vehicular:** *re-lated to automobiles*   [4]**Inkblots:** *in psychology tests, various patterns resembling spilled ink. Patients reveal aspects of their personalities by interpreting the patterns.*   [5]**four on the floor:** *a manual gear-shift system generally associated with sports cars*   [6]**heady:** *thrilling, exciting*   [7]**epitomize:** *to be a typical example of*   [8]**formidable:** *dif-ficult to defeat, impressive*

states;[9] those who buy American autos tend to come from union families and red states.[10]

Read My Ride

Our cars reflect not just who we are but also how we want others to see us. "Cars are the ultimate status symbol," says BJ Gallagher of Los Angeles, a consultant to automotive businesses. "But status lies in the eye of the beholder and varies with your peer group."

In high finance, cars so rare and pricey that they're made of what one expert calls "unobtainium"[11]—such as a Bentley or Maserati—telegraph fiscal[12] triumph. Among political activists, an environmentally correct Toyota Prius hybrid commands respect. For the young and well-wheeled, individuality rules. "You don't want to look like you're driving anybody else's car, especially your parents'," says Bobby Jones, a hip-hop lifestyle expert for a marketing company. "You want a car they'd never drive—like a Scion xB or Dodge Magnum—tricked out[13] to make a statement about you."

Car talk can be more subtle. A sports car hints of an inner James Bond. A woman in a pickup asserts anything-he-can-do competence. Midlife men—and increasingly women—in convertibles tell the world they still have a lot of life left in them. Drivers of retro-styled cars like the Mini Cooper or Chrysler PT Cruiser "are trying to recapture the exuberance that comes so easily when you're young and carefree," says Charles Kenny.

At any age or life stage, automotive messaging is "natural, normal and healthy," he adds. "Expressing a unique identity is what makes us human, and that's what our cars let us do."

7

8

9 IDENTIFY: Put a check mark next to each of the specific examples of cars in this paragraph.

10 ■ **IDEA JOURNAL:** Why do you think Americans tend to be so serious about the cars they drive?

[9]**blue states:** *states that tend to vote for Democratic candidates in national elections and are viewed as more liberal than red states*   [10]**red states:** *states that tend to vote for Republicans in national elections and are viewed as more conservative than blue states*   [11]**unobtainium:** *a word formed by combining* unobtainable *with* titanium, *an expensive metal*   [12]**fiscal:** *related to money*   [13]**tricked out:** *slang for "modified with fancy accessories"*

CHECK YOUR COMPREHENSION . . . .

1. Which of the following would be the best alternative title for this essay?
   a. "How to Choose the Car That's Right for You"
   b. "How Your Car Reflects Your Personality"
   c. "The Importance of Expressing a Unique Identity"
   d. "Environmentally Friendly Cars"

2. The main idea of this essay is that
   a. many people choose cars that make them feel powerful.
   b. the most important aspect of choosing a car is how it makes the buyer feel.
   c. a car often reveals something about its owner's self-image.
   d. cars today come in a wide variety of makes, models, and styles.

3. According to the essay,

    a. people often choose a car on the basis of irrational factors.

    b. most drivers don't care about the message that their car sends about them.

    c. in a perfect world we would all drive a car that looked like everyone else's car.

    d. most people want to drive a car that makes them appear different from everyone else.

4. If you are unfamiliar with the following words, use a dictionary to look up their meanings: *broadcasts, analyst, extension* (para. 1); *accessories, strategist* (2); *racier* (3); *rugged* (4); *status symbol, consultant* (7); *telegraph* (8); *subtle, exuberance* (9).

READ CRITICALLY . . . .

1. Do you think that Hales provides enough examples to support her main point? What other examples could she have used?

2. Hales divides her essay into two sections. What is the focus of each of these sections?

3. Throughout the essay, Hales quotes several people. Why do you think she chose these people and these particular quotations?

4. In paragraph 1, Carleton Kendrick says, "Your car is the best way of advertising who you are and how well you're doing." How do you respond to this statement?

5. Can you think of any examples in which a person's car does not reflect his or her personality? What other reasons might people have for choosing a particular car?

WRITE . . . .

■ **TIP:** For a sample illustration paragraph, see pages 77–78.

1. Using the cars that you, your family members, or your friends drive, test Hales's observations. Using specific examples from your own experiences, write about the relationship between the car a person drives and that person's personality and self-image.

2. Think about something else that can reflect its owner's personality—for example, a pet, a music system, or a piece of clothing. Like Hales, use many specific examples to show what the object can suggest about the owner's personality.

Tucker Carlson

You Idiot! If You Believe What You See on TV, All Men Are Morons

Tucker Carlson (b. 1969) hosts *Tucker* on MSNBC, a show in which he debates various news stories with people who hold different viewpoints. He is also a contributor to *Esquire* magazine and *The Weekly Standard*. Before beginning his television career, Carlson worked at *Policy Review* and the *Arkansas Democrat-Gazette*.

"You Idiot!" first appeared in *Reader's Digest* in 2003. Carlson wonders why so many television commercials portray men as stupid. He uses examples—which include commercials for soup, cars, and computers—to support his point that anti-male humor is becoming increasingly common and accepted.

GUIDING QUESTION
How are men portrayed in advertising, according to Carlson?

Imagine a new television ad from Dell computers. A woman, obviously a homemaker, sits wide-eyed in front of a computer screen, frantically clicking the mouse. "Why won't it work?" she moans and then begins to cry. Her husband strolls over to her, rolling his eyes, and with one deft[1] keystroke—voilà.[2] Everything's fixed. Then comes the voice-over: "Dell. So simple, even your wife can use it." 1

Actually, Dell would never run such an ad, nor would any computer company. Why? Because it plays to a negative stereotype of women, few of whom cry at the thought of using computers. If there's one thing the people who make television ads know, it's that unflattering stereotypes of women—as indecisive or shrewish[3] or mechanically inept[4]—are unacceptable in modern America. Put one on the air and you're likely to find yourself the target of a boycott,[5] or worse. 2

Racial or ethnic stereotypes, of course, have been rightfully out of bounds for decades, leaving advertisers with almost no one to make fun of. Except men. You can still mock them with impunity.[6] And advertisers do. 3

Unless you're particularly unlucky, the men portrayed in television advertising bear no resemblance to the actual men you know. The ones on television are dim, lazy, pompous,[7] and incompetent, sometimes lovable, but fundamentally ridiculous. They are clueless and insensitive. Useless lumps of flesh. Meaty doorstops. 4

Watch them: The husband in a Citibank spot is so cheap he tries to talk his wife out of using painkillers during childbirth. "Do you really need an epidural?"[8] he asks. "I've got ibuprofen right here." In a Hewlett-Packard 5

---

[1]**deft:** *quick and skillful* [2]**voilà:** *French for "see there"; used to call attention to an accomplishment* [3]**shrewish:** *ill-tempered, continually complaining* [4]**inept:** *unskilled, clumsy* [5]**boycott:** *a campaign urging consumers not to purchase a product* [6]**impunity:** *freedom from punishment* [7]**pompous:** *arrogant, conceited* [8]**epidural:** *an injection that numbs the lower half of the body during childbirth*

PREDICT: Pause after reading the second sentence of this paragraph. How do you think Carlson will answer the question? Why?

_____

_____

_____

REFLECT: Do you agree with Carlson's description of how men are portrayed in television ads? Why or why not?

_____

_____

_____

IDENTIFY: Put a check mark by the three companies Carlson gives as examples in paragraphs 5 and 6.

ad, the guy is so dull he can't make it through a store without color photos of the products he is supposed to buy: "A shopping list that won't confuse your husband."

In every possible way, the men portrayed in advertising don't measure up. A recent commercial for Heinz soup opens with a couple in bed, moments after sex. The man falls asleep almost immediately and begins snoring. The woman heads to the kitchen, where she's left a cup of soup cooking in the microwave. The timer rings. An announcer says: "Heinz microwavable soups — ready in just two minutes."

Clever as it is, it's hard to know if an ad like this really convinces consumers to buy Heinz soup. ("Heinz: for the woman whose husband is sexually inadequate.") On the other hand, it's likely that a steady diet of anti-male advertising does affect everyone's views of men. And since "men" is just another word for husbands, fathers, sons, and brothers, this is a problem.

What's more, the problem appears to be getting worse. Anti-male hostility in advertising no longer bubbles beneath the surface but floats atop it. A recent commercial for the Hummer promises that women who drive the massive SUV will be able to "threaten men in a whole new way." A couple of years ago, American Greetings, the card company, ran an ad with this joke: "Men are always whining about how we are suffocating them. Personally, I think if you can hear them whining, you're not pressing hard enough on the pillow."

Try to imagine what would happen if a greeting card company joked about murdering women. Or a car company mocked women drivers. Or if anybody at all said an unkind word about women's career choices or mothering skills or sexual prowess.[9] "It would be a modern heresy,"[10] says Christina Hoff Sommers, author of the book *The War Against Boys*. "You'd have to go to some gender reeducation seminar. It wouldn't be tolerated."

Yet men do tolerate it, every time they turn on the television to find parodies[11] of themselves haplessly[12] stumbling down the cereal aisle without color photographs, or accidentally driving to Guadalajara[13] because they're too stubborn to ask directions — the men of television advertising, acting like morons.

No one stages a boycott. Hardly anyone even complains, maybe because complaining is one thing most men don't do a lot of. Pardon the stereotype.

[9]**prowess:** *superior skill or ability* [10]**heresy:** *an opinion contrary to generally accepted beliefs, often religious beliefs* [11]**parodies:** *artistic works that make fun of someone or something* [12]**haplessly:** *pitifully* [13]**Guadalajara:** *a city in Mexico*

6

7

8

9

10

11

SUMMARIZE: In your own words, summarize Carlson's main point in this paragraph.

_____

_____

_____

■ **IDEA JOURNAL:** What other kinds of stereotypes have you seen in television commercials or programs?

CHECK YOUR COMPREHENSION . . . .

1. Which of the following would be the best alternative title for this essay?
   a. "Television Commercials: Harmless Entertainment"
   b. "Racial and Ethnic Stereotypes: A Thing of the Past"
   c. "Why Men Don't Complain"
   d. "Harmful Images of Men in Television Advertising"

2. The main point of this essay is that
   a. in many television commercials, men are made to look ridiculous.
   b. images of women in television advertising have improved over the years.
   c. television commercials should make fun of women as well as men.
   d. it is impossible to know the effect of stereotypes in advertising.

3. According to Carlson, racial and ethnic stereotypes are
   a. common in today's television advertisements.
   b. no longer seen in today's television advertisements.
   c. not as harmful as many people believe.
   d. are more common on television than stereotypes of women.

4. If you are unfamiliar with the following words, use a dictionary to look up their meanings: *frantically* (para. 1); *unflattering, mechanically, stereotype* (2); *dim, incompetent* (4); *ibuprofen, dull* (5); *inadequate* (7); *tolerated* (9).

READ CRITICALLY

1. According to Carlson, how are men often portrayed in television advertisements?

2. In your opinion, which of Carlson's examples best supports his main point? Why?

3. In paragraph 1, Carlson gives a fictional example. What point does he make with this example?

4. What do you think was Carlson's purpose in writing this essay?

5. How are the examples in paragraph 8 different from Carlson's earlier examples? What is significant about this difference?

WRITE

1. Expand on Carlson's main point using different examples drawn from your own television viewing. As he does, be sure to describe your examples fully.

   ■ **TIP:** For a sample illustration paragraph, see pages 77–78.

2. Think of another group that is stereotyped on television or in films. (Keep in mind that the stereotype does not necessarily have to be negative.) Write about this stereotyped group, focusing on specific examples as Carlson does.

36

Description

Each essay in this chapter uses description to get its main point across. As you read these essays, consider how they achieve the four basics of good description that are listed below and discussed in Chapter 8 of this book.

▪▪ FOUR BASICS OF DESCRIPTION

1. It creates a main impression—an overall effect or image—about the topic.
2. It uses specific examples to create the impression.
3. It supports the examples with details that appeal to the senses: sight, hearing, smell, taste, and touch.
4. It brings a person, place, or object to life for the readers.

Chitra Banerjee Divakaruni
Common Scents

Chitra Banerjee Divakaruni emigrated from Calcutta, India, to the United States in 1976, when she was nineteen. Working at a series of odd jobs—babysitting, slicing bread, washing laboratory glassware—to pay for her education, she earned a master's degree in English from Wright State University in Dayton, Ohio, and a Ph.D. from the University of California at Berkeley. Her first book of short stories, *Arranged Marriage*, won the 1996 American Book Award and the PEN Oakland Award. In addition to three books of poetry, three novels, two short-story collections, and a children's book, Divakaruni has written numerous essays and short stories.

The essay that follows appeared first in Divakaruni's column in the online magazine *Salon.com*. In it, Divakaruni explores the connection between memory and the sense of smell.

GUIDING QUESTION
How does the author use the sense of smell to describe aspects of her childhood?

■ **IDEA JOURNAL:** List some smells that transport you back to your own childhood.

It's a cool December morning halfway across the world in Gurap, a little village outside Calcutta where we've come to visit my mother. I sit on the veranda and watch my little boys, Anand and Abhay, as they play on the dirt road. They have a new cricket bat and ball, a gift from their grandma, but soon they abandon these to feed mango leaves to the neighbor's goat, which has wandered over. Abhay, who is two, wants to climb onto the goat's back. Anand, who is five and very much the big brother, tells him it's not a good idea, but Abhay doesn't listen.   1

Behind me the door opens. Even before I hear the flap-flap of her leather chappals,[1] I know who it is. My mother, fresh from her bath, heralded by the scent of the sandalwood soap she has been using ever since I can remember. Its clean, familiar smell pulls me back effortlessly into my childhood.   2

When I was young, my mother and I had a ritual every evening. She would comb my hair, rub in hibiscus[2] oil and braid it into thick double plaits.[3] It took a long time—there were a lot of knots to work through. But I was rarely impatient. I loved the sleepy fragrance of the oil (the same oil she used, which she sometimes let me rub into her hair). I loved, too, the rhythm of her hands, and the stories (each with its not-so-subtle moral) that she told me as she combed. The tale of Sukhu and Dukhu, the two sisters. The kind one gets the prince, the greedy one is eaten up by a serpent. Or the tale of the little cowherd boy who outwits the evil witch. Size and strength, after all, are no match for intelligence.   3

REFLECT: How do the details in this paragraph help you to understand Divakaruni's childhood and her relationship with her mother?

_____

_____

_____

_____

What is it about smells that lingers in our subconscious, comforting and giving joy, making real what would otherwise be wooden and wordy? I'm not sure. But I do know this: Every lesson that I remember from my childhood, from my mother, has a smell at its center.   4

IDENTIFY: Underline the sentence in paragraph 4 that provides the main or unifying idea for paragraphs 5–7.

The smell of turmeric,[4] which she made into a paste with milk and rubbed into my skin to take away blemishes, reminds me to take pride in my appearance, to make the best of what nature has given me.   5

The smell of the rosewater-scented rice pudding she always made for New Year is the smell of hope. It reminds me to never give up. Who knows— something marvelous may be waiting just around the bend.   6

Even the smell of the iodine she dabbed on my scraped knees and elbows, which I so hated then, is one I now recall with wry[5] gratitude. Its stinging, bitter-brown odor is that of love, love that sometimes hurts while it's doing its job.   7

Let me not mislead you. I wasn't always so positively inclined toward my mother's lessons—or the smells that accompanied them. When I first   8

IDENTIFY: Put Xs by the details that show the author's attempts to Americanize herself.

---

[1]**chappals:** *Indian footwear, sandals*   [2]**hibiscus:** *a large and colorful tropical flower*
[3]**plaits:** *braids*   [4]**turmeric:** *an East Indian plant that, in powdered form, is used as seasoning*   [5]**wry:** *showing a sense of humor about and acceptance of something unpleasant*

moved to the United States, I wanted to change myself, completely. I washed every last drop of hibiscus oil from my hair with Vidal Sassoon shampoo. I traded in my saris[6] for Levi's and tank tops. I danced the night away in discos and returned home in the bleary-eyed morning smelling of vodka and sweat and cigarettes, the perfume of young America.

But when Anand was born, something changed. They say you begin to understand your mother only when you become a mother yourself. Only then do you appreciate all the little things about her that you took for granted. Maybe that's true. Otherwise, that morning in the hospital, looking down at Anand's fuzzy head, why did I ask my husband to make a trip to the Indian store and bring me back a bar of sandalwood soap?   9

I have my own rituals now, with my boys, my own special smells that are quite different. (I learned early that we can't be our mothers. Most times, it's better to not even try.)   10

On weekends I make a big chicken curry with turmeric and cloves. Anand helps me cut up the tomatoes into uneven wedges; Abhay finger-shreds the cilantro[7] with great glee. As the smell of spices fills the house, we sing. Sometimes it's a song from India: *Ay, ay, Chanda mama*—come to me, Uncle Moon. Sometimes it's "Old MacDonald Had a Farm."   11

When the children are sick, I sprinkle lavender water on a handkerchief and lay it on their foreheads to fend off that other smell, hot and metallic: the smell of fever and fear.   12

If I have a special event coming up, I open the suitcase my mother gave me at my wedding and let them pick out an outfit for me, maybe a gold-embroidered kurta[8] or a silk shawl. The suitcase smells of rose potpourri.[9] The boys burrow into it and take deep, noisy breaths.   13

Am I creating memories for them? Things that will comfort them in the dark, sour moments that must come to us all at some time? Who knows—there is so much out of my own childhood that I've forgotten that I can only hope so.   14

"Watch out!" says my mother now, but it's too late. The goat, having eaten enough mango leaves, has decided to move on. He gives a great shrug, and Abhay comes tumbling off his back. He lies on the dirt for a moment, his mouth a perfect O of surprise, then runs crying to me. A twinge goes through me even as I hide my smile. A new lesson, this, since motherhood: how you can feel someone else's pain so sharply, like needles, in your own bones.   15

When I pick him up, Abhay buries his face in my neck and stays there a long time, even after the tears have stopped. Is he taking in the smell of my body? Is he going to remember the fragrance of the jabakusum oil that I asked my mother to rub into my hair last night, for old time's sake? I'm not sure. But I do know this—I've just gained something new, something to add to my scent-shop of memories: the dusty, hot smell of his hair, his hands pungent[10] with the odor of freshly-torn mango leaves.   16

PREDICT: What possible rituals might Divakaruni have with her own children?

_____

_____

REFLECT: How can a smell provide comfort?

_____

_____

_____

REFLECT: What does Divakaruni mean by the expression "scent-shop of memories"? Do you think the expression is an effective way for her to get her point across?

_____

_____

_____

_____

---

[6]**saris:** *garments worn by women in India, consisting of a piece of cloth wrapped around the waist and draped over the shoulder*   [7]**cilantro:** *leaves used as an herb in cooking*   [8]**kurta:** *a loose-fitting shirt worn in India*   [9]**potpourri:** *a mixture of dried flower petals with spices*   [10]**pungent:** *strong and sharp*

CHECK YOUR COMPREHENSION . . . .

1. Which of the following would be the best alternative title for this essay?
   a. "A Calcutta Childhood"
   b. "Childhood Memories"
   c. "Creating Rituals"
   d. "Scents: A Bridge to the Past"

2. The main idea of this essay is that
   a. scents have the power to evoke memories.
   b. we should all have childhood rituals.
   c. good scents create good memories.
   d. the lessons we learn in childhood never fade.

3. Why does Divakaruni create rituals with her sons?
   a. She wants them to experience different smells in their lives.
   b. She wants them to have structure in their lives as she did when she was a child.
   c. She wants them to learn about their Calcutta culture.
   d. She wants them to be able to associate smell with a comforting childhood ritual.

4. If you are unfamiliar with the following words, use a dictionary to check their meanings: *heralded* (para. 2); *subtle* (3); *blemishes* (5); *iodine, dabbed* (7); *inclined* (8); *fend* (12); *burrow* (13)

READ CRITICALLY . . . .

1. How would you describe the tone of this essay?

2. Describe how Divakaruni shifts between present and past in this essay.

3. What details does Divakaruni include in this essay to make the connection between scent and memories of her childhood?

4. What happened in Divakaruni's life that made her understand her mother?

5. Why did Divakaruni begin rituals with her own children?

WRITE . . . .

1. Write a paragraph or essay using a technique similar to the one Divakaruni uses in paragraph 3. That is, think of a particular ritual that you shared with someone, such as a parent. What smells were involved? How were those smells incorporated into the ritual? Think of rituals such as going to the beach, setting up a campsite, and so on.

■ **TIP:** For a sample description paragraph, see pages 79–80.

2. Explore your past and think of a particular smell from childhood that helps you recall a specific memory of an event or person. What memory or memories do you associate with that smell? As Divakaruni does, use descriptive details as you discuss both the smell and the memory it generates. Feel free to include the ideas you wrote about in your idea journal.

Gary Soto

The Jacket

Born in 1952 in Fresno, California, Gary Soto is an award-winning poet, memoir writer, and essayist. Much of his work reflects his experiences growing up as a Mexican American. His *New and Selected Poems* (1995) was nominated for the National Book award, and his memoir, *Living Up the Street* (1985), won an American Book Award. Among his many other honors, he has received the Andrew Carnegie Medal and the Levinson Award from *Poetry* magazine. His most recent book of poems is *Fire in My Hands* (2006). He has also written novels and books of poetry for young adults, including *Neighborhood Odes* (1992) and *The Afterlife* (2003), and he visits schools to promote reading.

In "The Jacket," first published in *Small Faces* (1986), Soto describes this piece of clothing chosen by his mother as an "ugly brother who breathed over my shoulder that day and ever since." The young Soto hated the jacket so much that he blamed it for everything wrong in his life.

GUIDING QUESTION
How well do you think Soto relates his feelings in this essay? How does he go about doing so?

My clothes have failed me. I remember the green coat that I wore in fifth and sixth grade when you either danced like a champ or pressed yourself against a greasy wall, bitter as a penny toward the happy couples. 1

When I needed a new jacket and my mother asked what kind I wanted, I described something like bikers wear: black leather and silver studs, with enough belts to hold down a small town. We were in the kitchen, steam on the windows from her cooking. She listened so long while stirring dinner that I thought she understood for sure the kind I wanted. The next day when I got home from school, I discovered draped on my bedpost a jacket the color of day-old guacamole.[1] I threw my books on the bed and approached the jacket slowly, as if it were a stranger whose hand I had to shake. I touched the vinyl sleeve, the collar, and peeked at the mustard-colored lining. 2

From the kitchen my mother yelled that my jacket was in the closet. I closed the door to her voice and pulled at the rack of clothes in the closet, hoping the jacket on the bedpost wasn't for me but my mean brother. No luck. I gave up. From my bed, I stared at the jacket. I wanted to cry because it was so ugly and so big that I knew I'd have to wear it a long time. I was a 3

---

[1]**guacamole:** *a green dip made of avocados that darkens when it is no longer fresh*

small kid, thin as a young tree, and it would be years before I'd have a new one. I stared at the jacket, like an enemy, thinking bad things before I took off my old jacket, whose sleeves climbed halfway to my elbow.

REFLECT: How would you have felt as a young person if you had to wear the jacket Soto describes?

I put the big jacket on. I zipped it up and down several times and rolled the cuffs up so they didn't cover my hands. I put my hands in the pockets and flapped the jacket like a bird's wings. I stood in front of the mirror, full face, then profile, and then looked over my shoulder as if someone had called me. I sat on the bed, stood against the bed, and combed my hair to see what I would look like doing something natural. I looked ugly. I threw it on my brother's bed and looked at it for a long time before I slipped it on and went out to the backyard, smiling a "thank you" to my mom as I passed her in the kitchen. With my hands in my pockets I kicked a ball against the fence, and then climbed it to sit looking into the alley. I hurled orange peels at the mouth of an open garbage can, and when the peels were gone I watched the white puffs of my breath thin to nothing.   4

I jumped down, hands in my pockets, and in the backyard, on my knees, I teased my dog, Brownie, by swooping my arms while making bird calls. He jumped at me and missed. He jumped again and again, until a tooth sunk deep, ripping an L-shaped tear on my left sleeve. I pushed Brownie away to study the tear as I would a cut on my arm. There was no blood, only a few loose pieces of fuzz. Damn dog, I thought, and pushed him away hard when he tried to bite again. I got up from my knees and went to my bedroom to sit with my jacket on my lap, with the lights out.   5

That was the first afternoon with my new jacket. The next day I wore it to sixth grade and got a D on a math quiz. During the morning recess Frankie T., the playground terrorist, pushed me to the ground and told me to stay there until recess was over. My best friend, Steve Negrete, ate an apple while looking at me, and the girls turned away to whisper on the monkey bars.[2] The teachers were no help: they looked my way and talked about how foolish I looked in my new jacket. I saw their heads bob with laughter, their hands half covering their mouths.   6

IDENTIFY: Underline the bad things that happened to Soto the first day he wore his jacket to school.

Even though it was cold, I took off the jacket during lunch and played kickball in a thin shirt, my arms feeling like braille[3] from goose bumps. But when I returned to class I slipped the jacket on and shivered until I was warm. I sat on my hands, heating them up, while my teeth chattered like a cup of crooked dice. Finally warm, I slid out of the jacket but put it back on a few minutes later when the fire bell rang. We paraded out into the yard where we, the sixth graders, walked past all the other grades to stand against the back fence. Everybody saw me. Although they didn't say out loud, "Man, that's ugly," I heard the buzz-buzz of gossip and even laughter that I knew was meant for me.   7

And so I went, in my guacamole-colored jacket. So embarrassed, so hurt, I couldn't even do my homework. I received C's on quizzes and forgot the state capitals and the rivers of South America, our friendly neighbor. Even the girls who had been friendly blew away like loose flowers to follow the boys in neat jackets.   8

I wore that thing for three years until the sleeves grew short and my   9

---

[2]**monkey bars:** *a piece of playground equipment with bars that children swing from*
[3]**braille:** *a system of writing for the blind that uses raised dots for letters that are "read" by the fingers*

SUMMARIZE: What did Soto miss during the three years he wore the jacket?

_____

_____

_____

■ **IDEA JOURNAL:** Write about a time when you blamed something or someone else for your unhappiness.

REFLECT: What do you think of Soto's mother's response? Why does Soto act as he does?

_____

_____

_____

forearms stuck out like the necks of turtles. All during that time no love came to me—no little dark girl in a Sunday dress she wore on Monday. At lunchtime I stayed with the ugly boys who leaned against the chainlink fence and looked around with propellers of grass spinning in our mouths. We saw girls walk by alone, saw couples, hand in hand, their heads like bookends pressing air together. We saw them and spun our propellers so fast our faces were blurs.

I blame that jacket for those bad years. I blame my mother for her bad   10 taste and her cheap ways. It was a sad time for the heart. With a friend I spent my sixth-grade year in a tree in the alley, waiting for something good to happen to me in that jacket, which had become the ugly brother who tagged along wherever I went. And it was about that time that I began to grow. My chest puffed up with muscle and, strangely, a few more ribs. Even my hands, those fleshy hammers, showed bravely through the cuffs, the fingers already hardening for the coming fights. But that L-shaped rip on the left sleeve got bigger; bits of stuffing coughed out from its wound after a hard day of play. I finally Scotch-taped it closed, but in rain or cold weather the tape peeled off like a scab and more stuffing fell out until that sleeve shriveled into a palsied[4] arm. That winter the elbows began to crack and whole chunks of green began to fall off. I showed the cracks to my mother, who always seemed to be at the stove with steamed-up glasses, and she said that there were children in Mexico who would love that jacket. I told her that this was America and yelled that Debbie, my sister, didn't have a jacket like mine. I ran outside, ready to cry, and climbed the tree by the alley to think bad thoughts and watch my breath puff white and disappear.

But whole pieces still casually flew off my jacket when I played hard,   11 read quietly, or took vicious spelling tests at school. When it became so spotted that my brother began to call me "camouflage," I flung it over the fence into the alley. Later, however, I swiped the jacket off the ground and went inside to drape it across my lap and mope.

I was called to dinner: steam silvered my mother's glasses as she said   12 grace; my brother and sister with their heads bowed made ugly faces at their glasses of powdered milk. I gagged too, but eagerly ate big rips of buttered tortilla that held scooped-up beans. Finished, I went outside with my jacket across my arm. It was a cold sky. The faces of clouds were piled up, hurting. I climbed the fence, jumping down with a grunt. I started up the alley and soon slipped into my jacket, that green ugly brother who breathed over my shoulder that day and ever since.

[4]**palsied:** _shrunken and trembling_

CHECK YOUR COMPREHENSION . . . .

1. Which of the following would be the best alternative title for this essay?
    a. "A Special Gift"
    b. "The Ugly Green Companion of My Youth"
    c. "How to Survive a Difficult Childhood"
    d. "Playground Bullies"

2. The main idea of this essay is that
    a. Soto blames his ugly jacket for his social difficulties and his poor grades.
    b. Soto believes his mother secretly agreed that the jacket was ugly.
    c. Soto wanted a leather jacket with studs and lots of belts but got something else instead.
    d. Soto will never make his children wear ugly clothing.

3. Over time, Soto's jacket
    a. made him feel grateful to his mother.
    b. no longer kept him warm.
    c. became more fashionable.
    d. began to fall apart.

4. If you are unfamiliar with the following words, use a dictionary to look up their meanings: *vinyl* (para. 2); *hurled* (4); *swooping* (5); *bob* (6); *paraded* (7); *propellers* (9); *vicious, camouflage, mope* (11).

READ CRITICALLY

1. Why do you think that Soto continued to wear the jacket?

2. How strong do you think the connection was between Soto's "bad years" (para. 10) and the jacket? Could there be other contributing factors?

3. Soto writes in his final paragraph that the jacket "breathed over my shoulder that day and ever since" (para. 12). What does he mean by "ever since"? Why did his experiences with the jacket have such lasting effects?

4. What senses does Soto appeal to in paragraph 7? What impression do these details create?

5. Throughout the essay, Soto makes imaginative comparisons using the words *as* and *like*—for example, "bitter as a penny" in paragraph 1 and "like a bird's wings" in paragraph 4. Reread the essay, underlining examples of such comparisons. What is their effect?

WRITE

1. Write about an article of clothing that had—or has—special significance to you, either positive or negative. Like Soto, be sure to describe the article in detail and to relate occasions when you wore it and how it made you feel.

■ **TIP:** For a sample description paragraph, see pages 79–80.

2. Soto's mother was obviously an important presence in his life. Write a description of an older family member or friend who continues to be important to you. Let readers see this person physically and understand his or her personality.

37

Process Analysis

Each essay in this chapter uses process analysis to get its main point across. As you read these essays, consider how they achieve the four basics of good process analysis that are listed below and discussed in Chapter 8 of this book.

▪▪ FOUR BASICS OF PROCESS ANALYSIS

1. It tells readers either how to do the steps of the process or to understand how it works.
2. It includes the major steps in the process.
3. It explains each step in detail.
4. It presents the steps in the order they happen (time order).

Cindy Chupack

The End

Born in Tulsa, Oklahoma, Cindy Chupack earned a journalism degree from Northwestern University. While working in advertising in New York City, she published her first humorous essay in *New York Woman*. Having caught the eye of a television producer who convinced her to pursue a career in comedy writing, Chupack went on to write for the programs *Coach* and *Everybody Loves Raymond*. She is best known, however, for her work as a writer and producer of HBO's *Sex and the City*, for which she earned three Golden Globes and an Emmy Award. She currently divides her time between New York and Los Angeles.

In "The End," Chupack explains some of the steps she believes men will go through to avoid a messy breakup.

GUIDING QUESTION
How would you describe Chupack's tone in the essay?

Men are good at a lot of things. Breaking up is not one of them. When a 1
woman want to break up with a man, she invites him over for dinner, cooks
his favorite dish, and tells him she's seeing his best friend. It's all very
straightforward and diplomatic. But men have this weird aversion[1] to endings. They prefer to take the passive mode, allowing the relationship to end
itself. Men can't be bothered with dramatic farewells, the questioning of
motive, discussions. They are bored. They want out. Good-bye.

I remember the first time a boy broke up with me. We were in the sev- 2
enth grade. He invited me over after school, said he just wanted to be
friends, then had his mother drive me home. It was all downhill from there.
In more recent years, a doorman informed me that my date was not coming down. Ever. A friend called her boyfriend and found out he had moved
to a new city. A coworker happened upon a personal ad placed by the man
she was dating.

SUMMARIZE: What point is
Chupack making with the
examples in this paragraph?
_____
_____
_____
_____

Every woman, with the possible exception of Cindy Crawford, has a 3
story like this. She may have dated the man a few weeks or a few years. They
may have shared a cab or an apartment. It doesn't matter. For some reason,
the man thinks that the decision to break up is none of her business. (Of
course, some women do the same thing. But then again, some women mud
wrestle.)

Often a woman senses a breakup brewing and tries to get the man to sit 4
down and fess up.[2] This is futile.[3] The average male gets this beam-me-up-
Scotty[4] look on his face as soon as you mention the word "discussion." He
avoids subsequent contact as if you were trying to serve him a subpoena.[5]
Then, when you finally work up the nerve to ask him what the heck is going
on, he pretends you're imagining the whole thing. It's all part of the game,
and evidently the winner is the one who can quit the game without ever talking about it.

PREDICT: Based on the first
two sentences, what do you
think Chupack will go on to
do in this paragraph?
_____
_____
_____

Some men admit they avoid confrontation because they're afraid we'll 5
cry. Of course we'll cry; we cry at Hallmark[6] commercials. What they don't
understand is that we're not crying because of them, we're crying because
now we have to get naked in front of someone else. It's enough already.

It's a rare and brave man who breaks up in person. Most likely he has 6
sisters and does volunteer work. He'll say things you've heard before: "I'm
unable to make a commitment. I don't have time to be the kind of boyfriend
you deserve." Then he'll add, "I hope we can eventually be friends. I'd really
miss your company." It doesn't matter if he's lying, telling the truth, or quoting something he read in a woman's magazine. At least he's trying.

Most men, however, think that even making a phone call to end a re- 7
lationship is excessive. "What's the point?" they want to know. The humane thing, they've decided, is not to call, but instead to disappear like the
Lone Ranger.[7] These men believe in "Close your eyes and make it go away."

[1]**aversion:** *strong dislike*   [2]**fess up:** *admit to something; confess*   [3]**futile:** *hopeless,
producing no result or effect*   [4]**beam-me-up-Scotty:** *expression drawn from the
1960s science fiction series* Star Trek, *in which crew members were instantly trans-
ported from a planet to the spaceship by an electronic beam*   [5]**subpoena:** *an order
to appear in court*   [6]**Hallmark:** *a greeting card company*   [7]**Lone Ranger:** *1950s television cowboy hero who wore a mask and rode off into the sunset at the end of each
episode*

REFLECT: How do you think Chupack wants readers to respond to this paragraph? How do you respond?

_____

_____

_____

_____

■ **IDEA JOURNAL:** Do you think women and men are as different as Chupack suggests in this essay? Why or why not?

REFLECT: What do you think of Chupack's closing sentence?

_____

_____

_____

_____

They believe in the Fifth Amendment.[8] They believe in absentee ballots.[9] They may ski black diamonds,[10] walk barefoot on hot asphalt, skydive for fun, but measured on their fear of confrontation, these guys are wimps.

They'll say they're going to the rest room and never return. Then they'll   8
meet friends for drinks and say, "She just doesn't get it," or "What do I have to do, spell it out for her?" It's not that we don't get it. After about three weeks of shampooing with the water off—just in case he calls—we get the picture. But we'd like to feel like more than simply a notch in somebody's bedpost. Stranded without an explanation, we sound like the neighbors of a murderer. "He seemed nice. Kind of kept to himself. This came as a complete surprise." Underneath, of course, we know.

You can spot a woman whose relationship is disintegrating[11] because her   9
answering machine gives hourly updates of her whereabouts. "I'm at work now, but I'll be home by seven." "I'm at aerobics." "I'm in the shower." Meanwhile, _his_ machine has the same message as always. "I'm not home. Later."

So what happens is this: you refuse to bow out gracefully, and he refuses   10
to confront. His only option is to make you so miserable that you break up with him. We're talking emotional terrorism. It's fun, easy, and gets results.

During this period he won't laugh at your jokes. He'll ask you out, then   11
act like you're imposing. He'll shred what's left of your confidence by saying, "You're wearing that?" He may even tell you he'd like to end the relationship, but continue sleeping with you. Then he'll act surprised when you bash in his headlights, stuff his favorite tie down the disposal,[12] and ignite his baseball card collection.

So what's the right way for a man to break up? I suggest the following   12
steps:

Step One: Choose a reason. Inevitably[13] your girlfriend will ask why   13
you're leaving, and you should be prepared to explain. If you know that your reason is petty and immature (I know a woman who broke up with a man because his nose looked like a penis), make up a nicer reason.

Step Two: Select a date that doesn't conflict with birthdays or   14
major holidays. "I didn't plan to break up with her on Valentine's Day," a male friend once explained. "It just happened to coincide."

Step Three: Talk to her. You're both adults. It might go surprisingly   15
smoothly.

Step Four: Hide your baseball cards.   16

[8]**Fifth Amendment:** _amendment to the U.S. Constitution that prevents an accused party from having to testify against himself or herself_   [9]**absentee ballots:** _votes cast by mail_   [10]**black diamonds:** _markers in ski areas that indicate the most difficult slopes_   [11]**disintegrating:** _falling apart_   [12]**disposal:** _a device in kitchen sinks for chopping up and disposing of food waste_   [13]**inevitably:** _certainly, without doubt_

1. Which of the following would be the best alternative title for this essay?
    a. "Why Women Are Better Friends than Men"
    b. "Breaking Up Can Be Fun"
    c. "Disappearing Act: The Male Approach to Breakups"
    d. "A Guide to Understanding Your Boyfriend"

2. The main idea of this essay is that
    a. breaking up a relationship is difficult for both women and men.
    b. sometimes it is impossible to know when a relationship is over.
    c. most women would rather not know the truth about a breakup.
    d. men generally avoid telling women that they are ending a relationship.

3. According to Chupack, one reason men avoid confrontation is that
    a. they don't want to be caught lying.
    b. they are afraid the woman will cry.
    c. they don't realize that women want to know the truth.
    d. they enjoy making their girlfriends miserable.

4. If you are unfamiliar with the following words, use a dictionary to look up their meanings: *diplomatic, motives* (para. 1); *brewing, evidently* (4); *confrontation* (5); *humane* (7); *stranded* (8); *aerobics* (9); *imposing, ignite* (11); *petty* (13); *coincide* (14).

1. What do you think is Chupack's purpose in writing this essay? Who might her intended audience be?

2. Reread paragraph 11, circling the transitional words. How does Chupack organize the steps of the process that she describes in this paragraph?

3. Do you think that Chupack is being entirely serious in this essay? Why or why not?

4. How does the process in paragraphs 13–16 differ from the process that Chupack describes throughout the rest of the essay?

5. In paragraphs 13–15, Chupack includes details about the first three steps of the process. Why do you think she provides no details for Step Four? What is the effect of this decision?

■ **WRITE**

1. Write about a pattern of behavior (aside from handling a breakup) that you think is more characteristic of men than of women or vice versa. Like Chupack, explain each step of the process using specific details drawn from your own experience or observations.

■ **TIP:** For a sample process analysis paragraph, see page 82.

2. Chupack writes about the end of a relationship. Write a process analysis paragraph or essay about the beginning of a relationship. What are the usual stages couples go through as they meet, get to know each other, and establish a romantic relationship? You may, if you wish, present this process humorously.

Real Simple *Magazine*

How to Save Gas

Founded in 2000, *Real Simple* is a popular lifestyle magazine. Focusing on helping readers make their lives easier, it offers tips and articles on everything from cooking a quick weeknight meal to organizing the messiest room in your house. In this article, the editors give tips on how to make the most of gas purchases. Although it was first published in August 2001, the article is even more relevant today as gas prices continue to increase and readers continue to become more and more concerned with ways to save gas money.

GUIDING QUESTION
How easy do you think it would be to follow the advice offered in this essay?

SUMMARIZE: In your own words, what is the main point of this paragraph?

The days of low gas prices are over, so it's time to stop complaining and   1
start doing things to cut our own gas consumption. The United States has long enjoyed low prices compared to other countries around the world, and as a result, we have learned to guzzle gas. Now that gas takes a bigger chunk of our money, we need to learn how to use less. It's pretty simple, really.

Slow Down

IDENTIFY: Underline the topic sentence of this paragraph.

When it comes to putting a cap on gas guzzling, how you drive is almost as   2
important as what you drive. "Fuel economy suffers at speeds higher than 60 and drops like a stone above 70," says Chris Grundler of the National Vehicle and Fuel Emissions[1] Laboratory, in Ann Arbor, Michigan. Adds Richard Beard, an associate professor at Utah State University who researches fuel efficiency, "Slowing from 70 to 55 can increase your miles per

[1]**emissions:** *pollution released into the air*

gallon by 15 percent." Putting the brakes on "jackrabbit starts" (stomping on the gas after a red light) cuts use by 25 percent, says Grundler, and cruise control[2] also saves fuel. Limit use of gas-chugging air conditioners and defrosters, and unload extra junk, since "you lose one mile per gallon or more for each 300 pounds," notes Beard. Avoid idling,[3] he advises: "One minute of idle is almost equal to starting the car." Finally, leave the car lot with the best gas hoarder[4] by consulting before you buy.

In the Garage

Inflate those tires. Soft tires slow you down and can cut gas mileage   3
by 10 percent or more, according to the tire-sales and research Web site www.tirerack.com. Follow the inflation instructions in your owner's manual or on the decal[5] at the inside edge of the driver's door. Ignore the numbers on the tire sidewall, as they are more general and not specific to your make of car. Aim to check your tire pressure once a week—at least once a month is crucial. Keeping tires properly inflated will also help you avoid rollover and other tire-related accidents.

Maintain the engine. A reduced air supply or a sluggish ignition can   4
cut into mileage. Change the air filter twice a year and the spark plugs every 50,000 miles. When you change the oil every 6,000 to 7,500 miles, have the mechanic check your cooling system, too. Even cars with computer-controlled engines, which need fewer tune-ups, require these chores.

Take a load off. Extra weight in the car can hurt mileage. Reduce the   5
clutter in your trunk by removing tools, golf clubs, and other weighty and hardly used items.

On the Road

Drive the thriftier car. If your family owns both a sport utility and a   6
sedan, get into the habit of taking the smaller vehicle whenever you can. By driving the Toyota Camry instead of the Ford Expedition[6] to the mall, you are saving about nine miles per gallon in suburban driving. After 20 10-mile trips, you'll have saved about $11.

Steer away from rush hours. Idling in bumper-to-bumper traffic   7
uses precious gas unnecessarily, and it pollutes more, too. Don't waste time in lines at the fast-food drive-through; go inside for your Extra Value Meal— and get extra value from your gas.

REFLECT: How practical do you find the advice in paragraph 7?

_____

_____

_____

_____

Before a Road Trip

To calculate what you can expect to spend on gas for a weekend getaway,   8
go to AAA's www.fuelcostcalculator.com, then type in your starting city, destination, and vehicle make, model, and year. Staying put? Go to www.gasbuddy.com, which will help you find the cheapest gas in your area. Driving those extra few miles to fill up might be well worth it.

---

[2]**cruise control:** *a device that automatically keeps a car moving at a certain speed*
[3]**idling:** *running the engine while a car is not moving*   [4]**hoarder:** *a person who saves a large quantity of something for future use; here, referring to a car that uses gas efficiently*   [5]**decal:** *sticker*   [6]**Toyota Camry...Ford Expedition:** *Camrys are compact cars while Expeditions are large sport utility vehicles that use a lot of gas*

■ **IDEA JOURNAL:** Think of another common product, and list some ways that people could save money on it.

Time Your Purchases

At any time, the price of a gallon of gas can vary by as much as 20 cents   9 within a metropolitan area, says Brad Proctor, founder of GasPriceWatch, a consumer-advocacy[7] Web site. To get the best bargain, avoid buying gas on weekends, when most people travel or run errands and gas stations raise prices accordingly. (Tip: Plan to take care of errands all at once instead of making extra trips.) Also, stay away from stations on toll highways, which charge high prices to their captive customers. If you can stick to pumping once a week, says Proctor, you can often find the best prices on Tuesdays.

Consider a Hybrid

For a real gas saver, consider the Toyota Prius, a hybrid gas-and-electric   10 sedan that gets about 55 miles a gallon, and feels like a car, not a golf cart. The competing two-seat Honda Insight gets more than 60 miles per gallon. "I wave at the people lined up for gas," says Dan Becker, energy and global-warming director of the Sierra Club[8] who drives a Prius, "and keep right on going."

[7]**consumer-advocacy:** *working to protect people who use certain products*   [8]**Sierra Club:** *an organization dedicated to protecting the environment*

CHECK YOUR COMPREHENSION . . . .

1. Which of the following would be the best alternative title for this essay?
   a. "The Expense of Gas Guzzling"
   b. "Finding a Gas-Efficient Automobile"
   c. "How to Save the Environment"
   d. "Using Gas Wisely"

2. The main idea of this essay is that
   a. drivers can do a number of things to spend less money on gasoline.
   b. the most important way to save on gasoline is to avoid buying it on weekends.
   c. cars use more gasoline when they are driven at higher speeds.
   d. good automobile maintenance does not help much in saving gas.

3. According to this essay, all of the following are ways of saving gas *except*
   a. reducing trunk clutter.
   b. avoiding idling in rush-hour traffic.
   c. keeping tires slightly deflated.
   d. driving at speeds lower than seventy miles per hour.

4. If you are unfamiliar with the following words, use a dictionary to check their meanings: *consumption* (para. 1); *guzzling, efficiency* (2); *crucial* (3); *sluggish* (4); *thriftier* (6); *metropolitan* (9).

READ CRITICALLY . . . .

1. Note the use of headings in this selection. How helpful do you find them?

2. Which is the longest paragraph in the essay? Which is the shortest? Why do you think some paragraphs are longer than others?

3. What assumptions do the writers make about their audience? How can you tell?

4. How effective do you find the use of quotations throughout the article?

5. Are you likely to change any of your driving-related habits because of this essay? If so, which ones and why? If not, why not?

WRITE . . . .

1. Write about some other tips to help readers save money on a different product. As with "How to Save Gas," offer specific advice and provide concrete benefits.

   ■ **TIP:** For a sample process analysis paragraph, see page 82.

2. Think of some area in which you consider yourself an expert. Write a paragraph or an essay offering advice to readers that will help them better accomplish something related to this area or subject.

. . . .

38

Classification

Each essay in this chapter uses classification to get its main point across. As you read these essays, consider how they achieve the four basics of good classification that are listed below and discussed in Chapter 8 of this book.

▪▪ FOUR BASICS OF CLASSIFICATION

1. It makes sense of a group of people or things by sorting them into useful categories.
2. It has a purpose for sorting.
3. It includes categories that follow a single organizing principle (for example, to sort by size, by color, by price, and so on).
4. It gives detailed examples or explanations of things that fit into each category.

Russell Baker

The Plot against People

Russell Baker (b. 1925) is a humorist and political writer whose work has been widely published in magazines, newspapers, and books. In 1979, Baker won a Pulitzer Prize for distinguished commentary based on his Observer column in the *New York Times*. He received a second Pulitzer Prize in 1983 for his auto-biography, *Growing Up*. In 2002, he published *Looking Back*, a collection of essays on public figures who influenced America—and Baker himself as he was growing up.

In the following essay, originally published in the *New York Times* in 1968, Baker uses classification to sort objects according to ways in which they make life frustrating.

GUIDING QUESTION
What are the three types of inanimate objects, and what examples does Baker provide of each?

Inanimate[1] objects are classified into three major categories—those that don't work, those that break down and those that get lost.

The goal of all inanimate objects is to resist man and ultimately to defeat him, and the three major classifications are based on the method each object uses to achieve its purpose. As a general rule, any object capable of breaking down at the moment when it is most needed will do so. The automobile is typical of the category.

With the cunning[2] typical of its breed, the automobile never breaks down while entering a filling station with a large staff of idle[3] mechanics. It waits until it reaches a downtown intersection in the middle of the rush hour, or until it is fully loaded with family and luggage on the Ohio Turnpike.

Thus it creates maximum misery, inconvenience, frustration and irritability among its human cargo,[4] thereby reducing its owner's life span.

Washing machines, garbage disposals, lawn mowers, light bulbs, automatic laundry dryers, water pipes, furnaces, electrical fuses, television tubes, hose nozzles, tape recorders, slide projectors—all are in league with[5] the automobile to take their turn at breaking down whenever life threatens to flow smoothly for their human enemies.

Many inanimate objects, of course, find it extremely difficult to break down. Pliers, for example, and gloves and keys are almost totally incapable of breaking down. Therefore, they have had to evolve a different technique for resisting man.

They get lost. Science has still not solved the mystery of how they do it, and no man has ever caught one of them in the act of getting lost. The most plausible[6] theory is that they have developed a secret method of locomotion[7] which they are able to conceal the instant a human eye falls upon them.

It is not uncommon for a pair of pliers to climb all the way from the cellar to the attic in its single-minded determination to raise its owner's blood pressure. Keys have been known to burrow[8] three feet under mattresses. Women's purses, despite their great weight, frequently travel through six or seven rooms to find hiding space under a couch.

Scientists have been struck by the fact that things that break down virtually[9] never get lost, while things that get lost hardly ever break down.

A furnace, for example, will invariably break down at the depth of the first winter cold wave, but it will never get lost. A woman's purse, which after all does have some inherent[10] capacity for breaking down, hardly ever does; it almost invariably[11] chooses to get lost.

Some persons believe this constitutes evidence that inanimate objects are not entirely hostile to man, and that a negotiated peace is possible. After all, they point out, a furnace could infuriate a man even more thoroughly by getting lost than by breaking down, just as a glove could upset him far more by breaking down than by getting lost.

1 ■ **IDEA JOURNAL:** What other objects might you classify and why?

2

3

REFLECT: What is Baker's purpose in suggesting that things knowingly take turns breaking down?

4

5 ————————————

————————————

————————————

6

7

8 IDENTIFY: In paragraph 8, check off examples of things that get lost.

9

10

11

---

[1]**Inanimate:** *not living*   [2]**cunning:** *scheming*   [3]**idle:** *doing nothing*   [4]**cargo:** *load (in this case, passengers)*   [5]**in league with:** *plotting or scheming with*   [6]**plausible:** *credible; likely*   [7]**locomotion:** *movement*   [8]**burrow:** *to tunnel into something*   [9]**virtually:** *almost*   [10]**inherent:** *referring to an essential trait*   [11]**invariably:** *without exception*

SUMMARIZE: Why are objects that don't work "the most curious of all"?

_____

_____

_____

_____

IDENTIFY: Underline the main point of paragraph 16.

Not everyone agrees, however, that this indicates a conciliatory[12] attitude among inanimate objects. Many say it merely proves that furnaces, gloves and pliers are incredibly stupid.   12

The third class of objects—those that don't work—is the most curious of all. These include such objects as barometers, car clocks, cigarette lighters, flashlights and toy-train locomotives. It is inaccurate, of course, to say that they never work. They work once, usually for the first few hours after being brought home, and then quit. Thereafter, they never work again.   13

In fact, it is widely assumed that they are built for the purpose of not working. Some people have reached advanced ages without ever seeing some of these objects—barometers, for example—in working order.   14

Science is utterly baffled[13] by the entire category. There are many theories about it. The most interesting holds that the things that don't work have attained[14] the highest state possible for an inanimate object, the state to which things that break down and things that get lost can still only aspire.[15]   15

They have truly defeated man by conditioning him never to expect anything of them, and in return they have given man the only peace he receives from inanimate society. He does not expect his barometer to work, his electric locomotive to run, his cigarette lighter to light or his flashlight to illuminate, and when they don't it does not raise his blood pressure.   16

He cannot attain that peace with furnaces and keys and cars and women's purses as long as he demands that they work for their keep.   17

[12]**conciliatory:** _having the aim of making peace_   [13]**baffled:** _confused_   [14]**attained:** _achieved; reached_   [15]**aspire:** _try for_

CHECK YOUR COMPREHENSION

1. Which of the following would be the best alternative title for this essay?
   a. "Why I Took a Hammer to My Car, Work Tools, and Furnace"
   b. "Three Types of Objects That Seek to 'Defeat' Humans"
   c. "Inanimate Objects Will Always Rule over Humans"
   d. "With Lost or Broken Objects, a Sense of Humor Is Key"

2. The main idea of this essay is that
   a. Because we own too many objects, we are certain to break them, lose them, or find that they do not work.
   b. Objects like pliers, purses, and gloves have been known to move from one place to another on their own, and no one can explain why.
   c. Objects can be classified as those that break down, those that get lost, and those that don't work; all of them cause frustration.
   d. A car will always break down at the worst possible time and place.

3. What category of items has "truly defeated man," according to Baker?
   a. inanimate objects
   b. objects that break down
   c. objects that get lost
   d. objects that don't work

4. If you are unfamiliar with the following words, use a dictionary to look up their meanings: *ultimately* (para. 2); *irritability* (4); *evolve* (6); *locomotion* (7); *determination* (8); *capacity* (10); *constitutes, hostile, negotiated, infuriate* (11); *barometers, locomotives* (13); *utterly* (15); *conditioning, illuminate* (16).

READ CRITICALLY

1. What do you suppose is Baker's purpose for classifying the items he does in the way that he does? Do you think he has achieved his purpose?

2. Evaluate Baker's use of examples. How does he develop each category he mentions?

3. Baker writes as if he is discussing a serious matter—something that "science" is concerned with. What are the effects of his tone and language in these cases? Is he really being serious?

4. Baker exaggerates in a few places in this essay. Where does he do this, and why do you think he does so? What effects did these exaggerations have on you as a reader?

5. In a couple of places, Baker says that objects seek to defeat humans. What do you think this defeat would consist of, based on your reading of the essay?

WRITE

1. Like Baker, classify people or things that interest you into groups (for example, friendships you've kept versus those you've dropped, or gifts you've loved versus those you've disliked). Then, write a paragraph that states the categories and gives examples of people or things in each one. If you used the Idea Journal tip on page 575, you might draw on some of your insights from that.

   ■ **TIP:** For a sample classification paragraph, see page 84.

2. In your view, what other types of objects are out to "defeat" us? Classify them into at least two groups and give examples for each group. Have fun, and think of details that will make your readers laugh.

Carolyn Foster Segal

The Dog Ate My Disk, and Other Tales of Woe

Carolyn Foster Segal (b. 1950) is an associate professor of English at Cedar Crest College in Pennsylvania, where she teaches creative writing, American literature, and film; she also serves as an adviser for the writing minor. In addition to teaching, Segal has published fiction, poetry, and popular and critical essays. She has recently written a series of eleven essays on academic life for the *Chronicle of Higher Education*.

The essay that follows classifies students' excuses for late course work. Segal notes, "I am not talking about all students or all excuses here. There are certainly legitimate—and sometimes devastating—reasons for missing a deadline; on the other hand, it's quite possible that a few readers might feel guilty." Her essay clearly touched a nerve with other instructors, hundreds of whom sent their own stories of student excuses to Segal after the piece appeared.

GUIDING QUESTION
What creative categories of student excuses does Segal present? Are the examples within each category concrete and specific?

■ **IDEA JOURNAL:** Can you recall a common excuse that you may have used in school or college in the past or have heard others use?

PREDICT: Pause here. Predict the type of family excuses Segal will give in this paragraph.

Taped to the door of my office is a cartoon that features a cat explaining to 1 his feline teacher, "The dog ate my homework." It is intended as a gently humorous reminder to my students that I will not accept excuses for late work, and it, like the lengthy warning on my syllabus, has had absolutely no effect. With a show of energy and creativity that would be admirable if applied to the (missing) assignments in question, my students persist, week after week, semester after semester, year after year, in offering excuses about why their work is not ready. Those reasons fall into several broad categories: the family, the best friend, the evils of dorm life, the evils of technology, and the totally bizarre.

The Family. The death of the grandfather/grandmother is, of course, 2 the grandmother of all excuses. What heartless teacher would dare to question a student's grief or veracity[1]? What heartless student would lie, wishing death on a revered family member, just to avoid a deadline? Creative students may win extra extensions (and days off) with a little careful planning and fuller plot development, as in the sequence of "My grandfather/grandmother is sick"; "Now my grandfather/grandmother is in the hospital"; and finally, "We could all see it coming—my grandfather/grandmother is dead."

Another favorite excuse is the "family emergency," which (always) goes 3 like this: "There was an emergency at home, and I had to help my family." It's a lovely sentiment,[2] one that conjures[3] up images of Louisa May Alcott's[4]

[1]**veracity:** *truthfulness*   [2]**sentiment:** *expression of feeling*   [3]**conjures:** *summons, creates*   [4]**Louisa May Alcott:** *a nineteenth-century American author best known for the novel* Little Women

little women rushing off with baskets of food and copies of *Pilgrim's Progress*, but I do not understand why anyone would turn to my most irresponsible students in times of trouble.

The Best Friend. This heartwarming concern for others extends beyond the family to friends, as in, "My best friend was up all night and I had to (a) stay up with her in the dorm, (b) drive her to the hospital, or (c) drive to her college because (1) her boyfriend broke up with her, (2) she was throwing up blood [no one catches a cold anymore; everyone throws up blood], or (3) her grandfather/grandmother died."

At one private university where I worked as an adjunct,[5] I heard an interesting spin that incorporated the motifs[6] of both best friend and dead relative: "My best friend's mother killed herself." One has to admire the cleverness here. A mysterious woman in the prime of her life has allegedly committed suicide, and no professor can prove otherwise! And I admit I was moved, until finally I had to point out to my students that it was amazing how the simple act of my assigning a topic for a paper seemed to drive large numbers of otherwise happy and healthy middle-aged women to their deaths. I was careful to make that point during an off week, during which no deaths were reported.

The Evils of Dorm Life. These stories are usually fairly predictable; almost always feature the evil roommate or hallmate, with my student in the role of the innocent victim; and can be summed up as follows: My roommate, who is a horrible person, likes to party, and I, who am a good person, cannot concentrate on my work when he or she is partying. Variations include stories about the two people next door who were running around and crying loudly last night because (a) one of them had boyfriend/girlfriend problems; (b) one of them was throwing up blood; or (c) someone, somewhere, died. A friend of mine in graduate school had a student who claimed that his roommate attacked him with a hammer. That, in fact, was a true story: it came out in court when the bad roommate was tried for killing his grandfather.

The Evils of Technology. The computer age has revolutionized the student story, inspiring almost as many excuses as it has Internet businesses. Here are just a few electronically enhanced explanations:

- The computer wouldn't let me save my work.
- The printer wouldn't print.
- The printer wouldn't print this disk.
- The printer wouldn't give me time to proofread.
- The printer made a black line run through all my words, and I know you can't read this, but do you still want it, or wait, here take my disk. File name? I don't know what you mean.
- I swear I attached it.
- It's my roommate's computer, and she usually helps me, but she had to go to the hospital because she was throwing up blood.
- I did write to the newsgroup, but all my messages came back to me.

[5]**adjunct:** *additional instructor*   [6]**motifs:** *patterns*

4

5

6   **IDENTIFY:** Underline the sentence in which Segal summarizes stories about the "evils of dorm life."

7

• I just found out that all my other newsgroup messages came up under a diferent name. I just want you to know that its really me who wrote all those messages, you can tel which ones our mine because I didn't use the spelcheck! But it was yours truley :) Anyway, just in case you missed those messages or dont belief its my writing, I'll repeat what I sad: I thought the last movie we watched in clas was borring.

REFLECT: How "bizarre" is the excuse presented in this paragraph? Is it too bizarre to be believable?

The Totally Bizarre. I call the first story "The Pennsylvania Chain Saw Episode." A commuter student called to explain why she had missed my morning class. She had gotten up early so that she would be wide awake for class. Having a bit of extra time, she walked outside to see her neighbor, who was cutting some wood. She called out to him, and he waved back to her with the saw. Wouldn't you know it, the safety catch wasn't on or was broken, and the blade flew right out of the saw and across his lawn and over her fence and across her yard and severed a tendon in her right hand. So she was calling me from the hospital, where she was waiting for surgery. Luckily, she reassured me, she had remembered to bring her paper and a stamped envelope (in a plastic bag, to avoid bloodstains) along with her in the ambulance, and a nurse was mailing everything to me even as we spoke. 8

That wasn't her first absence. In fact, this student had missed most of the class meetings, and I had already recommended that she withdraw from the course. Now I suggested again that it might be best if she dropped the class. I didn't harp on the absences (what if even some of the story were true?). I did mention that she would need time to recuperate and that making up so much missed work might be difficult. "Oh, no," she said, "I can't drop this course. I had been planning to go on to medical school and become a surgeon, but since I won't be able to operate because of my accident, I'll have to major in English, and this course is more important than ever to me." She did come to the next class, wearing—as evidence of her recent trauma—a bedraggled[7] Ace bandage on her left hand. 9

REFLECT: How do you imagine Segal reacted when she read this final excuse?

You may be thinking that nothing could top that excuse, but in fact I have one more story, provided by the same student, who sent me a letter to explain why her final assignment would be late. While recuperating from her surgery, she had begun corresponding on the Internet with a man who lived in Germany. After a one-week, whirlwind Web romance, they had agreed to meet in Rome, to rendezvous[8] (her phrase) at the papal[9] Easter Mass. Regrettably, the time of her flight made it impossible for her to attend class, but she trusted that I—just this once—would accept late work if the pope wrote a note. 10

[7]**bedraggled:** *messy, untidy*   [8]**rendezvous:** *to meet*   [9]**papal:** *relating to the pope of the Roman Catholic Church*

CHECK YOUR COMPREHENSION . . . .

1. Which of the following would be the best alternative title for this essay?
   a. "Computer Cop-Outs"
   b. "Homework Hassles"
   c. "How to Lie Effectively"
   d. "Excuses: The Old, the New, and the Creative"

2. The main idea of this essay is that

   a. students have never-ending and often bizarre excuses for not submitting required work.

   b. teachers often downgrade late assignments.

   c. the more bizarre excuse a student gives, the less likely that the teacher can prove the student is lying.

   d. teachers should issue strong warnings and penalties to prevent students from handing in assignments late.

3. Which excuse can students expand upon to get further deadline extensions?

   a. Best friend

   b. Technology

   c. Dorm life

   d. Family

4. If you are unfamiliar with the following words, use a dictionary to look up their meanings: *bizarre* (para. 1); *revered* (2); *enhanced* (7); *severed* (8); *harp*, *trauma* (9); *recuperating*, *whirlwind* (10).

READ CRITICALLY

1. How would you describe the tone of this essay?

2. Do Segal's categories seem logical and appropriate for the examples she provides?

3. Which category seems the most developed? The least developed?

4. What gives Segal authority to write about this subject?

5. What do you suppose Segal means by the phrase "the grandmother of all excuses" in paragraph 2?

WRITE

1. Think of another category that Segal could have included in this essay. Using that category, create a topic sentence and write a paragraph that provides concrete examples of student excuses.

   ■ **TIP:** For a sample classification paragraph, see page 84.

2. Consider one of your roles in life—as an employee, child, parent, boyfriend, girlfriend, and so on. Then, brainstorm and categorize excuses for not doing something that you are supposed to do as part of that role—for example, coming to work, doing assigned chores, and so on. Next, as Segal does, write a paragraph or an essay in which you present and develop each category with examples.

39

Definition

Each essay in this chapter uses definition to get its main point across. As you read these essays, consider how they achieve the four basics of good definition that are listed below and discussed in Chapter 8 of this book.

▪▪ FOUR BASICS OF DEFINITION

1. It tells readers what is being defined.
2. It gives a clear definition.
3. It gives examples to explain the definition.
4. It gives details about the examples that readers will understand.

Mitch Albom

What's Patriotic?

Born in Trenton, New Jersey, in 1958, Mitch Albom received a bachelor's degree in sociology from Brandeis University and master's degrees in law and business from Columbia University. Before becoming a writer, he briefly worked as an amateur boxer, nightclub singer, and pianist. Albom is currently a columnist for the *Detroit Free Press*, where he writes about both sports and general-interest issues. His book *Tuesdays with Morrie* (1997), based on his friendship with a terminally ill college professor, gained incredible popularity and was made into a television movie starring Jack Lemmon and Hank Azaria. More recently, Albom has published the novels *The Five People You Meet in Heaven* (2003), and *For One More Day* (2006). In his free time, he sings and plays the keyboard with the Rock Bottom Remainders, a rock band made up of famous writers including Stephen King and Amy Tan.

"What's Patriotic?" was first published in the *Detroit Free Press* on July 4, 2005. Albom answers the question in the title by describing the actions of a young man who died for a cause that he believed in.

GUIDING QUESTION
Where in the essay does Albom begin his definition? How does he go on to develop it?

1   Her son was dead. He died serving our country.

2   At this point, you're thinking "Iraq." But this young man never wore a helmet. He never carried a gun. His name was Andrew Goodman, and he was a white college student. Forty-one years ago, he went from New York City to Mississippi after hearing the Ku Klux Klan[1] firebombed a church. He tried to help.

3   He was murdered.

4   And yet, here is what Carolyn Goodman told me a few weeks ago when I asked if she regretted her son's devotion to civil rights:

5   "When he saw what was happening down there, he said, 'What is this? We're supposed to be living in a democracy where everyone can be together.'

6   "He couldn't believe it. I said, 'It's true, Andy, things like this happen in this country, too.' And he said, 'Look, I want to go down there.'

7   "Well, we couldn't talk about it at home and then say, 'Let others do it.'... [Our family] said if you believe in something and you feel it's right, do it."

8   Goodman went to Mississippi. He was shot to death—with two other civil rights workers—by a mob of white men on a rural road. They buried the bodies in an earthen dam. Mississippi Burning.[2] Four decades later, the murder was still being tried in court.

9   But Goodman's sacrifice was clear: It was patriotism.

10   On this Fourth of July weekend, it is worth asking ourselves what exactly is a patriotic act. Many define it as fighting a war. But that is too simplistic. In fact, such thinking is dividing this nation. People who support the war in Iraq paint themselves as "patriotic"—even if they're not the ones fighting it—and label others as subversive,[3] or anti-American.

11   It is smarter, and healthier, to see patriotism in more places than a foxhole.[4] One dictionary defines it as "love, support and defense of one's country." One encyclopedia calls it as "any selfless act that directly benefits the nation."

12   Under those definitions, wouldn't teaching for low wages in the inner city be a patriotic act? Isn't the education of our least fortunate children a deed that "directly benefits the nation"? How about keeping a factory open in the United States, even though profits may be more lucrative overseas? Isn't employing your countrymen, at the expense of more riches, "love and support" of your nation? How about volunteerism—at hospitals, soup kitchens, or house-building projects? Doesn't that better the country? Or pro bono[5]

1   **REFLECT:** What is your response to Albom's story of Andrew Goodman?

_____

_____

_____

_____

11   **IDENTIFY:** Underline the dictionary definitions of *patriotism* that Albom presents here.

12   **SUMMARIZE:** What point is Albom making with these questions? Form a brief definition of *patriotism* based on the examples in this paragraph.

_____

_____

_____

_____

[1]**Ku Klux Klan:** *a long-established, secretive organization violently opposed to equal rights for African Americans*   [2]**Mississippi Burning:** *a reference to the movie* Mississippi Burning *(1988), based on the investigation of Andrew Goodman's death*   [3]**subversive:** *seeking to weaken or overthrow a government*   [4]**foxhole:** *a small pit that protects soldiers from enemy fire*   [5]**pro bono:** *from the Latin* pro bono publico *("for the public good"); in this case, without charging a fee*

■ **IDEA JOURNAL:** Why do you think citizens of the United States are so divided over the concept of patriotism?

REFLECT: How do you respond to Albom's point in paragraph 14?

work by lawyers? Or volunteer firefighting? Or driving the elderly to polling places on Election Day? Or reacting when a church is firebombed?

The point is, there are many ways to love, defend, and honor your coun- 13 try. Just sticking a flag on your porch doesn't make you patriotic. And not everyone who joins the military gets an automatic "patriot" card.

We need to stop slicing this country in half, and saying those who sup- 14 port this act or this politician are "good" Americans, and the rest are not. Sometimes "dissent[6] is the highest form of patriotism." I didn't make that up. Thomas Jefferson did.

Andrew Goodman dissented from "acceptable" behavior in Mississippi. 15 And as a result, Carolyn Goodman hasn't seen or kissed her son in 41 years. When I heard her speak so proudly of his going down there, I wondered where that spirit of 1964 went. I remember those days, where we saw something wrong and felt compelled to do more than cluck our tongues.[7]

Today the nation turns 229 years old. And one thing hasn't changed in 16 all that time. Whether it's war, racism, poverty, or scooping soup, patriotism begins not when you boast that your country is better than others, but when you do something to make it so.

[6]**dissent:** *active disagreement, particularly involving political matters*   [7]**cluck our tongues:** *make disapproving noises*

CHECK YOUR COMPREHENSION . . . .

1. Which of the following would be the best alternative title for this essay?
   a. "War: The Ultimate Act of Patriotism"
   b. "Volunteering as an Act of Patriotism"
   c. "More Than One Way to Be Patriotic"
   d. "A Civil Rights Hero"

2. The main idea of this essay is that
   a. serving in the military is the highest form of patriotism.
   b. citizens who support the war are not truly patriotic.
   c. volunteers are the most patriotic citizens.
   d. patriotic people perform many different types of acts that benefit their country.

3. What, according to Albom, is a good example of patriotism?
   a. believing one's country is better than all others.
   b. displaying an American flag on one's porch.
   c. criticizing those who don't support the war in Iraq.
   d. teaching for low wages in the inner city.

4. If you are unfamiliar with the following words, use a dictionary to look up their meanings: *regretted, devotion* (para. 4); *lucrative, volunteerism, polling* (12); *compelled* (15).

1. Why do you think that Albom opens his essay with the story of Andrew Goodman? Why does he turn to Goodman again near the end of the essay?

2. Why do you suppose Albom chose to present the examples he offers in paragraphs 13–15 in the form of questions? What effect do these questions have on you as a reader?

3. Why do you think Albom quotes Thomas Jefferson in paragraph 14?

4. Reread the essay focusing on the one-sentence paragraphs. Do you find them effective? Why or why not?

5. What would you say was Albom's purpose in writing this essay?

1. Write about your own definition of *patriotism*. In what ways is your definition similar to and different from Albom's?

   ■ **TIP:** For a sample definition paragraph, see pages 86–87

2. The Declaration of Independence refers to the rights of "liberty" and "the pursuit of happiness," concepts fundamental to the American dream. Write a paragraph or an essay defining either *liberty* or *happiness*. Like Albom, use plenty of examples and explain how your definition of the concept may differ from that of other people.

Patrice Gaines
Healing the Wounds of Crime

As a young woman, Patrice Gaines survived physical and sexual abuse and served a prison term for possession of heroin. After overcoming her drug problem, she went on to become a Pulitzer Prize–winning reporter for the *Washington Post*. She has published two books about her struggles, *Laughing in the Dark: From Colored Girl to Woman of Color, a Journey from Prison to Power* (1995) and *Moments of Grace: Meeting the Challenge to Change* (1997). She now lectures at prisons and universities around the country, working to raise public awareness about the need for judicial reform.

"Healing the Wounds of Crime" originally appeared in *The Crisis*, a publication of the National Association for the Advancement of Colored People (NAACP). In the essay, Gaines defines the concept of restorative justice, explaining why it could be more effective for some crimes than traditional punishments.

In Lincoln, Nebraska, young offenders learn how to install replacement windows in burglarized homes. They listen as victims describe the pain the burglary caused them, and they glimpse the importance of contributing in a positive way to their community. This is restorative justice.   1

Restorative justice stresses that crime harms individuals and communities rather than the state. Those affected by crime—victims, community members, and offenders—are encouraged to play a role in the justice process. Rather than just punish the offender, the goal is to repair the emotional damage done by the crime.   2

Restorative justice programs first popped up in the United States during the 1970s, most of them involving mediation[1] between victim and offender. Now there are more than 400 of these mediation programs. Restorative justice can also involve offenders performing community service or paying financial restitution,[2] generally in addition to counseling or education. Some programs are a part of the court system; others are operated by nonprofit organizations and serve clients referred by the courts.   3

Restorative justice is widely used in New Zealand, Australia, and Japan. In some parts of Africa and in Native American communities disputes are settled in traditional ways that often embody the principles of restorative justice. In researching African practices, Morris Jenkins, an assistant professor of criminal justice at the University of Toledo, found that disputes are often mediated by elders or village chiefs, rather than by officers of the law. Also, because African definitions of family typically include people who are not blood relatives, calling a family together for mediation can mean much of the community is present.   4

"This philosophy is not a new concept, but one we've forgotten," says Dale R. Landry, one of the first African Americans to champion this approach to crime. Chairman of the Criminal Justice Committee of the Tallahassee Branch of the NAACP,[3] Landry observes, "As a kid, when I broke a window next door, my grandmother took me over there to apologize. I had to find a way to pay for the window—collect bottles or mow the grass. Restorative justice is a return to the values of our grandmothers."   5

Many African Americans now view these programs as a way to reduce the disproportionate[4] number of blacks and other people of color who are incarcerated[5] in the United States. "Restorative justice is probably the biggest hope I've seen in my lifetime," says Saleem Hylton, chief of alternative detention for the D.C. Youth Services Administration.   6

Most restorative justice programs are for juvenile offenders involved in less serious crimes such as property damage and simple assault. The offenders are often directed to participate in the programs as part of a court   7

SUMMARIZE: Write your own brief definition of restorative justice.

_____

_____

_____

_____

IDENTIFY: Underline the example in this paragraph that supports the opening topic sentence.

[1]**mediation:** *the process of trying to bring people into agreement*   [2]**restitution:** *repayment*   [3]**NAACP:** *the National Association for the Advancement of Colored People, an organization promoting civil rights for African Americans*   [4]**disproportionate:** *an amount different from what is considered normal*   [5]**incarcerated:** *jailed*

sentence. One notable program was designed by Theresa McBride, Norfolk (Virginia) Juvenile Court's first restorative justice coordinator. The Norfolk program features four possible ways of connecting offenders with the victim or community:

- victim-offender mediation, in which the persons involved meet face to face;
- victim-offender impact groups, in which offenders are taught to see how their crimes affect victims;
- neighborhood groups, through which offenders do community service, which helps them learn social skills and establish personal bonds; and
- job readiness programs, in which juveniles learn new vocational skills and get help finding a job.

"Restorative justice allows people to see each other's human sides," says McBride, who notes that she can't predict which victims or offenders will agree to mediation: Victims of atrocious[6] crimes often do, but religious people sometimes don't. "More offenders turn it down than victims," she notes. Overall, most victims say yes and, according to the comment cards they fill out, are generally extremely satisfied with the program.

McBride illustrates the potential power of restorative justice through the example of a teenage driver sentenced to the Norfolk program for leaving the scene of an accident. The sixteen-year-old wrote a letter of apology to his victim, and the program helped him find a job so he could pay $859 in restitution.

But it was the meeting between the teen and his victim that was unforgettable, McBride says: "They talked, and the woman shared how what hurt her most was that this young man saw she was hurt and left her." McBride quotes the victim as saying, "I am a Christian woman, and I want you to know that before Ms. McBride contacted me I had already forgiven you." When the woman asked the teen for a hug, the embrace lasted almost half a minute. The teen later told McBride, "This was nothing I expected, and everything I needed."

Restorative justice presents a radical alternative to the prevailing punitive[7] approach to juvenile justice, and where it has been tried, it seems to be embraced by the people involved. Take Tallahassee's Southside Project, in which the community helped determine what sanctions[8] offenders should receive. This project successfully facilitated[9] 106 juvenile cases (and cited only four failed efforts). When the state didn't renew the project's funding, the outraged community responded by reincorporating[10] it as a nonprofit organization, the Leon County Community Justice Center.

"We're in a crisis in the black community," says Dale Landry of the Tallahassee NAACP. "If we don't do something to stop what is going on, we won't be a free people, especially when youths are being charged with felonies and are losing the right to vote before they become adults. It is our community that is suffering. We are the only ones who can change this—and we should."

8

9

10 **PREDICT:** Given the first sentence in this paragraph, what do you think Gaines will do in the rest of this paragraph?

_____

_____

_____

11 _____

■ **IDEA JOURNAL:** Do you agree that restorative justice programs can be a good alternative to jail time? Why or why not?

12 **REFLECT:** What does this final paragraph suggest to you about Gaines's intended audience and purpose for writing?

_____

_____

_____

---

[6]**atrocious:** *especially awful* [7]**punitive:** *based on punishment* [8]**sanctions:** *negative consequences for violating a law* [9]**facilitated:** *helped out* [10]**reincorporating:** *reopening*

. . . .

1. Which of the following would be the best alternative title for this essay?
    a. "Crime and Punishment"
    b. "Crime Never Pays"
    c. "The Importance of Jail Time for Criminals"
    d. "Restorative Justice"

2. The main idea of this essay is that
    a. a disproportionate number of African Americans are serving time in prison in the United States.
    b. restorative justice programs bring criminals together with their victims to see the human cost of their crimes.
    c. the present approach to criminal justice in the United States relies too heavily on punishment.
    d. restorative justice programs can be so expensive that many states cannot afford to fund them.

3. Gaines makes that point that
    a. restorative justice is not a new concept but one that has traditionally been a part of many cultures.
    b. restorative justice is not a suitable approach for all criminals or for all crimes.
    c. restorative justice relies heavily on punishing offenders for the crimes they commit and on seeking revenge for their victims.
    d. restorative justice is an idea that has been very controversial within the African American community.

4. If you are unfamiliar with the following words, use a dictionary to look up their meanings: *embody* (para. 4); *philosophy* (5); *alternative, detention* (6); *establish, readiness, vocational* (7); *potential* (9); *embrace* (10); *radical, prevailing, cited, outraged* (11); *felonies* (12).

. . . .

1. Gaines opens with an example drawn from an actual restorative justice program. How effective do you find this opening strategy? Did it spark your interest to keep reading?

2. What examples does Gaines use to help her define restorative justice? Is her use of examples effective? Why or why not?

3. Reread paragraph 11, underlining the topic sentence. How does Gaines support this point in the rest of the paragraph?

4. Gaines offers numerous quotations throughout the essay. How do these help her define her term? In general, do you find the quotations effective? Why or why not?

5. After reading the essay, how well do you understand the concept of restorative justice? Is Gaines's definition clear? Why or why not?

WRITE . .

1. Define a term that is fundamental to another course you are studying or have studied. Give enough examples and details to explain the term. Like Gaines, you might also include historical background or quotations from experts. (If you use quotations, be sure to document them according to your instructor's preference.)

    ■ **TIP:** For a sample definition paragraph, see pages 86–87.

2. Define a concept that is important to your beliefs or culture. Make sure to explain and give concrete examples of the term. (Your culture may include your race, ethnicity, religion, or another group of people with whom you share common ideas and customs.)

40

Comparison and Contrast

Each essay in this chapter uses comparison and contrast to get its main point across. As you read these essays, consider how they achieve the four basics of good comparison and contrast that are listed below and discussed in Chapter 8 of this book.

▪▪ FOUR BASICS OF COMPARISON/CONTRAST

1. It has subjects (usually two) that are enough alike to be usefully compared or contrasted.
2. It serves a purpose — either to help readers make a decision about two subjects or to understand them.
3. It gives several points of comparison and/or contrast.
4. It uses one of two organizations: **point-by-point** or **whole-to-whole**.

Joseph Sobran

Patriotism or Nationalism?

Joseph Sobran is a journalist known for his conservative political views. Born in 1946, Sobran earned a bachelor's degree in English from Eastern Michigan University. After spending a few years pursuing graduate studies in Shakespeare and teaching English, Sobran took a position writing for the *National Review*, where he served as a senior editor for seventeen years. He now writes columns for newspapers around the country and has published several books including *Single Issues: Essays on the Crucial Social Questions* (1983), *Alias Shakespeare: Solving the Greatest Literary Mystery of All Time* (1997), and *Hustler: The Clinton Legacy* (2000).

In "Patriotism or Nationalism?" Sobran makes important distinctions between these two outlooks.

GUIDING QUESTION
What does Sobran see as the central difference between patriotism and nationalism?

This is a season of patriotism, but also of something that is easily mistaken for patriotism: namely, nationalism. The difference is vital.[1]

G. K. Chesterton once observed that Rudyard Kipling, the great poet of British imperialism,[2] suffered from a "lack of patriotism." He explained: "He admires England, but he does not love her; for we admire things with reasons, but love them without reasons. He admires England because she is strong, not because she is English."

In the same way, many Americans admire America for being strong, not for being American. For them America has to be "the greatest country on earth" in order to be worthy of their devotion. If it were only the second-greatest, or the nineteenth-greatest, or, heaven forbid, "a third-rate power," it would be virtually worthless.

This is nationalism, not patriotism. Patriotism is like family love. You love your family just for being your family, not for being "the greatest family on earth" (whatever that might mean) or for being "better" than other families. You don't feel threatened when other people love their families the same way. On the contrary, you respect their love, and you take comfort in knowing they respect yours. You don't feel your family is enhanced by feuding with other families.

While patriotism is a form of affection, nationalism, it has often been said, is grounded in resentment and rivalry; it's often defined by its enemies and traitors, real or supposed. It is militant by nature, and its typical style is belligerent.[3] Patriotism, by contrast, is peaceful until forced to fight.

The patriot differs from the nationalist in this respect too: he can laugh at his country, the way members of a family can laugh at each other's foibles.[4] Affection takes for granted the imperfection of those it loves; the patriotic Irishman thinks Ireland is hilarious, whereas the Irish nationalist sees nothing to laugh about.

The nationalist has to prove his country is always right. He reduces his country to an idea, a perfect abstraction, rather than a mere home. He may even find the patriot's irreverent[5] humor annoying.

Patriotism is relaxed. Nationalism is rigid. The patriot may loyally defend his country even when he knows it's wrong; the nationalist has to insist that he defends his country not because it's his, but because it's right. As if he would have defended it even if he hadn't been born to it! The nationalist talks as if he just "happens," by sheer accident, to have been a native of the greatest country on earth—in contrast to, say, the pitiful Belgian or Brazilian.

Because the patriot and the nationalist often use the same words, they may not realize that they use those words in very different senses. The American patriot assumes that the nationalist loves this country with an affection

1

2

3 REFLECT: Briefly describe your own view of America.

_____

_____

_____

4

5

6 IDENTIFY: Underline the main idea of this paragraph.

7

8 SUMMARIZE: In your own words, what is Sobran saying in this paragraph?

_____

_____

_____

9

---

[1]**vital:** *of life-and-death importance*   [2]**imperialism:** *the creation of an empire through the conquering of other countries*   [3]**belligerent:** *inclined to fight*   [4]**foibles:** *minor faults*   [5]**irreverent:** *disrespectful*

like his own, failing to perceive that what the nationalist really loves is an abstraction—"national greatness," or something like that. The American nationalist, on the other hand, is apt[6] to be suspicious of the patriot, accusing him of insufficient zeal,[7] or even "anti-Americanism."

When it comes to war, the patriot realizes that the rest of the world   10
can't be turned into America, because his America is something specific and particular—the memories and traditions that can no more be transplanted than the mountains and the prairies. He seeks only contentment at home, and he is quick to compromise with an enemy. He wants his country to be just strong enough to defend itself.

But the nationalist, who identifies America with abstractions like *freedom*   11
and *democracy*, may think it's precisely America's mission to spread those abstractions around the world—to impose them by force, if necessary. In his mind, those abstractions are universal ideals, and they can never be truly "safe" until they exist, unchallenged, everywhere; the world must be made "safe for democracy" by "a war to end all wars." We still hear versions of these Wilsonian[8] themes. Any country that refuses to Americanize is "anti-American"—or a "rogue nation." For the nationalist, war is a welcome opportunity to change the world. This is a recipe for endless war.

In a time of war hysteria, the outraged patriot, feeling his country under   12
attack, may succumb[9] to the seductions of nationalism. This is the danger we face now.

[6]**apt:** *having a tendency, likely*   [7]**zeal:** *passion*   [8]**Wilsonian:** *referring to President Woodrow Wilson (1856–1924), under whom the United States entered World War I* [9]**succumb:** *give in*

SUMMARIZE: What is Sobran contrasting in paragraphs 10 and 11?

_____

_____

_____

_____

■ **IDEA JOURNAL:** Would you consider yourself a patriot or a nationalist according to Sobran's definitions? Explain why.

CHECK YOUR COMPREHENSION

1. Which of the following would be the best alternative title for this essay?
   a. "Spreading America's Values around the World"
   b. "Loving America versus Admiring America's Strength"
   c. "How to Achieve World Peace"
   d. "Finding Humor in One's Country"

2. The main idea of this essay is that
   a. patriots love America for what it is, while nationalists insist that America must be strong and always right.
   b. nationalism is better than patriotism.
   c. patriots are more likely than nationalists to go to war to defend the abstract ideals of their country.
   d. nationalists love their country just as much as patriots do, but they may find patriots to be "anti-American."

3. The purpose of Sobran's final paragraph is

   a. to explain why nationalism can sometimes be appealing.

   b. to remind readers that the country is under attack.

   c. to suggest ways in which patriots and nationalists can get along better.

   d. to warn against the danger of acting like nationalists.

4. If you are unfamiliar with the following words, use a dictionary to check their meanings: *devotion, virtually* (para. 3); *enhanced, feuding* (4); *resentment, rivalry, traitors, militant* (5); *rigid* (8); *insufficient* (9); *transplanted, contentment, compromise* (10); *abstractions, impose* (11); *hysteria, outraged, seductions* (12).

READ CRITICALLY

1. Sobran writes in his first paragraph that the difference between patriotism and nationalism is "vital." What does he mean, and why does he think so?

2. In paragraph 4, Sobran compares patriotism to "family love." How helpful do you find this comparison in terms of understanding what he means by *patriotism*?

3. Why, according to Sobran, is it a problem to think of America in terms of "abstractions like *freedom* and *democracy*" (para. 11)?

4. Does Sobran use point-by-point or whole-to-whole organization? How effective do you find this pattern here?

5. This essay was written shortly after the terrorist attacks of September 11, 2001. Given this fact, what would you say was Sobran's purpose?

WRITE

1. In a paragraph or an essay, compare and contrast two opposing viewpoints on a particular political or cultural issue—for example immigration, censorship, steroid use in professional sports, or another issue that interests you. Like Sobran, you might set up your comparison and contrast in such a way that your own position on the issue is clear.

TIP: For a sample comparison/contrast paragraph, see pages 89–90.

2. In a paragraph or an essay, compare and contrast two people you know who have differing views on an issue. This can be a political, social, religious, moral, financial, or family issue. As you plan, keep in mind that you may want to consider similarities as well as differences.

Grace Hsiang

"FOBs" versus "Twinkies": The Language of Intraracial Discrimination

Born in San Jose, California, Grace Hsiang is a student at the University of California–Irvine, pursuing a double major in international relations and literary journalism. She is a writer for *Jaded*, a student magazine that aims to "build connections and bridge gaps between people of different ethnicities and ways of thinking." Her writing has also been published in *Youth Outlook* and *Pacific News Service*.

In "'FOBs' versus 'Twinkies,'" Hsiang relates her surprise at learning that much racial or ethnic harassment occurs not between groups but within them. She describes how some Asian Americans make distinctions between people who adopt mainstream American culture and those who resist it.

GUIDING QUESTION
What does Hsiang compare and contrast in this essay? How well do you think she distinguishes the two subjects?

■ **IDEA JOURNAL:** What kinds of discrimination have you witnessed or experienced in your life?

PREDICT: Having read this paragraph, what do you expect Hsiang will go on to do in the rest of the essay?

SUMMARIZE: In your own words, what point is Hsiang making in paragraphs 3 and 4?

Today in my sociology class, the teacher asked the students to volunteer 1 our own experiences with racism or ethnic harassment. I imagined the responses would once again feature the ongoing battle between white versus minority. Instead, to my surprise, most of the students told of being discriminated against and marginalized[1] by members of their own ethnic group.

In the Asian community, the slurs[2] heard most often are not terms such 2 as "Chink" or "Jap," but rather "FOB" ("Fresh Off the Boat") or "whitewashed" (too assimilated[3]). When Asian Americans hit puberty, they seem to divide into two camps, each highly critical of the other.

Members of the first cling to their ethnic heritage. They tend to be ex- 3 clusive in their friendships, often accepting only "true Asians." They believe relationships should remain within the community, and may even opt to speak their parents' native language over English in public.

Members of the second group reject as many aspects of Asian culture as 4 possible and concentrate on being seen as American. They go out of their way to refuse to date within the community, embrace friends outside their ethnic circle, and even boast to others about how un-Asian they are.

"My coworker is Vietnamese," nineteen-year-old Carol Lieu remarked, 5 "but she will yell at you if you speak it to her and pretend that she doesn't understand."

Second-generation Asian Americans often face pressure from their par- 6 ents, who believe that the privileges we are allowed in this country make us spoiled and ungrateful. Many of us very much want to belong to our par-

[1]**marginalized:** *made to feel different and less important*   [2]**slurs:** *insults*   [3]**assimilated:** *having taken on the practices of one's adopted culture*

ents' community, but we cannot completely embody one culture when we are living in another.

The pressures we face force many of us to feel we must choose one culture over another. We can either cling to our parents' ideology,[4] or rebel against it and try to be "American."

7 IDENTIFY: Underline the two options many Asian American teenagers feel are the only ones open to them.

The problems start when those who have made one choice discriminate against those who have made the other. I've heard ethnocentric[5] Asians speak with disgust about Asians who wear Abercrombie and Fitch[6] (which is viewed as the ultimate "white" brand), or make fun of those who don't know their parents' language. This perspective even made it into the recent hit movie *Harold and Kumar Go to White Castle*. John Cho's character complains about a girl who is pursuing him despite his lack of interest: She "rambles on about her East Asian Students Club or whatever. Then I have to actually pretend that I give a s——t or she calls me a Twinkie…yellow on the outside, white on the inside."

8

"People act disappointed that I can't speak Japanese fluently," a student of Mexican and Japanese ancestry in my sociology class complained this morning. "I don't see anyone giving me credit for speaking fluent Gaelic."[7]

9

On the other side, second-generation kids who refuse to assimilate are called FOBs. The cars they drive are derided[8] as "Rice Rockets," and their pastimes and ways of dressing are stereotyped as exclusively Asian. "We live in America," one freshman political science major recalls more assimilated friends telling her. "Don't bring your culture here."

10

Not all young Asian Americans buy into the dichotomy[9] between "FOBs" and "Twinkies." Many, like me, understand the term "Asian American" in all its complexity, and embrace all sides of our identity. Rather than identifying with one culture or another, my friends and I accept both.

11 REFLECT: How do you feel about the point Hsiang makes in this paragraph?

You should identify with your heritage "because that's who you are," Ricky Kim, founder of the online journal *Evil Monito*, has said. "But don't be ignorant of the culture you grew up in—that's being ungrateful."

12 _____
_____
_____

Asian Americans grow up experiencing enough difficulties living in a predominately[10] white country with the face of a foreigner. The gap between races is wide enough without drawing lines within ethnicities and communities. We can avoid this internal discrimination simply by recognizing that we are of two cultures—and that in itself creates a new culture that should be fully celebrated.

13

---

[4]**ideology:** *set of beliefs* [5]**ethnocentric:** *believing in the superiority of one's ethnicity* [6]**Abercrombie and Fitch:** *a fashionable clothing retailer popular with young people* [7]**Gaelic:** *ancient language of Ireland* [8]**derided:** *made fun of* [9]**dichotomy:** *sharp split* [10]**predominately:** *mostly*

CHECK YOUR COMPREHENSION . . . .

1. Which of the following would be the best alternative title for this essay?

    a. "An Unsolvable Problem: Conflicts within Ethnic Groups"

    b. "Proud to Be an Asian American"

c. "White Discrimination against Asian Americans"

d. "Differing Attitudes among Asian American Teenagers"

2. The main idea of this essay is that

a. many Asian American teenagers choose to embrace one of two strongly conflicting identities.

b. many young people feel they are discriminated against by members of their own ethnic identity.

c. some Asian American teenagers tightly hold on to their ethnic heritage.

d. Asian American teenagers should embrace their new American culture as much as possible.

3. According to Hsiang,

a. Asian Americans experience little discrimination from members of other ethnic groups.

b. parents of second-generation Asian Americans generally embrace the culture of their adopted country.

c. Asian Americans should recognize the importance of both their traditional and their adopted cultures.

d. many Asian American teenagers cannot speak their parents' native language.

4. If you are unfamiliar with the following words, use a dictionary to check their meanings: *harassment*, *discriminated* (para. 1); *cling*, *exclusive*, *opt* (3); *embody* (6); *ancestry* (9); *complexity*, *embrace* (11).

READ CRITICALLY . . . .

1. Does Hsiang's essay use point-by-point or whole-to-whole organization? Do you find this organization effective? Why or why not?

2. What sorts of examples does Hsiang offer here? How well do you think these examples help her develop her essay?

3. Reread paragraphs 3 and 4, underlining the topic sentences. How effective are the topic sentences?

4. In paragraph 11, Hsiang shifts the focus of her essay. What is this shift, and what does it suggest to you about Hsiang's larger purpose for writing?

5. Given your experiences and observations, explain whether you think the kind of internal discrimination that Hsiang describes occurs within other ethnic groups.

WRITE

1. Compare and contrast the differing attitudes among two clearly defined groups within your own ethnic culture. Like Hsiang, focus on the language that members of each group use to characterize the other.

2. Think of a commonly held stereotype that you believe does not accurately reflect the reality of a particular group of people. Then, compare and contrast that stereotype with your perception of the group. As Hsiang does, use specific examples to help make your meaning clear.

■ **TIP:** For a sample comparison/contrast paragraph, see pages 89–90.

41

Cause and Effect

Each essay in this chapter uses cause and effect to get its main point across. As you read these essays, consider how they achieve the four basics of good cause and effect that are listed below and discussed in Chapter 8 of this book.

▪▪ FOUR BASICS OF CAUSE AND EFFECT

1. The main point reflects the writer's purpose: to explain causes, effects, or both.

2. If the purpose is to explain causes, it gives real causes, not just things that happened before. For example, just because you ate a hot dog before you got the flu doesn't mean the hot dog caused the flu.

3. If the purpose is to explain effects, it gives real effects, not just things that happened after. For example, getting sick wasn't the effect of eating the hot dog; it just happened after you ate the hot dog.

4. It gives readers detailed examples or explanations of the causes and/or effects.

Steve Vaught

Walking for My Life

Steve Vaught, a thirty-nine-year-old father of two, felt that being overweight had become a burden to both his physical health and his mental well-being. Eager to change his life, he decided to walk across the country, leaving California in April 2005. Although he took several breaks along the way to spend time with his family, he crossed the George Washington Bridge into New York City on May 9, 2006. He lost about a hundred pounds along the way. He is currently turning his journal entries that he wrote during the trip into a book.

Told by Vaught to Candice Reed while walking across the Arizona desert, "Walking for My Life" first appeared in the *New York Times Magazine* in July 2005. Vaught explains how a car accident caused his depression and weight gain, and how he thinks his walk will help him to change his life.

GUIDING QUESTION
What is significant about the title of this essay?

When you first tell people that you're going to walk across the country, a lot of them are like, "Wow, that takes courage just to say it." Others are like, "You'll never make it." I weigh 400 pounds, and I'm carrying an 85-pound backpack, and so far, I've gone more than 300 miles. If I was going to quit anywhere, it would be out here in the desert—because this is not fun.

I am a thirty-nine-year-old married father of two great kids. But because I am fat, I am not happy, so I am walking across the United States from just outside San Diego to New York City to lose weight and to regain my life. It isn't only about the weight; I just feel that something is bound to change during this journey.

I haven't always been overweight. I used to be in the Marine Corps. I used to be an artist and a really funny guy. I was good-looking, living the good life in California. I had friends, belonged to a car club and chased girls.

But when I was twenty-five, I killed two people in an auto accident. They got off a bus at a bad intersection, and I didn't see them. I was charged with vehicular manslaughter[1] and spent ten days in jail. I'll never stop being sorry for what happened. I feel so bad for the families. But from that moment on, my life changed forever, too. Over the years, my depression grew, I gained this weight and I haven't been able to shake it since.

My wife, April, is the younger sister of a good friend. Her family stuck by me after the accident. We built up a friendship that later turned to love, and we were married. But depression is a horrible thing. It can make you forget about the good things in your life, like family, and make you concentrate on all the bad things. I used to own a towing company and managed some other places. More recently I've worked low-paying jobs for friends, but when you weigh this much, no one wants to hire you. So a year ago we moved in with April's mom.

When I told April about my idea to walk across the country, I thought she'd say I was crazy. Instead she said, "Well, go ahead." You know, I could have gone out and had my stomach stapled,[2] but that's not me—and she knew it. And what would that have fixed? I had to go full-bore[3] on this thing.

I didn't do much planning. I looked at some maps and charted a course on smaller roads instead of freeways. The people at a hiking-gear store advised me and gave me a backpack to use. And within a few weeks, I was walking down the road. I started on April 10 with a goal of reaching New York by October. I filled my pack with food, water and a tent, but I made room for two books, *Zen and the Art of Motorcycle Maintenance* and the

SUMMARIZE: In your own words, explain why Vaught decided to make this journey.

_____

_____

_____

_____

IDENTIFY: In paragraph 4, put a check mark next to each of the effects of Vaught's car accident.

¹**vehicular manslaughter:** *accidental death of others caused by the driver of a vehicle*
²**stomach stapled:** *a surgical procedure to reduce the size of the stomach and thus help with weight loss*   ³**full-bore:** *all the way*

REFLECT: Why do you suppose people along the way have been so helpful to Vaught?

_____

_____

_____

_____

■ **IDEA JOURNAL:** What would you most like to change about your life? How might you go about making such a change?

SUMMARIZE: What is Vaught's main point in this conclusion?

_____

_____

_____

*Odyssey.*⁴ A shoe company is giving me shoes. So far I've gone through nine pairs. A group of podiatrists⁵ is giving me shoe inserts, and I call them to report how I'm feeling. I have a cellphone, and that's pretty much the only way I can contact anyone if something goes wrong.

I'm averaging about 15 miles a day, and I think I'll walk even faster as   8
the weight comes off. I was weighed in Bullhead City, Arizona, and it looks as if I'm losing about four pounds a week. If I keep up this pace, I'll be in Winslow, Arizona in mid-July—as in that Eagles song: "Well, I'm a standin' on a corner in Winslow, Arizona, an' such a fine sight to see."

People can be very mean to someone who is as overweight as I am, but so   9
far only a handful of people have been unkind. People think I'm heroic, interesting or crazy, but almost everyone I've met has been helpful. I've had people open their houses to me. Occasionally I've taken them up on it, but mainly I camp outdoors, often under bridges. The few weeks I spent on Route 66 were tough; at one point I even ran out of water. It can get really boring. If you want to know your condition mentally, spend some time alone like this.

I think about the accident a lot out here, and I know it's not rational, but   10
sometimes I think I'm going to get my karmic retribution⁶ and be run over. I know the world doesn't work like that, but when a car comes too close to me, in those two or three seconds, I think: *This is it.*

That accident changed me. I'm full of self-loathing, and I lack self-   11
esteem. But I'm learning to take care of myself and survive. If I don't make it—and I don't even want to think about that—it will be because something unexpected happens, like an injury. And then what will probably happen, after a few years, is that I'll die. You don't see a lot of 400-pound fifty-year-olds. If I died at fifty, my kids would be eighteen and thirteen. That's a horrible time to lose your father.

You've got to be out of your skull to do something like this. But I can't   12
stand the thought of my kids without a father. I want to be healthy enough, physically and mentally, to be a good dad. If this is what it takes, then it's worth it. This walk is giving me back the discipline I once had. I'll make it. And when I do get to New York, I'll know that I'm not the failure that I've thought I was for the past fifteen years. I'm a determined man—once I finally make up my mind.

⁴*Zen and the Art of Motorcycle Maintenance* and the *Odyssey: two stories of heroic journeys, the first modern and the second classical*   ⁵**podiatrists:** *foot specialists* ⁶**karmic retribution:** *in some Eastern religions, the idea that one's actions affect what happens to him or her in the future*

CHECK YOUR COMPREHENSION . . . .

1. Which of the following would be the best alternative title for this essay?
   a. "The Causes and Effects of a Car Accident"
   b. "A Unique Way to Lose Weight"
   c. "How to Plan a Cross-Country Walking Trip"
   d. "A Journey to Find My Self-Esteem"

2. The main idea of this essay is that

    a. Vaught decides to undertake an ambitious walking trip to improve his mental and physical health.

    b. Vaught will never forgive himself for the auto accident that killed two people.

    c. Vaught realizes that he must lose weight if he is to see his children grow into adulthood.

    d. Vaught is surprised by how helpful people have been to him during his walking trip.

3. One important point Vaught makes is that

    a. gaining weight is always the result of depression.

    b. depression can destroy a person's life.

    c. deciding to make a cross-country walk is something that more people should do.

    d. most people lack the courage to make a cross-country walk.

4. If you are unfamiliar with the following words, use a dictionary to look up their meanings: *rational* (para. 10); *self-loathing, self-esteem* (11).

READ CRITICALLY . .

1. What is the purpose of paragraphs 3–5? Why do you suppose Vaught decided to include this background in his story?

2. What were the effects of Vaught's depression?

3. What effects does Vaught hope that his walking trip will have on his life?

4. What do you think of Vaught's wife's reaction to his plan? What does it suggest to you about their relationship?

5. How would you describe the tone of this essay?

WRITE . .

1. Write about a decision you've made that you hope will change your life in some way. Be sure, as in this essay, to describe the outcome you hope for. (Alternatively, you may describe a decision you made that has already changed your life.)

2. Have you ever attempted something or pursued an activity that other people found unusual? Write about what you did and how people responded to your actions.

■ **TIP:** For a sample cause/effect paragraph, see pages 92–93.

Ana Veciana-Suarez and Alexandra Alter

Life Unplugged

Born in Havana, Cuba, in 1956, Veciana-Suarez and her family fled Cuba when she was six years old and eventually settled in Miami, Florida. After graduating from the University of South Florida, Veciana-Suarez went on to write for the *Miami News* and the *Palm Beach Post*. She is currently a columnist for the *Miami Herald*. Her writing has won awards from professional organizations. She has also published a novel, *The Chin Kiss King* (1997), and an essay collection, *Birthday Parties in Heaven: Thoughts on Love, Life, Grief, and Other Matters of the Heart* (2000).

Alexandra Alter was born and raised in Saudi Arabia. She received both bachelor's and master's degrees in religious studies from Columbia University in New York City, where her primary focus was Asian religions and Sanskrit language. She also earned a master's in journalism from Columbia. She currently works as a religion writer for the *Miami Herald*.

In "Life Unplugged," Veciana-Suarez and Alter examine the effects of 2005's Hurricane Wilma on residents of South Florida. Without power for their televisions and computers, people were forced to turn to old-fashioned forms of entertainment.

GUIDING QUESTION

How did the people interviewed for this article cope with conditions following Hurricane Wilma?

REFLECT: How do you respond to this point about people's dependency on technology?

B aseball enthusiast Felix "Bibe" Vasquez had planned on one thing this 1 week: watching the World Series between the Houston Astros and the Chicago White Sox on his living room TV. Two of his compatriots[1]— Cubans Orlando "El Duque" Hernandez and Jose Contreras—were expected to be on the field and "I wanted to support a piece of my homeland."

Instead, Vasquez has been cleaning up his yard and standing in line for 2 ice. To add insult to injury, the radio station that would have aired the series in Spanish has been without power. He has been struggling to follow along in English. "It's not the same as TV, no matter what they say," he laments.[2]

Like hundreds of thousands of residents in South Florida, Vasquez, of 3 Allapattah, is learning to survive without the all-mighty power of electricity and the gadgets it fuels.

It's not easy. Most of us have become so dependent on technology—for 4 everything from communication to entertainment—that Life After Wilma feels as if we're living in the Stone Age.

"It's kind of like living in the old, old times," says Mike Cedeno, fifteen, 5 of South Dade. "It was fun at the beginning, but now it's lost its punch. I can't do anything."

Anything is what a typical teenager does these days: play video games, 6 instant message friends, talk on the cellphone. Cedeno figures he spends about three hours a day on some kind of screen under normal circum-

[1]**compatriots:** *fellow countrymen, in this case Cubans*   [2]**laments:** *says with great sadness and regret*

stances. Now? "I've been playing football outside with the neighborhood kids and some board games with family friends."

Steve Levitt of Kendall says, sure, he misses TV and Web surfing, but 7 he's having a hard time giving up "eating normal food. I don't even have ice for the drinks." On the plus side: The cool weather has eased the transition into a powerless world. "It's nice enough to spend some time outside."

For Maraya Rivera, seven, a second-grader at Kenwood Elementary, the 8 most difficult part of Life After Wilma has been doing without the Nickelodeon and Disney channels. So what's a young girl to do? "I go out more now and I'm coloring. But it's bo-ring."

No doubt power outages will condemn media-addicted people to inescapable boredom, but that may not be such a bad thing, said Richard 9 Louv, author of *Last Child in the Woods: Saving Our Children from Nature-Deficit Disorder.*

In Defense of Boredom

Louv, who argues children today are cut off from the natural world and have 10 become dependent on technology for entertainment, defends boredom as the muse of creativity. "We don't have enough boredom for kids now because they're so preoccupied," he said. "Their lives are so structured. If it isn't being shuttled to a play date, it's being shuttled to an organized sport or spending time in front of the computer."

In a culture that's allergic to idle behavior, power outages can provide 11 a rare opportunity to indulge in what Louv calls "dream time"—time away from technology, work, and sports. "Dream time is a scarce commodity[3] for kids as well as adults," Louv said. "If you don't have that, the chance that you're going to have a sense of creativity or a sense of wonder is diminished."

Idle time makes entrepreneurs[4] of some young people. Marcos Medina 12 and his two neighborhood pals in Kendall made $60 each cleaning up yards. "We cleared out the big branches, cut them all up and piled them in a neat pile," he explains. After he pocketed his earnings, he shot hoops with friends and—drum rolls, please—read a book for school. His take on life without technology: "It would have been very boring 100 years ago."

Michael Lopez, his fourteen-year-old neighbor, was well prepared this 13 time around. After suffering through a few TV-less days during Hurricane Katrina's aftermath, he badgered[5] his mother to buy a small battery-powered television set. He admits this may be overkill. "I think we're too dependent on technology," Michael muses. "It does everything for us. We forget how to do things ourselves."

Young people spend some 44 hours a week plugged into the Internet, 14 television, video games, movies and print media, according to a March 2005 study by the Kaiser Family Foundation, a nonprofit group that focuses on major health care issues. The study, which looked at recreational media use among 2,000 young people ages eight to eighteen, found that daily media consumption rose by an hour in the last five years, from 7½ hours to 8½

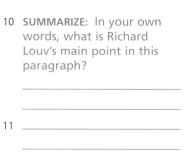

8 IDENTIFY: How would you describe the tone of the people quoted in paragraphs 5–8?

9 _____

_____

_____

_____

10 SUMMARIZE: In your own words, what is Richard Louv's main point in this paragraph?

_____

_____

11 _____

_____

14 IDENTIFY: Underline what you see as the most interesting or surprising statistics presented in this paragraph.

---

[3]**commodity:** *something useful and valued*   [4]**entrepreneurs:** *people who start up businesses*   [5]**badgered:** *talked into by asking over and over*

hours. The study also found an increase in media "multitasking": One in four young people reported surfing online while watching TV, for example.

"Monster Generator"

But it's not just young people who have become dependent on technology. 15 Their parents rely on it for work and communication. Henry Pfister of Wilton Manors in Broward bought a "monster generator" for his home to ensure that he would be able to power up both his business and home gadgets. An engineer and semiconductor salesman, he has been receiving work-related e-mail on his telephone and entertaining his neighbors in the evening. "Everybody's been coming over to eat, and we've been drinking a lot of wine," he adds jovially.[6]

Yet, for all their risks, natural disasters can provide an opportunity to 16 connect with the natural world in a profound way, author Louv said. "One of the good things about hurricanes and tornadoes, even though they do a lot of bad things, they break open your senses," he said. "The aftermath of that hurricane and all the things that come with this kind of intense weather, it seems to me this would be a great opportunity, having the television not work, having the video games not work, that may be a good thing."

It's been a good thing for Marcos Medina's mother, Terry. "Check out 17 my closets," she says with gusto.[7] "There's been a direct correlation between closet improvement and hurricanes this season."

For others, like Sonia Ramon of Miami Beach, power outages have 18 meant more family interaction. Without TV or Internet, "we walked on the beach and we hung out and we talked," she says. "There was nothing else to do, and that's probably a good thing."

[6]**jovially:** *cheerfully*   [7]**gusto:** *great enthusiasm*

PREDICT: Based on the first sentence, what do you think the authors will go on to do in this paragraph?

_____

_____

_____

_____

■ **IDEA JOURNAL:** What might you do to occupy yourself if your community lost power for an extended period of time?

CHECK YOUR COMPREHENSION . . . .

1. Which of the following would be the best alternative title for this essay?
    a. "Some Causes of Boredom among Teenagers"
    b. "Power Outage Reveals Technology Dependence"
    c. "The Dangers of Technology Addiction and What We Must Do about Them"
    d. "Preparing for a Power Outage"

2. The main idea of this essay is that
    a. before the invention of electricity, people must have been very bored.
    b. a power outage can be a good thing because it brings families together.
    c. it can be difficult but rewarding to adjust to an extended power outage.
    d. children like the excitement caused by a power outage.

3. One expert quoted in the article claims that
    a. time spent without technology can be a good thing for both children and adults.
    b. city governments need to work harder to restore power after storms.
    c. children today have a special relationship to the natural world.
    d. children today should have more structure in their lives.

4. If you are unfamiliar with the following words, use a dictionary to look up their meanings: *enthusiast* (para. 1); *condemn, inescapable* (9); *muse, preoccupied, shuttled* (10); *recreational* (14); *profound* (16); *correlation* (17).

READ CRITICALLY

1. What do you think is the writers' purpose in this essay?

2. The first two paragraphs of the essay introduce an example. Does the example make an effective opening? Why or why not?

3. What specific cause-and-effect relationships do the authors suggest here? How do they demonstrate these relationships? Do they succeed in making these relationships clear to you?

4. Note the number of paragraphs in which the writers use quotations. What is the purpose of these quotations? What is their effect?

5. Do you agree with the point made here that most Americans today are too addicted to technology? Why or why not?

WRITE

1. Write about what would happen in your family if your community faced an extended power outage. How would you occupy your time? You might discuss this question with family members and use quotations to develop your discussion.

    ■ **TIP:** For a sample cause/effect paragraph, see pages 92–93.

2. Choose a certain type of technology and write about its effects on society. Consider effects on individuals as well as effects on interactions among people. Like the authors of "Life Unplugged," you may wish to consider both positive and negative effects.

42

Argument

Each essay in this chapter uses argument to get its main point across. As you read these essays, consider how they achieve the four basics of good argument that are listed below and discussed in Chapter 8 of this book.

▪▪ FOUR BASICS OF ARGUMENT

1. It takes a strong and definite position.
2. It gives good reasons and evidence to defend the position.
3. It considers opposing positions.
4. It has energy from start to finish.

Children's Sports

David Oliver Relin
Who's Killing Kids' Sports?

Relin worries that youth sports are becoming too competitive. In "Who's Killing Kids' Sports?" from *Parade* magazine, he argues that the pressures placed on young athletes by adults can not only result in injuries and poor sportsmanship but also take all the fun out of the game.

GUIDING QUESTION
How does Relin answer the question he poses in his title?

REFLECT: How do you respond to the examples in paragraphs 1–4? Are these the types of examples that come to mind when you think of youth sports?

Two years ago, when he was still in high school, pro basketball prospect LeBron James inked an endorsement contract with Nike worth between $90 million and $100 million. Five days later, the $1 million contract Nike offered to Maryland soccer prodigy[1] Freddy Adu seemed almost ordinary, except for one detail—Freddy was just thirteen years old.

In the summer of 2003, Jeret Adair, a fifteen-year-old pitcher from Atlanta, started 64 games with his elite traveling baseball team—more than most pro players pitch in an entire season. After the ligament[2] in his elbow snapped, he had to undergo reconstructive surgery, a process once reserved for aging professional pitchers. In 2004, his doctor, James Andrews, performed similar surgery on fifty other high school pitchers.

Last March, Valerie Yianacopolus of Wakefield, Massachusetts, was sentenced to one year of probation, including fifty hours of community service, and ordered to watch a sportsmanship video after she was found guilty of assaulting an eleven-year-old boy who was cheering for the opposing team at her son's Little League game.

And in June, according to state police, Mark Downs, the coach of a youth T-ball[3] team near Uniontown, Pennsylvania, allegedly offered one of his players $25 to throw a baseball at the head of a nine-year-old disabled teammate so the injured boy wouldn't be able to play in an upcoming game. League rules mandate[4] that every healthy child play at least three innings. "The coach was very competitive," said State Trooper Thomas B. Broadwater. "He wanted to win."

A Sports Culture Run Amok[5]

Across the country, millions of children are being chewed up and spit out by a sports culture run amok. With pro scouts haunting the nation's playgrounds in search of the next LeBron or Freddy, parents and coaches are conspiring to run youth-sports leagues like incubators[6] for future professional athletes. Prepubescent athletes are experimenting with performance-enhancing drugs. Doctors are reporting sharp spikes in injuries caused by year-round specialization in a single sport at an early age. And all too often, the simple pleasure of playing sports is being buried beneath cutthroat competition.

"If I had to sum up the crisis in kids' sports," says J. Duke Albanese, Maine's former commissioner of education, "I'd do it in one word—adults."

Some adults, Albanese says, are pushing children toward unrealistic goals like college sports scholarships and pro contracts. According to National Collegiate Athletic Association (NCAA) statistics, fewer than 2 percent of high school athletes will ever receive a college athletic scholarship. Only one in 13,000 high school athletes will ever receive a paycheck from a professional team.

"There is a terrible imbalance between the needs kids have and the needs of the adults running their sports programs," says Dr. Bruce Svare, director of the National Institute for Sports Reform. "Above all, kids need to have fun. Instead, adults are providing unrealistic expectations and crushing pressure."

As a result, Svare says, at a time when an epidemic of obesity is plaguing the nation's youth, 70 percent of America's children are abandoning

IDEA JOURNAL: Do you think that youth sports are too competitive? Why or why not?

SUMMARIZE: What point does Relin make in paragraphs 8–9? What problem is he describing?

[1]**prodigy:** *a highly talented youth* [2]**ligament:** *a band of muscle tissue that connects bones* [3]**T-ball:** *a version of baseball adapted for young players in which the ball is batted from a stand rather than pitched* [4]**mandate:** *require* [5]**amok:** *wild* [6]**incubators:** *mechanisms or environments that help develop growing organisms*

organized sports by age thirteen. "The only way to reverse this crisis," Svare argues, "is to fundamentally rethink the way America's kids play organized sports."

Is Change Possible?

Many communities are trying to change the way they approach children's sports. Florida's Jupiter-Tequesta Athletic Association, facing a rash of violent behavior by sports parents, now requires them to take an online course on how to behave at their children's athletic events. School officials in Connecticut, concerned about the toll of too much focus on a single sport, instituted a statewide ban on students playing on a private travel team during the same season they play their sport in high school.   10

But no reform effort is more aggressive than that of the state of Maine, where educators, student athletes, and others have teamed up to launch a counterrevolution[7] called Sports Done Right. Led by J. Duke Albanese and Robert Cobb, dean of the University of Maine's College of Education, and funded by a federal grant secured by U.S. Senator Susan M. Collins, the project aims to radically remake Maine's youth-sports culture and provide a model that the rest of America might emulate.[8]   11

The Maine Challenge

Their first step is a sweeping campaign to dial down the kind of competition that leads many kids to drop out of sports at an early age. "I was a high school football coach—I know how badly communities want their teams to win," Albanese says. "We're not saying there's anything wrong with competition. We're saying what's appropriate at the varsity level is out of bounds in grade school and middle school. That's a time to encourage as many children as possible to play. Period."   12

To do that, the Sports Done Right team held statewide summit meetings before producing an action plan. It chose twelve school districts as the program's pilot sites, but so many other districts clamored[9] to participate that it is now under way in dozens more.   13

The program has identified core principles that it insists must be present in a healthy sports environment for kids, including good sportsmanship, discouragement of early specialization, and the assurance that teams below the varsity level make it their mission to develop the skills of every child on every team, to promote a lifelong involvement with sports.   14

Sports Done Right's second task is to attack the two problems it says are most responsible for the crisis in kids' sports—the behavior of parents and coaches.   15

Problem #1: Out-of-Control Adults

The behavior of adults has been at the center of the debate about reforming kids' sports ever since 2002, when Thomas Junta of Reading, Massachusetts, was convicted of beating Michael Costin to death during an argument at their sons' youth hockey practice. "I've watched adult civility in youth   16

PREDICT: Given the headings before paragraphs 10 and 12, what do you think Relin will go on to write about in this section?

_____

_____

_____

_____

IDENTIFY: Underline the "core principles" of a good sports program that are listed in this paragraph.

---

[7]**counterrevolution:** *an attempt to turn a situation completely around*   [8]**emulate:** *imitate*   [9]**clamored:** *called for loudly or insistently*

sports spiral downward since the early 1990s," says Doug Abrams, a law professor at the University of Missouri, who has tracked media reports of out-of-control sports parents for more than a decade. "At one time, adults who acted like lunatics were shunned[10] as outcasts. But today, they are too often tolerated."

REFLECT: To what extent do the examples in this section convince you that parents of student athletes are "out of control"?

The nearly one hundred Maine students *Parade* interviewed recited a litany[11] of incidents involving adults behaving badly, including examples of their own parents being removed from sporting events by police. Nate Chantrill, seventeen—a shot-putter and discus thrower at Edward Little High School in Auburn and a varsity football player—volunteers to coach a coed fifth-grade football team. "One game, a parent flipped out that we didn't start his daughter," Chantrill recalls. "He was screaming, using bad language and saying she's the best player out there. Parents take this stuff way too seriously. Fifth-grade football is not the Super Bowl. It's a place for your kid to learn some skills and have fun. One parent can ruin it for all the kids."   17

That's why each Sports Done Right district is holding training sessions to define out-of-bounds behavior at sporting events and requiring the parents of every student who plays to sign a compact promising to abide[12] by higher standards of sportsmanship.   18

Problem #2: Poor Coaching

Dan Campbell, who has coached Edward Little's track team to two state championships, says he sees too many of his peers pressing to win at all costs and neglecting their primary responsibility—to educate and inspire children. "One coach can destroy a kid for a lifetime," he says. "I've seen it over and over."   19

"I was at an AAU basketball game where the ref gave the coach a technical and threw him out of the game," says Doug Joerss, who was starting center on Cony High School's basketball team. "Then the coach swung at the ref. The kids ended up on the floor, getting into a huge brawl. You look up to coaches. Kids think, 'If it's OK for them to do it, it's OK for me to do it.'"   20

SUMMARIZE: According to the leaders of Sports Done Right, how can coaching quality be improved?

A campaign to improve the quality of coaching is at the center of Sports Done Right. "The most powerful mentors kids have are coaches," J. Duke Albanese says. "Coaches don't even realize the extent of their influence." He disparages[13] the national trend to offer coaches salary incentives based on their won-lost records. Instead, Sports Done Right recommends compensation based on their level of training. And each pilot school district is encouraged to send coaches to continuing-education classes in subjects like leadership and child psychology.   21

Exporting Good Sense

Educators in thirty states have requested more information from Sports Done Right. "We think a small place like Maine is a perfect place to get kids' sports culture under control," says Albanese. "And if we can do that,   22

---

[10]**shunned:** *avoided*   [11]**litany:** *a long, repetitive list*   [12]**abide:** *to comply with, act in obedience to*   [13]**disparages:** *criticizes*

maybe we can export the good sense Maine is famous for to the rest of the country."

An example of that good sense recently occurred at a Sports Done Right   23 pilot site. "An influential parent, a guy who volunteers to coach sixth-grade basketball, wanted the kids divided into an A and a B team, so he could coach just the elite kids," says Stephen Rogers, the principal of Lyman Moore Middle School. "I said we weren't going to separate the kids and discourage half of them. We were going to encourage all of our interested kids to play."

"But we won't win the championship," the parent complained.   24

"I don't really care," Rogers replied. "We're not talking about the   25 Celtics. We're talking about sixth-graders."

CHECK YOUR COMPREHENSION . . . .

1. Which of the following would be the best alternative title for this essay?
   a. "Resolving the Crisis in Children's Sports"
   b. "The Benefits of Competition in Children's Sports"
   c. "How Coaches Are Creating Problems in Children's Sports"
   d. "Why Kids Are Dropping Out of Sports Programs"

2. The main idea of this essay is that
   a. more and more children are dropping out of sports programs at an early age.
   b. the central problem in children's sports today is coaches who do not encourage intense competition.
   c. very few high school athletes will receive college athletic scholarships or play on professional teams.
   d. coaches and parents need to reduce the pressure on young athletes and lessen the focus on competition in youth sports.

3. In Relin's view, the primary role of children's coaches should be to
   a. create winning teams at all costs.
   b. create an atmosphere in which all team members enjoy participating in sports and have a chance to develop their skills.
   c. work with parents to see that only the most gifted athletes have a chance to play in children's sports.
   d. make sure that the best young athletes they work with have a chance at athletic scholarships and professional contracts.

4. If you are unfamiliar with the following words, use a dictionary to look up their meanings: *prospect, endorsement* (para. 1); *elite, reconstructive* (2); *conspiring, prepubescent* (5); *commissioner* (6); *epidemic, obesity, plaguing* (9); *radically* (11); *varsity* (12); *civility, lunatics, outcasts* (16); *compact* (18); *incentives, compensation* (21).

1. What is the purpose of the examples Relin offers in his opening four paragraphs? How do they help him make his point about children's sports today?

2. At the end of paragraph 9, Relin offers a quotation suggesting that we must "fundamentally rethink the way America's kids play organized sports." Does what he has written up to this point convince you of this? Why or why not?

3. Why do you think Relin devotes so much attention to the Sports Done Right program in Maine?

4. What is your response to Relin's use of headings? How helpful did you find them as you read?

5. How would you evaluate Relin's overall argument? How convincing do you think it would be to most coaches, parents of student athletes, and student athletes themselves?

1. Construct your own argument about children's sports. Depending on your viewpoint, you might write a response to Relin that argues against the central points he makes in his essay, you might write a letter to leaders in your community encouraging the kinds of reforms Relin advocates, or you might take a position somewhere in between. Just be sure that, like Relin's, your position is clear and developed with specific details.

■ **TIP:** For a sample argument paragraph, see page 95.

2. Write an argument about another problem that relates to young people. It could have to do with education, the media, health issues, the gap between generations, or another subject that interests you. Like Relin, be sure to establish that the problem exists and that a solution is possible.

David Brooks

Boys of Summer

David Brooks is a *New York Times* columnist, a senior editor at the *Weekly Standard*, and a contributing editor at *Newsweek* and the *Atlantic Monthly*. His books *Bobos in Paradise: The New Upper Class and How They Got There* (2000) and *On Paradise Drive: How We Live Now (and Always Have) in the Future Tense* (2004) are commentaries about American culture. Brooks was born in Toronto in 1961, and he grew up in New York City. He attended the University of Chicago, where he earned a degree in history. In addition to writing for numerous publications, Brooks has also appeared as a commentator on National Public Radio and the *NewsHour with Jim Lehrer*.

"Boys of Summer" was first published in the *New York Times* in July 2005. Brooks, having experienced it firsthand, defends the high-pressure environment of youth sports. He believes that a competitive traveling baseball team has given his son discipline, confidence, and the ability to cope with disappointment.

GUIDING QUESTION
Where does Brooks begin his specific argument for his position in this essay?

REFLECT: Do you agree that such parents' behavior is "insane"? Why, or why not?

_____

_____

_____

Every few weeks a newspaper or magazine will do an article on the professionalization[1] of youth sports. It will be about these insane parents who spend their weekends driving or flying around the country for tournaments; who spend $60 an hour so their little ones can get tutoring from former minor leaguers; who can be seen screaming on the sidelines as their children compete.

For the past seven years my family and I have been living that life. My son plays on a travel baseball team called the BCC Heat, which has meant countless nights at Comfort Inns across rural America, driving through ice storms to get to winter practices and an infinity of weekends spent sitting in blue folding chairs on the sidelines while the boys grapple[2] with the baseball gods.

Those of us involved in this sort of life can see why people object to the over-the-topness of it all: the $200 bats, the professional coaches, not to mention the sheer competitiveness of the games. There isn't a boy on this team who hasn't experienced, along with many moments of glory, crushing moments of defeat—the crucial strikeout, the game-altering error, giving up the season-ending grand slam—moments when tears come to even adolescent eyes and the parents on the sidelines sort of crumple inside at the sight of their child's pain.

PREDICT: Based on paragraph 4, what do you suppose Brooks will go on to do in the paragraphs that follow?

_____

_____

_____

_____

Yet this team, which ends one phase of its existence here in Sarasota at the A.A.U. Nationals before the boys go off to their different high school programs, has been one of the most fabulous experiences of our lives.

What the critics miss is the irrepressible[3] boyness of the kids, the rhythms of disciplined learning and exuberant[4] play. They compete practically as men in fourteen-year-old tournament baseball in the morning, and then they go off and organize their own stickball games on the beach until the sun goes down at night. They've played together as a unit for all these years—from when they were four feet tall until now, when some have passed six feet—and not a single boy has lost his love of baseball or his comrades.

IDENTIFY: Underline the words or phrases in paragraphs 6–7 that indicate the positive effects of playing competitive baseball.

They have a physical confidence about them now, which comes from knowing they have become good at something really hard. They have come into contact with coaches who commanded an authority that, frankly, surpasses that of many of their teachers; coaches who talk more directly about character, self-sacrifice, and discipline than other people in their lives or in

[1]**professionalization:** *treating amateur games with the same intensity as if they were professional* [2]**grapple:** *struggle* [3]**irrepressible:** *impossible to control* [4]**exuberant: high-spirited**

their culture. They have become members of the community of baseball, the oddballs, near-stars, and legends from Little League to the Hall of Fame, who speak a similar language and share a common attitude.

7   The attitude comes from the reality of the game, which is that the difference between a home run and a pop-up is minuscule. A pitcher dominates one day and is shelled the next. So the players, even our boys, develop this emotional resilience,[5] this fatalistic[6] ability to accept the good and the bad, which will serve them well in life.

8   The parents have a tougher time. There's almost a biological urge to want your child to be pre-eminent,[7] and to shelter him from setbacks. And yet we've developed an unarticulated[8] honor code for the team. Never lobby for playing time for your kid. Never speak ill of a teammate.

9   Human nature being what it is, everybody doesn't always live up to the code all the time, but we've become a tight community, enjoying and depending upon one another's company year after year.

10   We have seen loutish[9] coaches and parents who live through their kids' glory—the stuff of Little League cliché.[10] But that is rare. And there is no correlation between the quality of a team and the behavior of the parents. We have seen more bad sportsmanship at the local recreation level than at the national level.

11   Mostly we've seen boys experiencing the thrills of competition and the joy of being with teammates who share a common passion. We've seen boys who have matured not by being sheltered from challenges in order to protect their self esteem, but by being able to go out and play against the best. We've seen boys who were thrilled to be sixth at nationals last year and who responded to this year's lower finish by going to the hotel pool and doing back flips.

12   This team ... has turned them into remarkable young men.

[5]**resilience:** *ability to recover from misfortune*   [6]**fatalistic:** *related to the belief that humans are powerless to change the future*   [7]**pre-eminent:** *superior to all others*   [8]**unarticulated:** *unspoken*   [9]**loutish:** *rough, ill-mannered*   [10]**cliché:** *an overused expression or idea*

SUMMARIZE: Explain in your own words what Brooks is saying in this paragraph about "Little League clichés."

■ **IDEA JOURNAL:** How do you feel about competitive sports for young players? Has Brooks influenced your opinion in any way?

CHECK YOUR COMPREHENSION

1. Which of the following would be the best alternative title for this essay?
   a. "My Son, the Baseball Star"
   b. "The Joys of Coaching"
   c. "Why People Object to the Competitiveness of Youth Baseball"
   d. "The Thrill of Competition in Youth Baseball"

2. The main idea of this essay is that
   a. competitive sports are beneficial for young players.
   b. parents should take a greater interest in the sports their children participate in.
   c. people object to the competitiveness of youth sports because the games become all about the parents.
   d. it is hard for young players to experience defeat.

3. Brooks makes the point that, in his experience, bad behavior among parents and coaches is

    a. the worst problem facing youth sports.

    b. usually entertaining.

    c. rare.

    d. common.

4. If you are unfamiliar with the following words, use a dictionary to look up their meanings: *crucial, crumple* (para. 3); *comrades* (5); *surpasses* (6); *minuscule, dominates* (7); *lobby* (8); *correlation* (10).

READ CRITICALLY

1. Why does Brooks open his essay as he does? What is his point in describing the stereotype of young team players' "insane parents" as reported in the media?

2. What is the purpose of paragraph 4?

3. Where in the essay does Brooks consider opposing opinions? What kind of evidence does he offer to argue that they are not seeing the whole picture?

4. In paragraph 10, why do you suppose Brooks admits that there is some truth to critics' portrayals of coaches and parents? Do you think he goes on to counter these portrayals effectively? Why or why not?

5. Brooks repeats the phrase "we've seen boys" in all three sentences of paragraph 11. What do you suppose was the intended effect of this repetition? Do you think it achieves this effect?

WRITE

1. Think of an opinion held by many people that, based on your own experience, you think is wrong—or at least does not represent the whole picture. Then, write an argument in order to change the minds of people who hold this opinion. As Brooks does, use your own experience as evidence.

■ **TIP:** For a sample argument paragraph, see page 95.

2. Write an argument to convince readers that an activity you are familiar with is beneficial to those who participate in it. Like Brooks, describe those benefits specifically so that readers can understand them concretely.

Useful Appendices

Appendix A

Succeeding on Tests

Adam Moss
DeVry South Florida

This appendix will help you prepare for any testing situation, increasing your confidence and your chances of success.

Understand Testing Myths and Facts

One of many common myths about tests is that test makers create test questions that will trip you up. The fact is that they do not set out to do so. Here are some other myths, followed by the facts:

MYTH: Test makers pick obscure topics for reading passages to confuse you.

FACT: Test makers often avoid common topics because they don't want students who are familiar with those topics to have an unfair advantage.

MYTH: Tests often have hidden patterns, and if you can just figure out these patterns, you'll get a good score.

FACT: Tests answers rarely follow a pattern, and if they do, the pattern is often hard to figure out, and you'll waste time trying. The best strategy is good preparation.

MYTH: Some people are just good at taking tests and others are not.

FACT: Students who are good at tests are usually those who have learned to manage their anxiety and to be "test wise": They know what to find out about the test, they know how to study, and they know how to read and answer test questions. In other words, they are informed about and prepared for tests. You, too, can be a good test taker if you learn the strategies that are discussed in the pages that follow.

Understand What to Do before and during Tests

Before the Test

To do well on a test, take the time to gather information that will help you study effectively.

Ask Questions

Although your instructors won't give you the test questions in advance, most will give you general information that will help you prepare. Ask a few key questions, and write down the answers.

- What subjects are on the test, or what chapters are covered? If the test has more than one part, do you have to take all the parts or just some?
- What kinds of questions appear on the test? Question types include multiple choice, true/false, matching, short answer, and essay. Many tests combine several types of questions.
- How much time do you have for the entire test? How much time do you have for each section? Are there breaks between sections?
- Can you recommend what to review? The text? Handouts? Lecture notes? Something else?
- Is the test paper-and-pencil or computerized? If it will be paper-and-pencil, practice that format. If it will be computerized, practice that. In some cases, your teacher may be able to provide or refer you to sample tests on paper or on computer. See also the suggestions in the next section.
- What materials are you required or allowed to bring? Do you need a pen, a pencil, or both? Can you use notes or the textbook? Are you allowed to use a calculator? Do you need to bring an ID? Are you required to provide your own scratch paper?
- What score do you need to pass? If you do not pass, are you allowed to retake the test?
- For multiple-choice tests, will you be penalized for guessing answers?

Study Effectively

Once you have collected information about the test you are about to take, write out a plan of what you need to study and follow it. The following tips will also help you study effectively:

- Choose a good place to study. Find a straight-backed chair and table in the dining room or kitchen and study there, or study in the library or another quiet place with similar conditions. Be careful about studying in bed or on the sofa; you may fall asleep or lose concentration.

- Use test-specific study materials like preparation books and software, if they are available. These materials often include questions from actual tests and usually have full practice tests. Be sure to get an up-to-date book to ensure that any recent changes to the test are covered. Also, your instructor may have practice tests. Note that this textbook has sample tests at the end of each writing and grammar unit. Additionally, grammar practices are available at **<bedfordstmartins.com/ realskills>** and on a CD available with this book, *Exercise Central to Go.*

- Visit Web sites with practice tests. The following are some sites that have samples of tests required in certain states: the CUNY/ACT Basic Skills Test, **<www.lehman.cuny.edu/provost/enrollmentmgmt/ testing/act.html>**; the Florida College Basic Skills Exit Test, **<net2 .valenciacc.edu/mwhissel/Grammar/FCBSET/fcbset_wr_01c .htm>**; Florida's College Level Academic Skills Test (CLAST), **<www .dianahacker.com/writersref/add_clast.html>**; the Georgia Regents' Test, **<www2.gsu.edu/~wwwrtp/index94.htm>**; and the Texas Higher Education Assessment (THEA), **<www.thea.nesinc.com>**.

- Make up and answer your own test questions. Try to think like your instructor or the test writer.

- Take a test-preparation class if one is available. Many schools offer free or reduced-cost classes to students preparing for entrance or exit tests.

- If your test is going to be timed, try to do a sample test within a time limit. Grab an egg timer from the kitchen and set it for a time similar to that of the test.

- Use all the study aids available to you: chapter reviews, summaries, or highlighted terms in your textbook; handouts from your instructor; study guides; and so on. Also, many schools have writing centers that offer tutoring or study-skills worksheets. Check out your school's resources. Your tuition pays for these services, so you should take advantage of them.

- Learn what study strategies work best for you. Some students find that copying over their notes is effective because they are doing something active (writing) as they review the material. Other students find that reading their notes aloud helps them to remember the ideas. Still others find that drawing a concept helps them remember it.

- Study with other students in your class. By forming a study group, you can share each other's notes and ideas.

- Don't give up! Often, the key to preparing well is to study until you are sick of the material. Whatever pain you feel in studying hard will be offset by the happiness of doing well on the test.

Reduce Test Anxiety

Everyone gets test anxiety. The trick is to manage your nerves instead of letting them control you. Turn your nervousness into positive energy, which can sharpen your concentration. Also, the following tips can help:

- Study! Study! Study! No test-taking strategies or anxiety-reducing techniques can help if you do not know the material. Think about a job you do well. Why don't you get nervous when you do it, even under pressure? The answer is that you know how to do it. Similarly, if you have studied well, you will be more relaxed as you approach a test.

- Eat a light meal before the test; overeating can make you uncomfortable or sleepy. Consider including protein, which can help your brain work better. Do not consume too much caffeine or sugar, however. Be especially wary of soft drinks, because they contain both. Take a bottle of water with you if you are allowed to. Sipping water as you work will help you stay hydrated, especially during long testing periods.

- Take the test at a time that is good for you, if possible. For example, if you are a "morning person," take the test early in the day. With computerized testing, more and more schools offer flexible test schedules or individual appointments. If you can choose your testing time, do not take the test after a long day of work or if you are very tired.

- Get to the test early. Nothing is more stress-inducing than arriving late, and you might miss the valuable pre-test instructions. Also, you may not be allowed to take the test at all if you arrive too late.

- Resist the urge to discuss the test with others before you begin. Anxiety can be contagious, and others who are less prepared can make you needlessly nervous.

- Be sure to breathe deeply, in through your nose and out through your mouth. When you get nervous, your breathing becomes rapid and shallow. By controlling your breathing, you can reduce your nervousness.

- Think positive thoughts. Don't think about how terrible it will be if poor test scores keep you from getting accepted into school, advancing to the next class, or getting a new job. Instead, remind yourself of how much you know and how well prepared you are. Harness your energy and believe in yourself.

During the Test

■ **TIP:** For more tips on understanding test directions, see Chapter 2.

As the test begins, it's important to listen to any directions your instructor or test monitor gives. Resist the temptation to start flipping through the test as soon as you get it; if you're not paying attention, you might miss important instructions that aren't included in the written directions.

Also, it's important to monitor your time. Many test takers lose track of time and then complain, "I didn't have time to finish." Don't let that happen to you. After you have listened to the directions, survey the whole test, unless you are told not to do so. This way, you will know how many parts the test has, what kinds of questions are asked, and, in some cases, how many points each part or question is worth. Then, make a time budget.

Look at one student's time budget:

	MINUTES (55 TOTAL)
Part 1: 10 multiple-choice questions (2 points each)	5
Part 2: 10 fill-ins (3 points each)	10
Part 3: 2 paragraphs to edit (10 points each)	15
Part 4: 1 paragraph to write (30 points)	20
Final check of work	5

Here is a good strategy for taking this test:

1. Do items in Parts 1 and 2 that you know the answers to; don't spend time on items for which you don't know the answer immediately. (However, if you are not penalized for guessing, you may want to fill in answers; you can always change them later.)
2. Move on to Part 3, making all the edits you can and leaving at least twenty minutes for Part 4.
3. Write the paragraph for Part 4. Reread it to fix any problems you see.
4. Go back and try to answer any questions from Parts 1 and 2 that you were unsure of.
5. If you have time, do a final check of your work.

Do not work too slowly or too quickly. Spending too much time on questions can lead to "overthinking" and losing attention. You only have so much energy, so use it wisely. However, rushing is as big a problem as overthinking. Test designers sometimes make the first choice in a multiple-choice question appear correct, while the truly correct answer is presented later. This approach trips up students who don't take the time to read each question and answer carefully.

Understand How to Answer Different Types of Test Questions

The general strategies just described will help you on any test. However, it is equally important to develop strategies to attack specific types of questions. Following are some ways to approach typical kinds of questions.

Multiple Choice

- Read the directions carefully. Most tests allow only one answer choice per question, but some tests allow multiple responses.
- For each question, see if you can come up with an answer before looking at the answer choices.
- Be sure to read all answer choices. Answer A may seem correct, but B, C, or D may be a better answer.
- Use the process of elimination, ruling out those answers that you know are incorrect first. Your odds of guessing correctly will increase with every answer eliminated.
- Stick with your first choice unless you're sure it is wrong. Your initial thinking will often be correct.
- If there is no penalty for guessing, then go ahead and guess if you have to. If there is a penalty, then guess only when you can make an educated guess — that is, a guess based on having narrowed the choices.
- Many students fear the answers "all of the above" and "none of the above" for multiple-choice questions, but you can actually use them to your advantage. If you know that any single answer is correct, you can eliminate "none of the above"; likewise, if you know that any single answer is incorrect, you can eliminate "all of the above." If you know that more than one answer is correct, you can safely choose "all of the above."
- Be sure to interpret questions correctly. A question that asks "Which of the following is not true?" is actually asking "Which of the following is false?" Consider the following example.

    EXAMPLE

    Which of the following instruments does not belong in an orchestra?

    a. timpani

    b. cello

    c. electric guitar

    d. oboe

    The question is asking which instrument is *not* in an orchestra, but students who do not read carefully may miss the word *not* and choose incorrectly. The correct answer is *c*.

- Pay attention when there are two similar but opposite answers. The following question is based on a reading passage not shown here.

    EXAMPLE

    Which of the following is true based on the passage you have read?

    a. Drug abusers who enter treatment under legal pressure are as likely to benefit from it as those who enter treatment voluntarily.

b. Drug abusers who enter treatment under legal pressure are less likely to benefit from it than are those who enter treatment voluntarily.

c. Drug abusers who have committed crimes should be treated only in high-security facilities.

d. Drug abusers can overcome their addictions more easily if they get treatment in isolated facilities.

Answer options *a* and *b* say the opposite things, so one of them must be eliminated as incorrect. In this case, *a* happens to be the correct answer.

- Usually, you can eliminate two answers that say the same thing in different words. If one is true, the other must be too. Therefore, you cannot choose both of them, unless the test allows you to select more than one answer.

EXAMPLE

Upton Sinclair's novel *The Jungle* was famous for its stark view of what?

a. unsafe and filthy working conditions in the American meat-packing industry

b. the situation of poor and jobless Americans during the Great Depression

c. the events of the last days of the Vietnam War

d. working-class Americans and their plight during the Depression era

Answers *b* and *d* can clearly be eliminated because they contain the same idea. If one were to be correct, the other would automatically be correct as well. Eliminate these two choices. The correct answer is *a*.

- Keep in mind that longer and more detailed answers are often the correct ones. Test makers may put less time and effort into creating the wrong answer choices.

EXAMPLE

One role of hemoglobin in the bloodstream is to

a. fight disease.

b. bind to oxygen molecules and carry them to cells.

c. help form blood clots.

d. carry proteins to cells.

Answer choice *b* is the longest and most detailed answer, and it is the correct choice. Always be sure, however, to read every answer option, for it is not always the case that the longest one is correct.

- Be aware of absolute statements that include words like *all, always, every, everyone, never, none,* and *only.* They are rarely the correct answer. The following question is based on a reading passage not shown here.

EXAMPLE

Which of the following statements is true based on the reading passage?

a. Catheter-based infections are less treatable than other hospital infections.

b. Meticillin-resistant *Staphylococcus aureus* is always more serious than regular *Staphylococcus aureus.*

c. Meticillin-resistant *Staphylococcus aureus* is treatable, but fewer antibiotics work against it than against other staph infections.

d. Hand washing plays a small role in preventing the spread of staph infections.

Choice *b* contains the word *always,* suggesting that there are no exceptions. This is not true; therefore, *b* can be eliminated. The correct answer happens to be *c.*

True/False

- You have a 50 percent chance of guessing correctly, so it is usually wise to guess on true/false questions.
- There are usually more true answers than false answers on a test. Start with the presumption that an item is true, and then look for information that may make it false.
- If any part of a question is false, the whole question is false. Students tend to focus on just the true section.

EXAMPLE

True or false? In 1492, Christopher Columbus reached the new world with three ships: the *Nina,* the *Pinta,* and the *Santa Dominga.*

Even though most of this statement is correct, the mistake in the third name, which should read *Santa Maria,* is enough to make the whole statement false.

- Be aware that statements with absolute words like *all, always, never,* and *none* are usually false (see above).
- However, "possibility" words like *most, often, probably, some, sometimes,* and *usually* often indicate true answers.

EXAMPLE

True or false? Penguins usually live in cold climates.

Penguins do not always live in cold climates, and the word *usually* allows for these exceptions. This statement is true.

- Beware of cause-and-effect statements that may seem true at first but that show a false cause.

EXAMPLE

True or false? A koala bear is a marsupial because it eats eucalyptus leaves.

It is true that a koala is both a marsupial and eats eucalyptus leaves, but it not a marsupial *because* it eats eucalyptus leaves.

Reading Comprehension Questions

Reading comprehension questions are usually based on a paragraph (or paragraphs) that you have to read. Follow these tips for success:

- Read all the questions before reading the passage. This will help you pay attention to important points as you read.
- Understand that you must read for speed. Reading the passage is the number one time killer on tests. If you take too long to read, you will use up much of your time.
- On a related point, try to absorb whatever you can, and do not stop on any one word or idea. Chances are that the questions will not require a perfect understanding of the word(s) you are finding difficult.
- Take a leap of faith when answering reading comprehension questions. Do not agonize over a question, especially if you are fairly sure you know the right answer. In this case, take an educated guess and move on.

Essay Questions and Timed Writing Assignments

Many students think essay questions are harder than other types of questions, but they actually offer a little more flexibility because there is not just one, limited answer. There are, however, certain standards you need to follow. These are described in the following sections.

Understand the Essay Rubric

Most standardized or departmental essay tests have their own scales, called *rubrics*. Rubrics show what elements graders look for and rate in an essay answer or timed writing, and they often present the number of possible points for each element. Rubrics are often available from a college's testing center, writing center, or learning lab. Also, instructors often include scoring rubrics as part of the course syllabus.

Regardless of the particular rubric used, every essay test is graded based on similar fundamentals, described in the following chart.

Typical Rubric for an Essay Exam Answer
(what elements it may be graded on)

ELEMENT	CRITERIA FOR EVALUATION	SCORE/ COMMENTS
RELEVANCE	The essay should address the question completely and thoroughly. If there is more than one part to the question, the answer should address all parts.	Total points possible: [will vary] This essay's score:
ORGANIZATION	The essay should follow standard essay structure, with the following items: —an introduction with a clear and definite thesis statement —body paragraphs, each of which starts with a topic sentence and supports the thesis —a conclusion If a paragraph, as opposed to an essay, is called for, the paragraph should include a topic sentence followed by enough supporting sentences to back up the main point.	Total points possible: [will vary] This essay's score:
SUPPORT	The body paragraphs contain sufficient, detailed examples to support the thesis statement.	Total points possible: [will vary] This essay's score:
COHERENCE	The essay sticks to the thesis, with all support related to it. There are no detours. The writer uses transitions to move the reader smoothly from one idea to the next.	Total points possible: [will vary] This essay's score:
CONCISENESS	The essay does not repeat the same points.	Total points possible: [will vary] This essay's score:
SENTENCE STRUCTURE	The sentences are varied in length and structure; they are not all short and choppy.	Total points possible: [will vary] This essay's score:

ELEMENT	CRITERIA FOR EVALUATION	SCORE/ COMMENTS
SENTENCE GRAMMAR	The essay should not have any of the following: —fragments —run-ons or comma splices —errors in subject-verb agreement —errors in verb tense	Total points possible: [will vary] This essay's score:
CONSISTENCY	The essay should use consistent point of view and verb tense.	Total points possible: [will vary] This essay's score:
WORD CHOICE	The essay should use the right words for the intended meaning and demonstrate an understanding of formal, academic English, especially avoiding slang.	Total points possible: [will vary] This essay's score:
PUNCTUATION	The essay should use commas, periods, semicolons, question marks, and other punctuation correctly.	Total points possible: [will vary] This essay's score:
SPELLING	Most words should be spelled correctly.	Total points possible: [will vary] This essay's score:
LEGIBILITY	The essay should be readable. (If it's handwritten, the cross-outs should be neat.)	Total points possible: [will vary] This essay's score:
TOTAL SCORE:		

Understand the Question

Every writing test comes with a topic or set of topics from which you must choose. Read the topic(s) and directions carefully, and make sure you understand whether a single paragraph or a whole essay is required. Is there a minimum or maximum length for the paragraph or essay? How many words

■ **TIP:** When considering the length of your answer, be especially careful with paragraphs. Some test graders penalize short paragraphs, even if they are well written.

should it be? How much time do you have, and does that include prewriting time?

Then, read the question/topic carefully, looking for key words that tell you

- What subject to write on.
- How to write about it.
- How many parts your answer should have.

When you see the key words in the chart that follows, circle them.

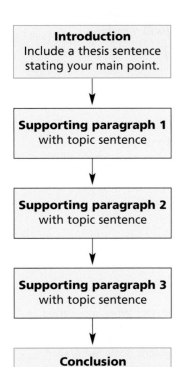

Common Key Words in Essay Exam Questions	
KEY WORD	**WHAT IT MEANS**
Analyze	Break into parts (classify) and discuss
Define	State the meaning and give examples
Describe the **stages of**	List and explain steps in a process
Discuss the **causes of**	List and explain the causes
Discuss the **effects/results of**	List and explain the effects
Discuss the **concept of**	Define and give examples
Discuss the **differences between**	Contrast and give examples
Discuss the **similarities between**	Compare and give examples
Discuss the **meaning of**	Define and give examples
Explain the **term**	Define and give examples
Follow/trace the **development of**	Give the history
Follow/trace the **process of**	Explain the sequence of steps or stages in a process
Identify	Define and give examples
Should	Argue for or against
Summarize	Give a brief overview of

Introduction
Include a thesis sentence stating your main point.

↓

Supporting paragraph 1
with topic sentence

↓

Supporting paragraph 2
with topic sentence

↓

Supporting paragraph 3
with topic sentence

↓

Conclusion

Follow Key Writing Steps, Using Standard Essay Structure

Once you understand the question or topic, plan your answer, using prewriting to get ideas and at least three major support points. (See Chapter 5.)

As you begin to write, bear in mind that your test essay, just like other essays you write, should have the parts shown in the chart on the left.

Follow this process to complete the essay:

1. Try to write a scratch outline based on your prewriting. This should include your thesis statement and at least three support points. The outline doesn't have to be in complete sentences.

2. Write an introduction, concluding with your thesis statement.

3. Write your body paragraphs. Each paragraph should begin with a topic sentence based on the support points you wrote for step 1. You should include at least three minor supporting details in each body paragraph.

4. Finish with a short concluding paragraph. It should refer back to your main point and make an observation.

5. If you have time, revise and proofread your essay, looking for any grammar errors and other issues from the rubric on pages A-10–A-11. Usually, it is acceptable to make corrections by crossing out words and neatly writing the correction above.

Sample Student Essays

Following are some sample essays written in response to a single exam topic. After each sample is an analysis of the student's work.

Here is the topic to which the writers were responding:

TOPIC: As we mature, our hobbies and interests are likely to change. In an essay of no more than five hundred words, describe how your interests have changed as you have gotten older.

A LOW-LEVEL ESSAY

I had many hobbies over the years. I use to play T-ball but I moved on to playing real Baseball. I played baseball for more than ten years finaly I became a pitcher for my High School varsity squad. The one hobby that I can think of that I use to have that I don't do anymore is riding bicycles. My friends and I cruised all over our neighborhood on our bicycles looking for trouble to get into all the time and once even running from the cops, who caught my friend Jimmy, who was the leader of our so called gang. When I got in high school, though I got another hobby which took all my time and money, my car was my new love. I got it when I was 17 and I put everything I had into it and I loved it almost as much as my girlfriend Kate. As you can see, by my senior year, my only hobbies were playing baseball for my school team and taking care of my sweet car.

> ■ **TIP:** Ask if you will be penalized for using contractions in writing for tests. Some graders won't care, but others might mark you down for this.

ANALYSIS

This response likely will not pass. It is a single paragraph, which is unacceptable given that the question requires an essay. It begins with a general thesis and has no real conclusion. The essay offers examples of hobbies but gives no supporting details about them, and it fails to clearly show the changes in interests over the years. The writer strays from the topic when discussing his gang and follows no pattern of organization. In addition, the writing lacks varied sentence structure and contains few transition words. There are a number of grammar and spelling errors, and the language is too informal for an essay.

A MID-LEVEL ESSAY

Everybody has some kind of hobby, whether it is playing piano, or skiing. People's hobbies change sometimes over the years as they change too. This is certainly true for me. I have had many hobbies over the years, and they have certainly changed.

As a child, I played T-ball, and I eventually moved on to playing real baseball. I played baseball for more than ten years; finally, I became a pitcher for my High School varsity squad, and I played during my junior and senior years. I am looking forward to pitching in the college ranks.

The one favorite hobby I used to have that I don't have anymore is riding bicycles. My friends and I cruised all over our neighborhood on our bicycles looking for trouble to get into all the time and once even running from the cops, who caught my friend Jimmy, who was the leader of our so called gang. I eventually outgrew this hobby, as it was replaced by a new more exciting vehicle.

When I got in high school, though I got another hobby which took all my time and money, my car was my new love. It is a Nissan 300 ZX, and it is black with a black interior. It had 16" rims and a sweet body kit. I got it when I was 17 and I put everything I had into it and I loved it almost as much as my girlfriend Kate.

As you can see, by my senior year, my only hobbies were playing baseball for my school team and taking care of my car. I once spent all my time riding my bicycle with my friends but I guess I've outgrown that. The one hobby that has lasted throughout my life is my love for baseball. I will probably play that until I am an old man.

ANALYSIS

This essay is better, showing a clearly identifiable introduction, body, and conclusion. There is a thesis statement that addresses the topic, but it could be more specific. The body paragraphs are generally cohesive, and the essay shows chronological (time order) development. However, the writing still strays from the topic in a few areas and could use several more transitions to help readers move smoothly from one paragraph to the next. This essay has fewer grammar and punctuation errors than the previous one, but the language is still too informal in spots. The essay's biggest problem remains a lack of supporting details about the hobbies and the changes in them over the years.

A HIGH-LEVEL ESSAY

Everybody has some kind of hobby, whether it is a craft, a musical instrument, or a sport. While some hobbies last a lifetime, many fade or appear at different times during our lives. Some people play sports as youngsters that they cannot play later in life, and some people adopt new hobbies as adults that they would never have enjoyed as a young person. This is certainly true for me. I have had many hobbies over the years, and as I have gotten older, they have changed. As I have grown, I have lost my interest in riding bicycles, gained a love for cars, and undergone some changes in the way I play baseball, the one hobby I have always enjoyed.

My earliest hobby was one that I outgrew some time during junior high school: riding bicycles with my friends. As a child, my bicycle was my only real means of independence. My friends and I rode all over our neighborhood, looking for trouble to get into and even tangling with the police on one occasion. As I got older and my friends began to get cars, this hobby faded and a new one emerged, featuring a new type of vehicle.

Working on my car is my new interest, and it is a hobby that grew from my love for my bicycle. The car is a Nissan 300 ZX, and it is black with a black interior, sixteen-inch rims, and a beautiful body kit. I got it when I was seventeen, and for the past two years, I have put all of my time and money into it. My high school friends joked that I loved it almost as much as my girlfriend, Kate. It offers me the same sense of freedom as the bicycle, and I feel the same pride in keeping it in perfect shape.

My one love that has remained throughout my life is baseball, but even that hobby has undergone some changes as I have matured. As a young child, I played T-ball and quickly grew to love it. I eventually moved on to playing real baseball and played second base and shortstop in Little League for more than ten years. After years of hard work, I became a pitcher for my high school varsity squad, and I pitched in the starting rotation for both my junior and senior years. I am looking forward to pitching in college and beginning a new stage in my baseball "career."

My hobbies have changed as I've matured, but in many ways, they have stayed the same. My first hobby, riding my bicycle, grew into my love for my car, and in many ways, the change from two wheels to four wheels reflects my growing maturity. My one lifetime hobby, baseball, has evolved as well, as I've lost the "T" and changed positions. One day, I may play another position or even another sport. However, like my love for speed, my love for competition will always define my hobbies.

ANALYSIS

This essay is clear, effective, and well-supported. All the essential elements are present, and the thesis is specific, clearly setting up the rest of the essay. The writer has described his hobbies in a clear chronological order, and he uses transitions effectively. The introduction and conclusion are reflective, and descriptions of the hobbies are detailed, using more varied and exciting language and sentence structure than the previous examples. The writing stays on topic throughout and answers the essay question thoughtfully and thoroughly.

Use *Real Skills* to Succeed on Standardized Tests

Many standardized, departmental, and state exams (like those listed on page A-3) test for the same basic skills, whether through multiple-choice questions, essay questions, or other items. Following is a list of typical skills tested, and where you can get help in *Real Skills*.

SKILL	CHAPTER IN *REAL SKILLS*
Writing/Essay Questions	
Using thesis statements and topic sentences (main ideas)	6, 8, 9
Using adequate and relevant support	6–9
Arranging ideas in a logical order	6, 8, 9
Writing unified sentences/paragraphs	7
Using effective transitions	7
Choosing appropriate words	25
Avoiding confused or misused words	26
Taking a position on an issue (typical in essay exams)	8
Reading	
Understanding readings	2 (and the Readings section of *Real Skills with Readings*)
Understanding purpose/audience	4
Identifying thesis statements and topic sentences (main ideas)	6, 8, 9
Identifying adequate and relevant support	6–9
Understanding word meaning	Appendix B
Grammar/Mechanics	
Using modifiers correctly	19
Using coordination and subordination correctly	22–23
Understanding parallel structure	24
Avoiding fragments	11
Avoiding run-ons and comma splices	12
Using standard verb forms/tenses	14–15
Avoiding inappropriate shifts in verb tense	20
Making subjects and verbs agree	13
Making pronouns and antecedents agree	17
Avoiding pronoun shifts in person	20

SKILL	CHAPTER IN *REAL SKILLS*
Maintaining clear pronoun references	17
Using proper case forms of pronouns	17
Using adjectives and adverbs correctly	18
Using standard spelling	27
Using standard punctuation	28–31
Using standard capitalization	32

Appendix B

Building Your Vocabulary

Patti Levine-Brown
Florida Community College

Building a good vocabulary helps you understand anything you read; write better papers and tests in college; communicate better with coworkers, bosses, and customers at work; and get people to see things your way in your everyday life. Students who are able to speak, write, and read effectively are likely to be successful in both their college and work careers, and in their personal lives.

There are several strategies you can use to build your vocabulary and increase your understanding of what you read.

Use Context Clues

Context clues are clues in a sentence or paragraph that suggest the meaning of a word you don't know. While reading, use the information you get from context clues to help you understand what a word means. Several of the most common context clues are described in the chart that follows.

In this chart, the words that you may not know are underlined in the "Examples" column. Read the "What It Is" column and the examples, and, using the context clues, guess the meanings of the words. The meaning is already provided for the first word.

TYPE OF CONTEXT CLUE	WHAT IT IS	EXAMPLES
DEFINITION/RESTATEMENT	A definition of the word is actually given. Definition/ restatement is often used in textbooks, particularly after a **boldfaced** or *italicized* word. Or the definition may be in parentheses. **Words that signal a definition/ restatement:** *are, defined as, is.*	• Students must avoid **plagiarism**, using someone else's work as your own. *Using someone else's work as your own* is a definition/restatement of *plagiarism*.
EXAMPLE	Giving illustrations, details, or other kinds of examples that make the meaning of a word clear. **Words that signal examples:** *for example, for instance, like, such as.*	• Misdemeanors, such as petty theft, trespassing, and vandalism, go on a person's record. The phrase *such as petty theft, trespassing, and vandalism* provides examples of *misdemeanors.* I think *misdemeanors* means _____ .
COMPARISON	Comparing something (finding similarities) to something else. **Words that signal comparisons:** *alike, as, like, similar.*	• She was as conspicuous as a bear in a church. *As* signals that the subject of the sentence, *she*, was like something: *a bear in a church.* I think *conspicuous* means _____ .
CONTRAST	Contrasting something (finding differences) with something else: The things being contrasted are opposites. **Words that signal contrasts:** *although, but, however, in contrast, not, unlike.*	• The house was once very well maintained, but now it is decrepit. The word *but* signals a contrast: The house is no longer well maintained. I think *decrepit* means _____ .

continued

TYPE OF CONTEXT CLUE	WHAT IT IS	EXAMPLES
RELATED WORDS	Finding words related to the one you don't know. If you know the meaning of the related words, you can guess the meaning of the word you don't know. **Words to look for:** *and* = similar, *because* = cause or reason, *but* = contrast, *however* = contrast.	• The teacher said my son's behavior was <u>incorrigible</u> and impossible. *And* signals that *incorrigible* is similar to *impossible.* I think *incorrigible* means _____. • Her expression is <u>dour</u>, but she is actually very funny. *But* signals that *dour* is unlike *funny.* I think *dour* means _____. • Geri's voice sounds <u>rasping</u> because she has strep throat. *Because* signals that strep throat caused Geri's voice to sound this way. Strep throat makes one's voice sound scratchy or rough. I think *rasping* means _____.

Many times, readings will have a variety of context clues that help the reader understand the author's point. While reading, make a note of any unfamiliar words. Then, see if you can figure out their meaning by using context clues. If you can't, look up the word's meaning in a dictionary.

Read the paragraph that follows, which is from an organizational communication textbook. Try to figure out the meaning of the underlined words using context clues, and write their meanings in the blanks that follow the reading. If you can't figure out the meanings of certain words, look them up in a dictionary.

The Meaning of Work

Some of the values being <u>espoused</u> today about work signal not a retreat from it but a transformation of its meaning—from <u>drudgery</u> to a source of personal significance and fulfillment. Employees want to feel that the work they do is worthwhile, not just a way to draw a paycheck. This trend is increasingly <u>pervasive</u>. For example, while white-collar workers and college students tend to view blue-collar workers as being motivated primarily by money, job security, and benefits, the most important <u>incentives</u> for workers at all levels include positive relationships with co-workers and managers. Also important are opportunities to participate in organizational decision-making. Without these major <u>determinants</u> of job satisfaction, worker stress and burnout may occur. Work has considerable social significance for Americans, who, despite increased concerns for balance, as a rule spend more time on the job than they do with their families.

> —Eric M. Eisenberg and H. L. Goodall,
> *Organizational Communication: Balancing Creativity and Constraint*

espoused: _____

drudgery: _____

pervasive: _____

incentives: _____

determinants: _____

Understand Word Parts

Knowing word parts—prefixes, suffixes, and roots—can help you break words down into smaller parts so that you can understand them.

A **prefix** is used at the beginning of a word to give the word a certain meaning.

DEFINITION: The prefix *sub* means under or below.

EXAMPLE: The patient's temperature was *subnormal*.

> [This means the temperature was lower than normal.]

DEFINITION: The prefix *hyper* means excessive or above normal.

EXAMPLE: He was in shock from the accident and began to *hyperventilate*.

> [This means he began to breathe unusually fast.]

A **suffix** is a word part at the end of a word.

DEFINITION: The suffix *ment* describes the state or quality of something.

EXAMPLE: As the drum roll started, the crowd's *excitement* was obvious.

> [*Excitement* is the state of being excited.]

DEFINITION: The suffix *ize* means to become a certain way.

EXAMPLE: Christmas has become very commercialized.

> [*Commercialize* means to become commercial.]

The **root** of a word is its base form.

DEFINITION: The root *wise* means informed or intelligent. Prefixes and suffixes added to this word change its meaning.

EXAMPLES:

wise + dom (suffix) = wisdom [The state of being wise]

un (prefix) + wise = unwise [Not wise]

DEFINITION: The root *ped* means foot (and sometimes leg).

EXAMPLES:

ped + al (suffix) = pedal [Something pushed with the foot]

centi (prefix) + pede (root with e ending) = centipede [Bug with many legs]

The following tables contain some common prefixes, suffixes, and roots. If you can't figure out the meanings of the words in the "Examples" column, look them up in a dictionary.

Prefixes

PREFIX	MEANING	EXAMPLES
a-	not	amoral
ad-	to; toward	adventure
ante-	before	anteroom
anti-	against	anti-aircraft
bi-	twice; two	biweekly; bipartisan
co-	together	cohabitate
de-	to decrease or go down	de-escalate
dis-	not; to undo	dissatisfied; dissemble
ex-	beyond; former	extend; ex-husband
hyper-	excessive	hyperactive
-il, -in, -ir	not	illiterate, insensitive, irrelevant
inter-	among; between	interstate
intra-	within, inside	intramural
mis-	not; mistaken or wrong	misinformed; mistrial
mono-	one	monotone
multi-	many, much	multiply
non-	not	nonsensical
per-	throughout	pervasive

PREFIX	MEANING	EXAMPLES
poly-	many	polymorphic
post-	after; behind	posterior
pre-	before	preview
re-	again; back	refinish; return
sub-	under, below	subordinate
super-	over, above	supersonic
tri-	three	triumvirate
un-	not	unable

Choose five prefixes and use them to make new words (not those given in the examples in the chart).

Suffixes

SUFFIX	MEANING	EXAMPLE
-able, -ible	capable of being or happening	achievable
-al	relating to	physical
-an	belonging to; from	Canadian
-ance, -ancy, -ence	state of being	dependence
-ant	state of being	defiant
-ard	one who is a certain way	coward
-dom	state of being or realm	kingdom
-ee	one who plays a certain role	trustee
-er	one who does a certain thing	speaker
-ful	full of	helpful
-fy	to make; to do	beautify; classify
-hood	a certain group or state of being	sisterhood
-ic	pertaining to; having a quality	mystic
-ier; -yer	one who does a certain thing	lawyer
-ion, -sion, -tion	a certain thing or quality	emotion
-ism	a certain thing or quality	capitalism
-ist	one who does a certain thing	physicist

continued

SUFFIX	MEANING	EXAMPLE
-ity	a certain thing or quality	minority
-ive	a certain thing or quality	captive; restive
-ize	to make something a certain way	sensitize
-less	without	helpless
-ment	a certain thing or quality	contentment
-ness	state of being	loneliness
-ology	study of	pathology
-or	one who plays a certain role	mayor
-ous	full of	famous
-phobia	fear of	claustrophobia
-ship	a certain thing or quality	seamanship
-tude	a certain thing or quality	attitude
-ward	in the direction of	eastward

Choose five suffixes and use them to make new words (not those given in the examples in the chart).

Roots

ROOT	MEANING	EXAMPLE
act	do	activate
alter	other	alternative
amor	love	amorous
ann	year	anniversary
anthrop	human	anthropological
aqua	water	aquamarine
audio	hear	auditorium
auto	self	automobile
belli; bellum	war	bellicose; antibellum
biblio	book	bibliomania
bio	life	biology
cap; capit	head	captain; capital
cardi	heart	echocardiogram
chrome	color	monochrome

ROOT	MEANING	EXAMPLE
cred	belief	credible
cycl	circle; cycle	cyclical
derm	skin	hypodermic
dict	speak	dictation
frater	brother	fraternize
geo	earth	geographical
gram; graph	write	grammar; graphic
hetero	different	heterogeneous
homo	same	homogenize
junct	join	junction
loc	place	locate
logue, log	speak; word	dialogue
mater	mother	maternal
micro	small	microcosm
mot; mov	move	motivate; movable
neo	new	neonatal
nym	name	synonym
orig	beginning	original
pater	father	paternity
path	feeling	empathy
ped; pod	foot; leg	pedestrian
photo	light	photograph
port	carry	portable
quer; ques; quiz	to ask	query; question; quizzical
rupt	break	disrupt
scop	view	microscope
scrib; script	write	scribble; manuscript
spect	look	inspect
tact	touch	tactile
terra	earth	terrarium
vac	empty	vacuum
ver	truth	verdict
voc	voice	vocal

Choose five roots and use them to make new words (not those given in the examples in the chart).

Use Vocabulary Resources

Another way to improve your vocabulary is to use a dictionary, a thesaurus, and glossaries to expand your knowledge of words.

A Dictionary

A dictionary includes word meanings, pronunciations, and more. Here is a sample entry.

Spelling and syllabication   Pronunciation   Part of speech   Definitions

pla • ce • bo (pluh-SEE-bo) *n.* **1a.** A substance containing no medication that is given to reinforce a patient's expectation to get well. **1b.** An inactive substance used as a control in an experiment. **2.** Something of no medical value that is used to reassure.

■ **TIP:** For more on dictionaries, see Chapter 25.

When using a dictionary to look up a word, whether you find the word in your reading or want to use it in your writing, carefully consider the context: the general meaning of the sentence or passage. The same word can have quite a different meaning depending on the context.

Glossaries

A **glossary** is a list of difficult or technical terms with definitions. Not all books have glossaries, but textbooks and technical manuals often do. Usually, glossaries appear at the end of books or at the end of chapters or units.

A Thesaurus

While trying to express your thoughts or feelings in writing, have you ever felt you were using the same words over and over again? Next time this happens, try using a **thesaurus**, a book of synonyms, words that have the same or similar meanings. For example, the word *efficient* has several synonyms: *proficient, professional, competent, resourceful, able, well-organized, economical, cost-effective, useful,* and *helpful.*

However, make sure you choose the right synonyms for the context of your writing, and avoid using a thesaurus just for the sake of picking out big or fancy words. Such words can make your writing sound odd or overly complicated.

Use Vocabulary Study Tools

To continue building your vocabulary, consider using a few study tools either alone or in a group.

Vocabulary Cards

Making your own vocabulary cards can help you learn and remember new words.

Image Cards

To make vocabulary cards with images, follow these steps:

- Print the word you do not know on the front of an index card (use one card for each word).
- Turn the card over and write the definition of that word on the back.
- Write a sentence using the word.
- Think of an image or symbol you can draw that will help you connect the word and its definition. Draw this next to the definition, using colored markers if you like. The idea is to come up with something that will trigger your memory in terms of the word's definition.

Mnemonic Cards

A **mnemonic** is a system of remembering things. For example, a common mnemonic for remembering how many days each month has is the saying "Thirty days hath September, April, June, and November..." Another example is the spelling rhyme "*I* before *e* except after *c* or when sounded like *a* as in *neighbor* or *weigh*." To make mnemonic cards, follow these steps:

- Print the word you do not know on the front of an index card (use one card for each word).
- Turn the card over and write the definition of that word on the back.
- Write a sentence using the word.
- Carefully examine the word and definition and try to come up with an acronym (a set of letters that stands for a group of words) that will help you remember the word and its definition. For example, the acronym used to remember the names of the Great Lakes is HOMES (Huron, Ontario, Michigan, Erie, Superior). An acronym used in this book to help you remember the coordinating conjunctions is FANBOYS (*for, and, nor, but, or, yet, so*). The idea is to come up with an idea that will trigger your memory in terms of the word's definition.

Whether you use image or mnemonic cards, keep the cards with you and refer to them between classes or at other free times. The more you refer to the cards, the better your chances of really learning and understanding the words and their definitions.

Vocabulary Games

Word games are a fun way to build your vocabulary. Here is one game you might try.

TEAMWORDS

- Your teacher will have created index cards with vocabulary words. These should be stacked and placed at the front of the room.
- Pick a student monitor.
- The rest of you should break into two teams, perhaps by counting off by twos.
- Each team should pick a captain.
- The monitor should take the index cards, pick one, and call the word out to the first team.
- The team will confer and give the team captain the meaning of the word.
- The team captain will then give the meaning to the monitor, who will determine whether the meaning is correct, checking a dictionary if necessary.
- If the meaning is correct, the team receives a point.
- The monitor will then select a word to give to the second team, and that team will go through the same procedure as the first team.
- If at any time a team does not know the definition of a word given to them, or if the captain gives an incorrect meaning, the opposing team is given a chance to answer.
- If the opposing team gives the correct meaning, this team gets the point.
- Keep playing until the monitor has used the whole stack of cards.

Look and Listen

Finally, be aware of words outside of the college classroom. When you're listening to the radio, watching television, or reading newspapers or online sites, make a note of words you don't know. If you can't understand them from the context in which they're used, look them up in a dictionary. Even if you do understand the general meaning from the context, add the word to a personal vocabulary list and try to use it in speech or in writing.

Appendix C

Getting a Job

This appendix will lead you through the steps of getting a good job—one that uses your skills and leads to a satisfying career.

Do Some Research

Before applying for specific jobs, find out about various kinds of jobs that are suited to your interests and skills. Many Web sites describe jobs, the skills they require, and typical salary ranges. For example, you can go to Monster.com or Jobsearch.com and browse for kinds of jobs you might be interested in.

Look for Internships

Many students find that an internship gives them good experience in a particular kind of job as well as connections within a company they might be interested in working in after graduation. Some internships are paid, while others are not; make sure you know whether an internship you are interested in is paying or nonpaying. Quite often, internships can lead to job offers, so even if an internship pays little or nothing, it may be worth taking. Many Web sites provide information about internships, including Internjobs.com and Collegeboard.com. (When you get to the College Board site, type "internships" into the search box.)

Find Out about Specific Companies

If you are interested in working for a specific company or have an interview there, get as much information as you can about the company by visiting its Web site or by calling and asking for an annual report or other information that is available to the public.

Prepare a Résumé

To apply for a job, you will need a good résumé. A model is included here, but you can also get help from two other sources: your college's placement office and a variety of Web sites. Do a Web search using the words "how to write a résumé," and many sites will appear. Your résumé should be simple and professional: Its purpose is to provide information, not to entertain the person to whom you send it. Try to keep your résumé to one page.

Following is an example of a résumé, with annotations indicating what each section is and what it should do. When you have prepared a résumé, make sure that you proofread it carefully; it is important that your résumé be error-free.

SAMPLE RÉSUMÉ

PAT GEMELLI
12856 Glover Street
Manchester, NH 03110
603-441-2248
pgemelli@hotmail.com

List full name and current contact information, centered.

OBJECTIVE	To work as a city probation officer in New Hampshire

Describe what job you are seeking and/or what skills you want to use. You can tailor the objective to different jobs you are applying for.

EDUCATION	Mill City College

Manchester, NH
Major: Criminal justice
B.S. degree to be granted in May 2006
Grade point average: 3.4
Courses taken included:
 Criminal Law
 Criminal Investigation
 Technology in Criminal Justice
 Evidence and Court Procedures
 Abnormal Psychology
 Sociology of the Family

Include college, major, degree, graduation date, and courses related to the position sought. You may also wish to include your grade point average.

EXPERIENCE

Youth Leader
September 1996 to present
Grace Unity Church, Manchester, NH
• Teach a variety of courses to high school students
• Lead regional seminars for students
• Perform outreach activities
• Counsel teens
• Work with families of teens to understand issues
• Designed a community service program

List relevant jobs and internships with dates and skills, putting the most recent experience first.

Internship
September 2005 to April 2006
New Hampshire Corrections Institution, Nashua, NH
• Worked in the warden's office, providing administrative assistance to warden
• Attended meetings with warden and prison guards
• Attended and took minutes for meetings with assistant warden and county parole officers
• Observed meetings between parole officer and one of his assigned parolees
• Worked as ad hoc member of prisoners' rights committee

Include any skills that are a plus, especially for a specific position.

SPECIAL SKILLS

Fluent in Spanish and Portuguese. Experienced with most PC and Macintosh computer programs and applications.

List anything that shows you are an active and involved person. Activities can distinguish you from other applicants, so do not be falsely modest.

OTHER ACTIVITIES

Volunteer, King City Soup Kitchen
Player, Gael's Adult Soccer League
Soccer coach, middle school intramural program

REFERENCES

Available on request

References are people who can speak favorably about your suitability for the job. Before you give anyone's name as a reference, be sure to ask the person if you may do so.

CHECKLIST: HOW TO WRITE A RÉSUMÉ

STEPS	HOW TO DO THE STEPS
☐ **Include your name and contact information.**	• Write your full name (no nicknames), address, telephone number, and e-mail address, centered, at the top of the page.
☐ **State your career objective, briefly and specifically.**	• Write an objective that is concrete (not, for instance, "to find an interesting position"). • Be prepared to modify your objective slightly to fit various positions you apply for or are interested in.
☐ **Describe your education.**	• List college(s), degree(s) received, and graduation date(s) (or date(s) when degrees will be awarded). • List any college honors (dean's list and so on). • If you have a good grade point average, include it. • List courses that are relevant to the position you are interested in.
☐ **Describe your experience.**	• Start with your most recent position. • List your title, the company name and location, and the dates of employment. • List your responsibilities and achievements, using active verbs (for example, **organized** *a youth retreat*). • Include both paid and unpaid positions, including internships.
☐ **Describe your special skills.**	• Include languages, computer skills, and other skills that could be relevant to the position and that can be demonstrated (for example, *Strong organizational skills: developed a mentoring program; Strong teamwork skills: served as part of team that . . .*).
☐ **Describe other activities or awards.**	• Include any activities that show you are an involved person, such as volunteer or community service activities, sports, and relevant hobbies.
☐ **Provide a list of references or state "References available on request."**	• Select people who can speak favorably about your qualifications. • Contact references before listing them.
☐ **Revise and edit your résumé.**	• Add other skills and experiences that will distinguish you from others. • Make sure there are no errors in spelling, grammar, or punctuation. • Ask someone else to read the résumé.

STEPS	HOW TO DO THE STEPS
☐ **Format and print your résumé.**	• Use a typeface that is simple and easy to read (not fancy), like Times New Roman. • Leave enough space between items so that the information is easy to read, not cramped. • Use **bold** to highlight key information. • Use a high-quality printer to print your résumé, and use high-quality paper that is white or a light, neutral color. The résumé must look professional.

A FINAL WORD: Never make up information for a résumé. Employers often check facts on résumés, and being caught in a lie will automatically eliminate you from consideration for a job.

Write a Cover Letter

When you send your résumé, include a cover letter. Although your résumé provides crucial information about your experience and skills, your cover letter is the first item a prospective employer sees, so it is an important piece of writing. It should be direct, telling the reader why you are interested in the job and what you have to offer. It should also be confident and enthusiastic, but professional, and written in formal English. For example, express your strong interest in the position and the organization, but avoid informal language such as "Working for your company would be awesome."

Following is an example of a cover letter, with annotations indicating what each section does. When possible, try to address your letter to a specific person. You may have to call the company to get the appropriate contact name. Verify that you have the correct spelling.

SAMPLE COVER LETTER

Full name and current contact information, centered, using same format as for résumé

PAT GEMELLI

12856 Glover Street

Manchester, NH 03110

603-441-2248

pgemelli@hotmail.com

Date of letter

May 4, 2006

Full name, position, department, and address of person being contacted

Richard Willey, Director
Human Resources
New Hampshire Department of Corrections
State Office Park West
8900 River Street
Concord, NH 03665

Dear Mr./Ms. and last name followed by a colon (:)

Dear Mr. Willey:

States position writer is interested in

I am interested in a position as a probation officer in New Hampshire, specifically in Nashua, Manchester, or Concord, our major cities.

Shows knowledge of organization

Has confident and enthusiastic tone

Having grown up in Manchester, I am committed to contributing to our state, specifically in efforts to both ensure the protection and safety of our residents and to rehabilitate convicts. My internship at the New Hampshire Corrections Institution in Nashua allowed me to participate in some of the very innovative and successful initiatives launched by the Department of Corrections. I believe strongly that my experience and education make me uniquely qualified for the position of New Hampshire probation officer, and I would be proud to serve in such a forward-looking organization.

Summarizes education and shows extra effort

This month, I will receive a bachelor of science degree from Mill City College, having maintained a 3.4 grade point average. I took advantage of the many courses offered by the college by taking an extra course load each semester. Doing so allowed me to fulfill all the criminal justice requirements and also to learn about areas that could benefit my work as a probation officer, such as psychology and sociology.

Cites specific skills; expresses enthusiasm

My experiences as a youth counselor and as an intern at NHCI, Nashua, have developed my abilities to communicate with others; to observe the blend of authority, objectivity, and compassion that make a good law enforcement officer; and to understand the role of sound teamwork in criminal justice. I am eager to further advance these skills and learn from others by working with professionals at the New Hampshire Department of Corrections.

Ends confidently and thanks the addressee

I have enclosed a résumé that provides more details about my education and experience. I believe I will be a good probation officer because I am motivated and certain of my career choice. I hope you will consider me as a candidate and look forward to speaking with you. Thank you for your consideration.

Sincerely,

Pat Gemelli

Pat Gemelli

CHECKLIST: HOW TO WRITE A COVER LETTER

STEPS	HOW TO DO THE STEPS (IF APPLICABLE)
☐ **Include your identifying information.**	• Put your name, address, telephone number, and e-mail address in a letterhead that is centered at the top of the page.
☐ **Write the date and address of your letter.**	• Write the date and skip two or three spaces. • Write the name, title, and address of the person you are writing to. Skip two more spaces.
☐ **Write your salutation.**	• Write Dear Mr./Ms./Mrs./Dr. and the person's last name. Put a colon (:) after the name. Skip two spaces.
☐ **Write the body of your letter.**	• In the first paragraph, state the position you are interested in. • In the body paragraphs, briefly but specifically state your qualifications, skills, and strengths. • In your final paragraph(s), restate your interest in the position, your enthusiasm, and your confidence in your ability to succeed in the position; indicate how the prospective employer can contact you; and thank him or her for considering you. Skip two spaces.
☐ **Write your closing.**	• Write *Sincerely* followed by a comma (,). Skip four spaces. • Type your name. • Sign your name, neatly, above your typed name.
☐ **Revise your letter.**	• Reread what you have written, and add anything that would strengthen your appeal to the prospective employer.
☐ **Edit your letter.**	• Carefully edit your letter, making sure that it has no errors in spelling, grammar, or punctuation.
☐ **Format and print your letter.**	• Make sure that the letter follows the standard format for a letter of application and includes all of the elements. • Use a high-quality printer and paper, or go to a copy shop to print your letter. It is important that it look clean, crisp, and professional. • Make a copy of your letter for your files.

Prepare for an Interview

When you are called in for an interview, be prepared. If you haven't already gone to the company's Web site, do so now, and learn as much as you can about the organization, its products and services, and its culture. (For example, is it a casual or formal workplace?) Search your library's holdings to see if the company has been written about in magazines or professional journals.

Rehearse Interview Questions

As confident as you may feel about your qualifications for a position, you should practice your answers to some typical interview questions so that you will respond to them well. As you form answers, always keep an interviewer in mind, remembering that he or she is looking for qualities that will benefit the company and fit the position for which you are applying. The following are ten common interview questions to which you should have answers:

1. *How would you describe yourself?*
   The interviewer wants to know about traits that would make you a valuable employee. Consider adjectives that describe positive traits, such as *honest, hardworking, intelligent, flexible, creative, motivated, good listener,* and so on.

2. *How would a friend describe you?*
   This question tries to get at your character. It gives you an opportunity to say lots of good things about yourself without feeling as if you're bragging. Take advantage of the opportunity, and use positive descriptions, like *born leader, great sense of humor, dedicated.*

3. *What are your greatest strengths/weaknesses?*
   When asked this question, you really want to describe your weaknesses as the flip side of a strength. So, for example, if you give *hardworking* as a strength, you might then give *sometimes a little driven* as a weakness. It's not really a weakness because it tells the interviewer that you push yourself.
   Here are some other examples of strengths that can also be (good) weaknesses:

STRENGTH		WEAKNESS
Motivated	→	Don't understand when others are negative about everything
Organized	→	Sometimes spend too much time helping others who are not organized
Hardworking	→	Impatient with slackers
Creative	→	Sometimes impatient with those who hold on to old ways of doing things for no good reason
Good communicator	→	Sometimes spend too much time trying to understand those who are poor communicators

4. ***Describe a problem that you solved.***
   The problem doesn't have to be a huge one, just one where you looked at a challenging situation and figured out how to deal with it. If you can think of a situation that involved other people, all the better. An example could be consulting with coworkers to figure out a better filing system for a disorganized office.

5. ***Name someone you admire and tell why.***
   Because you are in a business interview, avoid controversial political or religious figures. You might choose someone who has helped others, showed bravery, or changed the world in some way. If there is a member of your family you particularly admire, you can name that person, but make sure to describe concretely what that person did to make you admire him or her.

6. ***Name an accomplishment that you are proud of.***
   This doesn't have to be a minor miracle, just something you did that made you stand out. It could be achieving an athletic or academic success, committing to and sticking with something (like learning to play an instrument), or helping someone else in need. The point is to prove that you have traits that will be valuable in the workplace (stamina, commitment, ability to work well with others, and so on).

7. ***Describe your ideal job.***
   Obviously, you want to describe some elements of the job you're applying for. If you have particular skills that fit the job, mention how you would welcome an opportunity to use those skills. Also, you might say you're looking for a job that presents a challenge, an opportunity to learn, and an opportunity for advancement. Avoid mentioning things like a good salary, a nice office, good vacation benefits, and the ability to dress casually. Instead, stick to things that demonstrate your interest in doing a good job.

8. ***Why do you want to work here?***
   Mention some of the positive things you have learned about the company from your research. For example, you might point to the company's high-quality products, involvement in the community, or size (small enough or large enough to allow employees to learn and grow). Be as specific as you can, but keep your comments at a professional level, and avoid saying things like "It's close to my house."

9. ***Why should we hire you?***
   Many people have trouble with this question, but it's an important one, and it gives you a wonderful opportunity to sell yourself. Telling a prospective employer why you would be an asset to the company isn't bragging; it's a good way to reinforce your earlier descriptions of your strengths. Be as specific as possible, listing specific skills you have that will benefit the company. Also, re-emphasize your good qualities—for instance, your motivation, your willingness to work hard and solve problems, and so on. Know in advance what you will say to sell yourself.

10. ***Where do you want to be in five years?***

If you have researched the company, state a job that is a level or two above the one you're applying for. Be reasonable but optimistic. If you're applying for an entry-level job, it would be unrealistic to say, "I'd like to be president of the company." However, it would be realistic to say, "I'd like to be entering a management position." Then, say you hope that in five years you will have learned a good deal and will be able to apply your skills in a job that will challenge you and benefit the company. Again, avoid mentioning salary.

Have a Few Questions to Ask

At some point toward the end of the interview, the interviewer will probably ask if you have any questions. Based on what you know about the company or the general industry, have one or two questions to ask, such as "I read on the Web site that the company is planning to expand overseas. That's exciting. Can you tell me a little more about that?" or "What do you like best about working here?" Asking a couple of questions shows your interest and initiative.

As important as money is, salary isn't usually discussed in a first interview. The interviewer might ask you to specify an ideal salary range, and if you've done your homework about the job and comparable positions, you should be able to answer this question. If the interviewer doesn't mention salary and you haven't been able to determine a salary range for the position, you might ask what a general range for the position is.

Some Interview Tips

- Leave plenty of time to get to the interview, and try to arrive a few minutes early. If you have a morning interview, and you have trouble getting up early, ask a friend to call you. Do whatever you need to do to get to an interview on time; if you arrive late, you have already created a bad impression.

- Dress simply and professionally: no flip-flops, T-shirts, shorts, jeans, or too-short skirts. As a general rule, men should wear a light-colored, unwrinkled shirt, unwrinkled dress pants, and dress shoes with socks. If people in the type of job you're interested tend to dress conservatively, you should wear a jacket and tie as well. When in doubt, it's better to dress up than dress down. Women should wear an unwrinkled blouse, dress pants or a skirt, hose, and either flat shoes or shoes with modest heels. Avoid overly bright colors, elaborate hairdos, and lots of big jewelry. Both men and women should avoid heavy colognes. *Neat* and *conservative* are the code words for interview attire: You want to be remembered for your qualifications, not your unique look.

- Do not drink, eat, or chew gum while waiting for, or taking part in, an interview.

- When you meet the interviewer, stand up straight, walk toward him or her, and shake his or her hand. Your handshake should be firm, not wimpy, but not so firm that the person's hand is crushed.

- Look the interviewer in the eye, both during the greeting and as you respond to questions.

- During the interview, sit up straight; slouching is often perceived as sloppy—a characteristic that will turn off prospective employers. Try to create an impression of confidence and interest.

- When you speak, speak clearly while looking at the interviewer. Mumbling and avoiding eye contact give negative impressions that can wipe out all of your good qualifications.

- When the interview is at an end, thank the interviewer for his or her time, express your interest, and ask what the time frame for making a decision is. Ask whether there is any additional information that would help bolster your candidacy.

- Shake the interviewer's hand again, and walk away with good posture.

Follow Up after the Interview

Within twenty-four hours of your interview, write a thank-you note to the person or people with whom you spoke. Your sending such a note shows the interviewer(s) that you have the ability to follow up, a characteristic that is essential in business.

In the thank-you note, take the opportunity to restate your interest and enthusiasm, to mention your good fit with the position, and to say you look forward to joining the company. Depending on the culture of the organization, a typed letter, handwritten note, or e-mail can be appropriate. In any case, use formal English, and proofread what you write carefully. Make sure you spell the name of the interviewer(s) correctly.

PAT GEMELLI

12856 Glover Street

Manchester, NH 03110

603-441-2248

pgemelli@hotmail.com

May 19, 2006

Richard Willey, Director
Human Resources
New Hampshire Department of Corrections
State Office Park West
8900 River Street
Concord, NH 03665

Dear Mr. Willey:

Thank you for taking the time to talk with me about the position of probation officer for the New Hampshire Department of Corrections. Our interview confirmed my strong interest in the position, where I believe I could both learn and contribute a great deal.

I realize you have many responsibilities, and I do appreciate your time. If I can provide any further information, please contact me. I look forward to the opportunity to join the organization.

Sincerely,

Pat Gemelli

Pat Gemelli

If you have not heard from the company by the time a decision about the position was expected, write another note or e-mail, again stating your interest in the position and inquiring about the status of the decision. Once again, thank the interviewer for his or her time, and express your hope that you will become part of the organization.

Appendix D

Useful Forms

This appendix includes forms that you can use to generate ideas for, and plan, paragraphs and essays. First are a few blank diagrams that you can use if you want to try mapping/clustering as an idea-generating strategy. (See Chapter 5 for more details.) Next are outline forms for each type of essay covered in Chapter 8. Finally, we provide an essay outline form. (See Chapter 9 for more details.)

Mapping/Clustering Worksheet

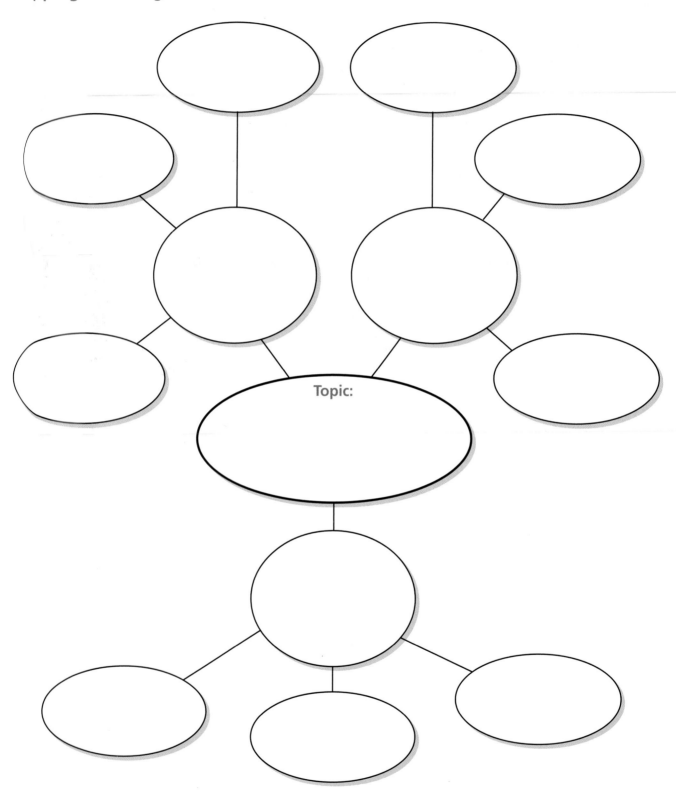

Mapping/Clustering Worksheet

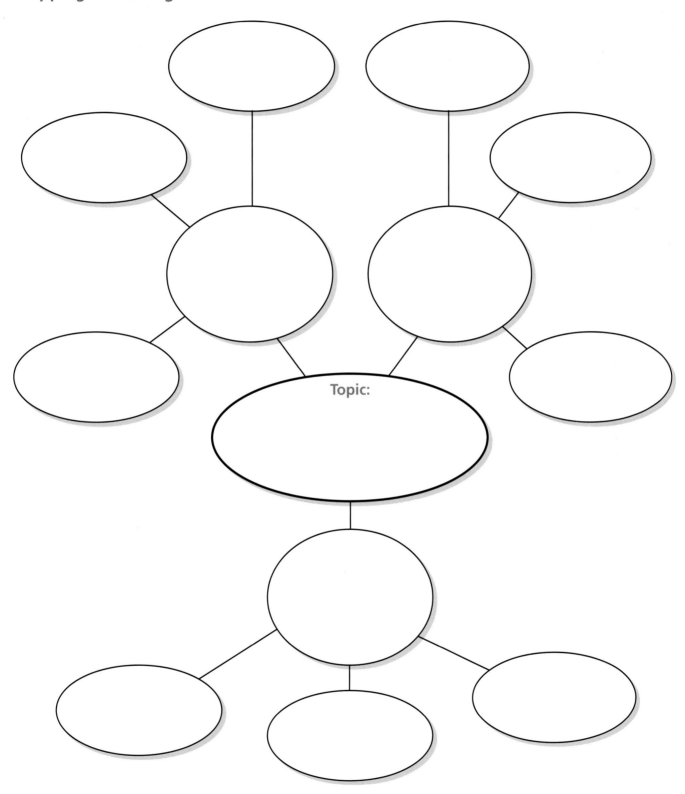

Topic:

Mapping/Clustering Worksheet

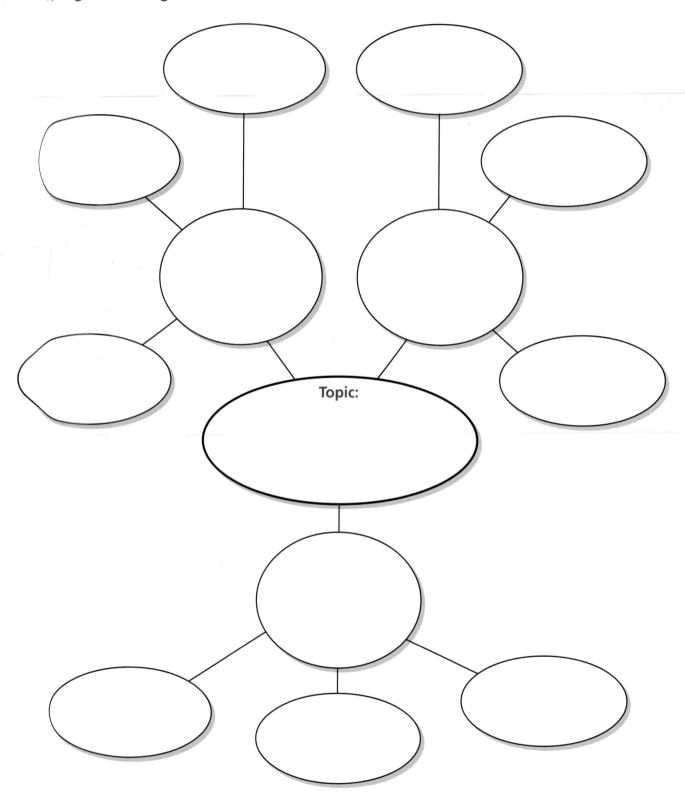

Topic:

Mapping/Clustering Worksheet

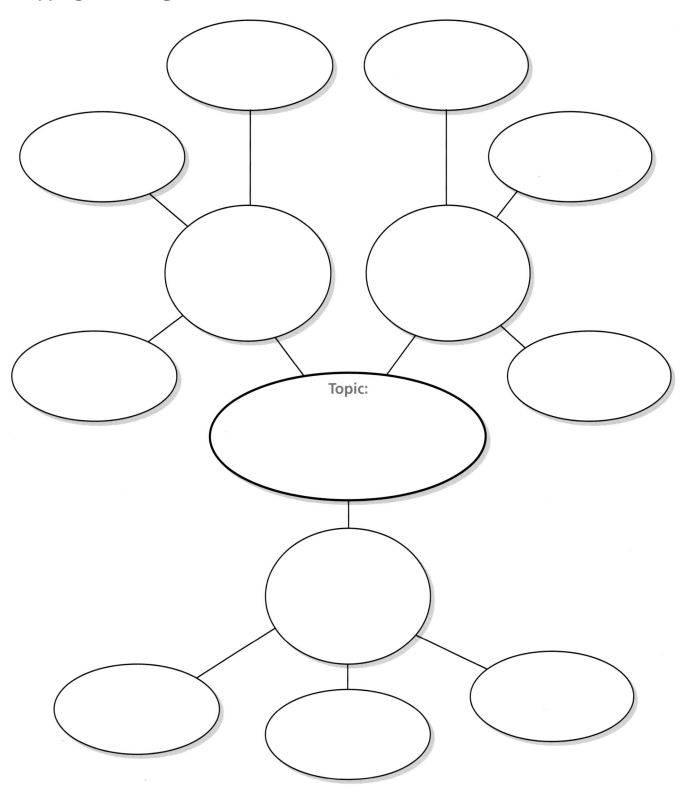

Mapping/Clustering Worksheet

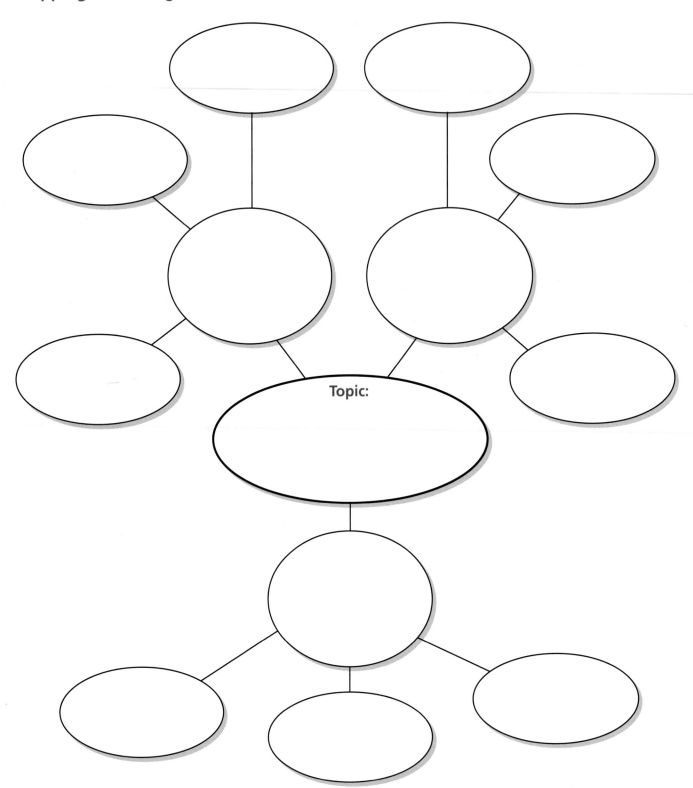

Paragraph Outlines

Narration

TOPIC SENTENCE: _____.

    FIRST EVENT: _____

        DETAILS: _____

    SECOND EVENT: _____

        DETAILS: _____

    THIRD EVENT: _____

        DETAILS: _____

CONCLUDING SENTENCE: _____.

Illustration

TOPIC SENTENCE: _____.

    FIRST EXAMPLE: _____

        DETAILS: _____

    SECOND EXAMPLE: _____

        DETAILS: _____

    THIRD EXAMPLE: _____

        DETAILS: _____

CONCLUDING SENTENCE: _____.

Description

TOPIC SENTENCE: _____.

    FIRST EXAMPLE: _____

        DETAILS: _____

    SECOND EXAMPLE: _____

        DETAILS: _____

    THIRD EXAMPLE: _____

        DETAILS: _____

CONCLUDING SENTENCE: _____.

Process Analysis

TOPIC SENTENCE: _____.

FIRST STEP: _____

EXPLANATION: _____

SECOND STEP: _____

EXPLANATION: _____

THIRD STEP: _____

EXPLANATION: _____

CONCLUDING SENTENCE: _____.

Classification

TOPIC SENTENCE: _____.

FIRST CATEGORY: _____

EXAMPLE/EXPLANATION OF WHAT FITS INTO THE CATEGORY: _____

_____

SECOND CATEGORY: _____

EXAMPLE/EXPLANATION OF WHAT FITS INTO THE CATEGORY: _____

_____

THIRD CATEGORY: _____

EXAMPLE/EXPLANATION OF WHAT FITS INTO THE CATEGORY: _____

_____

CONCLUDING SENTENCE: _____.

Definition

TOPIC SENTENCE: _____.

FIRST EXAMPLE: _____

DETAILS: _____

SECOND EXAMPLE: _____

DETAILS: _____

THIRD EXAMPLE: _____

DETAILS: _____

CONCLUDING SENTENCE: _____.

Comparison and Contrast

POINT-BY-POINT ORGANIZATION

TOPIC SENTENCE: _____ .

FIRST POINT OF COMPARISON/CONTRAST _____

SUBJECT 1: _____

SUBJECT 2: _____

SECOND POINT OF COMPARISON/CONTRAST _____

SUBJECT 1: _____

SUBJECT 2: _____

THIRD POINT OF COMPARISON/CONTRAST _____

SUBJECT 1: _____

SUBJECT 2: _____

CONCLUDING SENTENCE: _____ .

WHOLE-TO-WHOLE ORGANIZATION

TOPIC SENTENCE: _____ .

SUBJECT 1 _____

FIRST POINT OF COMPARISON/CONTRAST: _____

SECOND POINT OF COMPARISON/CONTRAST: _____

THIRD POINT OF COMPARISON/CONTRAST: _____

SUBJECT 2 _____

FIRST POINT OF COMPARISON/CONTRAST: _____

SECOND POINT OF COMPARISON/CONTRAST: _____

THIRD POINT OF COMPARISON/CONTRAST: _____

CONCLUDING SENTENCE: _____ .

Cause and Effect

TOPIC SENTENCE: _____ .

FIRST CAUSE/EFFECT: _____

DETAILS: _____

SECOND CAUSE/EFFECT: _____

DETAILS: _____

THIRD CAUSE/EFFECT: _____

DETAILS: _____

CONCLUDING SENTENCE: _____ .

Argument

TOPIC SENTENCE: _____ .

FIRST REASON: _____

DETAILS: _____

SECOND REASON: _____

DETAILS: _____

THIRD REASON: _____

DETAILS: _____

CONCLUDING SENTENCE: _____ .

Essay Outline

THESIS STATEMENT: _____ .

OTHER IDEAS FOR INTRODUCTORY PARAGRAPH: _____

_____

TOPIC SENTENCE 1: _____ .

SUPPORTING DETAILS (ONE SENTENCE FOR EACH DETAIL): _____

_____

TOPIC SENTENCE 2: _____ .

SUPPORTING DETAILS (ONE SENTENCE FOR EACH DETAIL): _____

_____

TOPIC SENTENCE 3: _____ .

SUPPORTING DETAILS (ONE SENTENCE FOR EACH DETAIL): _____

_____

CONCLUSION REMINDING READERS OF MAIN POINT AND MAKING AN OBSERVATION:

_____ .

Answers to Odd-Numbered Grammar Exercises

Chapter 10

Practice 10-1, page 119
Possible answers: **1.** mechanic **3.** She **5.** air conditioner **7.** baseball **9.** convertible

Practice 10-2, page 119
Answers: **1.** father **3.** he **5.** traveler **7.** You **9.** dad

Practice 10-3, page 120
Answers: **1.** These annoying insects **3.** The hungry pests **5.** Mosquitoes **7.** Their discovery **9.** These special chemicals

Practice 10-4, page 120
Possible edits: **1.** A digital camera was 30 percent off the regular price. **3.** The noisy store was packed with shoppers. **5.** The new camera is now his favorite toy.

Practice 10-5, page 121
Answers: **1.** Plural **3.** Plural **5.** Plural **7.** Singular **9.** Plural

Practice 10-7, page 124
Answers: **1.** ~~Without a doubt~~, crows are intelligent birds. **3.** Crows ~~from this region~~ violently attack other crows ~~for food~~. **5.** Curious ~~about this behavior~~, scientists ~~at the University of Washington~~ observed a group ~~of fifty-five crows~~. **7.** The crows are rough and aggressive while stealing ~~from distant relatives and nonrelatives~~. **9.** ~~Like most humans~~, these birds are nicer ~~to members of their family~~ than ~~to nonrelatives~~.

Practice 10-8, page 125
Answers: **1.** suggested **3.** drink **5.** developed **7.** go **9.** threatened

Practice 10-9, page 125
Answers: **1.** lost **3.** teased **5.** forgot **7.** replaces **9.** rejected

Practice 10-10, page 127
Answers: **1.** Melissa felt **confident** **3.** serves were **stronger** **5.** He seemed **serious and aggressive** **7.** Tennis was **great fun** **9.** she looked **determined**

Practice 10-11, page 128
Answers: **1. have** suffered **3. is** **5. has** doubled **7. can** double **9. should** watch

Practice 10-12, page 130
Answers and possible edits: **1.** Incomplete. The cost of my car insurance went up. **3.** Incomplete. The speed limit in my town is very slow. **5.** Incomplete. Even though my friends make fun of me, I always follow the speed limit. **7.** Incomplete. Another speeding ticket would raise my insurance even more. **9.** Complete.

Editing Reviews, pages 130–32
Answers and possible edits: **1.** (1) People ~~with obsessive-compulsive disorder~~ have rituals, or repeated behaviors. (3) These people may not feel ~~in control of their actions~~. (5) They feel less anxious ~~as a result~~. (7) People may clean their homes, their clothing, or themselves dozens or even hundreds ~~of times during the day~~. (9) Also, sufferers might repeat certain words, phrases, or expressions. **2.** (1) Your supervisor, Eduardo Lopez, recently met with me to talk about your projects. (3) I am pleased to inform you of a raise in your salary. (5) The raise will begin with your next paycheck. (7) You completed additional training by attending company classes. (9) You worked twenty hours of overtime. (11) When two members of your department retired, you helped complete their current projects. (13) You showed company spirit by organizing events for the company barbecue. **3.** (1) Although a teen's first car may be old and unreliable, she probably remembers it with affection. (3) It also represents freedom from parental controls. (5) It was an ancient, unattractive, canary-yellow Oldsmobile. (7) The poor thing was dented and rusty in spots. (9) My friends called it the "junk-mobile."

Chapter 11

Practice 11-2, page 138

Answers and possible edits: **1. Preposition:** Among. Among older people, those with close friends tend to live longer.   **3. Preposition:** Of. Having close family ties did not affect the life span of the people studied.   **5. Preposition:** Before. Before the study was published, many people believed that staying close to family members would help a person live longer.   **7. Preposition:** By. They gathered their data by interviewing the participants every year for the first four years of the study.   **9. Preposition:** About. This study sends a clear message about our older relatives and friends.

Practice 11-3, page 139

Possible edits: **1.** She wanted to spend some time by herself.   **3.** At those parties, she met some interesting new people.   **5.** She spent most of her time with a few close friends.   **7.** In the future, she would try to be more outgoing.   **9.** Through meeting new people and doing new things, she would form a new group of friends.

Practice 11-4, page 139

Possible edits: **1.** After eating a meal, you should wait for a while before going swimming.   **3.** At the pool, children wait impatiently for their food to digest.   **5.** From a review of the available statistics, it now appears that this warning is a myth.   **7.** With alcohol use involved, the story is different.   **9.** In California, forty-one percent of drowning deaths one year were alcohol-related.

Practice 11-6, page 142

Answers and possible edits: **1. Dependent words:** Even though. Correct.   **3. Dependent word:** Therefore. Correct.   **5. Dependent words:** so that. Correct.   **7. Dependent word:** when. They also steal ice cream cones from children when the kids are not careful.   **9. Dependent word:** Because. Correct.

Practice 11-7, page 142

Possible edits: **1.** I always owed a lot of money when I had the credit card.   **3.** Because the credit card made it so easy to borrow money, I could not control my spending.   **5.** I watched my spending carefully until I paid off my debt.   **7.** Unless a person has self-discipline, a credit card can be dangerous.   **9.** I like this card, which draws money from my checking account.

Practice 11-8, page 143

Possible edits: **1.** If a person is not very active, that person is likely to be overweight.   **3.** Although she has her own parking spot close to the door, she parks as far away as possible and takes the stairs instead of the elevator whenever she can.   **5.** When she walks to work, she keeps a pace of 3.7 miles an hour.   **7.** Correct.

Practice 11-10, page 145

Answers and possible edits: **1. –ing verb:** Working. Working an eight-hour shift six days a week, Einstein somehow found time to follow his true passion.   **3. –ing verb:** Remaining. Correct.   **5. –ing verb:** Reviewing. Reviewing inventions at the patent office might also have been helpful in keeping his mind active.   **7. –ing verb:** Refusing. The Nobel Prize committee found Einstein's theory of relativity too extreme, refusing Einstein the prize for that accomplishment.   **9. –ing verb:** Ignoring. Ignoring the committee, he mentioned it anyway.

Practice 11-11, page 146

Possible edits: **1.** Pretending he did not hear his roommate's loud typing, Shawn tried to fall asleep.   **3.** Then, he tried stuffing cotton in his ears.   **5.** Sounding like mice tap-dancing, the typing was impossible to ignore.   **7.** Smiling as he continued typing, Patrick didn't get the point.   **9.** Stopping his typing, Patrick apologized.

Practice 11-12, page 146

Possible edits: **1.** Tens of millions of Americans try online dating every year, making it one of the most popular paid services on the Internet.   **3.** Correct.   **5.** Looks were the most important personal feature, ranking first for both women and men.   **7.** Women who posted photos got higher interest, receiving twice as many e-mail responses than those who did not post photos.   **9.** Going beyond looks and income, most relationships last because of the personalities involved.

Practice 11-14, page 149

Answers and possible edits: **1. Verbal phrase:** To fuel. To fuel the rocket, he used zinc and sulfur from his chemistry set.   **3. Verbal phrase:** To prevent. Unfortunately, he should have used a stronger metal to prevent the burning fuel from melting the rocket.   **5. Verbal phrase:** To become. Correct.   **7. Verbal phrase:** To help build. To help build the rocket *SpaceShipOne*, Allen invested a large amount of money.   **9. Verbal phrase:** To find. What Allen learned as a businessman may have helped him to find the designer and test pilots who made *SpaceShipOne* a success.

Practice 11-15, page 149

Possible edits: **1.** To win a game against my sister, I needed help from a professional.   **3.** I needed to learn to hit the ball where my opponent cannot get to it.   **5.** To take care of the pain that developed in my elbow, I went to a physical therapist.   **7.** To avoid making the injury worse, I stopped playing tennis for a while.   **9.** To play well right after my elbow had healed, I had to practice extra hard.

Practice 11-16, page 150

Possible edits: **1.** To make cars more comfortable and convenient to drive, engineers have designed many high-tech features.   **3.** However, some seat heaters are programmed to switch off after fifteen minutes without warning the driver.   **5.** Correct.   **7.** Many people do not know that it is fairly easy to turn off some of a car's features.   **9.** Correct.

Practice 11-18, page 152

Possible edits: **1.** One major fast-food chain is making changes to its menu, like offering fresh apple slices.   **3.** The company is trying to offer its customers healthier food, such as fresh fruit and salads.   **5.** Many people are blaming fast-food companies for Americans' expanding waistlines, especially those of children.   **7.** This particular restaurant is discovering that healthy food can be profitable. It earns about 10 percent of its income from fresh salads.   **9.** Correct.

Editing Reviews, pages 153–55

Possible edits: **1** (1) Like doctors and physical therapists, nurses must study the structure of the body and the way it functions. (3) Studying how these elements of the body function is called *physiology*. (5) Correct. (7) A solid understanding of medical terminology is necessary to communicate with doctors about patients' disorders. (9) Most medical terms, however, can be broken into three parts. These parts are the prefix, the root, and the suffix.   **2.** (1) We hope that your company is pleased with the project we completed for you in January, two oak wall units. (3) Looking through our records, I realize that we have not received payment for the project. (5) We would appreciate immediate payment of the amount owed, which is $1,500. (7) Correct. (9) If you have any questions or concerns, please contact me at (817) 555-3499.   **3.** (1) As a longtime resident of 5 Rosemont Way in this city, I have seen my neighborhood decline. (3) The sidewalks are in serious disrepair and have caused several residents, such as my son, to injure themselves. (5) As a result, residents don't know the right time to leave out their trash. (7) Delete sentence. (9) Waiting at the bus in the morning darkness, my daughter is very afraid. (11) Thirty residents of the Rosemont neighborhood, including me, have organized to draw up a full list of our complaints.

Chapter 12

Practice 12-2, page 160
Answers: **1.** Run-on **3.** Comma splice **5.** Correct **7.** Comma splice **9.** Comma splice

Practice 12-3, page 162
Answers and possible edits: **1.** Comma splice. The *Cephalotes atratus* ant is common in Central and South America. It lives in trees about a hundred feet above the forest floor. **3.** Run-on. Most of the time, the ants do not fall straight to the ground; they land on the tree trunk instead. **5.** Comma splice. The ants do not want to fall to the ground; that can be a dangerous place for them. **7.** Comma splice. Researchers videotaped some falling ants. The video showed that the ants fall in three separate stages. **9.** Run-on. Next, the ant quickly adjusts its position; it lines up its stomach with the tree trunk.

Practice 12-4, page 163
Answers and possible edits: **1.** Correct. **3.** Comma splice. People want to be around likable coworkers; they make everyone feel better emotionally and physically. **5.** Run-on. For example, a likable person is friendly; he or she makes other people feel liked and welcome. **7.** Run-on. The likable person is also sensitive to other people's wants and needs. It makes people comfortable to feel understood. **9.** Correct.

Practice 12-6, page 166
Answers and edits: **1.** Most birds use their songs to attract mates, but the chickadee also sings for another reason. **3.** Chickadees are protective of their flock, so they use their song to warn other chickadees of danger. **5.** The chickadee's call can have a different number of "dees" at the end, and the number of "dees" sends a message to the rest of the flock. **7.** A call ending with many "dees" warns of a small enemy, and fewer "dees" signal a larger enemy. **9.** A call ending with a large number of "dees" brings many chickadees to the area to dive-bomb the enemy, and fewer "dees" draw fewer chickadees.

Practice 12-7, page 167
Answers and possible edits: **1.** Large discount chains are keeping toy prices low, so this makes it difficult for toy companies to make a profit. **3.** Today, many kids play video games, and they also spend a lot of time on the Internet. **5.** Some simple toys still become kids' favorites, but discount stores often copy these toys. **7.** The original toys often cannot compete against the cheaper copies. Correct. **9.** The company calls one of its creations "Money Man," and the doll looks like a company's chief financial officer with cash strapped around its waist.

Practice 12-8, page 168
Possible edits: **1.** Bette Nesmith Graham was a secretary in the 1950s, but her typing skills were poor. **3.** Correct. **5.** She soon needed more paint, for the other secretaries wanted to use the fluid, too. **7.** She started selling an improved fluid in 1956, and she called it Mistake Out. **9.** Correct.

Practice 12-10, page 170
Answers and edits: **1.** Even though most people understand the importance of a good night's rest, about half of all Americans do not get enough sleep. **3.** After you have had a long week with little sleep, you might sleep late on the weekend. **5.** Coffee, tea, and soda can keep you alert because they contain caffeine. **7.** Your pillow might be the problem if you have trouble sleeping. **9.** Because a supportive pillow is important for restful sleep, pillow experts suggest a simple test.

Practice 12-11, page 171
Answers and possible edits: **1.** Because few people can afford such expensive cars, some companies are offering them for rent. **3.** Since rental times are flexible, you can rent a fancy car for as short as a few hours or as long as several months. **5.** It may seem surprising, but 70 percent of the companies' renters are women. Correct. **7.** A Ferrari is like a racecar since the driver changes gears by pulling a pair of paddles behind the steering wheel. **9.** Because it goes so fast, the car has specially designed brakes. Correct.

Practice 12-12, page 172
Possible edits: **1.** When most people buy a new cell phone, they pay close attention to the phone's features. **3.** Some charities accept old cell phones when their owners no longer want them. **5.** Correct. **7.** Although most old cell phones are worth only $2 to $20, that is better than nothing. **9.** Correct.

Editing Reviews, pages 173–75
Possible edits: **1.** (1) Correct. (3) Apes have more complex brains than monkeys, and apes' brains are larger in relation to the size of their body. (5) This method of movement is called *brachiation*; the term comes from the Latin word for "arms." (7) Gibbons are good acrobats; they can cover up to fifty feet in one swing, at a speed of about thirty-five miles per hour. (9) Correct. **2.** (1) Because safety is a top priority at Alpha Chemical, the following visitor policy must be followed at all times. (3) Visitors must sign in at the front lobby, where they will receive a visitor's badge. (5) After they watch a brief safety film, visitors will be given protective eyewear, a lab coat, and any other necessary safety equipment. (7) Visitors must be accompanied by an employee at all times, and no children are allowed into the facility. (9) For security reasons, personal items such as purses and briefcases are not allowed in laboratory areas; these items must be left at the front desk or in personal office areas. **3.** (1) Correct. (3) Correct. (5) Correct. (7) Because the Olympics celebrate friendship and world peace, you might be shocked by the dark history of the first torch relay. (9) The games that year were held in Berlin, and Hitler believed the torch relay would show off the glory and power of Nazi Germany. (11) The torch is usually carried by runners, and the relays for several early Olympics were held entirely on foot. (13) The torch has been conveyed on horseback, steamboat, Indian canoe, and skis, and it has even traveled by satellite. (15) The nomination process is open to the public, and most people chosen to be torchbearers have shown some kind of heroism or made a positive contribution to their community.

Chapter 13

Practice 13-1, page 179
Answers: **1.** Jason jumps **3.** Signs tell **5.** doctors believe **7.** People want **9.** phone falls

Practice 13-2, page 179
Answers: **1.** You practice, we practice, she practices **3.** we play, I play, he plays **5.** he cleans, she cleans, they clean **7.** we lose, he loses, I lose **9.** I sing, they sing, he sings

Practice 13-3, page 180
Answers: **1.** spend **3.** write **5.** save **7.** appreciate **9.** help

Practice 13-5, page 184
Answers: **1.** is **3.** is **5.** are **7.** am **9.** are

Practice 13-6, page 186
Answers: **1.** has **3.** has **5.** has **7.** have **9.** have

Practice 13-7, page 187
Answers: **1.** does **3.** do **5.** do **7.** do **9.** does

Practice 13-8, page 188
Edits: **1.** My family has trouble finding time to eat dinner together. **3.** Our busy schedules are hard to work around, however. **5.** Scientists have found interesting benefits to such meals. **7.** According to this study, teenagers do less drinking and smoking if they eat with family members an average of five to seven times weekly. **9.** A teen girl is less likely to be anorexic or bulimic if she regularly eats meals with her family. **11.** Correct. **13.** Vegetables are certainly important, too, and children eat more of them when dining with their families. **15.** Correct.

Practice 13-10, page 191
Answers: **1.** Waves ~~from the bay~~ **hit** the dock hard. **3.** The people ~~on the deck~~ **grab** the rail for support. **5.** One ~~of the guests~~ **asks** the captain if it is safe to go out in this weather. **7.** The ride ~~across the bay~~ **goes** smoothly at first. **9.** The boats ~~on the water~~ **turn** back toward the dock.

Practice 13-11, page 191
Answers: **1.** Tips ~~that save money or improve comfort~~ **are** always welcome. **3.** Passengers ~~who volunteer to travel on a later flight~~ **receive** a free ticket. **5.** The people ~~who you sit near on a plane~~ **are** important to your comfort. **7.** A person ~~whose seat back is pushing into your knees~~ **is** very annoying. **9.** People ~~who want to avoid lost luggage~~ **carry** all their bags with them on the plane.

Practice 13-12, page 192
Answers and edits: **1.** Baby strollers ~~that you see today~~ are fancier than ever before. **3.** However, features ~~that increase the baby's comfort~~ are becoming more popular. **5.** Babies ~~who like to sleep in their strollers~~ are able to lie flat on their backs. Correct. **7.** A certain type ~~of these strollers~~ costs $850. **9.** One expert ~~on stroller marketing~~ makes an interesting point. Correct. **11.** Statements ~~that express something about the parents' lifestyle~~ are best. **13.** Strollers ~~that keep the baby very high off the ground~~ show the parents' desire to be close to their child.

Practice 13-14, page 194
Answers: **1.** or/makes **3.** and/run **5.** and/are **7.** or/is **9.** and/agree

Practice 13-15, page 195
Answers: **1.** and/ride **3.** or/buy **5.** or/make **7.** or/have **9.** nor/are

Practice 13-16, page 196
Edits: **1.** Diet and exercise are important parts of a healthy lifestyle. **3.** Doctors and nutritionists recommend starting every day with a healthy breakfast. **5.** A healthy lunch or dinner is easier to prepare than many people think. **7.** Correct. **9.** Most children and adults order the combination meal, even when they want only a hamburger.

Practice 13-18, page 198
Answers: **1.** thinks **3.** owns **5.** tells **7.** believes **9.** loves

Practice 13-20, page 200
Answers: **1.** Are you **3.** is it **5.** is/ride **7.** do you **9.** does everyone

Practice 13-21, page 201
Answers: **1.** is/lake **3.** are/keys **5.** are/cries **7.** is/phone number **9.** Are/trails

Practice 13-22, page 202
Edits: **1.** Here is the farm stand we were telling you about. **3.** Correct. **5.** Here are tomatoes loaded with flavor. **7.** Here is homemade ice cream fresh from the freezer. **9.** There is an apple pie that is still steaming from the oven.

Practice 13-23, page 202
Edits: **1.** Here are some common questions about traveling to New York City: **3.** How much do most hotels cost? **5.** Where do travelers on a tight budget stay? **7.** Correct. **9.** Correct.

Editing Reviews, pages 203–06
Possible edits: **1.** (1) Members of a law enforcement agency collect evidence before making an arrest. (3) Someone who has firsthand knowledge of a crime provides testimonial evidence. (5) Correct. (7) Other examples of physical evidence include drugs, weapons, and fibers from clothing. (9) The Fourth Amendment of the U.S. Constitution regulates the collection of evidence. (11) Correct. (13) In certain situations, an officer has the authority to search a car without a warrant. (15) Neither security nor freedom is worth sacrificing for the other, they believe. **2.** (1) The Volunteer Center of Northern Indiana wishes to apply for a Tri-State Foundation Community Development Grant. (3) The center supports volunteerism in the area by connecting various organizations with volunteers. (5) There are many people who are unsure about where to volunteer their time and energy. (7) The Volunteer Center seeks a $10,000 grant from the Tri-State Foundation. (9) The Volunteer Center now operates on an $800,000 annual budget. (11) Currently, however, no funds are used for training our volunteers or communications staff. (13) With a Tri-State Foundation Community Grant, we plan to train volunteers to communicate this information more effectively. (15) I look forward to your response. **3.** (1) There are few natural disasters more destructive than a hurricane. (3) Correct. (5) Correct. (7) In fact, some hurricanes have winds of up to 250 miles per hour near the eye. (9) Correct. (11) A wall of water called a storm surge builds up in front of a hurricane. (13) The violent waves and high water are extremely dangerous. (15) There are five categories of hurricanes. (17) A Category 1 hurricane has wind speeds of 74 to 95 miles per hour. (19) Roofs and trees are damaged during a Category 2 hurricane. (21) Anything over a Category 2 is considered a major hurricane. (23) With wind speeds over 150 miles per hour, a Category 5 hurricane results in widespread destruction. (25) There are several methods. (27) At other times, people fly small planes right into a hurricane. (29) Correct. (31) Anyone who understands the incredible power of hurricanes admires the bravery of these men and women.

Chapter 14

Practice 14-2, page 211
Answers: **1.** subscribes: present **3.** traveled: past **5.** relaxes: present **7.** learns: present **9.** carried: past

Practice 14-3, page 211
Answers: **1.** like; liked **3.** stays; stayed **5.** work; worked **7.** talk; talked **9.** agree; agreed

Practice 14-4, page 212
Answers: **1.** trusted **3.** stored **5.** turned, tried **7.** repeated **9.** worried **11.** estimated, recovered **13.** waited, called **15.** purchased, performed

Practice 14-6, page 214
Answers: **1.** ran **3.** began **5.** chose **7.** had **9.** gave

Practice 14-7, page 215
Answers: **1.** took **3.** got **5.** taught **7.** saw **9.** paid

Practice 14-8, page 215
Edits: **1.** A few years ago, I fell into debt. **3.** Through a quick Internet search, I found a company that sold printers at a very low cost.

5. Then, I understood the reason for the low prices. 7. I bought one of these printers from the company. 9. But over the last few years, my wonderful printer made me a believer in used products.

Practice 14-10, page 216
Answers: 1. was 3. were 5. was 7. were 9. was

Practice 14-11, page 216
Answers: 1. were 3. was, was 5. were 7. was 9. was

Practice 14-13, page 217
Answers: 1. have 3. had 5. had 7. had 9. had

Practice 14-14, page 219
Answers: 1. can 3. would 5. would 7. would 9. can

Practice 14-15, page 219
Answers: 1. can 3. could 5. would 7. can 9. would 11. will 13. can 15. will

Editing Reviews, pages 220–23
Edits: 1. (1) One late night in St. Louis, Missouri, in 1996, an elderly woman came out of a convenience store. (3) Correct. (5) Before she had time to respond, the attacker hit her with the gun and ran off. (7) In 1996, a group of social scientists studied eighty-six criminals like this one in St. Louis. (9) Many of the criminals were afraid of being caught. (11) When they thought about the risk of punishment, they would only work more quickly to finish the crime. (13) Many of them were broke and living on the streets. (15) But their day-to-day life was so difficult that they feared prison less than they feared being broke. 2. (1) Your advertisement for a personal private investigator, which I saw in the March 31 issue of *The Campbell Times*, caught my eye. (3) Last year, I graduated from Whitley University with a B.S. in administration of justice. (5) In particular, I gained extensive experience with high-technology surveillance equipment. (7) In addition to my classroom studies, last year I was an intern with a private investigation firm in San Francisco. (9) By the end of the internship, I could handle large cases on my own. (11) If a technique that I needed was not in the manual, I usually could figure out the problem myself. (13) Thank you for considering me for the position. 3. (1) The first humans used tools as early as 2.5 million years ago. (3) For most of human history, people simply ate with their fingers. (5) When Greek servers carved meat, food sometimes slipped and fell off the plate. (7) Around A.D. 700, royalty in the Middle East began to use forks at meals. (9) Correct. (11) The princess made people angry when she refused to eat with her fingers. (13) Correct. (15) Correct. (17) As in Italy, the tool was unpopular once again. (19) Today, forks can be made of expensive material, or they might be made of inexpensive plastic, aluminum, or steel.

Chapter 15

Practice 15-1, page 227
Answers: 1. have stayed 3. have worked 5. has remembered 7. have used 9. has learned

Practice 15-2, page 227
Edits: 1. Your friends have knocked on the door three times already. 3. You have washed the dishes every night this week. 5. Our supervisor has repeated the instructions four times. 7. I have wanted to speak with you all morning. 9. Since January, Lauren has needed a new car.

Practice 15-3, page 228
Answers: 1. has ordered 3. have bothered 5. have watched 7. has decided 9. has trained

Practice 15-5, page 231
Edits: 1. We have given ourselves plenty of time. 3. Dan has come

to class after all. 5. I have ridden horses for more than fourteen years. 7. So far, Melissa has caught no fish. 9. He has chosen you because of your honesty.

Practice 15-6, page 232
Answers: 1. have spent 3. has read 5. has eaten 7. have met 9. have fallen

Practice 15-8, page 235
Answers: 1. went 3. opened 5. has been 7. have played 9. have always wanted

Practice 15-9, page 236
Answers: 1. had 3. have become 5. learned 7. have complained 9. saw 11. have considered 13. has created

Practice 15-11, page 238
Answers: 1. had scared 3. saw 5. had gone 7. saw 9. tried

Practice 15-13, page 239
Answers: 1. has shown 3. have become 5. offered 7. had been 9. had come 11. made 13. settled 15. has added 17. have enjoyed 19. have noticed

Practice 15-14, page 241
Answers: 1. studied: active 3. ate: active 5. were drawn: passive 7. served: active 9. were given: passive

Practice 15-15, page 241
Edits: 1. Matthew got the tickets to the concert at the campground. 3. Sean did the driving. (**Or** Sean drove.) 5. He made several wrong turns. 7. Meanwhile, I prepared dinner. 9. While we waited for the concert to begin, several other friends joined us.

Editing Reviews, pages 242–45
Edits: 1. (1) Few scientific theories have created as much controversy as the theory of evolution. (3) The book presented evidence that Darwin had collected on a five-year voyage along the coast of South America. (5) Correct. (7) For more than a century now, people have been divided on whether evolution should be taught in public schools. (9) Earlier, in the small town of Dayton, Tennessee, a biology teacher named John T. Scopes had assigned a textbook that described the theory of evolution. (11) Earlier that year, a state law titled the Butler Law had banned the teaching of evolution, so Scopes was arrested. (13) Correct. (15) Ever since the Scopes trial, people have fought over the issue in courtrooms across the country. 2. (1) On Monday, a new database system was chosen and installed by the Information Technology Department. (3) After I read the user's manual, I attended the all-day training session on Tuesday. (5) I have made a lot of progress learning the system. (7) By the end of last week, I had logged thirty-five customer-service calls. (9) All the software problems were handled at the time of the call. (11) So far, I have resolved half of these calls. (13) I submitted service requests for the other five, but I have had no time to follow up on these requests yet. (15) I am certain the remaining problems will be resolved early next week. 3. (1) A recent study shows that Americans have started watching more sports on television rather than actually playing them. (3) Another reason may be that they might have been discouraged at some point in the past, so they have left the playing to the professionals. (5) Playing sports has always been and always will be better than watching them. (7) Throughout human history, people have gathered together to form teams. (9) Men have gone head-to-head against women. (11) Correct. (13) The health benefits speak for themselves. (15) Then, in the 1970s, scientists discovered endorphins, chemicals that produce a pleasant feeling after a workout. (17) Healthy people usually have less stress, a benefit that may add years to their life. (19) Cheering for the same team, for example, has brought people closer together and made friends out of enemies. (21) However, no one who has played in an exciting basketball game would argue that watching the sport is more thrilling than actually doing it.

Chapter 16

Practice 16-1, page 260
Answers: **1.** characters **3.** couches **5.** wishes **7.** pickles **9.** ashes

Practice 16-2, page 262
Edits: **1.** The people who arrived in Jamestown in 1607 were willing to face many difficulties. **3.** Among the group were craftsmen, soldiers, and breeders of animals, such as oxen. **5.** Correct. **7.** Captain John Smith pulled the survivors together and kept the colony going for many more days, until five hundred more people arrived. **9.** Correct.

Practice 16-3, page 263
Edits: **1.** Archaeologists have found loaves of bread in Egyptian tombs. **3.** Correct. **5.** Soon, however, men set up bread-baking shops, and bakeries were born. **7.** Good bread had to be white, which is why wives used wheat only from certain places. **9.** Correct.

Editing Reviews, pages 263–65
Edits: **1.** (1) In delivery rooms, doctors and nurses evaluate the health of newborns at one, five, and sometimes ten minutes following birth. (3) There are several quick ways to test a baby's initial health. (5) Correct. (7) A baby whose limbs are flexed and moving slightly receives one point. (9) Correct. **2.** (1) As you know, October 15 to December 31 is one of our busiest and most profitable seasons. (3) As a result, we need to have as many people as possible on the shipping floor during that period. (5) Correct. (7) If you are willing to work extra shifts, please notify your supervisor. (9) If you have any questions, please see your supervisor or call Human Resources at extension 15. **3.** (1) Every summer, carnivals come to many small towns across America. (3) However, many families still enjoy an old-fashioned day at the fair. (5) Ferris wheels, small roller coasters, and various spinning machines are among the most popular rides. (7) At the carnival's game booths players might throw darts at balloons or shoot fake guns at toy ducks. (9) Correct. (11) Between acts, there might be clowns and monkeys to keep the audience laughing. (13) However, most carnivals offer an embarrassment of riches.

Chapter 17

Practice 17-1, page 269
Answers: **1.** Pronoun: their; noun: bears **3.** Pronoun: it; noun: Garbage **5.** Pronoun: it; noun: bear **7.** Pronoun: him; noun: Jon Beckman **9.** Pronoun: they; noun: bears

Practice 17-2, page 272
Answers: **1.** Indefinite pronoun: Everyone; replacement: his or her **3.** Indefinite pronoun: Nothing; replacement: its **5.** Indefinite pronoun: All; replacement: their **7.** Indefinite pronoun: Some; replacement: their **9.** Indefinite pronoun: Some; replacement: their

Practice 17-3, page 273
Answers: **1.** his or her **3.** they spend **5.** his or her **7.** he or she is **9.** his or her

Practice 17-4, page 275
Answers: **1.** Antecedent: band; pronoun: its **3.** Antecedent: audience; pronoun: their **5.** Antecedent: band; pronoun: its **7.** Antecedent: dance troupe; pronoun: its **9.** Antecedent: team; pronoun: their

Practice 17-5, page 276
Answers: **1.** its **3.** its **5.** its **7.** their

Practice 17-6, page 277
Possible edits: **1.** The babysitter, Jan, and I were fascinated by *Twenty Thousand Leagues Under the Sea*, and Jan is now studying marine biology. **3.** I enjoy visiting the aquarium and have taken a biology class, but the class didn't focus on ocean life as much as I would have liked. **5.** Both space and the ocean are largely unexplored, and the ocean contains a huge proportion of all life on Earth. **7.** Jan says that marine biologists have found some very odd creatures in the ocean. **9.** According to marine biologists who made the discovery, the octopus looks like a piece of seaweed bouncing along the sand.

Practice 17-7, page 279
Edits: **1.** Fireworks were originally used by the Chinese to scare enemies in war. **3.** People who use paper fans to cool off should thank the Chinese for this invention. **5.** A counting device called the *abacus* was used for counting and led to the development of the calculator. **7.** The oldest piece of paper in the world was discovered near Xian, China. **9.** Chinese merchants were using paper money in the ninth century.

Practice 17-8, page 281
Possible answers: **1.** She **3.** our **5.** her **7.** her **9.** She

Practice 17-9, page 283
Answers: **1.** him **3.** me **5.** he **7.** me **9.** him

Practice 17-10, page 283
Edits: **1.** Correct. **3.** No one guessed that Calico Jack's new first mate was a woman, and she and the other pirates became friends. **5.** On one ship, she and Calico Jack discovered Mary Read, another female sailor disguised as a man. **7.** When Calico Jack learned of their friendship, he and Anne decided to let Mary sail on the *Vanity*. **9.** Anne and Mary were skilled pirates and fierce fighters, but the British Navy finally captured them and their pirate crew in 1720.

Practice 17-11, page 286
Edits: **1.** Other Texans may be more famous than he, but Lance Armstrong has accomplished so much. **3.** Few cyclists have won as many races as he. **5.** Against incredible odds, he survived surgery and chemotherapy for cancer and went on to compete against athletes who thought that they were better than he. **7.** Athletes are in awe of Armstrong's determination and know that he can perform better than they under extreme pressure. **9.** Cycling just seems to come more naturally to Lance Armstrong than to me.

Practice 17-12, page 287
Answers: **1.** who **3.** whom **5.** whom

Editing Reviews, pages 287–90
Possible edits: **1.** (1) Sometimes, students receive a grade for a course that is not what they expected. (3) Correct. (5) Correct. (7) The committee will issue its ruling after contacting the student and instructor for information. (9) No one is happier than we administrators when both parties feel they have been treated fairly. **2.** (1) On March 21, you asked Allegra Conti and me to look into purchasing a new color printer for our department. (3) Correct. (5) Both printers are also able to print labels, photographs, and overhead transparencies. (7) The FX 235 offers more flexibility for employees who have unique needs. (9) Correct. (11) We read several reviews of both printers, and everyone recommends the FX as his or her top choice in our price range. (13) Correct. (15) Please let us know when the company has made its decision. **3.** (1) The Internet is continually changing to meet the needs of the people who use it. (3) However, the Internet has become a place where people share their thoughts and opinions. (5) Blogs began as online diaries where people could regularly post their thoughts and links to favorite Web sites for friends and family. (7) Blogs cover every topic imaginable, including politics, current events, sports, music, and technology. (9) When a lot of people blog about a particular political or social controversy, the result is called a blogstorm. (11) Correct. (13) Because the site is a wiki, she and I were able to edit outdated facts and add new information.

Chapter 18

Practice 18-1, page 294
Possible answers: **1.** frightened **3.** striped **5.** happy **7.** angry **9.** cold

Practice 18-2, page 295
Possible answers: **1.** Modified word: ran; adverb: happily **3.** Modified word: dance; adverb: beautifully **5.** Modified word: walked; adverb: carefully **7.** Modified word: told; adverb: nervously **9.** Modified word: shouted; adverb: angrily

Practice 18-3, page 297
Answers: **1.** Modified word: enthusiastic; adverb: wildly **3.** Modified word: reviews; adjective: poor **5.** Modified word: film; adjective: unusual **7.** Modified word: fans; adjective: Serious **9.** Modified word: danced; adverb: happily

Practice 18-4, page 299
Answers: **1.** smarter **3.** more quietly **5.** briefer **7.** more patiently **9.** more thankful

Practice 18-5, page 300
Answers: **1.** richest **3.** proudest **5.** most sensible **7.** most bitter **9.** most impatiently

Practice 18-6, page 301
Answers: **1.** sweeter **3.** tastiest **5.** most surprised **7.** most popular **9.** more generously

Practice 18-7, page 302
Edits: **1.** This summer, my family and I went to the biggest amusement park in the state. **3.** My little sister bought the silliest red-and-yellow clown hat. **5.** Dad was hungry and got some chili that turned out to be saltier than he imagined. **7.** The line seemed to go on for miles, but it moved more quickly than we had expected. **9.** Everyone said it was the bumpiest ride ever invented.

Practice 18-8, page 303
Answers: **1.** Modified word: ingredients; modifier: good **3.** Modified word: written; modifier: well **5.** Modified word: dough; modifier: good **7.** Modified word: cook; modifier: well **9.** Modified word: recipes; modifier: good

Practice 18-9, page 304
Answers: **1.** Modified word: choice; modifier: better **3.** Modified word: beverage; modifier: best **5.** Modified word: choice; modifier: best **7.** Modified word: Doughnuts; modifier: worse **9.** Modified word: oatmeal; modifier: better

Editing Reviews, pages 305–07
Edits: **1.** (1) College tuition costs are higher than ever before. (3) The most common types of aid include scholarships, loans, and military aid. (5) Correct. (7) Government loans don't require credit checks, and they usually offer the lowest interest rates. (9) Finally, students can enroll in Reserve Officers Training Corps (ROTC) for funds, and veterans can also obtain good tuition benefits. **2.** (1) Thank you for interviewing me on Thursday and giving me such a thorough tour of your factory. (3) I was particularly impressed with the quality-control system. (5) Correct. (7) I would also enjoy the challenge of developing newer methods for increasing production and improving plant safety. (9) I hope you consider me a good candidate for your management team. **3.** (1) At military boot camps, new recruits receive physical and psychological training. (3) Recruits are pushed to learn new responsibilities and skills quickly. (5) Juvenile boot camps teach respect and discipline to teenagers who behave badly. (7) Boot camps that teach life skills or hobbies to adults offer a more pleasant environment than military or juvenile boot camps. (9) At the end of the camp, the best player gets to join the World Poker Tournament. (11) Golf camp participants take lessons from some of the greatest professional golfers. (13) Even Oprah is part of this latest fad. (15) The program consists of a strict diet and eight workouts a week. (17) Correct.

Chapter 19

Practice 19-1, page 312
Possible edits: **1.** I received an invitation in the mail to Mrs. Garcia's upcoming barbecue. **3.** Mrs. Garcia, who likes to barbecue, wanted to use her new grill. **5.** Losing track of time, I burned the beans. **7.** Mrs. Garcia fired up the grill with the extra-large cooking racks in her backyard. **9.** Correct.

Practice 19-2, page 313
Possible rewrites: **1.** In the first paragraph, the instructions explain how to install the fan's blades. **3.** Working in the garden, Lilly saw a beautiful butterfly. **5.** He nearly left the screen door open. **7.** Julia keeps a sweatshirt that is comfortable in her backpack. OR Julia keeps a comfortable sweatshirt in her backpack. **9.** James has nearly completed the entire lesson.

Practice 19-3, page 315
Possible edits: **1.** While I was practicing my song, my costume made a ripping sound. **3.** Correct. **5.** We checked the whole costume, but it was hard to see in the dimly lit dressing room. **7.** Worried, I heard the ripping sound still echoing in my head. **9.** Correct.

Practice 19-4, page 316
Possible edits: **1.** Arriving early, we got good seats for the concert. **3.** Wanting to be a gymnast, Carlo must practice every day. **5.** Frightened by the spider, I almost dropped my can of soda. **7.** I saw a strange parrot sitting on a perch in the pet shop. **9.** Bored with the movie, Gino turned off the television.

Editing Reviews, pages 317–19
Possible edits: **1.** (1) Hoping to make their streets safer, some communities are trying new crime-fighting programs. (3) Identifying the problems that are most important to the community, the police and the community set goals. (5) Because the police officers must be actively involved with the people in their precincts, the program requires a strong commitment. (7) Patrolling on foot rather than in cars, the police officers create a sense of security and community. (9) They are always looking for ways to establish better ties with the community. (11) Correct. **2.** (1) Correct. (3) Opening the word-processing program, I noticed the computer comes with version 5.0 rather than version 6.0. (5) Correct. (7) For the past five years, I have used MiHiTech for nearly all of my technology needs. (9) Correct. **3.** (1) Invented in 2001, iPods are now used by an estimated twenty-two million people. (3) If you look around any college campus, you will see iPods everywhere. (5) Music fans can keep thousands of songs by different artists in their pocket. (7) People who ride public transportation especially love their iPods. (9) Popular among athletes, iPods help many people enjoy their exercise more. (11) Correct. (13) If the trend continues, soon nearly everyone will have iPods.

Chapter 20

Practice 20-1, page 325
Answers: **1.** began **3.** submitted **5.** became **7.** began **9.** is

Practice 20-2, page 325
Edits: **1.** Correct. **3.** Correct. **5.** When my instructor gave the

sign to jump, we leaped out together and fell for what seemed like forever. **7.** After the parachute opened, I began a graceful and relaxing landing.

Practice 20-3, page 327
Possible edits: **1.** Whether a person has a new car or an old one, he or she can still take some steps to save gas. **3.** A driver should also make sure that his or her trunk is empty because extra weight causes the car to use more gas. **5.** People should not drive aggressively or fast if they want to improve gas mileage. **7.** I know that keeping the tires inflated improves my gas mileage. **9.** It tells drivers about correct tire inflation and gasoline quality so that their cars will be cheaper to run.

Editing Reviews, pages 328–30
Possible edits: **1.** (1) Around ten thousand years ago, early humans learned how to keep animals and grow crops. (3) The men used simple tools to hunt, while the women gathered wild fruits, vegetables, honey, and birds' eggs. (5) Hunter-gatherer societies typically consisted of about twenty to fifty people, and tasks were shared by all. (7) According to archaeologists, people treated each other equally in hunter-gatherer societies. (9) When agriculture spread throughout the world, the hunger-gatherer way of life mostly ended. **2.** (1) Correct. (3) Automobile manufacturers build cars, and then they sell them to customers. (5) Correct. (7) Correct. **3.** (1) As people answer phones, review e-mail messages, and respond to text messages, they become overwhelmed. (3) Worse, overuse of technology may lower people's IQ and damage their relationships. (5) In the study, workers who tried to juggle e-mail and voice-mail messages while working on other tasks scored lower on IQ tests. (7) Correct. (9) Correct.

Chapter 21

Practice 21-1, page 334
Possible edits: **1.** Recently, a <u>professor</u> found similarities between modern and ancient ghost stories. **3.** <u>Modern ghost stories</u> also have spirits of this color. **5.** Or <u>they</u> may bring a warning. **7.** In the scariest stories, <u>ghosts</u> want revenge. **9.** <u>These details</u> bring life to the tales.

Practice 21-2, page 337
Possible answers: **1.** He **3.** him **5.** His **7.** It **9.** I

Practice 21-3, page 340
Answers: **1.** cuts **3.** loves **5.** objected **7.** felt **9.** wonder

Practice 21-4, page 341
Rewrites: **1.** Does Sasha play baseball with her sister? **3.** Did Chris bait the hook on the fishing line? **5.** Did Rivka watch the tennis match?

Practice 21-5, page 344
Answers: **1.** holding **3.** crying **5.** playing **7.** doing **9.** going

Practice 21-6, page 345
Rewrites: **1.** Is Dan mowing the grass? **3.** Are you wearing a new dress? **5.** Was Chad working when you saw him?

Practice 21-7, page 349
Possible answers: **1.** would **3.** should **5.** cannot **7.** Can **9.** will

Practice 21-8, page 350
Rewrites: **1.** Can you tell me the secret? **3.** Should they leave the house before us? **5.** Would Cathy like to go sailing with us?

Practice 21-9, page 354
Answers: **1.** have/been **3.** have complained **5.** has discovered **7.** had never seen **9.** have opened

Practice 21-10, page 354
Possible answers: **1.** is rising **3.** produce **5.** have overwhelmed **7.** are melting **9.** will destroy **11.** can do **13.** do/drink **15.** could bring **17.** could start **19.** might/buy

Practice 21-11, page 356
Possible answers: **1.** might need **3.** Could/be **5.** vary **7.** might/call

Practice 21-12, page 358
Possible answers: **1.** working **3.** dreaming, making **5.** developing, ensuring **7.** being **9.** going

Practice 21-13, page 361
Answers: **1.** an **3.** no article **5.** the **7.** a **9.** a

Practice 21-14, page 361
Edits: **1.** In 2005, a national study about motherhood was released. **3.** As it turns out, mothers from around the country have many of the same attitudes and concerns. **5.** Likewise, most mothers believe that their role is an important one. **7.** They admit they had never experienced love so intensely before they had children. **9.** These women also had a few concerns. **11.** In fact, some felt less valued as mothers than they did before they had children. **13.** The biggest concerns of the mothers surveyed were education and safety.

Practice 21-15, page 364
Edits: **1.** Organizations such as the Centers for Disease Control are fighting against an HIV/AIDS epidemic in the rural United States. **3.** They might also be afraid of having their testing or HIV status discovered by the community. **5.** However, finding out their HIV status is the first step toward life-saving treatment for those who are infected. **7.** Correct. **9.** Correct.

Practice 21-16, page 365
Edits: **1.** As a child, I was totally confused by these statements, but I never asked him to explain them because I was scared of looking stupid. **3.** One day, when I was handing in an assignment to my teacher, I repeated one of my father's sayings to her. **5.** Correct. **7.** Correct. **9.** Correct.

Chapter 22

Practice 22-1, page 382
Possible answers: **1.** and **3.** or **5.** or **7.** and **9.** and

Practice 22-2, page 383
Possible edits: **1.** Teachers hear a variety of interesting excuses, yet some are more creative than others. **3.** The due date for a major term paper approaches, and distant relatives die in surprising numbers. **5.** A noble excuse always sounds good, so a student might claim that he had to shovel snow from an elderly neighbor's driveway. **7.** It's always best to be honest about a missed deadline, for students get caught more often than one would think. **9.** The professor did not accept the funeral excuse, and he did not allow the student to make up the missed quiz.

Practice 22-3, page 385
Edits: **1.** Homemade chocolate chip cookies are delicious; they're even better with a glass of cold milk. **3.** Fries have another natural partner; most people like to eat them with ketchup. **5.** A peanut butter sandwich is boring; a little jelly adds some excitement.

Practice 22-4, page 385
Possible edits: **1.** In January 1982, Steven Callahan set sail from the Canary Islands in a small homemade boat; however, the boat sank six days into his journey across the Atlantic. **3.** Alone on a five-foot inflatable raft, he knew his chances for survival were slim; however, he was determined to live. **5.** With his spear, Callahan was able to catch food; still, he lost a significant amount of weight. **7.** Several

ships passed Callahan; however, nobody on board saw him. **9.** For a total of seventy-six days, he drifted alone; then, three fishermen found him.

Editing Reviews, pages 386–89

Possible edits: **1.** (1) No change. (2/3) Most diabetes cases are classified as Type 2 diabetes; 90 to 95 percent of diabetics have this type of the disease. (5/6) In fact, diabetes is the fifth-deadliest disease in the United States, but it can be controlled or even prevented by careful attention to diet and exercise. (7/8) Patients should be encouraged to exercise for thirty minutes daily, and they should be taught how to plan meals according to the American Diabetes Association's Diabetes Food Pyramid. (9/10) It is also important for patients to practice proper foot and skin care, for diabetes can cause skin infections, particularly on the feet. (11) No change. (12/13) Smoking is especially dangerous for people with diabetes; consequently, smokers should be provided with resources to help them quit. (14/15) Living with diabetes is not easy, but patients can live long and healthy lives if they receive education and support in controlling the disease. **2.** (1) No change. (2/3) I am currently enrolled in the nursing program at Greenfield College, so this job would help me further develop skills in my field while letting me offer my services to your clients. (5) No change. (6/7) In my course work and practice, I learned to assist patients with basic hygiene procedures and meals; in addition, I monitored patients' vital signs and reported to the nurse on duty. (9/10) I bring a smile and a positive attitude to my nursing assistant duties, and my cheerful nature makes me a strong team member. (11/12) Finally, I am fluent in Navajo, English, and Spanish, so I would be able to speak with all of your clients and assist staff with translation if needed. (13) No change. (14/15) I am very interested in joining the team at Heart's Home Health, and I hope to hear from you. **3.** (1) No change. (2/3) Did your breakfast consist of coffee and a doughnut, or did you skip breakfast altogether? (5/6) This number may seem high; however, it's actually quite low compared to the forty-one million Americans who have pre-diabetes, a condition that puts people at risk for developing diabetes in the future. (7) No change. (9/10) Diabetics have two to four times the risk of dying of heart disease or having a stroke, and they are fifteen to forty times more likely to have a limb amputated. (11) No change. (12/13) People can use the categories of the American Diabetes Association's Diabetes Food Pyramid to select foods by calorie and sugar content; then, they can plan meals according to their needs and preferences. (15/16) The media have a strong influence in our lives, so advertising should promote a healthy diet instead of sugary, caffeinated sodas and greasy, salty fast foods. (17/18) Advertising has also promoted the idea that Americans can lose weight without work; instead, the message should be that exercise and a sensible diet are required—and worthwhile.

Chapter 23

Practice 23-1, page 394

Possible answers: **1.** If **3.** Although **5.** After **7.** so that **9.** because

Practice 23-2, page 395

Possible edits: **1.** Because we are obsessed with the lives of celebrities, they often have to fight for their privacy. **3.** Photographers follow celebrities around so that they can catch them in a newsworthy situation. **5.** After the press reported Jude Law and Sienna Miller's relationship problems, the couple spoke out about their love for each other (though they later broke up). **7.** Since Michael Jackson is constantly followed by photographers, he has reportedly disguised himself as a woman to escape the attention. **9.** Fascination with a celebrity can turn dangerous when an obsessive fan becomes a stalker.

Practice 23-3, page 396

Possible completed sentences: **1.** Whenever Vincent goes to the dentist, he has an anxiety attack. **3.** Because a hurricane is heading toward our city, many people are evacuating. **5.** Unless you turn the key all the way to the right, the door will not lock. **7.** Before I can go to the party, I must finish writing my term paper. **9.** George and Roxanne just bought a new fishing boat although they have never fished before.

Editing Reviews, pages 397–99

Possible edits: **1.** (1/2) When the explorer Christopher Columbus reached land in 1492, he did not realize just how lost he was. (3) No change. (4/5) When they were greeted by natives of the island, Columbus and his men mistakenly referred to them as Indians. (7/8) Although the Arawaks were friendly and welcoming, Columbus soon took some of them as prisoners, later bringing them back to Spain with him. (9) No change. (10/11) He mistakenly assumed that the islands were rich in gold because the Arawaks wore small gold ornaments in their noses. (13/14) In March 1493, Columbus returned to Spain, where he was greeted as a hero. **2.** (1/2) Since President Nixon made Columbus Day a federal holiday in 1971, our offices have always been closed on the second Monday of October. (3) No change. (4/5) Although this day will remain a federal holiday, with banks and post offices closed, it will no longer be a state holiday. (6/7) Because this is a state government office, Columbus Day will not be on our holiday schedule next year. (9/10) After the decision is announced next week, we will issue a revised version of our holiday schedule. (11) No change. (12/13) If this decision is made, the new holiday will fall in late September. **3.** (1) No change. (2/3) Even though I am a proud member of the Navajo tribe, I think there are more important issues to argue about. (5/6) Protests have been held and teams have been boycotted even though the players themselves are not responsible. (7) No change. (9/10) When I hear someone argue that certain team names are offensive, I am puzzled. (11) No change. (12/13) Before Europeans arrived on the continent, warriors were treated with great respect in native cultures, and they still are. (15/16) If a sports team wants to call themselves the Indians to represent their strength, I take the choice as a compliment. (17) No change. (18/19) Although there are numerous Native American tribes across the country, some people think of Native Americans as ghosts of the historical past, not as living people. (20/21) Because sports are meant to entertain, taking things too seriously just spoils the fun. (23/24) If some teams, however, want to wear respectful symbols of my pride and heritage, I say that they are welcome to do so.

Chapter 24

Practice 24-1, page 404

Answers and possible edits: **1.** Parts that should be parallel: sweet, silly, he was clumsy. On the television comedy *Gilligan's Island*, the title character was sweet, silly, and clumsy. **3.** Parts that should be parallel: a friendly farm girl named Mary Ann, there was a science teacher called Professor. The passengers included a friendly farm girl named Mary Ann and a science teacher called Professor. **5.** Parts that should be parallel: singing, to perform. Also on board was Ginger, an actress who liked singing and performing plays for the castaways. **7.** Parts that should be parallel: storms, wild animals, they were attacked by natives of the island. The seven castaways faced storms, wild animals, and attacks by natives of the island. **9.** Parts that should be parallel: tried, were failing. For three years they tried to escape the island, and for three years they failed.

Practice 24-2, page 406

Answers and possible edits: **1.** Comparison words: more time than; parts that should be parallel: To make a gift yourself, buying one. Making a gift yourself takes more time than buying one. **3.** Comparison words: more than; parts that should be parallel: homemade cookies, getting a new sweater. Most people appreciate homemade cookies more than a new sweater. **5.** Comparison words: not as expensive as; parts that should be parallel: Making a homemade gift, the purchase of commercial gifts. Making homemade gifts is generally not as expensive as purchasing commercial gifts. **7.** Comparison words: a better impression than; parts that should be parallel: Knitting a scarf, to buy an expensive one. Knitting a scarf will make a better impression than buying an expensive one. **9.** Comparison words: better than; parts that should be parallel: finding a rare book or an antique vase, to make a pot holder. Of course, sometimes finding a rare book or an antique vase is better than making a pot holder.

Practice 24-3, page 407

Answers and possible edits: **1.** Paired words: rather/than; parts that should be parallel: drive to Atlanta, to fly to Las Vegas. I would rather drive to Atlanta than fly to Las Vegas. **3.** Paired words: neither/nor; parts that should be parallel: gamblers, do we drink alcohol. My husband and I are neither gamblers nor drinkers. **5.** Paired words: rather/than; parts that should be parallel: go to Atlanta for a Braves game, be partying. Nevertheless, we would rather go to Atlanta for a Braves game than party in Las Vegas. **7.** Paired words: not only/but also; parts that should be parallel: cost less, it would be less stressful. As an added bonus, staying at home would not only cost less but be less stressful. **9.** Paired words: rather/than; parts that should be parallel: relax at home, going on a stressful vacation. My husband said that he would much rather relax at home than go on a stressful vacation.

Practice 24-4, page 408

Possible completed sentences: **1.** Our new kitten, Tiger, is not only curious but also energetic. **3.** During the day, we must either lock him in the bedroom or cover all the furniture. **5.** Still, having Tiger as my new friend is both a joy and an adventure.

Editing Reviews, pages 409–11

Possible edits: **1.** (1) Correct. (3) Resolving a domestic abuse call commonly involved "cooling off" the abuser by walking him around the block or talking to him privately. (5) Correct. (7) In some states, the criminal-justice system attempts to protect abuse survivors by pursuing cases even if the alleged victim does not show up in court or does not want to press charges. (9) For example, when they arrive on the scene, officers may find that the allegedly abusive spouse is absent or discover that the partner who made the call says that nothing happened. **2.** (1) Correct. (3) Rhonda defined domestic violence as abusive behavior between two people in an intimate relationship; it may include physical violence, economic control, emotional intimidation, or verbal abuse. (5) The company will also offer leave necessary for obtaining medical treatment, attending counseling sessions, or receiving legal assistance. (7) Correct. (9) Finally, if you know that a coworker is experiencing domestic violence, please consider asking if he or she would like to talk or suggesting our counseling resources. **3.** (1) In most divorce cases, joint child custody or generous visitation rights are in the best interests of the children. (3) As a result, many states now require training for judges, mediators, and other court workers who handle domestic violence cases. (5) A national study estimated that half of men who commit domestic violence not only abuse their wives but also abuse their children. (7) The abuser may exercise damaging emotional control over the children during visits, and such behavior may be either difficult to document or ignored by the court. (9) A judge can make visitations safer by limiting the length of visits and not allowing overnight stays. (11) Children should be sheltered from tension, conflict, and potential violence between parents as much as possible.

Chapter 25

Practice 25-1, page 424

Possible answers: **1.** synonym: a word that means the same thing as another **3.** concrete: a specific, material thing that can be distinguished by the senses **5.** wordy: containing too many or unnecessary words

Practice 25-2, page 425

Answers and possible edits: **1.** Vague words: interior design, nice. The lush plants and gorgeous fountains create a soothing atmosphere. **3.** Vague words: Pretty music. Relaxing jazz music is played on overhead speakers. **5.** Vague words: the coffee shop, great beverages. I enjoy visiting CC's Coffee for its rich, chocolatey mochas. **7.** Vague words: spa, many services. At the Serenity Spa, one can get manicures, pedicures, and massages. **9.** Vague words: Various entertainers. Local bands and theater groups perform on a small stage in the center of the complex.

Practice 25-3, page 427

Answers and possible edits: **1.** Slang: bummed. I am upset about the kitchen. **3.** Slang: trashed. The previous tenant damaged the dishwasher, and the rinse cycle doesn't work. **5.** Slang: cool. It would be much appreciated if you could correct these problems. **7.** Slang: freak me out. The mildew stains in the shower really make me uncomfortable. **9.** Slang: tick you off. I hope it does not bother you that I would like these problems taken care of as soon as possible.

Practice 25-4, page 428

Answers and possible edits: **1.** Wordy/repetitive language: are of the opinion. Many people think that romance novels follow a strict formula. **3.** Wordy/repetitive language: woman who is the heroine. The heroine should be strong, independent, and beautiful. **5.** Wordy/repetitive language: for the first time (or initially). When the hero and heroine initially meet, there is usually a conflict between them. **7.** Wordy/repetitive language: It is a well-known fact that. An obstacle will probably get in the couple's way and keep them apart. **9.** Wordy/repetitive language: Due to the fact that, conquer (or overcome). Because readers expect a happy ending, the characters must conquer all obstacles and live happily ever after.

Practice 25-5, page 430

Answers and possible edits: **1.** Cliché: stuck in a rut. Are you bored in your current job? **3.** Cliché: few and far between. You might think that dream jobs are uncommon. **5.** Cliché: near and dear to your heart. Find a skill that you enjoy using and that is important to you. **7.** Cliché: leave no stone unturned. Maybe your investigative skills are thorough. **9.** Cliché: playing with fire. Changing jobs may seem risky.

Editing Reviews, pages 431–33

Possible edits: **1.** (1) In the past few years, carbohydrates have been criticized by the media. (3) Some people decided that they would never eat pasta again. (5) Correct. (7) People should include healthy carbohydrates such as fruits, vegetables, and whole grains in their daily diets. (9) People can eat many types of foods as long as they do so in moderation. **2.** (1) It has come to my attention that some employees are upset about a lack of overtime hours. (3) I hope this memo will make it clear how overtime hours are assigned. (5) I rotate the names so that no one will become too exhausted. (7) This is an effective technique; it has worked successfully for the past ten years. (9) I hope that we all agree that this policy is as fair as possible. **3.** (1) Correct. (3) If they are working, going to school, and raising a family, they may be more likely to choose fast food than healthy, homemade meals. (5) The problem is not so serious for older students or those who live at home. (7) Students who live on campus can eat as much as they want in the cafeteria, at a friend's house, or at fast-food restaurants. (9) Correct. (11) Adjusting to an all new way of life is challenging. (13) Correct. (15) Keep a regular meal schedule and avoid eating too quickly. (17) Correct.

Chapter 26

Editing Reviews, pages 446–47

Edits: **1.** (1) Correct. (3) You're sure to do well if you do. (5) Correct. (7) In the past, students have rushed through the test and have regretted it. (9) Use that time well, and you can't lose. **2.** (1) Correct. (3) We hope that we will find a job for you soon. (5) Use a black or blue pen because it's much easier to read than pencil. (7) If you have references, please include their names and addresses on the back of the last page. (9) You will hear from a principal of the business within thirty days. **3.** (1) Mars in the springtime is not the most pleasant place to be. (3) The fun doesn't stop there, however. (5) You might find them under your desk or behind your computer monitor. (7) Springtime on Earth usually brings some extra wind, but you might not know that it does the same thing on Mars. (9) NASA's rover, *Spirit*, not only spotted them but took pictures of them too. (11) Watching a dust devil on film would certainly be much better than experiencing one in person. (13) Instead, dirt devils that have passed measurement equipment have been recorded as being several miles high and hundreds of feet wide. (15) Correct. (17) When it comes to dust devils, stick to the ones under your bed.

Chapter 27

Practice 27-2, page 453
Possible answers: **1.** chief **3.** grief **5.** sleigh

Practice 27-3, page 454
Answers: **1.** famous **3.** careful **5.** nicely **7.** dining **9.** senseless

Practice 27-4, page 455
Answers: **1.** saying **3.** easily **5.** beautiful **7.** laziest **9.** messiness

Practice 27-5, page 456
Answers: **1.** talking **3.** thundering **5.** tripped **7.** talented **9.** beginner

Practice 27-6, page 457
Answers: **1.** phones **3.** foxes **5.** echoes **7.** pencils **9.** dishes

Practice 27-7, page 458
Answers: **1.** biggest **3.** neglected **5.** needed, living **7.** unhappily **9.** running, playing

Practice 27-8, page 459
Edits: (1) When I stopped by my friend Vanessa's cubicle at work, I noticed a small vase of beautiful flowers and two boxes of chocolates sitting on her desk. (3) "I did," she admitted. (5) "I believe they help me while I'm thinking and writing," she said. (7) Correct. (9) Even my accounting tasks seemed easier than usual.

Editing Reviews, pages 460–62
Edits: **1.** (1) The Channel Tunnel, or Chunnel, is the rail tunnel connecting England and France. (3) To complete this huge construction, a partnership had to be formed between two countries with different languages, governments, and sets of laws and safety codes. (5) For years, it had viewed itself as a separate country from the rest of Europe. (7) Nevertheless, others saw the Chunnel as one of the best ways to truly bring together the two countries. (9) The Chunnel cost billions of dollars, averaging $5 million each day of construction. **2.** (1) I am writing in response to your classified ad in the *Baton Rouge Advocate*. (3) I believe I am the perfect person for the job. (5) I have worked at the front desk of three local businesses, where I greeted customers, answered phone calls, processed invoices, and managed the ordering of office supplies. (7) Correct. (9) Correct. **3.** (1) Ask many of today's college students what a muscle car is and you may receive a blank look in return. (3) Correct. (5) Correct. (7) Unfortunately, these vehicles had so much power that they could be deadly in the hands of inexperienced drivers. (9) Correct. (11) Correct. (13) Ford, Pontiac, and Dodge are making some new cars that will probably answer the wishes of some people who miss muscle cars. (15) Correct.

Chapter 28

Practice 28-1, page 474
Answers and edits: **1.** Items in series: cell phones, laptop computers, portable music players. Multitasking is easier than ever thanks to gadgets such as cell phones, laptop computers, and portable music players. **3.** Items in series: record players, black-and-white televisions, hula hoops. Sometimes, I miss the simpler days of record players, black-and-white televisions, and hula hoops. **5.** Items in series: ate lunch, watched the news, read a book. Earlier today, I ate lunch, watched the news, and read a book at the same time. **7.** Items in series: clean the house, cook dinner, watch the children. Tonight, I will clean the house, cook dinner, and watch the children. **9.** Items in series: driving, eating, seeing a movie. I try to avoid using my cell phone while driving, eating, or seeing a movie.

Practice 28-2, page 476
Edits: **1.** Many professions used to be dominated by men, and the majority of those men were white. **3.** Workplace diversity is now common, yet discrimination still occurs. **5.** Some respondents had been victims of prejudice over the previous year, or they had overheard others making intolerant statements. **7.** Age discrimination is another problem, for 20 percent of respondents reported prejudice against older workers. **9.** The American workforce is more diverse than ever before, and it will become even more diverse in the future.

Practice 28-3, page 477
Answers and edits: **1.** Introductory word: Yesterday. Yesterday, I accidentally stepped on a nail. **3.** Introductory word group: According to my doctor. According to my doctor, a shiny nail is just as likely to cause tetanus as a rusty one. **5.** Introductory word: Apparently. Correct. **7.** Introductory word group: Producing poisons that attack muscles all over the body. Correct. **9.** Introductory word: However. However, the vaccine's effects wear off after ten years.

Practice 28-4, page 480
Answers and edits: **1.** Appositive: a very nice lady. The owner, a very nice lady, is Francine Smythe. **3.** Interrupter: however. I have not, however, found any of Melville's books in her store. **5.** Appositive: always excellent bargains. Correct. **7.** Appositive: the basement. My favorite part of the shop, the basement, is dimly lit and particularly quiet. **9.** Interrupter: of course. The dim light is bad for my eyes, of course, but it gives the basement a cozy feel.

Practice 28-5, page 482
Answers and edits: **1.** Adjective clause: which look like sushi. The restaurant's dishes, which look like sushi, are made of paper. **3.** Adjective clause: that people can eat. Correct. **5.** Adjective clause: which are the main ingredients of the paper. Soybeans and cornstarch, which are the main ingredients of the paper, are also found in many other foods. **7.** Adjective clause: which changes daily. The chef sometimes seasons the menu, which changes daily, to taste like a main course. **9.** Adjective clause: who can afford the restaurant's high prices. Correct.

Practice 28-6, page 483

Edits: **1.** "It's not going to be the same here without you," she added. **3.** Alyson exclaimed, "It won't be the same not seeing you every day, though." **5.** "I think it would be a good idea," said Alyson, "if we had a going-away party for you." **7.** Correct. **9.** "Not really," I replied, "because I sure am sick of filing."

Practice 28-7, page 484

Edits: **1.** Michiko came here from Osaka, Japan, when she was four years old. **3.** I had my car's brakes fixed in July 2004 and in January 2005. **5.** The snowstorm hit St. Paul, Minnesota, on February 3, 2005. **7.** Leaving your job before June 2, 2005, caused you to lose your health benefits. **9.** I was driving to Houston, Texas, on May 4, 2001, to see my parents.

Practice 28-8, page 485

Edits: **1.** However, David, you cannot come with the rest of us. **3.** Ryan, please help me lift this box. **5.** Because I'm moving to Alaska, Kevin, you can have all of my Hawaiian shirts.

Practice 28-9, page 486

Edits: **1.** Yes, these curtains will brighten up the kitchen. **3.** Yes, I will vote for your proposal. **5.** Correct.

Editing Reviews, pages 486–88

Edits: **1.** (1) Marie, who went by the nickname Manya as a child, was finally on her way to her sister's home in Paris. (3) She was so filled with joy, however, that she didn't care. (5) For five years, she had sent her earnings from her work as a governess to Bronya, her sister, to put her through medical school. (7) At last, it was Manya's turn to continue her education. (9) She ate little, slept rarely, and studied every minute. **2.** (1) For the past five years, you have been one of our most valued employees. (3) You have been on time every day, and you rarely use your sick days. (5) He has told me that you are the best floor manager in the company and recommended you for a promotion. (7) Your new position, which begins next week, will pay an additional $4 per hour. (9) Correct. **3.** (1) When you first look up at the skyline of Malmö, Sweden, you might think you're dreaming. (3) However, you pinch yourself and find that you are wide awake. (5) On Saturday, August 27, 2005, a different kind of apartment building joined Malmö's skyline. (7) Over six hundred feet tall, the Torso is made of nine stacked cubes. (9) There is a full ninety-degree twist between the top and the bottom of the building. (11) Correct. (13) Already, Calatrava's building has won several awards. (15) He added, "I also wanted to deliver something technically unique." (17) The monthly rent payments are as high as $3,700, so the views had better be spectacular!

Chapter 29

Practice 29-1, page 492

Answers: **1.** my uncle's motorcycle **3.** the necklace's value **5.** my sisters' friendship

Practice 29-2, page 493

Edits: **1.** What happens when a galaxy loses one of its stars? **3.** This was astronomers' first discovery of a star escaping from a galaxy. **5.** It is currently about 196,000 light years from the galaxy's center. **7.** The star's official name is a long combination of letters and numbers, but some scientists call it the Outcast. **9.** This near miss could have increased the Outcast's speed.

Practice 29-3, page 495

Answers: **1.** there's **3.** it's **5.** you'll **7.** I'm

Practice 29-4, page 495

Edits: **1.** The little girl is dancing around the sidewalk, and she's certainly enjoying herself. **3.** When they take a seat next to me on the bus, I think that we're going to have a great time together. **5.** I can't hear my own thoughts because the girl is singing so loudly. **7.** Then there's a hand reaching across my book, and the girl's tearing a page out of it. **9.** I'm a mother myself, so I hope you won't think that I dislike all children.

Practice 29-5, page 496

Edits: **1.** The last two weeks' games had interesting scores. **3.** We win regularly because Renee, who spells her name with two e's, is so good. **5.** With a few months' practice, we'll get even better.

Editing Reviews, pages 497–98

Edits: **1.** (1) During this course, you'll be given four tests and eight quizzes. (3) You are allowed to take two makeup exams during the course's duration. (5) The other half of your grade will consist of points for attendance, participation, homework, and two research papers. (7) If you turn in others' work as yours, you will have to leave the class. (9) Correct. (11) Even if you don't get all A's, I hope this class will be a rewarding experience. **2.** (1) This addition to the employee handbook further describes the company's dress code. (3) Most of you already dress appropriately, but we've been questioned about certain kinds of clothing by a number of people. (5) Please note that jeans, sweatpants, shorts, and overalls aren't allowed. (7) Women's skirts and dresses must be at knee length or below. (9) Of course, these rules do not apply to each summer's company picnic. (11) Correct. **3.** (1) Correct. (3) Correct. (5) Correct. (7) Some termite homes have been around for more than fifty years and contain millions of occupants. (9) Correct. (11) Towers in rain forests, for example, are shaped like umbrellas to direct water away from the nest. (13) A tower's internal chambers and tunnels are very complicated. (15) They like to stay at home, leaving their amazing towers only to eat and mate.

Chapter 30

Practice 30-1, page 503

Answers and rewrites: **1.** Indirect. Dana noted, "Phoning is more personal than e-mailing." **3.** Direct. Dana answered that she didn't see the point of keeping a record of asking someone to dinner. **5.** Direct. Dana said that she didn't see his point. **7.** Indirect. Dana said, "I certainly remember."

Practice 30-2, page 504

Edits: **1.** Robert exclaimed, "I cannot believe that you quit a fantastic job as president of a huge advertising agency." **3.** Mr. Rivera continued, "I loved my job, but it left me with hardly any time to see my family." **5.** "I consider myself very lucky," Mr. Rivera responded. **7.** Mr. Rivera admitted, "I never pictured myself in this position, but now that I am, I can't imagine otherwise." **9.** Mr. Rivera laughed and then said, "I was exactly right, Gerry, and the most satisfying job I've ever had is the one I have now, being a stay-at-home dad."

Practice 30-3, page 505

Edits: **1.** "You used the TV all last night," Evi complained. **3.** "The show I'm watching," said Evi, "is just as important to me." **5.** "Each week," she said, "we signed up for time slots during which we had control of the television." **7.** "What did you do if you couldn't reach an agreement?" Evi asked. **9.** Evi thought it over and finally said that the two of them could probably compromise after all.

Practice 30-4, page 506

Edits: **1.** He told me that his idea for that title came from James Joyce's short story "The Dead," which was part of Joyce's book <u>Dubliners</u>. **3.** One of my band's most popular songs is "The Day of the Living Dead," which we wrote to honor our favorite old movie, <u>The Night of the Living Dead</u>. **5.** My doctor told me that our songs inspired him to write a story that he will call "The Death of Death," which he plans to submit to the <u>Atlantic Monthly</u> magazine.

Editing Reviews, pages 507–09

Edits: **1.** (1) Correct. (3) As the newly invented bicycle began to sweep the nation, the brothers opened a repair shop because they wanted to make sure people kept their new mode of transportation in good shape. (5) As Wilbur wrote in a letter to a friend, "The boys of the Wright family are all lacking in determination and push." (7) "I have some pet theories as to the proper construction of a flying machine," he wrote. (9) He reassured the experts at the Smithsonian that he and his brother were serious, not just simply curious. (11) Correct. **2.** (1) This afternoon, I spoke with Eileen Bosco about writing next month's feature article, tentatively titled, "Where's the Beef? Corpus Christi's Best Steakhouses." (3) She said that she would be glad to take on another project. (5) Correct. (7) Elaine recently finished several articles for <u>Texas Monthly</u> magazine, and I am concerned that they might hire her full-time. (9) Jenna Melton, who worked with Elaine on the diner article, told me, "Elaine is a talented food writer, and we should hire her as a staff writer if a position opens up." **3.** (1) Correct. (3) Correct. (5) "We treat a lot of patients who have tans and get skin cancer," said Richard Wagner, a physician at the University of Texas Medical Branch. (7) Correct. (9) Their results, published in the journal <u>Archives of Dermatology</u>, were far from conclusive but certainly fascinating. (11) Correct. (13) Correct. (15) Correct.

Chapter 31

Practice 31-1, page 513

Edits: **1.** He had visitors coming from as far away as Portland, Oregon; Butte, Montana; and Glasgow, Scotland. **3.** The two of them vacuumed; dusted; put out bowls for popcorn, chips, and nuts; and cleared out the refrigerator for drinks. **5.** In the end, they decided to play three games: find the orange, guess the number of pennies in a jar, and guess Manny's weight.

Practice 31-2, page 515

Edits: **1.** Because of her allergy, my wife and I always bring three things when we go on vacation with Courtney: medication, Courtney's medical information, and our doctor's emergency number. **3.** On our last vacation, a waitress made a serious mistake: she was not aware that the restaurant used peanut oil in a dish that we ordered. **5.** Luckily, Courtney responded immediately, and her next words made us all laugh: "Peanuts are not a friend."

Practice 31-3, page 516

Edits: **1.** Last year, I needed a new suit, but the suits I liked at stores were just too expensive (some outrageously expensive). **3.** This tailor, Mr. Shephard, measured me and had me try on several suits (at least six) to see what would work the best given my height and body type. **5.** Mr. Shephard was able to adjust the suit quickly (in about a week), and it looks great on me.

Practice 31-4, page 517

Edits: **1.** This study matched the percentage of people in an area who meet the exercise recommendations of the Centers for Disease Control and Prevention with weather reports from all over the United States. **3.** Several states with cool climates—Montana, Utah, Wisconsin, New Hampshire, and Vermont—had the highest percentages of people who met the exercise requirements. **5.** These unsurprising results—few people like to exercise in hot, humid weather—make me wonder why anyone even bothered to do this study.

Practice 31-5, page 518

Edits: **1.** She is certainly a high-achieving athlete, though. **3.** Although Becky has a go-getter attitude, she is immature and a poor

loser. **5.** Her league-leading statistics are proving that she has tremendous promise.

Editing Reviews, pages 518–21

Possible edits: **1.** (1) What caused Hermann Rorschach to look at ink spilled on paper and see it as a way to test people's mental health is a mystery; there is little doubt, however, that his invention is useful. (3) When patients look at the inkblots, they see different patterns—often, things that are quite unusual. (5) Correct. (7) Psychiatrists use the inkblots to help diagnose mental illnesses such as schizophrenia, obsessive-compulsive disorder, and multiple-personality disorder. (9) Sadly, the man who came up with this unique testing method did not live long enough to see it become widely used. (11) We have him to thank for a very important improvement in psychiatry: a better understanding of people's mental states. **2.** (1) This is a reminder about this Friday's company picnic (our first) at Shelton Community Park. (3) We need each person to bring some food to share: snacks, desserts, side dishes, casseroles, and salads. (5) Our tables will be set up by the east gate, and my nineteen-year-old son, Rob, will be directing you to the correct parking area. (7) Anyone who can't attend—and I hope there won't be anyone on this list—should let me know by the end of the day tomorrow. **3.** (1) Many people would complain if they had to spend an entire day at the mall; if it was the Mall of America, however, the story would be different. (3) There are places for people of all ages to spend time: more than five hundred stores; fifty restaurants; fourteen movie theaters with multiple screens, several concession areas, and great sound; eight nightclubs; a casino; a concert hall; and a bowling alley. (5) A four-story Lego Imagination Center shows what can be made with thousands of plastic bricks. (7) If this does not sound like enough fun, keep exploring. (9) The NASCAR Motor Speedway offers fast-paced excitement for racing fans. (11) In a new store called MinneNAPolis, shoppers are offered a unique service: the chance to take a nap. (13) My mother—a very tough woman to please—loves the Mall of America, and that says a lot.

Chapter 32

Practice 32-1, page 523

Edits: (1) Correct. (3) He also made people laugh when he stated, "Get your facts first, and then you can change them as much as you please." (5) People liked it best when Twain passed on comical advice, such as, "Be respectful to your superiors, if you have any."

Practice 32-2, page 526

Edits: **1.** My favorite classes at college are sociology, biology, and French. **3.** That class is taught by Professor John Sortensen, who happens to be my uncle. **5.** On weekends, I can catch the train into Los Angeles at the North Hollywood station, which is not far from where I live. **7.** The museum had a miniature courtroom showing the O. J. Simpson trial and tiny palaces furnished with chandeliers the size of rice. **9.** The city's restaurants are another reason to visit often, and so far I have tried Mexican, Japanese, Thai, Italian, Indian, Argentinian, and, of course, Chinese food.

Practice 32-3, page 527

Edits: (1) "I married your mother because I wanted children," said Groucho Marx in the movie *Horse Feathers*. "Imagine my disappointment when you arrived." (3) As a team, the Marx Brothers followed up with more Broadway hits, including *Animal Crackers*. (5) In their movie *Duck Soup*, Marx said to another character, "I got a good mind to join a club and beat you over the head with it." (7) Later, he brought *You Bet Your Life* to TV.

Editing Reviews, pages 528–30

Edits: **1.** (1) Correct. (3) Six of the eight weeks devoted to this unit will concentrate on the 1960s, when struggles for civil rights made daily headlines across the nation. (5) We will also examine the history of the Ku Klux Klan, the development of the National Association for the Advancement of Colored People, and the passage of the Civil Rights Act of 1964. (7) A final exam covering the course material will be given on December 15 in Howard Hall. (9) If you have any questions, please see me after class or during my office hours. **2.** (1) Correct. (3) 1429 Statler Blvd. (5) To be delivered on or before Saturday, September 19 (7) 12 copies of *The Scarlet Letter* by Nathaniel Hawthorne (9) Send by way of the Granger Distribution Company, Philadelphia, Pennsylvania **3.** (1) You can live in the same city for years and completely miss seeing a certain building. (3) However, can you imagine missing a four-hundred-foot waterfall? (5) In the autumn of 2003, a park ranger found a waterfall that somehow had been missed for decades. (7) He had no idea where to begin searching since the park covers 42,500 acres. (9) Correct. (11) Correct. (13) This time, the two of them found the falls, which were later named Whiskeytown Falls. (15) It is surrounded by deep ravines and thick undergrowth.

Acknowledgments, continued from page iv

Gary Soto. "The Jacket." From *Small Faces* and *The Effects of Knut Hamsun on a Fresno Boy: Recollections and Short Essays* by Gary Soto. Copyright © 1983, 2001 by Gary Soto. Reprinted by permission of Persea Books, Inc.

Elyzabeth Joy Stagg. "From the Welfare Rolls, a Mother's View." From *Newsweek*, August 23, 1999, p. 10. Copyright © 1999 Newsweek, Inc. Reprinted by permission. All rights reserved.

Brent Staples. "A Brother's Murder." First published in the *New York Times*, March 30, 1986. Reprinted by permission of the author.

Steve Vaught. "Walking for My Life." From the *New York Times Magazine*, July 10, 2005. Copyright © 2005 by the New York Times Company. Reprinted by permission.

Ana Veciana-Suarez and Alexandra Alter. "Life Unplugged." From the *Miami Herald*, October 29, 2005. Copyright © 2005 the Miami Herald. Reproduced with permission of the *Miami Herald* in the format Textbook via Copyright Clearance Center.

Photo Credits

Page 1: © Davis Barber/PhotoEdit
Page 33: © Dean Berry/Index Stock Imagery
Page 115: © Jeff Greenberg/The Image Works
Page 257: © Bill Aron/PhotoEdit
Page 377: © Will and Deni McIntyre / Photo Researchers, Inc.
Page 421: © John Cole/Photo Researchers, Inc.
Page 471: © Michael Newman/PhotoEdit
Page 539: © Mark Ludak/The Image Works

Index